WHY ANCIENT CHINESE POLITICAL THOUGHT MATTERS

Why Ancient Chinese Political Thought Matters

FOUR DIALOGUES ON CHINA'S PAST, PRESENT, AND FUTURE

DANIEL A. BELL

PRINCETON UNIVERSITY PRESS
PRINCETON & OXFORD

Published by Princeton University Press
41 William Street, Princeton, New Jersey 08540
99 Banbury Road, Oxford OX2 6JX

press.princeton.edu

GPSR Authorized Representative: Easy Access System Europe - Mustamäe tee 50, 10621 Tallinn, Estonia, gpsr.requests@easproject.com

ISBN 978-0-691-27980-0
ISBN (e-book) 978-0-691-27981-7
Library of Congress Control Number: 2025947015

British Library Cataloging-in-Publication Data is available

Editorial: Rob Tempio and Chloe Coy
Production Editorial: Jenny Wolkowicki
Jacket design: Katie Osborne
Production: Erin Suydam
Publicity: Alyssa Sanford and Kathryn Stevens
Copyeditor: Joseph Dahm

Jacket images: *(top to bottom)*: Mo Tzu © 2024 Caitlin Davis; Zhuangzi by Logic Images / Alamy; Confucius by Nastasic / iStock; Han Fei Zi by Naci Yavuz / Alamy

This book has been composed in Arno Pro

Printed in the United States of America

10 9 8 7 6 5 4 3 2 1

For Maman, who left this world in 2024, and my sister Valérie, who provided loving care until the "end"

CONTENTS

ACKNOWLEDGMENTS

IN 2002, I was offered an advance contract by Princeton University Press for a book to be titled *Talking About Politics: A Cross-Cultural Approach*. My book promised to fill an academic gap: all the major textbooks in English dealt almost exclusively with Western political theory ("Plato to Nato," as we used to say) and neglected great theorizing from non-Western traditions. I had proposed to write the book in dialogue form because my two previous books had been written in that form and readers found the final product more entertaining than the typical dry academic tome.[1] Plus, it made sense to use the dialogue form because ancient political thinkers often argued with each other and wrote dialogues to that effect. I also proposed to have the great political thinkers debate their theories in contemporary settings to show that their arguments shed light on today's political controversies.

Twenty-four years later, the gap remains and my book remains unwritten.[2] I did take a stab at writing but eventually realized the job was too big for me. Plus, new ideas about "cultural appropriation" might get in the way. How could a white male from Canada such as myself use the voice of, say, Frantz Fanon to argue against racism? What kind of chutzpah led me to think I could impersonate the voice of a Japanese feminist thinker to critique the oppression of women? Not to mention that I didn't have the language skills to read works in many of the world's languages or evaluate the quality of translations. I read English, Chinese, and French, but how could I propose to do justice to works written in, say, Arabic, Japanese, or German? So I dropped the project. I consoled myself with the thought that I'd written a few books for Princeton University Press since then, but deep down I still felt guilty about the unfulfilled promise.

Fortunately (or unfortunately), my editor at Princeton University Press found the contract from 2002. He said he liked the idea and urged me to revisit the project. But I knew I'd have to narrow it down. I'd been living in China for nearly three decades, working mainly in the field of Chinese political theory, and felt most comfortable writing about ideas in that domain. And since I feel part of Chinese culture, worries about "cultural appropriation" have less force (in my own mind). So I decided to keep the dialogue form as well as the idea of setting the dialogues in the modern world to show the relevance of ancient political arguments for contemporary challenges. But I'd stick to Chinese political theory written in the pre-Qin period, before China was unified in 221 BCE, the political context for China's most fascinating and influential political debates. I'd take those debates and set them in different parts of contemporary China and would try to be charitable and fair-minded to all sides. Here's the book that emerged from this process.

I owe much to my wonderful editor, Rob Tempio, who rescued this project (in modified form) from the realm of good ideas never implemented. Rob provided the book title and chapter headings and made valuable comments on the text. I'm also grateful to Paul D'Ambrosio and Li Chenyang for comments on earlier versions of chapters and to two anonymous referees who wrote constructive reports that allowed me to improve the manuscript.

The University of Hong Kong is an ideal place to research Chinese political theory because we have the experts, resources, academic freedom, comparative outlook, and community support to push the boundaries of the field in new and exciting directions. I'm grateful to university leaders and to the faculty of law and the department of philosophy for support. My colleagues Herman Cappelan, Jin Yutang, and Tang Siufu provided valuable comments on earlier drafts of chapters. I'm especially grateful to my colleague Justin Tiwald for excellent and detailed comments on an earlier draft of the whole manuscript. I'd also like to thank my research assistants—Li Yuzhen, Liang Ziying, Ngai Wing Sze Kitty, Tao Max Junbo, and Wang Tengqian—who found and organized material for the purpose of this book, as well as my postdoctoral researcher Li Dongyang and my doctoral student Tao Max Junbo (co-supervised with Justin Tiwald) for related discussion and insights. Special thanks to Max for helping with the bibliography. I'm most grateful to my brilliant spouse and colleague Wang Pei: our dialogues (and occasional arguments ☺) over mealtime have shaped almost every page of this book.

At the University of Hong Kong, I have taught an undergraduate common core course offered to the whole university, titled "Talking About Politics: Chinese Debates in Political Thinking, Past and Present," that draws on material from this book. Teaching this course (twice) to a broad range of intellectually curious students from different disciplines allowed me to identify the material that those without much background in Chinese political theory find to be particularly interesting and helped me refine the book. I served as my own teacher assistant for one tutorial group—which helped me to learn what students were really thinking—and I'm very grateful for the aid of other teaching assistants over the course of two years: Chen

Ruisi, Cheng Po San Sarah, Ding Zhuo, He Jingman, Ji Linfei, Tao Max Junbo (twice), and Wang Xinyu. Thanks too to Victoria Kwok, who helped to administer this course and other matters with efficiency and kindness.

An earlier draft of chapter 2 was presented at Sun Yat-sen University in Zhuhai in the form of a play: Jun-Hyeok Kwak was the chair, Li Yong played the part of Han Feizi, and I played Xunzi. Quite unexpectedly, the actors (including myself) became increasingly animated as we read the lines (we nearly came to blows), and we enjoyed great audience participation afterward. Chapter 2 was also presented at the University of Central Lancashire's Confucius Institute, with wonderful performances by Ed Griffith and Xin Liu. I highly recommend this way of engaging with the book!

WHY ANCIENT CHINESE POLITICAL THOUGHT MATTERS

Introduction

FOUR GREAT DEBATES OF CHINESE POLITICAL THOUGHT

CHINA'S POLITICAL thinking is rooted in its past. To understand Chinese politics, it is essential to understand the main themes of Chinese philosophy and history that serve as reference points for Chinese intellectuals and public officials in everyday conversation and political discourse. The political debates in the Spring and Autumn and Warring States periods (ca. 770–221 BCE) were, arguably, the most original, profound, and influential political debates in China's history. China had not yet been unified by the Qin dynasty in 221 BCE, and political theorists and the ancient equivalent of policy advisers roamed from state to state, seeking to influence rulers. Notwithstanding constant warfare, thinkers were surprisingly free to argue about political controversies. The founding members of schools that came to be known as Confucianism, Legalism, Daoism, and Mohism engaged in heated arguments about politics and good government. These debates recurred in different forms over the next two millennia and we can expect further iterations in the future.

I do not mean to imply that good understanding of these debates is sufficient to comprehend contemporary Chinese politics. Of course, there were diverse and fascinating political debates in subsequent Chinese history, and more recent imported theories such as socialism and democracy also shape Chinese political thinking and policymaking. But those seeking deeper knowledge of Chinese politics need to have a solid understanding of political theories from the pre-Qin period because they still serve as important reference points for Chinese intellectuals and political officials today: as background assumptions and ideals for much political thinking and policymaking in the twentieth century when China was shaped by the tradition of antitraditionalism and more explicitly the past several decades along with the revival of China's political traditions in academia and official political discourse.[1]

These ancient political debates are not well-known outside of China, and my book aims to remedy this gap of understanding. My aim is not to take sides in these debates but to be charitable and fair-minded to all sides and to familiarize readers with the most influential political thoughts and theories from ancient China using the words of the thinkers themselves.[2] For this purpose, I have written this book in dialogue form, and I draw mainly on the original thoughts and ideas of great political theorists from the pre-Qin period (in English translation). The dialogue form also has the advantage of showing the diversity of political thought in ancient China in an accessible and entertaining manner for the modern reader.

My book also aims to show that these ancient debates remain relevant today and for the foreseeable future. For this purpose, I have taken key strands of ancient political debates with lasting value—harmony versus freedom, law versus ritual, musical culture versus material welfare, and realism versus idealism in international relations—and apply them to policy questions of contemporary relevance. The debates are set in different parts of China in the near future, and the protagonists are (fictitious) descendants of the great political thinkers, which is not entirely implausible in a Chinese context because the descendants of Confucius and Mencius have family trees that extend to descendants in modern society who often take pride in the ideas of their ancestors. They argue about perennial political challenges such as whether moral obligations between family members need to be legally enforced, how to reduce corruption in government, whether the state should promote culture, and under what conditions the state should engage in warfare. The debates shed light not just on Chinese thinking but on political thinking more broadly: after all, what makes great thinkers great is that they proposed ideas that are relevant in different times and places and that can help us think about how to deal with modern-day political challenges.

The ancient Chinese works used for these dialogues were, of course, written in classical Chinese, and I rely on a mixture of my own translations and those by experts.[3] I have checked most of the translations against the original sources and selected those that seemed both relatively accurate and fluent in modern English, with occasional modifications.[4] For the general reader, I have provided brief introductions to the thoughts of the political thinkers before launching into the dialogues. For the experts, the notes provide references to secondary sources and point to alternative interpretations of some passages discussed in the main text.

Each chapter can be read more or less independently, depending on the reader's interests. The dialogues between descendants of the great thinkers are set in contemporary settings the descendants are committed to the thoughts of their ancestors, but they illustrate arguments with examples from recent history. Hence, the dialogues should be viewed as writings inspired by the great thinkers rather than unmediated interpretations of the original texts. But I remain relatively faithful to the key ideas in the sections on particular thinkers, so if the reader wants to learn the thoughts of individual thinkers, it is best to focus on the sections in chapters that discuss their thoughts using mainly their original words (in translation): for example, section 1 in chapter 1 discusses the views of Confucius in detail, and section 2 discusses the views of Zhuangzi in detail (the sections where the thinkers act as critics and the concluding sections in each chapter owe more to my own thinking). But I'd suggest that individual chapters be read from start to finish because they make sense only as a whole, and I provide somewhat surprising speeches at the end of each chapter.[5] Readers who want to have an overall sense of the thoughts of China's most influential political theorists from the pre-Qin era that set the terms for much of the political thinking in subsequent Chinese history should read the whole book.

The book leads off with a dialogue between Kong and Zhuang, descendants of Confucius (Kongzi) and the great Daoist thinker Zhuangzi. Both the Confucian and the Daoist traditions have been hugely influential in Chinese history, but they tend to pull in different directions: the Confucians argue for the importance of nourishing harmonious and humane social relations and educating talented and virtuous public officials, whereas Daoists emphasize an easygoing lifestyle with minimal social attachments. Confucians value constant self-improvement, hard work, and social and political responsibility, whereas the Daoist emphasis on carefree wandering has inspired countless artists, social recluses, and those who seek freedom from social stresses. Kong and Zhuang meet in a bar on a remote island in Hong Kong and argue about whether obligations between adult family members should be legally enforced. Kong allows for the possibility that the law can set constraints on freedom in order to promote harmonious ties between family members in such cases as the promotion of filial piety and the right to divorce. Zhuang appears to be more skeptical, but he might have a sudden change of mind.

The second dialogue considers how to minimize corruption in government, one of the perennial challenges in Chinese history. A descendant of the influential political thinker Han Feizi, who systematized China's Legalist tradition, argues that people cannot be motivated by moral concerns and that corruption can be curtailed only by means of harsh legal punishments that make public officials fearful of doing deeds that harm the state. The punishments need to apply to all without any discretion or mercy. A descendant of the Confucian thinker Xunzi, who was Han Feizi's teacher, agrees that people have a tendency to badness but argues that people can improve morally. If the aim is long-term reduction of corruption in government, only social rituals that make participants feel part of a community can succeed. Mr. Xun is not against legal punishments but argues they should be a last resort. The dialogue is heated and emotional, with the student seeming to call for the physical elimination of his teacher, but it ends with a banquet.

The third dialogue imagines a deliberative poll where ordinary citizens selected at random must decide whether the local community should fund a musical arts center. It takes place in a rural part of Shandong province rich in culture but poor in material resources. Mr. Mo, a descendant of Mozi, the founder of the Mohist school, argues that the community should spend scarce resources on supplying the material needs of the common people rather than funding musical arts. A descendant of the author of the *Yueji* (*Record of Music*) named Ms. Yue argues for funding the musical arts on the grounds that music is necessary for human flourishing. Music provides joy and forms the foundation for communal bonds that allow for policies that help the poor to be implemented without much resistance. The citizens deliberate at the end, but will their decision be respected by the powers that be?

The last dialogue is an acrimonious argument about the appropriate use of military power. I imagine a discussion between descendants of Mencius (Mengzi) and Shang Yang, a founder of the realpolitik Legalist school who is far more Machiavellian than Machiavelli himself. They argue over whether mainland China should invade Taiwan after it declares formal independence. Shang declares that an invasion should be carried out even if it involves cruel means, whereas Meng believes that war needs to be morally justified in terms of both cause and means, with the implication that Chinese rulers should be cautious about invading. The debate is carried out in the presence of the ruler, similar to ancient Chinese debates about war, and the chapter ends with a meeting of the Standing Committee of the Politburo where decision-makers discuss the possibility of invasion in view of the contrasting perspectives provided by the two thinkers.

The book ends with an *Atogaki* (afterword) explaining what's wrong with this book. I freely acknowledge that my method will not be to everyone's taste. Intellectual historians will fault me for plucking thinkers from their original context. Experts in Chinese philosophy may contest my interpretation of certain passages from classic texts. Normative theorists will object to the fact that I seek inspiration only from pre-Qin Chinese political thought. Some ideas of political theorists from ancient China that were meant to be deadly serious are discussed in a way that's sometimes lighthearted, which may turn off those who think humor shows a lack of respect for the greats. Oh well, it's hard to please everybody. But some students and scholars of China studies and comparative political theory as well as those who do not normally engage with Chinese politics and philosophy may enjoy this book. And if I'm lucky, a young intellectual rummaging in one of the world's few remaining libraries with physical books in fifty years' time will stumble upon this book and end up learning something about political debates from ancient China that may still be relevant for thinking about the challenges of the late twenty-first century.

1

On Harmony and Freedom

OR, SHOULD OBLIGATIONS BETWEEN FAMILY MEMBERS BE LEGALLY ENFORCED?

KONGZI (LATINIZED TO CONFUCIUS) is China's most influential thinker. He lived in the Spring and Autumn period (ca. 770–479 BCE) as old certainties were breaking down and "China" became divided into several states competing among each other for domination, though without (yet) the totalizing warfare of the Warring States period. Kongzi was born in the state of Lu (now part of Shandong province) and aimed to restore what he considered to be the beautiful and moral ways of the earlier Western Zhou dynasty. Kongzi served as a public official, but he left his native land after several political disappointments and roamed from state to state trying to persuade rulers to adopt his radical ideas for political reform.[1] He had even less success abroad and returned to Lu to pursue a life of teaching. His second choice proved to be his true calling, and today he is known as the teacher of teachers in China. Like Socrates, he never wrote down his ideas, but (fortunately for us) his students recorded his wisdom for posterity in *The*

Analects.[2] The sayings of Kongzi are somewhat elliptical but can be boiled down to the claim that the good life lies in nourishing harmonious and humane social relations, starting with the family and extending outward. The best life, for those with superior ability and (especially) virtue, lies in serving the community as a public official, and rulers should rely first and foremost on "soft power" in the form of ritual, moral exemplars, and persuasion, with legal punishment as a last resort.[3]

The Daoist thinker Zhuangzi, writing in the Warring States period (fourth century BCE), criticized the Confucian overemphasis on conventional morality and mainstream ways of life on the grounds it gives rise to hypocrites and posers. According to historian Sima Qian, Zhuangzi turned down a job offer from King Wei of Chu because he valued his personal freedom (or carefree way of life).[4] Rather than being bound by social ties and conventional morality, we should be skeptical about intellectual knowledge and claims of right and wrong expressed in ordinary language and let ourselves be carried by an inner power that flows with the Way. For the sage, it means internal freedom of heart and mind to the point that suffering from extreme hardship might not be experienced as hardship, similar to Stoic slaves who can transcend their social condition by feeling free "inside" in a state of unfreedom "outside." But Zhuangzi recognizes that it's much easier to be free if one is less attached to social entanglements in the earthly world, and the less the quest for recognition and reputation, the better:[5] politics in particular is a dangerous game, and the intellectual should steer clear to the extent possible. Similar to Buddhist ideas, the aim is to free oneself from social attachments that cause suffering (though Zhuangzi may have been more pessimistic regarding the possibility of completely transcending social relations). Hence, we can infer that Zhuangzi would oppose any state efforts to enforce family harmony, such as forcing adult children to support elderly parents and forcing people to stay married even if they seek to divorce.[6]

In this chapter, I imagine a discussion between a descendant of Kongzi named Kong and a descendant of Zhuangzi named Zhuang over whether moral obligations between family members should be legally enforced.[7] Kong is a professor of family law at the University of Hong Kong and argues that the law can back up moral obligations between family members. Accompanied by several of his students, Kong travels to the outlying island of Cheung Chau to try to persuade his old primary school friend Zhuang of his views. They meet in a bar. Zhuang is Hong Kong's most famous poet but shies away from any public events and lives as a recluse on the remote island. The two interlocutors present some key ideas and establish their philosophical orientations before addressing policy issues. Kong defends the ideal of social harmony and applies it to the family context: he thinks harmony should come from the heart but that legal and political institutions can be designed so as to facilitate the realization of the ideal. In practice, it means a legal obligation to provide material support for elderly parents and a lengthy waiting period with compulsory outside mediation before couples can break their marriage bond. Zhuang disagrees and opposes any attempt by the state to limit personal freedom. Kong's students Zizhang, Zigong, Zilu, Ran Qiu, Zihua, Zeng Xi, Zixia, and Yan Hui interject with questions and comments and provide mini-summaries along the way, all the while supplying both interlocutors with plenty of alcohol. Zhuang will fall unconscious on the table so as to enter (or exit) the dream world and then, in a hypnagogic state, will surprise Kong with his concluding statement.

1. Confucius on Harmony

The term "Confucianism" is somewhat misleading because it suggests that Confucius is the founding father of the tradition, similar to Buddha in Buddhism. In Chinese, however, there are no such misunderstandings because the thinker is called Kongzi ("Master Kong") and the tradition is called *Rujia* (School of the Gentle).[8] Kongzi himself viewed himself as the transmitter of an older tradition and went out of his way to emphasize that he taught nothing new: "I transmit rather than innovate. I trust in and love the ancient ways."[9] He loved the ways of the ancient Zhou and thought politics was in disarray in his own day. But Kongzi was not a blind follower of old ways. He reinterpreted ancient ideas to make them more relevant for his day: for example, the term *junzi* had referred to family members of aristocratic descent, but he (re)deployed the term to refer to those with superior ability and (especially) virtue. He deliberately did not supply full arguments to his students—"If I hold up one corner of a problem, and the student cannot come back to me with the other three, I will not repeat myself"[10]—because he thought they should think for themselves. He said different things to different students—appearing, at times, to contradict himself[11]—because he realized students have different needs and interests and need to be taught in unique ways. An ethical theory, however, does emerge from Kongzi's scattered sayings. He thinks we should aim to minimize the gap between what we want to do and what we ought to do, though it takes a lifetime of studying great works and training by such means as participation in rituals that clarify social roles and generate a sense of bonding. What we ought to do involves fulfilling our social roles, starting with the family, and extending outward, though with diminishing love and care as one moves further away from the circle of intimates. In a good society, people would strive for harmonious social relations, meaning that conflict would be dealt with in a nonviolent way and diversity would be respected if not celebrated. Diversity is important both for aesthetic reasons—it makes the world more beautiful—and for moral reasons—it opens up new possibilities of human flourishing. The best form of life involves serving the political community because those who exercise power can do the greatest good in the world, assuming they wield the power in morally justified ways. That's why Kongzi roamed from state to state trying to persuade rulers to improve their ways, though without much success. At the end of his life, he settled for the life of a teacher, though he didn't foresee that his ideas transmitted qua teacher would have such great influence (more so, arguably, than if had he achieved political success in his own day, with less time for teaching).

It took nearly four centuries, but his ideas finally had a political impact in the Han dynasty when Emperor Han Wudi (156–87 BCE), influenced by political adviser Dong Zhongshu, adopted Confucianism as the official government ideology. As often happens, Kongzi's ideas (and those of the two other most influential pre-Qin Confucians, Mengzi and Xunzi) became somewhat diluted once they were officially endorsed by power holders and Confucian morality became mixed with Legalist "realpolitik" for much of subsequent imperial Chinese history.[12] Nonetheless, the tradition continued to develop as an ethical system with critical power. During the Wei-Jin period that followed the Han, scholar-officials such as Wang Bi who identified with Confucianism sought to establish a Daoist-inspired Way that could provide order without Legalist policies that emphasize political control by means of rewards and punishments.[13] In the Song dynasty, great scholars such as Zhu Xi developed a strong metaphysical foundation for Confucian ethics, partly in response to the Buddhist challenge at the time, and sought to promote his ideas via a system of independent schools separate from the official examination system (though Zhu Xi's own critical vision became somewhat diluted when his interpretation of the Confucian classics became the content of imperial examinations for public officials in the Ming and Qing dynasties). The Confucian tradition came under attack after the collapse of the imperial system in 1912, when many Chinese intellectuals and reformers blamed the tradition for China's economic, scientific, and military "backwardness" relative to Western powers. The tradition of antitraditionalism reached its apogee in the Cultural Revolution when Kongzi was officially attacked by the Chinese state. To the surprise of many observers, however, Confucianism has mounted a huge comeback over the past four decades. Political leaders often invoke the tradition in official speeches, and the state-sponsored Confucius Institutes are meant to spread Chinese language and culture abroad. The opening ceremony of the Beijing Olympics in 2008 featured the saying from the *Analects* that welcoming friends from abroad is delightful (1.1), and the character for "harmony" (和) was showcased as representative of the best of Chinese culture (Marx was absent from the ceremony).[14] In academia, there has been a huge explosion of works on Kongzi and the Confucian tradition in Chinese, English, and other languages, along with work that compares the rich and diverse Confucian tradition with other traditions such as Legalism, Daoism, Buddhism, Christianity, liberalism, feminism, and socialism. Some of the work is intellectual history, and new archaeological records from over two millennia continue to be excavated to this day. Other works are more normative in orientation, with scholars drawing on the Confucian tradition for critical purposes and to put forward ideas for improving society. Notwithstanding increased censorship in mainland China, Chinese scholars are still relatively free to work out diverse interpretations of the tradition, though some predict that categorical endorsement of the Confucian tradition by the Chinese Communist Party would be the "kiss of death" for the academic development of the tradition because interpretations that deviate from the official interpretation would be banned (similar to what happened to Marxism in China).[15] Fortunately, there is still more academic freedom in Hong Kong compared to mainland China, and this dialogue is set in Hong Kong, on the assumption that things won't take a dramatic turn for the worse in the foreseeable future.

Let's now turn to the (fictitious) dialogue between descendants of Kongzi and Zhuangzi about whether moral obligations between adult family members can be legally enforced in such cases as filial piety and the commitment to maintaining marriage ties.

[Zhuang arrives at the bar for the prearranged meeting, twenty-five minutes late.]

Kong (gets up to greet his old friend): So happy to see you! "Is it not delightful to have friends come from afar?"[16]

Zhuang (suppressing his joy): Not so far. My home is a half hour walk from here. It has indeed been a long time. What have you been up to these years?

Kong: I'm an old man now and it's been quite a journey. Rather than tell the boring story—my jobs, my family, etc.—let me report a story of moral progress . . . (Zhuang assumes a skeptical expression) . . . "At fifteen, I set my mind upon learning; at thirty, I took my stance; at forty, I became free of doubts; at fifty, I realized the propensities of higher morality; at sixty, my ear was attuned; and at seventy, I could follow my heart's desires without overstepping the boundaries."[17] As I got older, my capacity for moral judgment improved and I could act better, morally speaking. Pardon me if this sounds pompous, but I've now reached the point where I can effortlessly do what I want without violating the standards of morality.

Zhuang: That took a long time. I recall you were quite the wild one, with a soft spot for alcohol. You said that you could "enjoy alcohol without limits."[18]

Kong (somewhat defensively): Yes, and though I had a good "drinking ability,"[19] I never drank "to the point of disorderliness."[20]

[Zigong serves fiery white liquor to both Kong and Zhuang. Kong tries to clink glasses but Zhuang fails to notice and downs his liquor. Kong performs the toasting ritual with his students, who lower their glasses as they clink the glass of their teacher.][21]

Zhuang: So why did it take so long to reach the point where there's no conflict between what you want to do and what you ought to do?

Kong: Well, I don't have to tell you that sexual impulses can get in the way of morality, especially for younger men. "In youth, [our] physical vitality has not settled, so the thing to guard against is lust."[22]

Zhuang: And did you succeed at guarding against lust?

Kong: It's not easy. Frankly speaking, "I've yet to meet anyone who loves virtue as much as sex."[23] . . . (Zeng Xi laughs) . . . Fortunately, old men like me are less enslaved by sexual desire. I'm still human—my desire for sex has not been completely extinguished—but it's easier to control and subordinate to morality, or at least, I no longer experience a conflict between the desire for sex and the desire for morality.

Zhuang: Eunuchs in Chinese history were notorious for power-hungry scheming and corrupt behavior. It seems castration didn't work if the aim was to promote moral behavior.

Kong: Of course, diminished sexual desire is not the whole story. How can we make moral progress? At the very least, we need to commit ourselves to learning from the great works of the past. Studying what the greats have thought and said can give us ideas to improve the way we lead our lives. And the more we read, the more ideas we have. Learning is a process of accumulating knowledge, including ethical knowledge, that ends only with death: "Be genuinely trustworthy and fond of learning, and adhere to the good Way firmly to death." . . . (looking at his students) . . . We must never slacken our efforts: "Learn as if you could not reach it fast enough, and as if you fear you might lose it again."[24]

Zhuang: I've lost most of what I learned. Perhaps it's my bad memory, which gets worse as I age.

Kong: But learning is not just an intellectual exercise: "Is it not satisfying to learn and then have occasion to practice what you have learned?"[25] It's a long process, but the main idea is not so complicated.

Zigong: Professor, "is there one word that one can practice throughout one's life?"

Kong: There are no magic tricks. But if we need to choose one word, "is it not 'reciprocity'? What you yourself do not desire, do not do onto others."[26]

Zilu: That doesn't sound so challenging: all I need to do is think about what I desire and do not desire and apply it to others.[27] Why can't young people do that? Professor, with all due respect, I'm not clear why it took you so long to reach the point where you could follow your heart's desire without overstepping the bounds of morality.

Kong (silent laugh): Zilu, it's much more complicated. Reciprocity is not a simple matter of applying our desires. Nor is reciprocity an abstract concept that applies to humans shorn of particularity. It's a relation between two social roles.[28] So reciprocity requires familiarity with the desires that are characteristic of social roles. And that takes a lifetime to learn. We need to experience various social roles to have a good sense of the specific desires that characterize those roles. It's not just that I should treat my son in the same way that I want my son to treat me. What I should do is treat my *father* in the same way I would want to be treated by my son. But it's not easy. I have my regrets. "I have not been able to serve my father as I demand my son. . . . I have not been able to serve my elder brother as I demand of my younger brother. I have not been able to do unto my friends first as I demand of them."[29] Still, one makes progress over time. We need to think about the moral demands of various social roles and do our best to adhere to those demands. But it's easier to think of those demands if we have occupied those social roles and experienced them in our own lives. And the elderly are more likely to have experienced different roles and forms of life that increase the capacity for moral judgment. We learn by participating in different roles and the wider the life experience, the greater the likelihood that one has developed the capacity for good moral judgment in this or that particular situation.

Zhuang (drily): I may have regressed from a moral point of view over the years, not sure how to explain that.

Kong: My dear friend, don't be too hard on yourself. But it's hard to progress if one leads the life of a recluse. "'Dwelling in seclusion in order to pursue one's aspirations, practicing rightness in order to realize the Way': I have heard such words, but have yet to see such a person."[30] We must stay socially engaged to progress. For one thing, it's a matter of deepening experience in particular roles: for example, as a teacher concerned with moral improvement, I learn from my mistakes and deal with a wide range of students and teaching materials, and I become a better teacher.

Zhuang: I tried teaching but didn't like it. The more I did it, the more boring and repetitive it became. I prefer writing poetry without any students to "instruct."

Kong (ignoring Zhuang's comment): It's also a matter of learning from new roles, some of which can be undertaken only later in life. Caring for elderly parents, for example, is a key aspect of learning by doing: "Filial and fraternal responsibility is the root of humaneness."[31] But the young can rarely practice filial piety: the parents care for the children rather than the other way around. Parents are more likely to need care as they get older, so it's usually adults that can really begin to seriously practice filial piety. And reverence for elderly parents extends to caring for them after they have already died: "Sacrifice as if [the spirits of your ancestors were] present, means that, when sacrificing to the spirits, you should comport yourself as if the spirits were present."[32]

Zhuang: What do you mean "as if" they were present? I like this idea of pretending, but do you really believe that our dead parents become "spirits"?

Kong: I have nothing to say about "spirits."[33] I have no idea what really happens after we die; understanding this life is complicated enough. In any case, we need to sacrifice to our parents, even after they passed away, with an attitude of appreciation and awe, the sort of attitude that can be extended to the world of the living. Again, however, it's not something available to young people with healthy parents. Only the elderly are likely to have the necessary experience that allows for the enlargement of empathy and humaneness.

Zhuang: It seems you've become more spiritual, and less political. It's all about self-improvement. What happened? You were very ambitious as a young man.

Kong: Well, I served in government, as you may know. But I failed to persuade rulers to support my plans for radical political reform inspired by the ways of the ancients. I still think politics is the highest calling: those in power have the power to do the greatest good, assuming, of course, that they are committed to morality. "One who excels in learning should then devote himself to official service." But "if the Way is not put into practice, I will set off upon the sea in a small raft." Basically, my view is that "if the Way is being realized in the world, then show yourself; if it is not, then go into reclusion."[34] I don't blame you for living in solitude, my friend, these are not the best of times. If our leaders are not committed to implementing the Way, there's no point in serving them. It's best to withdraw from public life.

Zhuang: But if they are implementing the Way, is there a need for advisers like you?

Kong: In an ideal world, I'd be superfluous: "If the Way were realized in the world, then I would not need to change anything." But morality is rarely all or nothing. Most of the time, the world is neither wholly good nor wholly bad, and we should try to make it better. So long as there's a bit of hope, one should serve the public if the opportunity presents itself. "To avoid public service is to be without a sense of right. . . . Exemplary persons take office in order to do what is right, even though they already know that the Way is not [yet] realized."[35] Even if it's impossible to serve at the highest level of government, there may be opportunities to serve at local levels.[36] And most rulers are partly good and partly bad. They can do better, so advisers committed to morality in politics can help to improve the status quo. Even if the rulers are sages, they need advisers to help them implement the Way.

Zhuang: Well, it may not be a bad thing that you didn't realize your political aspirations: most politicians are hypocrites and posers. The downside is that you missed out on fame and fortune.

Kong (somewhat defensively): People who go into politics should not be motivated by self-interest. "Exemplary persons seek the Way rather than food." Nor should they be motivated by the quest for power. Most people in politics, unfortunately, go in for the wrong reasons. "When they have not obtained what they want, they worry about how to get [power]. When they have got it, they worry about losing it. Whey they worry about losing it, there is nothing they won't do."[37] . . . (cautiously, lowers his voice) . . . Think of the certain leaders, they hang onto power far too long.

Zizhang: Professor, if I understand correctly, you believe in moral progress.[38] As one gets older, sexual desire gets less in the way of what we ought to do from a moral point of view, and we should morally improve so long as we remain actively committed to learning and we experience new roles and deepen our experience in particular roles. You also think we should go into politics if there is an opportunity to improve the world. But professor, "what must a person be like in order to be qualified to engage in government?"

Kong: "Uphold five excellences and banish four vices, a person like that may be engaged in government."

Zizhang: "What are the five excellences?"

Kong: "Exemplary persons are beneficent without being wasteful, they put people to work without causing resentment, they have desires but are not greedy, they maintain dignified ease without being arrogant, and they are commanding without being fierce."

Zizhang: "What is meant by being beneficent without being wasteful?"

Kong: "To benefit the people where they can be benefited, is this not beneficent without being wasteful? To choose those who can labor to put to work, who will have resentment? To desire humaneness and obtain humaneness, how is this being greedy? Exemplary persons, whether in dealing with many people or few, or with things great or small, dare not take them lightly, is this not having dignified ease without being arrogant? Exemplary persons dress their robes and caps correctly, adopt a respectful gaze, and have an air of dignity so people look upon them with awe: is this not being commanding without being fierce?"

Zizhang: "What are the four vices?"

Kong: "To execute those who have not been educated is called cruelty. To expect success from those who have not given advance counsel is called impetuous. To be tardy in issuing orders yet abruptly issue time limits is called detrimental. To be stingy when it comes to disbursing funds and rewarding people is called officious."[39]

Zhuang: How can you know all that if you didn't achieve the political success you had hoped for?

Kong: My friend, I've spent decades reading books on politics and history.

Zhuang: Oh, yes, of course. . . . (teasingly) . . . I suspect you're hoping that you'd be in one of them, that the history books of the future will mention you as well.

Kong: Well, I won't deny that. "The exemplary person is troubled by the possibility that his name will go uncelebrated after his death."[40]

Zhuang (shaking his head): So vain, so vain. . . .

Kong: My point is that one shouldn't seek fame in this life. One can achieve posthumous fame, assuming the Way, or part of it, eventually prevails.

Zhuang: You seem to be pursuing contradictory aims. Now you're old—as I am—and you say you can effortlessly act in accordance with the demands of morality. You just follow your desires and the right outcomes will magically emerge from your actions. Yet you also value politics as the highest vocation. But politics is a dirty business, it requires endless discussion among competing interests, reluctant compromise, twisting arms, threats, and maybe even some killing. It's not a business for a self-satisfied old man like yourself. It's time to say goodbye to politics, my friend.

Zigong (defending his professor): "Had [my professor] acquired control of a state or noble family, then, as they say: 'When he raised them up, they would stand; when he led them forward, they would advance; when he comforted them, they would come, and when he moved them, they would become harmonious.'"[41]

Kong (laughing): Please don't exaggerate, Zigong. I wish I had those abilities. But I do agree that political leaders should strive to secure social harmony among the people.

Zhuang: That sounds dangerous to me. North Korea seems like a harmonious society: everyone thinks alike and marches according to a common drum. Not sure I'd want to live in that kind of society.

Kong: Neither would I. By "harmony" I mean diverse elements that coexist peacefully, not blind sameness or uniformity. "Exemplary persons harmonize but do not conform, whereas the petty-minded conform but do not harmonize."[42] It's my Legalist enemies who seek ideological conformity,[43] but that's not what I mean by harmony.[44]

Zigong: Professor, I'm still not clear what you mean by "harmony."

Kong: It's easier to think clearly via examples from the past. Please recall what the Duke of Qi said in the *Spring and Autumn Annals*: "Harmony is like making soup. Water, fire, vinegar, minced meat and plum are used to cook the fish and meat. They are heated using firewood and brought into harmony by the chef, who uses the different flavors to achieve a balance, providing what is deficient and releasing what it excessive. The exemplary person eats the soup, and it will calm and settle his mind." The same goes for music. It's only beautiful if diverse notes are brought together in a harmonious way. Conversely, "who can listen to monotonic sound made by musical instruments?"

Zigong: That makes good sense! Bringing diverse things together, creating something new out of different parts, makes our world less boring and more beautiful. . . . But what does this have to do with politics?

Kong: Consider the relation between a ruler and a minister. "When the ruler's judgment is basically right, there may still be some reasons for opposing it. The minister offers the opposing reasons, in order to complete the rightness of the ruler. When the ruler's judgment is basically wrong, there may be reasons for thinking so. The minister offers the reasons for thinking so, in order to reject the ruler's wrong judgment."[45] The minister should allow for diverse views, including critical views, it's the only way to identify mistaken policies and allow for progress. Conversely, if the government is composed of conformist "yes-men," it's the end of the political system. "People have a saying, 'I take no joy in being a ruler, except that no one dares to oppose what I say.' If what the ruler says is good, and no one opposes him, is this not good? On the other hand, if what he says is not good, and no one opposes him, does this not come close to being a single saying that can cause a state to perish?"[46] In politics, "diversity in harmony" is a moral imperative: it allows for the government to correct its mistakes and it opens more possibilities, so that we can progress. It's too late for me, but if my students go into politics, I hope they will keep in mind the imperative to strive for social harmony.

Zhuang: You surprised me by coming with so many students. Are you sure they all want to go into politics to promote harmony?

Kong: I can't tell my students what to do. Why don't we ask them about their political ideals? My dear students, "if someone were to recognize your worth, what would you do?"

Zilu (replying immediately): "A state of a thousand [tanks], set in between powerful states, let us suppose that it also suffers from invading armies, and on top of that, is plagued by famine—if I were to govern it, in three years I could make the people courageous and have a sense of direction."[47]

Kong (smiling at Zilu): Ran Qiu, "what about you?"

Ran Qiu: "A state of sixty to seventy *li* square, or one of fifty to sixty *li* square—if I were to govern it, in three years I could make the people have adequate supplies. As for ritual propriety and the musical arts, they would have to wait for the arrival of exemplary persons."

Kong: "What about you," Zihua?

Zihua: "I am not saying that I can do it, but I am willing to learn. At the services of the ancestral temple, and at the meetings of sovereigns, dressed in ceremonial robes and a cap, I am willing to serve as a minor protocol officer."

Kong: Zeng Xi, "what about you?"

Zeng Xi (Slowing down the strumming of his zither, and as the final twang was fading, Zeng Xi laid the instrument aside and rose up.): "My wishes are different from what the other three have stated."

Kong: "What harm is in that? Each person speaks his own aspirations. That is all."

Zeng Xi: "In late spring, in full springtime regalia, I would like to take along five or six young men and six or seven boys, to bathe in the Yi River, enjoy the breeze in the Rain Altar, and then return home singing."

Kong (heaving a big sigh): "I am with [Zeng Xi]."

Zhuang: Me too! He aims to develop his inner cultivation rather than striving for concrete plans and showing commitment to politics. He appreciates nature and strives for "individual contact with the spirits of the universe."[48]

[Upset, Zilu, Ran Qiu, and Zihua go to the bar to order more drinks.]

Kong: Is that what you mean, Zeng Xi?

Zeng Xi (nervously): Not exactly, I experience joy with my friends, not alone. But why, professor, "did you smile at [Zilu]"?

Kong: "One must observe ritual propriety to govern a state, yet his words were not modest. That is why I smiled at him."[49]

Zeng Xi: "Was [Ran] Qiu not speaking of governing a state?"

Kong: "Who says a territory of sixty to seventy *li* square or fifty to sixty *li* square cannot be a state?"

Zeng Xi: "Was [Zihua] not speaking of governing a state?"

Kong: "Who else but rulers of states have to do with ancestral temples and meetings of sovereigns? If he took his aspiration as small, what would be considered big then?"[50]

Zeng Xi (relieved): That's my view, too. Just because we are not pulling the highest levers of the state doesn't mean that we don't care about political commitment. I bring my friends to swim and sing to forge the social harmony that my professor mentions as foundational to politics.[51]

Kong: Well put, Zeng Xi. Social harmony underpins trust between the leaders and the people and nothing matters more than trust for purposes of governance.

Zigong: Professor, can you elaborate? What is the key to good governance?

Kong: It's not too complicated. "Make sure there is sufficient food to eat, sufficient arms for defense, and that the common people trust their leaders."

Zigong: "If you had to give up one these three things, which should be given up first?"

Kong: "Give up the arms."

Zigong: "If you have to give up one of the remaining two, which should be given up first?"

Kong: "Give up the food. Death has always been with us, but a state cannot endure if the common people do not trust their leaders."[52] I like Zeng Xi's response because informal social interaction among intimates fosters social harmony and reduces the need for reliance on force and punishment to secure social order, and in turn the people are more likely to trust their leaders, which is the key to good governance in the long term. Strange as it may sound, good governance rests on singing, dancing, and swimming.

Zhuang: I'd add fishing to this list.

Zeng Xi: My professor's point is that social harmony is foundational: it's the necessary context for "higher" forms of morally defensible political activity. Zilu thinks he can govern the state and change it just by the force of his personality and correct policies, but he ignores the social harmony that can render those policies effective. Political commitment involves everything from governing the state to informal interaction among intimates, and the latter is, in some sense more foundational.

Kong: I'd add that music is especially important. It's an expression of harmony, and it generates a sense of harmony among participants. "What can be known about music is this: when it first begins, it resounds with a confusing variety of notes, but as it unfolds, these notes are reconciled by means of harmony, brought into tension by means of counterpoint, and finally woven together into a seamless whole. It is in this way that music reaches its perfection." Here too, I try to practice what I preach. Or, more precisely, I just do it. Whenever I "am singing in a group and hear something that I like, I ask to have it sung again, and only then would harmonize with it."[53]

Zhuang: My friend, I'm not sure we are so different. We all like to have a good time.

Zeng Xi (refilling Zhuang's empty cup): Mr. Zhuang, we do need to take seriously what my professor says about politics and harmony. Political actors need to do their best to promote "diversity in harmony" because it has aesthetic, moral, and political benefits. It makes the world more beautiful, it opens possibilities of human flourishing, and it allows for criticism of mistaken policies. Professor Kong says exemplary persons should go into politics, but if the times are not propitious, it's fine to seek social harmony at lower levels of society because it contributes to social trust and allows for progress toward a kind of political order that doesn't depend on force and fear of punishment. So even those who sing and dance and create joy among friends make an important contribution to politics!

Kong: Well put, Zeng Xi, but let me clarify: I didn't mean to imply singing is sufficient for producing a harmonious society. Even more important, at the base of a political community, is the family, it's where most people first learn about and practice morality. Those who fulfill family duties, who make the family more harmonious, are contributing to harmony in society. It's a political act: "in being a filial son and a good brother, one is already taking part in government."[54] Think about it: "If exemplary persons are kind to their relatives, the people will aspire to humaneness."[55] Harmonious families underpin harmonious societies, both because people in harmonious families "won't be fond of stirring up chaos"[56] and because they set a good model of harmony for people at large.

[Zilu, Ran Qiu, and Zihua return with drinks for the group.]

Zhuang: I'm not sure you want to go that route. I'd suggest freeing the self from commitments to the extent possible. Once we start having too many commitments, they will conflict and our lives will be miserable. Which commitment should have priority in cases of conflict, the family or the political community?

Kong: Yes, we can't escape conflict, it's part of the human condition, and we need to think about bringing diverse commitments into some sort of harmonious relation that minimizes the negative effects of conflict.

Zhuang: It's not so easy. Conflicts arise naturally and it's very hard to find ways of resolving them. For example, what if a family member breaks the law? It seems that you would have to choose between family harmony and harmony in the state.

Kong: In those cases, I think the better choice is usually to put family harmony first. The Duke of She told me, "Among my people there is one we call 'Upright Gong.' When his father stole a sheep, he reported him to the authorities." That's the view of the Legalists, for whom the state has priority over family obligations. It was realized in the Cultural Revolution, when children were encouraged to denounce their parents who were not "politically correct." You won't be surprised to hear that's not what I favor. "Among my people, those we consider 'upright' are different from this: fathers cover up for their sons, and sons cover up for their fathers. 'Uprightness' is to be found in this."[57]

Zhuang: It's upright to steal a sheep? Why would somebody want to steal a sheep?

Kong: Exactly, that's what we need to ask. It's not such a serious crime, and a loving child needs to ask what motivated the act rather than denouncing his father to the authorities. Perhaps the father suffers from Alzheimer's and thought he found his long-lost pet and the sheep can be returned to the owner. Perhaps it was a prank. If the father was hungry and stole the sheep for food, then the son should reflect upon why the father was on the verge of starvation: obviously the son wasn't fulfilling his duties of filial care. Or maybe the sheep wandered onto the family property and it had yet to be noticed by the father.[58] In any case, my main point is that the way to secure harmony starts with the family and state interference often undermines family harmony. We should err on the side of protecting the family from state interference if there is any doubt. My view should not be too controversial. For example, in common-law jurisdictions, including Hong Kong, we have "spousal testimonial privilege": with the exception of rare circumstances, spouses cannot be forced to testify against each other.[59]

Zilu: But professor Kong, you make it sound like the state should not be involved in family affairs. My view is that the state can help to promote obligations between family members.

Kong: I agree, to a certain extent. Parents have a legal obligation to care for their children. It's a moral obligation first and foremost, and the state need not use the strong arm of the law to enforce it, but I don't think there's any legal jurisdiction that would not punish parents if, say, they let their children starve to death. To protect children, moral obligations need to be backed up by law. Between adults, however, it's a different story. We need to be cautious about forcing adult members of the family to care for each other. Family harmony needs to come from the heart.

Zilu: Professor, as you know, here in Hong Kong, the government encourages the practice of at-home care for the elderly: adult taxpayers get a tax deduction if they live with elderly parents and grandparents for a period of at least six months, and they get a bigger break if it's continuous for a year.[60] Are you against that?

Kong: No. As a community, we strongly value filial piety and the government can sometimes help to nourish the practice via indirect methods that people do not find to be too burdensome.[61] So if the state provides tax breaks for maintaining the practice of at-home care of the elderly, and people are generally supportive of this policy, then it seems like a reasonable use of state power. But we need to be cautious about using force to secure family harmony. "If you guide the people with coercive regulations and keep them in line with punishments, the people will become evasive and will have no conscience. If, however, you guide them with virtue, and keep them in order by means of ritual, the people will have a conscience and will rectify themselves."[62] So if the state forces adult children to be filial, people may come to think of filial piety as something that's forced rather than being motivated by love, family members will become resentful of each other, and harmony between family members will be undermined.

Zilu (doing a quick internet search): Sometimes we need force. In mainland China, filial piety is compulsory. According to *The Law of the People's Republic of China on Protection for Rights and Interests of Older Persons,* "supporters of the elderly shall fulfill the obligations of providing for the elderly economically, taking care of them in daily life and comforting them mentally, and attend to their special needs."[63] This law aligns with the idea that adult children need to provide financial and emotional care for their elderly parents.

Kong: Well, that seems problematic. How can you force adult children to comfort their elderly parents mentally? Not all parents are ideal, unfortunately. "Rare are those who understand virtue."[64] In cases of dysfunctional family relationships, especially when children are in relationships with abusive parents, we can't expect adult children to comfort their elderly parents mentally or provide emotional support. Forcing them to do so won't be effective and it may be counterproductive; the adult children will become even more resentful.

Zixia: Professor Kong, I'm a bit confused. How exactly do you expect adult children to carry out the obligations of filial piety?

Kong: "It is the demeanor that is difficult. If there is work to be done, the young should shoulder the burden, and when wine and food are served, elders should take precedence, but surely filial piety consists of more than this."[65] If the adult child is not motivated by a willing heart while caring for his or her elderly parents, the internal emotional state will be revealed in his or her features. The state can't force people to be filial in this sense.

Zilu: But the law in mainland China also calls for "providing for the elderly economically." I think it's a good idea. Here in Hong Kong you see elderly people doing hard menial labor such as collecting cardboard boxes that they sell for pennies at recycling outlets. Shouldn't their adult children be forced to support their own parents?

Kong: Perhaps. If the elderly parents are in need, and if the adult children can afford it, then they can be forced to provide minimal material support.[66] I think Singapore more or less has the right balance and the law says nothing about mental or emotional support. According to the "Maintenance of Parents Act," residents aged sixty or above who are unable to subsist on their own can claim maintenance from their children. There is an assumption that since the parents supported their children when they were young, the elderly parents can claim something in exchange when they are elderly.

Zhuang: So it's okay for parents to sue their children for lack of maintenance. What if the children were abused or neglected when they were young?

Kong: According to the law in Singapore, the maintenance claim can be dismissed if the children can prove they were abused.[67]

Zhuang: What if the children don't like their elderly parents?

Kong: That's not relevant from a legal perspective. We can't expect the state to investigate the extent of loving relations between family members as a condition for material support.

Zhuang (gasps): The more I hear from you, the more I worry. How do you force adults to care for each other if they dislike each other?

Kong: Material support for elderly parents is the minimal obligation of filial piety. At the end of the day, adult children should be motivated by an affectionate bond for their parents that seems natural to them, and they can't be forced to do so. Again, the ultimate aim should be to nourish loving, harmonious bonds between family members. We need to be open minded about the role of the state interference: sometimes it can help, sometimes it can hurt. The point is to encourage, or at least not undermine, harmony between adult children and elderly parents. The same goes for relations between spouses: the government should aim to promote harmony between a married couple and if it involves legal constraints on, say, the right to divorce, then we need to allow for that possibility.

Zhuang (downing his cup): And what if there's no harmony between spouses?

Kong: Now, that's interesting. You may have heard I've been involved in a public debate in Hong Kong regarding change of the family law. Frankly, one of the reasons I came to see you is to enlist your support for the cause.

Zhuang: I'm afraid I don't follow the news.

Kong: Here's the issue. It's about divorce law. The surprise is that the law in Hong Kong is less liberal, in the sense that it imposes more constraints on individual freedom, compared to the law in mainland China. Some people in Hong Kong want to liberalize our law so that it conforms to that in mainland China, where people can easily get divorced so long as both spouses agree.[68] It's basically a right to divorce after a thirty-day "cooling-off period," which is much too short, almost like a right to instant divorce.[69] In Hong Kong, it's not so easy. Parties can divorce after a one-year separation with consent and after two years without consent.[70] But I think divorce should be made harder, not easier: once the marriage bond is broken, it's almost impossible to restore harmony in the family, and the effects for others—not least, the children in the marriage—are often disastrous. It's a recipe for chaos in society.

Zhuang (puzzled): I thought you were against the idea that the state can force people to be harmonious? How can there be social harmony if people are forced to be harmonious?

Kong: Indeed, we can't use legal punishments to secure social harmony. As I said, "If you guide the people with coercive regulations and keep them in line with punishments, the people will become evasive and will have no conscience."

Zhuang: So why would you want to use law to make people stay married if they want out?

Kong: Ideally, there would be no litigation. "In hearing civil litigation, I am no different from any other person. But if you insist on a difference, it is, perhaps, that I try to get the parties not to resort to litigation in the first place."[71] So, yes, in an ideal world, we'd all be exemplary persons and there would be no need for laws backed by legal punishments: "Someone who is broadly learned with regard to culture, and whose conduct is restrained by the rites, can be counted upon not to go astray." Unfortunately, we don't live in an ideal world. Not everyone is an exemplary person who "attacks the bad qualities in his or herself rather than the badness in others."[72] Many people prefer to attack their spouse if they experience conflict. It's not uncommon to go astray, if by that we mean adultery. Regrettably, petty-minded people can't always be motivated by virtue. Basically, there are two types of people: "Exemplary persons who are persuaded by what is right and petty persons who are persuaded by what is profitable."[73] And most people are not exemplary. So we still need laws as backup mechanisms in case people's behavior can't be regulated by conscience.

Zhuang: Sounds odd to me. Are there really two types of people? What evidence do you have to support such claims?

Kong: I frame it that way, but I don't mean to imply there are clear qualitative differences between people, and more importantly, people can improve. It's often a quantitative difference and the needle between other-regarding morality and self-interested profit can move one way or the other.

Zhuang: Is the difference between a quantitative difference and a qualitative difference a quantitative difference or a qualitative difference?[74]

Kong (laughs): That's a clever joke, my friend.

Zhuang: Are you an "exemplary person"?

Kong (modestly): I'm afraid not, though I strive to do my best, which gets easier as I get older, as mentioned. It's easier to improve intellectually than to improve morally. "When it comes to cultural refinement, I am no less than others. But as for becoming an exemplary person in practice, this is something I have not yet been able to achieve."[75] . . . (assumes a more somber expression) . . . I myself have divorced. I didn't set a very good example: my son and grandson also divorced.[76] So I do think we need laws regulating imperfect people in an imperfect society. But people should not be granted a right to instant divorce. They need to reflect upon their relation, do their best to restore family harmony, and if they fail after a certain period—say, two years—then they can divorce.[77]

Zhuang: Two years! I'm surprised you want to force people to stay together for that long! I thought you were against using the law to enforce morality, but it turns out you have authoritarian instincts. How can harmony be restored if it has already broken down?

Kong: Here too, I think we can learn from the past. In traditional China, mediation rather than litigation was the preferred means of dispute settlement in ordinary civil disputes.[78] Instead of judging the dispute and imposing a binding judgment on the parties, officials would mediate the dispute and search for a solution that was agreeable to the disputants. The ultimate aim was the reconciliation of the disputants to each other and hence the restoration of the family harmony that had been temporarily breached by the conflict. Of course, the government was not so sensitive to power imbalances in the past and sometimes the weaker parties in the dispute, especially women, felt coerced to agree. But today we have a better sense of how mediation can treat parties fairly, and spouses should be given the opportunity to sort out their differences, to improve mutual communication, understanding, and trust, and hopefully restore some sort of harmony, and perhaps even achieve a different and higher kind of harmony, before they break their marriage vows. In Hong Kong, solicitors advising clients on matrimonial proceedings are required to inform them of the availability of a mediation service. But Hong Kong law does not require parties to attempt mediation before the divorce cases go to court.[79]

Zhuang: And you think people should be forced to undergo mediation?

Kong: Yes, if the mediators are fair-minded and well-trained and if there is no domestic violence involved.[80] And the state should provide that service for free. Sometimes it takes a third party to remind couples of the ties that bind them together. That's what I've been arguing in the media, and I'm hoping you can join my efforts to make it harder, rather than easier, for spouses to divorce. But I'm not here as a missionary. I want to hear more from you. One can always learn from others. "When walking with two other people, I will always find a teacher among them. I focus on those who are good and seek to emulate them, and focus on those who are bad in order to be reminded of what needs to be changed in myself."[81] So, my friend, please correct me if I'm wrong.

Zhuang: Please correct me if I'm right.

Kong (laughing): I appreciate your dry humor. But I'm serious. Please tell more about your thoughts.

Zeng Xi (interjecting): But first, perhaps you will allow me to summarize my professor's view. Professor Kong thinks harmony in the family is foundational for harmony in society. Most people are not exemplary persons, so harmony doesn't always come naturally: hence, the state's laws should encourage harmony in the family and discourage people from taking actions that lead to disharmony.[82] Of course, at the end of the day, the desire to pursue harmony should come from the inside, so people cannot be forced indefinitely to maintain relationships on the grounds of social harmony. In the case of filial piety, it means that adult children can be forced to provide minimal material support for their parents, even if they feel estranged from their parents, but it would be ineffective or counterproductive to expect that the state can force adult children to serve petty-minded or abusive parents with a sincere, loving demeanor.[83] In the case of divorce law, it means that there should be a waiting period before spouses can divorce and the state can subsidize an experienced mediator to help spouses restore harmony in the family. If the mediator fails after a certain period of time, then people can divorce. The current divorce law in Hong Kong should not be liberalized; in fact, it needs to be toughened so as to allow for the possibility of restoring harmony in the family.

Zhuang (looking forlornly at his empty cup; Zeng Xi immediately refills it): Well, I'm not sure about that; or anything else, for that matter.

2. Zhuangzi on Freedom

The two classical texts of the Daoist tradition are the *Dao De Jing* (The Classic of the Way and Virtue) and the *Zhuangzi*. The *Dao De Jing* is more famous outside of China—according to one estimate, one new English translation is published every month!—but it is terse and brief to the point that anybody can find whatever they are looking for in the text.[84] Next to nothing is known about the supposed author Laozi, and the text may have been addressed to rulers who should govern with minimal interference of society and nature. The *Zhuangzi*, (partly) written around the time of Mengzi in the fourth century BCE, is far longer and richer, arguably from both a philosophical and a literary point of view. The *Dao De Jing* is not directly quoted in the *Zhuangzi*, but similar ideas regarding the Dao (Way) as an amoral, purposeless energy immanent in nature are found in both texts (in contrast to the Confucian view that the Way is a moral path that should serve as the standard for improvement of the human world). The *Zhuangzi* is a composite text of fifty-two chapters, though the first seven "Inner Chapters" have often been ascribed to the historical figure Zhuang Zhou.[85] The short biographical account of Zhuang Zhou by the Han dynasty historian Sima Qian portrayed him as a critic of Confucians and Mohists who refused to be polluted by political office.[86] The *Zhuangzi* is composed of humorous stories and parables that verge on the surreal, with the apparent aim of subverting conventional ways of thinking and moralizing. It is directed at the individual rather than the group or the ruling class and affirms detachment from social and cultural entanglements. To the extent there is a goal, it lies in the realization that there is no goal. All perspectives are relative, and ordinary language is vague and indeterminate. Conscious attempts to pursue morality and social harmony are doomed to fail. Ideally, the self and its projects should be erased to the point that "we" experience a sense of oneness with the ever-changing processes of nature.[87] Such spontaneous, purposeless wanderings are best experienced with maximum freedom from social or political attachments, and death, as yet another unexplained transformation, will be met with equanimity if not joy. Zhuangzi recognizes that we are inevitably bound with some entanglements, such as relations with parents and rulers, but it's possible to navigate social tasks by means of unselfconscious "going with the flow." At the highest levels of politics, however, it's best not to engage. It's not just that, Confucian-style, the political reformer should try to do what's right rather than being motivated by external rewards and seeking approval of others. Politics is a dangerous game, and the naive idealist will be made into minced meat by power hungry rulers: Zhuangzi tells amusing stories that illustrate (what we call today) the law of unintended consequences, of good intentions leading to bad results.

In contrast to the Confucian celebration of family life, attachments between family members are devalued by Zhuangzi, as in the case of an (in)famous passage where he sings joyfully after the death of his wife. It seems safe to infer that Zhuangzi would oppose laws that enforce family harmony and curtail people's freedom to be alone (as we will see, however, Zhuangzi has a way of surprising us). In subsequent Chinese history, Confucian theorizing about the importance of family harmony became mainstream and Zhuangzi's views were relegated to the margins (as, perhaps, he would have wanted). But the text's memorable turns of phrase and vivid imagery had huge impact on succeeding generations of writers, painters, and artists (not to mention failed bureaucrats). Buddhists in China and (later) Japan, especially members of the Zen (Chan) school, were inspired by the non sequiturs and absurdities designed to explore the inadequacies of language,[88] and perhaps more broadly the aim of dissolving the ego/self into nothingness (though, in Zhuangzi's case, without the promise of nirvana). In contemporary China, the *Zhuangzi* often shapes the life plan (or lack thereof) of artists, hermits, rebellious teenagers, and eccentrics, but even those pursuing mainstream ways of life engage with the text: every aspiring university student needs to memorize and interpret the stories of the transforming fish and the dreaming butterfly as preparation for the university entrance examination. Academics widely admire the *Zhuangzi* as a unique work of great genius, and there has been an explosion of translations and interpretations over the past two decades in both English and Chinese.[89]

And now, back to the dialogue.

Zhuang (looking at his old friend): You are I are different. Or perhaps not. You value social relations. I look to Liezi. He "could ride the wind and go soaring around with cool and breezy skill, but after fifteen days he came back to earth. As far as the search for good fortune went, he didn't fret and worry. He escaped the trouble of walking, but still had to depend on something to get around. If he had only mounted on the truth of Heaven and Earth, ridden the changes of the six breaths, and thus wandered through the boundless, then what would he have to depend on?"[90]

Kong (puzzled): I'm not sure I understand. . . .

Zhuang (downing his cup of liquor): I'm not sure *I* understand . . .

Kong (turning to his student): Yan Hui, does this make any sense to you? . . . (turning to Zhuang) . . . "Hui learns one thing and understands ten. I learn one thing and only understand two."[91]

Yan Hui (blushes): Professor, I'm just a student.

Kong: "The young should he held in awe. After all, how do we know that those who come after us will not surpass our contemporaries?"[92] Go on, Yan Hui, try to make sense of what Mr. Zhuang is saying.

Yan Hui (refilling Zhuang's cup of liquor): Perhaps Mr. Zhuang means that we should withdraw from this world. It's best to be as independent as possible and not be tormented by the petty worries of mere mortals. Instead of joining the rat-race—striving for wealth and power, always comparing ourselves to others and trying to best self-perceived rivals—we should turn away from the desires of the social world. . . . (looking at the other students who are busy with their cell phones) . . . Concretely, it might mean tuning-out from social media.

Kong (laughs): If that's what it means, I'm all in favor. But we need to distinguish between good desires for harmonious social relations and bad desires for selfish purposes. And we need learning and education to make such distinctions; it doesn't come naturally. Do you agree, Zhuang?

Zhuang: "When sages wander, knowledge is a curse, restrictions are paste, favors are a patch, and effort is for trade. Sages do not plan, so why do they need knowledge? They do not cut, so why do they need paste? They have nothing to lose so why do they need favors? They're not buying, so why do they need trade? In these four ways, they feed at Heaven. Feeding at Heaven they are nourished by Heaven. Once nourished by Heaven, why do they need other people? They have human form, but not human essence. Since they have human form, they flock with people. Since they lack human essence, right and wrong do not get to them. Infinitesimally small, they flock with people. Indescribably large, they complete their Heaven alone."[93]

Kong: I love your poetic language, but I'm not sure what you mean.

Zhuang: I'm not sure what I mean.

Kong: Yan Hui, I need your help.

Yan Hui (refilling Zhuang's cup): Here too, perhaps Mr. Zhuang means to suggest that the ideal life is free of social entanglements. Even if we can't really escape being with people, we should be detached from the cares of this world. We should seek our own happiness alone, without depending on other people.

Kong: But how can we live alone? We are social animals—like lions, we live in communities and unlike tigers, who spend most of their adult lives alone—and the task is to improve the quality of our communal relations, not to somehow transcend our social nature.

Zhuang (downing another drink): "In the mountains of far-off Guyi there lives a spiritual person, whose skin and flesh are like ice and snow, who is gentle as a virgin. He does not eat the five grains but sucks in the wind and drinks the dew; he rides the vapour of clouds, yokes flying dragons in his chariot, and roams beyond the four seas."[94]

Kong: Ok, if I understand you correctly, we should live like hermits in mountains who are not subject to any social constraints and who merge with the Way of nature to the point that we can transcend ordinary bodily urges. But that sounds so mysterious to me: who can realize that kind of fantastical life? And I still don't understand what's wrong with social relations. When I look outside of myself, I see ties to my family, my friends, my community: they provide meaning to my life. When I look inside, all I see is vast emptiness.[95]

Zhuang: Yes, that's beautiful! "The perfect person has no self."[96]

Kong (shaking his head): My point is that social relations are the source of meaning in our lives. Why do you object to relations with other people, it's such a strange view.

Zhuang: I recall wandering by the edge of the Diaoling reserve when I "saw a strange magpie flying up from the south. Her wings were seven feet across and her eyes were an inch around. She jumped into [my] forehead and then crashed into a chestnut grove. [I] said: 'What kind of bird is this, with such magnificent wings that don't get it anywhere and such big eyes that can't see?' Hitching up [my] robes and tiptoeing forward, [I] pursued it, bow in hand. [I] saw a cicada forgetting itself in a pretty bid of shade. A praying mantis took advantage of the cover to grab for it, forgetting its own body at the sight of gain. The strange magpie was right behind, eyeing the prize and forgetting the truth. [I] shuddered, 'Eeeee! Things certainly entangle one another, each one dragging in the next!' [I] threw down [my] bow and ran back the way [I] came—but the warden of the grove saw and pursued [me], cursing. . . . The grove warden took me for a poacher!"[97]

Kong (laughing): That's a good story! If I you understand correctly, we should be free of entanglements because you think they are harmful, they inevitably make us suffer. Even those who think they have power will end up being taken advantage of by those with even more power at some point. So best to avoid any social entanglements, it's much safer that way. We should care only for our self-preservation and not worry about other people. With all due respect, I think it's a pessimistic outlook. Of course, social relations can go wrong, but when they go right—when they are harmonious and characterized by mutual care and love—our lives flourish more than when we are alone.

Zhuang: "He who wants to do anything for his body had best abandon the world. By abandoning the world, he can be without entanglements. Being without entanglements, he can be upright and calm. . . . The sage is calm but not because he declares calmness good. None of the ten thousand things are enough to rattle his heart, so he is calm."[98]

Kong: Let me see if I understand. It's not just that freedom from entanglements reduces the risk of suffering harm at the hands of other people. You claim that such freedom can also make us calm because we won't be affected by the goings-on of the social world. Without any attachments, we are safe from influence, so our hearts are calm. Maybe so. But again, I still think you're missing out on something important. Social relations often bring us joy! They make life worth living! Don't you love life? Only the dead are without social attachments.

Zhuang: Yes, they are very lucky. I once had a dream, I was talking to a skull who told me, "You chatter like a rhetorician and betray all the entanglements of a living man. The dead know nothing of these! . . . Among the dead there are no rulers above, no subjects below, and no chores of the four seasons. With nothing to do, our springs and autumns are as endless as heaven and earth. A king facing south on his throne could have no more happiness than this!" [I] couldn't believe this and said, "If I got the Arbiter of Fate to give you a body again, make you some bones and flesh, return to your parents and family and your old home and friends, you would want that, wouldn't you?" The skull frowned severely, wrinkling in a brow. "Why would I throw away more happiness than that of a king on a throne and take on the troubles of a human being again?"[99]

Kong: It's a dream, my friend. If you really believed that the dead are happier than the living because they don't have any social attachments, why not end your life?

Zhuang: Why bother? The time will come, why interfere with this process? I neither "rejoice in life nor look on death as a calamity. . . . I received life because the time had come; I will lose it because the order of things passes on. Be content with this time and dwell in this order and then neither sorrow nor joy can touch you."[100]

Kong: You claim that social relations do not matter to you, but I wonder if that's really the case. I don't mean to be personal, but I heard you were married and your wife passed away. Did you not experience sorrow at your loss?

Zhuang: At first, yes. But then I felt some happiness. I recall my friend Huizi "came to convey his condolences, he found [me] with my legs sprawled out, pounding on a tub and singing. 'You lived with her, she brought up your children and grew old,' [he] said. 'It should be enough simply not to weep at her death. But pounding on a tub and singing—this is going too far, isn't it?' [I] replied: 'You're wrong. When she first died, do you think I didn't grieve like anyone else? But I looked back to her beginning and the time before she was born. Not only the time before she was born, but the time before she had a body. Not only the time she had before she had a body, but the time before she had a spirit. Another change and she had a body. Another change and she was born. Now there's been another change, and she is dead. It's just like the progression of the four seasons, spring, summer, fall, winter. Now she's going to lie down peacefully in a vast room. If I were to follow after her bawling and sobbing, it would show that I don't understand fate. So I stopped.'"[101]

Kong (gasps): You seem to have a superhuman ability to overcome your emotions. . . .

Zhuang: Why should I care about my emotions? I came to look at it from the perspective of my deceased wife. She has simply transformed to something else, and who knows, she may be happier without any entanglements from this world.[102]

Kong: My friend, are you serious? Or is this another joke? . . . (turning to Yan Hui) . . . Yan Hui, please explain.

Yan Hui (refilling Zhuang's glass): Perhaps Mr. Zhuang means that death is simply a transformation from one kind of energy to another. Nothing to worry about. When it happens, it happens, and we should accept death with equanimity. Conversely, if we are too attached to social relations, we will experience sorrow and unhappiness when those relations are broken, such as when a loved one dies. So better to free oneself from entanglements as much as possible. The benefits of an unencumbered life seem to be clear: we won't suffer at the hands of others who have power over us, we will become calm and free of worry, and we won't fear death. But I agree with my professor that it's a pessimistic outlook on life. If I had to choose between the serenity that comes from a "spiritual freedom" floating above and beyond this-worldly social entanglements and the joy that comes from harmonious social relations, I'd choose the latter, even if broken relations also bring sorrow. I don't mean to be rude, but Mr. Zhuang's perspective, frankly, may also be immoral. If a person withdraws from the social world, how can he or she be useful to society?

Zhuang: My friend Huizi said to me, "I have a big tree called *shu*. Its trunk is too gnarled and bumpy to apply a measuring line to, its branches too twisty to match up to a compass or square. You could stand it by the road and no carpenter would look at it twice. Your words, too, are big and useless, and so everyone alike spurns them." [I] replied, "Maybe you've never seen a wildcat or a weasel. It crouches down and hides, watching for something to come along. It leaps and races east and west, not hesitating to go high or low—until it falls into the trap and dies in the net. Then again there's the yak, big as a cloud covering the sky. It certainly knows how to be big, although it doesn't know how to catch rats. Now you have this big tree and you're distressed because it's useless. Why don't you plant it in Not-Even-Anything Village, or the field of Broad-and-Boundless, relax and do nothing by its side, or lie down for a free and easy sleep under it? Axes will never shorten its life, nothing can ever harm it. If there's not use for it, how can it come to grief and pain?"[103]

Kong: Well, of course you're right in the sense that trees useless to humans are likely to have a longer life. But don't you think humans have an obligation to be useful to society?

Zhuang: "There's Crippled Shu—chin stuck down in his navel, shoulders up above his head, pigtail pointing at the sky, his five organs on the top, his two thighs pressing his ribs. By sewing and washing, he gets enough to fill his mouth; by handling a winnow and sifting out the good grain, he makes enough to feed ten people. When the authorities call out the troops, he stands in the crowd waving good-bye; when they get up a big work party, they pass him over because he's a chronic invalid. And when they are dolling out grain to the ailing, he gets three big measures and ten bundles of firewood. With a crippled body, he's still able to look after himself and finish out the years Heaven gave him. . . . Everybody knows the use of the world, but nobody knows the use of the useless!"[104]

Kong: Isn't there something wrong about somebody who selfishly evades social obligations by claiming to be useless? Or somebody who almost seems to take pride in the fact he can live out a longer life because he is useless to society? Personally, I admire the government officials who "are dolling out grain to the ailing." Let me put it this way: do you deny that we have an obligation to make the world a better place, to alleviate suffering and promote social harmony to the extent possible?

Zhuang: I don't know what it means "to make the world a better place." By what standard do we judge moral progress? "What do words rely on, that we have right and wrong? How can the Way go away and not exist? How can words exist and not be acceptable? When the Way relies on little accomplishments and words rely on vain show, then we have the rights and wrongs of the Confucians and the Mohists. What one calls right the other calls wrong; what one calls wrong the other calls right."[105]

Kong (trying not to be offended): It's more than that. We try to give reasons for our views. We try to show that Mohists have a narrow understanding of human flourishing and that their aspiration to impartial behavior in everyday life violates our deepest commitments to intimate social relations.[106]

Zhuang: Have you ever convinced a Mohist? As I see it, it's just a silly argument between different perspectives. Both sides take their own views as the moral truth and argue endlessly from and for their limited perspectives. "Haven't you ever heard about the frog in the caved-in well? He said to the great turtle of the Eastern Sea, 'What fun I have! I come out and hop around the railing of well, or I go back in and take a rest in the wall where a tile has fallen out. When I dive into the water, I let it hold me up under the armpits and support my chin, and when I slip about in the mud, I bury my feet in it and let it come up over my ankles. I look around at the mosquito larvae and the crabs and polliwogs and I see that none of them can match me. To have complete command of the water of one whole valley and to monopolize all the jobs of the caved-in well—this is the best there is!'"[107]

Kong (laughs): That's a good one. Of course, we all have our limited perspectives. But unlike frogs, we can recognize that we have limited perspectives. Humans can only dwell in specific places, occupy a specific situation and obtain limited knowledge. These are trivial truths. But we need to take the implications seriously. You seem to think that we can't distinguish between better and worse perspectives. But we can. Those who are aware of their limitations are better than those who aren't. We always need to be open to the possibility that we may be wrong and that we can learn from others. As I said, "When walking with two other people, I will always find a teacher among them."[108]

Yan Hui: It also means that the ruler should be aware of his limitations and make comprehensive use of public officials with diverse backgrounds and talents to help correct for the necessary limitations of any one person's perspectives.[109]

Kong (lowers his voice): Indeed, some rulers seem to have an inflated self-image. I do worry about leaders with personality cults.

Yan Hui: I'm planning a trip.

Kong: "Where are you going?"

Yan Hui: "I'm going to [North Korea]."[110]

Kong (alarmed): "What will you do there?"

Yan Hui: "I have heard that the ruler of [North Korea] is very young. He acts in an independent manner, thinks little of how he rules his state, and fails to see his faults. It is nothing to him to lead his people into peril, and the dead are reckoned by swampfuls like so much grass. His people have nowhere to turn. I have heard you say, Professor, 'Leave the state that is well ordered and go to the state in chaos! At the doctor's gate are many sick men.' I want to use these words as my standard, in hopes that I can restore his state to health."

Kong: "Ah, you will probably go and get yourself executed, that's all. . . . Though your virtue may be great and your good faith unassailable, if you do not understand people's spirits, though your fame may be wide and you do not strive with others, if you don't understand people's minds, but instead appear before a tyrant and force him to listen to sermons on benevolence and righteousness, measures and standards—this is simply using other people's bad points to parade your own excellence. You will be called a plaguer of others. He who plagues others will be plagued in turn. You will probably be plagued by this man."

Yan Hui: I agree that it would be dangerous to try to convert an evil tyrant like Adolf Hitler. And that if I were to lecture him about morality, I'd probably end up getting myself killed. But perhaps the ruler of North Korea has some seeds of goodness within him. . . .

Zhuang (joining forces with Kong): "Suppose he is the kind who actually delights in worthy men and hates the unworthy—then why does he need you to try to make any difference? You had best keep your advice to yourself. Kings and dukes always lord it over others and fight to win the arguments. You will find your eyes growing dazed, your color changing, your mouth working to invent excuses, your attitude becoming more and more humble, until in your mind you end up by supporting him."[111] That's what happens to do-gooders: they start off with good intentions, but end up being corrupted by power and money. It's not just about politics. I had students who like poetry, but they ended up studying law because they wanted to help those suffering from injustice. They took out loans, and ended up working as corporate lawyers, initially because they needed the money to pay back the loans and later because they liked the comfort of the "good life."[112]

Kong: I wouldn't worry about Yan Hui succumbing to the temptations of power and money. "Virtuous indeed is Yan Hui! He has simple meals, only drinks cold water, and lives in a humble alley. While others would find such living unbearable, Yan Hui remains cheerful. What a virtuous person!"[113] But I share Zhuang's concern that he could get killed if he "speaks truth to power."

Yan Hui: That's not my intention, Professor.

Kong: "You must have some plan in mind. Come on, tell me what it is."

Yan Hui: "If I am grave and empty-hearted, diligent and of one mind, won't that do?" If it's not the right occasion, I won't say anything. I will wait till the ruler trusts me and if he's in a good mood, I can gently try to move him along the path of morality.

Kong: "Goodness, how could *that* do? You may put on a fine outward show and seem very impressive, but you can't avoid having an uncertain look on your face, any more than an ordinary man can. And then you try to gauge this man's feelings and seek to influence his mind. But with him, what is called 'the virtue that advances a little each day' would not succeed, much less a great display of virtue! He will stick fast to his position and never be converted. Though he may make outward signs of agreement, outwardly he would never give it a thought! How could such an approach succeed?" Either your facial expression will give you away—he will know you disagree with his immoral ways, even if you keep quiet—or he will ignore what you advise, even if you gain his confidence and he pretends to agree. Why should he listen to you?

Yan Hui: "Well then, suppose I am inwardly direct, outwardly compliant, and do my work through the examples of antiquity. . . . By being outwardly compliant, I can be a companion of people. Lifting up the tablet, kneeling, bowing, crouching down—this is the etiquette of a minister. Everybody does it, so why shouldn't I? If I do what other people do, they can hardly criticize me. . . . By doing my work through the examples of antiquity, I can be the companion of ancient times. Though my words may in fact be lessons and reproaches, they belong to ancient times and not to me. In this way, though I may be blunt, I cannot be blamed. This is what I mean by being a companion of antiquity. If I go about it this way, will it do?" The ruler will think of me as a compliant and respectful public official who draws inspiration from antiquity rather than a critic who criticizes policies on the basis of his own moral standards.

Kong: "Goodness, how could that do? You have too many policies and plans and you haven't seen what is needed. You will probably get off without incurring any blame, yes. But that will be as far as it goes. How do you think you can actually convert him?" So, yes, it's a good idea to appeal to antiquity if one is genuinely inspired by the past and believes past ideas and policies can help address needs of the present. But if it's just a strategic appeal to history with the aim of converting the ruler, either he will see through you or, if you are lucky, he will ignore your advice if it conflicts with the imperatives of power as he sees it.

Yan Hui: "I have nothing more to offer. May I ask the proper way?"

Kong: As I said, "If the Way is being realized in the world, then show yourself; if it is not, then go into reclusion." Don't go to North Korea, at least not now. I think Zhuang would agree with me, for once.

Zhuang: Actually, I disagree. I think Yan Hui should go. But on one condition. . . . (looking at Yan Hui) . . . "You must fast!"[114]

Yan Hui: "My family is poor. I haven't drunk wine or eaten strong foods for several months. So can I be considered as having fasted?"

Zhuang: "That is the fasting one does before a sacrifice, not the fasting of the mind."

Yan Hui: "May I ask what the fasting of the mind is?"

Zhuang: "Make your will one! Don't listen with your ears, listen with your mind. No, don't listen with your mind, but listen with your spirit. Listening stops with the ears, the mind stops with recognition, but spirit is empty and waits on all things. The Way gathers on emptiness alone. Emptiness is the fasting of the mind."

Yan Hui: "Before I heard this, I was certain that I was Hui. But now that I have heard it, there is no more Hui. Can this be called emptiness?" . . . But why do you think "I" should go to North Korea?

Zhuang: "You may go and play in [the ruler's] bird cage, but never be moved by fame. If he listens, then sing; if not, keep still. Have no gate, no opening, but make oneness your house and live with what cannot be avoided. Then you will be close to success."

Yan Hui: If I understand correctly, you think "I," whoever that may be, should go to North Korea without the intention of converting the ruler. "I" should wander about, go with the flow, and if the occasion presents itself, then "I" can do the appropriate thing. And "I" should also leave open the possibility of being "converted," or at least, of learning something that can change "my" original perspective. Concretely, perhaps, it means "I" should go as a tourist without any preconceived notions and stay away from politics.

Kong (laughs): If that what it means, then I have no objection. . . . (looking at Zhuang) . . . But I still find it strange that you think he should go to North Korea. Why not simply withdraw from all social obligations, as you argued earlier? Isn't freedom from all entanglements your ideal?

Zhuang: I'm not sure I have any ideals. I never said we can completely transcend our entanglements. I was married, as you know, and I have some friends. I need to work with my publisher and go in town to get groceries. Not to mention the necessary attachments to our parents and the political community. "In the world, there are two great restraints: one is fate and the other is duty. That a son should love his parents is fine—you cannot erase this from his heart. That a subject should serve his ruler is duty—there is no place he can go and be without his ruler, no place he can escape to between heaven and earth. These are the great restraints. Therefore, to serve your parents and be content to follow them anywhere—this is the perfection of filial piety. To serve your ruler and be content to do anything for him—this is the peak of loyalty."[115]

Kong: Now I'm truly baffled. Before you were arguing for freedom from entanglements. Now you praise filial piety and loyalty to the ruler and you say we should blindly follow parents and rulers. Is that a really a good thing?

Zhuang: It is neither good nor bad. We find ourselves with some entanglements that cannot be escaped. But we can deal with them. "To serve your own mind so that sadness or joy do not sway or move it; to understand that you can do nothing about and to be content with your fate—this is the perfection of virtue. As a subject and a son, you are bound to find things you cannot avoid. If you act in accordance with the state of affairs and forget about yourself, then what leisure will you have to love life and hate death? Act in this way and you will be all right."[116]

Kong: It sounds quite abstract. What does it mean to "act in accordance with the state of affairs and forget about yourself"?

Yan Hui: Perhaps Mr. Zhuang means that we should accept certain social roles, but still remain detached from them. Even if we can't really be hermits, we can live as though we are hermits.[117]

Kong: Is that what you mean, Zhuang?

Zhuang: Yes and no.

Kong (frustrated): Can you illustrate your view with an example?

Zhuang: "Follow the middle; go by what is constant, and you can stay in one piece, keep yourself alive, look after your parents, and live out your years. Cook Ding was cutting up an ox for Lord Wenhui. At every touch of the hand, every heave of his shoulder, every move of his feet, every thrust of his knee—zip! zoop! He slithered the knife along with a zing, and all in perfect rhythm, as though he were performing the dance of the Mulberry Grove or keeping time to the Jingzhou music." The ruler said: "Ah, this is marvelous! Imagine skill reaching such heights." Cook Ding laid down his knife and replied: "What I care about is the Way, which goes beyond skill. When I first began cutting up oxen, all I could see was the ox itself. After three years, I no longer saw the whole ox. And now—now I go at it by spirit and don't look with my eyes. Perception and understanding have come to a stop and spirit moves where it wants. I go along with the natural markup, strike in the big hollows, guide the knife through the big openings, and follow things as they are. So I never touch the smallest ligament or tendon, much less the main joint. . . . However, whenever I come to a complicated place, I size up the difficulties, tell myself to watch out and be careful, keep my eyes on what I'm doing, work very slowly, and move the knife with the greatest subtlety until—flop! The whole thing comes apart like a clod of earth crumbling to the ground. I stand there holding the knife and look all around me, completely satisfied and reluctant to move on, and then I wipe off my knife and put it away."[118]

Kong: That's a beautiful story, and it shows the greatness of an artisan who has mastered a craft after years of training, to the point that he can unselfconsciously perform a difficult skill with grace and ease. But what does this have to do with our discussion about politics?

Yan Hui: Professor, it looks like a state-sponsored ritual that needs to be performed for the ruler. Such occasions can be awkward, if not dangerous for the public official who thinks too much and makes mistakes. In this case, the official butcher finds the path of least resistance: he does what needs to be done, he has mastered the intricacies of ritual performance while staying "in one piece."[119] It's a safe and effective way to engage in politics. Is that what you mean, Mr. Zhuang?

Zhuang (downing his cup of "white liquor"): I'm not sure what I mean.

Yan Hui (looking at his teacher): Perhaps Mr. Zhuang's point is that politics involves dealing with disharmony. Things go wrong in the real political world, and we need to think about how to make them work more harmoniously. Mr. Zhuang posits the ideal of a public official who unselfconsciously and effortlessly performs an assigned task with skill and beauty. But even if we agree on the ideal—say, a society where people are trained to the point they can act like Cook Ding—we need to deliberate about what kind of laws and educational institutions generate desired outcomes, which involves arguments about competing policies, goals, and allocation of scarce resources. We need to consider diverse viewpoints, allow for criticism, reflect on one's faults, and think about how to improve things. So, yes, we can agree on the ideal, but perhaps the bigger challenge is to devise and implement appropriate measures for dealing with nonideal situations where things don't work so smoothly and harmoniously.

Kong: Well put, Yan Hui. . . . And let's draw implications for divorce law, if you don't mind. In the case of marriage, the question is what to do when things seem to break down between spouses. I suggested that we need a long waiting period before divorce can be finalized, during which skilled, state-appointed mediators can help the couple deal with conflict and restore or create a new kind of "diversity in harmony." Of course, there's no guarantee of success, but at least we should try. Zhuang, I wonder if you can join our cause? You had a long and seemingly successful marriage, and frankly, you'd have more credibility than a divorced man like myself. Your voice might help to tip the balance in public debate.

Zhuang: I was once asked to go into government. I happened to be fishing that day, and I told the officers, "I've heard Chu has a sacred turtle. It's been dead three thousand years and the king keeps it wrapped and boxed and stored up in his ancestral hall. Now, would that turtle rather have its bones treasured in death, or be alive dragging its tail in the mud?" The two officers said, "It would rather be alive dragging its tail in the mud." [I] replied, "Go! I'll keep my tail in the mud, too. . . ."[120]

Kong (laughs): You're very amusing my friend. But I'm not asking you to join the government, only to join the public debate. And there is no risk to you, the stakes are not so high. It won't interfere with your fishing. I'm just asking if you can help with the cause of changing the divorce law in Hong Kong so people will think twice about exiting from a married relation.

Zhuang: If people want to exit from social entanglements, they should have freedom to do so. I don't think the state should interfere by forcing people to stay together who don't want to be together. Sometimes, people fight over the silliest things. We're no different than animals. I recall a monkey trainer who "was passing out nuts. He said: 'You get three in the morning and four at night.' The monkeys were all angry. 'All right,' he said, 'you get four in the morning and three at night.' The monkeys were all pleased."[121]

Kong (laughs): That's a good story, but it supports what I say. The monkey trainer is like a good mediator who helps spouses to look at things from a new, more harmonious perspective without changing the material facts, so to speak.

Zhuang: Well, usually things change from one extreme to another, we just need to accept that and let it go. "When men get together to put their strength in games of skill, they start off in a light and friendly mood, but usually end up in a dark and angry one and if they go on too long they start resorting to various underhanded tricks. When men meet at some ceremony to drink, they start off in an orderly manner, but usually end up in disorder, and if they go on too long they start indulging in irregular amusements. It is the same with all things. What starts off being sincere usually ends up being deceitful. What was simple in the beginning acquires monstrous proportions in the end."[122] Same goes for marriage. Even if it starts off as a loving relation, the emotion won't last. It often ends up in hate, and then it's time to part ways.

Kong: Such a bleak outlook! I don't mean to get too personal, but why didn't you divorce if love turns into hate?

Zhuang: Why bother? I don't believe there are superior alternatives. But if others want to exit from entanglements, who are we to try to restrain them from doing so? Some entanglements are unchosen, like our relation with parents and to our political community, but marriage is a chosen entanglement, and people should be free to exit.

Kong: But there's substantial evidence that married people are happier.[123] Shouldn't we do our best to encourage people to stay in relations that make them happier?

Zhuang: "What ordinary people do and what they find happiness in—I don't know whether such happiness is in the end really happiness or not. I look at what ordinary people find happiness in, what they all make a mad dash for, racing around as though they couldn't stop—they all say they're happy with it. I'm not happy with it and I'm not unhappy with it. In the end is there really happiness or isn't there? I take inaction to be true happiness, but ordinary people think it is a bitter thing. I say: the highest happiness has no happiness."[124]

Kong: I really don't understand. If happiness is not important to you, what about "diversity in harmony"? Surely we can agree that it's better for people to be in a harmonious relationship, if possible.

Zhuang: "The torch of chaos and doubt—this is what the sage steers by."[125]

Kong (losing patience): What does that mean? I thought you preferred "going with the flow," and now you say you prefer chaos. Chaos is what makes life more difficult for people. I realize you value freedom from entanglements, but how can people lead carefree lives in chaotic societies?

Yan Hui: Perhaps Mr. Zhuang means that ordinary people strive for a wrongheaded form of "happiness" and "harmony," and the sage seeks to sow doubt and chaos regarding those goals. The sage needs to rise above those ordinary pursuits, to free him or herself from social entanglements to the extent possible, and to merge with the formless, amoral Way. Is that right, Mr. Zhuang?

Zhuang: What's right, and what's wrong? "Is there really any difference or isn't there? How is the Way obscured that there are true and false? How are words obscured that there are 'right' and 'wrong'?"[126]

Kong: If I understand correctly, we somehow need to transcend a way of thinking that distinguishes between what's true and what's false and between what's right and what's wrong. I must confess I find it hard to understand your perspective. Perhaps we should just stop talking. Do you stand for anything?

Zhuang: "I mean people not letting in good and bad to hurt them. . . . (repeating himself, slurring his words). . . When sages wander, knowledge is a curse, restrictions are paste, favors are a patch, and effort is for trade. Sages do not plan, so why do they need knowledge? They do not cut, so why do they need paste? They have nothing to lose, so why do they need favors? They're not buying, so why do they need trade? In these four ways, they feed at Heaven. Feeding at Heaven, they are nourished by Heaven. Once they are nourished by Heaven, why do they need other people?"[127]

Kong: My friend, let me be blunt. It's true that we can get hurt in the real world. But the solution is not exiting from social entanglements. Even if that leads to a kind of inner happiness, it's not right. Pursuing contentment for oneself is selfish. How can you deny that we have a moral obligation to help others in need?

Zhuang: "When the spring dries up and the fish are stranded together on land, they spit moisture at each other and soak each other in the foam, but they would be better off forgetting each other in the Yangzi or the Lakes."[128]

Kong: Of course, fish who are about to die should just accept their fate. Some attempts to help people can be futile. But sometimes we can make a positive difference, and we shouldn't dismiss those possibilities out of hand. There is evidence that good mediators can rescue seemingly bad marriages, so why not give it a try?

Zhuang: Interfere, interfere, that's all I hear. "Follow the natural and do not help life along. . . . A good swimmer can master it because he forgets the water."[129]

Kong: Mmh, perhaps babies are the best swimmers in your sense—they unselfconsciously know how to swim. But once they grow up, they start thinking about the water, they forget how to swim, and they drown if they find themselves in water without having made conscious efforts to learn how to swim. . . . (pause) . . . My friend, please forgive me if this sounds unfair, but I wonder if you want us to regress to a state of babyhood. Newborns are completely spontaneous and unselfconscious, they are unconcerned with the ways of the world, they make no distinctions between right and wrong, and they experience a pure, unadulterated sense of satisfaction and oneness with the world once their basic needs are met. They have no responsibility for others. They couldn't care less if the rest of the world is chaotic.[130]

Zhuang (first little smile of the day): That's beautiful, thank you, I hadn't thought of that. You think we make moral progress as we grow older, I look to babies as exemplars. . . . [Zhuang empties his fifth glass of "white liquor" and falls asleep, his head on the table, arms flapping on the side]. . . . He "dreams of being a butterfly, showing off and doing as he pleased, unaware of being Zhuang. Suddenly, he awoke, drowsily, Zhuang again. And he could not tell if it was Zhuang who had dreamed the butterfly or the butterfly dreaming Zhuang."[131]

3. A Harmonious Outcome?

[A few minutes later]

Kong: Are you back?

Zhuang (in a hypnagogic state): "You" implies an "I." Am I an "I"? "We say 'I.' But how do I know what I mean by 'I'?"[132]

Kong (smiling): Let me answer from my perspective: You're my friend, Zhuang! You temporarily left us for the dream world. We were discussing whether moral obligations between family members should be legally enforced. In the case of married couples who seek to part ways, we had agreed to disagree. I argued that there should be a waiting period with compulsory mediation before spouses can get divorced, but you argued that people should be free of entanglements to the extent possible and the state should not interfere if people want to free themselves of entanglements.

Zhuang: Ridiculous! Why would "I" say that? In fact, "I" agree with your proposal.

Kong (puzzled): You surprise me yet again.

Zhuang: Why marry? Why would anyone want to get entangled for the long term with another person? The best way to make that absurd institution obsolete is to make it as hard as possible to get out of it! With harsh divorce laws, fewer people will want to get married. So the harsher the divorce laws, the better!

Kong (laughs): That's a good one! . . . (Zeng Xi is about refill Zhuang's glass but Kong intervenes). . . . No more alcohol for the adult baby. 😵

2

On Law and Ritual

OR, HOW TO COMBAT CORRUPTION?

IN THE Warring States period (ca. 476–221 BCE) political theorists roamed from state to state, trying to persuade rulers to adopt their ideas. It was also a time of remarkable openness: otherwise ruthless rulers, not knowing how to deal with chaos and conflict, often welcomed intellectual exchanges with roaming scholars, and the debates of the time inspired political thinking for much of subsequent Chinese history right up to the modern era. In terms of domestic policy, the great political thinkers of the Warring States period condemned corrupt and self-interested public officials who contributed to the weakness (if not the downfall) of the state, but they had radically different ideas about how best to combat corruption. Xunzi and his student Han Feizi both wrote long works in the third century BCE that systematized political ideas into coherent systems. Xunzi wrote an eclectic and wide-ranging work with a Confucian moral foundation, whereas Han Feizi systematized the ideas of amoral realist thinkers into what came to be known as the Legalist school. They shared the assumption that people have a natural tendency to selfishness, but Xunzi argued that people can be morally improved by means of education and rituals that provide bonds between people not solely based on kinship. Han Feizi was skeptical about the possibility of moral improvement in a context where people compete for scarce resources: he argued that corruption and the pursuit of self-interest can be curbed only by means of a bureaucratic system that promotes and demotes public officials strictly according to performance of assigned roles and with clear and uniform laws backed by harsh punishments that keep commoners in line.

The self-proclaimed First Emperor Qin Shihuang drew on Han Feizi's ideas to build the world's first complex bureaucratic regime, but the dynasty collapsed after only fifteen years. In subsequent Chinese history, rulers continued to struggle with the question of how to build up an effective bureaucracy without excessive corruption. When President Xi Jinping assumed power in 2012, corruption had reached a tipping point that threatened to undermine the whole political system, and he launched the longest and most systematic anticorruption campaign in Communist Party history. Over two million public officials have been punished for corruption since then, spreading fear throughout the whole political system.[1] In this chapter, I imagine a debate between descendants of Xunzi and Han Feizi on the best way to combat corruption in contemporary China. I also imagine that the Jixia Academy in (what is now) Shandong province—a leading institution for political debates in the Warring States period where Han Feizi is said to have studied with Xunzi—has been rebuilt and serves as the site for the debate.[2] The debate is moderated by a chair who summarizes positions and puts forward her own views (of a more liberal orientation), in the style of chairs of academic events in China who are typically more active compared to the supposedly neutral "umpires" in the West. I begin with Han Feizi, since the current anticorruption campaign seems to have been mainly inspired by Legalist ideas,[3] then move on to Xunzi's criticisms of harsh Legalism and defense of ritual as a way of combatting corruption.[4]

1. Han Feizi on Law

Han Feizi (ca. 280–233 BCE) is the most renowned thinker of the Legalist school. He is the only major Warring States thinker from a noble family background, yet he argued for policies designed to destroy aristocratic families and other local centers of power that threatened to undermine unity at the top. Due to a serious stutter, he could not effectively communicate his proposals, so (luckily for us) he wrote his ideas in book form. Han Feizi was sent as an envoy from his native state of Han to the Qin state and may have tried to persuade the Qin ruler to adopt his ideas, but he was jailed by Prime Minister Li Si—another of Xunzi's students—and forced to drink poison rather than be subject to an excruciating death by torture. Han Feizi argued that the end of politics is to make the state into a strong economic and military power, particularly in a time of constant warfare when states faced a choice between survival and destruction. Whatever works to strengthen the state is fine, and morality is useless for this purpose. The legal system and the bureaucratic apparatus should be aligned with people's selfish nature: most people are motivated by the quest for pleasure and fear of harm, and the state should reward people for doing what's good for the state and ruthlessly punish those who harm it. Any societal forces that conflict with the imperative to strengthen the state should be exterminated.

Han Feizi took various ideas of amoral realist thinkers and built them up into a coherent political philosophy. From Shang

Yang, he developed the idea that clear and uniform laws (*fa*) backed by harsh punishments are necessary to keep common people's selfish tendencies in check and to make them do things that serve the public interest, meaning whatever strengthens the state.[5] From Shen Buhai, he borrowed the idea that administrative techniques (*shu*) could be used to control public officials and ensure that they serve the public interest rather than private or family interests. From Daoist thinkers, he incorporated the idea that the ruler should rarely intervene in political affairs, both because the state is weakened by arbitrary intervention and because the ruler would leave himself open to manipulation by ministers if he showed his likes and dislikes.[6] Han Feizi illustrated his arguments with colorful stories so extreme in their cynicism that Machiavelli seems like a softhearted moralist by comparison.[7] Like that of Shang Yang, his thought largely disappeared from official discourse after the Han dynasty (206 BCE–220 CE) because Confucians were appalled by Legalist amorality, but Han Feizi made a big comeback in the chaotic years of the twentieth century, and his ideas continue to be debated in both Chinese academia and political circles.[8]

Okay, let's turn to the debate!

Chair: Welcome to Jixia Academy. It is a great honor to preside over our first debate in twenty-two hundred years. I'd like to thank the Shandong government for providing the resources that allowed us to rebuild the academy. Today's debate, as you know, is about how best to combat corruption in government and society at large. The debaters are Professor Xun, Chief Libationer of the Jixia

Academy,[9] and his student, Han Fei.[10] Professor Xun, please go first.

Xun: I'd rather let my student go first. As Kongzi said, students should be regarded with awe because they will surpass us eventually.[11]

Han: Thank you, professor. I'm sure we agree that corruption—let's define it as the wrongful misuse of public power for private or family interests—needs to be eliminated.[12] "If wicked ministers, even though they have not produced any accomplishments, enjoy safety and profit, then corrupt officials will come to the fore. This is the beginning of the downfall of the state."[13] We need to strongly oppose the practice of *maiguan* [buying posts]. If "the ruler's kinsmen and elder statesmen beg titles and stipends from the ruler and then sell them to their subordinates in order to gain wealth and profit for themselves . . . [and] people who have sufficient money and influence may buy posts for themselves and become honored, and those who have friends among the ruler's attendants may make use of their special pleading to win important positions . . . [and] we find officials stealing posts to which they have no right and intriguing with foreign powers, neglecting their duties and cultivating people of wealth. . . . This is the mark of a doomed state!"[14]

Xun: Yes, I agree.

Han: The question is how to combat corruption. The state must be wealthy and powerful with the capacity to put down private scheming. And what are "the methods for achieving wealth and power"?[15] As I see it, we need commitment to the law: "He who can put an end to private scheming and make people uphold the public law will see his people secure and his state well-ordered; he who can block selfish pursuits and enforce public law will see his armies growing stronger and his enemies weakening." The ruler must enforce the law without exceptions: "An enlightened ruler will make certain that the ambitions of his ministers do not roam beyond the bounds of the law. . . . They are permitted to make no move that is not in accord with the law. Laws are the means of prohibiting error and ruling out selfish motives; strict penalties are the means of enforcing orders and disciplining inferiors. . . . If law does not command respect, then all the ruler's actions will be endangered. If penalties are not enforced, then evil will never be surmounted. . . . One should use laws to govern the state, disposing of all matters on their basis alone."[16]

Xun: I agree that laws are important, but they are not sufficient. We need public officials of good character to ensure that they don't misuse public resources for their own benefit.

Han: We need good laws, not good people. "When a sage governs a state, he does not wait for people to be good in deference to him. Instead, he creates a situation in which people find it impossible to do wrong. If you wait for people to be good in deference to you, you will find that there are no more than ten good people within the borders of your state. But if you create a situation in which people find it impossible to do wrong, the entire state can be brought into compliance. In governing, one must use what is numerous and abandon what is scarce. Therefore, the sage does not work on his virtue, he works on his laws."[17]

Xun: Surely there's also a role for moral education?

Han: "The law provides the only education; there are no words of learned masters, the civil officers are the only teachers."[18]

Xun: Do you really mean to deny that people can improve? Why should we always assume the worst of people?

Han: "Wisdom is a matter of man's nature and long life is a matter of fate, and neither human nature nor fate can come from others. . . . To try to teach people to be humane and righteous is the same as saying you can make them wise and long-lived."[19] People pursue their own self-interest and there's nothing we can do to change that. "The natural aspirations of the people are such that they all move toward security and benefit and avoid danger and poverty."[20]

Xun: That's such a stunted view of human nature. The great sages of the past governed mainly by virtue, not by means of laws that prevented wrongdoing. Why can't we seek inspiration from the great rulers of the past?

Han: "The Confucians and Mohists all claim that the former kings loved everyone in the whole world equally, and looked upon the people like parents look upon their own children. . . . But if one holds that when ruler and subject are like father and son there will always be order, this implies that there is never any disorder between fathers and sons. In the nature and disposition of human beings nothing is more primary than the love of parents for their children. All children are loved by their parents, and yet children are not always well behaved. Even if one loves a child deeply, how does that prevent the child from being unruly?"[21]

Xun: I'm glad to hear that you recognize some form of love.

Han: Yes, but family love is dangerous for the state. "There was a man of Lu who accompanied his sovereign to war. Three times he went into battle, and three times he ran away. When Kongzi asked him the reason, he replied, 'I have an aged father and, if I should die, there would be no one to take care of him.' Kongzi, considering the main filial, recommended him and had him promoted to a post in the government. Thus we see that a man who is a filial son to his father may be a traitorous subject to his lord."[22]

Xun: That story sounds like a fabrication. In any case, it makes sense to exempt those who care for elderly parents from conscription if no one else can provide the care. Even states like Israel exempt single children from military service.

Han: My point is that "the love of the former kings was not greater than that of parents for their children, so if children are not always well-behaved even when they are so loved, how could the people have been made well-ordered simply by loving them? . . . Humaneness cannot be relied on to secure order."[23] Only law, backed by harsh punishment, works.

Xun: The great sages of the past did secure order by means of virtue, they didn't rely on laws with harsh punishments.

Han: The great sages could govern with virtue because people were few and goods were plentiful. But then we had population growth. Nowadays, "the people are plenty and while commodities and goods are few. People work laboriously, but provisions are scanty. Hence, the people compete."[24] It's absurd to use old ways to govern the present. "The sage does not expect to follow the ways of the ancients or model his behavior on an unchanging standard of what is acceptable. He examines the affairs of the age and then makes his preparations accordingly. Among the people of Song there was a farmer who had a stump in the middle of the field. One day, a rabbit running across the field crashed into the stump, broke its neck, and died. Seeing this, the man put aside his plow and took up watch next to the stump, hoping that he could get another rabbit like this, and he soon became the laughing-stock of the entire state of Song. Now if one wants to use the government of the former kings to bring order to the people of the current age, this is all just so much stump-watching."[25]

Xun (laughs): That's a colorful story, but nobody's arguing for stump-watching. Of course we can't govern entirely by virtue in an age of material scarcity. But you're arguing for the opposite: governing entirely by law, with no room for virtue.[26] Think of the contemporary situation. We tried your methods with the campaign against corruption: millions of officials have been subject to harsh punishment because of corrupt practices. I do not deny it has worked to a certain extent. Public officials are less openly corrupt and there is less buying of government posts. Ordinary citizens perceive the system as less unfair because it's now possible to access public services without paying bribes and gifts to bureaucrats. That said, the campaign has been highly selective: our ruler has removed his political enemies but his allies have been largely spared.[27] Not to mention the disastrous side effects of the campaign. Today, public officials think almost all the time about what can go wrong, to the point that decision-making has become virtually paralyzed. And the anticorruption drive has created huge numbers of political enemies who may be rooting for the downfall of leaders, if not the whole political system.[28] So the Legalist campaign may have worked, at least in part, in the short term, but it may well lead to the downfall of the state! There's no end in sight, and the more it lasts, the more the state is in danger!

Han: The problem is not with Legalism per se. The problem is that the campaign has been *insufficiently* Legalist. Not just any kind of law will deter bad behavior. Yes, the punishment must be strict, even for small offenses. So far so good. But the law must be equally applied to all, regardless of social status. "The law does not make exceptions for those who are noble, just as the ink-line does not bend around that which is crooked. The wise cannot excuse themselves from what the law commands, and the brave do not dare oppose it. The punishment of transgressions does not bypass the great ministers."[29] As you said, however, some public officials close to the center of power have been spared. "If the enlightened ruler forgave penalties the corrupt minister will find it easy to do wrong . . . those who make genuine errors must always be punished, even if they are close and cherished."[30] The laws must be strict, but they must be consistently applied. "When assigning penalties, it's best to make them heavy and inescapable, so that the people will fear them,"[31] including those close to the ruler. Not only that. The laws should be clear and easy to understand. "Language that is subtle or mysterious is something that even the wisest people find difficult to understand. So if when making laws for the masses, you use language that even the wisest people find difficult to understand, then no one will comprehend or follow your laws."[32]

Xunzi: Admittedly, the anticorruption campaign has not been driven by anything that looks like consistent adherence to law.

Han: Exactly. The campaign has strengthened discipline inspection work while marginalizing legal institutions, with the result that some corrupt high party officials are treated leniently by disciplinary authorities and minor corruption cases committed by low- and midlevel officials are treated harshly by legal institutions.[33] People worry about sinking into a black hole without knowing what they did wrong. Far from strengthening the rule of law, the current campaign undermines it.[34] To repeat: yes, the punishments must be harsh to deter corrupt behavior, but laws must also be clear, easy to understand, and consistently applied. We need more Legalism, not less.

Xun: I still don't think you're getting to the heart of the problem. We can't eliminate corruption simply by relying on law. Even the best kind of legal institutions won't work if people are not committed to morality. Laws are not enough to stop people from doing bad things. Corruption in government can't be eliminated entirely by relying on fear of being punished.

Han: I may have overstated things. Laws can constrain wicked behavior by common people. For public officials in a complex bureaucratic system, however, we also need appropriate administrative methods to limit corruption. First, ministers should not be "free to be enforce the laws as they please. . . . If the ruler lends even a little of his power to others, then superior and inferior will change places. Hence it is said that no ministers should be allowed to borrow the power and authority of the ruler."[35] Second, political factions should not be allowed to form. "When relationships are profuse and confederates are numerous, so that cliques and factions flourish both inside and outside the state, then even if a minister commits a great transgression, he will have ample means to cover it up. . . . [Thus], the corrupt and wicked ministers will enjoy security and profits even though they have not produced any achievements."[36] Worse, it could spell the end for the ruler: "The only reason the ministers do not assassinate their sovereign is that their parties and cliques are not strong enough. Hence, if the ruler loses an inch, his subordinates gain a yard."[37] The ruler needs to atomize the ministers so they can't accumulate power by gathering in groups.

Xun: And like the laws, these methods and tactics for controlling ministers should be clear and transparent? But if they are clear to the ministers, they will find a way to circumvent them if they can get away with it. It won't prevent corruption.

Han: Exactly! So some methods to control ministers must not be too open! "As for such techniques, they are hidden in the chest. It is that through which you match up the various ends and from your secret place steer the ministers. Therefore, laws are best when they are clear, whereas techniques should not be seen." Such techniques include to "issue edicts and make wily dispositions, . . . keep your knowledge to yourself and ask for advice, . . . and say the opposite of what you mean and do the opposite of what you intend."[38] With these techniques, the ruler can keep the ministers atomized and guessing about the ruler's intentions; they can't form factions to misappropriate the resources of the state or subvert the ruler. "Hide your tracks, conceal your sources, so that your subordinates cannot trace the springs of your action."[39]

Xun: Now I'm confused. It will be hard for the bureaucracy to get any work done if administrative methods are kept secret.

Han: Some methods need to be open. In the bureaucracy, it is important to "assign one man to each office and do not let people talk to each other."[40] There needs to be an absolutely clear bureaucratic division of labor, with no overlap. "A clear-sighted ruler ensures that different positions do not interfere with one another, and thus there is nothing to dispute. He ensures that officials do not hold more than one post [and] that multiple people do not have responsibility for the same achievements."[41] Moreover, ministers should be rewarded strictly according to performance of assigned tasks, not according to reputation. "If a ruler distributes rewards based on reputation, and hands out penalties based on slander, those people who covet rewards and hate penalties will abandon the public law and carry our private schemes, colluding with one another in order to advance their mutual interests."[42] Public officials should be rewarded if they accomplish the assigned task and punished if they don't. "If the ruler of people wishes to put an end to wickedness, then he must be careful to match up names with results, that is to say, words and deeds. The ministers come forward to present their proposals, the ruler assigns them tasks on the basis of their words, and then concentrates on demanding the accomplishment of the task. If the accomplishment fits the task, and the task fits the words, then he bestows a reward; but if they do not match, he doles out punishment."[43]

Xun (skeptical): It all sounds very scientific. I can understand why the ruler would want to punish public officials who don't do what they are supposed to do, but what if they do more than the assigned task?

Han: That's a recipe for disaster. "Once in the past Marquis Zhao of Han got drunk and fell asleep. The keeper of the royal hat, seeing that the marquis was cold, laid a robe over him. When the marquis awoke, he was pleased and asked his attendants, 'Who covered me with the robe?' 'The keeper of the hat,' they replied. The marquis thereupon punished both the keeper of the royal hat and the keeper of the royal robe. He punished the keeper of the robe for failing to do his duty, and the keeper of the hat for overstepping his office. It was not that he did not dislike the cold, but he considered the trespass of one official upon the duties of another to be a greater danger than cold. Hence an enlightened ruler, in handling his ministers, does not permit them to gain merit by overstepping their offices, or to speak words that do not tally with their actions. Those who overstep are condemned to die; those whose words and actions do not tally are punished. If the ministers are made to stick to their proper duties and speak only what is appropriate, then they will be unable to band together in cliques to work for each other's benefit."[44]

Xun (shocked): Surely you don't believe what you're saying. If well-intentioned ministers are "condemned to die" just because they step outside of their assigned roles, I can assure you that will quickly doom the state. Nobody will take any initiative in response to new situations. What if a minister happens to come across a piece of information that, say, terrorists are about to blow up the presidential palace: should she not report that information if it's not part of her job description?[45]

Han: Such cases are exceptionally rare. We shouldn't change administrative methods just because of some imaginary scenarios.

Xun (exasperated): Not only do you assume the worst of common people, you also assume the worst of public officials. Do you really mean to deny that the political system can benefit by selecting and promoting public-spirited officials with some discretion to exercise their own moral judgment? Surely we should seek out public officials who are less likely to be corrupt?

Han: There are too few of them. "The inborn dispositions and nature of people are such that the worthy are few while the unworthy are numerous."[46] We can't build a bureaucratic system on the assumption most public officials won't be selfish. "Now, there are no more than ten officials in the whole world who are virtuous and honest, and yet the offices within the borders of a single state number in the hundreds [of thousands]. So if one insists on employing only officers who are virtuous and honest, there will not be enough people to fill the offices of the state. And if there are not enough people to fill the offices of the state, those promoting order will be few while those promoting disorder will be numerous. Therefore, the Way of an enlightened ruler is to unify the laws and not seek after wisdom, to establish the proper methods and not yearn for honesty. In this way, the law will not be defeated and the offices will all be free of corruption and treachery."[47]

Xun: You still don't get the point. Fear isn't sufficient to rein in public officials, and law isn't sufficient to secure public order. As Kongzi famously said, "If you guide the people with coercive regulations and keep them in line with punishments, the people will become evasive and will have no conscience. If, however, you guide them with virtue, and keep them in order by means of ritual, the people will have a conscience and will rectify themselves."[48] If the ruler relies only on harsh laws and administrative injunctions, people will seek to evade them as soon as they get a chance to do so. The best way to secure order is to win people's hearts and minds.

Han: "Those who don't understand the art of governing always say, 'One must win the hearts of the people.' If one could bring about order simply by seeking to win the hearts of the people . . . all one would have to do is listen to the people. But the wisdom of the people cannot be used because their minds are like the minds of infants. If an infant's . . . boils are not lanced, the swelling will become worse. Nevertheless, when an infant's boils are lanced, someone has to hold the infant while its loving mother takes care of these things, and the infant will scream and cry endlessly because it does not understand that enduring this little bit of discomfort will bring about a great benefit. . . . Those above draw up penal codes and establish heavy penalties in order to put an end to wickedness, but the people think their superiors are being harsh."[49] So, yes, harsh laws are not popular but the ruler needs to implement them for the people's long-term interest.

Xun: You have zero faith in the good sense of the people and you think public officials should not be selected on the basis of virtue, but you have tremendous faith in the virtue and wisdom of the ruler who can design laws and administrative methods that benefit the long-term interest of the people.

Han: I don't expect too much of a ruler. The ruler should not be too virtuous. In fact, a humane ruler can harm the state. "When a humane individual is in power, those below will be unrestrained and think little of violating prohibitions and laws. They will look to luck and be lazy, and will hope for good things from their superior."[50] Kindness is the road to ruin: "Being kind means that you cannot bear to inflict suffering. . . . If [the ruler] cannot bear to inflict suffering, [he] will not execute criminals; if [he] likes giving presents, [he will] reward people without waiting for them to deserve it. If criminals are not punished and undeserving people are rewarded, how can [the ruler] not come to ruin?"[51]

Xun (skeptical): Okay, so you think the ruler should not be kind to the people. . . . (pause) . . . But you did allow for the possibility of family love. At minimum, the ruler can be kind to loved ones.

Han: Absolutely not! The ruler cannot be family oriented! In fact, he should worry most about relatives and heirs apparent who "stand to profit by his death. Prepare as you may against those who hate you, calamity will come to you from those who love you."[52] The ruler must learn not to love. He must be able, not humane. And we only need one able ruler aided by "officers with sage-like understanding."[53] Once the machine is in place, so to speak, it will run by itself. Public officials will stick to their roles and the people will submit to the law. Then subsequent rulers need not interfere. "When names and results match, the ruler need do nothing more and the true aspect of all things will be revealed. . . . The Way lies in what cannot be seen, its function in what cannot be known. Be empty, still, and idle, and from your place of darkness observe the defects of others."[54] The point is to maximize the power of the state, not the private advantage of the ruler.[55]

Xun: It sounds like a miserable life for the ruler as well: he cannot get love from anybody and he must hide himself and refrain from any enjoyment.[56]

Han: Indeed. "The ruler must not reveal his desires; for if he reveals his desires, his ministers will put on a mask that pleases him. He must not reveal his will; for if he does so his ministers will show a different face. So it is said: Discard likes and dislikes and the ministers will show their true form; discard wisdom and wile and the ministers will watch their step. . . . The enlightened ruler reposes in nonaction, and below his ministers tremble with fear."[57] The system will work well even with mediocre rulers. If the mediocre rulers "hold to the law and depend on the power of the position, there will be order; but if they abandon the power of position and turn their backs on the law, there will be disorder."[58] The important thing is for rulers to refrain from interfering with the system; if they show their desires, they can be manipulated by their underlings.

Xun (baffled): So if I understand correctly, you propose to put in place a system that's in no one's interest. Everybody will work for the sake of increasing the wealth and power of the state. If it succeeds, everyone will be miserable. The people will live in fear of the law and the ministers will live in fear of the ruler. Even the ruler will lead a miserable life: he will be cut off from family, friends, and ministers, and with no freedom or power to act on his desires.

Han: Yes, "in effect, laws and policies are inimical to the private interests of the officials and the common people."[59] And the ruler must learn to rein in his private desires. In the short term, no one benefits. The point is to secure order, whatever the cost and without any show of mercy. "Once, when Qin had a great famine, Marquis Ying petitioned His Majesty, saying 'The grass, vegetables acorns, dates, and chestnuts in the Five Parks are sufficient to save the people. May Your Majesty give them out?' In reply King Zhao Xiang said, 'in accordance with the law of our country the people shall be rewarded for merits and punished for crimes. Now, if I give out the vegetables and fruits of the Five Parks, I will in so doing reward men of merit and no merit equally. To be sure, to reward men of merit and no merit equally leads to disorder. Indeed, instead of giving out the products of the Five Parks and thereby inviting confusion, we may as well discard the fruits and vegetables and thereby maintain order.'"[60]

Xun (raises voice): That is so inhumane! Are you completely insensitive to people's suffering? Nobody deserves to die as a result of natural calamities, how can you call that "merit"? The whole underlying purpose of the law should be to benefit the people! But you say the government should starve the people in order to maintain some sort of legal system that supposedly secures political order![61]

Han (unfazed): But eventually, everyone will benefit! Once the system that strengthens the public interest of the state is in place, there will be no corruption in government because officials fulfill their assigned roles, and there will be no need to implement harsh punishments because people are made aware of laws that prevent wicked behavior. "When no one in the world harms one another, this is the pinnacle of good governance."[62] So the sage should "rectify laws clearly and establish penalties severely in order to rescue everybody from chaos, rid the whole world of misfortune, prohibit the strong from exploiting the weak and the many from oppressing the few, enable the old and the infirm to die in peace and the young and orphans to grow freely, see to it that the frontiers are not invaded, . . . and that there be no worry about being killed in war or taken prisoner. Such are the greatest achievements. Yet the stupid people do not understand it and condemn it as draconian. . . . Severe penalties and heavy convictions are hated by the people, but the state can only be ordered by them. . . . The sage who makes laws in the state is always acting contrary to the prevailing opinions of the age, but is in accord with the Way."[63]

Xun (upset): Perhaps I'm one of the "stupid people." I still don't understand how we are supposed to get from cruel means that establish a quasi-totalitarian society where everybody serves the state out of fear to the utopian goal where peace and order reign on earth and the political community serves the interests of the weak and the needy. More likely, the people will feel great resentment at the cruel means and they will rebel whenever possible. And the ministers will find ways to sabotage the "machine"; they won't be satisfied sticking to one narrowly defined bureaucratic role. Even the ruler will rebel against being kept in a "gilded cage." Still, for the sake of argument, let's concede that we reach your account of utopia. What happens when a new situation arises that requires new policies? We can't predict the future except for one thing: it will look very different. You yourself said the ruler should change with the times. But if the ruler is hidden, how can he promulgate new laws and policies?

Han: Artificial intelligence could help with the adjustments. With AI's help, I'm more confident than ever that the system can work. Still, the ruler should be prepared to exercise power on rare occasions, if absolutely necessary. "The ruler does not try to work side by side with his people, [so] they respect the dignity of his position." The ruler accumulates mystique and dignity precisely by being "godlike in his isolation,"[64] so on the rare occasions he does have to interfere, he will be able to make the necessary changes to the "computer." Power can be increased precisely by doing nothing most of the time.

Xun (baffled): Can you give an example from history to support this claim?

Han: Think of Deng Xiaoping. After the chaos of the Cultural Revolution, he rebuilt a bureaucratic state by reestablishing the college entrance exam and meritocratic ways of assessing public officials. He was a far better Legalist than Chairman Mao, notwithstanding Mao's invocation of the Legalist tradition.[65] But Deng laid in the background and rarely intervened in public. And when he did intervene—as in 1992, when he praised Shenzhen's model of market-driven economic reform—he succeeded in mobilizing the whole country to enact necessary change. If he had been front and center as a leader, he couldn't have been as effective.

Xun: But corruption exploded under Deng! I thought you said Legalism is necessary to prevent corruption!

Han: Again, the problem was too little Legalism, not too much. If Deng had implemented very harsh punishments even for minor misuses of public resources, backed by administrative techniques that atomized public officials, corruption could have been controlled.

Xun (frustrated): I think you're still not getting my point. Even in an ideal Legalist society with well-designed laws and administrative methods, there will be a need for human judgment, especially in hard cases when rules conflict and new situations arise. How to interpret the law is not always clear, nor is it always clear whether and when to adhere to a particular law. And for those cases, it helps to have leaders and ministers with good moral character who are more likely to know when and how to break or bend the rules. Conversely, if government officials are not committed to the public interest, they will often find ways to get around the laws, no matter how stiff the punishments.[66]

Han: Well, most of the time, the laws will work without any need for human judgments. The law is the law. And I worry more about roaming scholars who instill doubt in the law than about rare cases when the law may not be so clear. In the disordered state, "its scholars praise the ways of the former kings and imitate their humaneness and righteousness, put on a fair appearance and speak in elegant phrases, thus casting doubt upon the laws of the time and causing the ruler to be of two minds. . . . If the rulers do not wipe out such vermin . . . they should not be surprised, when they look about the area within the four seas, to see states perish and ruling houses wane and die."[67] The state needs to purge troublemaking scholars.

Xun (losing control): So you think I—your teacher!—should be wiped out!!! How can I teach such students!!!

Han: Professor, if I'm successful, I'd also be superfluous. There would be no need for political advisers like me. But I care more about laws that benefit the state than my own private interest.

Xun (angrily): Who believes that! You think you're the only sage and the rest of us should blindly obey what you say! You. . . .

Chair (interrupting): Please let's calm down. Han is an original thinker but with a moral compass that seems seriously out of whack. He proposes an elaborate system of harsh laws and bureaucratic methods designed to strengthen the wealth and power of the state and to reduce corruption and private misuses of resources. Such measures might be effective in times of chaos, but the price seems too high: the people and the ministers will live in fear and the ruler himself cannot do the things that make him happy.

Han (interrupting): The ruler can set laws that more or less make him happy, so long as they don't diminish the power of the state. And fear is only necessary at the start. Eventually people will internalize the laws and once they do so, they no longer need to fear them, so long as they are law-abiding.[68]

Chair: But you don't persuasively show how we can transition to a peaceful and orderly society where the laws and methods work on behalf of the people. And even your ideal society would make no room for things that make life seem worth living: culture, intellectual curiosity, travel, and celebration of diversity. It's quite a terrifying vision. Let's hear what Professor Xun has to say about the best way to reduce corruption of the state.

2. Xunzi on Ritual

Xunzi (ca. 310-238 BCE) is regarded as the most realist of the Confucian thinkers. He criticized Mengzi's view that people have a tendency to goodness, arguing the opposite. He argued for the "realist" position that legal punishments are necessary to maintain social order in nonideal societies. In contrast to Mengzi (Latinized name Mencius), who favored humane monarchs and did not distinguish between hegemons and tyrants, Xunzi argued that "second-best" hegemons who build trust with allies can be effective in international relations. Xunzi is the most "secular" of Confucian thinkers, with few appeals to mystical phenomena and obscure metaphysics. But Xunzi's work is still grounded in Confucian moral foundations. He argued that people can be morally improved by means of education, good teachers, and rituals that create bonds between people, and he argued that the use of law should be minimized to the extent possible. The more the ruler relies on laws rather than rituals, the less ideal the society.[69] Xunzi acknowledged that strong leaders such as the Qin ruler could achieve short-term political and military success by means of "Legalist" laws and policies, but he said they were doomed to long-term failure because people would be resentful and find a way to rebel and circumvent laws given the chance to do so.

Xunzi's writing style is clear, systematic, and argumentative—he repeatedly names his opponents—and his work is close in style to "Western" philosophy of a more analytical bent. The book is unquestionably a great work of political theorizing, perhaps the greatest in the Chinese tradition and certainly a work that should be part of all courses that introduce the greats of political theory in diverse traditions from around the globe. But Xunzi was largely purged from the Confucian tradition once Mengzi's work was canonized as a Confucian classic in the Song dynasty, and he was expunged from sagehood status in 1530 (more than 450 years after he had been enshrined in 1084).[70] In the twentieth century, Xunzi's thought has made a huge academic comeback in both China and the West.[71] Among reform-minded government officials in China, Xunzi is increasingly viewed as a great thinker who provides politically realistic theorizing that is informed by Confucian morality. High-ranking officials have penned works directly inspired by Xunzi's thought.[72] In Lanling, a city in southern Shandong province with Xunzi's memorial grave site, local officials and scholars are still fighting to have his statue officially reinstated in Confucian temples (without success so far, I regret to report).[73]

Okay, let's return to the debate:

Xun (regaining composure): What's most important is to have public spirited officials in government who won't be corrupt even when application of the law is unclear or when nobody is watching over them. How to increase the possibility that good officials rule the people? Ritual matters more than law because only ritual can change people's hearts. "Ritual and rightness are called orderly. Whatever is not ritual and rightness is called chaotic. Thus, the exemplary person is one who orders ritual and rightness. He does not order what is not ritual and rightness."[74]

Han: Fine words, but it won't work in times of chaos.

Xun: "If the state is chaotic, will the [exemplary person] not order it? I say: Bringing order to a chaotic state does not mean employing the chaos in order to order it. One eliminates chaos and replaces it with order. Bringing cultivation to a corrupt person does not mean employing his corruption in order to cultivate him. One eliminates corruption and replaces it with cultivation. As such, the exemplary person eliminates the chaos: he does not order the chaos. He eliminates corruption; he does not cultivate corruption. The proper employment of the term 'to order' is as when one says that the exemplary person 'does what is orderly and does not do what is chaotic, does what is cultivated and does not do what is corrupt.'"[75] The only way to create a political order where public officials serve the common good rather than themselves is to employ public officials who have been properly educated. They must serve the public because they want to, not because they are forced to.

Han: How can you "cultivate" such individuals? You seem to have a very optimistic view of human nature.

Xun: Not at all. "People are born with a tendency to badness."[76] If people blindly follow their bodily natures and indulge their natural inclinations, aggressiveness and exploitation are sure to develop, resulting in cruel tyranny and poverty. "Humans are born with desires. When they have desires but do not get the objects of their desire, then they cannot but seek some means of satisfaction. If there is no limit to their seeking, then they cannot help but struggle with each other. If they struggle with each other then there will be chaos, and if there is chaos then they will be impoverished."[77]

Han: I agree with that. That's why we need strict laws to control people.

Xun: But you dogmatically deny that people can change for the better. My view is that "people can be made good by deliberate effort."[78]

Han: Sounds quite mysterious to me. I certainly wouldn't construct a political order on the assumption people can morally improve. It's a fool's errand.

Xun: Why so pessimistic? People can be transformed by means of rituals. "The ancient [exemplary rulers] hated chaos, and so they established rituals and rightness in order to divide things between people, to civilize their desires, and to satisfy their seeking. They caused desires never to exhaust material goods, and material goods never to be depleted by desires, so that the two support each other and prosper. This is how ritual arose."[79] We can learn to regulate our natural desires so there is a better fit between what we want to do and the goods available in society, resulting in social peace and material well-being. Rituals provide bonds not based solely on kinship that allow people to partake of the benefits of cooperative social existence in larger-scale societies.[80]

Han (baffled): You think social rituals are sufficient to change people's selfish nature?

Xun: No. We need to start with a commitment to learning from the sages of the past. "Where does learning begin? Where does it end? I say: Its order begins with reciting the classics, and ends with studying ritual. Its purpose begins with becoming a well-bred person and ends with becoming a sage. If you truly accumulate effort for a long time, then you will advance. Learning proceeds until death, and only then does it stop. And so, the order of learning has a stopping point, but its purpose cannot be given up even for a moment. To pursue it is to be human, to give it up is to be a beast."[81] It's a difficult process that requires lifelong commitment. Of course, we need good teachers too, at least at the initial learning stage.[82] "Since people have a tendency to badness, they must await teachers and proper models, and only then will they correct. . . . Without teachers or proper models for people, they will be deviant, dangerous, and not correct. . . . Among people of today, those who are transformed by teachers and proper models, who accumulate culture and learning, and who make ritual and righteousness their path, become exemplary people. Those who give rein to their natural tendencies and inborn dispositions, who take comfort in being utterly unrestrained, and who violate ritual and righteousness, become petty people."[83] With good teachers and models, rituals can do their transformative work.

Han: You seem to place a lot of faith in teachers and models. I guess it didn't work with me. . . . (laughs at his own joke) . . . But I still don't understand how ritual is supposed to improve people, especially if the aim is to make them more public spirited. Look at the rituals today: members of the mafia have elaborate rituals to induct new members of their criminal organizations and crazed football fans sing chants that demonize opposing teams. How do such rituals contribute to the public interest?

Xun: Indeed. We need to differentiate between good and bad rituals.[84] Good rituals change people's character for the better: they make people less selfish and more committed to the public interest. Let's call them "public-spirited rituals." I will use the word "ritual" in that sense.[85]

Chair: Professor Xun, please say more. What are the features of rituals that are beneficial to the public, and how can they help to reduce corruption in government?

Xun: Let me respond to the first question first. Good rituals must promote a long-lasting sense of care and community among participants with the possibility of extending the bonding to those who do not directly participate in the ritual. So first, the rituals must be social, they must involve more than one person. For example, Rafael Nadal's elaborate pregame "rituals" are presumably meant to help him relax before an anxiety-producing tennis match,[86] but they do not have any positive effect beyond himself. Or think of tattoos: today they are done as a means of individual expression and do not necessarily have socially beneficial effects; in the past, however, tattooing rituals were done for the purpose of bonding people to the community.[87] I favor the social form of tattooing. The village wine ceremony is another example of a social ritual that makes people feel as one: "Young and old take a drink from [the wine cup] in order of age. At the conclusion the tankard is rinsed and washed. In this way we know that it is possible for junior and senior to drink together without anyone being left out."[88] By means of this ritual, all members of the community, whatever their social status, establish bonds that extend beyond the ritual itself. They benefit not just those with more social power, but also those at the bottom of social hierarchies.

Han: I don't see how promoting drunkenness can help to limit people's selfish desires. Let's organize a banquet and see what happens: those at the bottom of hierarchies will feel forced to placate their bosses, women will be sexually harassed, etc.

Xun (sighs): We can't just invent rituals out of thin air. It's not a matter of personal choice. Again, "the ancient [exemplary rulers] hated chaos, and so they established rituals and rightness in order to divide things between people and to civilize their desires." The main point of ritual is to regulate what people do and transform their desires so they become civilized. The sage rulers of the past were careful to invent and promote rituals that serve socially beneficial purposes. We should follow the rituals handed down to us by the great sage rulers and that have proven to be socially beneficial over the course of time.

Han: Is there a historical record of such sage rulers who invented "good" rituals?

Xun (somewhat awkwardly): It was a long time ago, we don't have a clear idea of the past, especially the long-distant past. "Culture persists for a long time and then expires; regulations persist for a long time and then cease. The authorities in charge of preserving models and arrangements do their utmost in carrying out ritual but lose their grasp. And so I say: if you wish to observe the tracks of sage rulers, then look to the most clear among them. . . . If you wish to understand the ancient ages, then examine the way of the Zhou. If you wish to understand the way of the Zhou, then examine the exemplary people whom their people valued. Thus it is said: Use the near to know the far." The rituals of the Zhou rulers are the only ones we can adequately reconstruct since they are not too distant in time. As archaeological records surface, we may uncover more evidence of good rituals that predate the Zhou dynasty. In any case, "the sage is one who makes himself the measure."[89] The correct rituals are correct because they have succeeded at achieving desirable social purposes over hundreds if not thousands of years and sage-like interpreters have the capacity to discern these patterns even without a clear view of the origin of the rituals.[90]

Han: So we should blindly follow the rituals of the past, like the man who waits for the rabbit to hit a tree,[91] just because sage-like interpreters tell us to do so. But what worked in the past won't necessarily work now. Even if rituals served desirable purposes in the past, there is no reason to think they will do so now. Look around you: fewer and fewer people follow traditional rituals, or rituals of any sort, and when they do so, it's due to social pressure; such rituals rarely have transformative effect. That's why we tend to think of rituals as "empty": the form is there, without any emotion.

Xun: Good rituals involve emotion and form: "Rituals reach their highest perfection when both emotion and form are fully realized."[92] Again, the main point of ritual is to civilize our animal natures, and if people are just going through their outward routines without any emotion, they are not likely to transform their natures. A ritual needs to involve, or trigger, an emotional response, so that it will have an effect on the participants both during and beyond the ritual itself. That's why the great sage rulers of the past invented music to accompany the rituals: "They caused the progression, complexity, intensity, and rhythm of the music to be sufficient to move the goodness in people's hearts. . . . When music is performed in the ancestral temple and the rulers and ministers, superiors and inferiors, listen to it together, none fail to become harmoniously respectful. . . . It is sufficient to lead people in a single unified way, and is sufficient to bring order to the myriad changes within them."[93] There's a good reason why in Chinese, as you know, we often say "rituals and music" (*liyue*), as though the two are inseparable. Beautiful music engages with the emotions and helps to ensure that rituals have their transformative effect.

Han: My point is that we shouldn't blindly copy rituals from the past. They may have been effective in an age of plenty when people had nothing better to do than participate in drinking activities accompanied by pleasant music, but they won't help much today, in an age of limited resources and when people are at each other's throats. Your hero Kongzi advocated a three-year mourning period for dead parents. Surely you don't advocate restoration of such rituals from the past?

Xun: I do! Something happened in modern society: rituals that provided community have been replaced by a cult of the self,[94] and the ones left over are often too short to do their work. We do need to restore effective rituals from the past! It's worth asking, "What is the reason for the three-year mourning period? I say: It takes measure of people's dispositions and establishes a proper form for them. . . . It is a method that is to be neither adapted nor changed."[95] It's necessary to have a long ritual "when a wound is colossal. When pain is profound the recovery is slow. The three-year mourning period is a form established with reference to emotions; it is the means by which one conveys the acme of one's pain."[96] Such deep emotions threaten to throw our lives completely out of whack, and rituals provide suitable forms for their expression and they work best if they last a long time.

Han: But why three years? It seems completely arbitrary! Do you deny rituals can change with the times?

Xun: Of course not. Those who lack the energy to complete mourning rituals should be given leeway: "After the age of fifty, one is not to perform the mourning ritual in its entirety. After the age of seventy, it is only the wearing of the mourning garments that is to be kept."[97] In times of COVID, people were deprived of traditional ways of mourning, but end-of-life rituals were too important to omit and they often took new forms, even if they involved health risks to the participants:[98] some things matter more than good health! So we should do our best to maintain and restore traditional rituals, but the details can be changed according to context: "Rituals rely on valuables and goods to make offerings, use distinctions between noble and base to create forms, vary the quantity to make distinctions, and elaborate or simplify to render each their due. . . . Thus, exemplary persons can make the elaborate forms of ritual more florid or its simplified form leaner, but they dwell in the mean of its main course."[99] The forms of rituals can vary from community to community—"the people of Lu use cups as a tribute, the people of Wei use vats, and the people of Qi use containers made of hide"[100]—but they still serve the same purpose. The relatively intelligent and socially minded person who is aware of the main point of ritual—to civilize emotions and create a sense of community that extends beyond the ritual itself—can adjust the details of the ritual in accordance with the situation so that rituals are made to serve their point. To be effective, as mentioned, they must engage the emotions, and the effect should be long lasting.

Han: And you can just pick and choose the rituals that serve that purpose.

Xun: No! We should look to rituals that worked in the past. The longer they lasted, the more likely they were effective at generating social bonds between people. And whatever the true origin of the rituals, what matters is that people come to believe, as mentioned, that the rituals were established by sage rulers of the past. If people believe the rituals originated with the great sage rulers of the past, the rituals will be endowed with an aura of "sacredness" that increases the likelihood people care for and follow them. If they are grounded in tradition, they also help to bind people in an intergenerational community.

Han: You certainly place a lot of faith in history, even if it's distorted for your purposes.

Xun: We should also look to findings that transcend their historical context. "There is one measure in ancient times and the present."[101] Social science findings about rituals that generate social bonds can help us to identify those measures. For one thing, rituals that bind people together tend to be performed regularly. If they are performed with high frequency, like national anthems sung every day at school, they can bind the people to the community even if they are not very spectacular or particularly exciting. Other sorts of rituals can bind people for the long term by means of emotionally intense and extravagant practices that imprint in people's memory, if not their bodies: think of "coming-of-age" circumcision rituals for teenage boys, or fire-walking rituals performed by certain tribes. Rituals that are extremely difficult and time-consuming to perform, such as three-year mourning rituals, also serve to cement social glue.[102] Mourning rituals should not be too easy to carry out: "Wearing the mourning garments, propping oneself on a crude cane, dwelling in a lean-to, eating gruel, and using a rough mat and earthen pillow are the means by which one ornaments the utmost hurt."[103]

Such rituals both express intense emotional pain and leave a lasting imprint that binds those who participate in the rituals.

Han: Like the hazing rituals in fraternities or cutting off parts of fingers to initiate people into criminal gangs. I can see why they would leave a lasting imprint, but I can't see how they help with social bonding at large, much less combating corruption in government.

Xun (sighs): Again, the social rituals must be carefully designed and practiced so that they generate a broader sense of community.

Chair: Professor Xun, you repeatedly emphasize the importance of mourning rituals. Even if they serve to help to moderate the emotions of those who grieve the death of loved ones, how can they help society at large? Please recall, the question we are discussing is how best to combat corruption in government. How can mourning rituals help with that?

Xun: If we care about long-term effectiveness, the only way to combat corruption is to make people more public spirited and sensitive to the suffering of others. If our government officials are more public-spirited, they will be more willing to serve the public and less likely to misuse public resources for their own selfish purposes. How to change the motivation of public officials so they care more about the public interest? Again, the best mechanism is to change them via social rituals that have proven to be effective for that purpose. That's why I emphasize rituals involving proper treatment of the dead. The dead, for obvious reasons, are the least capable of protecting their interests. They are, quite literally, the worst off of the worst off. Hence, those with power—the living—need to be trained by means of certain rituals to treat them with love and respect. It is important to adorn the corpse because, "if the corpse is not adorned, it becomes hideous, and if it is hideous, no grief will be felt." The corpse must be gradually moved further away each time it is adorned because "if kept close at hand, one begins to scorn it; when having it close at hand makes it the object of scorn, one begins to weary of it; when one wearies of it, one forgets one's duty to it; and if one forgets one's duties, then one no longer shows proper respect." The ritual should be gradually phased out so that it allows for a smooth transition to everyday life, "whereby he cares for the needs of the living."[104] The moral effect is clear: if the ritual is done properly, it cultivates an altruistic outlook—the living care for the dead, and the dead cannot reciprocate; it's a pure form of caring for others. Then altruism can be extended to those who need care in the world of the living. We can be sure that public officials who undergo such rituals will care for the people and not be corrupt!

Han (laughing): My professor thinks that forcing people to care for dead bodies is the way to combat corruption in government.

Xun: Not forced. Moral education, and perhaps social pressure, can help at the start because some people only discover the value of rituals after they partake of them. But rituals should be noncoercive; they should not be forced upon people.

Han: Why? If rituals are so great, why not make them legally compulsory?

Xun (sighs): Rituals won't have transformative effects if people feel forced to partake of the rituals. Fear of punishment is not likely to produce the sorts of emotions that generate a sense of community. If people engage in rituals because they feel forced to, the rituals are likely to become empty displays of form and devoid of the sorts of other-regarding emotions. To repeat: "Rituals reach their highest perfection when both emotion and form are fully realized." People should perform rituals because they want to, not because they have to, so that they can generate emotions that involve care for the needy.

Han: So you deny that people should be punished for doing bad things? I thought you saw a role for law.

Xun (sighs): It's not either/or, dear student. Laws may be necessary as backup when rituals fail to do their work. But generally speaking, there is a trade-off, and the more society relies on social rituals to regulate people, the better off the society. Let's distinguish between different ways of exercising power: "There is the power to inspire awe that comes from the [moral] Way and virtue. There is the power to inspire awe that inspires awe that comes from being harsh and stringent." These can be arranged in order of desirability. In the best kind of society, "ritual and exemplary music are cultivated. Social divisions and rightness are made clear. Government policies and acts are timely. Concern for and benefit for the people are manifest." In the less desirable Legalistic society, ritual and exemplary music are not cultivated but "nevertheless, the ruler's prohibitions and penalties against those who are violent are stringent. His execution of those who do not submit are thoroughgoing. The punishments and penalties that he assigns are hefty and can be trusted to be applied, and the executions and killings that he commands are fierce and certain to be carried out, falling upon people as swiftly as a clap of thunder striking them or a collapsing wall crushing them."[105]

Han: That's my kind of power! Surely it's better than a society without any laws.

Xun: Yes, in the worst kind of society "there is the power to inspire awe that comes from being wild and reckless. . . . The ruler lacks a heart that is concerned for the people, he makes no effort to benefit the people, and instead he daily practices ways that create chaos among people. . . . When things are like this, then those below will definitely conspire secretly and move in a surge to abandon their superior." So I don't deny that Legalist practices may be necessary in a nonideal world if the alternative is tyranny and chaos. But too much Legalism is not stable. Here too, people will rebel eventually, and corruption can get out of hand because public officials will misuse public resources if they think they can get away with it. Harsh punishments cannot be used indefinitely, and once the ruler relaxes a bit, "he will have no way to keep hold of subordinates."[106] So that's why I favor a society ruled mainly by ritual, and "if one discards the rituals, this is getting rid of the markers. And so, the people become lost and confused and fall into disasters and troubles. This is why punishments and penalties become profuse."[107] There is, one might say, an inverse correlation between the use of rituals and the use of punishments in society.[108] The best form of society would secure social order without any coercion.

Han: My teacher tends to slip into flights of utopian fancy. Do you think we can implement an ideal society now, or do we have to wait for something like Karl Marx's higher communism where people can do as they see fit because advanced machinery does all the necessary work, there is material abundance, no more social classes, and the state would have withered away?

Xun: We cannot do away with social hierarchy. Here too, rituals can help because they specify different treatment for different people. "Ritual is a means of nurture. The exemplary person not only obtains its nurturing, but also loves its distinctions. What is meant by 'distinctions'? I say: 'It is for noble and lowly to have their proper ranking, for elder and youth to have their proper distance, and for poor and rich, humble and eminent to have their proper weights.'"[109] Good rituals involve common social practices that treat people differently, but they generate a sense of community among people including special concern for the well-being of those with less power. Putting rituals into practice means "treating the eminent in a respectful way, fulfilling one's duties to the old, behaving with fraternal courtesy towards one's elders, treating the young with affection, and being kind to the humble."[110] So yes, there is a social hierarchy, but in a society that practices rituals those with power will come to care about the needs and interests of those with less power.

Han (shaking his head): But the ultimate aim is to do away with legal punishments?

Xun: As things stand, it's not possible. Resources are limited and we need punishments to constrain those who would take more than their fair share. Most people, given the chance to do so, will try to satisfy their immediate desires and pursue their private interests regardless of the impact on the public interest. They must be constrained from doing so by means of legal punishments.

Han: Here we agree.

Xun: But I think everyone has the capacity to be virtuous. The problem is that it takes deliberate effort and most people have neither the time nor the inclination to do so. Luckily, a minority of educated people can be made to understand the function of ritual, become more fully transformed by participating in rituals, and develop refined moral sensibilities. "One consolidates one's grip on well-bred people by means of ritual."[111] In a nonideal society, "the [minor] officials on up must be regulated by ritual and exemplary music [but] the masses and commoners must be controlled by laws and regulations."[112] It's important to "use ritual to treat those bearing goodness, and use punishment to treat those bearing badness, then the worthy and unworthy will not be jumbled up, and what is right and what is wrong will not be confused."[113] So we must find a way to elevate the worthy, to select and promote public officials who can be regulated by ritual regardless of family background: "Let us inquire into how to conduct the government. I say: Promote the worthy and the capable without waiting for them to rise through the ranks. Dismiss the unfit and the incapable without waiting for even a single moment. . . . Even the grandsons of kings, dukes, gentry, and the grand ministers, if they cannot submit to ritual and rightness, should be assigned the status of commoners. Even the sons and grandsons of commoners, if they accept culture and learning, correct their person and conduct, and can submit to ritual and rightness, should be assigned the status of prime minister, gentry, or grand ministers."[114] What we need is a political meritocracy, where everyone has an equal opportunity at the start, and the political system should then select and promote those with above average ability who can be transformed into relatively virtuous public officials by means of learning and ritual.[115] That's the best way to combat corruption in the long term.

Chair (skeptically): Is that what we have in China?

Xun: It's an ideal that informs our political system, but as mentioned we still depend too much on fear of harsh punishment to control corruption. Things have improved somewhat since the start of the anticorruption campaign, but I worry that the old ugly practices will resurface once things loosen up. That said, there are some good indications of progress, such as the establishment of a new Confucian academy in Qufu—as you know, ground zero for Confucian culture in China—which aims to train public officials from the whole country in the Confucian classics so they learn about the importance of clean government.[116]

Han (sarcastic tone): And does that work? Are graduates of this academy in Qufu less likely to be corrupt?

Xun: I'm not sure. Frankly, if it were up to me, I'd suggest sending more officials to our newly reestablished Jixia Academy. Rather than didactic lectures, we'd rely more on the debate format so that attendees can witness the beauty and diversity of our political thought and come to their own conclusions, which is more likely to leave a lasting imprint. We'd also emphasize regular participation in rituals—eating, drinking, and singing—meant to generate a sense of community and inculcate a public-spirited work ethic. The more we rely on transformation by ritual and a compelling form of education as means to reduce corruption, the more we are assured of long-term success. Singapore may be an even better example: they rigorously select and promote public officials according to superior ability and virtue who then show commitment to clean government by means of such rituals as wearing white shirts in public. As a result, Singapore is now one of the least corrupt governments in the world.

Han (laughter): But they rely on harsh punishments! In Singapore, the Corrupt Practices Investigation Bureau investigates cases of corruption and strictly implements harsh punishments on those caught.[117] Lee Kuan Yew's view of human nature was as pessimistic as mine, and he thought people could be controlled only by fear.[118] It's pure Legalism. Of course, it also helps that they offer the world's highest salaries to their public officials. It has nothing to do with rituals and rightness.

Xun: It's not so simple. For one thing, the high salaries are intensely controversial in Singapore, and they are cut when public officials do not perform well. A recent case shows that even highly paid ministers can be corrupt.[119] Today, the ruling People's Action Party fully acknowledges that public officials should be motivated at least partly by the ethos of public service and sacrifice,[120] not just by selfish material interests and fear of being caught for immoral behavior. And the "Legalist" mechanism designed to catch malfeasance still reports to the prime minister, who is, in effect, above the law. It wouldn't work without a leader at the very top who sets a good example. In any case, it's much easier to control corruption in small and wealthy countries, where people know others more intimately and resources are relatively plentiful.[121] In China, it's a different story. The salaries of public officials are too low. It is important to "advance honors and rewards in order to encourage them."[122] I've heard cases of public officials who accepted bribes because they needed more money to pay for the health care of sick elderly parents. Higher salaries and better health benefits would minimize such ethical dilemmas. But greed won't disappear even with plentiful resources, and there will always be competition for higher status and powerful positions. At the end of the day, we can control corruption only when public officials feel a duty to serve the public and when corruption comes to be seen as something deeply shameful. What I'm saying is nothing new. The Han dynasty Emperor Wendi rid penal law of some of its most brutal and mutilating punishments in 167 BCE. When he found out that some of his officials were taking bribes, instead of hauling them before judges, he opened his own private coffers and showered them with further gifts of gold and cash to make them feel ashamed about their behavior.[123] We can question his methods, but he was right that corruption can be eliminated only when public officials feel ashamed about misusing public resources for private gain.

Chair: Professor Xun, let's assume that we succeed in selecting and promoting high-quality public officials who "submit to ritual and rightness." Will the system work if the rest of the population is purely self-serving and prone to corruption? It would be a challenge for any government, no matter how virtuous, to rule over a nation of devils: if the commoners have no commitment to paying taxes and find ways of evading their civic duties, for example, the state might collapse, no matter how virtuous the public officials. Shouldn't rituals aim to transform the general public, not just the ruling elite?

Xun: Yes, of course. Public officials need to set a good model for commoners. As Kongzi famously put it, "If you desire goodness, the people will be good. The virtue of a superior is like the wind; the virtue of the common people is like the grass. When the wind blows over the grass it will surely bend."[124] I do think "the humane person likes to instruct and demonstrate to people."[125] So yes, we should promote rituals and rightness in society at large and they will have some effect on commoners. Even an executed convict is entitled to mourning rituals that have positive effects on "his wife and children."[126] Still, we need to be realistic. Some people are "incapable of following the way of enlightened sage rulers,"[127] and they need to be controlled by legal punishments, as my student favors. If people follow their instincts, it will lead to disaster. "To be as noble as the Son of Heaven and to be so rich as to possess the whole world—these are what the natural dispositions of people are all alike in desiring. However, if you followed along with people's desires, their power could not be accommodated and goods would not be sufficient. Accordingly, for their sake the sage rulers established ritual and rightness in order to divide the people up and cause there to be rankings of noble and base. . . . This is the way to achieve community life and harmonious unity." Commoners must be restrained to avoid chaos and conflict and we need humane public officials who will, "for the sake of the whole population, consider the long run and reflect on consequences in order to protect them for ten thousand generations."[128] In politics, there's nothing more important than selecting and promoting high-quality public officials more likely to "submit to ritual and rightness."

Chair: Professor Xun, I do worry about your political elitism. Why can't we promote such egalitarian rituals as one person, one vote? We know that single votes are not likely to affect the outcome of elections, but people participate in voting rituals because they feel it's their moral duty to do so, and the ritual in turns generates a sense of community and public spiritedness.[129] That's one reason the least corrupt countries tend to be electoral democracies.

Xun: I'm not so sure. We need to compare large countries at similar levels of economic development. Electoral democracies such as Indonesia and India are perceived as far more corrupt than China.[130] And the big problem with our village elections, as you know, is that they are so corrupt.[131] Voting rituals do not always, or even usually, have the transformative effect we hope for. Perhaps they are too infrequent and lacking in emotional intensity. The deeper problem is that one person, one vote tends to erase distinctions—rituals, as mentioned, need to distinguish "between the noble and the lowly." With egalitarian voting rituals, the most incompetent and debased people think they have equal ability to make morally informed political judgments. Commoners rarely vote according to the public interest, and they often select leaders with no political experience who appeal to people's worst emotions.[132]

Han (smiles): Here, I fully agree with my teacher. It seems completely reckless to place faith in commoners, as though they will magically come up with informed political judgments. We need harsh laws, ruthlessly applied with no mercy, to control people's worst instincts.

Chair: Well, I didn't mean to suggest that voting rituals per se are sufficient to transform people into public-spirited citizens. We also need civic institutions such as the jury system where people participate in politics in a deeper way and on a more regular basis. Alexis de Tocqueville and John Stuart Mill both saw the jury as a school of public virtue: ordinary people learn to pay attention to others, deliberate about just outcomes, and take responsibility for their collective choices.[133] I also favor such practices as deliberative polling: randomly selected citizens, advised by experts, learn to make informed political judgments in the public interest. We tried such experiments in China and we need more of them, if the concern is to promote public spiritedness at large.[134]

Xun: Perhaps. But we need to be realistic. I don't think we need to aim so high with the general public. I doubt that commoners can be made to think and act in the public interest on a consistent basis. What you suggest involves changing people's minds. But rituals change people's feelings, that's easier to do. Rituals bring forth a "community without communication," to borrow Byung-Chul Han's felicitous phrase.[135] They come to be seen as enjoyable and "make people's hearts agreeable" by means of collective activities such as dancing, music, chanting, and moving in tandem, without requiring much conscious thinking or understanding or intellectual exchange.[136] Commoners can partake of rituals and get some moral benefits without really understanding the process: "the social divisions contained in the *Odes* and *Documents* and in the rituals and music are not something an ordinary person will understand."[137] Frankly, commoners often misunderstand where rituals come from—"To the exemplary person, they are part of the human way, to common people, they are something pertaining to spirits"[138]—but it doesn't matter so long as they partake of the rituals and change somewhat. If we want to promote a degree of public spiritedness among commoners, I'd suggest relying primarily on rituals rather than highly intellectualized deliberations in juries and town halls. But for public officials, we should aim higher: they should have a love of learning and good understanding of the function of ritual propriety and an above average attachment to the public interest, along with a sense of shame that will prevent wrongdoing even when nobody is looking or the law is silent.

Chair: Well, thank you both, it seems like a good time to wrap up. Professor Xun does not deny the necessity of legal punishments to prevent corruption. Nor does he deny the importance of providing positive incentives for good behavior, such as higher salaries for public officials. But he argues that only a strong commitment to serving the public can reduce the risk of corruption in the long term and that social rituals can make people more public-spirited. The political system should aim to select and promote high-quality public officials with the love of learning and the ability and motivation to be transformed by rituals so they become committed to the public interest and not be swayed by short-term desires and private interests. For commoners, the demands are not so high, but it is nonetheless important to restore and reinvent rituals so that people come to experience a sense of social bonding and care for the humble, as opposed to being left in their natural state where they compete without any restraints for social status and scarce resources.

---

3. The Banquet

Xun: It has been a long day. As Chief Libationer of the Jixia Academy, it is my obligation to host a drinking ritual followed by a banquet. In accordance with our anticorruption campaign, the Jixia Academy cannot provide alcohol at public expense, so I've brought a bottle of twenty-year-old *maotai* from my cellar. Admittedly, it was a gift from the "good old corrupt days."

Han (laughs): I must recognize that corruption has some benefits.

Xun: Well, the main benefit is that traditional drinking rituals generate a sense of social bonding,[139] which we desperately need after this heated debate. Frankly, if it were up to me, I'd allow for alcohol to be provided at public expense.

Chair: Professor Xun, you must have a good "drinking ability"!

Xun (relaxing a bit): Well, I'm more than willing to partake of social drinking, but my "drinking ability" is quite poor.[140] Plus, I might not remember tonight's festivities if we go overboard. The ritual won't be effective if it doesn't leave a lasting imprint.

3

On the Uses of Art

OR, SHOULD THE COMMUNITY SUBSIDIZE CULTURE?

THE WARRING STATES period (ca. 476–221 BCE) was a time of constant upheaval when different political thinkers argued for various governmental priorities. Legalist thinkers such as Shang Yang argued for the priority of victory in war and defended policies that led to military conquest, even if they required cruel means.[1] The Mohists—groups of soldiers, artisans, and mechanics inspired by the thoughts and ideals of Mozi ("Master Mo")—argued for defensive warfare and against aggressive warfare, similar to Mengzi (Mencius).[2] The moral foundation of Mohist thought is similar to modern-day consequentialist thinking: a policy is justified if and only if it promotes benefits and avoids harm for the majority of people.[3] What Mohists meant by "benefit" was quite basic: provision of material needs such as food and clothes and the avoidance of physical pain and hardship. So they argued, in populist mode, against extravagant funeral mourning rituals by the ruling classes on the grounds that they wasted resources that should go to benefit the common people. For the same reason, Mozi objected to expensive musical performances that diverted resources away from what we would today call poverty alleviation. The Confucian thinker Xunzi, writing toward the end of the Warring States period, explicitly criticized such Mohist outlooks. His work contains repeated attacks on the Mohists (he attacks other schools of thought, but most of his venom is directed at the Mohists), including a chapter that argues for the importance of musical arts,[4] because, combined with rituals, they can transform people's self-interested tendencies into other-regarding morality.[5] His defense of the musical arts was followed up by the *Record of Music* (*Yueji*), author unknown, which expands on some themes in Xunzi's essay, including a detailed discussion of the nature and benefits of exemplary music. Such debates are still highly relevant today, especially in relatively poor societies that must make hard choices about how to distribute scarce resources.

In this chapter, I imagine a debate between a descendant of Mozi and a descendant of the author of the *Yueji* called Yue over whether a township in southern Shandong province should fund a new cultural center.[6] The debate is set in rural Zaozhuang, somewhere between Lanling, site of Xunzi's memorial grave, and Tengzhou, site of the Mozi Memorial Hall.[7] It is a relatively poor part of Shandong province, but rich in culture, and I will imagine a deliberative poll where randomly selected citizens (mainly farmers, in this case) are asked to deliberate about whether the community should fund the proposed cultural center (He Baogang and others organized successful deliberative polls that allowed for participatory budgeting in a township in Zhejiang province,[8] so it is not implausible to imagine such polls taking place in Shandong province). Like most deliberative polls, the randomly selected citizens are advised by expert panels to help ensure that informed deliberations take into account the advantages and disadvantages of different possibilities. In this case, the first expert called to the panel is a descendant of Mozi, who argues against the proposed cultural center. He is followed by a (female) descendant of the author of the *Yueji*, who argues for the center. Mo and Yue argue with each other, and the panel is moderated by a professor at Shandong University, who does his best to summarize the positions in a fair-minded way. The chapter ends with a decision by randomly selected citizens along with an account of what happened after the decision was taken.

1. Mozi's Critique of Music

The *Mozi* is a collection of essays and (imaginary?) dialogues compiled by the disciples of Mozi ("Master Mo") about whom little is known. Mozi criticized Kongzi (Confucius) and was criticized in turn by Mengzi, suggesting he lived sometime in the fifth century BCE. The Mohists then developed into different schools inspired by the thoughts and ideals of the "founding father" and flourished in the Warring States period. The writing style of the *Mozi* is argumentative, repetitive, and relatively straightforward (if not pedestrian), without the literary flourishes, vivid metaphors, and compelling stories of Mengzi and other great thinkers and writers from the Warring States period. The text argues for an objective moral standard—to promote what is beneficial to the world and avoid what it harmful—to be used to resolve social and political controversies. In practice, it means adhering to the dictates of Heaven's Will that provides an account of morality for human beings (with Mozi as the interpreter of Heaven's Will)[9] and of "ghosts" and "spirits" who act as the agents of Heaven's Will by rewarding the worthy and punishing the wicked. Institutionally, Mozi defends the ideal of a humane and compassionate monarch who rules over the whole world, a political meritocracy that promotes and demotes public officials according to ability and virtue regardless of family background, and policies inspired by the ideal of "universal love" that aim to treat everybody equally (here Mozi explicitly criticizes Confucians who argue for "graded love" that varies with the level of intimacy). Policymakers should avoid aggressive warfare and promote economic wealth, a large population, and social order that benefits commoners. Mozi was explicitly critical of the Confucian fondness for elaborate and wasteful rituals that, he said, diverted resources from people's basic needs. He also caricatured Confucian outlooks on the grounds they justified a fatalistic attitude to life, arguing instead that human effort can and should contribute to improving society.[10]

Such ideas were hugely influential in the Warring States period, which is why Xunzi devoted so much time and effort to rebut them. The strict, almost cult-like nature of the Mohists also made them a fearsome force: they were highly disciplined and lived in quasi-poverty in accordance with their moral principles. At least some were paramilitary organizations that may have been threatening to the political authorities, and after the Han dynasty the Mohists largely disappeared from view, with the exception of Daoists, who incorporated Mozi into the pantheon of immortals.[11] Another explanation for their disappearance is that some of their ideas, such as the need for impartial government that has priority over family ties, were absorbed by Xunzi and the Legalists. It may also be that their ideals were both too extreme and too pedestrian. On the one hand, impartiality may be a desirable ethic for government officials, but the ideal of universal love is too demanding as an everyday morality, given strong attachments to family and friends. On the other hand, the somewhat vulgar concern with material well-being at the cost of cultural pursuits was rejected by mainstream Confucians in subsequent history. For Confucians, the state can and should provide for basic material welfare, but it doesn't follow that human beings do not also have a fundamental need to lead rich and flourishing lives informed by culture and musical arts. That said, Mohism has made a comeback of late in academia. Some scholars continue to seek inspiration from Mozi's highly original ideal of universal love (or care)[12] and the commitment to devising practical ways of addressing the material needs of common people. Others are impressed by the Mohist concern for rational argumentation and argue that the school contributed to ancient Chinese science and developed the earliest form of logical reasoning in the Chinese tradition.[13] In mainland China, an academic school termed New Mohism has emerged over the past few decades that takes the revival of Mohism as its mission and promotes such values as thriftiness, impartiality, and international peace by means of modern interpretations of Mohist texts.[14]

Now, let us move to the debate!

Moderator: Mr. Mo, you go first. What is the case against the proposed culture center for the musical arts? It seems like a good idea for our community to showcase local musical talent. But why are you against it, Mr. Mo?

Mo: Let's start with the basics. We need to apply moral standards to judge policy choices. What do we mean by morality? "It is the job of the humane person to work to promote what is beneficial to the world and to eliminate what is harmful."[15]

Yue: I agree with that.

Mo: But the reality is obviously very different. We need to ask, "At the present time, what produces the greatest harm to the world? Great states attacking small states, large fiefs producing disorder in smaller fiefs, the strong oppressing the weak, the many tyrannizing the few, swindlers cheating the simple, and the noble treating the humble with contempt—these are all examples of doing harm to the world."[16]

Yue: Again, hard to disagree, at that level of abstraction.

Mo: So we need to "inquire into the cause of these various harms. What has produced them? Are they born from loving others and benefiting others? Everyone would certainly say that that is not the case and would want to say instead that they are born from hating others and harming others. When we can then classify those in the world who hate others and harm others, will we say they are examples of 'being impartial' or 'being partial'? Everyone will surely say being partial. It is just such partiality in dealing with others that bears as its fruit the greatest harms to the world. This is why partiality is wrong."[17]

Moderator: You mean that rulers should aim to be impartial.

Mo (excited). Yes! "Suppose there are two rulers: one who maintains impartiality and one who maintains partiality. And so, the ruler who maintains partiality would say, 'How can I possibly regard the well-being of my myriad subjects as I do my well-being? This is profoundly at odds with the way people in the world feel.' . . . And so, when his subjects are hungry, the partial ruler does not feed them. When his subjects are cold, he does not clothe them. When his subjects are ill, he does not nurture them. And when his subjects die, he does not bury them. This is what the partial ruler says and what he does. But this is not what the impartial ruler says nor how he acts. The impartial ruler says, 'I have heard that in order to be an enlightened ruler in the world, one must first worry about the well-being of the people and then worry about oneself. Only in this way can one be an enlightened ruler.' And so, when the impartial ruler's people are hungry, he feeds them. When his people are cold, he clothes them. When his people are ill, he nurtures them. And when his people die, he buries them. This is what the impartial ruler says and what he does."[18]

Yue: I agree that rulers should aim to be impartial; they should care first and foremost about the well-being of their citizens, instead of misusing power for their own interests and that of family members. That's why we need to select and promote public officials with superior ability and virtue.

Mo: Exactly! "In a state where there are worthy people, good order will be secure, and in a state where there are few worthy people, good order will be tenuous. This is why the proper work of [great rulers] is to increase the number of worthy people in their states. Since that is the case, what is the best way to go about increasing the number of worthy people? . . . [The worthy] must be rewarded and esteemed, revered and praised; then one can succeed in increasing the number of worthy men in one's state. . . . In ancient times, when the sage-monarchs ruled, they promoted the virtuous and honored the worthy. Even someone who worked as a farmer, artisan, or merchant—if they had talent, they were promoted, given high rank, and a handsome salary, entrusted with responsibility, and empowered to have their orders obeyed. And so, at that time, rank was awarded on the basis of virtue, work was assigned according to office, reward was distributed according to the amount of labor done, and salary allotted in proportion to the effort expended. And so, officials were not guaranteed constant nobility and people did not have to perpetually remain in a humble state. Those with ability were promoted, those without ability were demoted."[19]

Yue: Yes, those were the good old days, when we had something close to an ideal political meritocracy. I agree with the ideal. Public officials with superior ability and virtue should be promoted regardless of family background.

Mo: But it's not just empty talk. "What I have been talking about here is not just some notion or theory. In ancient times, when Kings Wen and Wu ruled, they allocated everything equitably, rewarding the worthy and punishing the wicked without showing any partiality to their relatives or brothers. . . . The humane ruler promotes the righteous and does not turn away the poor and the humble. . . . When the ruler's relatives heard this, they retired and thought to themselves, 'At first, we could rely on being the ruler's kin, but now the ruler promotes the righteous and does not turn away those far removed. This being the case, we too must be righteous.' When those far removed from the ruler heard this, they too retired and thought to themselves, 'At first, we thought that being far removed from the ruler meant we had nothing to rely upon, but now the ruler promotes the righteous and does not turn away those removed from him. This being the case, we too must be righteous.'"[20] Good models can inspire righteous behavior; we need to restore such models.

Yue: Yes, I agree that virtuous behavior among public officials can help to promote morality in government more broadly, just as corruption can be contagious among less-than-virtuous public officials.

Mo: It's not limited to the government. Virtue can spread to the whole community! When the officials were righteous and ruled with impartiality, "The word spread to those serving in distant cities and outlying regions, to the sons of nobles serving within the court, to all within the capital, and out to the common people throughout the four corners of the kingdom. Hearing this, they all strove to be righteous!"[21]

Yue: Mr. Mo, here we may part ways. Let's be realistic. We can't expect common people to be impartial at all times, or even most of the time. In my own case, frankly speaking, I won't treat my mother's neighbor the same way I treat my own mother. I'm just a humble scholar, not a government official, so please forgive me if I prioritize the well-being of my family over that of others.

Mo: That's exactly the problem! The desire for partiality is the ultimate cause of harm in the world! We must "replace partiality with impartiality . . . how then can we replace partiality with impartiality? . . . If people regarded other people's states in the same way that they regard their own, who then would incite their own state to attack that of another? For one would do for others as one would do for oneself. If people regarded other people's cities in the same way that they regard their own, who then would incite their own city to attack that of another? For one would do for others as one would do for oneself. If people regarded other people's families in the same way that they regard their own, who would then incite their own family to attack that of another? For one would do for others as one would do for oneself. And so, if states and cities do not attack one another and families do not disrupt and steal from other another, would this be a harm to the world or a benefit? Of course, one must say it is a benefit to the world."[22]

Yue: Mr. Mo, a political theory must be both desirable and realistic. In theory, if we are all impartial all the time, as you suggest, we might live in a utopian world of harmonious order. But that wasn't psychologically realistic in the past and it's not realistic now. As mentioned, I agree that public officials should aim to be impartial when they perform their public duties. The state should select and promote public officials with above average virtue in the sense of being willing to serve the public in an impartial way and laws and incentives should reward impartial behavior and punish partial behavior in the form of nepotism and corruption. But common people will usually be partial to their communities and their families. That's how the real world works and we must work within those constraints. You won't persuade me that I should treat foreigners the same way I treat fellow citizens, that I should care for people living in different cities the same way I care for fellow "city-zens," not to mention treating my mother the same way I treat my neighbor's mother or treating my child the same way I treat other children.

Mo: But that's what we should aim for! "The impartial person says, 'I have heard that in order to be a morally superior person in the world, one must regard the well-being of one's friends as one regards one's own well-being; one must regard the parents of one's friends as one regards one's own parents. Only in this way can one be a morally superior person.' . . . Let us consider the case of a filial son who seeks what is beneficial for his parents. Does a filial son who seeks what is beneficial for his parents want other people to care for and benefit his parents or does he want other people to dislike and steal from his parents? According to the very meaning of filial piety, he must want other people to care for and benefit his parents. Given this, how should one act in order to bring about such a state of affairs? Should one first care for and benefit the parents of another, expecting that they in turn will respond by caring and benefiting one's own parents? Or should one first dislike and steal from other people's parents, expecting that they in turn will respond by caring and benefiting one's own parents? Clearly one must first care for and benefit the parents of others in order to expect that they in turn will respond by caring for and benefiting one's own parents. And so, for such mutually filial sons to realize unlimited good results, must they not care for and benefit other people's parents? Or should they let it be the case that filial sons are the exception and not the rule among the people of the world?"[23]

Yue (baffled): I really can't understand what you are saying. You present a false dichotomy between loving care for a stranger's parents and stealing from them. But isn't it more realistic to expect that one cares more for intimates, with some love for others, but with decreasing intensity along with increasing distance? You mention the relation between adult sons and elderly parents, but it's even more clear in the case of caring for one's own children: how strange to expect that I would care more for other people's children than for my own children! I've never met a mother who thinks that way! Plus, why do you think that I should care for my neighbor's mother first on the expectation that my neighbor will reciprocate by caring for my mother? With all due respect, that wouldn't work. For one thing, my mother would be upset that I'm not favoring her. She would think that I'm not a filial daughter (you keep on talking about sons and fathers but please don't forget that women do most of the caring for needy family members).[24] Second, I have no reason to expect that my neighbor will reciprocate: that would only work in some sort of ideal Shandong-style kibbutz where people care for other people's needy relatives in loving ways over and above their own relatives, but in the real world such expectations are, to say the least, unrealistic.

Mo: It's realistic, but we need better role models. "Now as for impartially caring for and benefiting one another, such things are incalculably beneficial and easy to practice. The only problem is that there are no morally superior people who take delight in them. If only there were superiors who delighted in them, who encouraged their practice through rewards and praise, and threatened those who violate them with penalties and punishments, I believe that the people would take to impartially caring for and benefiting one another just as naturally as fire rises up and water flows down. One could not stop these things from being practiced anywhere in the world."[25]

Moderator: My dear scholars, please don't forget what we are supposed to be discussing: whether our community should fund a musical arts center. So far, the discussion has been quite theoretical. You both seem to agree that the task of government is to promote the well-being of the people and that policymakers should aim to treat people with impartiality. You also agree that public officials should be promoted based on their ability and willingness to serve the people, that good-quality officials should be rewarded with high social status and decent salaries, that poor-quality public officials should be demoted, and that this kind of political meritocracy should operate regardless of family or partiality. But you disagreed when it comes to applying this ethic of impartiality to everyday life, outside of government. Mr. Mo thinks it can and should be done, with the help of good role models, and Ms. Yue argues it's unrealistic and violates some deeply held intuitions about family love. Now let me ask you: what does any of this have to do with the question I've asked you to answer?

Mo: I was getting to that. A very real problem with excessive devotion to a partial form of filial piety—those who care more for their parents than for the parents of other people—is that it leads common people to bankruptcy and wealthy members of the community to spend their resources on lavish funerals and extravagant mourning rituals rather than spreading their wealth to needy members of the community. Consider what happened in ancient China. When we implemented "the teachings of those who followed and upheld lavish funerals and prolonged mourning, then in mourning for a king, duke, or high official, they prescribed that there be several inner and outer coffins, a deep grave, many layers of burial clothes, elaborately and intricately embroidered funeral shrouds, and a massive burial mound. Among common men and women this exhausted the resources of the entire family. And even a feudal lord had to empty his entire treasury before the appropriate amount of gold, jade, and pearls could adorn the body and the proper quantities of silk, carriages, and horses could fill up the tomb."[26]

Yue (laughs): You're fond of attacking straw men! Yes, there may have been such elaborate funerals in the past, but they are rare today, with the possible exception of funeral ceremonies for members of deceased royal families, as in the United Kingdom. And in such cases, what they spend on funerals will likely be compensated by the amount of tourist dollars injected in the economy.

Mo: Lavish spending for funeral ceremonies is a still problem in China, especially among wealthy people in rural areas.[27] Excessive mourning is equally worrisome. "Mourners are to cry and wail irregularly, at all times of the day and the night, and to sound as if their sobs are choked off. . . . They are to dress in sackcloth, allow their tears to run down without wiping them away, and live in a mourning hut made of straw, sleeping upon a rush mat and using a lump of dirt as their pillow. . . . Should monarchs, dukes, and other great people follow such practices, they would not be able to come early to court and retire late in order to hear litigation and carry out the affairs of government. . . . Should farmers follow such practices, they would be unable to go out to the fields and return home late in the order to carry out the plowing, planting, and tending of crops. . . . And so lavish funerals entail burying a great deal of wealth, and prolonged mourning entails prohibiting people from pursing their vocations for an extended period of time."[28]

Yue: Of course I agree that funerals and mourning practices should not plunge people into poverty. Who argues otherwise? In any case, Mr. Mo completely ignores an important function of mourning rituals: they generate a sense of community among participants and cause the powerful to care for the needy.[29] Let me elaborate. . . .

Moderator: Ms. Yue, you will get your turn. Please let Mr. Mo finish his thought.

Mo: My point is that people should be moderate in caring for dead relatives. "A coffin three inches thick is adequate for the decaying bones. Three layers of clothes are adequate for the decaying flesh. The grave should be dug to a depth that does not strike water but that also does not allow fumes to escape to the surface. The burial mound should only be high enough to clearly mark the spot. There should be crying as one sees the departed off and as one comes back from the grave. But as soon as people have returned to their homes, they should resume their individual livelihoods. There should be regular sacrificial offerings made to extend filiality to one's parents."[30] To repeat, I'm not against filial piety. But filial duties should be practiced in moderation, especially in the case of the wealthy and powerful who tend to go overboard and waste scarce resources rather than helping the common people in need.

Moderator (losing patience): Mr. Mo, please address the question we are supposed to discuss today. What does any of this have to do with funding for the musical arts?

Mo: It's obvious: The principle of moderation should be extended to the performance of musical arts! As mentioned, "it's the job of the humane person to work to promote what is beneficial to the world and to eliminate what is harmful. . . . When such a humane person makes plans for the sake of the world, it's not to provide beauty for people's eyes to see, pleasures for their ears to hear, sweetness for their mouths to taste, or a place they will find comfortable to dwell in. If providing these would diminish or deprive the people of the materials required for their clothing and food, the humane person will not do it." That's why I say: "Making music is wrong!"[31]

Yue: My friend, how can you deny that music is pleasurable? As you know the character for music— 乐 (*yue*)—is the same as the character for pleasure or joy. Surely it's not a coincidence. Maybe the Taliban wants to ban music because such pleasures are bad for the soul, but that' s not our view here in China.

Mo: I do not deny that music can be pleasurable. I do not condemn music because "the sounds of bells, drums, zithers, and pipes are not pleasing." The problem is that music does not "accord with the practices of the sage-monarchs of old and does not promote the benefit of the people in the world today."[32]

Yue: Your appeals to the past are misleading. The sage-monarchs had music.

Mo: Yes, but "it amounted to so little, it was like being altogether without music." After that, music became so elaborate and that led to chaos. "The more elaborate musical performances become, the more government order diminishes. From this it can be seen that music is not something that should be used to govern the world."[33]

Yue: Music doesn't have to "govern the world," but it can provide enjoyment. How can you deny that the musical arts do not benefit the people today? Most people love music!

Mo: Too much love for music is precisely the problem: "If the state is infatuated with music and besotted with wine, then [we should] argue against the musical arts."[34] And we need to ask: who loves music? In our context—a relatively poor, largely rural community in Shandong province—the elites love music, but we need to focus on people's basic needs, and the government should not be funding musical performances. "These days, when . . . persons of high rank engage in the manufacture of musical instruments, it's not as simple as collecting rainwater or digging up a little dirt. Rather, they must heavily tax the people in order to enjoy the sounds of bells, drums, zithers, and pipes."[35]

Yue: But people are willing to be taxed to build cultural centers because music brings pleasure to them.

Mo: That' s not what people here care about![36] . . . (looking at the deliberative jury) . . . I speak on the behalf of the poor! Why should we fund luxurious entertainment for the rich! It's a complete waste of taxpayer's money![37] "The present use of musical instruments imposes three hardships upon the people. Because of the expenditures involved in producing such instruments, those who are hungry are unable to get food, those who are cold are unable to obtain clothing, and those who toil are not afforded a chance to rest. These are the three greatest hardships the people worry about. But what if we play the great bells, strike up the drums, sound the zithers, blow the pipes, and dance with shields and battle axes? Will this enable the people to procure food or clothing?"[38]

Yue: Maybe not, but what's wrong if people listen to music on their iPhones? It may not bring them their next meal but it brings them some pleasure.

Mo: That's not what we are debating! The question is whether the people should be taxed to build a musical arts center in our community. . . . "If we look to see whether heavily taxing the people to produce the sounds of great bells, drums, zithers, and pipes promotes the benefit of the people of the world and eliminates what is harmful to them, we see that it offers no such help. . . . Musical performances are wrong!"[39]

Yue: You make it seem like there is a necessary trade-off between funding for musical performances and providing food for the people. But we can afford a cultural center in our community to promote our local music arts.

Mo: The musical arts are expensive. "In ancient times, Duke Kang of Qi found excitement and delight in the performance of the Dance of Wan. The performers of the dance were not permitted to wear coarse and simple clothing nor could they eat plain or common food because it was said that 'if their food or drink is not fine, their faces and complexions will be unworthy to look at. If their clothing is not fine, their figure and movements will be unworthy of view.' And so, their food had to be only the finest grains and meats and their clothing had to be only embroidered silk. They never worked to produce their own food and clothing but were always supported by the work of others." The same is true today. "These days, when kings, dukes, and great people put on musical performances, they divert vast resources that could be used to produce food and clothing for the people. . . . Making music is wrong!"[40]

Yue: Again, you're attacking a straw man. We don't have to pay for very expensive instruments and costumes and feed our performers with bird's nest and shark fin soup. We can put on modest performances that suit our budget, and building the center won't bankrupt our community.

Mo: Even if we find the funds to build the center, it will take people away from farming! Where will we get our food? It takes a great deal of energy to perform music and dance, and who do you think will perform our local music? It will be "people in their prime, for their ears and eyes are sharp and clear, their limbs are nimble and strong, the sounds they produce are harmonious, and they can follow the complicated turns in the performance. If they employ [people in their prime] to make music, then they must abandon their work of plowing, planting, and cultivation." And other farmers will waste time listening to music. "If farmers delight in musical performances and spend their time listening to them, they will not be able to go out to the fields at dawn and return at dusk, plowing, planting, cultivating, and reaping great harvests of grain and other produce. As a result, the supply of food will be insufficient." That's why I say, "Making music is wrong!"[41]

Yue: Okay, I get your point, you don't have to repeat yourself so much.

Mo: It's not just that! If we go ahead with this plan, our local officials won't spend as much time doing what they are supposed to do, namely, serving the people! Public officials will "take pleasure in music and spend their time listening to it, they certainly will be unable to arrive in court early and leave late, hear lawsuits, and manage the government—and this is why nations fall into chaos and their altars of soil and grain are imperiled. . . . [They] will certainly be unable to expend the strength of their limbs and exhaust their mental powers, within the court, by managing the bureaus and treasuries and, outside the court, by collecting taxes at borders and markets and by gathering beneficial products from the forested hills and low-lying wetlands, all of which should fill the granaries and state treasuries—and this is why the granaries and treasuries are not full. . . . If one were to ask what caused great people to waste the time they could have spent hearing governmental affairs, . . . we would answer: Music!"[42]

Yue: These slippery slope arguments are not very persuasive. Why do you think that public officials listening to some music will cause them to neglect their duties? They can be good officials most of time, and listen to some music in their time off.

Mo: Yes, it's a slippery slope! Once the seal of desire is broken, it will get out of control.[43] . . . (looking at female members of the deliberative jury) . . . Perhaps it's modest at the start, but the Confucians like Ms. Yue "concoct elaborate and lavish ritual and musical performances to delude other people. . . . They rely on other people's households to fatten themselves and other people's fields for the liquor they drink. . . . They are fond of musical performances and engage in lewd conduct with others."[44] What Ms. Yue proposes, in effect, is a return to the bad old corrupt days of the 1990s, when public "servants" went to sing and dance with beautiful hostesses at karaoke bars, all at public expense!

Yue (offended): How can you say that! That's not at all what I have in mind. . . .

Mo (interrupting): Today, there are also karaoke bars for women. If we promote music, female officials will go to karaoke bars with male models.

Yue (rendered temporarily speechless): But . . . that's ridicu . . .

Mo: We must oppose public funding for music! . . . (turning to the deliberative jury) . . . It's worth keeping in mind that the natural world is not sufficient to provide our goods, so we need to work hard and be frugal. "Humans certainly are different from the various kinds of birds, beasts, and bugs that one can find in the world today. The various birds, beasts, and bugs rely upon their feathers and fur for their clothing, their hoofs and claws for their leggings and shoes, and grass and water for their food and drink. And so even if [they] do not plow and cultivate the land and do not spin and weave, these creatures are still assured of having food and clothing. Humans differ in this respect. Those who labor upon the land survive, while those who do not, perish. If exemplary persons do not exert themselves in pursuing their duties at court, then the laws and administration will fall into chaos. If the commoners do not exert themselves in carrying out their work, there will not be enough material goods."[45] So we must divert our energies and resources to what's important—securing the means of life—because it doesn't come naturally. If we use public funds for musical arts, it's a recipe for disaster!

Moderator: Thank you, Mr. Mo. You strongly favor moderation and oppose spending resources on such activities as expensive and time-consuming funeral and mourning rituals because they come at the cost of providing basic needs for the people. Similarly, you oppose musical performances because they come at the cost of people's basic needs, especially food and clothing. You do not oppose music per se, nor do you deny that it brings people some pleasure, but you think our community cannot afford a cultural center meant to showcase local musical performances. And even if we do find the funds for the center, you worry that people will waste too much time on music and things will get out of hand: farmers will enjoy music rather than farm for food, and public officials will be infatuated by elaborate and lewd musical performances rather serving the public. As a result, the people won't have enough food, clothes, and other basic necessities. They will remain poor, even worse than animals who can get by without much effort. Now, Ms. Yue, your turn. Please tell us why you think we should find a cultural center that promotes local musical arts.

2. Xunzi/Yueji's Defense of Music

Xunzi (ca. 310–238 BCE) and Mozi shared a commitment to universal rule by a humane monarch supported by public officials meritocratically selected regardless of family background. Xunzi also opposed aggressive warfare on the grounds it could not lead to long-term victory since the occupied people will rebel as soon as they get a chance to do so. Like Mozi, he developed an argumentative style that directly engages with opposing views. But Mozi was his main opponent, and Xunzi hammered away at their differences. Whereas Mozi claimed that it was relatively easy (if not natural) for humans to follow the dictates of morality, Xunzi argued it requires great effort. People are born with a tendency to badness that can be overcome only via a lifelong devotion to learning with the aid of great teachers as well as participation in social rituals that generate a sense of community among participants.[46] Those rituals should be accompanied by musical arts that directly engage with the emotions so as to unify hearts and help with the transformative process. Hence, Xunzi was strongly critical of Mozi for neglecting the importance of the musical arts, and he wrote a whole essay titled *Discourse on the Musical Arts* that was meant (at least partly) to counter Mozi's essay *Against the Musical Arts*.

For this dialogue, I draw on Xunzi's *Discourse on the Musical Arts* as well as the chapter *The Record of Musical Arts* (*Yueji*) that comes from the (later) Han dynasty text *The Book of Rites* (*Liji*). This chapter almost directly copies sections of Xunzi's chapter (there wasn't much concern with plagiarism in ancient China, or to put it more positively, authors were less concerned with taking credit for their own works and worried less about seeking direct inspiration from the great thinkers of the past),[47] but it insightfully elaborates some of Xunzi's points about the socially beneficial effects of "good" music and the harmful effects of "bad" music.[48] My own view, for what it is worth, is that if the renowned Song dynasty Confucian Zhu Xi had selected *The Record of Musical Arts* as one of the four Confucian classics instead of the *Doctrine of the Mean* (*Zhongyong*, also from *The Book of Rites*), which lends itself to flights of metaphysical speculation at the cost of social and political engagement[49]—and if the former rather than the latter text had been part of the imperial examination curriculum in the Ming and Qing dynasties—the Chinese world would have been better off. But perhaps it's not too late to revive this hugely important text.

And now, back to the dialogue. . . .

Yue (recovering her composure): Well, let's first point out that Mr. Mo has an oddly malleable view of human nature. He thinks people will change for the better—meaning that they will be committed to an ethic of impartiality and to doing good in the world—simply by force of argumentation and by following role models.[50] But this is absurdly optimistic. It's not so easy to change human nature, or, to be more accurate, the tendencies of human nature. To improve people, we need to engage with their emotions.

Mo: Yes, I agree. Fear works. That's why people need to believe in ghosts and spirits that "can reward the worthy and punish the wicked. Now if we could just persuade the people of the world to believe that ghosts and spirits can reward the worthy and punish the wicked, then how could the world ever become disordered?"[51]

Yue: The problem, of course, is that not everybody believes in ghosts and spirits.

Mo (looking at the deliberative jury): That's a problem for intellectuals. "Why not try going into a district or village and ask people there? If, in the course of human history, from ancient times up to the present, there really are people who have seen ghostly or spiritual entities or heard the sounds of ghosts or spirits, then how could one say that ghosts and spirits do not exist. . . . If the people turn to licentiousness, violence, rebellion, theft, or robbery and use weapons, poisons, water, or fire to attack travelers on the roads and byways and rob their carriages, horses, coats, and furs in order to profit themselves—there are ghosts and spirits who will see them!"[52]

Yue: As people become more educated, they are less likely to believe in ghosts and spirits that punish wrongdoing and I hope the jury doesn't fall for those rhetorical tricks.

Mo: "If it were the case that ghosts and spirits do not really exist, then in offering sacrifices, all we would be doing is expending resources of wine and millet. . . . These offerings would still be a means for welcoming and bringing together close family and gathering together and increasing fellowship among people living out in the villages and towns."[53]

Yue (laughs): It seems you're not persuaded yourself about the existence of ghosts and spirits, so I suspect you'll have a hard time persuading others. But you're on to something important. Rituals such as offerings for ancestors can be transformative. Here is the process. "People are born with a tendency to badness." If people blindly follow their bodily natures and indulge their natural inclinations, aggressiveness and exploitation are sure to develop, resulting in cruel tyranny and poverty. But "people can be made good by deliberate effort."[54] By participating in social rituals, people come to feel a sense of oneness that makes them other-regarding and sensitive to the needs of others. Rituals provide social bonds that allow for cooperative social existence.[55]

Mo: Rituals are more likely to be effective if people believe in ghosts and spirits that oversee social activities and reward good people and punish the wicked.

Yue: That's not so important. What matters is that rituals engage with the emotions, which is why they are usually accompanied by music that stirs the heart. Think about our village rituals. "When music is performed in the ancestral temple and the ruler and ministers, high status and low status, listen to it together, none fail to become harmoniously respectful. When it is performed within the home and [parents and children and elder and younger siblings] listen to it together, none fail to become harmoniously affectionate. And when it is performed in the village, and old and young people listen to it together, none fail to become harmoniously cooperative. Thus, music observes a single standard in order to fix its harmony, it brings together their playing in order to ornament its rhythm, and it combines their playing in order to achieve a beautiful pattern. It is sufficient to lead people in a single, unified way, and is sufficient to bring order to the myriad changes within them."[56] Without music, in other words, rituals won't be so effective. Rituals are typically hierarchical—they specify different roles for people with different social status. But music makes the participants feel as one. "Music unites that which is the same, and ritual distinguishes that which is different. Together the combination of ritual and music governs the human heart." But "[Mr. Mo] denounces these things"![57]

Mo: You exaggerate the effect of music. Music doesn't always stir my heart. I do not get moved by elevator music.

Yue: Mr. Mo, I didn't mean to imply that all music stirs the heart. But generally speaking, "music is joy,[58] an unavoidable human disposition. So, people cannot be without music; if they feel joy, they must express it in sound and give it shape in movement. The way of human beings is such that changes in the motions of their nature are completely contained in these sounds and movements."[59]

Mo: As I said, I do not deny that music can bring joy. The problem is that it doesn't always lead to "harmonious cooperation." When adolescents listen, to, say, the Sex Pistols, it makes them want to tear down the whole system.

Yue: So we must distinguish between different kinds of music! "If music is dissolute and dangerous, then the people will be dissolute, arrogant, vulgar, and base. If they are dissolute and arrogant then they will cause chaos. If they cause chaos and struggle with each other, then the state's soldiers will be weak and its fortifications vulnerable, and rival states will put them in danger."[60]

Mo: So we agree. Not only is music a waste of money, it can endanger the whole community.

Yue: But we need to promote good music that guides the emotions in a positive way! "People cannot be without joy, and their joy cannot be without shape, but if it takes shape and does not accord with the moral Way, then there will inevitably be chaos. The ancient sage-monarchs hated such chaos, and therefore they established the sounds of the *Ya* and the *Song* in order to guide them. They caused the sounds to be enjoyable without being dissolute. They caused the patterns to be distinctive without being degenerate. They caused the progression, complexity, intensity, and rhythm of the exemplary music to be sufficient to move the goodness in people's hearts."[61]

Mo (sarcastically): The sounds of the *Ya* and the *Song*? Please remind me what that sounds like.

Yue: Regrettably, those sounds have been lost to history. But the principle is the same: exemplary music that stirs the heart can lift people out of their self-interested orbit and make people feel as one. The effect is clear in the case of soldiers: every army knows that soldiers should be made to regularly sing in unison because they are motivated by stirring music. "Sounds and music enter into people deeply and transform people quickly."[62] Of course, the effect is even stronger when the music is accompanied by movement. "In taking up the shields and axes of the war dance and rehearsing its motions, their appearance becomes majestic. In proceeding according to the markings and boundaries of the dance stage and conforming to the rhythm of the accompaniment, their ranks and formations become ordered, and their advances and retreats become uniform."[63] So exemplary musical arts have the effect of motivating soldiers and making them more willing to fight for the community.

Mo: Like those American soldiers in *Apocalypse Now,* who listened to Wagner's *Ride of the Valkyries* as they went on shooting sprees from helicopters in Vietnam. They killed anything that moved with great joy, including innocent civilians. You sound like "an apologist for aggression and warfare."[64] It's fine to "slaughter the population, and force the common people to scatter,"[65] so long as the soldiers are moved by beautiful music.

Yue (upset): Of course that's not my view. I don't deny that beautiful music can be put to bad uses: Beethoven's Ninth Symphony was used to celebrate the fall of the Berlin Wall and also to glorify Hitler on his birthday in 1942.[66] So music that inspires people must to tailored to morally desirable purposes. "If one uses music to conduct punitive expeditions abroad, then there will be none who do not submit."[67] The cause must be in accordance with the Way and the means of warfare must be just. War starts and ends with music: "When one hears the sound of the drums, advance. When one hears the sounds of the gongs, withdraw." But soldiers cannot be made to commit unjust acts during the war itself. "The general will not accept a command from the ruler [if it means] mistreating the common people." Soldiers need to adhere to principles such as "Do not kill the old and feeble. . . . In all cases of executions, one is not to execute the common people."[68] Still, we need to recognize that some forms of warfare are justified and we need motivated soldiers ready and willing to defend the community. Exemplary music, accompanied by movement, ensures that if "people are harmonious and uniformly ordered, then the state's soldiers will be vigorous and its fortifications will be solid, and rival states will not dare to touch it."[69] So the state needs the musical arts to unify people, generate a sense of community, and inspire soldiers willing to die for that community. Mr. Mo wants to ban musical arts from public spaces, but that will weaken our military, leading to the collapse of the political community!

Mo: I'm more concerned with the well-being of the people. You're concerned with the strength of the state, which is why you favor taxing the people for musical activities that supposedly strengthen the state.

Yue: I'm also concerned with the well-being of the people! How can people benefit if the state is weak and vulnerable to attack by other states?

Mo: I think the state should spend its resources first and foremost on material welfare that benefits the weak and oppressed. Today, "the strong plunder the weak, the many tyrannize the few, swindlers cheat the stupid, the noble treat the humble with disdain, and there is widespread acceptance of bandits and robbers—none of this can be stopped. Given this, were we to deal with them by striking great bells, beating the singing drums, strumming the lutes and zithers, blowing the pipes and mouth organs, and brandishing shields and axes, how could we obtain anything that would produce good order. . . . Were one to lay heavy exactions on the peoples in order to [make music], nothing good would come of it."[70] How can music stop the strong from bullying the weak?

Yue: Here too, we can't do without music! "Music is something in which the sages delighted, for it has the power to make good the hearts of the people, to influence the people deeply, and to reform their manners and customs with facility. Therefore, the sage-monarchs of the past guided the people with ritual and exemplary music, and the people became harmonious and congenial." Again, it must be the right kind of music that guides emotions in a positive way. If it's bad music, the social effect will be disastrous: "Whenever bad sounds arouse people, a perverse vital energy responds to them from within. When this perverse vital energy takes form, then chaos results from it." But with exemplary music, "the common people will all rest secure in their dwellings and delight in their villages, and are entirely satisfied with their leaders." In other words, exemplary music provides social harmony that lets common people lead decent lives, free of oppression and misery. Conversely, without music, or with the wrong kind of music, there will be disorder and conflict, and "the common people will not be secure in their dwellings, will not delight in their villages, and will be dissatisfied with their leaders."[71] In times of chaos, "the strong entrap the weak, the many harm the few, the clever cheat the foolish, the bold bully the timid, those with ailments and illness are not cared for, the old, the young, the orphans and the widows and widowers are not accommodated."[72] So we both care about protecting the interests of weak and vulnerable people, but the best way to do so is to promote exemplary music that generates social harmony and avoids chaos.

Mo: Isn't it just better to provide more direct material welfare for the people? What you say is so abstract, it's hard to figure out what it means in practice.

Yue: Well, consider the village drinking ceremony. On the one hand, the ritual instantiates social hierarchies: "The guest of honor offers a toast to the host, the host offers a toast to the guests of the second rank, and the guests of second rank offer toasts to the rest of the guests, and the young and seniors each drink in turn according to their rank and age." It's important to "give face" to the powerful. But the ritual "treats appropriately those junior and senior without leaving anyone out" and beautiful music helps to cement a sense of oneness: "The singers enter, ascend, and sing three songs, and the host offers them wine. The *sheng* players enter, play three pieces, and the host offers them wine. The singers and musicians take turns performing separately three times and then perform together three times."[73]

Mo: I don't see the point of rituals with drunken musicians.

Yue (sighs): The ritual regulates drinking and we "know that it is possible to gather in harmony and joy without becoming dissolute."[74] "The ritual protocol is to take one drink per offering so that guests and hosts toast one another a hundred times and drink all day without being able to get drunk. . . . This is how food and drink can unite people in merriment, how exemplary music leads people to conform to virtue, and how the rites stop people from over-indulging."[75] And the ritual ends up benefitting those of lower status. With good food and fine wine people are happy, the music makes the participants feel as one, and those with power and wealth come to care about the needs of the less fortunate. So music-infused rituals bring great pleasure to participants, and they benefit not just those with more social power, but also those at the bottom of social hierarchies. Do you want to ban such ceremonies because they come with music?

Mo: Such rituals are expensive and the positive social effects are too uncertain. People need to be moderate and, more important, the state should encourage thriftiness. The state should not waste money sponsoring rituals with "exemplary music."

Yue: "Mr. Mo worries very conspicuously about insufficiency for the whole world. However, insufficiency is not a common disaster facing the world. . . . The greens and vegetables can grow so as to fill up whole swamps. Beyond these, in a single season the six domestic animals and other beasts can become [so numerous] as to fill up every available cart. . . . Instead, the common disaster facing the world is that chaos harms it. . . . Why don't we inquire together into who it is that makes it chaotic? I take it that Mr. Mo's rejection of music will cause the world to be chaotic and Mr. Mo's advocacy of frugal expenditure will cause the world to be impoverished. This is not an attempt to slander him. It's simply that his teachings cannot avoid these results. If at his greatest Mr. Mo had possession of the whole world, or if at the least he had possession of a single state, he would have people uncomfortably wearing coarse clothes and eating bad food, and though they might be sad, he would deny them music. If it were like this, then the state would be starved. If the state is starved, then rewards would not work. . . . He would put foremost and regard with merit toils that are laborious and bitter, dividing up the word evenly with the commoners and making equal all merit for labors."[76] We'd be back to the Cultural Revolution, where everyone is equally miserable and equally poor! Is that what we want?

Mo (pauses): Well . . . no. . . . In those times, they wasted government money on Jiang Qing's "eight model revolutionary operas" that were supposed to provide political education for the ignorant masses.

Yue: That's perhaps the only good thing we can say about the Cultural Revolution. By means of such operas, people became more sensitive to the ravages of patriarchy and class tyranny. Female soldiers were celebrated in the *Red Detachment of Women*—based on a true story of a band of female Communist guerrilla fighters in remote Hainan island—and it inspired women to fight against oppression.[77]

Mo: Our community is poor. We should focus our energies on providing material benefits for the people rather than subsidizing "politically correct" forms of music.

Yue: But without music, there is no joy, no social harmony, only chaos and violence, the state won't be effective and people will be poor. . . . "If the methods of Mr. Mo are put into practice, then the whole world will exalt frugality but will only become poorer. The people will denounce fighting but will only struggle with one another more each day. They will engage in laborious and bitter toils, bent over and exhausted, but will only increasingly fail to have accomplishments. Melancholy and sorrowful, they will denounce music but will only grow less harmonious by each day."[78]

Mo: Stop it! My only argument is that the state should not sponsor music!

Yue: You still don't understand: exemplary music is necessary for good government! "To lack beautiful things and ornaments will leave one incapable of uniting the people, to lack wealth and generous endowments will leave one incapable of managing one's subordinates, and to lack strength and the power to inspire awe will leave one incapable of stopping those who are violent and overcoming those who are brutal. Thus, the former sage-monarchs were sure to strike great bells, beat sounding drums, blow on reeds and pipes, and play lyres and zithers, in order to fill up their ears. They were sure to have carving, polishing, engraving and inlay, insignias and ornaments, in order to fill up their eyes. They were sure to have fine meats and good grains, the five flavors and the various spices, in order to fill up their mouths. Only afterward did they increase their personnel, set up official posts, promote rewards, and make strict punishments. . . . When rewards and punishments inspire awe, then the worthy can be gotten to advance and the unworthy can be gotten to withdraw, and the capable and incapable can be accorded their proper offices. . . . Thus, if the methods of Confucians are truly put into practice, then the whole world will be peaceful and prosperous! Put to work, the people will accomplish great things. Striking bells and beating drums, they will be harmonized. . . . One will obtain harmony among humankind!"[79]

Mo: Harmony among humankind! What does any of this lofty talk have to do with taxing farmers to subsidize a local community center for the musical arts?

Moderator: Yes, I do think we need to take stock and move the discussion forward. Ms. Yue argues that music stirs the heart. But she argues we must distinguish between different kinds of music. Bad music makes people rebellious and violent and leads to social chaos. Good music—exemplary music—regulates our emotions in a positive way and, combined with ritual, can make people less selfish and more concerned with the common good. It unifies people's hearts, leads to harmonious communities that protect the weak from oppression, and motivates soldiers to protect the state from attack. Exemplary music can be used by the state to create a sense of community that makes the powerful care for the worst off and makes it possible for the government to implement policies that lift people out of poverty without too much opposition. It's not just that material well-being and musical enjoyment are both important. Ms. Yue makes the stronger argument that material well-being can't be fulfilled without the musical arts because the latter provides the sense of community that underpins effective policies benefitting those who need material resources. Music is not sufficient to generate a robust sense of solidarity with the poor and downtrodden—teachers and moral examples can help, and music should usually be combined with ritual—but music, even in small doses, can be quite motivational compared to, say, pure argumentation or fear of punishment. Now, however, I'd like Ms. Yue to focus more directly on the question we are supposed to be discussing: why should our community subsidize a center for the local arts?

Mo: Exactly! . . . (looking at the jury) . . . Why should the state tax poor farmers for a cultural center? If Ms. Yue is so keen on this goal, let her find a wealthy philanthropist who can pay for her preferences!

Yue: I do not know of any such philanthropist, and even if there is one, the work of musical education is too important to be left to the private sector. We need both a publicly funded center to promote musical arts and a leader—let's call her the "Music Master"—with the task to select and disseminate exemplary music. "The work of the Music Master is to cultivate government regulations and orders, to keep watch over poetry and artistic form, to prohibit perverse music, and to smoothly cultivate these tasks at the appropriate times, so as to prevent barbarian, vulgar, and deviant tunes from daring to disorder the refined pieces."[80]

Mo: It sounds like you want to bring back Jiang Qing and her "eight model operas" and to prohibit other music.

Yue: Don't be silly. What I propose is not very different than what the foreigners call "Music Director." The Music Director of the Metropolitan Opera in New York, for example, has the task of selecting beautiful and uplifting classical operas for modern-day audiences. In our context, we need public support for a Music Master with the ability and motivation to select and disseminate great music from the past. To be frank, we can't leave it to the free market because much of new music is vulgar and deviant and it easily captures the desires of people without developed musical tastes. "Those who know musical sounds but don't understand exemplary music, these are common people! Only exemplary persons understand music. . . . Exemplary people rejoice in attaining the moral Way, whereas petty people rejoice in fulfilling their desires."[81] Such new music immediately engages with people's desires, without any moral filter. "In the new music, [the singers and dancers] advance and retreat without any regular order, the music corrupts [people] in order to promote the utmost form of vileness. . . . Such music cannot be modeled on the moral ways of antiquity."[82]

Mo: It sounds like you want to promote classical music on the supposed grounds it's morally uplifting and to ban "vulgar and deviant" new music. In the West, archconservatives such as Allan Bloom and Roger Scruton similarly argued for more promotion of classical music and they denounced "decadent" rock music.[83] So you want us to pay for a cultural center that promotes Bach and Mozart?

Yue: We need a Music Master with the ability and motivation to make fine-grained distinctions. Not all classical music from the West is good from a moral point of view: Think of Mozart's *Don Giovanni*, which can be used to promote sexual exploitation of women. I'm reminded of a scene from the film *Babette's Feast*: an older male French opera singer uses this music to seduce an innocent young farming woman in rural Denmark. The music may be beautiful, but the moral effects are perverse. Ideally, we should promote music that is beautiful—it brings joy to the performers and the audience—and also makes the people feel harmonious. Recall what Kongzi said about *shao* music: "The *shao* music is both superbly beautiful and superbly good. . . . Once I heard the *shao* music, I couldn't appreciate the taste of meat for three months; after that, I had no idea music can reach such heights!"[84]

Mo: But we no longer know anything about *shao* music! You keep on appealing to long lost music! . . . (looking at the deliberative jury) . . . Why should our community support a center and a music master to promote music that no longer exists?

Yue: I don't mean to deny that modern performers can also produce some exemplary music.

Mo: Like the *Red Detachment of Women*?

Yue: It doesn't have to be so didactic. Songs such as Michael Jackson and Lionel Richie's "We Are the World" inspire people to care about famine in distant lands. John Lennon's song *Imagine* breaks down socially constructed barriers between nations. As a moral globalist, you should welcome such music and frankly, it does more good in the world than your lectures on impartiality.

Mo (offended): Where is your empirical evidence for such claims? . . . (pause) . . . But now that I think about it, there may be a case for a center that exclusively promotes music proven to increase commitment to the virtue of impartiality.

Yue: That's not what I mean. Even seemingly simple love songs can lift people out of their selfish orbits. Think of Deng Lijun (Teresa Teng). Her songs, inspired by Tang dynasty poetry, were popular thirty years ago in China, they are still popular today, and they will still be popular one hundred years from now. It's impossible not to be moved while listening to, say, "The Moon Reflects my Heart."[85] It's widely sung in karaoke bars as a way of generating positive emotions between performers. I met my husband that way: he overheard me singing the song and joined in, we made it a spontaneous duet. It reminds me of what Kongzi said: when he heard people singing, and they sung well, he "asked them to sing again and then joined in their harmony."[86] With exemplary music, performers try to be sensitive to each other's styles while being aware of their own roles, and together they create beauty and "diversity in harmony"[87] beyond the capacity of any one individual. Thanks to "The Moon Reflects my Heart," my husband and I fell in love!

Mo (rolls his eyes): Well, if the song is so great, it will survive without public support. Why do you want our community to subsidize a center to promote Deng Lijun's songs?

Yue: My point is not that the center should promote particular songs. The Music Master should select exemplary music according to certain principles that fit appropriate times and places. The main point of exemplary music "is to provide a sense of togetherness . . . [and] a sense of togetherness leads to mutual care." Governing by means of exemplary music aims for a community where "there are no rebellious people, the [regional power holders] submit willingly, the weapons and armor are not used, the five punishments are not implemented, and the people are free from worry."[88]

Mo: I still don't see what kind of music can lead to that kind of utopian society. It sounds so mysterious and I hope our jury doesn't fall for those fine words.

Yue: It's not mysterious. People respond to musical sounds in different ways. "When delicate and fading musical sounds are made, the people will be sad and sorrowful. When expansive and harmonious yet slow and level, sophisticated and decorative yet simple rhythmic music expressions are made, the people will be content and happy. When unrefined, active, shocking, and bold beginnings, along with arousal of the whole body and expansive and indignant musical expressions are made, . . . the people will be firm and resolute. When straightforward and upright, unyielding and correct, serious and honest musical sounds are produced, the people will be solemn and respectful. When broad, rich, well-rounded, smoothly accomplished and harmoniously activated musical sounds are produced, the people will be kind and loving. When undisciplined, one-sided, biased, scattered, never-ending, and over-flowing musical sounds are produced, the people will be indulgent and disorderly."[89] The task of the Music Master is to select and disseminate exemplary music based on the musical sounds most likely to contribute to a society informed by joyful social relations and mutual affection. The truly outstanding interpreter of the musical arts can create new exemplary music appropriate for the times.[90] The Music Master also needs to be sensitive to context. "The five emperors in their different times did not follow the exemplary music of their predecessors."[91] If a society, for example, is very unjust and "angry" music like the *Red Detachment of Women* can motivate people to overcome oppression, then the Music Master can select music that generates such "negative" emotions.[92] But the long-term aim should be communal harmony: "Ordering ethical relations without worry is the nature of exemplary music and joy, happiness, affection, and care are its functions. . . . Exemplary music unifies everyone in care through different musical patterns."[93]

Mo: You have supreme faith in the ability of a "Music Master" to invent, select, and promote music that transforms people in a positive way. And you make these claims about the moral effects of music without any empirical evidence!

Yue: Do you deny that the music people listen to reflects their mood? At the level of whole societies, the same holds true. Think about it. "The musical sounds in periods of good governance are peaceful and joyful and the political administration is harmonious. The musical sounds in periods of chaotic government are bitter and angry and government policies are perverse. The musical expressions of the doomed state are mournful and regretful and its people experience great hardship."[94] Wouldn't you worry if, say, violent, racist, and sexist music were to become highly popular in China?[95]

Mo: Yes, I would. But I don't think "good" music can transform people for the better. You're making a causal claim that music can change people for the better, not simply arguing that we can tell the mood of the people by what kind of music they listen to. People in a certain mood may select music that reflects their mood, but it doesn't mean that music *causes* people to change for the better.

Yue: What I say isn't controversial. Capitalists know full well that music can affect people's feelings, and eventually, behavior. TV advertisements are accompanied by catchy tunes that make people have positive associations with the products so that people are more likely to buy them. Suspenseful music in horror films increases the anxiety level of the viewer, thus satisfying the desire to be scared. DJs feel the "vibe" of the crowd and try to make people feel as one, or sometimes they adjust to create more elevated "vibes" that make people appreciate new musical perspectives and enjoy less commercial music.[96] Plus, there is much empirical evidence that playing and listening to music can have desirable effects: neuroscience research shows that some music has the effect of unifying people.[97] Music can literally change the brain, which is why it's so important to select and promote the right kind of music.

Mo: Sounds dubious to me. And if there is an effect, it is probably stronger on the performer than the listener. But you're proposing a cultural center that is supposed to mainly benefit listeners. Even if there is an effect on listeners, does it really produce lasting change?

Yue: Those are certainly interesting questions that require further research. But so long as we are persuaded that music can have some positive transformative effect, we should identify and promote exemplary music that leads to communal harmony.

Mo (frustrated): I still don't understand what kind of music can lead to such beautiful outcomes.

Yue: It's for the Music Master to decide. All we can do is provide the principles that should inform her choices. Again, it's not as unusual as it sounds. All major centers for the musical arts are led by musical directors who select music that expresses both beauty and morality. Conversely, they deselect bad music: bad in an aesthetic sense, moral sense, or both. You won't hear punk music in Beijing's National Center for the Performing Arts.

Mo: But we're not a major center! We are a small community and we can't afford grandiose musical arts, even if it leads to the good consequences you describe.

Yue: Yes, I agree. As I said, context matters. The emotions elicited by exemplary music are the same, but the Music Master needs to select music "paired with appropriate times and occasions."[98] In this community, it doesn't have to be too high-brow: local musicians can play sweet sounding songs like "Go Home Often and Have a Look"[99] that remind people of their obligations of filial piety. Such songs are especially important now that many elderly people need family care. Of course, we should include folk music from southern Shandong, in accordance with what moves the people here. People are often inspired by local artists. Plus, we need to recover some of the exemplary music of our ancestors so as to encourage a strong sense of cultural pride and intergenerational solidarity. We also have an obligation to preserve some of our exemplary musical arts for the sake of future generations who will benefit from cultural vibrancy.[100]

Mo: Can you provide an example of exemplary music from Shandong?

Yue: Again, it's the task of the Music Master to select appropriate music.

Mo (contemptuous laughter, turning to jury): Please don't get fooled by any of this! If we pay for this center and its "Music Master," we are sure to lose money!

Yue: Of course, there's an initial investment but cultural centers often end up making money in the long run. If they are run well and spread a message of beauty and harmony, they will attract both local support and visitors from outside.[101] . . . The problem with Mr. Mo is that he aims both too high and too low. He thinks people can change simply by the force of argumentation and fear of ghosts and spirits, and does not recognize that changing people can be difficult: we need to engage with the emotions in a serious way, and music is necessary for that task. On the other hand, he seems satisfied with an orderly society where people are poor and culturally illiterate. Here I think we should aim higher—for a relatively wealthy community characterized by beauty and "diversity in harmony"—and an arts center that promotes exemplary music can help us to realize that ideal.

Moderator: Thank you, Ms. Yue. You argue for both a cultural center and a music director who will have the task of selecting musical arts that make people joyful and promote communal harmony. Such music, ideally, would have a proven track record in the past of engaging and regulating the emotions in ways that lead to mutual care, though Ms. Yue allows for the possibility that some modern music may also have this function. The center should emphasize local musical arts that move people in our community and make us proud of our past heritage and transmit the best of our culture to future generations. And even if the musical center loses money at first, it may still become a profitable enterprise if it proves to be successful at putting on performances that make people happy and harmonious. I think we have a good sense of the arguments on both sides of the question. Thank you both, Mr. Mo and Ms. Yue. Now the deliberative jury will discuss among themselves and come up with a recommendation.

3. The Decision

Moderator: After extensive deliberations, our randomly selected citizens have decided not to fund the musical arts center. They agree it's desirable in principle, but our township is too poor to afford it now and we should spend our resources on social welfare for needy people. In the long term, as our township becomes wealthier, we can revisit this proposal.

[Several weeks later, a new party secretary has been appointed, and he must decide whether to implement the decision of the deliberative opinion poll. He discusses with the moderator.]

Moderator: Mr. Secretary, the decision, taken after extensive deliberations with views from both sides of the question, was to not fund the musical arts center.

Party Secretary: That's surprising! Other townships have such centers, why can't we have one? I don't need to remind you that public officials in Shandong are promoted partly on their ability to promote the best of our cultural traditions.

Moderator: The deliberators—mainly farmers—agreed it's a good idea for the long term, but now we must focus on the welfare of the poor in our township.

Party Secretary (scoffs): Those farmers are quite clever. Why don't they want a cultural center? It all comes down to money. They think the price we offered for expropriation of their land is too low. They know we need their land to build the center, and they are holding out for a better price. Plus, they need time to build a second floor on their homes so they can claim more for the extra space when it comes time for expropriation. We can't wait, let's build it now.

Moderator: Mr. Secretary, the decision was taken with full information of both sides of the question. I think we need to respect their decision.

Party Secretary: How much did we pay for this "deliberative poll"?

Moderator: Only 148,000 yuan.

Party Secretary (raises voice): Are you kidding me! What a waste of money! We will never do that thing again. And we will build the musical arts center.

Moderator: But Mr. Secretary. . . .

Party Secretary: That's the conclusion. We won't talk about this again.

4

On the Morality of Warfare

OR, HOW TO THINK ABOUT THE USE OF MILITARY POWER?

IN THE Tang dynasty (618–907 CE)—perhaps the most open, vibrant, and multicultural period in China's history—it was common for the imperial court to host debates between Confucians, Daoists, and Buddhists on the pressing issues of the time. The emperor or empress would let them discuss policy suggestions from different points of view.[1] In modern China, the government hosts debates on foreign policy between hawkish and dovish scholars at Zhongnanhai to help decision-makers formulate policies based on different perspectives.[2] In this chapter, I imagine a debate a few years from now between a policy adviser who is a descendant of the Legalist thinker Shang Yang named Shang and a descendant of the Confucian scholar Mengzi (Latinized name Mencius) named Meng. I also imagine a situation where the United States makes firmer commitments to defend Taiwan and a proindependence government in Taiwan is on the verge of declaring formal independence. The two thinkers offer different perspectives on the morality of warfare in the context of debating the question of whether mainland China should invade Taiwan. The president moderates the debate.

Both Shang Yang and Mengzi wrote their works in the fourth century BCE of the Warring States period, a time of constant and increasingly brutal warfare. It was also a time when the ancient equivalent of policy advisers could roam from state to state with the aim of influencing rulers. Almost all thinkers of the time partook of the ideal of a politically unified and peaceful world ruled by a humane monarch,[3] but they had different ideas of how to get there, with Shang Yang and Mengzi on opposite ends of the political spectrum. The two thinkers exemplify what has come to be known as the debate between "realists" and "idealists" in international relations.[4] Shang Yang is openly amoral and favors whatever leads to military success: the more cruelty the better, if that is what it takes to win (he is the most extreme of the "realist" thinkers in the Chinese tradition).[5] Mengzi argues for morality in politics and favors warfare only if it is informed by moral ends and means.[6] Shang Yang was more politically successful than Mengzi, who, like Kongzi (Latinized name Confucius), had to settle for a life of scholarship and teaching as a second choice after rulers failed to take his advice. Their writing styles are very different: *The Book of Lord Shang* is blunt, curt, and humorless, whereas the *Mengzi* is a work of literary genius, with florid metaphors and memorable sayings that continue to be used in modern Chinese.[7] What's common is that both works open with debates: in the case of Shang Yang, he debates policy options with other advisers in the presence of a ruler, and in the case of Mengzi, he openly criticizes a ruler who engages in war for the purpose of territorial gain and proposes a moral approach to warfare as an alternative.[8] Let's start with what Shang Yang has to say, followed by Mengzi, and ending with a decision on whether to go to war by China's ruling Standing Committee of the Politburo.

1. Shang Yang on Amoral Warfare

Shang Yang (ca. 390–338 BCE) was perhaps the most influential statesman in preimperial China.[9] Like other roaming policy advisers of the Warring States era, he left his home state (of Wei) for another state where rulers might be more receptive to his advice. He ended up in the state of Qin, which he served as a senior statesman. Shang Yang argued that states in his day faced a stark choice between survival and dismemberment. Rather than appeal to a golden age of peace and material abundance for inspiration, rulers should disregard traditional morality and do whatever is necessary to strengthen the state. For that purpose, the state must rely on force at home and abroad. At home, the state should promote agriculture so it has enough food for its people and its army. Those not fighting should direct their energies to agriculture and "useless" professions—such as merchants, scholars, and musicians—need to be ruthlessly purged. The state's foreign policy should aim to build a strong military with the capacity to defend the state and invade and take over the territory of other states. Shang Yang thought that people are selfish and naturally dislike hard agricultural work and fighting to the death on the battlefield, and they should be kept ignorant of other possibilities. The whole system should be designed so people come to see it's in their self-interest to farm and to fight: people can be molded into farmers and soldiers by means of laws backed with harsh punishments (hence the label "Legalist") and a reward system that provides incentives for effective farmers and soldiers. For success in warfare, Shang Yang suggested an objectively meritocratic system that promotes soldiers according to the number of decapitated heads of enemy fighters.

Such policy advice was adopted by the Qin state, and it eventually succeeded in unifying the territory that came to be known as China with Qin Shihuang as the self-proclaimed First Emperor in 221 BCE. The dynasty proved to be short lived (only fifteen years), and the First Emperor went down in history as a cruel dictator. Shang Yang himself came to a sorry end—death by dismemberment and execution of his family—similar to the unhappy fate of other Legalist thinkers. The Legalist school continued to be influential in Chinese political history, but it was basically purged from official discourse after the Han dynasty largely because it was regarded as too amoral by Confucians who dominated the intellectual landscape.[10] In the twentieth century, however, Legalism made a comeback. Mao himself dedicated his first essay to Shang Yang, and Legalists were positively viewed during the Cultural Revolution (1966–1976) that attempted to smash Confucianism and other forms of traditional morality. Today, the slogan *fuguo qiangbing* (rich state, strong military)—first used by Shang Yang—is memorized by students in primary school and plastered on posters all over China (in shortened form *fuqiang*), usually in the most prominent position among the eleven other "core socialist values." Scholars in mainland China and outside contribute more dispassionate works about Shang Yang and his legacy.[11]

Okay, let's turn to the debate!

President: Welcome, dear scholars. As you know, we face a dire situation now. The United States has basically abandoned the One China policy. If Taiwan declares formal independence, we will face strong pressure to launch an invasion. I know we all favor a unified country, including Taiwan. But the question is whether we should use force to achieve this aim. Let's hear from your perspectives. Mr. Shang, please start.

Shang: We need to go in now. Hit them fast and hard.

Meng (gasps): Why? There will be hundreds of thousands of casualties, maybe more, with the risk of nuclear war.[12] Even in the best-case scenario, it will be a bloody battle with no clear prospect of a "win" and our economic development will be set back by decades. What's the hurry?

Shang: We haven't fought a war since 1979. Our military needs practice, and the longer we wait, the rustier we become. We're strong now, but "when a strong state is not engaged in warfare, poison infiltrates its intestines; rites, music, and parasitic affairs are born and [the state] will surely be dismembered."[13]

Meng: I also worry about dismemberment. But shouldn't we try other means first? There will be a huge cost to our people and maybe the whole world! War should always be a last resort.

Shang: War should be the first resort. Let's not waste time on useless diplomacy. "What makes the state powerful and the ruler respectable is force."[14] Nothing else works, and I'm sorry if this hurts your feelings. We go in, show who's in charge, and they will come around. After we passed the National Security Law in Hong Kong, the "democrats" folded quickly, and now there's no more threat of independence or political "reform" supported by foreign powers.

Meng: Taiwan is not Hong Kong. It's more instructive to look at what happened when Russia tried to invade Ukraine: they were bogged down for years, with hundreds of thousands of casualties and the country became a pariah state. The same thing will happen to us if we invade Taiwan: even worse, I say! President Putin invaded because Ukraine was not a member of NATO and he knew the United States wouldn't send military forces to help defend Ukraine. Taiwan, in contrast, is supported by the United States, and they are likely to intervene if we try to invade. Not to mention that invading Ukraine was supposed to be straightforward: Russia, with its far larger and experienced military, expected to easily conquer its neighbor by marching over mostly flat land. And look what happened! In our case, we'd have to invade an island by crossing a stormy sea, followed by urban warfare and operations on rugged mountainous terrain, fighting against an enemy assisted by the world's most powerful military.[15] Not to mention that the Taiwanese would be highly motivated to defend what they regard as their homeland, which makes a difference in war, as the case of Ukraine shows.[16] There's no way we can win in the short term, whatever "winning" means here.

Shang: Agreed. We need to be prepared for long-term warfare.

President: Mr. Shang, do you have a plan for the long term?

Shang: I do. But we need to change the way our people think. They have become too soft and complacent.

When the people "beautify their appearance, obtain food through talk, contact superiors to avoid farming and fighting, and contact foreign powers to get official positions, then the state is endangered."[17] All they care about now is enjoyment and comfort; they need to be prepared for a more difficult life.

President: I agree. People are too lazy now. All this "lying flat" stuff is worrisome. "Happiness must be achieved through hard work."[18] If you want happiness, you must struggle.

Shang: Indeed. If we want to win the war, we need to be prepared to "eat bitterness."[19] So here's the plan. We strengthen the state and weaken the people. "When the people are weak, the state is strong; when the people are strong, the state is weak. Hence, the state that possesses the Way devotes itself to weakening the people." We focus on the basics, starting with food security. Once we invade, the West will try to cut us from world markets, so we need to be self-sufficient. Without food, we can't feed our soldiers. "He who excels at ruling the state does not neglect agriculture, even if his granaries are full; he does not indulge in talk, even if the state is large and the population is plentiful: then the people will be simple and committed to agriculture and warfare."[20]

President: Mr. Shang, what you suggest sounds like a primitive economy. Don't we need an advanced economy that supports our military with the latest technology?

Shang: Yes, and once we control Taiwan's chip industry, it will help us to win the war.

Meng: If we go to war, Taiwan will become a Gaza-like rubblescape! Even if we "win," there won't be anything left.

Shang: We will rebuild. In any case, let's not overrate technology. We can win with a highly motivated fighting force, even if the enemy has technological superiority. We defeated the KMT, even though they had more advanced weapons provided by the United States. The same goes for our Vietnamese comrades, who defeated the world's most high-tech military machine. At the end of the day, winning in war comes down to two kinds of people: farmers who support the warriors and soldiers who do the fighting. "The means by which the state prospers are agriculture and warfare."[21]

Meng: It sounds like you want to make us into a North Korea–style country of farmers and fighters. But Chinese people care about many other things.

Shang: Yes, so like I said, we need to change what the people care about. What we have now is a recipe for disaster. "When the state has rites and music, *Poems* and *Documents*, goodness and self-cultivation, filiality and fraternal obligations, uprightness and argumentativeness—when it has these ten, superiors cannot cause [the people] to fight, and [the state] will surely be dismembered to the point of final collapse." At the moment, "the powerful and eminent diligently study *Poems* and *Documents* and then follow foreign powers; the petty and insignificant become merchants and peddlers, engage in skillful arts, and all thereby escape agriculture and warfare. If the people consider this a proper teaching, how can one avoid farmers becoming ever fewer and soldiers ever weaker?"[22]

President: So how can we make the people into effective soldiers, Mr. Shang?

Shang: Two means: punishments and rewards. I fully recognize that most people dislike suffering and hard work. "When the government does what the people detest, the people are weak; when the people are weak and are weakened further, the army's strength is multiplied." So we must make people do what they detest. They especially hate the prospect of violent death at the hands of enemies. "As for war: it is something the people hate." So soldiers need to be made to hate something even worse: death by torture for deserters and their families. "If the [soldiers] are afraid of death, a thousand people gather around them; they are admonished then punished beneath the walls by tattooing and the cutting off of their noses."[23] "People should be grouped in squads of five and ten, and supervise each other, bearing mutually binding responsibility. Those who fail to report villainy will be cut in two at the waist."[24] With such punishments in place, the army will be strong. "Among the people of a powerful state, fathers send off their sons, elder brothers send off their younger brothers, wives send off their husbands, and all say: 'Do not come back without achievements!' They also say: 'If you violate the [military] law and disobey orders, you will die, and I shall die. Under the canton's control, there is no place to flee from the army ranks, and migrants can find no refuge.' To order the army ranks: link them into five-man squads, distinguish them with badges, and bind them with orders. Then there will be no place to flee, and defeat will never ensue. Thus, the multitudes of the three armies will follow orders as [water] flows [downward], and even facing death they will not turn back. . . . When you enter a state and observe its governance, you know that he whose people are usable is powerful. How can I know that the people are usable? When the people look at war as a hungry wolf looks at meat, the people are usable."[25]

Meng (gasps): You think that people can be made to "look at war as a hungry wolf looks at meat" only because they fear something worse?

Shang: That's not sufficient. We also need an effective reward structure. "He who is able to [distinguish himself at] war will pass through the gates of riches and nobility."[26] People crave for riches and reputation and those rewards should go to the most effective soldiers.

Meng: What do you mean by "effective soldiers"?

Shang: My friend, please don't pretend to be so naive. We all know that war is about killing enemy soldiers. We need an objective standard for promotion and demotion that strengthens our fighting force. It's simple: the number of severed enemy heads. The more, the better. Those who kill more people should be promoted. "He who is able to attain one head of an armored soldier should be promoted to one rank; his field should be increased by one *qing*; his house plot should be increased by one *mu*. For every rank, he is granted the right to appoint one retainer, and then he is allowed to become a military or civilian official."[27]

Meng: You give new meaning to the word "head counting." It's not only cruel, it's unworkable, which is worse from your perspective. If soldiers only care about their self-interest, they will fight among themselves to cut off heads.

Shang: Of course, soldiers need to be supervised by their superiors. At higher levels, we need group head counting:

"For every fifty men there is a platoon leader; for every hundred men, a centurion. In battle, centurions and platoon leaders are not allowed to cut off heads [individually]; when [the battalion] gets thirty-three heads or more, they have fulfilled the quota, and the platoon leaders and centurions are granted one rank." "In attacking a besieged fortress, [an army] that is able to cut off eight thousand heads and more has fulfilled the quota. In a battle on an open field, [an army] that is able to cut off two thousand heads and more has fulfilled the quota."[28] Let's not forget the Qin state more or less implemented this objective kind of military meritocracy, which led to the Qin's military success against other warring states.[29] We unified China by such cruel means, I regret to report.[30] And that's what we need to unify China today.

Meng: It's odd that you look to China's most cruel period for inspiration. Things are different today, fortunately.

Shang: Are they really? Think of the Americans reporting body counts as a measure of success in the Vietnam War. Or the Ukrainians proudly announcing the number of dead Russian soldiers.

Meng: But you propose cutting off heads! Such barbarity!

Shang: Only the heads of enemy combatants. No need to cut off the heads of civilians.[31] Agreed, it's hard to tell in the bloody aftermath of battle. We need an objective system to ensure it's the heads of enemy combatants. Soldiers need to be supervised by their superiors. Officers and higher officials must check the number and identity of severed heads: "After the battle, when [severed] heads are exposed, they are checked for three days; if the general has no doubts, he delivers ranks of merit to soldiers and officers."[32]

Meng: Cutting off heads! Exposing heads! Even our worst enemies don't do that!

Shang: Do you want to win, or don't you? "He whose army performs whatever the enemy does not perform is strong; he who in [military] affairs advances whatever the enemy is ashamed of benefits."[33] To terrify the enemy, we need to be crueler than they are. Think of Tony Poe, a paramilitary officer from the CIA's special activities division, who waged the "Secret War" in Laos by using human ears to record the number of enemies his troops had killed: he sent these ears back to his superiors as proof of the efficacy of his operations. He also dropped severed heads from helicopters into enemy-controlled territory to terrorize the villagers.[34] What brilliance!

Meng: But the Americans lost the war in Vietnam! How can you praise such cruel tactics?

Shang: They lost because they did not systematically apply such tactics. The Qin's victory over other states in the Warring States period is a better example. It worked for them and it will work for us now.

Meng: How can we gain the hearts and minds of people in Taiwan with such tactics? They will regard us as barbarians. When Russia invaded Ukraine with their cruel tactics, the whole country turned against them. And what you propose is infinitely worse!

Shang: Once we achieve total victory, they will come around. Look at what happened to Japan: after two nuclear bombs that killed hundreds of thousands of civilians, the country folded and now they are happy to be military subordinates to their former enemies. It's a similar story in Germany: the British and the Americans bombed the city of Dresden, tens of thousands of civilians were killed in the firestorm, a few months later the Nazis were completely defeated, and Germany went to the other side(s). Basically, the use of cruel means that terrified local populations was successful. Or think of the American war on Vietnam—they killed one million soldiers and two million civilians, and now the Vietnamese often side with the Americans against us, even though we are supposed to be fellow communists. People will side with whoever brings them benefit. "The people follow after benefit as water flows downward; it has no preference among the four directions. The people do only whatever brings them benefit, and the benefit is granted by their superiors."[35] So long as we are the superiors, regardless of how we get there, the people will follow us.

President: That's interesting. Mr. Shang argues that we should go in now with as much force as possible. Even if we face difficulties in the short term, we can triumph in the long term if we change the incentive structure of our people: they should be rewarded for fighting and farming and ruthlessly punished if they fail to comply. And we need a military meritocracy that rewards soldiers according to battlefield success. It might seem excessive, but our Russian friends, arguably, did something similar. They transformed their country into a war economy and since they have more "usable" people they could pursue the war for years and achieve some sort of victory. Yes, it was cruel, but it worked.

Meng: But Mr. President, my interlocutor has such a stunted view of human nature! Surely people care about more than bare survival. And why can't our rulers appeal to the best of human nature? . . . (looking at Shang) . . . We had compassionate rulers in antiquity and society was peaceful and harmonious, why don't you look to the best of the past for inspiration?

Shang: Because we need to adjust to changing circumstances. "Rituals and laws are fixed according to the times: regulations and orders are all expedient; weapons, armor, utensils, and equipment, all are used according to the utility. Hence, I say: there is no single way to order the generation; to benefit the state, one need not imitate antiquity." In the past, perhaps, "the people were few, whereas trees and animals were plenty . . . the [ruler] used neither punishments nor regulations, yet there was order; arms and weapons were not set up." But times have changed. "The people multiplied, and they were engaged in particularity and malignity, there was turmoil. At that time, the people began seeking victories and forcefully seizing [each other's property]." Today, people compete for limited resources which leads to social conflict, hence the need for a state with harsh laws to prevent social chaos: "in the task of relying on laws, nothing is more urgent than eradicating villainy: the root of eradicating villainy is nowhere deeper than in making punishments stern."[36]

Meng: But that can't work for the long term. If your father regularly beats you to a pulp allegedly for your own long term good, will you forgive him? People will eventually resent harsh punishment and they will rebel. The self-proclaimed First Emperor Qin Shihuang took this kind of advice—he burned books, executed scholars, and terrified the people with harsh punishments—and his dynasty lasted only fifteen years.

Shang: Yes, he was outstanding; it's unfortunate he didn't live longer. Our First Emperor unified China, crushed the feudal aristocracy, built a network of roads and canals, standardized the language as well as the currency, measurements, and weights. He started the Great Wall. Basically, he built the world's first modern bureaucracy, with the boundaries and administrative system that shaped the rest of Chinese political history. What a great leader! But he didn't have time to finish his work, his heir was not so outstanding, and the dynasty collapsed into chaos after his death.

Meng: So you think we should complete Emperor Qin's project?

Shang (excited): Exactly! It's not too late. But we need to change: "now all rulers and ministers of [this] calamitous age act in a petty way, . . . appropriating the authority of their office so as to benefit their private [interests]. That is the reason the state is endangered." So we need to put in place a system where rulers and ministers "cannot forget the law for a single moment. Destroy and smash cliques and glibness, restrict and eradicate [empty] talk, rely on law, and [attain] orderly rule. Let the officials preserve nothing but the law; then even the crafty will not be able to act villainously. Let the people be rewarded nowhere but in warfare; then even when endangered they will not dare act deceitfully." "In general, the rule of the clear-sighted ruler relies on force, not on kindness . . . this is called the law." Once we have this kind of legal system, it will work almost by itself. We need impartial laws backed by harsh punishments that people obey unflinchingly—and it doesn't depend on the quality of the public officials.[37]

Meng: But surely government works best when public officials have above average virtue?

Shang: Quite the opposite, in fact: it's better if officials are villains: "When the good are employed, the people are attached to their relatives; when villains are employed, the people are attached to regulations. Those who are harmonious and cover up for each other are 'good'; those who are separate and regulate each other are 'villains.' When the 'good' are commended, transgressions are concealed; when 'villains' are appointed, crimes are punished. When transgressions are concealed, the people overcome the law; when crimes are punished, the law overcomes the people. When people overcome the law, the state is in turmoil; when the law overcomes the people, the army is strong." Villains in power ruthlessly enforce the law, with no room for mercy or family love, and people won't cover up for each other. That's what we want. "When a one-thousand-[tank] state is able to preserve itself and a ten-thousand-[tank] state is able to reinforce itself in war, then even if the sovereign is [as bad as] Jie, he will not be able to bend an inch to surrender to the enemy." Even if the ruler himself is a villain, the system will work! I understand this kind of advice may not be welcome. "Yet one who is not a sage should not speak, and heeding the sage is difficult."[38]

President (visibly upset): What do you mean when you say the ruler is a "villain"? Perhaps this kind of system has no need for sage-like political advisers.

Shang (nervously touching his neck): In the future, perhaps, not now. We still need outstanding rulers and advisers to build up the system.

Meng: You're not answering my point. Nobody likes to live under such a harsh regime. People will resent it, and they will rebel once they get the chance to do so. That's what happened to the Qin dynasty,[39] and fortunately we never had another experience with this kind of totalitarian regime that terrifies the population by means of harsh punitive laws.

Shang: I do not propose to keep this system in place forever. In fact, the long-term aim is to do away with punishment: "one eradicates punishments with punishments." By "killing and punishing, [the ruler eventually] returns to virtue."[40]

Meng: I don't understand.

Shang: It should be obvious. If we establish the right kind of punitive laws to control people there will be no need to implement the laws. "When penalties are implemented, inflict [heavy] punishments on light [offenses], then light [offenses] will not come, and heavy [ones] will not arrive." "When punishments are heavy and criminals mutually responsible, the people dare not try [to break the law]. When the people dare not try, there are no punishments. Hence, the prohibitions of the former kings, such as [carrying out] executions, cutting off feet, or branding the face, were imposed not because they sought to harm the people but only to prohibit depravity and stop transgressions. So, to prohibit depravity and to stop transgressions nothing is better than to make punishments heavy. When punishments are heavy and [criminals] are inevitably captured, then the people dare not try [to break the law]. Hence, there are no penalized people in the state." Of course, the laws must be understood if the people are to internalize them. When "nobody suffers capital punishment, it is not because they have abolished capital punishment. Rather the laws are clear and easily understandable, and law officials and clerks are established as teachers to direct [the people] to understand [the law]. The myriad people all understand what should be avoided and what should be pursued. They should avoid disaster and pursue good fortune: all will thereby govern themselves."[41] To sum up, here's the plan. We establish a military meritocracy, and we win the war. At home, we establish a clear and simple legal system with harsh punishments even for light offenses, and eventually there will be no need to enforce the laws. Mr. Meng. we probably agree on the end—a harmonious world where people govern themselves—but we simply disagree about how to get there.[42]

Meng (laughs): And people say I'm too idealistic! Even if we "win" the war by means of cutting off tens of thousands of enemy heads, do you really expect that rulers will strive to establish a peaceful order afterward? Look at what happened to your hero, the self-proclaimed First Emperor. After he unified China, he promised that "warfare will never arise again,"[43] yet he continued with the same military and economic organization that exploited his subjects until his dying days.[44] Violence corrupts, and absolute violence corrupts absolutely.

Shang: Maybe you're the cynical one. There are plenty of examples of rulers who promoted peace after winning in war. In ancient India, Emperor Ashoka expanded his state via brutal warfare, including a war against Kalinga that left at least 100,000 dead. After his empire was unified, he adopted Buddhism and advocated nonviolence and rule by moral power rather than the brute force of domination.[45] There are more modern examples. Nikita Khrushchev participated in Stalin's bloody purges and put an end to mass murder in politics after he took over. Rulers will change with the times, for better or worse.

Meng: So you think we can establish a peaceful society with self-governing citizens overseen by a virtuous ruler once we reunify with Taiwan?

Shang: Not so long as we have other enemies. They will find new ways to keep us down. We need to achieve global dominance that puts an end to all military threats. And it will take a long time for the people to fully internalize the law so it becomes second nature.

Meng: How long?

Shang: "If the state engages in the One [agriculture and warfare] for one year, it will be strong for ten years; if it engages in the One for ten years, it will be strong for one hundred years; if it engages in the One for one hundred years, it will be strong for a thousand years; he who is strong for a thousand years will become a humane ruler."[46]

Meng (laughs): A thousand years! Mr. President, my opponent can't be serious. He proposes to implement a totalitarian state that will magically wither away after one thousand years. Meanwhile, the weakened people will do nothing but farming and fighting. They will live in a state of fear and be kept ignorant of other possibilities. It's a society with no kindness or family love, no intellectuals or artists, no market economy, and no concern for the quality of public officials. It's inhuman. It's inhumane.[47]

President: Perhaps. But there may be some lessons for times of chaos and warfare, especially if the very survival of the state is at stake. In wartime, we do need a military meritocracy and a legal system that ruthlessly punishes wrongdoing. And the long-term aim—once we reestablish peace—is a society where people internalize the law and there is hardly any need to enforce it. Mr. Meng, let's hear your ideas about how to unify our country.

2. Mencius on Just and Unjust War

Mengzi (ca. 372–289 BCE) is regarded as the most idealistic among the Confucian thinkers. He argued that people are born with a tendency to goodness and flourish with supportive social and political conditions. Mengzi argued forcefully for an ideal world of global peace ruled by a humane sage king who relies on rites and moral power rather than coercion. But Mengzi was writing at a time of ruthless competition for territorial advantage between warring states, and it shouldn't be too surprising that he attempted to provide practical, morally informed guidance for this context. He was severely critical of rulers who launched ruthless wars of conquest simply to increase their territory and engage in economic plunder. Ideally, rulers should rely on moral power, but Mengzi did not counsel nonviolent resistance against tyrants who respond only to the language of force. In domestic policy, he is famous for sanctioning the killing of despotic rulers (which helps to explain why the first ruler of the Ming dynasty censored his work). In foreign policy, Mengzi argues that states can legitimately defend themselves against invaders if rulers have the people's support, similar to modern ideas of self-defense. More surprisingly, he argues that "punitive expeditions" (*zheng*) similar to modern ideas of humanitarian intervention can be justified if the aim is to bring peace and humane rule to foreign lands, so long as particular conditions are in place: the conquerors must try to liberate the people who are being oppressed by tyrants, the people must welcome the conquerors, the welcome must be long lasting, civilians must not be killed, and the humanitarian interventions must be led by potentially virtuous rulers with the world's support.[48]

Mengzi is the second most influential thinker in the Confucian tradition after Kongzi (Confucius) himself. Confucianism became a state-sponsored ideology in the Han dynasty (202 BCE–220 CE), but Mengzi's writings were not yet dominant. In the Tang dynasty, Confucian thought was revived partly in response to Buddhist influence, and the thinker Han Yu (768–824) praised Mengzi as the "most pure" of the followers of Kongzi.[49] The Confucian revival intensified in the Song dynasty (960–1279 CE)—again, partly in response to the perceived ideological challenge from Buddhism—and Mengzi's interpretation of Confucianism was made into the orthodox version by Neo-Confucians at the time. The great Confucian interpreter and synthesizer Zhu Xi (1130–1200 CE) grouped Mengzi's text as one of the classic *Four Books* that subsequently became part of the examination curriculum for aspiring public officials in the Ming and Qing dynasties. In the twentieth century, Confucian defenders of democracy found sprouts of democratic thinking in

Mengzi's "people-centered" thought,[50] and defenders of socialism found inspiration in Mengzi's idea that the state has an obligation to secure the material well-being of the people and to distribute land in a fair way.[51] Today, Mengzi's ideas on just war are hotly debated in academia both in China and outside and social critics invoke them to evaluate the morality of contemporary wars and to draw implications for Chinese foreign policy.[52]

Okay, back to the debate!

Meng: I agree on the goal. The political ideal is a unified world without any territorial boundaries. The only way to settle the world is "through unity." And this world should be governed by a humane ruler who relies on virtue, not force. "A humane ruler is one who, practicing compassion and humanity, resorts only to moral power." He will be strongly opposed to violence. "If there is [a ruler] who is not fond of killing, then the people of the whole world will crane their necks to watch for his coming! In such a case, the people will turn to him like water flowing downwards!"[53]

President (looking at his watch): Mr. Meng, please be more practical. I don't want to take over the whole world, notwithstanding what some crazy hawks in the United States say.[54] I just want to reunify our country with Taiwan. How do you propose we do that?

Meng: "There is a way to gain the whole world. It is to gain the people, and having gained them one gains the whole world. There is a way to gain the people. Gain their hearts, and then you gain them."[55]

President (impatiently): Mr. Meng, I just said I don't want to take over the whole world! And I doubt I could do so even if I tried. Maybe the Americans want to impose their political system on the rest of the world, but that's not our way.

Meng (taking off his glasses, looking at his notes): I understand. There's no hurry. But the general lesson applies. The use of force against a weaker party is not justified. "Allegiance which is gained by the use of force is not allegiance of the heart—it is the allegiance which comes from imposing upon weakness. Allegiance which is gained by the exercise of moral power is true allegiance. It is the response of joy felt deeply in the heart."[56] We can't unify our country without gaining the hearts of the people. And we can't gain the hearts of the people of Taiwan by going to war against them.

Shang: We tried everything else—economic benefits, educational exchanges, mass tourism, prolonged negotiations—and none of it worked. The longer we wait, the more they turn against us. They are "de-Sinicizing" their educational system,[57] and the longer it lasts, the less they will identify with our country. Only force works. Once we win, they will come around. The losers eventually accept their fate.

Meng: It may lead to World War III! We will all lose if we go to war against Taiwan. "In wars to gain land, the dead fill the plains. In wars to gain cities, the dead fill the cities. This is known as showing the land the way to devour human flesh. Death is too light a punishment for such men. Hence, those skilled at war should suffer the most severe punishment."[58]

Shang: Let's just abolish our military and open the gates to our enemies. Your principled opposition to war is both absurd and dangerous.[59]

Meng: I'm not opposed to war in principle. True, "the *Spring and Autumn Annals* acknowledges no just wars."[60] But wars in other contexts may be just.

Shang (smiles): Good. We call it a just war and then we go in. We win and we impose a treaty and make it seem like both sides agree to the outcome, just like the foreigners did to us in the nineteenth century.

Meng (looking at the President): Please do not let yourself be drawn into a bloody war of conquest simply to increase our territory and engage in economic plunder. . . . (turns to Shang) . . . "Those who serve rulers today promise to enlarge their landholdings and enrich their treasures and arsenals. They are called 'good ministers' but in antiquity they would have been called 'plunderers of the people.' To enrich a ruler who is neither attracted to the Way nor inclined toward humaneness is to enrich a Jie [an evil king]. Some promise to negotiate advantageous treaties for their ruler so that he will be successful in war. These too, are called 'good ministers' but in antiquity they would have been called 'plunderers of the people.'"[61]

Shang (irritated): Let's refrain from personal insults. Your pie-in-the-sky theorizing won't get us anywhere. We can win with the overwhelming use of force. We throw everything at them with the exception of nuclear weapons and they will succumb.

Meng (looking at the President): Wars of conquest are disastrous for all parties concerned, including the conqueror's loved ones. Consider what happened to Emperor Qin's descendants. And before that, "King Hui of Liang was the antithesis of humaneness. The man of humaneness brings upon the things he does not love the things he loves. But the man who is not humane brings upon the things he loves, the things he does not love. . . . [He] ravished his own people for the sake of territory and went to war. When defeated, he tried again and again and fearing that he might not succeed he drove the son he loved to fight and his son was sacrificed. This is what I mean by 'bringing upon the things he loves, the things he does not love.'"[62] There are more recent examples. Think of what happened to Adolf Hitler. He lost everything, including his lover. They married in the bunker, then he killed her and killed himself.

Shang: But you deny that it was wrong to use force against Adolf Hitler? I somehow doubt he would have responded to the love you're calling for.

Meng: Mr. Shang, I'm not so naive. Everyone has the potential to be good but it doesn't mean everyone will turn out that way. Even perfect humaneness will not always be reciprocated: if someone responds to humaneness with bad treatment, the exemplary person will conclude that his interlocutor is an "utter reprobate." In the Warring States era, almost all the leaders were bad: "The five hegemons offended against the humane rulers; the lords offended against the hegemons; and the counsellors offended against the lords." So if a territory is invaded by moral reprobates, wars of self-defense can be justified. People can, will, and should defend themselves from unjust invaders. Even if the invaded territory appears to be much weaker, it will triumph if the people willingly fight for it. If a small territory is attacked by a would-be hegemon, then the ruler of that territory can justifiably mobilize the people for military action. Remember that Teng was small state, wedged between Qi and Chu. In such cases, the ruler was right to "dig deeper moats and build higher walls and defend them shoulder to shoulder with the people."[63] When the Japanese invaded us, we were right to defend ourselves. Same goes for the Vietnamese when they were invaded by the French and the Americans, the Afghans when they were invaded by the Soviets and the Americans, and the Ukrainians when they were invaded by the Russians. The "weak" parties all resisted, often successfully, because the leaders gained the hearts of the people. The same thing will happen if we invade Taiwan: and they will have much of the world's support. We can't unify our country until we gain the hearts of the people. At the moment, I regret to report, we have yet to gain the hearts of the Taiwanese.

Shang: But it doesn't mean they will fight. In Hong Kong, there was a massive exodus of "democrats" after we imposed the National Security Law and those who stayed behind learned to live with the system. We imposed more patriotic education and they came to like our country. In Taiwan, the mandatory military service is outdated and impractical.[64] They are sissy boys. They will flee rather than cut off heads.

Meng: In antiquity, people did flee. "When King Tai lived in Bin, the Di tribes invaded his territory. He offered them furs and silk but still could not get rid of them. He offered them horses and hounds but still could not get rid of them. He offered them pearls and jade but still could not get rid of them. Whereupon he gathered the elders of his people and told them, 'The Di tribes want to take our land. I have heard it said, a humane ruler does not allow the people to be harmed interfering with the things upon which their livelihood depends. It will do you less harm to have no ruler [than to be deprived of your land]. I am going to leave this place.' He left Bin, crossed the Liang mountains, and built a city at the foot of Mount Qi and settled there. The people of Bin said, 'A man of humaneness indeed! We cannot do without him,' and they followed him, as if to a market."[65]

Shang (self-satisfied): Good plan. The Taiwanese government flees to the United States and establishes some sort of community there, to be followed by those who can't accept the new reality. The ones who stay will become part of our political community. That's fine too, I'm glad we agree.

Meng: We don't agree! Such an outcome is highly unlikely today, when territorial boundaries are more rigid compared to the Warring States period. Plus, it would be reckless to plan on such an eventuality. The Russians probably thought Ukrainian President Zelensky would flee after the invasion, but he stayed behind and rallied the people to his side. To repeat: we cannot use force to invade Taiwan!

Shang: We'll never get Taiwan back without a war. You say people can and should defend their territory if it's attacked by a larger power. But you oppose offensive warfare. That's a recipe for failure!

Meng: I'm not opposed to offensive warfare—or what I call "punitive expeditions"—in principle. States can legitimately invade other states if the aim is to bring about global peace and humane government.[66] Certain conditions, however, must be in place. Most important, the "conquerors" must try to liberate people who are being oppressed by tyrants. "These [tyrants] take the people away from their work during the busy seasons, making it impossible for them to till the land and so minister to the needs of their parents. Thus, parents suffer cold and hunger while brothers, wives, and children are separated and scattered. These [tyrants] push their people into pits and into water. If you should go and punish such [tyrants], who is there to oppose you? Hence it is said, 'the humane person has no match.'" The liberated people will be grateful: "When a major power attacks another and its armies are greeted by the people with baskets of rice and bottles to drink, what other reason can there be than the people are fleeing from water and fire [i.e., tyranny]." But I'm not a blind idealist. In the nonideal world, the tyrants are not likely to go down without a fight and moral power may not work against truly wicked oppressors. The liberation of people may require murdering the tyrant: the humane ruler "killed the tyrant and comforted the people, like the fall of timely rain, and the people rejoiced."[67]

Shang: We label them tyrants and kill the leaders. Good idea.

Meng: It's not just a matter of labels: they must be doing bad things. We can only launch humanitarian rescue missions when tyrants deprive the people of basic means of subsistence.[68] People can and should be moral, but there is no point promoting moral behavior if people are worried about their next meal. Without basic means of subsistence, people will go morally astray: "The people will not have dependable feelings if they are without dependable means of support. Lacking dependable means of support, they will go astray and fall into excesses, stopping at nothing. To punish them after they have fallen foul of the law is to set a trap for the people. How can a humane ruler allow himself to set a trap for the people? Hence when determining what means of support the people should have, a clear-sighted ruler ensures that they are sufficient for the care of parents and for the support of wives and children, so that the people will always have sufficient goods in good years and escape the danger of perishing in bad years; only then does he drive them towards goodness."[69] Depriving the people of their means of support will lead to internal strife, and it will be impossible to secure the peace. At minimum, then, the ruler striving for peace and humane rule must ensure that the people are well fed. Hence, the first obligation of government is to secure the basic means of subsistence of the people. By extension, the worst thing a government can do—the most serious violation of "human rights," so to speak—would be to be deliberately deprive the people of the means of subsistence, by killing them, not feeding them, not dealing with a plague, and so on. A ruler who engages in such acts is an oppressive tyrant and punitive expeditions against such rulers would be justified.

Shang: But the Taiwanese government isn't starving the people. In fact, the people there are relatively prosperous compared to the poor parts of China. And there seems to be growing support for formal independence. Surely a declaration of formal independence is cause for war? It will lead to chaos, and we need to liberate them from such tyranny.

Meng: I don't support independence—we should strive for unity, as I said—but we shouldn't launch a war just because people declare independence. We must win back their hearts and that can't be done by force.

President: Mr. Meng, I'm glad to hear you don't oppose war in principle. In a nonideal world, you support the right of people to defend themselves from invaders. But you claim that offensive warfare is only justified to liberate a people who are being starved to death by a tyrant. A declaration of independence is not a legitimate reason for invasion. But even our enemies disagree with what you say! In the United States, when the South tried to declare independence, the North launched a civil war to maintain unity.

Meng: But the South practiced slavery, which is a form of tyranny.[70] The government of Taiwan may not be perfect, but it's not a tyranny, and we don't have just cause to invade. Even if the ruler is a tyrant, we need to make sure other conditions for punitive expeditions have been met. The invading state has to be led by a humane ruler. If the aggressor state is led by an "utter reprobate,"[71] then obviously it's no improvement.

President (trying to conceal his anger): You're fond of giving lectures to rulers, Mr. Meng.

Meng: Everybody has the seed of virtue within them. "If others do not respond to your love with love, look into your own humaneness; if others do not respond to your attempts to govern them, look into your own wisdom; if others do not respond to your courtesy, look into your own respect." I realize it's asking for a lot, but it's not impossible. "A humane ruler must arise every five hundred years, and in between there will arise one from whom an age takes its name."[72]

President: Thank you for your advice, Mr. Meng. As it happens, my name is in the constitution and people refer to our age by my name. And even if I'm not a humane ruler in your eyes, we don't have the luxury of waiting five hundred years for someone better. Nor do I have time to improve my morality. I'm not a religious leader. I wish I had time for more self-cultivation, but I'm very busy trying to solve our country's problems.

Meng: Self-cultivation is helpful for politics too. "Look into yourself whenever you fail to achieve your purpose. When you are correct in your person, the whole world will turn to you." With the world's support, we can launch a punitive expedition against Taiwan. Recall the punitive expedition led by King Tang: "The *Book of History* says, 'In his punitive expeditions Tang began with Ge.' The whole world was in sympathy with his cause. When he marched on the east, the western tribes complained. When he marched to the south, the northern tribes complained. They said, 'Why does he not come to us first?'"[73]

Shang (contemptuous laughter): This is absurd. We need to wait till we gain the trust of the whole world before we invade Taiwan!

President: Indeed. It's our country, our sovereignty, it's not the business of the rest of the world.

Meng: But potentially bloody war needs to be endorsed by the world. In this case, it means that we should get the approval of the United Nations. Plus, we're more likely to succeed with such approval. The first Gulf War in 1991 was a just war authorized by the United Nations, similar to "a guilty duke punished by the Son of Heaven." It was like a "punitive expedition by a higher authority attacking a lower one."[74] In the 2003 invasion of Iraq, by contrast, the United States said it was using force to exercise humaneness, that is, acting as both a humane authority and a hegemon. But the Second Gulf War was not the same, because without the authorization of the United Nations, the United States used force under the pretext of humaneness, and it maintained its geopolitical, national security, and economic interests in the name of promoting democracy in the Middle East. It was obviously acting as a global hegemon, and it failed miserably.[75]

Shang: I can assure you the United States will use its veto on the Security Council to counter whatever plans we have for an invasion. It's a recipe for inaction.

Meng: We do need to wait until we have just cause to invade. And once we go in, we need to make sure we have the people's support. The people must demonstrate, in concrete ways, the fact that they welcome the conquerors. Again, we can turn to the past for inspiration: "When King Wu attacked Yin, he had over three hundred war chariots and three thousand warriors. He said, 'Do not be afraid. I come to bring peace, I am not an enemy of the people.' And the sound of people knocking their heads on the ground was like the toppling of the mountain."[76]

Shang (sarcastic tone): Well, that will comfort the Americans. You say they were wrong to go into Iraq in 2003 but they were greeted as liberators from tyranny.

Meng: The welcome must be long-lasting, not just immediate. The real challenge is to maintain support for the invading forces after the initial enthusiasm.[77] Even punitive expeditions that were initially justified can go bad. That's what happened after the 2003 invasion of Iraq, and it's an old pattern. Recall what happened when the state of Qi invaded Yan. "The people welcomed the army with baskets of rice and bottles of drink. But [the Qi army] killed the old, bound the young, destroyed the ancestral temples: how can they have expected the people's [lasting] approval?"[78] It's a common pattern: first the invaders are greeted as liberators but then they act as occupiers, and they lose the people's support.

Shang: Mr. Meng, you have things backward. People usually oppose invaders, but they will be accepted when people lose all hope of repelling them. We use maximum force and eventually we will win their "hearts," whatever that means. People will follow whoever brings them benefits, that's what we know from experience.

Meng: We can know much more than that. We cannot gain the hearts of the people if we carry out the war in an unjust way. When the Nazis tried to bomb Londoners into submission, it only hardened their determination to fight back. The same thing happened to us when the Japanese carried out the Nanjing massacre, killing hundreds of thousands of civilians. How can invaders gain the hearts of people by killings civilians? "To kill a single innocent person is not to be humane."[79] If we kill civilians, we will never be greeted as liberators.

Shang (exasperated): Show me a war where civilians have not been killed. . . . (turns to President) . . . Mr. President, it's time to end this "debate." Mr. Meng's "theory" is an elaborate justification for inaction. He raises the bar for invasion so high to ensure that we will never launch a war.[80] We can only send an army if the Taiwanese are killed, enslaved, or starved by their leaders: that's not going to happen. We can only send an army once we're led by a sage ruler with the world's support: that's not going to happen. And even if we go in, we must be welcomed by the whole people both at the start and for the long term, and we're supposed to carry out the war without any collateral damage: that's not going to happen.

Meng: Mr. President, the key is to implement humane government at home. You cultivate yourself and "employ the good and the wise in high positions, . . . lower taxes for traders, . . . abolish tariffs at border stations, and [abolish taxes on farming and land]. . . . If you truly execute these five measures, the people of the neighboring states will look up to you as their father and mother."[81] The ultimate justification for rule is the well-being of the people, both at home and abroad.[82] Once you provide for the people's well-being, they will come into our fold.[83] We can't force unity, it's morally wrong. And even if we are successful at first, it won't work for the long term; the people will disobey once they get a chance. "When people submit to force they do so not willingly but because they are not strong enough. When people submit to the transforming influence of morality, they do so sincerely, with admiration in their hearts. An example is the submission of the seventy disciples of Kongzi. *The Odes* say, 'From east, from west, from north, from south, there was none who did not submit.'" I realize some of this may sound idealistic, but we need ideals to judge what's right and what's wrong and to evaluate what counts as political progress and regress, even recognizing there will always be a gap between the ideal and the practice. In reality, perhaps there will never be a perfectly just war. "There are only cases of one war not being quite as bad as another."[84] But we should do our best to minimize the badness of war and we need to educate our soldiers, generals, and political leaders so that they are more likely to abide by the standards of just warfare.[85]

President: Thank you both. It seems you agree on the end—unification of our country with Taiwan—but you disagree on the means. Shang says we need to cut off people's heads and Meng says we need to win their hearts. These are two extreme views. But thank you for your contributions. We will "consider, consider."[86]

---

3. Politburo Meeting

[The next day, the President chairs a meeting of the Standing Committee of the Politburo.]

President: You have read notes on the debate. This Shang fellow is a sociopath, but we will need people like him once we go in. And we will go in if they declare independence; if we don't it will be chaos and there will be similar demands in Tibet, Xinjiang, and the rich parts of China. It will be the mother of all civil wars, the foreigners will try to carve up China again, and the battles of the Warring States period will seem like minor skirmishes in comparison. We have to maintain unity, by force if necessary.

Prime Minister: What if they don't declare independence?

President: Then we consider attacking when our enemies are busy with something else, like in 1962: we invaded India when the United States was preoccupied with the Cuban Missile Crisis.[87] Or we go in when they least expect it. In any case, there's no huge hurry. We can wait till the United States becomes less dependent on Taiwan for chip technology; they'll dump their "allies" once the cost is too high. Meanwhile, we prepare the ground by psychological warfare. It's amazing that Shang and Meng, despite their differences, had hardly anything to say about deception and covert operations.[88] Then we do a naval blockade and cut off the internet. And once we attack, it's full force; they need to know we are serious about winning.

Prime Minister: So once we go in, we follow Shang's recommendations?

President: No! We let him blog, and we will come off as moderate in comparison. Of course, we can't let him raise his own army. I'm still surprised our friend up north could make such an elementary mistake.

Prime Minister: So we follow Meng's recommendations?

President: Don't be silly. Meng has a good heart, but he's too self-righteous. And it's not the right time for this sort of utopian thinking. His words will bring comfort to our enemies. Look into his family finances, invite him for tea,[89] whatever. Just find a way to silence him.

Prime Minister: For how long, Mr. President?

President (impatiently): I don't know, a thousand years! Don't bother me with such details. What was the next item on the agenda? Climate change?

Prime Minister: Yes, Mr. President, as you know, it all happened much faster than we expected. Half of Shanghai is now under water and we have nearly eight million internal refugees. We plan to send them up north, give them small plots of land, and they can survive that way.

President: Good. That will help with our food security. "The rice bowls of the Chinese people must be firmly in our own hands. Our rice bowls should be filled mainly by Chinese crops."[90] Let's never forget: "Only when agriculture is strong can the state be strong."[91]

ATOGAKI

What's Wrong with This Book?

AN *ATOGAKI* is an "afterword" that Japanese authors commonly use to set forth the flaws, fallacies, logical lapses, and factual lacunae in the book they have just written.[1] As an intellectual masochist, I feel a need to borrow this practice. In this *Atogaki,* I imagine a dialogue where I'm invited to discuss my book on a podcast titled *Bad Books Network* (*BBN*), which is the (fictitious) evil twin of my favorite podcast, the *New Books Network* (*NBN*). On the *NBN,* authors are invited to discuss their books with kind and charitable hosts who hardly ever raise critical points.[2] On the *BBN,* the author is pilloried by the host who finds nothing of value in the book being discussed. Okay, let's move to the dialogue:

Host: Thank you for joining us. It's difficult, frankly, to get authors to participate in the *Bad Books Network.*

Author: Well, as they say, any publicity is good publicity.

Host: Let's see about that. So, tell me, why did you decide to write this awful book?

Author: My original plan was to write a book that covers the debates between great political theorists in different parts of the world so as to expand the corpus of political theory classics beyond the best of the West. But I realized I took on too much so I decided to limit myself to the greats from China's history before the country was unified in 221 BCE, when many of China's most profound, original, and influential political debates took place.

Host (laughs): That's quite a change! Your original idea was fantastic. What you ended up with is a survey of political debates from a slice of China's history. Why should we care about that?

Author: Political theory in the Anglophone world is still too West-centric. If I can help to familiarize readers with the most influential political debates in the history of the world's second most powerful country, I'd still have performed a valuable job.

Host: Even if we stick to China, you didn't choose the most influential political theorists. Why not select Dong Zhongshu, who provided the intellectual basis for justifying political rule in the Han dynasty and much of subsequent imperial history, or Zhu Xi, the "St. Thomas Aquinas of China" who systematized the Confucian tradition and provided commentaries that set the agenda for the education of public officials in the Ming and Qing dynasties?

Author: I have to draw the line somewhere. And what's interesting about the Spring and Autumn and Warring States periods, before China was unified, is that there were diverse schools—or, at least, different ways of thinking that subsequently came to be labeled and classified as "schools"—composed of great political thinkers who engaged in heated political debates with each other. They agreed on the ideal of a unified political community, but they disagreed fundamentally about how to get there and on the role of the state, not to mention deep disagreements on ethical ideals and conceptions of the good life. I think there's this image in much of the world of China as a kind of monolithic political entity where political elites tend to think and act alike, and I wanted to counter this stereotype and bring to life the diversity of political views in ancient China that helped shape political thinking for the rest of Chinese history, and the best way to do that is to put the thinkers in explicit debate with each other.[3]

Host: Even if you limit yourself to pre-Qin history, you left out key political thinkers and texts such as Laozi and Sunzi. Laozi is the most translated text from pre-Qin China. Surely Sunzi's *The Art of War* is more influential than, say, Mencius's views on morally justified warfare. Yin and Yang are central concepts in Chinese philosophy and you say nothing about how they shaped Sunzi's perception of the world and how they continue to shape political thinking in recent times.[4] For one thing, Mao's *On Protracted War* owes much to Sunzi's text and it helps to explain his strategy repelling Japanese invaders in the 1930s and 1940s.[5] Or you could have discussed the *Zuo Zhuan* [*The Commentary of Zuo*], which anticipates modern ideas about just war, including humanitarian intervention.[6]

Author: I had to make certain judgments. I don't think that Laozi is as original and profound as Zhuangzi, though perhaps the former was more politically influential. Sunzi's text is quite sketchy; it doesn't compare to the detailed argumentation in Shang Yang and Mencius. The *Zuo Zhuan*, a narrative history, is less explicitly normative in orientation than the thought of Mencius. I selected the thinkers that put forward original, profound, and politically influential ideas. Plus, the texts you mention are less argumentative, the "opponents" are unclear, and it's harder to get a good dialogue with a worthy opponent out of them. In any case, I don't mean to imply that my choices cover the whole of great pre-Qin political thinking. My aim is to shed light on some of the great political debates in pre-Qin history—the ones I think are most original, profound, and influential—but I recognize other scholars may come to different judgments and I welcome efforts to show that other works can and should be part of the debate about great political ideas from the pre-Qin era.

Host: If you aim to shed light on the political debates in pre-Qin history, why not present the debates as they took place at the time, instead of plucking the thinkers completely out of context and setting the debates in the modern world? You radically distort the original meaning of what was said!

Author: If I've misapplied them or distorted what the thinkers where really saying, please let me know. True, I imagine that their descendants have knowledge of the modern world, but I stick to the main arguments of the ancient thinkers. I try not to make the descendants say things that conflict with what the thinkers actually said. I do my best to be faithful to the arguments as they were discussed at the time.

Host: You're not faithful to the arguments! You present highly contestable interpretations of passages as fact. For example, in the long passage from the *Analects* where Confucius asks his students about their ideals, you claim that Confucius affirms Zeng Xi's supposedly political point about the importance of social harmony for good government. But that's going way beyond the text! A much more straightforward interpretation of Zeng Xi's ideal affirms a life of spontaneous joy over a life of politics, the very view you criticize in your book![7] You're actively misleading readers!

Author: I'm ready to defend my interpretation. I don't think it's plausible that Confucius would be affirming an apolitical ideal, and my interpretation coheres with the rest of the text where he suggests the best life involves serving the community *qua* public official.

Host: Whatever. At the very least, you should admit you put forward highly contestable views. And your cheating gets even more blatant: You even change the names of states from the original sources to states that didn't exist at the time, such as North Korea!

Author: If there's enough in common between the ancient and the modern setting to make the argument more compelling to the contemporary reader, then I make the change, but I explain why I did so in the notes. I've selected mainly arguments that have applicability beyond their original context and I left out points that seem obviously out of date, such as the infamous line in the *Analects* that compares women to "petty people."[8] Remember, what makes political thinkers great is that they came up with ideas that may still be relevant in different times and places and that can help us think about present-day concerns. Philosophy has to grapple with new challenges to stay in good health and carry on. Imagine if die-hard intellectual historians or Hellenistic philosophers had argued that Platonic thought couldn't be used to address the challenge of the new monotheistic religions in the early medieval period on the grounds that we need to respect the purity of Plato in his original context: they would have killed off Platonism as a living philosophical system![9] We don't say Plato's *Republic* should be read as simply expressing political ideas that should be confined to their time. His great genius lies in the fact that his work has a lot to offer for those of us thinking about justice and the good life today.

Host: But we wouldn't take Plato and put him in dialogue with people in the modern world!

Author: Actually, Rebecca Newberger Goldstein's awesome book titled *Plato at the Googleplex* does just that. She takes "Plato" and has him debate others in contemporary settings on such eternal questions as the nature of love and the meaning of life.[10] I'm inspired by her approach, though I take less creative license than she does in the sense that I rely more on quotations from the original sources.

Host: I still think you should stick to the debates in their original settings. If the aim is to familiarize readers with their ideas, why take the risk of distorting what they say by teleporting them to completely different times and places?

Author: I'm not sure about "completely different." For one thing, the debates are all set in China, where there is substantial cultural continuity. Arguably, it makes even more sense to invoke debates from pre-Qin China, when different states competed for supremacy, than from the works of political thinkers writing in imperial times when China was unified and viewed itself as the center of the civilized world. That's one reason I think political debates from pre-Qin China are especially relevant for today's China.

Host: So the book is only written for Chinese people. The rest of us need not read the book.

Author: Well, you can skip this book if you think your tradition has nailed down all the eternal truths about the good life and justice and other traditions are fundamentally misguided. But if you think there's room for improvement, then you can ask yourself to what extent these arguments and insights might be for relevant for "us," not just for "them."[11] It would be crazy to rule out the possibility that these ancient Chinese debates may be relevant for thinking about political challenges in the rest of the world, and I deliberately draw on themes such as the morality of warfare that seem to pose challenges across time and space.

Host: Make up your mind. Before you said the book is written for the Chinese context, and now you say political argumentation by ancient Chinese thinkers has universal reach. You can't have it both ways.

Author: Yes I can. Their arguments may be relevant outside of China, but it's easier to make the case for continuing relevance in China. It goes without saying that China is a political community with a long history. Chinese intellectuals tend to have a deep sense of history and regularly invoke ancient ideas and events to think about the present-day challenges. This continuity can take very concrete forms: for example, descendants of Confucius and Mencius trace family history to their great ancestors and are often proud defenders of their ideas in contemporary settings. So it's not completely crazy to imagine descendants of Confucius and Mencius, with knowledge of the modern world, in dialogue with other political thinkers in today's China.

Host: But Daoists, Legalists, and Mohists don't have family trees that go back to great ancestors! Yet you imagine that their descendants are part of the modern political debates.

Author: Yes, admittedly, I've taken some creative license here.

Host: But you distort what they say! Your "creative license" implies they all care about family ancestry! Would Zhuangzi want to establish a long family line? He'd probably regard such an effort as vainglorious and superficial. Not to mention that the families of Legalists such as Shang Yang were wiped out as part of collective punishment; how could their descendants have survived to this day?

Author (hesitates): Mmh, admittedly, you have a point there.

Host: And then you have a female descendant of Yue mouthing parts of the *Yueji*, as though the texts were written by females! I realize you're trying to be politically correct by including more female voices, but the effect is to sanitize the patriarchal history of China! Only men wrote what you call "great" texts; there were no female writers, and we shouldn't cover up this ugly reality!

Author: I'm not sure I agree. Mu Jiang was a sixth-century BCE female philosopher of the *Book of Changes*.[12] Ban Zhao was an influential female philosopher and historian in the first century. But I didn't include them because their ideas were not so political. In the case of Ban Zhao, her assertions of the value of female servility obviously seem out of date.[13] Still, I welcome efforts to bring their ideas to light. Also, females can now be part of the Kong (Confucius) family tree, so it's not implausible to imagine female descendants of the great thinkers defending the ideas of their ancestors in contemporary settings. In any case, I want to remind you, my aim is not merely to present the ideas of the great political thinkers from ancient China. I want to show that their ideas, or at least some of their ideas, are still relevant today. So I take some creative license for this purpose.

Host: Okay, so you admit intellectual historians would be horrified by your approach. You seem to be motivated more by normative concerns: you pick and choose ideas that still seem relevant today, whatever that means. But normative political theorists will be equally horrified. If you want to present strong arguments, say, about the morality of warfare, why not select the best possible arguments? Who today would defend Shang Yang's view that soldiers should be promoted on the basis of the number of decapitated heads of enemy soldiers?

Author: As I explain in the text, there is a rough parallel with "realists" today who measure success in warfare by the number of dead enemy soldiers. The technology has changed, but the basic idea is similar. And I think it's important to put such ideas in dialogue with defenders of morally justified warfare such as Mencius.

Host: But why choose Mencius? Why not have Shang Yang in dialogue with, say, Michael Walzer's views on just warfare?

Author: I think Mencius offers the most defensible theory of morally justified warfare; it has advantages compared to Michael Walzer's theory.[14] At the very least, philosophers who are influenced by theorizing from the Western tradition(s) should welcome new contributions on present-day concerns inspired by non-Western thought. Philosophy, like it or not, is an increasingly global dialogue. Plus, in this case, the debate is set in China, and Mencius's theory is more psychologically compelling in a Chinese context. People tend to take pride in the theories of their ancestors, and so their theories have more motivational force.

Host: Well, that's convenient. Mencius provides the best theory from a normative perspective, and it's the theory most likely to motivate Chinese people. But why would a normative theorist argue along those lines? The normative theorist will try to defend the best theory and there's no reason to limit oneself to the theories of one thinker.

Author: Again, my aim is to present the ideas of the great Chinese political thinkers from ancient China and to show that their ideas are still relevant today. I do not rule out the possibility that other theories may be even more interesting and relevant today. Traditions such as Buddhism and Marxism shape much contemporary Chinese political thinking and may be more defensible in some respects. But that's for other books to explore. Admittedly, I try to balance two aims that may be somewhat in tension with each other. If my sole aim were to present ancient ideas, then it might indeed work best by presenting the ideas as they were argued about in the original settings. If my sole aim were to present and defend the best possible political theories, then I probably wouldn't limit myself to pre-Qin theorizing and I might defend arguments that conflict with those put forward by great thinkers of the past. But I have two aims, which places limits on what I can do. I don't do "pure" history, obviously, but neither do I do "pure" philosophy. I concede that.

Host (laughs): That's quite a concession! The problem is that you do neither well. Intellectual historians and normative political theorists will both left shaking their heads! Not to mention your use of the dialogue form, which even further obscures what you are trying to do. In fact, it allows you to conceal your own viewpoint. I can never figure out where you yourself stand in these mini-dialogues.

Author: My aim—I guess it's my third aim—is to stimulate further reflection on the part of readers, not to tell them what to think. I'm not trying to defend my own position.

Host: But what is your own position?

Author: I do have some strongly held beliefs, but I try to be fair to all sides. A dialogue, as I see it, implies a certain willingness to treat an interlocutor with respect and show willingness to learn from the other's viewpoint. I didn't write this book to spread what I take to be "the truth." My aim, to repeat, is to encourage readers to do their own thinking, and for this purpose I selected political controversies where there seem to be reasonable arguments from different perspectives. It's up to the reader to choose which "side" he or she wants to stand on.

Host (losing patience): But which side are *you* on? It's dishonest to conceal your own position!

Author: Well, if you must know, I'm generally sympathetic to Confucian political ethics, but I think Daoists, Legalists, and Mohists also make some reasonable arguments. I'm afraid I hold many contradictory viewpoints and I struggle to make sense of them. If I express ambivalence and uncertainty, it's because that's where I really stand.

Host: And is that all you're trying to communicate to readers? Do they really need to read your book if that's where they're going to end up?

Author: I hope the reader will have learned some thought-provoking ideas developed by great political thinkers in the Chinese tradition. My book can open up new possibilities, new horizons.

Host: But the most likely outcome is that readers will be left even more confused than when they started off!

Author: What if I've succeeded in casting doubt on previously unquestioned dogmas about right and wrong? Isn't that a kind of success?

Host: If that's the aim, I suggest the reader go straight to Zhuangzi, no need to read your book.

Author: Zhuangzi is not the only great thinker in pre-Qin China. I encourage readers to learn about a broad range of political argumentation developed in great Chinese classics.

Host: Can you, in all honestly, recommend your book to readers? If Anglophone readers want to read the Chinese classics, why not read the works translated by experts with helpful introductions to the historical context and the main ideas, such as Eric L. Hutton's excellent translation of the complete works of the *Xunzi*, which you plundered for your book?[15]

Author: I'm not sure if "plunder" is the right word. I referred to his translations with proper academic references and indicated when and where I made modifications. In any case, I'd encourage readers to consult the Chinese classics, either in original or in translated form or both. But most readers won't have the patience to read whole works.

Host: In that case, why not simply ask readers to read excerpts of the Chinese classics, such as the collection of readings edited by Philip J. Ivanhoe and Bryan W. Van Norden, *Readings in Classical Chinese Philosophy*, which you also plundered for your book?[16] Why do people need to read your book?

Author: Perhaps it's an enjoyable read? My book presents the ideas of the greats in a relatively entertaining format.

Host: Entertainment! Surely we should read the classics to learn from them, not to be "entertained." People can read comic books to be entertained. And now that I think of it, the reader can turn to graphic narratives that present the ideas of the Chinese classics with humorous illustrations, such as the *Illustrated*

Library of Chinese Classics by your own publisher.[17] That's a much more entertaining format than your book. And if the aim is to interest those without much prior knowledge of classical Chinese political thinking, your book is still not accessible enough. The reader will need to consult works that explain key thinkers and basic concepts in more detail. Not to mention that experts won't have much to learn from your book. Your book is too complicated for beginners and too simple for experts.

Author: For experts, I try to elaborate and qualify arguments in the notes, and the translation issues discussed in the notes may be of interest. And the main text does contain some innovative interpretations and applications, if I can say so myself. For beginners, I begin each section that introduces the life, thought, and influence of the thinker, and they can look at the notes for references to more works if they happen to be interested in a particular topic. Ideally, the reader would read more than one work on the Chinese classics. My book can be read in conjunction with works that explain basic concepts in Chinese philosophy in some depth, such as Roger Ames's *A Conceptual Lexicon for Classical Confucian Philosophy*, Zhang Dainian's *Key Concepts in Chinese Philosophy*, and the edited work by Wan-yee Li and Yuri Pines, *Key Words in Chinese Culture*.[18]

Host: But why should they read your book? What's different about your approach?

Author: I try to show the lasting value of the ideas by discussing implications for present-day challenges.

Host: You're not the only one doing that. There are better works out there that draw implications for today, such as Michael Puett and Christine Gross-Loh's excellent book, *The Path: What Chinese Philosophers Can Teach Us About the Good Life*. I'd also recommend the comprehensive volume, *Why Traditional Chinese Philosophy Still Matters: The Relevance of Ancient Wisdom for the Global Age,* edited by Ming Dong Gu.[19]

Author: My book is more political in orientation; it addresses different issues.

Host: I'd recommend other books on Chinese classics that draw political implications for the modern world, such as Sor-Hoon Tan's *Confucian Democracy: A Deweyan Reconstruction,* Jiang Qing's *A Confucian Constitutional Order: How China's Ancient Past Can Shape Its Political Future,* Joseph Chan's *Confucian Perfectionism: A Political Philosophy for Modern Times,* Bai Tongdong's *Against Political Equality: The Confucian Case,* Kim Sungmoon's *Confucian Constitutionalism: Dignity, Rights and Democracy,* Chenyang Li's *Reshaping Confucianism: A Progressive Inquiry,* and Elena Ziliotti's *Meritocratic Democracy: A Cross-Cultural Political Theory*. I'd also recommend Roel Sterckx's *Chinese Thought from Confucius to Cook Ding,* which more or less covers the same period you cover and shows why ideas from classical Chinese thought matter today; Colin Lewis and Jennifer King's *Contemporary Politics and Classical Chinese Thought,* which shows the relevance of classical Chinese thought for contemporary challenges in liberal democracies; and the collection *Adventures in Chinese Realism: Classic Philosophy Applied to Contemporary Issues,* edited by Eirik Lang Harris and Henrique Schneider, which is an intriguing effort to draw political implications from the Legalist tradition.[20] All these books show how ancient Chinese philosophy can help us to think about political challenges in contemporary society. And they do it more systematically than your book. Again, please tell our listeners why anyone would want to read your book.

Author: My book is written in dialogue form. As I said, I want readers to think for themselves, not to promote a particular viewpoint.

Host: Yes, I got that point, but you're not sincere. Why not simply ask readers to read the classics and think for themselves instead of lecturing them about implications for today?

Author: I'm not "lecturing them." I argue for two contrasting possibilities, and I try to be fair to both "sides." That's the benefit of the dialogue form.

Host: So readers get to pick one of two possibilities you offer them. You're still cutting off thinking. Why not follow Confucius's model: make some pithy points and let the students fill in the rest? Or ask students to discuss the ideas with a teacher who doesn't seek to impose an interpretation about the contemporary value of the great classics. Such approaches would show more respect for readers than whatever you're trying to push in your book.

Author (hesitates, momentarily speechless): But my approach is original! There's no other book that. . . .

Host (interrupting): I have no further questions. Thank you for joining the interview on *Bad Books Network*. We'd normally ask authors about their next bad book, but frankly, I'm not very interested.

NOTES

Acknowledgments

1. See my books *Communitarianism and Its Critics* (Oxford: Clarendon Press, 1993) and *East Meets West: Human Rights and Democracy in East Asia* (Princeton: Princeton University Press, 2000).

2. Fred Dallmayr's edited book *Comparative Political Theory: An Introduction* (New York: Palgrave Macmillan, 2010) is a valuable effort to help fill this gap. In my view, however, the book is still too specialized to engage undergraduates, not to mention the general reader (and I say this as one of the contributors).

Introduction

1. To ensure dissemination of the classics among educated elites, the national university examination (*gaokao*) tests for knowledge of Confucius, Mencius, Xunzi, and Zhuangzi. Students preparing for the examination need to memorize parts of those texts as well as "correct" interpretations (of course, once they get into university, they can argue about alternative interpretations).

2. In this book, I do not seek to evaluate the pros and cons of China's political system. Two of my previous works—*The China Model: Political Meritocracy and the Limits of Democracy* (Princeton: Princeton University Press, 2015) and (coauthored with Wang Pei) *Just Hierarchy: Why Social Hierarchies Matter in China and the Rest of the World* (Princeton: Princeton University Press, 2020), chaps. 2–3—were normative efforts to evaluate China's political system.

3. I wouldn't call myself an expert translator, but I've done an intensive course in classical Chinese and devoted hundreds of hours to translating works by Confucius, Mencius, Xunzi, and the *Yueji* over the past couple of decades, so I'm at least good enough to judge what counts as a good translation.

4. Noted as "modified" in the notes.

5. For some strange reason, I have a desire to entertain the reader. I'm tempted to blame (or credit) my (late) father Don Bell, a writer who won the Stephen

Leacock Award for the best book of humor written in English by a Canadian writer for his book *Saturday Night at the Bagel Factory* (Toronto: McLelland and Stewart, 1972).

Chapter 1

1. See Sima Qian, *史记* [Records of the Grand Historian] (Beijing: Zhonghua Book Company, 1959), books 33, 47.

2. The last five books of the *Analects* (books 16–20) are less reliably attributed to Kongzi the person. Since Kongzi didn't say much about harmony (和, *he*) in the *Analects*, I will draw on other works that fill in his ideas in a way that (I think) is faithful to his original vision, though mainly sticking to sayings that were attributed (if not reliably) to Kongzi. I draw the line at the Kongzi quotes from the *Zhuangzi* because the author's intent seems to be to satirize Kongzi or use Kongzi to mouth his own ideas rather than be faithful to Kongzi's original vision.

3. In 2012, eminent political thinker Joseph Nye, who popularized the term "soft power," visited Shandong University. At a meeting with professors (I was one of them), Nye opened by (modestly) asking if there was anything he said about "soft power" that Kongzi hadn't said. People laughed nervously, knowing that the answer may be negative, and we moved on to the next topic.

4. Zhuangzi does not directly invoke the word "freedom" (自由), and there are diverse ways of interpreting his ideas by invoking the (modern) idea of freedom. My interpretation of Zhuangzi's freedom as "freedom from social entanglements" is inspired by Tao Jiang, *Origins of Moral-Political Philosophy in Early China* (Oxford: Oxford University Press, 2021), chap. 5. I recognize, however, that Jiang's interpretation draws mainly from Anglophone academia (Paul J. D'Ambrosio, "The Zhuangzi: Personal Freedom and/or Incongruity of Names?," *Philosophy East and West* 73, no. 2 [2023]: 463). For alternative interpretations of Zhuangzi's account of freedom, see Christine Abigail L. Tan, *Freedom's Frailty: Self-Realization in the Neo-Daoist Philosophy of Guo Xiang's Zhuangzi* (Albany: State University of New York Press, 2024); Karyn Lai, "Freedom and Agency in the *Zhuangzi*: Navigating Life's Constraints," *British Journal in the History of Philosophy* 30, no. 1 (2022): 3–23; Chen Yun, *自由之思:庄子"逍遥游"的阐释* [The Idea of Freedom: An Interpretation of Zhuangzi's "Carefree Wandering" (Hangzhou: Zhejiang University Press, 2020); He Hua and Yan Jiafeng, "论庄子的自由观及其当代价值: 以'逍遥游'为例" [On Zhuangzi's View of Freedom and Its Contemporary Value: Taking "Carefree Wandering" as an Example], *Journal of Huangshan University* 21, no. 1 (2019): 34–37; Mercedes Valmisa, "The Happy Slave Isn't Free: Relational Autonomy and Freedom in the Zhuangzi," *Philosophy Compass* 14, no. 3 (2019): 1–15; Chen Yun, *庄子哲学的精神* [The Spirit of Zhuangzi's Philosophy] (Shanghai: Shanghai People's Press, 2016),

chap. 2; Bao Qinggang, *反思与重构：郭象"庄子注"研究* [Reflection and Reconstruction: Research on Guo Xiang's "Commentary on Zhuangzi"] (Nanjing: Nanjing University Press, 2013), chaps. 2–4; Wang Furen, "论庄子的自由观：庄子'逍遥游'的哲学阐释" [On Zhuangzi's View of Freedom: A Philosophical Interpretation of Zhuangzi's "Carefree Wandering"], *Hebei Academic Journal* 29, no. 6 (2009): 39–46; Wan Yonghua, "庄子自由观论析" [An Analysis of Zhuangzi's View of Freedom], *Journal of Nanjing Forestry University (Humanities and Social Sciences Edition)* 6, no. 1 (2006): 36–40. And a century earlier, Yan Fu argued that Zhuangzi was a defender of "the spirit of freedom" (自由精神); see Huang Kewu, "严复晚年思想的一个侧面：道家思想与自由主义之会通" [An Aspect of Yan Fu's Late Thought: The Connection Between Daoist Thought and Liberalism], in *严复思想新论* [New Essays on the Thought of Yan Fu], ed. Liu Guisheng, Lin Qiyan, and Wang Xianming (Beijing: Tsinghua University Press, 1999), 270.

5. In book 1, Zhuangzi famously says that the sage does not rely on *ming* (名), which can be translated as "reputation" or "fame" but can refer more broadly to "identity" (Paul J. D'Ambrosio, "Ming as 'Identity' in Early Chinese Thought: Examining Laozi 44," *Philosophy East & West* 72, no. 1 [2022]: 92).

6. I do not mean to imply that Kongzi and Zhuangzi's ideas were rigidly separated in people's minds in subsequent Chinese history. In practice, educated Chinese often appealed to the thoughts of both thinkers (and, more generally, to both Confucian and Daoist traditions), either in combination or at different times. For a fascinating account of a late nineteenth- and early twentieth-century self-identified Confucian who also invoked the *Zhuangzi*, see Henrietta Harrison, *The Man Awakened from Dreams: One Man's Life in a North China Village* (Stanford, CA: Stanford University Press, 2005).

7. There is a genealogical record from Kongzi to today's Kong family, and members of the Kong family with a more direct descent from Kongzi have the honor of being buried in the Kong family cemetery (孔林) in Qufu, the oldest family cemetery in the world. In my experience, many members of the Kong family are committed to the thought of Kongzi as expressed in the *Analects*, so it is not far-fetched to imagine a descendant of Kongzi defending Kongzi's ideas in a contemporary setting. There are, however, no known descendants of Zhuangzi, so I hope the reader will pardon the fictitious license. In this dialogue, I try to be faithful to the views of the "real" Kongzi and the "real" Zhuangzi, but when "Zhuang" and "Kong" act as critics, I tend to resort to straightforward argumentation as opposed to pithy sayings (in the case of the "real" Kongzi) and metaphors and surreal stories (in the case of the "real" Zhuangzi). I also recognize that my interpretations may be controversial, and I try to flag some alternative interpretations in the notes.

8. Here I borrow Heiner Roetz's translation of *Rujia*. A more literal translation is "School of the Learned."

9. Confucius, *The Analects, with Selections from Traditional Commentaries*, trans. Edward Slingerland (Indianapolis: Hackett, 2013), 7.1.

10. Confucius, *Analects*, trans. Slingerland, 7.8 (modified).

11. See, e.g., 11.22, where he gives seemingly opposite advice to two different students.

12. See Zhao Dingxin, *The Confucian-Legalist State: A New Theory of Chinese History* (Oxford: Oxford University Press, 2015).

13. Alan Chan, "Neo-Daoism," in *The Stanford Encyclopedia of Philosophy* (Summer 2019 ed.), ed. Edward N. Zalta, https://plato.stanford.edu/archives/sum2019/entries/neo-daoism.

14. The Chinese government deemphasized the Maoist emphasis on class conflict after the Cultural Revolution and did a complete U-turn under the Hu Jintao administration, which emphasized the importance of a "harmonious society" (和谐社会), meaning that peaceful means (rather than violent class struggle) should be employed to restore harmony in society and between humans and nature. In contemporary China, "harmony" (和谐) is one of the "core socialist values" taught in schools and plastered on public notices. Over the past couple of decades, Chinese scholars have written academic works arguing for the relevance of Confucian harmony in contemporary society: see, e.g., Chenyang Li, *The Confucian Philosophy of Harmony* (London: Routledge, 2014); Xinzhong Yao, "The Way of Harmony in the *Four Books*," *Journal of Chinese Philosophy* 40, no. 2 (2013): 252–68; Yao Fulin, "建构和谐: 略谈孔子思想的现代价值" [The Construction of Harmony: A Brief Discussion on the Modern Value of Kongzi's Thought], *Journal of Historiography*, no. 3 (2010): 7–9; Liu Bing, "中国传统文化中的和谐思想及其当代价值" [Harmony in Traditional Chinese Culture and Its Contemporary Value], *Theory Journal*, no. 7 (2009): 78–81. For an argument that similar ideas of harmony exist in other Chinese traditions, see Shao Hanming and Qi Si, "'和而不同': 儒道释和谐思想分疏及其当代启示" ["Harmony But Not Sameness": Harmonious Ideas in Confucianism, Taoism, and Buddhism and Contemporary Implications], *Journal of Tianjin Normal University (Social Sciences)*, no. 5 (2007): 13–19. For a study that compares the virtue of harmony in different traditions around the world, see Chenyang Li and Dascha During, eds., *The Virtue of Harmony* (Oxford: Oxford University Press, 2022). For an effort to measure the Confucian idea of "diversity in harmony" (和) between family members, citizens, countries, and humans and nature in different countries, see Daniel A. Bell and Yingchuan Mo, "Harmony in the World 2013: The Ideal and the Reality," *Social Indicators Research* 118, no. 2 (2014): 797–818.

15. See Peng Guoxiang, "Inside the Revival of Confucianism in Mainland China: The Vicissitudes of Confucian Classics in Contemporary China as an Example" (https://archiv.oriens-extremus.org/49/OE49-10.pdf).

16. Confucius, *Analects*, 1.1 (the translations are mine unless indicated otherwise). The term "朋" literally means "acquaintance" or "companion" rather than "friend," but it has almost universally been translated as "friend," so I follow that convention here.

17. Confucius, *The Analects of Confucius: A Philosophical Translation*, trans. Roger T. Ames and Henry Rosemont Jr. (New York: Ballantine Books, 1998), 2.4 (modified). 天 is usually translated "Heaven," but doing so invites Christian connotations, so I translate it as "higher morality," which seems appropriate in this context (in Xunzi, by contrast, the invocations of 天 do not have strong moral connotations).

18. Confucius, *Analects*, 10.8.

19. The term 酒量 (*jiu liang*) is often used at meals and banquets in mainland China and refers to one's capacity for drinking alcohol.

20. Confucius, *Analects*, 10.8.

21. In toasting rituals of Confucian-influenced Shandong province, the lower status person lowers his or her glass relative to the glass of the higher status person as a way of showing respect. If the toasters are of roughly equal status, they will often mock-fight to clink the other's glass at a lower level, which often leads to laughter and smiles as they struggle to be the more modest "winner" (see, e.g., https://b23.tv/eeqlxeS or, for a more extreme, clearly satirical video, https://b23.tv/YZUqyNB).

22. Ni Peimin, *Understanding the Analects of Confucius: A New Translation with Annotations* (Albany: State University of New York Press, 2017), 16.7 (modified).

23. Confucius, *Analects*, 9.18 (the same line is repeated in 15.13).

24. Ni, *Understanding the Analects of Confucius*, 8.13, 8. 17.

25. Confucius, *Analects*, trans. Slingerland, 1.1.

26. Confucius, *The Analects of Confucius*, in Paul R. Goldin, *The Art of Chinese Philosophy: Eight Classical Texts and How to Read Them* (Princeton: Princeton University Press, 2020), 15.23.

27. I thank Justin Tiwald for the formulation of this objection.

28. For a strong defense of Confucian role ethics, see Roger T. Ames, *Confucian Role Ethics: A Vocabulary* (Hong Kong: Chinese University of Hong Kong Press, 2011).

29. Confucius as quoted in *The Doctrine of the Mean* (13), in Goldin, *Art of Chinese Philosophy*, 39. Here I follow Goldin's interpretation of 恕 (*shu*, reciprocity) in *The Art of Chinese Philosophy*, 38–39.

30. Confucius, *Analects*, trans. Slingerland, 16.11.

31. Confucius, *Analects*, 1.2.

32. Confucius, *Analects*, trans. Slingerland, 3.12 (modified).

33. See Confucius, *Analects*, 7.21.

34. Confucius, *Analects*, trans. Slingerland, 19.13, 5.7. 8.13.

35. Confucius, *Analects*, trans. Slingerland, 18.6, 18.7 (modified).

36. In the late Qing dynasty, the central government seemed to be hopelessly corrupt and in a position of irreversible decline, so scholar-officials increasingly directed their attention to local affairs. Daniel Barish, *Learning to Rule: Court Education and the Remaking of the Qing State, 1861–1912* (New York: Columbia University Press, 2022), 1–2, 8–9.

37. Ni, *Understanding the Analects of Confucius*, 15.32, 17.15 (modified).

38. For an alternative argument that there is no clear distinction between the "moral" and the "non-moral" in the *Analects*, see Paul D'Ambrosio, "The Ethics of Contingency: An Alternative (to) Morality in the *Analects*," *Religions* 14, no. 11 (2023): 1367. And for a more radical argument that casts doubt on the whole idea that Kongzi is a moralist, see Wayne Alt, "A Non-Moral Interpretation of *The Original Analects of Confucius*," *Sino-Platonic Papers*, no. 330 (2023), https://sino-platonic.org/complete/spp330_confucian_morality_analects.pdf.

39. This long exchange between Kongzi and Zizhang is drawn from translations by Ni Peimin and Edward Slingerland of *The Analects of Confucius*, 20.2 (modified). The passage, however, contains unusually detailed instructions in response to a student's questions, suggesting it may not be the "original" Kongzi who preferred to let students think for themselves.

40. Confucius, *Analects*, trans. Slingerland, 15.20 (modified).

41. Confucius, *Analects*, trans. Slingerland, 10.25 (modified).

42. Ni, *Understanding the Analects of Confucius*, 13.23. There may be a language issue here. In Chinese, the distinction between *he* (harmony) and *tong* (sameness/conformity/uniformity) is well-known to every intellectual, but in English it is easy (compared to Chinese) to conflate harmony and sameness/conformity/uniformity, especially when the idea of harmony is invoked in a political context (see Li, *Confucian Philosophy of Harmony*, esp. chap. 1). So I translate *he* as "diversity in harmony."

43. See chapters 2 and 4.

44. For an argument that Confucian harmony is a viable ideal in pluralistic societies marked by a diversity of worldviews, see David B. Wong, "Soup, Harmony, and Disagreement," *Journal of the American Philosophical Association* 6, no. 2 (2020): 139–55.

45. Quoted in Kam Por Yu, "The Confucian Conception of Harmony," in *Governance for Harmony in Asia and Beyond*, ed. Julia Tao, Anthony B. L. Leung, Martin Painter, and Chenyang Li (London: Routledge, 2009), 17 (modified).

46. Confucius, *Analects*, trans. Slingerland, 13.15.

47. I've taken the liberty of translating 乘 (*sheng*) as "tanks" rather than "chariots." The basic idea is the more 乘, the greater the military power of the state, so tanks are the modern-day functional equivalent of chariots.

48. In her best-selling work on the *Analects*, Yu Dan explicitly invokes this passage (独与天地精神往来) from chap. 7 of the *Zhuangzi* to make sense of Zeng Xi's words. I criticize her depoliticized interpretation of the Confucian ideal in *China's New Confucianism: Politics and Everyday Life in a Changing Society* (Princeton: Princeton University Press, 2008), app. 1.

49. Elsewhere, Kongzi says that "realizing harmony is the most valuable function of ritual propriety" (*Analects of Confucius*, 1.12). For more on ritual, see chapter 2, section 2.

50. This exchange between Kongzi and four of his students is the longest passage in the *Analects* (11.26). I have modified the translation by Ni Peimin.

51. I do not know of any interpreters who attribute a homoerotic dimension to Zengxi's ideal of swimming and singing with "five or six young men and six or seven boys," but the bonding between men and boys in an ancient Greek context had political implications: the gymnasium was the setting for institutionalized (or legitimate) pederasty and such bonding served the purpose of the *polis* by strengthening harmonious bonds in society at large. Conversely, those who wanted to atomize political society and break these bonds attempted to close gymnasia. As Thomas F. Scanlon puts it, these "hotbeds of pederastic bonding" were threatening to tyrants because they could give rise to coup attempts: one "famous example of tyrannical repression of gymnasia is that of Aristodemus of Cymae (died 524) who, seeking to discourage a 'noble and manly spirit,' closed all gymnasia and forced all youths reared in the city to dress and wear long hair in the fashion of girls" (Scanlon, *Eros and Greek Athletics* [Oxford: Oxford University Press, 2002], 268).

52. This exchange between Kongzi and Zigong is drawn from *The Analects of Confucius: A Philosophical Translation*, trans. Ames and Rosemont, 12.7 (modified).

53. Confucius, *Analects*, trans. Slingerland, 3.23, 7.32 (modified). For more on Confucianism and music, see chapter 3, section 2.

54. Confucius, *Analects*, trans. Slingerland, 2.21.

55. Ni, *Understanding the Analects of Confucius*, 8.2 (modified).

56. Confucius, *Analects*, 1.2.

57. Confucius, *Analects*, trans. Slingerland, 13.18.

58. For a similar point, see Erin M. Cline, *The Analects: A Guide* (Oxford: Oxford University Press, 2022), 169.

59. Colin Manchester, "Wives as Crown Witnesses," *Cambridge Law Journal* 37, no. 2 (1979): 249–251.

60. GovHK, "Allowances," https://www.gov.hk/en/residents/taxes/salaries/allowances/allowances/allowances.htm.

61. This statement implies that some communities do not strongly value filial piety and that the government should not promote the ideal in such communities.

The real Kongzi seemed to argue for an ethical perspective that all civilized communities should adopt. On the other hand, he also appeals to classical works and history to justify his views, and perhaps he would have allowed for different rankings of values had he known about other civilized communities (in the sense that they have a long history and works regarded as classical texts that set out an ethical vision) such as ancient Athens with contrasting value rankings. So it is not implausible to assume that if Kongzi were around today, he would defend the value of filial piety only in communities (1) that strongly value the ideal, such as East Asian communities with a Confucian heritage (as opposed to, say, Canada, where it is not widely assumed that adult children have a strong obligation to care for and revere their elderly parents and ancestors) and (2) where the ideal has a long history and grounding in works regarded as classical texts.

62. I draw on and modify the translations of this famous passage in the *Analects* (2.3) by Edward Slingerland and Paul Goldin. I follow Goldin's unusual translation of 耻 as "conscience" rather than "shame" (*Art of Chinese Philosophy*, 43) because it more closely (in my view) expresses Kongzi's point that people should be encouraged to regulate themselves by means of internal moral standards rather than be motivated by fear of punishment.

63. World Health Organization, "Law of the People's Republic of China on the Protection of Rights and Interests of the Elderly," https://extranet.who.int/mindbank/item/4741. This law is quoted and discussed in Wang Pei, "Confucian Filiality Revisited: The Case of Contemporary China," *Philosophy and Social Criticism*, October 18, 2024, 6, https://doi.org/10.1177/01914537241288471.

64. Confucius, *Analects*, 15.4.

65. Confucius, *Analects*, trans. Slingerland, 2.8 (modified). My interpretation of this passage follows that of Slingerland (11).

66. Here I follow Wang, "Confucian Filiality Revisited," 6.

67. Puay Ling Lim, "Maintenance of Parents Act," https://www.nlb.gov.sg/main/article-detail?cmsuuid=d2328927-c580-4088-8d74-268caaff635b.

68. Jason Tian, *Family Laws and Regulations Report 2025 China*, International Comparative Legal Guides, 2025, https://iclg.com/practice-areas/family-laws-and-regulations/china.

69. Ministry of Civil Affairs, Government of China. *民政部关于贯彻落实《中华人民共和国民法典》中有关婚姻登记规定的通知* [Notice of the Ministry of Civil Affairs on the Implementation of the Marriage Registration Provisions in the Civil Code of the People's Republic of China], https://www.gov.cn/zhengce/zhengceku/2020-12/04/content_5567010.htm.

70. Kelly Merris, "'No-Fault Divorces' in England and Wales: Is Hong Kong Ready to Follow Suit?," *Hong Kong Lawyer*, March 2023, https://www.hk-lawyer.org

/content/%E2%80%9Cno-fault-divorces%E2%80%9D-england-and-wales-hong-kong-ready-follow-suit.

71. Confucius, *The Analects (A Bilingual Edition)*, trans. D. C. Lau (Hong Kong: Chinese University of Hong Kong Press, 2000), 12.13 (modified).

72. Confucius, *Analects*, trans. Slingerland, 6.27, 12.21 (modified).

73. Ni, *Understanding the Analects of Confucius*, 4.16 (modified).

74. This is a variation of a philosophical joke I heard in my graduate student days.

75. Confucius, *Analects*, trans. Slingerland, 7.33 (modified). See also 14.28.

76. See Yutang Lin, "Confucius as I Know Him," *China Critic* 4, no. 1 (1931): 5–9, http://www.chinaheritagequarterly.org/030/features/030_confucius.inc, and Alexa Olesen, "Confucius: China's Most Famous Single Dad," *Tulsa World*, August 24, 2014, https://tulsaworld.com/opinion/alexa-olesen-confucius-chinas-most-famous-single-dad/article_2a607960-2457-54da-b2c8-f2594122478f.html. Such views are contested: see Yang Chaoming, "孔子'出妻'说及相关问题" [Confucius's Alleged Repudiation of His Wife and Related Problems], *Qilu Journal* 2 (2009): 10–14.

77. For an argument that a "cooling-off period" helps to reduce the divorce rate in China, see Guo Junwei, "离婚冷静期制度实施中的价值冲突与衡平" [Value Conflict and Balance in the Implementation of the Divorce "Cooling-Off Period" System], *Journal of Northeast Normal University (Philosophy and Social Sciences)*, no. 6 (2021): 137–143.

78. Haiyan Lee, *A Certain Justice: Toward an Ecology of the Chinese Legal Imagination* (Chicago: University of Chicago Press, 2023), 22–26, 270–271. But Philip Huang argues that Qing dynasty courts generally did not mediate and that mediation in contemporary China comes from the Maoist period (Huang, "Court Mediation in China, Past and Present," *Modern China* 32, no. 3 [July 2006], https://doi.org/10.1177/0097700406288179).

79. This paragraph draws on Albert Chen, "Mediation, Litigation, and Justice: Confucian Reflections in a Modern Liberal Society," in *Confucianism for the Modern World*, ed. Daniel A. Bell and Hahm Chaibong (Cambridge: Cambridge University Press, 2003), 257–287.

80. The latter condition is necessary because judicial mediation "in the name of harmony" often serves to undermine the rights of battered women in divorce cases. Xin He and Kwai Hang Ng, "In the Name of Harmony: The Erasure of Domestic Violence in China's Judicial Mediation," *International Journal of Law, Policy and the Family* 27, no. 1 (2013): 97–115.

81. Confucius, *Analects*, trans. Slingerland, 7.22.

82. The Apology Ordinance, which aims to "promote and encourage the making of apologies with a view to preventing the escalation of disputes and facilitating their

amicable resolution" (https://www.elegislation.gov.hk/hk/cap631) but that does not constitute an admission of the person's liability in connection with the matter, is another "gentle" manifestation of the commitment to harmony in Hong Kong's legal system.

83. Zeng Xi was known for his devotion to filial piety (he composed and edited the *Classic of Filial Piety* under the direction of Confucius, the legend goes), and it seems safe to assume he would endorse Kong's defense of the ideal.

84. Victor H. Mair, *Wandering on the Way: Early Taoist Tales and Parables of Chuang Tzu* (Honolulu: University of Hawai'i Press, 1994), xiii. Mair refers to the *Dao De Jing* as "a kind of Taoist fast food."

85. For a counterargument, see Esther Klein, "Were the 'Inner Chapters' in the Warring States? A New Examination of Evidence About the *Zhuangzi*," *T'oung Pao* 96 (2011): 299–369. For the sake of simplicity, I will continue to refer to Zhuangzi as a person who authored the whole text.

86. All we know about Zhuang Zhou comes from Sima Qian's brief bio written more than two centuries after he died (for a translation, see Mair, *Wandering on the Way*, xxxi–xxxii).

87. Given that emphasis on erasure of the self, it should not be surprising that the author(s) of the *Zhuangzi* do not affirm their identity or identities (the author[s] of the text had a sense of humor, which may also explain why Kongzi is sometimes invoked as a defender of ideas that clearly seem anti-Confucian). It's worth noting that Kongzi himself, notwithstanding his reputation as a stern old moralist, also had a developed sense of humor: see Christoph Harbsmeier, "Confucius Ridens: Humor in *The Analects*," *Harvard Journal of Asiatic Studies* 50, no. 1 (1990): 131–161.

88. Mair, *Wandering on the Way*, xliii–xliv.

89. Usage of the word "Zhuangzi" has dramatically increased over the past two decades in both Chinese (https://books.google.com/ngrams/graph?content=%E5%BA%84%E5%AD%90&year_start=1800&year_end=2019&corpus=en-2019&smoothing=3) and English (https://books.google.com/ngrams/graph?content=zhuangzi&year_start=1800&year_end=2019&corpus=en-2019&smoothing=3).

90. Zhuangzi, *Basic Writings*, trans. Burton Watson (New York: Columbia University Press, 2003), chap. 1, p. 26.

91. Confucius, *Analects*, trans. Slingerland, 5.9 (modified).

92. Confucius, *Analects*, 9.23.

93. Zhuangzi, trans. Paul Kjellberg, in *Readings in Classical Chinese Philosophy*, 3rd ed., ed. Philip J. Ivanhoe and Bryan W. Van Norden (Indianapolis: Hackett, 2023), chap. 5, p. 249.

94. Zhuangzi, *The Inner Chapters*, trans. A. C. Graham (Indianapolis: Hackett, 2001), chap. 1, p. 46 (modified).

95. It could be argued that social ties also lie "inside" as memories, but the Confucian would add that social relations constantly need to be nourished via "outside" activities such as rituals.

96. This famous line from chapter 1 of the *Zhuangzi*—"至人无己"—can be taken to mean that the perfect person should strive not to be overly attached to the self rather than (as in Buddhism) positing an ideal of completely transcending the self (I thank Paul D'Ambrosio for this point).

97. Zhuangzi, trans. Kjellberg, in *Readings in Classical Chinese Philosophy*, 3rd ed., chap. 20, p. 263. Zhuangzi does not refer to himself as "I" in the text, so I change the original here by inserting an "I" (if translators insert an "I" in other passages, I keep it as translated).

98. Zhuangzi, *Basic Writings*, trans. Watson, chap. 19, p. 121, and Zhuangzi, trans. Kjellberg, in *Readings in Classical Chinese Philosophy*, 3rd ed., chap. 19, p. 257.

99. Zhuangzi, *Basic Writings*, trans. Watson, chap. 18, pp. 116–117. See also Zhuangzi, trans. Kjellberg, in *Readings in Classical Chinese Philosophy*, 3rd ed., chap. 2, p. 237.

100. Zhuangzi, *Basic Writings*, trans. Watson, chap. 17, p. 100 and chap. 6, p. 81.

101. Zhuangzi, *Basic Writings*, trans. Watson, chap. 18, p. 115 (modified).

102. Zhuangzi's reaction to the death of his wife is not unique: Celtic wakes can involve music and drinking and laughter in celebration of the life of the deceased (Nicholas Collender, "The Irish Wake—Ireland's Most Enduring Tradition," https://irishurns.com/the-irish-wake-irelands-most-enduring-tradition). But the reasons for the joyful response differ. In Zhuangzi's case, he seems happy because his wife is free of social entanglements and may be transformed to a better condition.

103. Zhuangzi, *Basic Writings*, trans. Watson, chap. 1, pp. 29–30. See also chap. 4, pp. 57–58.

104. Zhuangzi, *Basic Writings*, trans. Watson, chap. 4, pp. 61–62 (modified). Elsewhere, Zhuangzi tells stories that suggest the aim is not uselessness per se but rather to open oneself to original and unconventional conceptions of usefulness. Chris Fraser, *Late Classical Chinese Thought* (Oxford: Oxford University Press, 2023), 130.

105. Zhuangzi, *Basic Writings*, trans. Watson, chap. 2, p. 34.

106. See chapter 3.

107. Zhuangzi, *Basic Writings*, trans. Watson, chap. 17, pp. 108–109. In the text, this story is told by Prince Mou of Wei.

108. Confucius, *Analects*, 7.22.

109. Such views were explicitly put forward by Daoist-inspired thinkers in the Huang Lao tradition (see the discussion in Bell and Wang, *Just Hierarchy*, 100–101), but they are compatible with the Confucian view that we can always learn from others and that good policymaking requires diverse viewpoints and exposure of mistakes.

110. I take the liberty of changing "Wei" to "North Korea," which may the closest modern equivalent to the ancient state of Wei in this dialogue. In the *Zhuangzi* (*Basic Writings*, trans. Watson, chap. 4, pp. 49–53), it is a dialogue between Kongzi and his student Yan Hui, but it seems safe to assume that Zhuangzi is using Kongzi to express his own views. That said, it also seems safe to assume that the views expressed in the early part of the dialogue would also be endorsed by Kongzi given his view that "if the Way is being realized in the world, then show yourself; if it is not, then go into reclusion" (8.13). My interpretation of the different stages of this dialogue has been inspired by Justin Tiwald and Richard Kim's excellent podcast (Justin Tiwald and Richard Kim, "Episode 4: Persuasion," in *This Is the Way: Chinese Philosophy Podcast*, https://www.listennotes.com/da/podcasts/this-is-the-way/episode-4-persuasion-Y_Ha6vIr53K/), though I provide a different interpretation of the final piece of advice.

111. I've changed "Kong" to "Zhuang" here because Kong is not likely to think that Yan Hui can be corrupted by power (because Kongzi had a high estimation of Yan Hui's ability to remain moral even in a state of poverty).

112. Here I borrow from ideas expressed in Tiwald and Kim's podcast.

113. Confucius, *Analects*, 6.11.

114. The discussion of the "fasting of the mind" is more distinctly "Zhuangzian," so I change "Kong" to "Zhuang" at this point in the dialogue.

115. Zhuangzi, *Basic Writings*, trans. Watson, chap. 4, p. 55 (modified).

116. Zhuangzi, *Basic Writings*, trans. Watson, chap. 4, p. 55.

117. I thank Justin Tiwald for this point.

118. Zhuangzi, *Basic Writings*, trans. Watson, chap. 3, pp. 45–46.

119. I borrow this political interpretation of the Cook Ding passage from Jiang, *Origins of Moral-Political Philosophy in Early China*, 329–330. For an alternative political interpretation of this passage, see the creative video "Butcher Ding: A Slaughter Ballet" with a script by Hans-Georg Moeller (https://www.youtube.com/watch?v=vGtgGz5SsY0).

120. Zhuangzi, trans. Kjellberg, in *Readings in Classical Chinese Philosophy*, 3rd ed., chap. 17, p. 260.

121. Zhuangzi, trans. Kjellberg, in *Readings in Classical Chinese Philosophy*, 3rd ed., chap. 2, p. 233.

122. Zhuangzi, *Basic Writings*, trans. Watson, chap. 4, p. 56.

123. See, e.g., Olga Khazan, "Take a Wife . . . Please! Why Are Married People Happier than the Rest of Us?," *Atlantic*, August 31, 2023.

124. Zhuangzi, *Basic Writings*, trans. Watson, chap. 18, p. 114.

125. Zhuangzi, *Basic Writings*, trans. Watson, chap. 2, p. 38.

126. Zhuangzi, trans. Kjellberg, in *Readings in Classical Chinese Philosophy*, 3rd ed., chap. 2, p. 232.

127. Zhuangzi, trans. Kjellberg, in *Readings in Classical Chinese Philosophy*, 3rd ed., chap. 5, p. 249.

128. Zhuangzi, *Inner Chapters*, trans. Graham, chap. 6, p. 90.

129. Zhuangzi, trans. Kjellberg, in *Readings in Classical Chinese Philosophy*, 3rd ed., chap. 5, p. 249, and chap. 19, p. 262. Zhuangzi has Kongzi say the second line, but it's clearly something Zhuangzi would endorse.

130. In the *Dao De Jing* (*The Classic of the Way and Virtue*), chap. 55, Laozi explicitly praises the Way of the baby: "One who possesses virtue in abundance is comparable to a newborn baby. Poisonous insects will not sting it, wild animals will not pounce on it, birds of prey will not swoop down on it. Its bones are weak and its sinews supple yet its hold is firm" (quoted in Roel Sterckx, *Chinese Thought from Confucius to Cook Ding* [Milton Keynes, UK: Pelican Books, 2019], 182).

131. Zhuangzi, trans. Kjellberg, in *Readings in Classical Chinese Philosophy*, 3rd ed., chap. 2, p. 238.

132. Zhuangzi, trans. Kjellberg, in *Readings in Classical Chinese Philosophy*, 3rd ed., chap. 6, p. 255. Zhuangzi uses "Kongzi" to make this point, but I assume it's Zhuangzi's point and not something the real Kongzi would say.

Chapter 2

1. Jin Keyu, *The New China Playbook: Beyond Socialism and Capitalism* (New York: Viking, 2023), 129.

2. The Jixia Academy is the ancient Chinese equivalent of Plato's Academy (see Wang Zhimin and Eleni Karamalengou, eds., *稷下学宫与柏拉图学园: 比较研究论集* [The Jixia Academy and Plato's Academy: A Collection of Comparative Research] (Beijing: SDX, 2021). In 2022, archaeologists discovered the exact site of the Jixia Academy (Kevin McSpadden, "Archaeologists Discover Centre for Greatest Chinese Philosophers During Warring States Period from over 2,000 Years Ago," *South China Morning Post*, March 17, 2022, https://www.scmp.com/news/people-culture/article/3170781/archaeologists-discover-centre-greatest-chinese-philosophers), and my hope is that a rebuilt academy will host political debates as in ancient times.

3. In the early days of the anticorruption drive, academics developed the argument that Han Feizi's ideas can be used to curb corruption in government (see, e.g., Xu Keqian, "私德, 公德与官德: 道德在韩非子法家学说中的地位" [Private Morality, Public Morality, and Official Ethics: The Position of Morality in Han Feizi's Legalist Theory], *Research in the Traditions of Chinese Culture*, no. 4 [2013]: 68–73). In my (limited) experience with senior political leaders, they say (off the record) that the campaign has been inspired by Legalist-style harsh measures since nothing else can effectively deal with the urgent problem of corruption in government.

4. The debate about whether law/methods (法) or ritual (礼) is more effective at preventing wrongdoing is a recurring theme in Chinese history: for an account of the debates in the Song dynasty, see Su Jilang and Su Shoufumei, 有法无天 [Law Without Heavenly Order] (Hong Kong: Chinese University of Hong Kong Press, 2023), 289–290.

5. The character *fa* (法) as employed by Han Feizi can be translated as law, standards, or methods depending on the context, but here I draw mainly on the uses that most closely approximate "law."

6. See Burton Watson's introduction to his translation of Han Feizi, *Basic Writings* (New York: Columbia University Press, 2003).

7. Han Feizi's amoralism is frequently compared to that of Machiavelli; see, e.g., Sun Xiaochun, "韩非与马基雅维利非道德政治观评议" [A Commentary on Han Fei and Machiavelli's Amoral Political Views], *Jilin University Journal (Social Sciences Edition)*, no. 5 [1997]: 53–59.

8. For an argument that the government openly and consistently draws on Legalism for inspiration, see David K. Schneider, "China's New Legalism," *National Interest*, no. 143 (2016): 19–25; and Jianying Zha, "China's Heart of Darkness: Prince Han Fei and Chairman Xi (Prologue)," *China Heritage*, July 2020, https://chinaheritage.net/journal/chinas-heart-of-darkness-prince-han-fei-chairman-xi-jinping-prologue/.

9. The real Xunzi, according to Sima Qian, was Chief Libationer of the Jixia Academy (Sima Qian, 史记, book 74), and here I imagine the same is true of his descendant.

10. I've deleted the honorific *zi*, which tends to be added to the names of great Chinese thinkers after they die.

11. *Analects of Confucius*, 9.23.

12. It is possible to misuse state resources for good reasons, e.g., if the state policies are generally unjust and an upright public official illegally misappropriates public resources to help the poor. Or else one can imagine that an official misuses public resources out of fear, e.g., if the system as a whole is corrupt and a leader puts pressure on an otherwise upright subordinate to join in the corruption. But here I define corruption as wrongful misappropriation of public resources for selfish individual or family interests, which fits the usage of the term by Han Feizi and Xunzi.

13. Han Feizi, *Basic Writings*, trans. Watson, chap. 6, p. 23 (modified).

14. Han Feizi, *Basic Writings*, trans. Watson, chap. 9, p. 48 (modified).

15. *Han Feizi*, trans. Eirik L. Harris, in *Readings in Classical Chinese Philosophy*, 3rd ed., ed. Philip J. Ivanhoe and Bryan W. Van Norden (Indianapolis: Hackett, 2023), chap. 40, p. 356.

16. Han Feizi, *Basic Writings*, trans. Watson, chap. 6, pp. 22, 27 (modified).

17. *Han Feizi*, trans. Joel Sahleen, in *Readings in Classical Chinese Philosophy*, 2nd ed., ed. Philip J. Ivanhoe and Bryan W. Van Norden (Indianapolis: Hackett, 2001), chap. 50, p. 357.

18. *Han Feizi*, trans. Sahleen, in *Readings in Classical Chinese Philosophy*, 2nd ed., chap. 50, p. 347.

19. Han Feizi, *Basic Writings*, trans. Watson, chap. 50, pp. 127–128.

20. *Han Feizi*, trans. Sahleen, in *Readings in Classical Chinese Philosophy*, 2nd ed., chap. 50, p. 350.

21. *Han Feizi*, trans. Sahleen, in *Readings in Classical Chinese Philosophy*, 2nd ed., chap. 50, p. 341.

22. Han Feizi, *Basic Writings*, trans. Watson, chap. 49, p. 107.

23. *Han Feizi*, trans. Sahleen, in *Readings in Classical Chinese Philosophy*, 2nd ed., chap. 50, p. 341.

24. Quoted in Bai Tongdong, "The *Han Feizi* and Its Contemporary Relevance," in *Dao Companion to China's Fa Tradition*, ed. Yuri Pines (Cham: Springer, 2024), 650.

25. *Han Feizi*, trans. Sahleen, in *Readings in Classical Chinese Philosophy*, 2nd ed., chap. 50, p. 340. In pre-Qin writings, the people of Song were often the butt of jokes.

26. See Hou Wailu, *中国古代思想学说史* [History of Ancient Chinese Thoughts and Theories] (Shenyang: Liaoning Education Press, 1998), 263.

27. See Peng Wang, *The Chinese Mafia: Organized Crime, Corruption, and Extra-Legal Protection* (Oxford: Oxford University Press, 2017), 190–191.

28. I can testify both to the effectiveness and to the drawbacks of the anticorruption campaign from my own experience serving as a public official: see my book *The Dean of Shandong: Confessions of a Minor Bureaucrat at a Chinese University* (Princeton: Princeton University Press, 2023), chap. 4.

29. *Han Feizi*, trans. Sahleen, in *Readings in Classical Chinese Philosophy*, 2nd ed., chap. 43, p. 322.

30. *Han Feizi*, trans. Sahleen, in *Readings in Classical Chinese Philosophy*, 2nd ed., chap. 12, p. 317.

31. *Han Feizi*, trans. Sahleen, in *Readings in Classical Chinese Philosophy*, 2nd ed., chap. 50, p. 343.

32. *Han Feizi*, trans. Sahleen, in *Readings in Classical Chinese Philosophy*, 2nd ed., chap. 50, p. 345.

33. Fu Hualing, "China's Striking Anti-Corruption Adventure: A Political Journey Towards the Rule of Law?," *University of Hong Kong Faculty of Law Research Paper*, no. 1 (2016): 18, https://hub.hku.hk/bitstream/10722/223185/1/Content.pdf.

34. For an argument that Han Feizi theorizing on law is similar to Lon Fuller's account of the "internal morality of law," see Kenneth Winston, "The Internal

Morality of Chinese Legalism," *Singapore Journal of Legal Studies* 2005 (December 2005): 313–347. But if the "rule of law" refers to an ideal of law as superior to the will of rulers, along with its institutional manifestation in the form of an independent judiciary, then Han Feizi's Legalism is obviously very different.

35. Han Feizi, *Basic Writings*, trans. Watson, chap. 16, p. 90.

36. *Han Feizi*, trans. Sahleen, in *Readings in Classical Chinese Philosophy*, 2nd ed., chap. 12, pp. 318–319.

37. Han Feizi, *Basic Writings*, trans. Watson, chap. 8, p. 40.

38. Quoted in Bai Tongdong, "*Han Feizi* and Its Contemporary Relevance," 664–665.

39. Han Feizi, *Basic Writings*, trans. Watson, chap. 5, p. 17. Han Feizi suggests that the need for underhanded techniques to uncover corruption extends to public officials at lower levels of government: "When Bu Pi was serving as a county magistrate, he discovered that the royal inspector was corrupt . . . and he had a beloved concubine. Bu Pi accordingly ordered his young servant to make love to her, in order to discover the inspector's secrets" (Han Feizi, *In Praise of Regulations: A New Translation of the Han Feizi*, trans. Olivia Milburn, forthcoming, chap. 30).

40. Han Feizi, *Basic Writings*, trans. Watson, chap. 5, p. 17.

41. *Han Feizi*, trans. Harris, in *Readings in Classical Chinese Philosophy*, 3rd ed., chap. 7, p. 341.

42. *Han Feizi*, trans. Sahleen, in *Readings in Classical Chinese Philosophy*, 2nd ed., chap. 12, p. 318.

43. Han Feizi, *Basic Writings*, trans. Watson, chap. 7, p. 31.

44. Han Feizi, *Basic Writings*, trans. Watson, chap. 7, pp. 30–31.

45. For a similar objection, see Eirik Lang Harris, "Constraining the Ruler: On Escaping Han Fei's Criticism of Confucian Virtue Politics," *Asian Philosophy* 23, no. 1 (2013): 57.

46. *Han Feizi*, trans. Harris, in *Readings in Classical Chinese Philosophy*, 3rd ed., chap. 27, p. 349.

47. *Han Feizi*, trans. Sahleen, in *Readings in Classical Chinese Philosophy*, 2nd ed., chap. 50, p. 346.

48. *Analects of Confucius*, 2.3 (see chap. 1).

49. *Han Feizi*, trans. Sahleen, in *Readings in Classical Chinese Philosophy*, 2nd ed., chap. 50, p. 358.

50. *Han Feizi*, trans. Harris, in *Readings in Classical Chinese Philosophy*, 3rd ed., chap. 40, p. 357.

51. Han Feizi, *In Praise of Regulations*, trans. Milburn, chap. 30.

52. Han Feizi, *Basic Writings*, trans. Watson, chap. 16, pp. 87–88.

53. *Han Feizi*, trans. Sahleen, in *Readings in Classical Chinese Philosophy*, 2nd ed., chap. 50, p. 358.

54. Han Feizi, *Basic Writings*, trans. Watson, chap. 5, pp. 15, 16–17.

55. See Peter Moody, "The Legalism of Han Fei-tzu and Its Affinities with Modern Political Thought," *International Philosophical Quarterly* 19, no. 3 (1979): 329.

56. For a similar point, see Philip J. Ivanhoe, "Hanfeizi and Moral Self-Cultivation," *Journal of Chinese Philosophy* 38, no. 1 (2011): 41.

57. Han Feizi, *Basic Writings*, trans. Watson, chap. 5, pp. 15, 16.

58. *Han Feizi*, trans. Sahleen, in *Readings in Classical Chinese Philosophy*, 2nd ed., chap. 49, pp. 330-31.

59. Han Feizi, *Basic Writings*, trans. Watson, chap. 13, p. 82.

60. Quoted in Sungmoon Kim, "Virtue Politics and Political Leadership: A Confucian Rejoinder to Hanfeizi," *Asian Philosophy* 22, no. 2 (2012): 188–189.

61. See Kim, "Virtue Politics and Political Leadership," 189, for a similar point.

62. *Han Feizi*, trans. Harris, in *Readings in Classical Chinese Philosophy*, 3rd ed., chap. 7, p. 341.

63. Quoted in Bai Tongdong, *Supplement Materials* (forthcoming), 5–6.

64. Han Feizi, *Basic Writings*, trans. Watson, chap. 8, pp. 38, 39.

65. For a similar argument, see Bai Tongdong, "*Han Feizi* and Its Contemporary Relevance," 672.

66. For similar points, see Fraser, *Late Classical Chinese Thought*, chap. 2; Bryan W. Van Norden, "Han Fei and Confucianism: Towards a Synthesis," in *Dao Companion to the Philosophy of Han Fei*, ed. Paul R. Goldin (Dordrecht: Springer, 2013); Justin Tiwald, "On the View That People and Not Institutions Bear Primary Credit for Success in Governance: Confucian Arguments," *Journal of Confucian Philosophy and Culture*, no. 32 (2019): 81–82; and Harris, "Constraining the Ruler," 50–51, 57.

67. Han Feizi, *Basic Writings*, trans. Watson, chap. 49, pp. 117–118.

68. I thank Bai Tongdong for this point (email communication).

69. The ideal of ritual (礼) is central to Confucian philosophy—three of the *Thirteen Classics* are dedicated specifically to ritual (Chenyang Li, *Reshaping Confucianism: A Progressive Inquiry* [New York: Oxford University Press, 2024], 74)—but I discuss Xunzi's interpretation of ritual because he systematically spelled out the implications for political order (and disorder).

70. Chin-shing Huang argues that Xunzi should be (re) enshrined on the grounds that he meets the two main standards for enshrinement: "the candidate's importance to the development of Confucian learning and its current relevance" (Huang, *Confucianism and Sacred Space: The Confucius Temple from Imperial China to Today*, trans. Jonathan Chin with Chin-shing Huang [New York: Columbia University Press, 2020], 168).

71. According to Paul Goldin (writing in 2007), Xunzi "has been the subject of more books published in English over the past two decades than any other Chinese

philosopher, vastly outstripping Mencius" (Goldin, "Xunzi and Early Han Philosophy," *Harvard Journal of Asiatic Studies* 67, no. 1 [2007]: 137).

72. See, e.g., Wang Meng, *治国平天下:"荀子"解读* [Ruling the Country and Providing Peace in the World: An Interpretation of Xunzi] (Jiangsu: People's Press, 2023) and Pan Yue, *战国与希腊* [The Warring States Period and (Ancient) Greece], http://theory.people.com.cn/n1/2020/0603/c40531-31734074.html. Wang Meng is a well-known Chinese writer who served as Minister of Culture from 1986 to 1989, and Pan Yue is one of China's most scholarly public officials (with a doctorate in history) and served as the Minister of the National Ethnic Affairs Commission.

73. See my book *Dean of Shandong*, 92.

74. Quoted in Eirik Lang Harris, "Han Fei on the Problem of Morality," in *Dao Companion to the Philosophy of Han Fei*, ed. Paul R. Goldin (Dordrecht: Springer, 2013), 115n12 (modified).

75. Quoted in Harris, "Han Fei on the Problem of Morality," 115n12 (modified).

76. The phrase 人之性恶 (23.1) is usually translated as "people's nature is bad (or evil)," but since people can improve it is not meant to be a claim about a permanent, unchangeable human nature, so I translate the phrase as "tendency to badness." Kurtis Hagen translates 恶 as "crude" ("Xunzi and the Nature of Confucian Ritual," *Journal of the Academy of Religion* 71, no. 2 [2003]: 372), which is appropriate because Xunzi allows for the possibility that "nature" can be shaped in different ways. However, Xunzi means to contrast 恶 with 善 (good), so I think "bad" is more accurate.

77. *Xunzi: The Complete Text*, trans. Eric L. Hutton (Princeton: Princeton University Press, 2014), chap. 19, p. 201 (slightly modified).

78. *Xunzi*, 23.1.

79. *Xunzi*, trans. Hutton, chap. 19, p. 201 (modified).

80. Donald J. Munro, *A Chinese Ethics for the New Century: The Ch'ien Mu Lectures in History and Culture, and Other Essays on Science and Confucian Ethics* (Hong Kong: Chinese University of Hong Kong Press, 2005), 112.

81. *Xunzi*, trans. Hutton, chap. 1, p. 5 (modified). The opening chapter of the Xunzi—"An Exhortation to Learning"—is well-known to university students in China because they need to memorize it as preparation for the national university entrance examinations.

82. Siufu Tang, "Ritual as Skill: Ethical Cultivation and the Skill Model in the Xunzi," in *Skills in Ancient Ethics: The Legacy of China, Greece and Rome*, ed. Tom Angier and Lisa Raphals (London: Bloomsbury, 2022), 226.

83. *Xunzi*, trans. Hutton, chap. 23, pp. 248–249 (modified).

84. Xunzi does not explicitly distinguish between good and bad rituals. He uses the term 礼 (*li*, ritual) invariably to mean something good, but what follows is what he likely would have said had he been asked to make that distinction. The next few

paragraphs draw on my "Hierarchical Rituals for Egalitarian Societies," in *Ritual and the Moral Life: Reclaiming the Tradition*, ed. David Solomon, Ping-Cheung Lo, and Ruiping Fan (Dordrecht: Springer, 2012), chap. 11.

85. In practice, some rituals may be partly bad and partly good. For example, rituals such as communal cheering and chanting at sporting events may be bad in the sense that they promote dislike (if not hatred) of another team and its supporters, but they may be good if they serve to channel communal energies away from more destructive and violent activities such as warfare.

86. See Dimitris Xygalatas, *Ritual: How Seemingly Senseless Acts Make Life Worth Living* (New York: Little, Brown Spark, 2022), 61–63.

87. For a similar point, see Byung-Chul Han, *The Disappearance of Rituals: A Topology of the Present*, trans. Daniel Steuer (Cambridge: Polity, 2020), 20.

88. *Xunzi II*, trans. John Knoblock (Changsha: Hunan People's Publishing House, 1999), chap. 20, p. 667.

89. *Xunzi*, trans. Hutton, chap. 5, pp. 35–36.

90. I thank Justin Tiwald for this argument (email communication).

91. See part 1 of this dialogue.

92. *Xunzi II*, trans. Knoblock, chap. 19, p. 611.

93. *Xunzi*, trans. Hutton, chap. 20, p. 218.

94. See Han, *Disappearance of Rituals*, chap. 2.

95. *Xunzi*, trans. Hutton, chap. 19, p. 213.

96. Quoted in Paul Goldin, "Xunzi," in *Stanford Encyclopedia of Philosophy* (Fall 2018 ed.), ed. Edward N. Zalta, https://plato.stanford.edu/archives/fall2018/entries/xunzi.

97. *Xunzi*, trans. Hutton, chap. 27, p. 291.

98. Xygalatas, *Ritual*, 246–247.

99. *Xunzi II*, trans. Knoblock, chap. 19, p. 615 (modified). See Lee Wilson, "Confucianism and Totalitarianism: An Arendtian Reconsideration of Mencius Versus Xunzi," *Philosophy East & West* 71, no. 4 (2021): 994.

100. *Xunzi II*, trans. Knoblock, chap. 18, p. 571.

101. *Xunzi*, trans. Hutton, chap. 5, p. 36.

102. Xygalatas, *Ritual*, chap. 4.

103. *Xunzi*, trans. Hutton, chap. 19, p. 213.

104. *Xunzi II*, trans. Knoblock, chap. 19, pp. 623–625 (modified). Knoblock translates "久而平，所以优生也" into "with the passage of life he resumes the ordinary course of life, whereby he cares for the needs for the living," which points to the social benefits of the ritual. Hutton translates the phrase as "the reason that only over a long time does he gradually return to his regular routine is to properly adjust his life" (*Xunzi*, trans. Hutton, chap. 19, p. 209). Hutton's interpretation seems too

individualistic in orientation, given Xunzi's repeated emphasis on the transformative effects and social benefits of ritual.

105. *Xunzi*, trans. Hutton, chap. 16, pp. 163–164 (modified).

106. *Xunzi*, trans. Hutton, chap. 16, p. 164.

107. *Xunzi*, trans. Hutton, chap. 27, p. 291.

108. For a similar point, see Lou Yulie, *中华文化的感悟* [Insights into Chinese Culture] (Beijing: Commercial Press, 2021), 15–16.

109. *Xunzi*, trans. Hutton, chap. 19, p. 201 (modified).

110. *Xunzi II*, trans. Knoblock, chap. 27, p. 859.

111. *Xunzi*, trans. Hutton, chap. 15, p. 162.

112. *Xunzi*, trans. Hutton, chap. 10, p. 85 (modified).

113. *Xunzi*, trans. Hutton, chap. 9, p. 68.

114. *Xunzi*, trans. Hutton, chap. 9, p. 68 (modified). Here Xunzi agrees with the Mohists who first proposed the ideal of political meritocracy, where officials are promoted on the basis of ability and virtue, as opposed to earlier Confucians, who were willing to accommodate familial ties in the appointment of public officials (see Tao Jiang, *Origins of Moral-Political Philosophy in Early China*, 394).

115. For a systematic discussion of Xunzi's defense of political meritocracy, see Gan Chunsong, *儒家政治哲学大纲* [An Outline of Confucian Political Philosophy] (Beijing: Peking University Press, 2025), chap. 10.

116. For more information on the 山东济宁政德教育干部学院 (Shandong Jining Academy for the Education of Virtuous Public Officials), see http://gbzdjy.jiningdq.cn/.

117. See CPIB, "Singapore's Corruption Control Framework," https://www.cpib.gov.sg/about-corruption/prevention-and-corruption/singapores-corruption-control-framework/.

118. See Fareed Zakaria, "A Conversation with Lee Kuan Yew," *Foreign Affairs*, March/April 1994, https://www.foreignaffairs.com/articles/asia/1994-03-01/conversation-lee-kuan-yew-0.

119. Wee Kek Koon, "How Singapore Transport Minister's Corruption Case Has Put Focus on High Pay of Ministers and Recalls Imperial China, Where Paying Officials to Be Honest Failed," *South China Morning Post*, February 3, 2024, https://www.scmp.com/magazines/post-magazine/short-reads/article/3250554/how-singapore-transport-ministers-corruption-case-has-put-focus-high-pay-ministers-and-recalls.

120. Benjamin Wong, "Political Meritocracy in Singapore: Lessons from the PAP Government," in *The East Asian Challenge for Democracy*, ed. Daniel A. Bell and Chenyang Li (New York: Cambridge University Press, 2013), 299–300. See the discussion in my book *The China Model: Political Meritocracy and the Limits of Democracy* (Princeton: Princeton University Press, 2015), 121–124.

121. The top eight countries in Transparency International's Corruption Perception Index are all small (the largest is the Netherlands, with 17.5 million people): Transparency International, "Corruption Perceptions Index," 2023, https://www.transparency.org/en/cpi/2022.

122. *Xunzi*, trans. Hutton, chap. 9, p. 81.

123. See Sterckx, *Chinese Thought*, 264–265.

124. *Analects of Confucius*, 19.12.

125. *Xunzi*, trans. Hutton, chap. 4, p. 29 (modified).

126. *Xunzi*, trans. Hutton, chap. 19, p. 207.

127. *Xunzi*, trans. Hutton, chap. 19, p. 39 (modified).

128. *Xunzi*, trans. Hutton, chap. 4, pp. 29–30 (modified).

129. For a similar argument, see Li, *Reshaping Confucianism*, 91.

130. Transparency International, "Corruption Perceptions Index."

131. See, e.g., Andrew Wedemen, "Village Elections and Grassroots Corruption in China," *Taiwan Journal of Democracy* 13, no. 2 (2018): 107–129.

132. Liu Anting argues that Xunzi is China's earliest defender of democracy because of his famous statement "从道不从君" ("follow the moral way, not the way of the ruler") (Liu Anting, "'隆礼尊贤而王'— 荀子礼治论" [Honoring Rituals and Respecting the Worthy [Can Make One a] Humane Monarch: Xunzi's Theory of Ritual Order], *Confucius Studies*, no. 2 [2008]: 48), but if democracy means (at minimum) the idea that commoners should have a say in politics, then there is no evidence that Xunzi was a democrat.

133. See Albert W. Dzur, *Punishment, Participatory Democracy, and the Jury* (Oxford: Oxford University Press, 2012), chap. 4.

134. James S. Fishkin, Baogang He, Robert C. Luskin, and Alice Siu, "Deliberative Democracy in an Unlikely Place: Deliberative Polling in China," *British Journal of Political Science* 40, no. 2 (2010): 435–448, https://www.researchgate.net/profile/Baogang-He/publication/248665977_Deliberative_Democracy_in_an_Unlikely_Place_Deliberative_Polling_in_China/links/547476d70cf245eb436ddf53/Deliberative-Democracy-in-an-Unlikely-Place-Deliberative-Polling-in-China.pdf. See chapter 3 for a fictitious case.

135. Han, *Disappearance of Rituals*, 1.

136. *Xunzi*, trans. Hutton, chap. 27, p. 292. For a similar point supported by scientific findings, see Xygalatas, *Ritual*, 99–103.

137. *Xunzi*, trans. Hutton, chap. 4, p. 30. Xunzi's program for transformation through learning the Confucian classics is quite demanding: for details, see Wang Zheng, "礼与法— 荀子与法家根本差异" [Ritual and Law: The Fundamental Differences between Xunzi and Legalism], *History of Chinese Philosophy*, no. 4 (2018): 36–37.

138. Quoted (modified) in Mark Berkson, "Xunzi as a Theorist and Defender of Ritual," in *Ritual and Religion in the Xunzi*, ed. T. C. Cline III and Justin Tiwald

(Albany: State University of New York Press, 2014), 248. See Berkson's discussion of "The Hierarchy of Understanding" (248–250).

139. For detailed discussion of Shandong-style drinking rituals, see Bell and Wang, *Just Hierarchy*, 1–7.

140. Claims and questions about "drinking ability" (酒量, *jiu liang*) often lead off banquets in Shandong province, and even heavy drinkers modestly assert that their "drinking ability" is not great.

Chapter 3

1. See chapter 4, section 1.

2. Similar but not identical: for an essay on the commonalities and differences in the just war thinking of Mengzi and Mozi, see Cui Huabin and Daniel A. Bell, "墨子和孟子的战争伦理思想比较" [A Comparison of Mozi's and Mengzi's Theories of War], *Culture, History, and Philosophy*, no. 1 (2021): 96–104.

3. See Bryan Van Norden, *Virtue Ethics and Consequentialism in Early Chinese Philosophy* (Cambridge: Cambridge University Press, 2009), chap. 3; Chris Fraser, "Mohism," in *The Stanford Encyclopedia of Philosophy* (Fall 2024 ed.), ed. Edward N. Zalta and Uri Nodelman, https://plato.stanford.edu/archives/fall2024/entries/mohism; and Hui-chieh Loy, "Xunzi Contra Mozi," in *Dao Companion to the Philosophy of Xunzi*, ed. Eric L. Hutton (Dordrecht: Springer, 2016), 356–357.

4. The term 乐 (*yue*) in both Mozi and Xunzi refers to music as well as dance and poetry and other arts that often accompanied music. In the Confucian "six arts" (六艺) *yue* is one of the arts. So I translate 乐 as "musical arts," though at times I use "music" as shorthand.

5. In addition to attacking Mohists, Xunzi also developed his theory on musical education in response to Daoist criticisms of early Confucian thought: see Wang Kai, "美善相乐：生命哲学视域下的荀子乐论精神" [Beauty, Goodness, and the Musical Arts: On the Spirit of Xunzi's Musical Theory from the Perspective of the Philosophy of Life], *Journal of Beijing Normal University*, no. 4 (2018): 125–131. On the differences between Xunzi and Zhuangzi on music, see Guido Kreis, "Xunzi and Zhuangzi on Music: Two Ways of Modeling the Ethical Significance of Art," *Journal of Chinese Philosophy* 50, no. 1 (2023): 64–80.

6. Yue (乐) is still a common family name in China.

7. I have visited both sites, and local guides were proud defenders of the ideals of the respective thinkers, as though they were still fighting ideological battles from the Warring States period. The guide of the Mozi Memorial Hall explicitly cast Confucian contributions in a negative light on the grounds that Mozi, from nonelite social origin, favored commoners, whereas Confucians favored the aristocracy (my spouse

Wang Pei and I were accompanied by an otherwise coolheaded descendent of Kongzi, who was fuming after the visit). The guides of Xunzi's Memorial Grave hosted a grand banquet for myself and some graduate students where they movingly argued for the rehabilitation of Xunzi in China's Confucian temples and blamed Mengzi and Mozi for Xunzi's "cancellation" from the Song dynasty onward.

8. He Baogang, "Deliberative Participatory Budgeting: A Case Study of Zeguo Town in China," *Public Administration and Development* 39, no. 3 (2019): 144–153; Fishkin et al., "Deliberative Democracy in an Unlikely Place," 435–438. Local-level electoral democracy has been curtailed since President Xi Jinping centralized power and sought to reestablish party control at the grassroots level (Ben Hillman, "The End of Village Democracy in China," *Journal of Democracy* 34, no. 3 [2023]: 52–76, https://muse.jhu.edu/pub/1/article/9004330), but the government continues to develop nonelectoral forms of political representation and deliberative participation at the local level (Zhongyuan Wang and Su Yun Woo, "Deliberative Representation: How Chinese Authorities Enhance Political Representation by Public Deliberation," *Journal of Chinese Governance* 7, no. 4 [2021]: 583–615).

9. Ian Johnson, otherwise sympathetic to Mozi's thought, notes that "Master Mo takes Heaven's intention, as defined by himself, to be his standard by which to judge the conduct of regimes and individuals" ("Introduction," in *Mo Zi: The Book of Master Mo*, trans. Ian Johnson [London: Penguin Classics, 2013], xix).

10. I say "caricatured" because Confucians shared the view that human effort is necessary to improve society. Mozi's criticism may have been better directed at Zhuangzi-style Daoism (see chapter 1).

11. See Chris Fraser, "Introduction," in *Mozi: The Essential Mozi*, trans. Fraser (Oxford: Oxford University Press, 2020), xiii, and Jeffrey Riegel and John Knoblock, "Introduction," in *Mozi 墨子: A Study and Translation of the Ethical and Political Writings*, trans. Knoblock and Riegel (Berkeley: Institute of East Asian Studies, 2013), 18–21.

12. Even Burton Watson, who can barely hide his distaste for Mozi's "singular monotony of sentence pattern, and a lack of wit or grace that is atypical of Chinese literature," recognizes that doctrine of universal love is an original contribution to Chinese thought ("Introduction," in *Basic Writings of Mo Tzu, Hsun Tzu, and Han Fei Tzu*, trans. Burton Watson [New York: Columbia University Press, 1963], 15, 9).

13. See Fenrong Liu and Jialong Zhang, "New Perspectives on Moist Logic," *Journal of Chinese Philosophy* 37, no. 4 (2010): 605–621, and Riegel and Knoblock, "Introduction," 13–14.

14. Sun Junheng and Li Yue, "新墨学的兴起和前景" [The Revival and Future Prospects of New Mohism], *Journal of Early Chinese Philosophers*, no. 2 (2013): 321–328. Others defend Mozi on the grounds that his arguments against music made

sense in the Spring and Autumn and Warring States periods as a critique of rulers who oppressed the people by sending them to war and wasted resources on musical arts for their own enjoyment rather than implementing policies that benefited the people (Zhuang Hui, "墨子'非乐'思想辨析" [An Analysis of Mozi's "Against the Musical Arts"], *Dongyue Tribune* 24, no. 3 [2003]: 128–130).

15. *Mozi*, trans. Knoblock and Riegel, chap. 32, p. 275. This translation is useful because it has the original in (classical) Chinese, followed by an English translation, but I also rely on the smooth translation by Philip J. Ivanhoe, in *Readings in Classical Chinese*, 3rd ed., ed. Philip J. Ivanhoe and Bryan W. Van Norden (Indianapolis: Hackett, 2023). I switch back and forth based on my preferences: for example, I prefer Ivanhoe's translation 人 rendered as "person," not "man" (which is not inconsistent with the grammar, though ancients, admittedly, often had only men in mind), and in the Knoblock and Riegel translation I prefer the translation of 仁者 as "humane person" rather than "the benevolent." I make only slight modifications to the translations, e.g., rendering 高士 as "morally superior" rather than "superior" because 高 is meant to suggest moral desirability, and I translate 圣王 as "sage-monarch" rather than "sage-king" to leave open the possibility that there were female sage-monarchs (admittedly pre-Qin thinkers may have had only male monarchs in mind, but as far as I know they did not rule out the possibility of female monarchs).

16. *Mozi*, trans. Knoblock and Riegel, chap. 16, p. 156 (modified).

17. *Mozi*, trans. Knoblock and Riegel, chap. 16, p. 156 (modified).

18. *Mozi*, trans. Ivanhoe, chap. 16, p. 68.

19. *Mozi*, trans. Ivanhoe, chap. 16, pp. 59–61.

20. *Mozi*, trans. Ivanhoe, chap. 16, pp. 71, 60.

21. *Mozi*, trans. Ivanhoe, chap. 16, pp. 60–61.

22. *Mozi*, trans. Ivanhoe, chap. 16, p. 66 (modified).

23. *Mozi*, trans. Ivanhoe, chap. 16, pp. 67 (modified), 71.

24. Wang Pei, "Confucian *Ren* Ethics Revisited: A Feminist Perspective," *China Review* (forthcoming).

25. *Mozi*, trans. Ivanhoe, chap. 16, pp. 72–73.

26. *Mozi*, trans. Ivanhoe, chap. 25, pp. 77–78 (modified).

27. See, e.g., Su Liya, "Chinese Funeral Costing US$1.5 Million with Heavy Drinking and Fireworks Display Sparks Debate on Value of Lavish Ceremonies," *South China Morning Post*, May 13, 2022, https://www.scmp.com/news/people-culture/article/3177575/chinese-funeral-costing-us15-million-heavy-drinking-and.

28. *Mozi*, trans. Ivanhoe, chap. 25, pp. 78–79.

29. See chapter 2, section 2.

30. *Mozi*, trans. Ivanhoe, chap. 25, pp. 84–85.

31. *Mozi*, trans. Knoblock and Riegel, chap. 32, pp. 275–276.

32. *Mozi*, trans. Ivanhoe, chap. 32, p. 99 (modified).

33. *Mozi*, trans. Knoblock and Riegel, chap. 32, pp. 275–276.

34. *Mozi*, trans. Knoblock and Riegel, chap. 49, p. 379 (modified).

35. *Mozi*, trans. Ivanhoe, chap. 7, pp. 78, 77 (modified).

36. Needless to say, China does not have an electoral mechanism that might allow for the majority of voters to decide such matters, nor does it carry out referenda to assess and implement preferences. But opinion polling can, to a certain extent, reveal what the people think and care about (Wenfang Tang, *Public Opinion and Political Change in China* [Palo Alto, CA: Stanford University Press, 2005]).

37. See Keping Wang, *Chinese Culture of Intelligence* (Beijing: Foreign Language Teaching and Research Press / Palgrave Macmillan, 2019), 249; Ma Yue, "节用与非乐: '墨子' 平均主义思想研究" [Thrift and "A Condemnation of the Musical Arts": An Analysis and Research on Mozi's Egalitarianism], *Journal of the Staff and Workers' University*, no. 6 (2019): 20–21; and Qu Hongqi, "墨子 '非乐论' 辨析" [An Analysis of Mozi's "Against the Musical Arts"], *Journal of Shandong University*, no. 6 (2002): 62–64. The latter two scholars are sympathetic to Mozi's argument against hedonism and luxury in the context of relatively corrupt and poor societies.

38. *Mozi*, trans. Ivanhoe, chap. 32, pp. 99–100 (modified).

39. *Mozi*, trans. Ivanhoe, chap. 32, p. 100.

40. *Mozi*, trans. Ivanhoe, chap. 32, p. 101 (modified).

41. *Mozi*, trans. Ivanhoe, chap. 32, pp. 100, 102 (modified). Here I use square brackets to indicate that I go somewhat beyond the text because I translate 丈夫 as "people in their prime" rather than "men" or "husbands." In modern China, both men and women engage in farming activities, so it no longer makes sense to invoke the ancient gender-based division of labor when men did the farming (outside) and women did the weaving (inside the home).

42. *Mozi*, trans. Knoblock and Riegel, chap. 32, p. 281 (modified).

43. Here I borrow the formulation of So-Jeong Park, "Danger of Sound: Mozi's Criticism of Confucian Ritual Music," *Philosophical Forum* 51, no. 1 (2020): 55.

44. *Mozi*, trans. Knoblock and Riegel, chap. 39, pp. 315, 316, 321 (modified).

45. *Mozi*, trans. Ivanhoe, chap. 32, p. 100.

46. See chapter 2, section 2.

47. The precise dating of the *Yueji* is controversial: see Haun Saussy, "Music and Evil: A Basis of Aesthetics in China," *Critical Inquiry* 46, no. 3 (2020): 489; Scott Cook, "Introduction," in Cook, "*Yueji* 乐记—Record of Music: Introduction, Notes and Commentary," *Asian Music* 26, no. 2 (1995): 8–9; and Scott Cook, "Xun Zi on Ritual and Music," *Monumenta Serica* 45, no. 1 (1997): 2–3. I am not an expert in intellectual history, but I am more persuaded by the argument that the *Yueji* came after

Xunzi because the former does not engage with Mozi (Mohism was less influential in the Han, hence no need to bother responding to it) and the *Yueji* provides a metaphysical discussion of the underpinnings of exemplary music that is lacking in Xunzi's essay (such abstract theorizing was more typical of Han thinking; I do not draw on this aspect of the *Yueji* in this dialogue because such claims as exemplary music reflects the natural order are highly controversial today). Another key difference is that the *Yueji* does not invoke Xunzi's claim that humans have a tendency to badness, suggesting it was written in more peaceful and hopeful times (compared to the late Warring States period).

48. The nineteenth-century Sinologist and missionary James Legge translated the "Record of Musical Arts" (available free online: https://ctext.org/liji/yue-ji), but it has numerous errors. More recently, Scott Cook produced a much better translation for the first two thirds of the text, though the last third is translated in summary form (Cook, "*Yueji* 乐记—Record of Music"). In 2023, I joined an informal reading group on the *Yueji* with colleagues at the University of Hong Kong—Jin Yutang, Meng Tiantong, Tang Siufu, Justin Tiwald, Wang Pei, Yang Lili—and I draw on our translation of the *Yueji* in this chapter (we plan to publish our translation one day). If I quote from the *Yueji* without any reference to a translation, it means that I draw on our translation.

49. The *Yueji* was widely discussed among Song Confucians (I thank Justin Tiwald for this information), but (one speculates) Zhu Xi selected the *Zhongyong* as one of the four classics because it helped for the purpose of meeting the challenge of Buddhism by showing that Confucianism has a rich metaphysics too.

50. Xunzi's student Han Feizi defended the other extreme: that it's almost impossible to change human nature (see chapter 2, section 1).

51. *Mozi*, trans. Ivanhoe, chap. 31, pp. 89–90.

52. *Mozi*, trans. Ivanhoe, chap. 31, pp. 90, 98.

53. *Mozi*, trans. Ivanhoe, chap. 31, p, 98.

54. *Xunzi*, 23.1.

55. For more detailed discussion of Xunzi's defense of ritual, see chapter 2, section 2.

56. *Xunzi*, trans. Hutton, chap. 20, p. 218 (modified, including the passage in square brackets that has been changed—going beyond the text—to make it gender neutral).

57. *Xunzi*, trans. Hutton, chap. 20, p. 221. I've taken the liberty of translating 墨子 as "Mr. Mo" and will not use square brackets in the rest of the dialogue.

58. The original in Chinese is 夫乐者, 乐也. Here Xunzi may be playing on a pun because (as mentioned in the previous section) the same character 乐 means both music (or the musical arts) and joy (or happiness).

59. *Xunzi,* trans. Hutton, chap. 20, p. 218 (modified).

60. *Xunzi,* trans. Hutton, chap. 20, pp. 219–220.

61. *Xunzi,* trans. Hutton, chap. 20, p. 218 (modified). For a more detailed discussion of the ancient music that Xunzi favored and opposed, see Lei Yongqiang, "荀子乐教思想新论" [A New Analysis of Xun's Thoughts on Musical Education], *Dongyue Tribune* 7 (2018): 12–19.

62. *Xunzi,* trans. Hutton, chap. 20, p. 219.

63. *Xunzi,* trans. Hutton, chap. 20, pp. 228–229 (modified).

64. *Mozi,* trans. Knoblock and Riegel, chap. 18, p. 177.

65. *Mozi,* trans. Knoblock and Riegel, chap. 19, p. 183.

66. Daniel K. L. Chua, *Music and Joy: Lessons on the Good Life* (New Haven, CT: Yale University Press, 2024), 27.

67. *Xunzi,* trans. Hutton, chap. 20, p. 219.

68. *Xunzi,* trans. Hutton, chap. 15, pp. 152–154.

69. *Xunzi,* trans. Hutton, chap. 20, pp. 218–219. Mengzi developed a theory of just cause similar to modern-day just war theory (see chapter 4, section 2), but Xunzi had more to say about justice in war (see chapter 4, note 79).

70. *Mozi,* trans. Knoblock and Riegel, chap. 32, p. 277 (modified).

71. *Xunzi,* trans. Hutton, chap. 20, pp. 220, 219, 220 (modified). Note that I side with John Knoblock's translation of the passage 不足其上矣 (*Xunzi,* trans. Knoblock, chap. 20, p. 655), except that I translate 上 as "leader" rather than "superior."

72. *Yueji,* 8.

73. *Xunzi,* trans. Hutton, chap. 20, pp. 222–223.

74. *Xunzi,* trans. Hutton, chap. 20, p. 223.

75. *Yueji,* 25.

76. *Xunzi,* trans. Hutton, chap. 10, pp. 88–89.

77. In January 2024 I attended a performance of *Red Detachment of Women* by the National Ballet of China in Hong Kong. I was surprised that the emotions generated by the ballet still had a strong effect on the audience. After the evil landlord had been shot and presumably killed by one female soldier and fell into a ditch, other soldiers joined in and continued to shoot the dead landlord, and the crowd broke into enthusiastic applause (personally I thought it was overkill).

78. *Xunzi,* trans. Hutton, chap. 10, p. 91.

79. *Xunzi,* trans. Hutton, chap. 10, p. 90.

80. *Xunzi,* trans. Hutton, chap. 20, p. 220.

81. *Yueji,* 5, 32.

82. *Yueji,* 42.

83. James Harold, "On the Ancient Idea That Music Shapes Character," *Dao* 15, no. 3 (2016): 347–348. It is worth noting that some music that we now recognize as

classical, such as Mozart's music, was viewed as dangerous and decadent new music in its own time (R. Taggart Murphy, "The Real Threat to Classical Music," *Compact*, January 8, 2024, https://compactmag.com/article/the-real-threat-to-classical-music).

84. *Analects of Confucius*, 3.25, 7.14.

85. The literal translation of her song "月亮代表我的心" is "The Moon Represents My Heart."

86. *Analects of Confucius*, 7.32. Kongzi also seemed to appreciate more popular music outside of formal ritual settings (see Peter Yih-Jiun Wong, "The Music of Ritual Practice—An Interpretation," *Sophia* 51, no. 2 [2012]: 244n6).

87. The Chinese character 和 (*he*) is best translated as "diversity in harmony" (see chapter 1, section 1).

88. *Yueji*, 10, 11.

89. *Yueji*, 27.

90. Ming Dong Gu, "The Ethical Turn in Aesthetic Education: Early Chinese Thinkers on Music and Arts," *Journal of Aesthetic Education* 50, no. 1 (2016): 109–110.

91. *Yueji*, 15.

92. This claim, admittedly, goes beyond the text in the *Xunzi* or the *Yueji*, but the influential Neo-Confucian thinker Zhu Xi argued that anger can be justified in certain circumstances if it is "mirror-like" in the sense that it reflects the anger-worthy events in front of it and does not transfer to other objects and situations where it is not warranted (Kwong-loi Shun, "On Anger: An Essay in Confucian Moral Psychology," in *Rethinking Zhu Xi: Emerging Patterns Within the Supreme Polarity*, ed. David Jones and He Jinli [Albany: State University of New York Press, 2015], https://www.klshun.com/wp-content/uploads/2015/11/On-Anger-An-Essay-in-Confucian-Moral-Psychology-Preprint.pdf). For a contemporary argument that "bad" emotions can be productive in certain contexts, see Krista K. Thomason, *Dancing with the Devil: Why Bad Feelings Make Life Good* (New York: Oxford University Press, 2023).

93. *Yueji*, 15, 12.

94. *Yueji*, 3.

95. In the Han dynasty, the emperor sent out messengers "who strolled the streets and collected songs. These airs were then presented to the music master who arranged them according to the musical standard pitches in order to make them audible to the Son of Heaven; therefore, the ruler knew the realm without leaving the door" (Martin Kern, "The Poetry of Han Historiography," *Early Medieval China* 10–11, no. 1 [2004]: 34). Such practices can be seen as early forms of opinion polls that assess national mood.

96. I thank my son Julien, who works as a DJ in Hong Kong and other locations, for this point.

97. See Larry S. Sherman and Dennis Plies, *Every Brain Needs Music: The Neuroscience of Making and Listening to Music* (New York: Columbia University Press, 2023), and Harold, "On the Ancient Idea That Music Shapes Character," 346.

98. *Yueji*, 12. See also Meilin Chinn, "Only Music Cannot Be Faked," *Dao* 16, no. 3 (2017): 346–347.

99. 常回家看看 (https://www.youtube.com/watch?v=bj5ftKgPG-8).

100. For a version of the latter argument, see Ronald Dworkin, "Can a Liberal State Support Art?," reprinted in Dworkin, *A Matter of Principle* (Cambridge, MA: Harvard University Press, 1985), 221–233.

101. For an argument that public investment in cultural centers can lead to long-term economic benefits in the Hong Kong context, see Ilnur Minakhmetov, "Hong Kong's West Kowloon Cultural District Deficit Is an Investment Opportunity, Not a Loss," *South China Morning Post*, November 24, 2023, https://www.scmp.com/comment/letters/article/3242530/hong-kongs-west-kowloon-cultural-district-deficit-investment-opportunity-not-loss.

Chapter 4

1. The one female empress in Chinese imperial history—Empress Wu Zetian, who officially promoted Buddhism—ruled in the Tang dynasty.

2. In 2010, an official from the Ministry of Foreign Affairs told me of this practice. I do not know if such debates continue under President Xi.

3. See Yuri Pines, *The Everlasting Empire: The Political Culture of Ancient China and Its Imperial Legacy* (Princeton: Princeton University Press, 2012), 16–19.

4. The Melian Dialogue (416 BCE) in Thucydides's *The History of the Peloponnesian War* "is often cited as the first 'Realist-Idealist' debate" (Johanna Hanink, *How to Think About War: An Ancient Guide to Foreign Policy (Thucydides)* [Princeton: Princeton University Press, 2019], 163), but there were similar debates around the same time in ancient China. Arguably, the "Realist-Idealist" debates in ancient China are more systematic and diverse. For overviews, see Wm. Theodore de Bary and Irene Bloom, eds., *Sources of Chinese Tradition*, 2nd ed., vol. 1 (New York: Columbia University Press, 1999), pt. 1, and Ralph D. Sawyer, ed., *The Seven Military Classics of Ancient China* (New York: Basic Books, 2007).

5. The *Guanzi*, for example, is regarded as a "Legalist" (or realist) text, but its military thought is less amoral: See Fang Yunxiang, "商鞅, 管仲军事思想的法家渊源与异同" [The Legalist Origins, Differences, and Similarities of the Military Thought of Shang Yang and Guan Zhong], *Jiangxi Social Sciences*, no. 4 (2020): 32–38.

Guan Zhong's more moderate military thinking may have had longer-term influence in Chinese history (Yang Ling, *先秦法家思想比较— 以"管子","商君书","韩非子"为中心* [A Comparison of Pre-Qin Legalist Thought: Focusing on the *Guanzi, The Book of Lord Shang,* and *Han Feizi*] [doctoral thesis, Zhejiang University, 2005], 170).

6. It could be argued that Mozi was even more "extreme" in his idealism: He argued that only defensive war is justified, whereas Mengzi allowed for morally justified offensive warfare under certain circumstances (see Ting-mien Lee, "Interstate Relational Ethics: Mengzi and Later Mohists in Dialogue," *Religions* 14, no. 5 [2023]: 659). I select Mengzi for this debate because his views have been more influential in Chinese history (and also because I think his views are more defensible).

7. My personal favorite is 揠苗助长, which literally means pulling up rice shoots to make them grow faster. It has come to mean that trying to rush things or solve problems right away is often counterproductive, and I try to remind myself of this saying every time a slower approach and "going with the flow" is more likely to be effective.

8. Xunzi's essay on military affairs (chapter 15) similarly opens with a debate between a defender of realpolitik (Lord Linwu) and Xunzi in the presence of a ruler (King Xiaocheng of Zhao). Both Lord Linwu and King Xiaocheng seem to end up persuaded by Xunzi's "well spoken" arguments in favor of morality in warfare, which suggests the debate may not be entirely realistic. Later in the chapter, Li Si—Xunzi's "Legalist" student who went on to serve as prime minister in the state of Qin—joins a debate with Xunzi and there is no sign that he was persuaded, which may be more realistic.

9. Yuri Pines, "Introduction," in Shang Yang, *The Book of Lord Shang: Apologetics of State Power in Early China*, ed. and trans. Pines, abridged ed. (New York: Columbia University Press, 2019), 16, 22–23.

10. The "Salt and Iron debate" in the Han dynasty is the last recorded official debate between Legalists and Confucians (see "The Debate on Salt and Iron," trans. Patricia Ebrey, in *Chinese Civilization: A Sourcebook*, ed. Patricia Ebrey [New York: Free Press, 1993], 60–63).

11. See Pines, "Introduction." For a mainland Chinese scholar who explicitly argues that Shang Yang's Legalism should inform China's modernization, see Xiao Bofu, "商鞅法治理论及其现代借鉴" [Shang Yang's Theory of the Rule of Law and Its Modern Application], *China Law*, no. 2 (2002): 152–163.

12. Cindy Yu and Charles Parton, "Why China Won't Invade Taiwan," *Spectator*, June 5, 2023, https://www.spectator.co.uk/podcast/why-china-wont-invade-taiwan/.

13. *Book of Lord Shang*, 4.2. My quotes of Shang Yang are from Yuri Pines's fluent translation of *The Book of Lord Shang* (no changes unless otherwise indicated, with the exception of some changes of verb tenses).

14. *Book of Lord Shang*, 25.4.

15. Andrew Scobell and Lucy Stevenson-Yang, "China Is Not Russia, Taiwan Is Not Ukraine," United States Institute of Peace, March 4, 2022, https://www.usip.org/publications/2022/03/china-not-russia-taiwan-not-ukraine.

16. Phillips O'Brien, "The War That Defied Expectations," *Foreign Affairs*, July 27, 2023, https://www.foreignaffairs.com/ukraine/war-defied-expectations.

17. *Book of Lord Shang*, 13.3.

18. The sentence is quoted is the official translation of President Xi's words "要幸福就要斗争" (http://www.xinhuanet.com/english/2021-08/11/c_1310121056.htm). The next sentence is a more literal translation.

19. "Eat bitterness" is a literal translation of the common Chinese expression 吃苦 (*chi ku*), which refers to the ability to suffer without complaint.

20. *Book of Lord Shang*, 20.1, 3.3.

21. *Book of Lord Shang*, 3.1.

22. *Book of Lord Shang*, 4.3, 3.3.

23. *Book of Lord Shang*, 20.10, 19.9.

24. Quoted from the *Records of the Historian* (*Shiji*)'s account of Shang Yang's reforms in the Qin state (from Pines, "Introduction," 16).

25. *Book of Lord Shang*, 18.3.

26. *Book of Lord Shang*, 17.4.

27. *Book of Lord Shang*, 19.6.

28. *Book of Lord Shang*, 19.3, 19.5.

29. See Ye Zicheng, "商鞅的创新精神与秦国对大国的超越" [Shang Yang's Innovative Spirit and the Surpassing of the State of Qin over Large States], *Frontiers*, no. 8 (2012): 34–44; Pines, "Introduction," 20–22; Hu Bingquan, "论商鞅的军事思想— 读'商君书'浅议" [A Discussion of Shang Yang's Military Thought—A Brief Interpretation of "The Book of Lord Shang"], *Journal of Hebei University (Philosophy and Social Sciences)*, no. 4 (1980): 42; and Xie Naihe, "商鞅强秦的道与术" [Shang Yang's Way and Technique to Strengthen Qin], http://paper.people.com.cn/rmlt/html/2018-03/20/content_1887771.htm.

30. Tong Weimin estimates that Qin soldiers in three military campaigns led by General Bai Qi beheaded almost 900,000 enemy combatants (Tong Weimin, "On the Composition of the 'Attracting the People' Chapter of the Book of Lord Shang," *Contemporary Chinese Thought* 47, no. 2 [2016]: 144). According to Ping-Cheung Lo, "Modern scholarship tends to agree that among the various reasons for Qin's rise to a superpower is the fact its people had a 'reputation for ruthlessness in war'" (Lo, "Warfare Ethics in Sunzi's *Art of War*? Historical Controversies and Contemporary Perspectives," *Journal of Military Ethics* 11, no. 2 [2012]: 119).

31. This is a charitable interpretation of Shang Yang's proposal. Yuri Pines suggests that exposing severed heads and checking them for three days was done partly out

of concern about killing innocent people (Pines, "A 'Total War'? Rethinking Military Ideology in the Book of Lord Shang," *Journal of Chinese Military History* 5 [2016]: 122–123), but he does not refer to an explicit passage in the text that shows Shang Yang cares about protecting civilians.

32. *Book of Lord Shang*, 19.6.

33. *Book of Lord Shang*, 4.1.

34. NPR, "'America In Laos' Traces the Militarization of the CIA," *Fresh Air*, January 23, 2017, https://www.npr.org/2017/01/23/511185078/america-in-laos-traces-the-militarization-of-the-cia.

35. *Book of Lord Shang*, 23.3.

36. *Book of Lord Shang*, 1.4, 18.1, 7.1, 7.6.

37. See chapter 2, section 1 for a similar view.

38. *Book of Lord Shang*, 14.4, 25.3, 9.4, 9.5, 5.2, 25.4, 15.6. I changed "chariot" to "tank" to modernize the passage (see also chapter 1, note 47).

39. Xunzi, writing at the height of the Qin's power, more or less predicted its downfall: "The method based on brute strength reaches an impasse. The method based on *yi* [appropriateness and justice] goes through. How can I say this? I say: The state of Qin is just what I mean. In its strength and power, it exceeds Tang and Wu. In its breadth and bulk, it exceeds Shun and Yu. Nevertheless, its worries and troubles are innumerable. Full of apprehension, it constantly fears that all under Heaven will unite and combine the roll over it" (*Xunzi*, trans. Hutton, chap. 16, p. 169).

40. *Book of Lord Shang*, 4.8, 7.5. Yuri Pines leaves open the possibility that such passages were added by Shang Yang's followers to soften his philosophy by showing that violence and oppression should be viewed as means to establish a truly moral world rather than as ends in themselves (Pines, "From Historical Evolution to the End of History: Past, Present and Future from Shang Yang to the First Emperor," in *Dao Companion to the Philosophy of Han Fei*, ed. Paul R. Goldin [Dordrecht: Springer, 2013], 35).

41. *Book of Lord Shang*, 13.5, 17.3, 26.6.

42. For a similar view, see Zeng Zhenyu, "'以刑去刑': 商鞅思想新论" ["Eradicating Punishment with Punishment": A New Perspective on Shang Yang's Thought], *Journal of Shandong University (Philosophy and Social Science Edition)*, no. 1 (2013): 32–41.

43. Quoted in Pines, "Introduction," 84.

44. See Xu Yunliang, "商鞅变法的'战时法治'特征及其启示" [The Characteristics and Inspiration of the "Rule of Law in Wartime" of Shang Yang's Reforms], *Journal of the Beijing Institute of Administration*, no. 3 (2011): 118–121, and Pines, "From Historical Evolution to the End of History," 42.

45. See Patrick Olivelle, *Ashoka: Portrait of a Philosopher King* (New Haven, CT: Yale University Press, 2024).

46. *Book of Lord Shang*, 3.7. I translate 王 in this context as "humane ruler," though "humane monarch" may be a more literal translation.

47. Such negative evaluations of Shang Yang's legacy were widely articulated by thinkers in the Han dynasty: for an overview, see Zeng Zhenyu, "Shang Yang as a Historical Personality and as a Symbol," *Contemporary Chinese Thought* 47, no. 2 (2016): 73–76.

48. For more detailed argumentation, see my book *Beyond Liberal Democracy: Political Thinking for an East Asian Context* (Princeton: Princeton University Press, 2006), chap. 2.

49. Bryan Van Norden, "Mencius," in *The Stanford Encyclopedia of Philosophy* (Winter 2024 ed.), ed. Edward N. Zalta and Uri Nodelman, https://plato.stanford.edu/archives/win2024/entries/mencius.

50. See, e.g., Larry Lai, "Mencius and the New Confucianism's Pursuit of Democracy," in *Dao Companion to the Philosophy of Mencius*, ed. Xiao Yang and Kim-chong Chong (Cham, Switzerland: Springer, 2023), 281–303, https://link.springer.com/chapter/10.1007/978-3-031-27620-0_15.

51. See, e.g., my book *Beyond Liberal Democracy*, chap. 9.

52. See the references in this section, below.

53. *Mengzi*, 1A.6, 2A.3, 1A.6. The translations of Mengzi are based on W. A. C. H. Dobson's translation of *The Works of Mencius* (London: Oxford University Press, 1963) and D. C. Lau's translation of *Mencius, Vol. 1 and Vol. 2* (Hong Kong: Chinese University Press, 1984). I have modified most of these translations.

54. See, e.g., Gordon G. Chang, "Confessions of a China Apologist," *New Criterion*, May 2023, https://newcriterion.com/issues/2023/5/confessions-of-a-china-apologist.

55. *Mengzi*, 4A.10.

56. *Mengzi*, 2A.3.

57. See, e.g., http://www.news.cn/english/2021-10/13/c_1310242355.htm and the examples in my book *Beyond Liberal Democracy*, 182–183.

58. *Mengzi*, 4A.14.

59. For an argument that Mengzi's view on war needs to be supplemented with positive regard for martial virtues (as a means to strengthen the country), see Yang Chuanzhao and Zhao Minli, "孟子武德思想及其现代价值" [Mengzi's View of Martial Virtues and Its Contemporary Relevance], *Qilu Journal*, no. 6 (2018): 18–23. Wang Guoliang criticizes Mengzi for neglecting the need to train the military and supply it with advanced weaponry: Wang Guoliang, "王道如何战胜霸道: 孟子正义战争与和平思想引论" [How Humane Authorities Can Overcome Hegemons:

An Introduction to Mengzi's Thoughts on Just War and Peace], *Journal of the Communist Party School of Ningbo* 37, no. 1 (2015): 44–49.

60. *Mengzi*, 7B.2. Mengzi is the first recorded thinker to use the term 义战, which can be translated as "appropriate/righteous/just war" (Ping-cheung Lo, "Gratian and Mengzi: Pioneer Works in the Christian and Confucian Just War Traditions," *Journal of Religious Ethics* 48, no. 4 [2020]: 706).

61. *Mengzi*, 6B.9.

62. *Mengzi*, 7B.1.

63. *Mengzi*, 4B.2, 6B.7, 1B.13.

64. Eric Cheung, "'If War Breaks Out . . . I Will Just Become Cannon Fodder': In Taiwan, Ex-Conscripts Feel Unprepared for Potential China Conflict," *CNN*, January 20, 2023, https://edition.cnn.com/2023/01/20/asia/taiwan-mandatory-military-service-conscription-intl-hnk-dst/index.html.

65. *Mengzi*, 1B.15.

66. For an argument that Mengzi's idea that "humaneness overrides sovereignty" is still relevant today, see Bai Tongdong, "仁权高于主权— 孟子的正义战争观" ["Humaneness Overrides Sovereignty—On Mengzi's View of Just War], *Social Sciences*, no. 1 (2013): 131–139, and Bai Tongdong, *Against Political Equality: The Confucian Case* (Princeton: Princeton University Press, 2019), chap. 8.

67. *Mengzi*, 1A.5, 1A.10, 1B.11.

68. For an argument that material welfare alone is not sufficient moral justification for Mengzi's theory of humanitarian intervention, see Sungmoon Kim, "Mencius on International Relations and the Morality of War: From the Perspective of Confucian 'Moralpolitik,'" *History of Political Thought* 31, no. 1 (2020): 52–56. Kim argues that Mengzi's "moral-political metaphysics of Heaven" is equally important, but perhaps we can agree that the deprivation of the means of subsistence is a necessary condition (and also that Mengzi's "metaphysics" is not so persuasive today). In a later work, Kim argues that Confucian humanitarian intervention must be transformed into a democratic theory to be justified in the modern world ("Confucian Humanitarian Intervention? Toward Democratic Theory," *Review of Politics* 79, no. 2 [2017]: 187–213), but I will have to register my disagreement: if, say, intervention by a nondemocratic government in China can help to rescue millions of people from starvation in North Korea without substantial costs, then such an intervention would be justified.

69. *Mengzi*, 1A.7.

70. Mengzi did not explicitly identify slavery as a characteristic of tyranny, but other characteristics include deprivation of people's livelihoods, murder, and torture (Summer B. Twiss and Jonathan Chan, "Classical Confucianism, Punitive Expeditions, and Humanitarian Intervention," *Journal of Military Ethics* 11, no. 2 [2012]: 87),

and we can infer that slavery would also count as a moral evil that could justify punitive expeditions.

71. *Mengzi*, 2B.8. Mengzi's term here for what I translate as "humane ruler" is 天吏, which can be more literally translated as "an officer appointed by heavenly power." In the case of Xunzi, he argues that a "hegemon"—less good than a humane ruler but better than an "utter reprobate" tyrant—who has the trust of allies can also undertake punitive military action (see Summer B. Twiss and Jonathan Chan, "The Classical Confucian Position on the Legitimate Use of Military Force," *Journal of Religious Ethics* 40, no. 3 [2012]: 457–458).

72. *Mengzi*, 4A.4, 2B.13.

73. *Mengzi*, 1B.11.

74. *Mengzi*, 7B.2.

75. This paragraph draws on Gong Gang's critique (in Chinese) of the 2003 invasion of Iraq that appeals to Mengzi's theory of just war (Gong Gang, "谁是全球伦理的带刀侍卫?" [Who Is the Sword-Wielding Bodyguard of Global Ethics?], http://news.sina.com.cn/o/2003-09-16/15511754323.shtml).

76. *Mengzi*, 7B.4.

77. Xunzi is more explicit: "To capture and take over others is something that it is easy to be capable of doing, but it is solidifying and consolidating one's grip that is the hard part" (*Xunzi*, trans. Hutton, chap. 15, p. 162).

78. *Mengzi*, 1B.11.

79. *Mengzi*, 7A.33. Perhaps because Mengzi felt that war is so distasteful, even when it is necessary, he was unwilling to think through in great detail the implications of going to war beyond an aversion to killing civilians. In contrast, the more hard-nosed Xunzi, writing in the most brutal period of the Warring States period with frequent large-scale massacres of civilians, did go into detail, and he proposed moral guidelines meant to apply once "the drum of war sounded," similar to those of contemporary theorists of just warfare, such as not executing prisoners, not engaging in the massacre of defenders of a city, and not trampling down people's crops (see *Xunzi*, trans. Hutton, chap. 15, pp. 154–155).

80. Kurtis Hagen argues both Mengzi and Xunzi can be viewed as just war theorists who offer criteria so demanding that they cannot ordinarily be satisfied ("Mencius and Xunzi on the Legitimate Use of Offensive Force: A Pacifistic Critique of Recent Just War Interpretations," *Philosophy Compass* 17, no. 6 [2022]: e12831).

81. *Mengzi*, 2A.5.

82. See Sungmoon Kim, *Theorizing Virtue Politics: The Political Philosophy of Mencius and Xunzi* (Cambridge: Cambridge University Press, 2020), 198. Note, however, that Mengzi's ideal of politics *for* the people does not translate into support for politics *by* the people (the idea that common people have sufficient political agency to

govern themselves). Even Mengzi's supposed justification for a "right to rebellion" falls short: the people can participate in rebellion but should not be permitted to decide for themselves when rebellion is warranted (see Justin Tiwald, "A Right of Rebellion in the Mengzi?," *Dao* 7, no. 3 [2008]: 269–282).

83. See Zhang Qiwei, "孟子的军事哲学思想初探" [A Preliminary Analysis of Mengzi's Military Philosophy], *Qilu Journal*, no. 4 (1989): 54–59. It is difficult not to read this paper against the backdrop of the June 4, 1989, killings in Beijing, which clearly went against Mengzi's advice of how to gain the hearts of the people.

84. *Mengzi*, 2A.3, 7B.2.

85. As it happens, "the People's Liberation Army studies pre-modern Chinese military thought intensely and PLA Press has published many studies on pre-modern Chinese military thought for their peers and students to read. The government and the military need to endorse some ethics of war, and because they are reluctant to endorse Western notions, it is inevitable that they must retrieve it from Chinese traditions" (Lo, "Warfare Ethics in Sunzi's *The Art of War*?," 123–124).

86. This is a literal translation of 考虑, 考虑, which usually means that the advice will be rejected.

87. I borrow from Lyle Goldstein's sober voice on this podcast: Kaiser Kuo, "Wargaming a Taiwan Invasion Scenario: Lyle Goldstein on the CSIS Wargame 'The First Battle of the Next War,'" https://thechinaproject.com/podcast/wargaming-a-taiwan-invasion-scenario-lyle-goldstein-on-the-csis-wargame-the-first-battle-of-the-next-war/.

88. In contrast, Sunzi's *The Art of War* (ca. fifth century BCE) promotes deception and espionage and "knowing the enemy" as key for achieving victory in war with the minimum use of force.

89. An "invitation for tea" is code for informal political scolding. In practice, however, it can assume different forms: in Shandong province, for example, informal political scolding can take place after a sumptuous banquet and endless glasses of *bai jiu* (I was once on the receiving end of such scolding).

90. Speech given by Xi Jinping at the Central Rural Work Conference, December 23–24, 2013 (https://www.chinastory.cn/ywdbk/english/v1/detail/20190719/1012700000042741563517384580290837_1.html). For a historically informed analysis of how China ensures food security for its people, see Dongsheng Explains No. 6, "How Is China Ensuring Food Security for 1.4 Billion People?," https://dongshengnews.org/en/china-ensuring-food-security/.

91. Speech given by Xi Jinping at the Central Rural Work Conference, December 26, 2022 (https://www.bjreview.com/China/202212/t20221226_800316716.html).

Atogaki

1. I first learned about the *Atogaki* from T. R. Reid's book, *Confucius Lives Next Door* (New York: Random House, 1999), which includes an *Atogaki*.

2. New Books Network, https://newbooksnetwork.com.

3. For another example of a contemporary author who puts great thinkers from the pre-Qin period in explicit debate with each other, see Zhang Xianglong, *儒家哲学史讲演录, 第二卷: 从"春秋"到荀子* [Lectures on the History of Confucian Philosophy, Vol. 2: From the "Spring and Autumn" Period to Xunzi] (Beijing: Commercial Press, 2019), 365–368. Zhang has Mengzi and Xunzi debating about human nature. The dialogue form is also used extensively by Liu Zhexin in a series of popular books on Chinese political culture. His latest book is a discussion of the history and philosophy of China's imperial examination system (Liu Zhexin, *漫话科举* [Talking About the Imperial Examination System] [Beijing: Learning Press, 2024]). Liu's works are accessible and entertaining guides to diverse perspectives on Chinese political culture and they are used to train public officials in China (though the discussion of contemporary politics is constrained by official narratives).

4. LitCharts, "Yin and Yang: Theme Analysis," https://www.litcharts.com/lit/the-art-of-war/themes/yin-and-yang.

5. See Samuel B. Griffith, "Introduction," in *Sun Tzu, The Art of War*, trans. Griffith (Oxford: Clarendon Press, 1963).

6. Walter Lee, *Principles and Laws in World Politics: Classical Chinese Perspectives on Global Conflict* (Singapore: World Scientific, 2022), 180–185, 232–236.

7. In addition to the Yu Dan passage mentioned in chapter 1, note 43, see Edward Slingerland's interpretation of 11.26 in Confucius, *Analects, with Selections from Traditional Commentaries*, 124.

8. "Women and petty persons are particularly hard to manage" (*Analects of Confucius*, 17.25). This line comes from the last five books that are less reliably attributed to Kongzi himself.

9. I borrow this point from Justin Tiwald (email communication).

10. Rebecca Newberger Goldstein, *Plato at the Googleplex: Why Philosophy Won't Go Away* (New York: Vintage Books, 2014).

11. See Owen Flanagan, *The Geography of Morals: Varieties of Moral Possibility* (Oxford: Oxford University Press, 2017), 21.

12. Huang Yushun, "穆姜: 易学第一女哲" [Mu Jiang: The First Female Philosopher of the *Book of Changes*], *Studies on the Book of Changes*, no. 3 (2024), https://www.chinakongzi.org/xsyj/xmcg/202406/t20240625_573908.htm.

13. Paul R. Goldin, *After Confucius: Studies in Early Chinese Philosophy* (Honolulu: University of Hawai'i Press, 2005), 112–118.

14. I defend this argument in my book *Beyond Liberal Democracy*, 43–51.

15. *Xunzi*, trans. Hutton.

16. Philip J. Ivanhoe and Bryan W. Van Norden, *Readings in Classical Chinese Philosophy*, 3rd ed. (Indianapolis: Hackett, 2023).

17. Illustrated Library of Chinese Classics, https://press.princeton.edu/series/the-illustrated-library-of-chinese-classics.

18. Roger T. Ames, *A Conceptual Lexicon for Classical Confucian Philosophy* (Albany: State University of New York Press, 2022); Zhang Dainian, *Key Concepts in Chinese Philosophy*, trans. Edmund Ryden (Beijing: Foreign Languages Press, 2002); Wai-yee Li and Yuri Pines, eds., *Key Words in Chinese Culture* (Hong Kong: Chinese University of Hong Kong Press, 2020).

19. Michael J. Puett and Christine Gross-Loh, *The Path: What Chinese Philosophers Can Teach Us About the Good Life* (New York: Simon & Schuster, 2016); Ming Dong Gu, ed., *Why Traditional Chinese Philosophy Still Matters: The Relevance of Ancient Wisdom for the Global Age* (Abington: Routledge, 2018).

20. Sor-Hoon Tan, *Confucian Democracy: A Deweyan Reconstruction* (Albany: State University of New York Press, 2004); Jiang Qing, *A Confucian Constitutional Order: How China's Ancient Past Can Shape Its Political Future*, trans. Edmund Ryden (Princeton: Princeton University Press, 2012); Joseph Chan, *Confucian Perfectionism: A Political Philosophy for Modern Times* (Princeton: Princeton University Press, 2013); Bai Tongdong, *Against Political Equality*; Kim Sungmoon, *Confucian Constitutionalism: Dignity, Rights and Democracy* (Oxford: Oxford University Press, 2023); Chenyang Li, *Reshaping Confucianism*; Elena Ziliotti, *Meritocratic Democracy: A Cross-Cultural Political Theory* (Oxford: Oxford University Press, 2024); Roel Sterckx, *Chinese Thought*; Colin J. Lewis and Jennifer King, *Contemporary Politics and Classical Chinese Thought* (Oxford: Oxford University Press, 2025); Eirik Lang Harris and Henrique Schneider, eds., *Adventures in Chinese Realism: Classic Philosophy Applied to Contemporary Issues* (Albany: State University of New York Press, 2022).

SELECTED BIBLIOGRAPHY

Alt, Wayne. "A Non-Moral Interpretation of *The Original Analects of Confucius*." *Sino-Platonic Papers*, no. 330 (2023). https://sino-platonic.org/complete/spp330_confucian_morality_analects.pdf.

Ames, Roger T. *A Conceptual Lexicon for Classical Confucian Philosophy*. Albany: State University of New York Press, 2022.

———. *Confucian Role Ethics: A Vocabulary*. Hong Kong: Chinese University of Hong Kong Press, 2011.

Bai, Tongdong. "The *Han Feizi* and Its Contemporary Relevance." In *Dao Companion to China's Fa Tradition*, edited by Yuri Pines, 645–676. Cham: Springer, 2024.

———. *Against Political Equality: The Confucian Case*. Princeton: Princeton University Press, 2019.

———. "仁权高于主权— 孟子的正义战争观" [Humaneness Overrides Sovereignty—On Mengzi's View of Just War]. *Social Sciences*, no. 1 (2013): 131–139.

———. *Supplement Materials*. Forthcoming.

Bao, Qinggang. *反思与重构: 郭象 "庄子注" 研究* [Reflection and Reconstruction: Research on Guo Xiang's "Commentary on Zhuangzi"]. Nanjing: Nanjing University Press, 2013.

Barish, Daniel. *Learning to Rule: Court Education and the Remaking of the Qing State, 1861–1912*. New York: Columbia University Press, 2022.

Bell, Daniel A. *The Dean of Shandong: Confessions of a Minor Bureaucrat at a Chinese University*. Princeton: Princeton University Press, 2023.

———. *The China Model: Political Meritocracy and the Limits of Democracy*. Princeton: Princeton University Press, 2015.

———. *China's New Confucianism: Politics and Everyday Life in a Changing Society*. Princeton: Princeton University Press, 2008.

———. *Beyond Liberal Democracy: Political Thinking for an East Asian Context*. Princeton: Princeton University Press, 2006.

———. *East Meets West: Human Rights and Democracy in East Asia*. Princeton: Princeton University Press, 2000.

———. *Communitarianism and Its Critics*. Oxford: Clarendon Press, 1993.

Bell, Daniel A., and Chaibong Hahm, eds. *Confucianism for the Modern World*. Cambridge: Cambridge University Press, 2003.

Bell, Daniel A., and Chenyang Li, eds. *The East Asian Challenge for Democracy*. New York: Cambridge University Press, 2013.

Bell, Daniel A., and Yingchuan Mo. "Harmony in the World 2013: The Ideal and the Reality." *Social Indicators Research* 118, no. 2 (2014): 797–818.

Bell, Daniel A., and Wang Pei. *Just Hierarchy: Why Social Hierarchies Matter in China and the Rest of the World*. Princeton: Princeton University Press, 2020.

Bell, Don. *Saturday Night at the Bagel Factory*. Toronto: McLelland and Stewart, 1972.

Chan, Alan. "Neo-Daoism." In *The Stanford Encyclopedia of Philosophy* (Summer 2019 ed.), edited by Edward N. Zalta. https://plato.stanford.edu/archives/sum2019/entries/neo-daoism.

Chan, Joseph. *Confucian Perfectionism: A Political Philosophy for Modern Times*. Princeton: Princeton University Press, 2013.

Chang, Gordon G. "Confessions of a China Apologist." *New Criterion*, May 2023. https://newcriterion.com/issues/2023/5/confessions-of-a-china-apologist.

Chen, Yun. *自由之思: 庄子 "逍遥游" 的阐释* [The Idea of Freedom: An Interpretation of Zhuangzi's "Carefree Wandering"]. Hangzhou: Zhejiang University Press, 2020.

———. *庄子哲学的精神* [The Spirit of Zhuangzi's Philosophy]. Shanghai: Shanghai People's Press, 2016.

Cheung, Eric. "'If War Breaks Out . . . I Will Just Become Cannon Fodder': In Taiwan, Ex-Conscripts Feel Unprepared for Potential China Conflict." *CNN*, January 20, 2023. https://edition.cnn.com/2023/01/20/asia/taiwan-mandatory-military-service-conscription-intl-hnk-dst/index.html.

Chinn, Meilin. "Only Music Cannot Be Faked." *Dao* 16, no. 3 (2017): 341–354.

Chua, Daniel K. L. *Music and Joy: Lessons on the Good Life*. New Haven, CT: Yale University Press, 2024.

Cline, Erin M. *The Analects: A Guide*. Oxford: Oxford University Press, 2022.

Collender, Nicholas. "The Irish Wake—Ireland's Most Enduring Tradition." https://irishurns.com/the-irish-wake-irelands-most-enduring-tradition.

Confucius. *The Analects, with Selections from Traditional Commentaries*. Translated by Edward Slingerland. Indianapolis: Hackett, 2013.

———. *The Analects of Confucius*. Translated by Arthur Waley. London: Routledge, 2012.

———. *The Analects of Confucius: A Philosophical Translation*. Translated by Roger T. Ames and Henry Rosemont Jr. New York: Ballantine Books, 1998.

Cook, Scott. "Xun Zi on Ritual and Music." *Monumenta Serica* 45, no. 1 (1997): 1–38.

———. "*Yueji* 乐记—Record of Music: Introduction, Notes and Commentary." *Asian Music* 26, no. 2 (1995): 1–96.

CPIB. "Singapore's Corruption Control Framework." https://www.cpib.gov.sg/about-corruption/prevention-and-corruption/singapores-corruption-control-framework/.

Cui, Huabin, and Daniel A. Bell. "墨子和孟子的战争伦理思想比较" [A Comparison of Mozi's and Mengzi's Theories of War]. *Culture, History, and Philosophy*, no. 1 (2021): 96–104.

Dallmayr, Fred, ed. *Comparative Political Theory: An Introduction*. New York: Palgrave Macmillan, 2010.

D'Ambrosio, Paul J. "The Ethics of Contingency: An Alternative (to) Morality in the *Analects*." *Religions* 14, no. 11 (2023): 1367.

———. "The Zhuangzi: Personal Freedom and/or Incongruity of Names?" *Philosophy East and West* 73, no. 2 (2023): 458–466.

———. "Ming as 'Identity' in Early Chinese Thought: Examining *Laozi* 44." *Philosophy East & West* 72, no. 1 (2022): 79–98.

De Bary, Wm. Theodore, and Irene Bloom, eds. *Sources of Chinese Tradition*. 2nd ed. New York: Columbia University Press, 1999.

Dworkin, Ronald. *A Matter of Principle*. Cambridge, MA: Harvard University Press, 1985.

Dzur, Albert W. *Punishment, Participatory Democracy, and the Jury*. Oxford: Oxford University Press, 2012.

Ebrey, Patricia, ed. *Chinese Civilization: A Sourcebook*. New York: Free Press, 1993.

Fang, Yunxiang. "商鞅, 管仲军事思想的法家渊源与异同" [The Legalist Origins, Differences, and Similarities of the Military Thought of Shang Yang and Guan Zhong]. *Jiangxi Social Sciences*, no. 4 (2020): 32–38.

Fishkin, James S., Baogang He, Robert C. Luskin, and Alice Siu. "Deliberative Democracy in an Unlikely Place: Deliberative Polling in China." *British Journal of Political Science* 40, no. 2 (2010): 435–448. https://www.researchgate.net/profile/Baogang-He/publication/248665977_Deliberative_Democracy_in_an_Unlikely_Place_Deliberative_Polling_in_China/links/547476d70cf245eb436ddf53/Deliberative-Democracy-in-an-Unlikely-Place-Deliberative-Polling-in-China.pdf.

Flanagan, Owen. *The Geography of Morals: Varieties of Moral Possibility*. Oxford: Oxford University Press, 2017.

Fraser, Chris. "Mohism." In *The Stanford Encyclopedia of Philosophy* (Fall 2024 ed.), edited by Edward N. Zalta and Uri Nodelman. https://plato.stanford.edu/archives/fall2024/entries/mohism.

———. *Late Classical Chinese Thought*. Oxford: Oxford University Press, 2023.

Fu, Hualing. "China's Striking Anti-Corruption Adventure: A Political Journey Towards the Rule of Law?" *University of Hong Kong Faculty of Law Research Paper*, no. 1 (2016). https://hub.hku.hk/bitstream/10722/223185/1/Content.pdf.

Gan, Chunsong. *儒家政治哲学大纲* [An Outline of Confucian Political Philosophy]. Beijing: Peking University Press, 2025.

Goldin, Paul R. *The Art of Chinese Philosophy: Eight Classical Texts and How to Read Them*. Princeton: Princeton University Press, 2020.

———. "Xunzi." In *The Stanford Encyclopedia of Philosophy* (fall 2018 ed.), edited by Edward N. Zalta. https://plato.stanford.edu/archives/fall2018/entries/xunzi.

———, ed. *Dao Companion to the Philosophy of Han Fei*. Dordrecht: Springer, 2013.

———. "Xunzi and Early Han Philosophy." *Harvard Journal of Asiatic Studies* 67, no. 1 (2007): 135–166.

———. *After Confucius: Studies in Early Chinese Philosophy*. Honolulu: University of Hawai'i Press, 2005.

Goldstein, Rebecca Newberger. *Plato at the Googleplex: Why Philosophy Won't Go Away*. New York: Vintage Books, 2014.

Gong, Gang. "谁是全球伦理的带刀侍卫?" [Who Is the Sword-Wielding Bodyguard of Global Ethics?]. http://news.sina.com.cn/o/2003-09-16/15511754323.shtml.

GovHK. "Allowances." https://www.gov.hk/en/residents/taxes/salaries/allowances/allowances/allowances.htm.

Gu, Ming Dong, ed. *Why Traditional Chinese Philosophy Still Matters: The Relevance of Ancient Wisdom for the Global Age*. Abington: Routledge, 2018.

———. "The Ethical Turn in Aesthetic Education: Early Chinese Thinkers on Music and Arts." *Journal of Aesthetic Education* 50, no. 1 (2016): 95–111.

Guan, Zhong. *Guanzi*. https://ctext.org/guanzi.

Guo, Junwei. "离婚冷静期制度实施中的价值冲突与衡平" [Value Conflict and Balance in the Implementation of the Divorce "Cooling-Off Period" System]. *Journal of Northeast Normal University (Philosophy and Social Sciences)*, no. 6 (2021): 137–143.

Hagen, Kurtis. "Mencius and Xunzi on the Legitimate Use of Offensive Force: A Pacifistic Critique of Recent Just War Interpretations." *Philosophy Compass* 17, no. 6 (2022): e12831.

———. "Xunzi and the Nature of Confucian Ritual." *Journal of the Academy of Religion* 71, no. 2 (2003): 371–403.

Han, Byung-Chul. *The Disappearance of Rituals: A Topology of the Present*. Translated by Daniel Steuer. Cambridge: Polity, 2020.

Han, Feizi. *Han Feizi: Basic Writings*. Translated by Burton Watson. New York: Columbia University Press, 2003.

———. *In Praise of Regulations: A New Translation of the Han Feizi*. Translated by Olivia Milburn. Forthcoming.

Hanink, Johanna. *How to Think About War: An Ancient Guide to Foreign Policy (Thucydides)*. Princeton: Princeton University Press, 2019.

Harbsmeier, Christoph. "Confucius Ridens: Humor in *The Analects*." *Harvard Journal of Asiatic Studies* 50, no. 1 (1990): 131–161.

Harold, James. "On the Ancient Idea that Music Shapes Character." *Dao* 15, no. 3 (2016): 341–354.

Harris, Eirik Lang. "Constraining the Ruler: On Escaping Han Fei's Criticism of Confucian Virtue Politics." *Asian Philosophy* 23, no. 1 (2013): 43–61.

———. "Han Fei on the Problem of Morality." In *Dao Companion to the Philosophy of Han Fei*, ed. Paul R. Goldin. Dordrecht: Springer, 2013.

Harris, Eirik Lang, and Henrique Schneider, eds. *Adventures in Chinese Realism: Classic Philosophy Applied to Contemporary Issues*. Albany: State University of New York Press, 2022.

Harrison, Henrietta. *The Man Awakened from Dreams: One Man's Life in a North China Village*. Stanford, CA: Stanford University Press, 2005.

He, Baogang. "Deliberative Participatory Budgeting: A Case Study of Zeguo Town in China." *Public Administration and Development* 39, no. 3 (2019): 144–153.

He, Hua, and Yan Jiafeng. "论庄子的自由观及其当代价值: 以'逍遥游'为例" [On Zhuangzi's View of Freedom and Its Contemporary Value: Taking "Carefree Wandering" as an Example]. *Journal of Huangshan University* 21, no. 1 (2019): 34–37.

He, Xin, and Kwai Hang Ng. "In the Name of Harmony: The Erasure of Domestic Violence in China's Judicial Mediation." *International Journal of Law, Policy and the Family* 27, no. 1 (2013): 97–115.

Hillman, Ben. "The End of Village Democracy in China." *Journal of Democracy* 34, no. 3 (2023): 52–76. https://muse.jhu.edu/pub/1/article/900430.

Hou, Wailu. *中国古代思想学说史* [History of Ancient Chinese Thoughts and Theories]. Shenyang: Liaoning Education Press, 1998.

Hu, Bingquan. "论商鞅的军事思想— 读'商君书'浅议" [A Discussion of Shang Yang's Military Thought—A Brief Interpretation of "The Book of Lord Shang"]. *Journal of Hebei University (Philosophy and Social Sciences)*, no. 4 (1980): 42.

Huang, Chin-shing. *Confucianism and Sacred Space: The Confucius Temple from Imperial China to Today*. Translated by Jonathan Chin with Chin-shing Huang. New York: Columbia University Press, 2020.

Huang, Kewu. "严复晚年思想的一个侧面: 道家思想与自由主义之会通" [An Aspect of Yan Fu's Late Thought: The Connection Between Daoist Thought and Liberalism]. In *严复思想新论* [New Essays on the Thought of Yan Fu], edited by Liu Guisheng, Lin Qiyan, and Wang Xianming, 261–283. Beijing: Tsinghua University Press, 1999.

Huang, Philip C. C. "Court Mediation in China, Past and Present." *Modern China* 32, no. 3 (July 2006). https://doi.org/10.1177/0097700406288179.

Huang, Yushun. "穆姜: 易学第一女哲" [Mu Jiang: The First Female Philosopher of the Book of Changes]. *Studies on the Book of Changes*, no. 3 (2024). https://www.chinakongzi.org/xsyj/xmcg/202406/t20240625_573908.htm.

Hutton, Eric L., ed. *Dao Companion to the Philosophy of Xunzi*. Dordrecht: Springer, 2016.

Illustrated Library of Chinese Classics. https://press.princeton.edu/series/the-illustrated-library-of-chinese-classics.

Ivanhoe, Philip J. "Hanfeizi and Moral Self-Cultivation." *Journal of Chinese Philosophy* 38, no. 1 (2011): 31–45.

Ivanhoe, Philip J., and Bryan W. Van Norden, eds. *Readings in Classical Chinese Philosophy*. 3rd ed. Indianapolis: Hackett, 2023.

———, eds. *Readings in Classical Chinese Philosophy*. 2nd ed. Indianapolis: Hackett, 2001.

Jiang, Qing. *A Confucian Constitutional Order: How China's Ancient Past Can Shape Its Political Future*. Translated by Edmund Ryden. Princeton: Princeton University Press, 2012.

Jiang, Tao. *Origins of Moral-Political Philosophy in Early China*. Oxford: Oxford University Press, 2021.

Jin, Keyu. *The New China Playbook: Beyond Socialism and Capitalism*. New York: Viking, 2023.

Kern, Martin. "The Poetry of Han Historiography." *Early Medieval China* 10–11, no. 1 (2004): 23–65.

Khazan, Olga. "Take a Wife . . . Please! Why Are Married People Happier than the Rest of Us?" *Atlantic*, August 31, 2023. https://www.theatlantic.com/ideas/archive/2023/08/does-marriage-make-you-happier/675145/.

Kim, Sungmoon. *Confucian Constitutionalism: Dignity, Rights and Democracy*. Oxford: Oxford University Press, 2023.

———. "Mencius on International Relations and the Morality of War: From the Perspective of Confucian 'Moralpolitik.'" *History of Political Thought* 31, no. 1 (2020): 33–56.

———. *Theorizing Virtue Politics: The Political Philosophy of Mencius and Xunzi*. Cambridge: Cambridge University Press, 2020.

———. "Confucian Humanitarian Intervention? Toward Democratic Theory." *Review of Politics* 79, no. 2 (2017): 187–213.

———. "Virtue Politics and Political Leadership: A Confucian Rejoinder to Hanfeizi." *Asian Philosophy* 22, no. 2 (2012): 177–197.

Klein, Esther. "Were the 'Inner Chapters' in the Warring States? A New Examination of Evidence About the *Zhuangzi*." *T'oung Pao* 96 (2011): 299–369.

Kline, T. C., III, and Justin Tiwald, eds. *Ritual and Religion in the Xunzi*. Albany, NY: State University of New York Press, 2014.

Kreis, Guido. "Xunzi and Zhuangzi on Music: Two Ways of Modeling the Ethical Significance of Art." *Journal of Chinese Philosophy* 50, no. 1 (2023): 64–80.

Kuo, Kaiser. "Wargaming a Taiwan Invasion Scenario: Lyle Goldstein on the CSIS Wargame 'The First Battle of the Next War.'" https://thechinaproject.com/podcast/wargaming-a-taiwan-invasion-scenario-lyle-goldstein-on-the-csis-wargame-the-first-battle-of-the-next-war/.

Lai, Karyn. "Freedom and Agency in the *Zhuangzi*: Navigating Life's Constraints." *British Journal in the History of Philosophy* 30, no. 1 (2022): 3–23.

Laozi. *Dao De Jing*. https://ctext.org/dao-de-jing.

Lee, Haiyan. *A Certain Justice: Toward an Ecology of the Chinese Legal Imagination*. Chicago: University of Chicago Press, 2023.

Lee, Ting-mien. "Interstate Relational Ethics: Mengzi and Later Mohists in Dialogue." *Religions* 14, no. 5 (2023): 659.

Lee, Walter. *Principles and Laws in World Politics: Classical Chinese Perspectives on Global Conflict*. Singapore: World Scientific, 2022.

Lei, Yongqiang. "荀子乐教思想新论" [A New Analysis of Xun's Thoughts on Musical Education]. *Dongyue Tribune* 7 (2018): 12–19.

Lewis, Colin J., and Jennifer King. *Contemporary Politics and Classical Chinese Thought*. Oxford: Oxford University Press, 2025.

Li, Chenyang. *Reshaping Confucianism: A Progressive Inquiry*. New York: Oxford University Press, 2024.

———. *The Confucian Philosophy of Harmony*. London: Routledge, 2014.

Li, Chenyang, and Dascha During, eds. *The Virtue of Harmony*. Oxford: Oxford University Press, 2022.

Li, Wai-yee, and Yuri Pines, eds. *Key Words in Chinese Culture*. Hong Kong: Chinese University of Hong Kong Press, 2020.

Lim, Puay Ling. "Maintenance of Parents Act." https://www.nlb.gov.sg/main/article-detail?cmsuuid=d2328927-c580-4088-8d74-268caaff635b.

Lin, Yutang. "Confucius as I Know Him." *China Critic* 4, no. 1 (1931): 5–9. http://www.chinaheritagequarterly.org/030/features/030_confucius.inc.

Liu, Anting. "'隆礼尊贤而王'— 荀子礼治论" [Honoring Rituals and Respecting the Worthy [Can Make One a] Humane Monarch: Xunzi's Theory of Ritual Order]. *Confucius Studies*, no. 2 (2008): 48–55.

Liu, Bing. "中国传统文化中的和谐思想及其当代价值" [Harmony in Traditional Chinese Culture and Its Contemporary Value]. *Theory Journal*, no. 7 (2009): 78–81.

Liu, Fenrong, and Jialong Zhang. "New Perspectives on Moist Logic." *Journal of Chinese Philosophy* 37, no. 4 (2010): 605–621.

Liu, Zhexin. *漫话科举* [Talking About the Imperial Examination System]. Beijing: The Learning Press, 2024.

Lo, Ping-cheung. "Gratian and Mengzi: Pioneer Works in the Christian and Confucian Just War Traditions." *Journal of Religious Ethics* 48, no. 4 (2020): 689–729.

———. "Warfare Ethics in Sunzi's *Art of War*? Historical Controversies and Contemporary Perspectives." *Journal of Military Ethics* 11, no. 2 (2012): 114–135.

Lou, Yulie. *中华文化的感悟* [Insights into Chinese Culture]. Beijing: Commercial Press, 2021.

Ma, Yue. "节用与非乐: '墨子' 平均主义思想研究" [Thrift and "A Condemnation of the Musical Arts": An Analysis and Research on Mozi's Egalitarianism]. *Journal of the Staff and Workers' University*, no. 6 (2019): 20–21.

Mair, Victor H. *Wandering on the Way: Early Taoist Tales and Parables of Chuang Tzu.* Honolulu: University of Hawai'i Press, 1994.

Manchester, Colin. "Wives as Crown Witnesses." *Cambridge Law Journal* 37, no. 2 (1979): 249–251.

McSpadden, Kevin. "Archaeologists Discover Centre for Greatest Chinese Philosophers During Warring States Period from Over 2,000 Years Ago." *South China Morning Post*, March 17, 2022. https://www.scmp.com/news/people-culture/article/3170781/archaeologists-discover-centre-greatest-chinese-philosophers.

Mengzi. *Mencius.* Vols. 1–2. Translated by D. C. Lau. Hong Kong: Chinese University Press, 1984.

———. *The Works of Mencius.* Translated by W. A. C. H. Dobson. London: Oxford University Press, 1963.

Merris, Kelly. "'No-Fault Divorces' in England and Wales: Is Hong Kong Ready to Follow Suit?" *Hong Kong Lawyer*, March 2023. https://www.hk-lawyer.org/content/%E2%80%9Cno-fault-divorces%E2%80%9D-england-and-wales-hong-kong-ready-follow-suit.

Minakhmetov, Ilnur. "Hong Kong's West Kowloon Cultural District Deficit Is an Investment Opportunity, Not a Loss." *South China Morning Post*, November 24, 2023. https://www.scmp.com/comment/letters/article/3242530/hong-kongs-west-kowloon-cultural-district-deficit-investment-opportunity-not-loss.

Ministry of Civil Affairs, Government of China. *民政部关于贯彻落实《中华人民共和国民法典》中有关婚姻登记规定的通知* [Notice of the Ministry of Civil Affairs on the Implementation of the Marriage Registration Provisions in the Civil Code of the People's Republic of China]. https://www.gov.cn/zhengce/zhengceku/2020-12/04/content_5567010.htm.

Moeller, Hans-Georg. "Butcher Ding: A Slaughter Ballet." https://www.youtube.com/watch?v=vGtgGz5SsY0.

Moody, Peter. "The Legalism of Han Fei-tzu and Its Affinities with Modern Political Thought." *International Philosophical Quarterly* 19, no. 3 (1979): 317–330.

Mozi. *Mo Zi: Mozi: The Essential Mozi*. Translated by Chris Fraser. Oxford: Oxford University Press, 2020.

———. *The Book of Master Mo*. Translated by Ian Johnson. London Penguin Classics, 2013.

———. *Mozi 墨子: A Study and Translation of the Ethical and Political Writings*. Translated by John Knoblock and Jeffrey Riegel. Berkeley: Institute of East Asian Studies, 2013.

Munro, Donald J. *A Chinese Ethics for the New Century: The Ch'ien Mu Lectures in History and Culture, and Other Essays on Science and Confucian Ethics*. Hong Kong: Chinese University of Hong Kong Press, 2005.

Murphy, R. Taggart. "The Real Threat to Classical Music." *Compact*, January 8, 2024. https://compactmag.com/article/the-real-threat-to-classical-music.

Ni, Peimin. *Understanding the Analects of Confucius: A New Translation with Annotations*. Albany: State University of New York Press, 2017.

NPR. "'America In Laos' Traces the Militarization of the CIA." *NPR*, January 23, 2017. https://www.npr.org/2017/01/23/511185078/america-in-laos-traces-the-militarization-of-the-cia.

O'Brien, Phillips. "The War That Defied Expectations." *Foreign Affairs*, July 27, 2023. https://www.foreignaffairs.com/ukraine/war-defied-expectations.

Olesen, Alexa. "Confucius: China's Most Famous Single Dad." *Tulsa World*, August 24, 2014. https://tulsaworld.com/opinion/alexa-olesen-confucius-chinas-most-famous-single-dad/article_2a607960-2457-54da-b2c8-f2594122478f.html.

Olivelle, Patrick. *Ashoka: Portrait of a Philosopher King*. New Haven, CT: Yale University Press, 2024.

Pan, Yue. "战国与希腊" [The Warring States Period and (Ancient) Greece]. http://theory.people.com.cn/n1/2020/0603/c40531-31734074.html.

Park, So-Jeong. "Danger of Sound: Mozi's Criticism of Confucian Ritual Music." *Philosophical Forum* 51, no. 1 (2020): 49–65.

Peng, Guoxiang. "Inside the Revival of Confucianism in Mainland China: The Vicissitudes of Confucian Classics in Contemporary China as an Example." https://archiv.oriens-extremus.org/49/OE49-10.pdf.

Pines, Yuri. "A 'Total War'? Rethinking Military Ideology in the Book of Lord Shang." *Journal of Chinese Military History* 2 (2016): 97–134.

———. *The Everlasting Empire: The Political Culture of Ancient China and Its Imperial Legacy*. Princeton: Princeton University Press, 2012.

Puett, Michael J., and Christine Gross-Loh. *The Path: What Chinese Philosophers Can Teach Us About the Good Life*. New York: Simon & Schuster, 2016.

Qu, Hongqi. "墨子'非乐论'辨析" [An Analysis of Mozi's "Against the Musical Arts"]. *Journal of Shandong University*, no. 6 (2002): 62–64.

The Record of Musical Arts [*Yueji*]. In *The Book of Rites* [*Liji*]. https://ctext.org/liji/yue-ji.

Reid, T. R. *Confucius Lives Next Door*. New York: Random House, 1999.

Saussy, Haun. "Music and Evil: A Basis of Aesthetics in China." *Critical Inquiry* 46, no. 3 (2020): 482–495.

Sawyer, Ralph D., ed. *The Seven Military Classics of Ancient China*. New York: Basic Books, 2007.

Scanlon, Thomas F. *Eros and Greek Athletics*. Oxford: Oxford University Press, 2002.

Schneider, David K. "China's New Legalism." *National Interest*, no. 143 (2016): 19–25.

Scobell, Andrew, and Lucy Stevenson-Yang. "China Is Not Russia, Taiwan Is Not Ukraine." United States Institute of Peace, March 4, 2022. https://www.usip.org/publications/2022/03/china-not-russia-taiwan-not-ukraine.

Shang, Yang. *The Book of Lord Shang*. https://ctext.org/shang-jun-shu.

———. *The Book of Lord Shang: Apologetics of State Power in Early China*. Abridged ed. Translated by Yuri Pines. New York: Columbia University Press, 2019.

Shao, Hanming, and Qi Si. "'和而不同': 儒道释和谐思想分疏及其当代启示" ["Harmony But Not Sameness": Harmonious Ideas in Confucianism, Taoism, and Buddhism and Contemporary Implications]. *Journal of Tianjin Normal University (Social Sciences)*, no. 5 (2007): 13–19.

Sherman, Larry S., and Dennis Plies. *Every Brain Needs Music: The Neuroscience of Making and Listening to Music*. New York: Columbia University Press, 2023.

Shun, Kwong-loi. "On Anger: An Essay in Confucian Moral Psychology." In *Rethinking Zhu Xi: Emerging Patterns Within the Supreme Polarity*, edited by David Jones and He Jinli. Albany: State University of New York Press, 2015. https://www.klshun.com/wp-content/uploads/2015/11/On-Anger-An-Essay-in-Confucian-Moral-Psychology-Preprint.pdf.

Sima, Qian. 史记 [Records of the Grand Historian]. Beijing: Zhonghua Book Company, 1959.

Solomon, David, Ping-Cheung Lo, and Ruiping Fan, eds. *Ritual and the Moral Life: Reclaiming the Tradition*. Dordrecht: Springer, 2012.

Sterckx, Roel. *Chinese Thought from Confucius to Cook Ding*. Milton Keynes, UK: Pelican Books, 2019.

Su, Jilang, and Su Shoufumei. 有法无天 [Law Without Heavenly Order]. Hong Kong: Chinese University of Hong Kong Press, 2023.

Su, Liya. "Chinese Funeral Costing US$1.5 Million with Heavy Drinking and Fireworks Display Sparks Debate on Value of Lavish Ceremonies." *South China Morning Post*, May 13, 2022. https://www.scmp.com/news/people-culture/article/3177575/chinese-funeral-costing-us15-million-heavy-drinking-and.

Sun, Junheng, and Li Yue. "新墨学的兴起和前景" [The Revival and Future Prospects of New Mohism]. *Journal of Early Chinese Philosophers*, no. 2 (2013): 321–328.

Sun, Xiaochun. "韩非与马基雅维利非道德政治观评议" [A Commentary on Han Fei and Machiavelli's Amoral Political Views]. *Jilin University Journal (Social Sciences Edition)*, no. 5 (1997): 53–59.

Sunzi. *The Art of War*. https://ctext.org/art-of-war.

———. *Sun Tzu, The Art of War*. Translated by Samuel B. Griffith. Oxford: Clarendon Press, 1963.

Tan, Christine Abigail L. *Freedom's Frailty: Self-Realization in the Neo-Daoist Philosophy of Guo Xiang's Zhuangzi*. Albany: State University of New York Press, 2024.

Tan, Sor-Hoon. *Confucian Democracy: A Deweyan Reconstruction*. Albany: State University of New York Press, 2004.

Tang, Siufu. "Ritual as Skill: Ethical Cultivation and the Skill Model in the Xunzi." In *Skills in Ancient Ethics: The Legacy of China, Greece and Rome*, edited by Tom Angier and Lisa Raphals. London: Bloomsbury, 2022.

Tang, Wenfang. *Public Opinion and Political Change in China*. Palo Alto, CA: Stanford University Press, 2005.

Thomason, Krista K. *Dancing with the Devil: Why Bad Feelings Make Life Good*. New York: Oxford University Press, 2023.

Tian, Jason. *Family Laws and Regulations Report 2025 China*. International Comparative Legal Guides, 2025. https://iclg.com/practice-areas/family-laws-and-regulations/china.

Tiwald, Justin. "On the View That People and Not Institutions Bear Primary Credit for Success in Governance: Confucian Arguments." *Journal of Confucian Philosophy and Culture*, no. 32 (2019): 65.

———. "A Right of Rebellion in the Mengzi?" *Dao* 7, no. 3 (2008): 269–282.

Tiwald, Justin, and Richard Kim. "Episode 4: Persuasion." In *This Is the Way: Chinese Philosophy Podcast*. https://www.listennotes.com/da/podcasts/this-is-the-way/episode-4-persuasion-Y_Ha6vIr53K.

Tong, Weimin. "On the Composition of the 'Attracting the People' Chapter of the Book of Lord Shang." *Contemporary Chinese Thought* 47, no. 2 (2016): 138–151.

Twiss, Sumner B., and Jonathan Chan. "The Classical Confucian Position on the Legitimate Use of Military Force." *Journal of Religious Ethics* 40, no. 3 (2012): 447–472.

———. "Classical Confucianism, Punitive Expeditions, and Humanitarian Intervention." *Journal of Military Ethics* 11, no. 2 (2012): 81–96.

Valmisa, Mercedes. "The Happy Slave Isn't Free: Relational Autonomy and Freedom in the Zhuangzi." *Philosophy Compass* 14, no. 3 (2019): 1–15.

Van Norden, Bryan. "Mencius." In *The Stanford Encyclopedia of Philosophy* (Winter 2024 ed.), edited by Edward N. Zalta and Uri Nodelman. https://plato.stanford.edu/archives/win2024/entries/mencius.

———. *Virtue Ethics and Consequentialism in Early Chinese Philosophy*. Cambridge: Cambridge University Press, 2009.

Wan, Yonghua. "庄子自由观论析" [An Analysis of Zhuangzi's View of Freedom]. *Journal of Nanjing Forestry University (Humanities and Social Sciences Edition)* 6, no. 1 (2006): 36–40.

Wang, Furen. "论庄子的自由观: 庄子 '逍遥游' 的哲学阐释" [On Zhuangzi's View of Freedom: A Philosophical Interpretation of Zhuangzi's "Carefree Wandering"]. *Hebei Academic Journal* 29, no. 6 (2009): 39–46.

Wang, Guoliang. "王道如何战胜霸道: 孟子正义战争与和平思想引论" [How Humane Authorities Can Overcome Hegemons: An Introduction to Mengzi's Thoughts on Just War and Peace]. *Journal of the Communist Party School of Ningbo* 37, no. 1 (2015): 44–49.

Wang, Kai. "美善相乐: 生命哲学视域下的荀子乐论精神" [Beauty, Goodness, and the Musical Arts: On the Spirit of Xunzi's Musical Theory from the Perspective of the Philosophy of Life]. *Journal of Beijing Normal University*, no. 4 (2018): 125–131.

Wang, Keping. *Chinese Culture of Intelligence*. Beijing: Foreign Language Teaching and Research Press / Palgrave Macmillan, 2019.

Wang, Meng. *治国平天下: "荀子" 解读* [Ruling the Country and Providing Peace in the World: An Interpretation of Xunzi]. Jiangsu: People's Press, 2023.

Wang, Pei. "Confucian Filiality Revisited: The Case of Contemporary China." *Philosophy and Social Criticism*, October 18, 2024. https://doi.org/10.1177/01914537241288471.

———. "Confucian *Ren* Ethics Revisited: A Feminist Perspective." *China Review* (Forthcoming).

Wang, Peng. *The Chinese Mafia: Organized Crime, Corruption, and Extra-Legal Protection*. Oxford: Oxford University Press, 2017.

Wang, Zheng. "礼与法— 荀子与法家根本差异" [Ritual and Law: The Fundamental Differences Between Xunzi and Legalism]. *History of Chinese Philosophy*, no. 4 (2018): 36–37.

Wang, Zhimin, and Eleni Karamalengou, eds. *稷下学宫与柏拉图学园: 比较研究论集* [The Jixia Academy and Plato's Academy: A Collection of Comparative Research]. Beijing: SDX, 2021.

Wang, Zhongyuan, and Su Yun Woo. "Deliberative Representation: How Chinese Authorities Enhance Political Representation by Public Deliberation." *Journal of Chinese Governance* 7, no. 4 (2021): 583–615.

Watson, Burton, trans. *Basic Writings of Mo Tzu, Hsun Tzu, and Han Fei Tzu*. New York: Columbia University Press, 1963.

Wedemen, Andrew. "Village Elections and Grassroots Corruption in China." *Taiwan Journal of Democracy* 13, no. 2 (2018): 107–129.

Wee, Kek Koon. "How Singapore Transport Minister's Corruption Case Has Put Focus on High Pay of Ministers and Recalls Imperial China, Where Paying Officials to Be Honest Failed." *South China Morning Post*, February 3, 2024. https://www.scmp.com/magazines/post-magazine/short-reads/article/3250554/how-singapore-transport-ministers-corruption-case-has-put-focus-high-pay-ministers-and-recalls.

Wilson, Lee. "Confucianism and Totalitarianism: An Arendtian Reconsideration of Mencius Versus Xunzi." *Philosophy East & West* 71, no. 4 (2021): 981–1004.

Winston, Kenneth. "The Internal Morality of Chinese Legalism." *Singapore Journal of Legal Studies* 2005 (December 2005): 313–347.

Wong, David B. "Soup, Harmony, and Disagreement." *Journal of the American Philosophical Association* 6, no. 2 (2020): 139–155.

Wong, Peter Yih-Jiun. "The Music of Ritual Practice—An Interpretation." *Sophia* 51, no. 2 (2012): 243–255.

World Health Organization. "Law of the People's Republic of China on the Protection of Rights and Interests of the Elderly." https://extranet.who.int/mindbank/item/4741.

Xiao, Bofu. "商鞅法治理论及其现代借鉴" [Shang Yang's Theory of the Rule of Law and Its Modern Application]. *China Law*, no. 2 (2002): 152–163.

Xiao, Yang, and Kim-chong Chong, eds. *Dao Companion to the Philosophy of Mencius*. Cham, Switzerland: Springer, 2023.

Xie, Naihe. "商鞅强秦的道与术" [Shang Yang's Way and Technique to Strengthen Qin]. http://paper.people.com.cn/rmlt/html/2018-03/20/content_1887771.htm.

Xu, Keqian. "私德, 公德与官德: 道德在韩非子法家学说中的地位" [Private Morality, Public Morality, and Official Ethics: The Position of Morality in Han Feizi's Legalist Theory]. *Research in the Traditions of Chinese Culture*, no. 4 (2013): 68–73.

Xu, Yunliang. "商鞅变法的 '战时法治' 特征及其启示" [The Characteristics and Inspiration of the "Rule of Law in Wartime" of Shang Yang's Reforms]. *Journal of the Beijing Institute of Administration*, no. 3 (2011): 118–121.

Xunzi. *Xunzi: The Complete Text*. Translated by Eric L. Hutton. Princeton: Princeton University Press, 2014.

———. *Xunzi: I–II*. Translated by John Knoblock. Changsha: Hunan People's Publishing House, 1999.

Xygalatas, Dimitris. *Ritual: How Seemingly Senseless Acts Make Life Worth Living*. New York: Little, Brown Spark, 2022.

Yang, Chaoming. "孔子 '出妻' 说及相关问题" [Confucius's Alleged Repudiation of His Wife and Related Problems]. *Qilu Journal* 2 (2009): 10–14.

Yang, Chuanzhao, and Zhao Minli. "孟子武德思想及其现代价值" [Mengzi's View of Martial Virtues and Its Contemporary Relevance]. *Qilu Journal*, no. 6 (2018): 18–23.

Yang, Ling. *先秦法家思想比较— 以 "管子," "商君书," "韩非子," 为中心* [A Comparison of Pre-Qin Legalist Thought: Focusing on the *Guanzi*, *The Book of Lord Shang*, and *Han Feizi*]. Doctoral thesis, Zhejiang University, 2005.

Yao, Fulin. "建构和谐: 略谈孔子思想的现代价值" [The Construction of Harmony: A Brief Discussion on the Modern Value of Kongzi's Thought]. *Journal of Historiography*, no. 3 (2010): 7–9.

Yao, Xinzhong. "The Way of Harmony in the *Four Books*." *Journal of Chinese Philosophy* 40, no. 2 (2013): 252–268.

Ye, Zicheng. "商鞅的创新精神与秦国对大国的超越" [Shang Yang's Innovative Spirit and the Surpassing of the State of Qin over Large States]. *Frontiers*, no. 8 (2012): 34–44.

Yu, Cindy, and Charles Parton. "Why China Won't Invade Taiwan." *Spectator*, June 5, 2023. https://www.spectator.co.uk/podcast/why-china-wont-invade-taiwan/.

Yu, Kam Por. "The Confucian Conception of Harmony." In *Governance for Harmony in Asia and Beyond*, edited by Julia Tao, Anthony B. L. Leung, Martin Painter, and Chenyang Li, 15–36. London: Routledge, 2009.

Zakaria, Fareed. "A Conversation with Lee Kuan Yew." *Foreign Affairs*, March/April 1994. https://www.foreignaffairs.com/articles/asia/1994-03-01/conversation-lee-kuan-yew-0.

Zeng, Xi. *The Classic of Filial Piety*. https://ctext.org/xiao-jing.

Zeng, Zhenyu. "Shang Yang as a Historical Personality and as a Symbol." *Contemporary Chinese Thought* 47, no. 2 (2016): 69–89.

———. "'以刑去刑': 商鞅思想新论" ["Eradicating Punishment with Punishment": A New Perspective on Shang Yang's Thought]. *Journal of Shandong University (Philosophy and Social Science Edition)*, no. 1 (2013): 32–41.

Zha, Jianying. "China's Heart of Darkness: Prince Han Fei and Chairman Xi (Prologue)." *China Heritage*, July 2020. https://chinaheritage.net/journal/chinas-heart-of-darkness-prince-han-fei-chairman-xi-jinping-prologue/.

Zhang, Dainian, and Edmund Ryden. *Key Concepts in Chinese Philosophy*. New Haven, CT: Yale University Press, 2002.

Zhang, Qiwei. "孟子的军事哲学思想初探" [A Preliminary Analysis of Mengzi's Military Philosophy]. *Qilu Journal*, no. 4 (1989): 54–59.

Zhang, Xianglong. *儒家哲学史讲演录, 第二卷: 从 "春秋" 到荀子* [Lectures on the History of Confucian Philosophy, Vol. 2: From the "Spring and Autumn" Period to Xunzi]. Beijing: Commercial Press, 2019.

Zhao, Dingxin. *The Confucian-Legalist State: A New Theory of Chinese History*. Oxford: Oxford University Press, 2015.

Zhuang, Hui. "墨子'非乐'思想辨析" [An Analysis of Mozi's "Against the Musical Arts"]. *Dongyue Tribune* 24, no. 3 (2003): 128–130.

Zhuangzi. *Basic Writings*. Translated by Burton Watson. New York: Columbia University Press, 2003.

———. *Chuang-Tzu (Zhuangzi): The Inner Chapters*. Translated by A. C. Graham. Indianapolis: Hackett, 2001.

Ziliotti, Elena. *Meritocratic Democracy: A Cross-Cultural Political Theory*. Oxford: Oxford University Press, 2024.

INDEX

How to Develop Your Mind and Spirit for exploits

SSB Series

Book 2

Adiari Captain

How to Develop Your Mind and Spirit for Exploits
Spirit, Soul and Body (SSB) Series: Book 2

Published by Agape Lifecare Books
Pretoria
books@agapelifecare.com

ISBN 978-0-620-81233-7
eISBN 978-0-620-81236-8

2 4 6 8 10 9 7 5 3 1

Layout and cover design by Boutique Books
Printed in South Africa by Digital Action

E-Book Format:
How to Develop Your Mind and Spirit for Exploits (SSB Book 2) is also available in various electronic versions. To access the ebook format, visit: http://www.agapelifecare.com/books.

Also, more hardcopies (paperback) of the book can be obtained from your local bookshops or contact: http://www.agapelifecare.com/books.

Dedication

I DEDICATE THIS BOOK TO my kids, Charis, Phoster, and Sophia, and their generations yet unborn, that they may seek for greater light in the pages of the Bible on how God has wired the tripartite nature of man (spirit, soul, and body) for continuous success, and that by such knowledge they can escape the corruption of this present life and enjoy a life of bliss with their Creator in Christ Jesus. Indeed, that is my prayer for this lawless generation and the progenies yet unborn.

How to Develop Your Mind and Spirit for exploits

Abbreviations

AMP = Amplified Bible
CEB = Common English Bible
CEV = Contemporary English Version
Chpt = Chapter
ERV = Easy-to-Read Version
ESV = English Standard Version
EXB = Expanded Bible
GNT = Good News Translation
HCSB = Holman Christian Standard Bible
ICB = International Children's Bible
ISV = International Standard Version
KJV = King James Version
LEB = Lexham English Bible
NABRE = New American Bible (Revised Edition)
NASB = New American Standard Bible
NET = New English Translation
NIRV = New International Reader's Version
NIV = New International Version
NKJV = New King James Version
NLV = New Life Version
NLT = New Living Translation
RSV = Revised Standard Version
SSB=Spirit, Soul and Body
TLB = The Living Bible
Voice = The Voice Bible
WYC = Wycliffe Bible

Alphabetical Listing of the 66 books of the Bible and their Abbreviations					
Book	**Abbreviation**	**Book**	**Abbreviation**	**Book**	**Abbreviation**
Acts	Act.	James	Jam.	Nehemiah	Neh.
Amos	Amo.	Jeremiah	Jer.	Numbers	Num.
1 Chronicles	1Chr.	Job	Job	Obadiah	Oba.
2 Chronicles	2Chr.	Joel	Joe.	1 Peter	1Pet.
Colossians	Col.	John	Joh.	2 Peter	2Pet.
1 Corinthians	1Cor.	1 John	1Joh.	Philemon	Philem.
2 Corinthians	2Cor.	2 John	2Joh.	Philippians	Philip.
Daniel	Dan.	3 John	3Joh.	Proverbs	Pro.
Deuteronomy	Deu.	Jonah	Jon.	Psalms	Psa.
Ecclesiastes	Ecc.	Joshua	Jos.	Revelation	Rev.
Ephesians	Eph.	Jude	Jude	Romans	Rom.
Esther	Est.	Judges	Judg.	Ruth	Rut.
Exodus	Exo.	1 Kings	1Kin.	1 Samuel	1Sam.
Ezekiel	Eze.	2 Kings	2Kin.	2 Samuel	2Sam.
Ezra	Ezr.	Lamentations	Lam.	Songs of Songs	Son.
Galatians	Gal.	Leviticus	Lev.	1 Thessalonians	1The.
Genesis	Gen.	Luke	Luk.	2 Thessalonians	2The.
Habakkuk	Hab.	Malachi	Mal.	1 Timothy	1Tim.
Haggai	Hag.	Mark	Mar.	2 Timothy	2Tim.
Hebrews	Heb.	Matthew	Mat.	Titus	Tit.
Hosea	Hos.	Micah	Mic.	Zechariah	Zec.
Isaiah	Isa.	Nahum	Nah.	Zephaniah	Zep.

Contents

Section 2: How to Develop Your Spirit for Exploits – The Force of Vision

Section 3: How to Develop Your Spirit for Exploits – The Force of Faith

Declaration and Acknowledgment

All the stories reproduced in this book are true-life occurrences. However, the names of the persons involved were changed to preserve the identities of the individuals, except in few cases in which the story has actually been published with the full disclosure of identity or in any other public domain.

I wish to thank the numerous permissions we received from relevant quarters while compiling the materials of this book. Especially, I would like to thank my wife and children who have been the first students I have used to refine most of the thoughts in this book. The principles in this book are not new because principles are eternal laws of creation. However, the unveiling knowledge of some of these principles are quite novel as they came via creative illumination from the Holy Spirit, the Greatest Teacher, over the more-than-30 years of my spiritual walk with God. My family were usually the first students to practice the illuminated teachings. As you study this book, may you find the creative illumination that will enrich your life and drive you towards successful accomplishments beyond the confines of your perceived limitations.

PREFACE

IN 1980, WHILE IN PRIMARY school, two of my schoolmates, Jude and Cheif, were given corporal punishment by the school labour master, Mr. Claudius. The offence they had committed was that they were caught picking mango fruits in the bush when they were supposed to be in class. I still remember how we would taunt the boys for leaving the classes to pick bush mangoes. The corporal punishment meted out was to clean up some sections of the fields around the school premises.

Jude came with a sharp cutlass while Cheif had a blunt heavy machete. Jude finished his cleaning within the same day while Cheif finished his on the third day despite that they both had the same measured portions of fields with same type of grass on them. Cheif was expected to have finished his cutting long before Jude because he was much muscular, athletic, and appeared stronger than Jude.

Jude and Cheif represent the two classes of humans on earth. One is the unsuccessful class, whose dreams and aspirations have been frustrated. For this class, life seems to be one resistance to another as nothing appears to be working well. All the lofty desires they had while growing up as children and young adolescents seem to have died. After attaining some minimal level of success, it was like all hell was let loose on them to halt any further advancement. Disappointments and frustrations have gradually but progressively grounded them to a halt, and now they have resigned themselves to 'fate.'

The other class are the individuals whose desires have been met, and new goals have been set and again achieved. To them, it is a continuous progress and advancement. Everything they do seems to prosper. Like any other humans, they do have their challenges and disappointments; nonetheless, their advancement was never impeded to a halt. The interesting thing about this class is that only a very few number of people belong here while the majority of people belong to the earlier category.

Is life unfair? Does God love some people and favour some more than others? Why is it only few people tend to have their desires met while many others are always met with frustrations? These are common questions in the heart of many people.

The truth is that we live in a structured world. Our universe is quite methodological, being governed by laws. Sadly, the majority of people are ignorant of these laws of operation, and ignorance of a law is not an excuse. This book is a continuation of the previous one: *Spirit, Soul and Body – a Concise Analysis of the Human Nature (SSB Book 1).* It unveils the operation of the laws of success. In this book, you'll learn about the mind functionalities, and how to access creativity, and the secret of genius. The book introduces you to the mind activation principle, the three greatest forces that rule the world and how to harness these forces to make advancement in life. Other significant topics include how to harness sexual energy for life success, and much more. In this book, you'll study how individuals utilised the laws of success to forcefully advance their endeavours to become great achievers in their fields.

This book makes an interesting study, one that promises to be your companion in your earthly journey. Don't just browse through it, rather study it diligently to be wise, and practise these principles that will cause your heart desires to come to fruition.

Section 1

How to Develop Your Mind for Exploits

CHAPTER 1
THE POTENCY OF THE MIND

ON 27TH AUGUST 1858, ABOUT a century following the advent of the industrial revolution, Edwin Laurentine Drake (AD 1819-1880), also known as Colonel Drake, discovered petroleum in Titusville of Pennsylvania, USA; hence, becoming the first American to successfully drill for petroleum oil. That exploration and discovery changed the face of energy production and utilisation not just in the USA but across the globe. For the next 25 years after the oil discovery, men jostled about with personnel and machines, trying to conquer the industry. Standard Oil, pioneered by John D. Rockefeller, emerged the arrowhead and dominated the oil industry.

Rockefeller's wealth grew astronomically as he meticulously built his industry. Historians, anthropologists, and industrialists have written a lot about this character that, not only ruled the oil industry globally, but stood as a symbol of capitalism of industrial age. His rise from an obscurity, a village lad born to an impostor father and a dedicated Christian mother, to a global prominence, sounds more or less as a fairy tale, making those who never knew him to cast sentimental aspersions with awful veneration on his personality. Interestingly, the driving quality of Rockefeller's success was the robustness of his spirit man and his astute mind. He wasn't the best brains in the class during his school days or the best intellect in the oil industry. However, he had developed his spirit and sharpened his mind to such a degree that would dominate his physical world. One experience to clearly illustrate this is the Lima Oil.

THE 19TH CENTURY STORY OF THE LIMA OIL

At its infancy, the oil industry had been haunted by two nightmares – either the oil would dry up, thus starving their refineries and network of pipelines; or the oil would soon become irrelevant as the source of energy. *"At one panicky executive-committee meeting in the early 1880s, it was even suggested that Standard Oil should exit the business and enter something more stable. After listening quietly to such defeatist talk, Rockefeller stood up, pointed skyward, and intoned, 'The Lord will provide.' Rockefeller tended to see a heavenly design in all things and was convinced that the Almighty had buried the oil in the earth for a purpose,"* wrote Chernow Ron in *The Titan.*

During this period, specifically in May 1885, a dramatic event occurred in Lima, the headquarters city of Allen County, Ohio, United States. The event was the discovery of oil in and around this city. By December of 1885, more than 250 derricks had sprouted in and around the town, spilling across the borders into Indiana. But soon, hope gave way to despair because the newly discovered Lima oil was found to be chemically unmarketable because of its high sulphur contents that not only increased the cost of production but also had a pungent, irritating smell, spreading an unwanted thin film over lamps, making it unfit for the domestic use of its kerosene. In addition, the Lima petroleum contained less kerosene, the most useful refined component of crude oil as at then.

With all these challenges, many investors that hoped to reap from the new-found oil were disappointed. Many lost hope and looked for willing buyers of their share of investment. But not Rockefeller. *"It seemed to us impossible that this great product had come to the surface to be wasted and thrown away; so we went on experimenting with every process to utilize it,"* said Rockefeller in the heat of corporate despair about the Lima oil. One experiment he did to solve the challenges of the Lima oil was to import Mr. Herman Frasch, a distinguished, German-born chemist, unarguably the best in his time, with a marching order to banish the deadly odour from Lima oil and turn it into a marketable product.

While Frasch became neck-deep in his assignment, Standard Oil executive board was thrown into frenzy, dichotomous dilemma: Should the company buy up the shares of the willing sellers with the assumption that Frasch would succeed or should they wait until Frasch had come up with ways of converting the oil into marketable product? The problem with the first option was that Frasch was not showing any sign of success in his assignment, hence, if they should go ahead and make purchases, they could end up with millions of unsellable barrels of oil that would dim the future of the company. However, if they chose the second option, they ran the risk of losing Lima oil market to competition.

Faced with this dilemma, the executives chose to tow the 'safest' route by waiting for Frasch to come up with rays of hope of success on how to convert the Lima oil to marketable product. But Rockefeller's insight came into play. He refused to tow the myopic road of his board members. He would bring up the topic again and again in their board meetings, with each time receiving a resounding 'NO' answer from his board members. At every meeting, Rockefeller would propose the immediate purchase of the Lima oil leases, but each time was blocked by the board.

After several weeks of bringing up the same topic but kept meeting resistance, at one meeting Rockefeller decided to do the unthinkable. *"I will build this improvement out of my own funds and underwrite it for two years,"* Rockefeller replied in his cool calculated manner while piercing at the heated temper of the board members in the room. *"At the end of that time if it is a success the company can reimburse me. If it is a failure, I will take the loss,"* he finally laid out his thoughts, pledging three million USD (equivalent to about 60 million USD in 2016 rate). That caught the board members unawares.

There was dead silence in the room, the kind that even a pin drop could be heard, as the board members sat in contemplative awe. Across the table sat Charles Pratt, a thin man with calculative demeanours and the strongest opposition to Rockefeller's idea of outright purchase of Lima oil. Whether influenced by Rockefeller's unflinching resolve or realising that they would lose out, Charles Pratt broke the silence and announced, "If that's the way you feel about it, we'll go it together. I guess I can take the risk if you can."

That sealed the deal. For the next two years, Standard Oil invested millions of dollars in purchasing and expanding their influence into Lima and Ohio in general. To many minds, this was a gamble, which could bring down the fortunes of the company, and possibly destroy the company's future. But for Rockefeller, it wasn't a gamble. His insight had nerved him to believe that was the profitable way to go. *"Once Rockefeller had an insight, it often gripped him with the irresistible force of an epiphany,"* wrote Chernow Ron.

That insight paid off in no small measure. In October 1888, Frasch finally got the desired result; he discovered methods on how to remove the odour and the stain associated with Lima oil, thereby turning it into a marketable product. The joy of Standard Oil knew no bounds. Soon the company launched the largest refinery, Whiting Refinery, in Indiana, that processed 36000 barrels of crude oil daily. The refinery became a wonder to the world for many years, with Standard Oil dominating the Lima oil production for those numbers of years, profiting immensely from it for more than a decade and which refocused the company for global supremacy in the industry.

Fig.1: Whiting Refinery is a sprawling 1400 acre (5.7 km2) complex, located in Whiting Indiana, spanning into the neighbouring cities of southeast Chicago. The refinery was established in 1889 by John D. Rockefeller's Standard Oil of Indiana, reaping from the proceeds of Lima Oil. By the mid-1890s, the Whiting plant had become the largest refinery in the United States, handling 36000 barrels of oil per day and accounting for nearly 20 percent of the total U.S. refining capacity. In 1998, British Petroleum (BP) merged with Amoco (formerly Standard Oil of Indiana) to form BP Amoco plc, now BP plc. In 2013, BP plc completed a multi-billion dollar modernization project of the Whiting refinery, making it the largest refinery in the Midwest as well as BP's largest refinery in the world with a production capacity of up to 430000 barrels a day, enough gasoline each day to fuel 6 million cars!

INSIGHT – AN OUTPUT OF ROBUST SPIRIT AND KEEN MIND

Insight is a word that has become common in science and business circles. It is one word that can spell a difference in the outcome of our life endeavours. John D. Rockefeller's ability to correctly decipher the future prospects of Lima oil, while others in the industry had written it off, was due to a keen insight.

A man with a keen insight sees what others do not. The question will then be: 'what is an insight?' Most importantly, how can one develop a keen insight and utilise it to achieve one's heart desires? As you study through the pages of this book, you'll undoubtedly come to know about insight and, more especially, how to develop it for maximum gain in life. The caution here is that you should take time to study and not just browse through the book if you sincerely desire to benefit from it. Some may find the answers in the first chapter, others in the second, and so on.

Man is a tripartite being; he is primarily a spirit being, possesses a soul, and lives in a physical body. Just as the human body can be divided into systems, the human spirit, sometimes referred to as the spirit man, consists of three systems or components – the heart, eido centre, and censor. The soul is the outer covering, the cocoon, which houses the spirit man. The functional expression, the software, of the soul is called the mind, which has five faculties or systems – the emotion, imaginative, intellect, memory, and willpower. For a clearer understanding, see the book, *Spirit, Soul and Body – A Concise Analysis of the Human Nature (SSB Book 1),* by this same author. With the eido centre of the human spirit, an individual can perceive, discern, or 'see' beyond the physical senses. Such perceived, discerned, seen information is received by the heart of the spirit man and is judgmentally weighed by the censor to determine its significance.

In other words, the spirit man can perceive information which is, hitherto, not detected by the body senses. Such perceived information is then passed onward to the faculties of the mind, where it is processed into an intelligible idea. That is, a combination of the functions of the human spirit and the mind is what produces such intelligible idea, which is referred to as insight.

Etymologically, insight is from two words: 'inside' and 'sight.' Simply put, insight means 'having an inside sight.' The 'inside sight' here refers to the inner knowing by the action of the eido centre, and such inner knowing is then refined by the mind. Rockefeller's eido centre could perceive the bright prospects of Lima Oil. His mind processed the perceived information, refining it more clearly into an acceptable, workable idea. Hence, in his heart and mind, Rockefeller had seen the huge profits from the Lima Oil even though all available statistics pointed otherwise.

Indeed, the more robustly developed the human spirit and the more refined the mind, the sharper is insightful perception. A combination of the functions of the spirit man and the mind produces insight. That is, insight is an output of a robust spirit and a keen mind. A well-developed spirit is not the religious farce that goes all around us. A well-developed spirit is a robustly fecund spirit. Such a person is productive. His heart and eido centres know how to receive superior thought from the spiritual and physical environments, and such thought is then processed by his astute mind into a refined idea for execution in the physical world. That is the secret of Mr. Rockefeller and any other true success story in any industry!

CHAPTER 2
THE MIND – LINK BETWEEN THE PHYSICAL AND SPIRITUAL WORLDS

IN 1950, SHORTLY AFTER THE Korean War began, Kim Woo-Choong was an undernourished 12-year-old refugee who earned just enough money delivering newspapers to buy food for his widowed mother and his brother and sister. Despite such circumstances, Kim had a dream in his heart. Deep within him, he saw riches of financial fortunes and not poverty.

He later wrote, *"I did not have a single coin in my pocket, but I had dreams... making a product that is the finest of its type in the world. I treasure this dream, no matter what the product may be. It could be anything, so long as it becomes renowned as the finest of its kind in the world – like a Parker pen or a Nikon camera. It does not matter so long as they say that it was made by Kim Woo-Chong and that it is the best of its kind."*

Thus, with his heart he conceived dreams of becoming an entrepreneur of world's renown. But if he stopped on just dreaming, such a vision, no matter how sound, would never become a reality. From the heart of the spirit man, the dream must pass down to the mind for rationalisation. It was in his mind that Kim was able to rationalise the step-by-step approach to actualising his vision. His mind broke the dreams down into workable, practical steps. Thus, he wrote:

"We lived in the Changchung-dong section of Seoul then, and I had to walk two hours to Yonsei University, which was more than six miles away. I did not have a single coin in my pocket, but I had dreams. I still cannot forget the feeling that would come over me when I stepped

out of the library late at night, or when I looked up at the sky on the long trudge home. It seemed like the world was mine, that I could just wrap the universe up in my arms. Nothing seemed impossible to me. The vitality of youth was in me, and it filled my heart with dreams. There was nothing that could stop me."

If you are a dreamer; Kim's story would have been quite familiar to you. When a dream permeates to the mind and it is processed into practical steps, it generates the propulsive force of faith that drives a man beyond expectation. Kim's heart dreams had passed down to his mind, where they had been processed into workable, practical steps that triggered his faith beyond words.

In 1967, Kim took a practical step by establishing a small trading company in pursuance of his dreams. Seventeen years later, the small trading company had grown into a giant multinational conglomerate, the Daewoo Group, employing more than 85,000 people in Korea and 60 overseas offices.

Daewoo's brand products include motor vehicles, textiles, ships, computers, home appliances, chemicals, leather goods, robots, fibre optics, machinery and consumer electronic goods. The company's nearly eight billion US dollars in sales in 1984 catapulted the relatively infant Daewoo Group into Number 48 position on Fortune magazine's International 500 list. His company's unprecedented success story earned Kim the International Chamber of Commerce's 1984 award as the world's best businessman, a kind of Nobel Prize for entrepreneurs that is presented by the King of Sweden once every three years.

Prior to the financial crisis that gripped much of East Asia beginning July 1997, Daewoo was the second largest conglomerate in Korea after Hyundai Group, followed by LG Group and Samsung. Notwithstanding its seemingly strong overseas branch office spread, the company easily plummeted under the weight of the crisis heavily. It caved in because of its hollow financial structure as events later revealed Daewoo as an unstable Group. It had to sell off nearly 50 division corporations to focus only on the major companies. There were about 20 divisions left under the Daewoo Group, some of which survived until today as independent companies. Kim was plunged into unduly huge debts that earned him an arrest and a sentence of 10 years in jail in 2006. He was however pardoned after a few months by the South Korean government on personal recognition of his towering contribution to economic growth of the country in particular and Asia in general.

Kim's success is a testimony of the power of a dream in the heart of a man that has undergone processing in the mind. He wrote in his book, *Every Street is Paved with Gold, the following words*:

> *"Of all the things that youth brings with it, dreams are the most important. People with dreams know no poverty, for a person is as rich as his or her dreams. Youth is the time of life when, even if you do not own a thing, you have nothing to envy if you have dreams. History belongs to dreamers. Dreams are the power for changing the world. I will bet that all the people who are shaping world history today had big dreams when they were young. But nowadays I often hear that young people no longer have dreams about the future. Or that the dreams they do have are fixed only on the present. If that is true, then nothing could be sadder for the individuals, and even more so for the nation."*

Kim concludes with these words:

> *"History belongs to dreamers. Only nations that have people with dreams, people who try to make dreams come true, and people who share dreams can be leaders of world history. Your dreams have to be as pure and as clear as spring water. And such dreams have to be big dreams. You have to carry the universe with you in your heart, and your dreams have to be as big as the universe itself. A philosopher once said that youth without dreams is the same as psychological suicide. So dream dreams that are pure and bright and big" (Woo-Choong and Louis, 1992).*

With his mind, Kim could see his future clearly, and that triggered the propulsive power of faith that jerked his physical body into action to actualise the dreams. Indeed, the mind is the link between the spiritual and the physical worlds. With the heart of the spirit, a man conceives dream, which are processed by the mind and then executed by the body organs.

***Fig*.2: Former Daewoo Group Headquarters building (now Seoul Square Building), the power of dreams in the heart being processed by the mind of man.**

WEALTH – FUNCTION OF DEGREE OF MIND DEVELOPMENT

Indeed, the mind is the link between the spiritual and physical worlds. With his spirit, a man relates with the spiritual world. The received thoughts from the spiritual world are processed by the mind for execution by the body in the physical world. In other words, the keenness of the mind determines how much of the information received in the spiritual world becomes relevant and productive for the individual. For instance, vision, faith and love – the three greatest forces that rule the world – originate from and are perceived in the heart of the spirit man, but it is the mind of the soul that processes the vision, articulates the acts of faith, and processes the power of love into a driving force for physical execution.

The Manual of Life, the Bible, repeatedly teaches the crucial place of the mind for a successful living. For instance, analysis of the Third Epistle of John verse 2 clearly reveals this:

> *"Beloved, I wish above all things that thou mayest prosper and be in health even as your soul propereth" (3 Joh.2 KJV).*

The above Scripture mentions three points:
(i) '*I wish above all things that you may prosper*':
This is the thought of God for humans He has created in His image and likeness. Remember that John the Beloved, who penned down these words, was under divine inspiration; he wrote as being directed by the Spirit of God. The letter was addressed to Gaius, apparently a Christian leader in the first Century Church. However, the letter was not an expression of divine thought for Gaius alone. Gaius was only an avenue by which God unveils His thought for humanity. Thus, it is a spiritual message of blessing in the heart of God for man.

(ii) '*Be in health*':
God's thought for man is not just for man to prosper spiritually but this prosperity must materialise so that it can be seen physically here on earth. Health is the spiritual wealth translated into physical, tangible wealth. Health is wealth. In other words, the spiritual message of prosperity will only become relevant when it is physically transmuted into physical, tangible wealth.

(iii) '*Even as your soul prospers*':
Take note of the subordinate conjunction - 'even as', in the Scripture. It means for the spiritual wealth that God has blessed man with to become physical wealth, the soul must prosper. The term soul in the Scripture is from the Greek word *psyche*, which is occasionally translated as 'mind' (see SSB Book 1). The mind is the functional expression of the soul. Thus, the translation of the spiritual endowments into material prosperity is dependent on the prosperity of the mind.

That is, the more developed a man's mind is, the higher is his ability to translate unseen wealth into physical reality. That explains why many Christians do not experience physical prosperity. They may be good prayer warriors, living a committed and disciplined lifestyle, good Christian leaders with unrivalled holy living, yet remain grossly impoverished in material blessings. On the other hand, it also explains why a man, who knows nothing about spiritual growth and development and may not even believe in God, yet is able to amass stupendous amount of material blessings. Indeed, the development of our mind is crucial to our success in life. In other words, wealth of all forms is a function of the degree of mind development of the individual. Therefore, I encourage you to keep reading this book in order to discover the intricacies, the laws, and their application that govern mind growth and development.

A TWO-WAY COMMUNICATION

There is a two-directional passage of information across the mind, viz.

Downgraded Communication

This is when thought is passed down from the heart of the spirit to the mind for processing. All thoughts projected from the spiritual world that enter the heart, alongside those thoughts independently originated by the heart of the spirit man, pass from the heart to the mind for processing. It is this mental processing function of the downgraded thoughts that convert the thoughts into functional ideas for execution by the body.

Upgraded Communication

In addition, information received from the physical world by the body senses pass to the mind for processing.

In many instances, thoughts can also be projected directly into the mind of a man from spirit beings, and this is referred to as **thought projection** in psychiatry. Whether the information passes onto the mind from the body senses or it is projected directly into the mind; once it is in the mind, the information will undergo processing as far as the capability of the person's mental prowess into an idea.

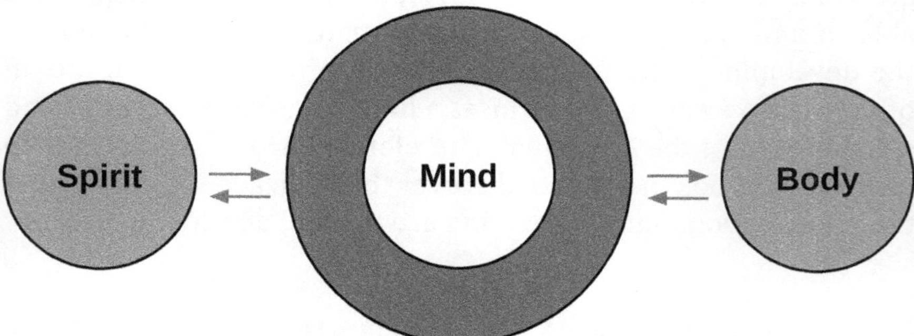

***Fig.3*: The Mind – the Central Processor between the Spiritual and Physical realms**

MIND – THE CENTRAL PROCESSOR

The role of the mind in life's accomplishments cannot be over-emphasised. Being a medium between the spiritual world and the physical world, the mind is central to every degree of man's life achievements. Without the mind, all the products from the spirit man cannot be transmuted or converted into physical substances. Also, without the mind, information obtained from the physical world cannot be processed into usable substances for productive execution. The mind is the central processor that processes spiritual messages from the spirit realm for physical execution as well as information from the physical world for profitable execution.

"WITHOUT YOUR MIND I CAN DO NOTHING"

As this chapter rounds up, it is interesting to note the inspired word of Apostle Paul about the power of the mind in the Epistle of Philemon. The epistle, known simply as Philemon, is one of the books of the New Testament. It is written by Apostle Paul, co-authored by Timothy, while in a Roman prison in about AD 61. The letter was addressed to Philemon, a wealthy man and a leader in the Colossian church. Philemon might have converted to Christianity through Paul's ministry in Ephesus.

The highlight of the letter was Apostle Paul's plea on behalf of Onesimus, a runaway slave of Philemon. Apparently, Onesimus became regenerated and converted to Christianity after coming in contact with Paul in prison. Following the conversion, Paul decided to send Onesimus back to his master, Philemon, with an enclosed letter, pledging to personal pay any charges:

> *"If he has cheated you or owes you anything, charge it to my account. With my own hand I write: I, Paul, will pay you back. But don't forget that you owe me your life. My dear friend and follower of Christ our Lord, please cheer me up by doing this for me" (Philem.1:18-20 CEV).*

Notice something of great interest: Onesimus' changed character won the affection of Apostle Paul.

> *"I beg you to help Onesimus! He is like a son to me because I led him to Christ here in jail. Before this, he was useless to you, but now he is useful both to you and to me. Sending Onesimus back to you makes me very sad. I would like to keep him here with me, where he could take your place in helping me while I am here in prison for preaching the good news" (Philem.1:10-13 CEV).*

Because of such a changed character and usefulness, Apostle Paul would have been glad to keep Onesimus with him. However, he made it very clear that without the consenting mind of Philemon, he wouldn't dare do otherwise.

> *"But without thy mind [gnōmē] would I do nothing ..."*
> *(Philem.1: 14 KJV).*

That is the power of the mind. The Greek term for 'mind' in this Scripture is *gnome*, which means cognition or reasoning. *Gnome* is one of the expressions of the Intellectual Faculty of the mind, and more specifically it is one of the expressions of the Ideological Unit of the Intellectual Faculty (see the book: SSB Book 1). Thus, *gnome* means 'to agree, to purpose, to arrive at a decision, be at one accord.' In other words, Apostle Paul told Philemon that without the latter consenting mind, he wouldn't be able to proceed any further with the matter at hand.

This inspired statement spoken to Philemon was a revelation of the power of the mind in the running of our affairs. Philemon was only a channel through which the Creator reveals the created potency of the mind of man. As you conclude this chapter, always remember that your mind is essential in your quest for success in life. Without your mind, neither God nor any other being can cause you to make advancement and success in life. Indeed, without your mind, even your spirit man and body cannot produce success in your life. That is the potency of our mind! It, therefore, behoves on you to feed your mind appropriately and adequately in order for it to grow, develop and be sharpened for exploits.

Chapter 3
Mind Development – Key to Life Success

The mind is the functional expression of the soul; it is the software of the soul. The mind consists of five systems or faculties: emotion, imaginative, intellect, memory, and willpower (see SSB Book 1). The development of your mind is the key to your success in life. Your altitude in life is directly proportional to the development of the faculties of your mind.

Each of the five faculties of the mind can be developed independently. For instance, an individual who preoccupies his effort in suffocating the emotional faculty (as it is seen in many religions), will undoubtedly have a weakened emotional faculty. Academia hinges on development of the intellect, hence, many academics have well developed intellectual faculty. On the other hand, many artists have well developed imaginative faculty because they repeatedly feed and exercise this faculty.

The implication of this is that a poorly developed faculty of the mind doesn't mean the other faculties of your mind are not developed. The development of each faculty depends on how you feed and exercise that faculty. That should tell us to be wary of the so-called tests for intelligent quotient (IQ). These tests are not true reflections of the power of one's mind. A low IQ today does not mean a low IQ throughout the person's life. In fact, most of the IQ test questions focus more on the intellect faculty with little or no consideration given to the other four faculties of the mind. IQ test is a biased assessment of the astuteness and power of the mind.

THOMAS EDISON'S MIND AND SCHOOL DROPOUTS

After repeated observations, the teacher of Thomas Edison made a mistake. He wrote to Edison's parents that their seven-year-old son was "too stupid to learn anything." The teacher advised that Thomas be withdrawn from the school since, according to him, Thomas had no intelligent capacity to succeed in life. Thomas' mother, Nancy Edison, the devout daughter of a highly respected Presbyterian minister and an educator in her own right, promptly withdrew Thomas from school and began to 'home-school him.'

How wrong the teacher was! This same Edison turned out to be one of the most celebrated scientists and inventors of all time. In AD 2012, about 81 years after Edison's death, Life magazine honoured him as Man of the Millennium, a person who brought more value to the human race than any other, literally giving us our modern world and standards of living. His four great inventions were recorded sound, motion pictures, the electric light bulb and utility industry, and corporate R&D labs from which new products continue to flow in abundance.

Thus, because Thomas' intellect faculty was not properly harnessed by his early formal schooling does not in any way mean that Thomas was 'too stupid to learn anything' or his mind faculties were incapable of growth and development in other fields of endeavour.

Furthermore, the reason many school dropouts turn out to be great industrialists and financiers has a lot to do with mind development and growth. They dropped out from school because they chose not to sharpen their intellect faculty with academic stuff. They wanted to use business information to sharpen their intellect. That never made them less intelligent than the professor who developed his intellect using academic information.

What this means is that the information we concentrate and feed our mind with, determines how and to what degree our mind will develop. If you feed and regularly exercise your mind with academic substance, you'll turn out to be academically intelligent, but may not be developed in other areas of intelligence that receive less attention. Hence, that doesn't make you less intelligent than the individual who has developed his intellect using artistic information. This is important information no parent should overlook in guiding their wards in the right direction of career choice. The place of vision, talents, passion is very crucial in the choice of career, and this is discussed in this book.

Fig.4: Thomas Edison

In AD 1854, the teacher of Thomas Edison wrote to Edison's parents that their seven-year-old son was "too stupid to learn anything."

How wrong the teacher was! This same Edison turned out to be one of the most celebrated scientists and inventors of all time, as he gave the world our modern electricity light, a testimony of the power of mind development!

THE TRUE ESSENCE OF EDUCATION

Our world, especially developing African countries, is crazy about paper qualifications in form of certificates, diplomas, and degrees. Modern education has promoted the value of these paper qualifications, in most cases, over the knowledge that should be associated with such qualification. Because of emphasis on paper qualification, getting jobs, social status and recognition have become synonymous with paper qualification. These have driven men and women to acquire these paper qualifications by all means, some even fraudulently.

I remember a lecture class we had about a year to our graduation from the medical school. The professor of surgery asked the class:

> *"How many of you will want the medical degree at this stage without waiting for the completion of the remaining academic year?" Over ninety per cent of the class raised their hands. The professor was alarmed. "Does it mean you don't care about the knowledge that you still need to acquire in order to become good medical practitioners? Does it mean you are only thinking of the social prestige and financial blessings of a medical degree," the Professor lamented. Of course, the school never graduated any of us until we satisfied the full requirements of the medical school training.*

The important lesson here is that because of emphasis on paper qualification, modern education has forced the society to give more accolades to individuals with chains of degrees, not minding whether or not they have the requisite knowledge that their paper qualifications demand. As such, fake nursery, primary, secondary, and tertiary institutions that offer fake certificates now exist all over the world.

Nonetheless, we can never cheat the laws of the universe. Paper qualifications alone can never produce outstanding results in any field. Having an engineering degree does not guarantee a success in engineering field. What counts is the individual's ability to produce good works. In other words, until we begin to transmute theoretical knowledge into practical reality, our paper qualifications will remain a failure. There are many professors of academics who are failures, all they know is to quote theories and works of others, and yet they never publish any paper of originality that contributes to the advancement of their field.

On the other hand, there are many people with less academic endowments but great achievements. That is to say, in any field you choose, your target should not just be to acquire the paper qualification, but to acquire the knowledge in that field that will cause you to generate outstanding contributions in that field. If you are an accountant, your target shouldn't be to sit down and count money. Have you thought about how to create new knowledge in the banking and financial system? The world will only reward you to the extent that you introduce problem-solving changes that impact lives positively. Financial gains are directly proportional to one's contribution to solving other people's problems; and your degree of contribution depends on the degree of growth and development of your mind.

WHY SOME PERSONS ARE MORE BLESSED THAN OTHERS IN THE SAME CAREER

Every individual wants success in his or her chosen career. Nevertheless, not all individuals in the same chosen career achieve the same level of success. How much success, recognition, and influence we command in any career is dependent not on our paper qualifications. Paper qualifications may only grant you influence and recognition within your office and nothing more. Larger society only recognises how much changes you bring to bear on the lives of people. That is the Law of Seedtime and Harvest. The more you sow into people's lives, the more blessings you reap in your chosen career.

True education is to enlighten our minds for productive usage in our chosen careers. My high school principal often admonished us: 'Don't just go through the school; let the school also go through you.' If a man desires paper qualification, let his dominant intent be to acquire the knowledge behind the paper qualification he possesses. That will enable him to unleash his potentials in that field. The mind is built and developed by the knowledge a man acquires and puts in practice!

Chapter 4
The Power of the Mind: Faculty of Intellect

An analysis of the functions of each of the five faculties of the mind will give a deeper understanding of the power of the mind on the success of an individual. As mentioned in the previous chapter, the mind has five faculties, each wielding enormous power on the outcome of our lives.

POWER OF FACULTY OF INTELLECT

The intellectual faculty is the rationalisation centre of the mind. It is the faculty for analysis and synthesis of information that comes into the mind. The intellectual faculty consists of three units – Conceptualisation, Reactive, and Ideological Units. Thoughts from the heart of the spirit man enter the mind usually via the Conceptualisation Unit. Thus, the Conceptualisation Unit of the Intellectual Faculty acts as the reservoir of the mind for thought reception.

The power of the Conceptualisation Unit should never be underrated. Thought from the heart of man or the heart of any other spirit being can be projected directly into the human mind. Psychiatrists refer to this as ***thought insertion***. The thought will appear first in the Conceptualisation Unit, and because such thought has not yet undergone any form of processing, the projected thought will appear as if it is originating from the mind of the individual.

This has caused a great deal of confusion in deciphering the origin of thought, especially for Christians who desire to please God.

Evil thoughts will project into the mind of a Christian from negative spirits like the demons, and such thoughts appear first in the Conceptualisation Unit of the Intellect Faculty of his mind. With the thoughts appearing in the Conceptualisation Unit, the individual may consider them to be his thought. As his regenerated spirit desires to please his Heavenly Father, the individual will start feeling guilty for considering such evil thoughts, not realising they were originally not his thoughts and, as such, can be cast down.

THE STORY OF KENNETH'S DISCOVERY

Kenneth became a born again Christian in 1982. One battle he fought gallantly was the feeling of guilt as a result of immoral thoughts. When immoral thoughts flashed into his mind, he never knew they weren't coming from the heart of his spirit man. Because the thoughts often appeared as if originated from within his heart, he would feel guilty for thinking such immoral thoughts. Kenneth spent considerable amount of time praying and asking God for forgiveness each day for thinking the immoral thoughts. He would feel good within himself after praying for forgiveness. However, the moment he had finished the prayer of forgiveness, soon another immoral thought would flash into his mind again. The continuous battle to keep a clean thought-life and conscience wearied him and he started thinking: 'maybe I am only deceiving myself to lead a good Christian life as required by God in the Scriptures.'

Then he stumbled on a truth. One day as an immoral thought flashed into his mind, he just shouted out, rebuking it in Jesus Name. Surprisingly, the thought faded away from his mind immediately he did that. That kept him thinking. It made him to realise that those immoral thoughts weren't really coming from his heart, but projected by unclean demonic spirits into his mind. Then, he didn't know he had just discovered the Law of Faith (see Chapter 32). This law has a lot to do with the use of our tongue. With the tongue we cast down every imagination or thought that exalts itself against the knowledge of God.

> *"For the weapons of our warfare are not carnal, but mighty through God to the pulling down of strongholds; casting down imaginations, and every high thing that exalteth itself against the knowledge of God, and bringing into captivity every thought to the obedience of Christ" (2Cor.10:4,5 KJV).*

The power of the Conceptualisation Unit of the Intellectual Faculty has wrecked much havoc in the lives of many people with sincere motive. It makes them to believe that the evil thoughts projected into their mind were originated from their hearts, triggering the emotional faculty to produce the feeling of guilt. An intense guilty feeling has driven many people into committing unwholesome activities. Indeed, many cases of extreme penitence we read about in the story of great saints like Augustine of Hippo (AD 354-430) and Martin Luther (AD 1483-1546) were directly due to the deceptive influence of the Conceptualisation Unit (see SSB Book 1).

However, we should not allow the power of the Conceptualisation Unit of the Intellectual Faculty to hold us ransom. Adequate knowledge is what brings about liberation. Such knowledge includes the awareness that we can cast down unwholesome thought and disallows it from taking root in our mind and heart. Study the Scriptures for yourself to allow them to guide you. For instance, when you fall into sin and pray for forgiveness, the Blood of Christ has wiped the sins away. It means God has forgiven you. If God has forgiven you, you should also forgive yourself and any one that might have wronged you. Any guilty feeling that crops up in your mind after you have prayed for forgiveness is not of God. Cast it down by the application of the Law of Faith. Refuse to accept the guilty feeling; never allow it to hold you in ransom. Use your tongue to speak peace and quietness into your mind.

FROM CONCEPTUALISATION UNIT TO REACTIVE UNIT

From the Conceptualisation Unit the projected thought passes into the Reactive Unit of the intellectual faculty. The Reactive Unit is the centre for analysis and synthesis of thoughts. The keenness of the Reactive Unit shows how well developed the mind is. The so-called intelligent quotient tests are actually tests of the Reactive Unit of the intellectual faculty. The more keen the Reactive Unit, the more intelligent we perceive the individual.

To sharpen the Reactive Unit depends on how we feed and exercise it. The food we feed the Reactive Unit with is what determines how it grows and develops. For instance, if we feed our Reactive Unit with theoretical academic information but with no relevant financial information, we will develop academically but languish in penury. Lack of financial intelligence explains why many professors of Economics are poor. With their theoretical academic information on wealth, some of these Economics professors sharpen and hone the Reactive Unit of their intellectual faculty; but because they lack the practical financial intelligence to transmute theoretical knowledge into practical financial gains, they remain financially poor.

Individuals who know the power of the Reactive Unit of the Intellectual Faculty of the mind often exercise it for their benefits. For instance, individuals who know that the Reactive Unit of their intellectual faculty can analyse and synthesize information to generate results, don't take rash decisions and they don't believe in impossibilities. They give time for their Reactive Unit to search around for solutions during which they keep an open mindedness, refusing to allow thoughts of impossibility to settle or take root in their mind. When emotions of fear attempt to break into their mind, they shut them out through the principle of autosuggestion, which is a significant aspect of the Law of Faith. The story of Henry Ford does illustrate this vividly.

PRINCIPLES BEHIND HENRY FORD'S SUCCESS

Millions of people around the world read the story of Henry Ford and admire his success. But many never bother to understand the principles behind Ford's success. In 1902, Henry Ford had conceived a thought. It was to make a horseless cart – an automobile, available and cheaper to Americans. But he was plagued, so to say, with what the ignoramus will call handicaps or limitations. Firstly, Ford was raised as a poor farmer with little formal education. He only had less than six years of formal education; he wasn't a trained automobile engineer. Secondly, no one had ever produced cars in mass quantities as he had thought of; hence, there was no strong past success to emulate. Thirdly, he was financially handicapped to embark on such a gigantic project. Each of these three challenges was strong enough to stop most men from advancing onwards with their dreams; but not so with Mr. Ford. He never believed in impossibilities. He never allowed fear to paralyse his mind into inaction.

To circumvent his handicaps, he formed a mastermind team with others that had what he needed. He teamed up with Alexander Y. Malcomson, a Detroit-area coal dealer; John and Horace E. Dodge (the Dodge brothers); Malcomson's uncle John S. Gray; Malcolmson's secretary James Couzens; and two of Malcomson's lawyers – John W. Anderson and Horace Rackham. These together formed Ford's mastermind team, which was translated into a physical company, the Ford Motor Company. The team hired engineers and mechanics to work for them.

To achieve his dream, in 1928 Henry Ford decided to produce his famous V8 motor; it would be an engine with the entire cylinders cast in one block. He instructed his engineers to produce a design for the engine, and this was done and placed on a paper. But the bad news was that this was never a popular design and his engineers agreed it was an 'impossible task' to cast an eight-cylinder gas engine block in one piece. However, Henry Ford's response was:

"Produce it anyway."

"But, it's impossible," they replied.

"Go ahead, and stay on the job until you succeed; no matter how much time is required," Ford insisted.

He ordered Engineer C. James Smith to lead a team to start work on a V8 engine. The engineers went ahead; they couldn't do otherwise if they must continue working in the Ford Motor Company.

Six months came and went, and another six months! At the end of the year, Ford made an assessment, but there was no sight of success. During this period, Chevrolet introduced its first six-cylinder engine. That invigorated and drove Henry Ford beyond words. Meanwhile, both Edsel Ford (Henry Ford's son, who later became the President of Ford Motor Company after his father's retirement in 1919) and production manager Charlie Sorenson, pushed strongly for Ford Motor Company to introduce its own six-cylinder engine car; Henry Ford's sole concession was to authorise some preliminary development work with no commitment to production. He was not interested in any six-cylinder engine; in his mind, Ford Motor Company would have a V8 or nothing.

In 1929, with intention to give more drive to the V8 project, Ford assigned Fred Thoms to gather and dismantle rival designs to study the existing state of the art. In fact, counting Jimmy Smith's early work, Ford had a total of four different teams working on the V8 at different times, all under Henry Ford's personal supervision and each largely unaware of each other's efforts. Each team was micromanaged by Henry Ford himself, who, to many minds, often complicated the engineers' work with his arbitrary and sometimes irrational whims! Ford's perception was that if he must birth something new, he had to behave differently from the conventional ideas. Thus, even though Ford Motor Company had engineering teams assigned to develop the engine, Ford was completely monitoring and engaging; indeed, many of the ideas and innovations were Henry Ford's.

Another year had come and gone, yet no visible sign of success! To invigorate the work, Henry Ford assigned Arnold Soth to start over in May 1930, resulting in a completely new 299 cu. in. (4905 cc) engine with a 60-degree bank angle rather than the theoretically ideal 90 degrees. This too proved unworkable; the narrow vee angle created balance problems and lubrication was hopelessly inadequate because Henry Ford forbade the use of an oil pump. Despite another failure, Henry Ford was so adamant and insistent that he nearly fired Engineer Gene Farkas for taking it upon himself to design a pump not in line with the vision of V8.

When no success was in sight, instead of giving up, and acting on the principle of perseverance, which he learnt from his mentor and friend, Thomas Edison, Henry Ford again dissolved the team and established yet another team of engineers. The team was led by Carl Schultz, working with Fred Thoms and Ray Laird to start over largely from scratch. As before, every detail was dictated by Henry Ford himself and he allowed his engineers little leeway, strenuously opposing any deviation from his specifications. The engineers worked from sketches and engineering drawings and machined the parts. The work was gruelling, continuing seven days a week, and engineers rarely left even to sleep.

Undaunted and intransigent, Henry Ford and his engineers forged on tirelessly. To forestall leakage of company secret and progress to competitors, Henry Ford barely allowed his own employees to talk to each other about the project.

Finally, in 1932, under Henry Ford's direct watchful eyes, Schultz, Laird, and Thoms produced two prototype engines, one of 299 cu. in. (4.9 L) displacement and the other 233 cu. in. (3.8 L). Both were 90-degree V8 with three main bearings. They used an L-head ('flathead') layout with both intake and exhaust valves in the block, hence, the popular name Ford Flathead V8. The block itself was cast as a single piece. Thus, the dream of a V8 engine car with the entire cylinders cast in one block was realised.

The Ford flathead V8 was perfectly in tune with the cultural moment of its introduction, leading the way into a future of which the Ford Motor Company was a principal architect. Ford Motor Company made the Ford flathead V8 affordable to the emerging mass market consumer for the first time. It was the first independently designed and built V8 engine produced by Ford for mass production, and it ranks as one of the company's most important developments. Henry Ford had put Americans on wheels and revolutionised the process of mass production. Thus, it became a phenomenal success. The Ford flathead V8 was licensed to other producers. It was used for cars by Simca in France till 1961 and in Brazil till 1964 while in the Simca Unic Marmon Bocquet military truck till 1990.

***Fig*.5: Ford Flathead V8**

Henry Ford saw no impossibility to the realisation of his vision. That is the Law of Faith. His faith allowed him to persist. That is the Principle of Perseverance, an integral step in the exercise of the Law of Faith (see Chapter 32). By persevering and refusing to give in to negative emotions of doubt and fear, Henry Ford was allowing the Reactive Unit of the intellectual faculty of his mind to search out a solution. The activated Reactive Unit stimulated his spirit man for creative ideas, which finally came. Indeed, patience is a virtue, and time is an invaluable resource in the use of our mind.

THINKING VERSUS WORRYING

The Reactive Unit of the intellect faculty is essential for rationalisation. Rationalisation is a significant component of the processing function of the mind. To rationalise is to think or brood over an issue. It is like a hen incubating over its eggs until they hatch. Productive thinking is the process of incubating over a matter until it hatches the desired results.

However, note that to think is not to worry. The two (thinking and worrying) are completely different. To worry is to be agitated due to fear, but to think is to rationalise for a solution. To worry is to be reactive to an event while to think is to be proactive to an event. Worry does not generate solutions to problems whereas thinking seeks for a solution; worry magnifies fears while thinking magnifies faith. Worry focuses your mind on the purported problems while thinking focuses your mind on possible solution. Thus, worry is a negative, retrogressive thought while thinking is a positive, progressive thought.

Table 1: Differences Between Thinking and Worrying		
	Thinking	**Worrying**
Definition	Mind rationalisation for a solution	Mind agitation from fear of a problem
Outcome	Magnifies faith	Magnifies fears
Responsiveness	Proactive to an event	Reactive to an event
Object of interest	Focuses on unravelling possible solutions	Focuses on purported problems
Kind of thought	Positive, progressive thought	Negative, retrogressive thought

FROM REACTIVETO IDEOLOGICAL UNIT

From the Reactive Unit, the processed thought passes unto the Ideological Unit of the intellectual faculty. The processed thought in the Ideological Unit will become impressed in the mind. That is, it becomes implanted just as a fertilised embryo becomes implanted in the uterus. Such an implanted processed thought is what is called an *idea*.

Not all embryos grow into full term foetuses (some foetuses are spontaneously miscarried or aborted); in the same way, not all ideas grow into fruition. For the idea to grow into fruition, the mind must have agreed or accepted the thought. Those ideas that do not make intelligible sense to the mind are often rejected and discarded. Those ideas that make intelligible sense to the mind are passed onward to the other faculties of the mind.

Chapter 5
The Power of the Mind: Faculty of Imagination

What made Henry Ford to be insistent despite several times he was told by his team of engineers that it was impossible to cast an eight-cylinder gas engine block (V8) in one piece? The answer lies in the power of imaginative faculty! In his mind's eye, Ford had already seen the V8 motor driving on the streets of America.

Indeed, an important truth we must never forget is that God creates us to believe what we see. We may doubt what we hear, smell, taste and feel. But we don't doubt what we see. Indeed, 'seeing is believing.'

However, the 'seeing' here does not refer to the optical eye. It refers to the inner eye. The Imaginative Faculty is the eye of the mind just as the Eido Centre is the eye of the Spirit. With the Eido Centre we can see into the world of the spirit and receive messages. Such received messages are then passed to the mind for processing. Once in the mind, the intellectual faculty rationalises the message and forwards it to the imaginative faculty. The message in the imaginative faculty is presented in a pictorial format, creating a vivid impression in the mind.

WE DON'T DOUBT WHAT WE SEE!

As a way of illustrative analysis, let's examine what happened to Henry Ford. His spirit man was, no doubt, stimulated to receive creative thoughts, possibly by reason of his association with his friend, Thomas Edison. The creative thought must have been generated in his heart and passed to the eido centre of his spirit, where he could see vision of his V8. The creative thought in Ford's eido centre would appear in pictorial format. However, these pictorial images in the eido centre were not yet processed, hence, were really not yet intelligibly assimilated.

From the eido centre of Henry's spirit man, the creative thought then passed down to his mind, where his intellectual faculty must have rationalised the possibility of its actualisation. The creative thought had, thus, been rationalised into a workable idea, which was then transmitted to Henry's imaginative faculty. In the imaginative faculty, the creative idea appeared in pictorial forms, making Henry Ford to see clearly the V8 already driving on the streets of America.

The difference between the pictorial images in the eido centre of the spirit man and the pictorial images in the imaginative faculty of the mind is that the ones in the eido centre are not yet processed, hence, will not be very clear and intelligible to the individual unlike the pictorial images in the imaginative faculty that have been processed into more intelligible form. This explains why when we see a vision, it is often not very clear and meaningful until we sit down and analyse the vision, then it becomes quite clear, intelligible, and usable. Sadly, many people who receive or see visions don't realise this truth. Every vision you receive should be subjected to mind processing for it to become clear, intelligible, and applicable.

In other words, with his mind's eye, Henry Ford had already seen the end of his project even before it was physically available on earth. He couldn't doubt what he saw. Hence, failure was not an option. He burnt the bridge by refusing to produce anything else including the six-cylinder motor. He tried to communicate the vision to his team of engineers, but because they never saw what he saw, the engineers struggled to become identified with Henry Ford's dream. This is one of the dilemmas of visioners. Because others don't see what the visioner saw, they often find it difficult to go along with the vision of the visioner. Hence, oftentimes, visioners find themselves walking alone! That is one of the unpleasant prices to be paid for being a visioner; heroes walk alone It behoves on the visioner to try to communicate his vision in clear terms to his team and motivate and drive the team to go along with his vision, which task is often a difficult and gruesome one as shown by Ford's story.

The inner visual sense is so unique in the operation of the Law of Faith. You cannot muster adequate faith to push an idea into materialisation if you don't 'see' the success of the idea in your mind. The Faculty of Imagination of your mind is what makes the processed idea 'see-able.' Once you can see the idea clearly, intelligibly and practicably, you'll never doubt the success of the idea. You'll become more than persuaded to run with the vision despite what people will say or do; your faith will become charged up to realise what you see.

The last year of Jesus earthly ministry was an interesting and eventful one. At about age 33 years, Jesus had already seen His sacrificial death, burial, and resurrection. He knew beyond all doubts that He was to pass through that route. As a visioner, Jesus saw the glory ahead, hence, that empowered His faith to go through the torture of gruesome death!

> *"He (Jesus) was willing to die a shameful death on the cross because of the joy he knew would be his afterwards; and now he sits in the place of honour by the throne of God" (Heb.12:2 TLB).*

He told His disciples on three different occasions about His death. The first prediction was recorded in Mak.8:31-33, Mat.16:21-23, and Luk.9:21,22. The second prediction was recorded in Mak.9:30-32, Mat.17:22,23 and Luk.9;43-45; while the third prediction was reported in Mak.10:32-34, Mat.20:17-19 and Luk.18:31-33. He also told the Jews the same thing at various times (Joh.8:21; 12:23). Incidentally, no one understood Him. Even when Moses and Prophet Elijah appeared to Jesus on the Mount of Transfiguration to discuss His death, burial and resurrection, the disciples Peter, James and John who were there and heard the discussion, didn't understand Jesus (Luk.9:28-36). When Jesus, again, mentioned these coming events, Peter was ready to forbid Him from ever discussing such impending horrors. The disciples never saw the vision that Jesus had; hence, they found it difficult to go along with the vision of the Master.

Thus, when Jesus finally died and was buried, the disciples were all discouraged; they abandoned the cause, and went their separate ways. However, when they SAW the risen Lord Jesus, all doubts and fears disappeared and great faith took over as they powerfully witnessed and attested to His death, burial and resurrection; many of these disciples even allowed themselves to be killed for what they saw and knew was true. The witnessing soon shook the world and established the Church of God that is still thriving – over 2,000 years later (see SSB Book 6). Indeed, there is power in *vision* – we don't doubt what we see!

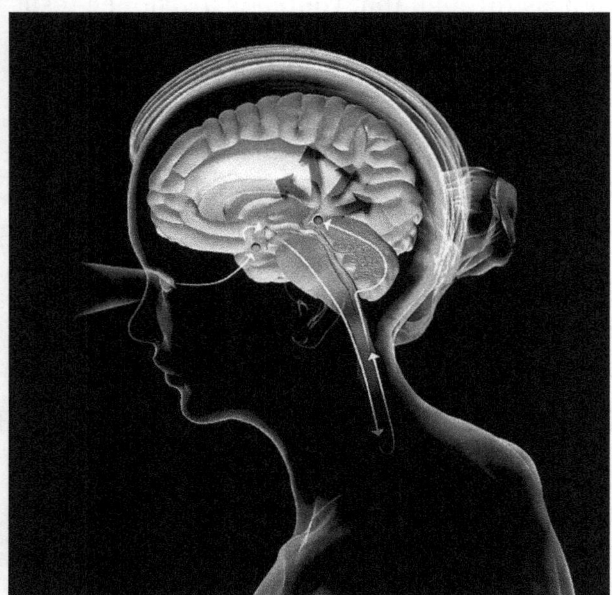

***Fig*.6: Indeed, an important truth we must never forget is that God creates us to believe what we see. We may doubt what we hear, smell, taste and feel. But we don't doubt what we see. Indeed, 'seeing is believing.'**

However, the 'seeing' here does not refer to the optical eye. It refers to the inner eye. Once you can 'see' an idea clearly, intelligibly and practicably, you'll never doubt the success of the idea.

POWER OF IMAGINATION – INTERESTING STORY

An interesting story of the power of imagination is told in Genesis chapter 11. After Noah's Flood, people started to multiply again on earth. Since they all spoke one language, there was easy flow of communication amongst them. Their leader, apparently Nimrod the great hunter (see SSB Book 4), conceived an idea, which became vivid in his mind. The idea was communicated in clear terms to others:

> *"Come, let's build a great city for ourselves with a tower that reaches into the sky. This will make us famous and keep us from being scattered all over the world" (Gen.11:4 NLT).*

They started implementing their idea by burning bricks, quarried stones and made mortars ready to build. That action attracted God, who *"came down to look at the city and the tower the people were building"* (Gen.11:5 NLT).

On inspecting the building project, God, who created humans and knew the human frame, uttered a profound statement of truth that reveals the power of imagination:

> *"And the Lord said, Behold, they are one people and they have all one language; and this is only the beginning of what they will do, and now* ***nothing they have imagined they can do will be impossible for them****" (Gen.11:6 AMPC).*

Indeed, 'nothing you have imagined you can do will be impossible for you.' The imaginative faculty exudes power that turns impossibility to possibility. How this works is that the imaginative faculty converts ideas into pictorial format for visualisation. The visualised image in our mind triggers the force of faith, and with faith all things are possible. Such vivid image eliminates fears and doubts since we don't doubt what we see.

What Nimrod and his people were doing was against divine plan for man to spread across the earth; it was not God's plan for man to be confined to one region of the earth. The only way God could thwart this plan of Nimrod and his people was to stop the flow of communication of the vision among them. God did this by giving them different languages so that the people couldn't understand each other any longer. By so doing, confusion set in and the flow of communication of ideas was interrupted. That was how the Tower of Babel project was thwarted by divine hand.

The lesson here is that individuals who have learnt to utilise the imaginative force of the mind at will often bath in creativity and innovation, making them to rise in the pinnacle of success. That is one secret of the so-called geniuses. In fact, if you underrate the power of the Imaginative Faculty, you'll end up living an average life, quite below your potentials.

Chapter 6
The Power of the Mind: Faculties of Memory, Willpower and Emotions

All the five faculties of the mind play dominant impact in the outcome of our lives. The power of the faculties of the intellect and imagination on our lives has been discussed in the two previous chapters. This chapter reviews briefly the power of the faculties of memory, willpower, and emotions.

THE POWER OF FACULTY OF MEMORY

The memory faculty is the storage centre of the mind. Its power lies in the fact that it is a supply centre for the other four faculties of the mind. The memory faculty is the storage bank for the myriad information that comes to us. In some cases, such information is not required immediately. However, when needed, the mind has a way of recalling the information from its storage bank.

A good memory is a great asset. In fact, most times intelligence is measured by not just the rationalising keenness of the intellectual faculty, but how fast and well an individual is able to recall past information. Brilliance at school has more to do with the memory faculty; the more a student is able to recall what he studies, the higher his chances of passing his exams.

The memory faculty consists of three units or components – *Registration, Storage and Retrieval units* (see the SSB Book 1, for detailed discussion). These units appear to have unlimited elastic capacity for receiving, storing, and retrieving information.

However, despite the unlimited elastic capacity of the mind for information reception, storage and retrieval, the mind gets tired from monotony. Flooding the mind with a particular pattern of information will cause saturation end-point, where the mind won't be interested in further assimilation of that particular pattern of information. This is referred to as ***memory block*** or ***memory fatigue***.

Memory fatigue occurs when the memory faculty is actively engaged and bombarded with a particular type of information with no room for recreation. This occurs a lot among students, who want to force in all the information without recourse to recreation. Indeed, recreational exercises free the mind from its preoccupied information and allow it to imbibe new sets of information. The good news is that memory block is usually a temporal thing, and it goes away once the mind is rested a bit.

Mind fatigue is not only seen in students but also at places of work. Doing a particular assignment over and over a time can induce mind fatigue. When mind fatigue occurs, productivity is lowered. Hence, intelligent managers design their work schedule to allow time each day for other activities. Unnecessary strictness to work schedules and study timetables has been shown to reduce efficiency and effectiveness. Indeed, 'all work without play makes Jack a dull boy.' A stitch in time saves nine!

THE POWER OF FACULTY OF WILLPOWER

Our willpower is what finally determines what gets done. This is because the willpower faculty is what energises our body to initiate and take the necessary steps in line with the vision of our heart and mind. It is of no use entertaining an idea that eventually would not be executed. How much we are motivated to execute our ideas is dependent how much of the force of faith has been stimulated. The ultimate drive of the force of faith is to push our willpower into action and the willpower compels our body to take the corresponding steps. If you are not motivated enough to take action steps in line with your idea, it simply means you are yet to see clearly the benefits such an execution of the idea will bring into your life, and such an idea will not come to fruition because no action has been taken to bring it to pass.

The willpower of the mind is usually the last lap in the processing function of the mind. By the time the idea has been processed through the mind and gets to the willpower faculty, it means it is time for execution. The willpower faculty energises the human body to initiate the corresponding steps that will force the idea into materialisation. A weak willpower for a particular idea is often due to lack of motivation, which is borne from lack of faith to drive for execution, and the lack of faith is as a result of lack of clarity of the vision, such as clarity of the benefits of what the idea holds.

THE STORY OF KARON

Karon was a primary and secondary schoolmate of mine, whose love for flying knew no bounds. We grew up together; his house was opposite ours. In those days, you could literally hear the song of a desire to be a pilot on Karon's lips at all times. Incidentally, the resources to pursue this dream were not lacking as Karon's father was among the richest in the state/province. That was between 1970s and 1990s.

Sadly, Karon's dream died with him as he failed to attain his desire of becoming a pilot. Like it happens to many, Karon's ambition to fly the aircraft was swept away by the exigencies of life he exposed himself to – remarkably, excesses of youthful exuberance. He could not focus on his studies; he was more into partying and socializing. By mid-90s, Karon found himself increasingly driven away from his life dream.

This was not because he lacked the intelligence, opportunities, or wherewithal to determinably pursue his desire of becoming a pilot. His ordeal was simply lack of the discipline or willpower to focus and pursue his dream. In his innermost being, Karon knew what to do in life, which was to become a pilot; but he lacked the resolute willpower of the mind to carry out his heart's desire.

Indeed, Karon's chances of realising his ambition to fly the aircraft became increasingly remote as he entered his late 20s. The last time I heard from him was in early 1990s while we sat in my room in the medical hostel, where he was still inundating me with his dream of becoming a pilot; yet he was still not ready to cut down his excessive youthful exuberance and face his dream. It turned out a dream that would remain unfulfilled; a dream that would be buried with the dreamer! Karon died, having contracted the dreaded HIV infection with its complications. His dream was buried with him and never saw the light of the day to bless humanity! His family was utterly devastated. What a painful outcome! All because he failed to cultivate the willpower of his mind to discipline his body for pursuit of his heart's desire.

THE POWER OF FACULTY OF EMOTIONS

As discussed in SSB Book 1, love, joy, peace and all other fruits of the spirit are deposits in the heart of the spirit man. However, these deposits in the heart of man are expressed through the mind of the soul. The emotional faculty specifically expresses this varied range of emotions.

All the basic human emotions of the soul can be grouped into five classes: ***Adrenergic, Apathetic, Decelerating, Exhilarating,*** and ***Penitential*** emotions (see SSB Book 1). The expressions of these emotions have untold impact on our lives. Many have taken decisions in the height of emotional instability and ended up regretting all through their lives.

Many men and women have been sentenced to prison because of regrettable actions done in a fit of uncontrolled anger. Many great accomplishments have been raced down by the rage of men.

Many women have destroyed their homes and their lives due to uncontrolled emotion of jealousy.

THE SAD STORY OF EMPEROR NERO'S LIFE

When Nero (AD 37-68) ascended to the throne as Emperor of Rome, he had a challenge – poor control over his emotions. With absolute power, his lack of emotional control led to an epiphany of rage and jealousy that resulted in the tyrannical killings almost unrivalled in human history. In fits of rage, he executed his mother, Agrippina, his wife, Octavia, his stepbrother, Britannicus, a number of his senators, and an unaccounted number of Christians.

According to the Roman historian, Gaius Suetonius Tranquillus (c. AD 69-122), Nero *"showed neither discrimination nor moderation in putting to death whomsoever he pleased"* (The Lives of the Twelve Caesars – *the Life of Nero* 37.1) during his reign. His lack of emotional control not only ruined his governance but also ended up killing him at age 30 when he committing suicide, the first Roman emperor to ever do so.

Indeed, inappropriate application of emotions unleashes mayhem, destruction, and even death. The opposite is true when emotions are controlled and directed for productive venture; positively channelled emotions have the power to drive a man along the path of his vision unto success. Emotions have power, never doubt that.

THE MIND HAS NO LIMIT

In summary, the forces of the mind are very crucial to our success in life. Any thought that flows through the intellect, imagination, memory, and willpower faculties, only becomes an energetic idea when it is mixed with appropriate emotions from the Faculty of Emotion. That is, thought will remain a plain and plastic idea until it is given feelings to it. An emotionalised thought is what awakens the dormant, restful mind. Napoleon Hill vividly captures the power of emotions on human's life when he writes:

> *"The world is ruled, and the destiny of civilisation is established, by the human emotions. People are influenced in their actions, not by reason so much as by 'feeling.' ...All thoughts which have been emotionalised (giving feeling) and mixed with faith, begin immediately to translate themselves into their physical equivalent or counterpart...Thoughts which are mixed with any of the feelings of emotions, constitute a 'magnetic' force..."*
>
> *(Think and Grow Rich, 1938, pages 48,51,184).*

Simply put, there is more to the mind of man than we all know. Napoleon submits his conclusion by succinctly articulates the power of the mind on a man's life with this statement:

> *"There are no limitations to the mind except those we acknowledge" (Think and Grow Rich, page 65).*

Indeed, the day a man realises his mind has no limit and that the only limitation is the one he places on himself, he'll be setting himself free to explore the rich endowments enclosed within his nature by his Creator.

Chapter 7
Mind Activation

THE MIND IS IN A restful state until it is activated. The restful mind is the ***Inertial Mind***. One common trait with the human nature is that we all love comfort zone. No one will like to be dislodged from his comfort zone, where he feels his life has attained some level of success and equilibrium. But without venturing out from that comfort zone, how can we access better things that still lie in our destiny path?

An inertial mind is at its comfort zone. 'Inertia' comes from the Latin word *iners*, which literally means 'idleness or sluggishness.' A man with an inertial mind is one who feels contented with his status quo. In other words, he is unable to see the next level of a higher calling. If he does see the next level, he is passive, docile and unwilling to make the required movement that will place him in that higher level.

The characteristic of an inertial mind is that it resists any change to its uniform motion. Such a mind is idle and sluggish, which is the state of many people. Humans are created for continuous advancement; we are created to continuously make progress. However, the fallen human nature is often pleased with an inertial mind.

DANDISON'S BUNGALOW

The truth is that our comfort zone today becomes a discomfort tomorrow if we don't move with time. While growing up in the 1970s, Mr. Dandison's bungalow stood out in shining white, adorned with colourful brick walls. Amidst some zinc houses and patched mud huts, Dandison's house sparkled out. It was built with the colonial era taste, beautiful and glittering to our young eyes in the town, Ataba, where we grew up. As kids, we would dream and would talk how we would have such a beautiful 'edifice' someday! I still remember how Mr. Dandison would rest at the balcony and wave out to passers-by, apparently savouring the accolades his beautiful house had generated.

By the early 80s, new houses surfaced in the town. No one seemed to notice the beauty of Dandison's house again. Mr. Dandison had repainted his house to adorn it with more beauty. However, the truth was that the newer houses outclassed Dandison's house in sophistication, quality, and beauty so much that no amount of refurbishing could make Dandison's house comparable with these new ones. It was either that Mr. Dandison would have to accept the new downgraded status of his house or build a new house to match the modern taste if he still wanted to be a reference point.

Dandison's house was a graphical illustration of our life destinies. A man who chooses to remain at a spot and does not take the appropriate steps to advance in his life endeavours is relegating his mind to inertia. Soon he'll realise that time has passed on and his comfort zone has become increasingly discomforting.

SUBCONSCIOUS MIND

A thought process that is emotionalised (given feeling to) has the capacity to stimulate the restful, inertial mind into an active state. In other words, the mind remains restful and even dormant until an emotionalised thought acts on it. Plain, unemotional thoughts do not activate the mind.

However, once a thought process is given feeling, such emotionalised thought acts on the mind, activating it into a dynamic state. An activated mind is a dynamic mind; it is a mind that is energetic and productive. An activated mind has the capacity to interact with the world of the spirit, which interaction often results in productivity. Simply put, an activated mind is what is popularly referred to as the ***subconscious mind*** (or ***subconsciousness***, for short). That is, an activated mind is one that has been awoken from its inertial state; it is an inertial mind stimulated into a subconscious state.

SIGNIFICANCE OF MIND ACTIVATION

When a man 'sees' his bright future, he becomes restless until he takes practical steps that will propel him into that future. The stronger the emotions evoked in him by the foreseen future, the more agitated he becomes to see it accomplished. Until the future becomes a reality, he remains restless. What triggers such restlessness and agitation in him is his activated mind.

As a young boy, I was a voracious reader. Before I knew how to read at age seven, I always took my Bible to my Papa, as we used to call our dad, to read it for me. My dad would read some interesting stories about some Bible characters. However, he noticed my keen interest, and apparently was not comfortable with my excitement about Bible stories, hence, stylishly would give excuses for not reading the Bible stories for me. At the Anglican Church I attended, I would pummel the Sunday school teacher with questions and questions in our children class about Jesus, Heaven and the Bible.

Thankfully, by age seven, I could read and understand a bit. By age nine, my vocabulary had increased and I could understand most things that I read. With that feat, it was like the world was open before me! I read and read everything I could see. I had covered the

Bible from Genesis to Revelation page to page by age nine and again at age 10. At Easter and Christmas periods when we often received gifts like clothes from parents and other family members, I would bargain with my dad to rather buy me books as gifts.

As I read, I never knew that the words would impact on me. I enjoyed reading biographies. Stories of great achievers like Biblical Moses, David, and Jesus Christ, and non-Biblical characters like Albert Einstein, Thomas Edison, William Shakespeare, Charles Dickens and many other popular characters impacted me. I started 'seeing' a future beyond my present environments. I saw beyond the poverty, limitation, disease, etc. that encompassed around me. The more I read, the clearer I saw. I became so motivated and excited about the bright future I saw that I started making statements that earned me ridicule from my schoolmates. Statements like: "As God sent Jesus to salvage the world, so I am sent to my generation;" "I am special;" and such utterances. My classmates in the primary school would laugh, but they never knew I wasn't joking.

The future I saw propelled me to rise forward. When apparently there was no physical way, yet the foreseen future kept me restless. Without such clear sight, I would have been in the village with my mates bemoaning my 'fate.' One of the 'future' I saw was to become a medical doctor. Based on my background and circumstances, there was practically no way such dream could be realised. There was no ready source of finances to pursue the dream. I was not able to attend a good school, and there were no teachers for some science subjects in my school at that time. Moreover, I often went hungry for lack of food, a situation worsened by the sudden death of my dad – the family breadwinner.

Nonetheless, the clear future I saw elicited such powerful emotions in me. The emotions stimulated my mind into hyperactivity not to accept the status quo and the circumstantial limitations. Indeed, the power of my activated mind could be so strong that I would become physically restless, tossing up and down and moving about my room agitatedly, speaking words of power and hope to myself. In a few times that my brothers saw me in such mood, they thought I was going crazy. That is the power of an activated mind. It keeps you restless until you move in the direction of the 'seen' future.

The point here is that no matter the awesomeness of a vision, it will remain mere thought in the heart of the visioner until it is passed down to his mind for processing into a functional idea. Once such a processed idea becomes emotionalised (that is, mixed with appropriate emotions), it is then capable of activating the mind into its subconscious state. It is the activated mind that triggers the needed faith from the heart of man to bring the vision into physical reality.

Great achievers, so-called geniuses, operate at the level of subconsciousness. Such great achievers have discovered how to activate their minds and, hence, tune into their subconsciousness from where they derive their inspiration and creativity. Indeed, if you really desire to have outstanding achievements in life, you must understand and know how to activate or tune your mind into its subconscious state.

Chapter 8
How to Activate the Mind

THE MIND CAN BE ACTIVATED by a conscious act. Great achievers in various fields of human endeavours have learnt to do this. You don't need to wait for 'something' to activate your mind for you; you can do that by conscious practice. Conscious activation of the mind is achieved principally by the practice of ***meditation***.

Through meditation, the Reactive Unit of the intellect faculty of the mind is stimulated to analyse and synthesize facts that will birth a specific thought, referred to as an idea. As the meditation process continues, the birthed idea is converted into a visual image in the imaginative faculty; that is, the idea becomes pictorial. The pictorial idea stimulates the appropriate emotions. The emotionalised idea or thought can activate the mind, and an activated mind inspires the force of faith to galvanise the mind's willpower faculty, which in turn energises the body into taking the necessary corresponding steps that ultimately result in the desired solution.

WHAT IS MEDITATION?

Meditation is the repeated pondering over a matter until illumination is achieved. To meditate is to deliberately ponder, consider, or contemplate on an issue until the desired answer is obtained. Meditation is akin to the feeding process of ruminant animals.

Most herbivorous ruminant animals like goats have four stomachs – rumen, reticulum, omasum, and abomasum. The rumen is the first stomach and it is connected directly with the oesophagus (throat). When eating their vegetable meal, they chew it as much as they can and as fast as their mouth can carry. The chewed food, usually not properly masticated, first goes to their first stomach, the rumen, where it is partially degraded by some enterobacteria and enzymes that are found there to form semi-solid masses popularly known as cud.

During resting, the cud will be drawn up or regurgitated from the rumen back to the mouth by the process of retro-peristalsis. With its tongue and palate, the ruminant animal will squeeze out the fluid from the cud and re-swallow the fluid while the solid masses are then chewed into more fine particles before they are swallowed again. This whole process of chewing, swallowing, regurgitation, re-chewing and re-swallowing is referred to as *rumination*.

Ruminant animals may spend up to eight hours per day in rumination, depending on the type of feed. The animals derive immense benefits from the rumination phenomenon as it reduces the particle sizes of the feed through re-chewing thereby allowing the food materials to be easily accessible to the microorganisms and to pass out of the rumen to the three remaining stomachs for easy digestion, absorption and assimilation. In addition, rumination allows the animals to eat as much as they can and store the food away for a time when it will be required for energy production and cellular maintenance of the body.

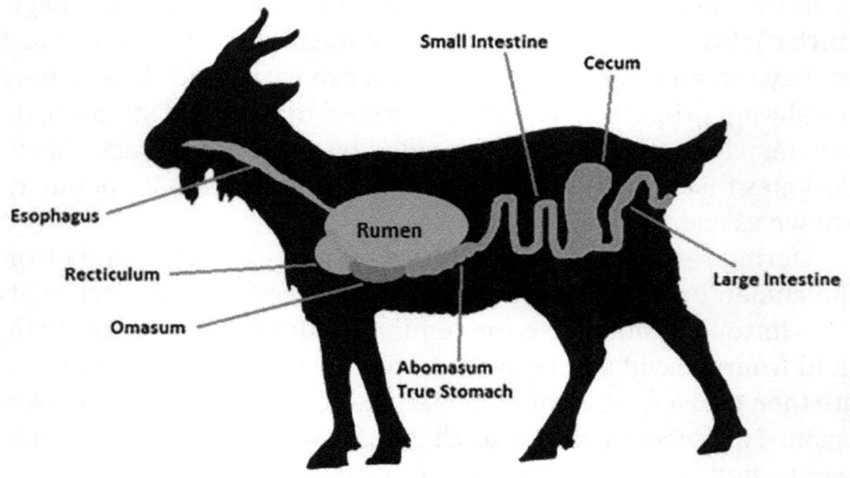

***Fig.*7: The Basic Anatomy of an herbivorous ruminant animal, e.g. goat, showing the rumination pathway. Ruminant animals may spend up to 8 hours per day in rumination, which is the process of chewing, swallowing, regurgitation, re-chewing and re-swallowing. Simply put, meditation is rumination.**

MEDITATION – KEY FOR ACTIVATING THE MIND

Simply put, meditation is rumination. It is the process of chewing, swallowing, regurgitation; re-chewing and re-swallowing of the information cud until the mind becomes illuminated. Illumination refers to the activation of the mind to procure the needed solution. An illuminated mind is an activated mind.

Meditation is the key for activating the mind to search for an answer. The Bible says a lot about the significance of meditation in the pursuit of success.

> *"This Book of the Law shall not depart from your mouth, but you shall meditate [hagah] in it day and night, that you may observe to do according to all that is written in it. For then you will make your way prosperous, and then you will have good success" (Jos.1:8 NKJV).*

Again, meditation gives illumination. An illuminated mind is an activated mind. The Hebrew word for meditation in the Old Testament Scriptures is *hagah* while the Greek term for meditation in the New Testament Scriptures is *meletao*.

Hagah occurs 25 times in 24 verses in the Old Testament Scriptures while *meletao* occurs 3 times in 3 verses in the New Testament Scriptures; their multiple occurrences underscore the significance of meditation in human's drive for success.

Chapter 9
The Three Phases of Meditation for Mind Activation

THE TRUTH THAT THE MIND can be activated by a conscious act into its subconscious state cannot be overemphasized. Meditation is the principal means for mind activation. According to the Scriptures, meditation (Hebrew: *hagah* or Greek: *meletao*) has three components or phases:

PHASE ONE MEDITATION: STUDY

This means to think, analyse, synthesize, weigh, or devise. Phase one meditation is when an individual sits down and seriously considers the matter; it is when the individual critically and unbiasedly studies the matter at hand. He allows his mind to go wild, thinking or contemplating on the situation.

> *"Think [meletao] on these things. Devote your life to them so that everyone can see your progress" (1Tim.4:15 ISV).*

> *"The heart of the righteous studies [hagah] how to answer, but the mouth of the wicked pours forth evil" (Pro.15:28 NKJV).*

Nothing is really impossible in life! That is the truth of life. Impossibility simply means our inability to critically study the situation through critical thinking analysis and synthesis. What we don't know today only reveals the limited depth of our knowledge.

As we become adept in knowledge, what we don't know suddenly pales away. For instance, before 1796, man did not have an answer to the draconic smallpox that killed a minimum of 300 million people in each century until the invention of immunization by Edward Jenner (1749-1823) in 1796. The knowledge of immunisation suddenly allowed the smallpox to be eradicated in 1979 from the world.

Today the only places where smallpox could be seen in the world are the Centers for Disease Control and Prevention in Atlanta, USA, and the State Research Center of Virology and Biotechnology Vector in Koltsovo, Novosibirsk Oblast, Russia, where some pus samples of smallpox are kept in highly secured laboratories. These pus samples of smallpox are reminders to humanity that nothing is impossible; what is impossible today is because of our ignorance. Tomorrow, as we acquire more inspirational knowledge, we'll look back and laugh at our past ignorance.

Practising Phase One Meditation

For Phase One Meditation to be productive, you need to do the following:

(i) Practise inner quietness
This involves maintaining inner tranquillity. Consciously practise inner quietness. Man is inbuilt with the ability to exercise control. Take your eyes off from the environmental turmoil, and practise being still in your inside. At first, it may seem difficult; but as you persist, you'll learn the beauty of being in control of yourself and not allow situations to overwhelm you. One way I do this is to fill my day with the Presence of God. I study my Bible and inspired books of my mentors that deal on the challenges I face. I talk to God in prayers, speak to my spirit, soul, and body, telling them what I need. I talk to the environments and negative forces using my authority in Jesus Name. These put me in total control of my day. It makes me

not to be agitated and fearful. Maintaining inner tranquillity is the first step to obtaining answers to challenges.

A rowdy and crowded mind cannot focus and contemplate adequately. Learning to maintain quietness in your inner self is a virtue that every successful person cultivates and practices. All great achievers, without exception, are individuals who know the value of inner tranquillity. They don't jump into conversation because everyone is talking. They maintain a quiet disposition, and many ignorant people misconstrue such quietness to be anti-social. Indeed, heroes walk alone. One reason for this lonesomeness in heroes is the practice of quietness.

(ii) Maximise *Ruwach* Time

A number of crucial decisions are often made in the quietness of the day, which is usually early hours of the morning or at dusk. Most of great mind illumination occurs at this period: early morning (from 00H00 to about 06H00) or at dusk (from 18H00 to 24H00). In other words, from 6pm to 6am is often a crucial moment in decision making. Study through the Scriptures, and you'll see that major life-changing decisions and events occur at this time interval, such as the followings:

- the Fall of Man in the Garden of Eden occurred at this time (Gen.3:8)
- God's covenant with Abraham that would bring the desired Messiah was made at this time (Gen.15:12-20)
- the destruction of the immoral cities of Sodom and Gomorrah took place at this time (Gen. chpt. 19)
- Moses' encounter with God that delivered divine mandate for Israel's liberation from a 430-year slavery was at this time (Exo. chpt. 3)
- God's judgment on the Egyptian gods and Egyptian firstborns that finally liberated the Israelites from the 430-year slavery was made at this time (Exo. chpt. 12)

- the introduction and establishment of the Ten Commandment that formed the constitution of Israel was at this time (Exo. chpt. 34)
- the Fall of Samson took place at this time (Judg.16:1-21)
- Jesus made the most important decision in His earthly ministry of choosing His twelve disciples at this time after spending all night praying to decipher the will of God on who to choose (Luk.6:12-16)
- crucial miracles and teaching of Jesus occurred at this time (Joh.8:2).
- crucial decision of Satanic human agents to arrest Jesus was made at this time (Mat. chpt. 26)
- Jesus Last Supper and the institution of the Communion Table were made at this time (Mat.26:20-30)
- the burial of Jesus occurred at this time (Mat.27:57-60)
- the resurrection of Jesus occurred at this time (Mat.28:1-10; Mak.16:1-8)
- the Ascension of Jesus occurred at this time (Act. chpt. 1).
- the Birth of the Church with the outpouring of the Holy Ghost happened at this time (Act. chpt. 2)
- Paul's second missionary journey, which was the most productive of his three missions, was unveiled to him by the Holy Ghost during this time (Act.16:6-10). In fact, there is every reason to believe that his ordination as the missionary to the Gentiles took place at this time (Act.13:1-3).

We can go on and on. Most likely, the first human Adam arrived on earth between 6am and 6pm, and the second human, Eve, must have also arrived on earth at this time. Gideon, David, and indeed, all great heroes of faith utilised this time period in advancing their life courses. In the same manner, negative forces tend to hold sway during this time period. For instance, most occult manipulations take place at this time.

Obviously, these events and many others did not occur at this time by chance. God who created the universe knows the significance of this time period (6pm to 6am). I refer to this time period as the *Ruwach* Time. Ruwach is a Hebrew word translated severally such as 'cool of the day (Gen.3:8), spirit (Gen.6:3), breath (Gen.7:15), wind (Gen.8:1), and mind (Gen.26:35).' Ruwach Time is a crucial time period for any individual who wants to maximise his destiny spiritually, mentally, and physically. Abraham, Isaac, Moses, and indeed, all great heroes of faith were individuals who utilised Ruwach Time for their benefits.

> *"And Isaac went out to meditate in the field* ***in the evening****; and he lifted his eyes and looked, and there, the camels were coming"*
> *(Gen.24:63 NKJV).*

> *"Now it was during this time that Jesus went out to the mountain to pray, and he* ***spent all night*** *in prayer to God. When* ***morning*** *came, he called his disciples and chose twelve of them, whom he also named apostles" (Luk.6:12,13 NET).*

Significant Lesson

The significant lesson here is that it pays greatly to invest your meditation moment at this Ruwach Time, especially when you are faced with important decision or searching for an answer to a boggling life issue. At such moment, it is not the period to sleep all through the night. It is time to wake up and utilise the *Ruwach Time.*

Great achievers are never lazy. They don't sleep all through the nights each day. An interesting observation is that employees generally are the ones that sleep all through the nights. Employers of labour, captains of industries, and outstanding inventors of note maximise the night season and early morning hours. They make crucial decisions during *Ruwach Time.* This observation is a powerful insight, and the decision is left to an individual to determine which group he must belong to, either an employee or an employer of labour.

The Bible encourages the maximisation of *Ruwach Time* for advancement in life. Check up the following Scriptures:

> *"The Lord God has given me his words of wisdom so that I may know what I should say to all these weary ones.* ***Morning by morning he wakens me and opens my understanding to his will****" (Isa.50:4 TLB).*

> *"Day unto day utters speech, and* **night unto night reveals knowledge***" (Psa.19:2 NKJV).*

> *"I love them who love me; and* ***they who wake up early to seek me, shall find me****" (Pro.8:17 WYC).*

PHASETWO MEDITATION: IMAGINE

To Meditate is also translated as 'to imagine' in the Scriptures.

> *"They also that seek after my life lay snares for me: and they that seek my hurt speak mischievous things, and imagine [hagah] deceits all the day long" (Psa.38:12 KJV).*

> *"Who by the mouth of thy servant David hast said, Why did the heathen rage, and the people imagine [meletao] vain things?"*
> *(Act.4:25 KJV).*

Phase One Meditation involves the conscious stimulation of the intellectual faculty while Phase Two Meditation is the conscious stimulation of the imaginative and emotional faculties of the mind. That is, whereas the Phase One Mediation targets primarily the intellectual faculty, Phase Two Meditation targets both the imaginative and emotional faculties.

The Aspects of Phase Two Meditation

Thus, there are two aspects of Phase Two Meditation:

(a) Pictorialisation of Thought
To practise Phase Two mediation, consciously let your mind try to visualise the issue as you ponder over it. Just as Phase One is a conscious determination to reflect on an issue, in the same way Phase Two requires conscious reflection. However, whereas Phase One is reflection focused on intellectual analysis and synthesis, Phase Two focuses on visualisation and emotionalisation of thoughts.

In those days when it was practically impossible for me to gain admission into medical school, one exercise I often engaged in was to close my eyes and see myself as a doctor working in a big hospital. Sometimes I would spend a considerable part of my afternoon swimming in an ocean of visual perception of becoming a medical doctor. As I repeatedly did this, I realised that my mind was strongly becoming influenced to believe that the dream of becoming a doctor was, after all, realisable.

Indeed, Phase Two is when you let the faculty of imagination of your mind to become stimulated by consciously trying to hold a picture of the thought or information in your mind. In other words, through meditation, the imaginative faculty is stimulated to create a visual image of the thought. At first the whole exercise may be difficult, especially if you have been living in a sensual realm of feelings for a long time of your life without paying close attention to your mental and spiritual development. But if you really desire to be successful and to go beyond your present circumstance, then you have no option than to pay the price of this required sacrifice. Simply put, you just have to be practising this exercise until you have mastered the process. By repeatedly engaging in meditation, you are stimulating your dormant mind, and it will grow with such usage. If you don't give up, you'll be pleasantly surprised how well you have developed mentally.

(b) Emotionalisation of Thought
During my teenage years, after my father had died and there was no seeming way to realise my dream, I would close my eyes and picture the fulfilment of my dream. As I closed my eyes and pictured myself a doctor, I realised my emotions were being stimulated also. Such exercises would arouse my emotions beyond measure. I became more and more passionate about the thought of becoming a medical practitioner, and a driving force would be generated in me that pushed me to believe nothing on earth could stop the realisation of my dream. Then I didn't quite understand it: the truth was that I was activating my mind for the realisation of my dream of becoming a medical practitioner by thought pictorialisation and emotionalisation, which collectively constitute the Phase Two Meditation.

Joe in Nazi Camp

When Joe was captured and incarcerated by the Nazis in a concentration camp in Germany, he had a wife and two young children left behind. Every morning, he and the other prisoners would be marched out and subjected to inhumane treatment. Being beaten with rods and military boots, hard manual labour, verbal and psychological abuse coupled with perennial hunger and poor hygiene, these gruesomely horrific hardships started having grave toll on their minds. Every day a prisoner died and the rest would be forced to bury the dead in shallow grave and abandon the corpse to rot away. Many lost all hope of survival. Their willpower was shattered as they constantly witnessed each day a prisoner perished away.

However, Joe's willpower could not be broken. He held a vision in his mind. According to him, he would picture himself being reunited with his wife and two children. He would see with his mind eye a lovely family life, embraced and being embraced by his wife, two children, and well-wishers. This visualisation would rouse up strong emotions in him, causing him to have the faith that he would be reunited with his family. At the height of inhuman degradation in the concentration camp, he would recoil into this visual and emotional exercise, bathing in the euphoria that energised his survival willpower. This would temporally make him to be numb to the hardship and frustrations. At the end, virtually all the prisoners in that camp died, and only less than 5 percent survived the gruesome ordeal. Joe was one of the survivors from this camp!

The Unfathomable Capabilities of the Mind

The human mind and spirit have unfathomable capabilities, far more than we think. When triggered, such enormous capabilities can be utilised for survival and advancement. Phase Two Meditation is one sure way to trigger the unfathomable capabilities of the human mind and spirit. The visual capability coupled with appropriate emotions can trigger the unquenchable force of faith. It is by this exercise that many great achievers were able to transmute their desires into physical profits, and rise from penury to affluence. By it, we can obtain our hearts desires and it can harden us up in the day of battle.

To stimulate the emotional faculty, the mind must first see and like what it sees. If you cannot see with your mind's eye and have a liking for what you see, it will be difficult to muster faith to pursue the idea. Interestingly, repeated visualisation has a way of whipping up appropriate emotions with time. For example, there are many people that got married and soon thought that they had made a mistake. Love has died and all forms of affection in a relationship have faded. However, when such individuals meditate on what they actually need in marriage, focusing on the good qualities, even if they were infinitesimal, of their mate and picture a good lovely marriage, with time the mind will pick up appropriate emotions, and affection can be restored in such relationships. This has worked a great deal for many couples, and that leads to the concept of autosuggestion, which is the Phase Three of Meditation.

PHASE THREE MEDITATION: UTTER

Meditation also involves to repeatedly utter, mutter, speak, or roar.

> *"But when they arrest you and deliver you up, do not worry beforehand, or premeditate [meletao] what you will speak. But whatever is given you in that hour, speak that; for it is not you who speak, but the Holy Spirit" (Mar.13:11 NKJV).*

> *"My lips shall not speak wickedness, nor my tongue utter [hagar] deceit" (Job 27:4 KJV).*

Phase One Meditation is rationalisation, Phase Two is visualisation and emotionalisation, while Phase Three is verbalisation. Verbalisation means to speak forth or to utter. It can mean muttering under your breath, contemplative musing or moaning of words. As you become intoxicated with the idea, the emotions can drive you beyond words like a crazy individual and roaring like a young lion over its prey. That is the power of meditation!

> *"For thus hath the LORD spoken unto me, Like as the lion and the young lion roaring [hagah] on his prey, when a multitude of shepherds is called forth against him, he will not be afraid of their voice, nor abase himself for the noise of them: so shall the LORD of hosts come down to fight for mount Zion, and for the hill thereof" (Isa.31:4 KJV).*

In those days of physical helplessness with no visible human assistance forthcoming in the pursuit of my medical dream, as I meditated, visualising myself becoming a medical practitioner, the picture would be so intoxicating and the emotions so driving. I would be literally tossed about, speaking under my breath with words like: "I must become a doctor," "No force in hell can stop me," "I enter medical school and graduate as a medical practitioner," .... Sometimes the emotions would be so driving that I would blast out in high tone, roaring like a lion, anyone seeing me at that time would think I was getting nuts. I usually practised the meditation all alone when no one was around to distract me. At one evening, I never knew my dad was standing behind me while I got enthralled roaring out. When I realised his presence he looked so disturbed, apparently wondering what I was doing because I was mixing the words with the Holy Ghost-induced 'speaking in tongues.' It was during those moments that I made a desperate vow to give to God all of my first salary as a doctor once I graduated; a vow I fulfilled.

Indeed, the power of visualisation and emotionalisation can be so driving and pushing that it would force the mouth to start speaking words beyond your natural comprehension. Any man that had been gripped by the Force of Faith, which was triggered by the visualisation and emotionalisation of meditation, would confirm to you how driving it could be, especially when such faith is rooted in the Scriptures and engineered by the Spirit of God. Never underrate the power of meditation as a prerequisite for triggering the force of faith.

Warning: Never allow your tongue to utter words not in harmony with the visualised thought, for that will send conflicting messages to your mind and spirit, and this deadens the force of faith. Meditation is the practice that disciplines your tongue to utter words that line up with the visualised thought.

> *"For my mouth shall speak [hagah] truth; and wickedness is an abomination to my lips" (Pro 8:7 KJV).*

Autosuggestion

In psychology, Phase Three of meditation is what is known as *autosuggestion*, and it is when you consciously insert words of your desire into your mind by speaking to yourself. For the words to be effective and efficient; that is, be able to activate the mind into its subconscious state, they must have four characteristics:

- personalised
- specific
- forceful
- emotionalised

That is, words that will activate the mind must be personalised (in first person pronouns like 'I'), must be specific, must use forceful words such as 'must,' and be able to elicit emotions in the individual. An example is: "I must enter medical school this year and graduate as a medical doctor in six years from today." This was actually one of the statements I was making in those days. They were highly emotionalised words to me then.

Emotionalised words are words given appropriate feelings to. Napoleon Hill wrote:

> *"Plain, unemotional words do not influence the subconscious mind" (Think and Grow Rich, 1938, page 67).*

The emotionalised words being triggered by the vision of becoming a doctor activated my mind and stimulated my heart to trigger the force of faith. Indeed, an activated subconscious mind does interact with the spiritual world to trigger the force of faith in the heart of the spirit man. The force of faith energised my body into taking practical actions. Although I didn't quite understand at that time, I was actually triggering the Law of Faith to work in my favour. Obviously, the Spirit of God in me was pushing me to utilise the Law for my benefit. In other words, operation of the Law of Faith involves the three realms of man – spirit, soul (mind), and body.

Autosuggestion works because it triggers the Law of Faith. Autosuggestion is a component practice of meditation and it is one clear way of activating the mind. Even individuals who know nothing about God practise this principle and it works for them, how much more you that have been regenerated and is indwelled by the Holy Spirit of God? Principles are principles, and once any man meets the terms of the principle, he reaps the benefits of the principle. Napoleon Hill wrote:

> *"Your ability to use the principle of autosuggestion will depend, very largely, upon your capacity to concentrate upon a given desire until that desire becomes a burning obsession"*
>
> *(Think and Grow Rich, 1938, page 68).*

Chapter 10
The Interaction Between the Mind and the Spirit

For many individuals, the discussion about spirit is only relegated to religion. But that is where many people are wrong. Faith, creativity and similar powers of the mind only come from the spiritual reality. Faith is not only in religion; it is central to any meaningful achievement. Without faith, no great feat can be realised in life. Psychologists give faith various names such as confidence, assurance, trust, etc

Every human is principally a spirit being. The spirit being consists of three components – censor, heart, and eido centre. Each of these three components carries specific deposits. Faith, love, etc. are deposits in the heart (see SSB Book 1). These deposits are tools for actualising the life purpose of one's existence. Interestingly, these rich deposits in the spirit man can only be released when the spirit is stimulated. For instance, faith in the heart of the spirit man will only be triggered into action when the heart is stimulated appropriately.

MIND ACTIVATION AND HEART STIMULATION

Of significant interest is the fact that what stimulates the spirit man to release its spiritual contents is the activated mind. An inertial mind cannot stimulate the spirit man. Indeed, this truth cannot be overemphasized: *it is the activated mind, which is the subconscious state of the mind, that has the capacity to stimulate the spirit man.*

This knowledge explains why people who have nothing to live for are often destitute of creativity. When a man does not have something that triggers excitement in him, something he excitedly looks forward to, such a man will be unable to ascend into the creative realms because creativity emanates from the heart of the human spirit. Martin Luther King Jr. concisely puts it this way:

> *"If a man has not discovered something that he will die for, he isn't fit to live"* (Address at the Freedom Rally in Cobo Hall, 1963).

An excited mind is the activated mind. It is such an activated mind that has the capacity to stimulate the spirit to release its contents. This is not a theoretical knowledge but powerful information that great achievers have employed to attain great success. Read on to have a good knowledge of this all-important discussion in the field of success.

RESPONSIBILITY FOR OUTCOME OF LIFE

The contents of the human mind occur as information or thought, which is processed to form ideas. An activated mind simply holds not just an idea but a highly emotionalised idea. This active emotionalised idea from the activated mind is what stimulates the spirit man to release its contents. In other words, when a man's mind is activated, the activated mind releases its emotionalised idea, which stimulates the spirit man to release its spiritual forces. This is discussed further in subsequent chapters.

The important lesson here is that since we can consciously activate our mind through meditation, it means we can consciously stimulate our spirit man to release its qualities. That is, if faith is a requisite qualification for success and faith is released from the stimulated spirit, you actually determine the degree and strength of faith you muster to actualise your vision. A vision that drives a man is a vision that excites or activates his mind, and such an activated mind is what will stimulate the spirit of the man to search for creative ideas and generate the necessary force of faith to actualise the vision. That explains why any man with a pulsating vision is a man of faith and creative innovations. Such a man is unstoppable as the world parts way for him to pass.

In Summary

Here is the summary of the discussion thus far: genuine meditation involves emotionalisation of thought, which activates the mind into its subconscious state; the activated mind processes the emotional thought into an emotionalised idea that can stimulate the spirit man. That is the functional relationship between the mind (soul) and the spirit.

Indeed, this truth cannot be overemphasized: it is the activated mind that stimulates the spirit. In other words, a man who has learnt to activate his mind will continuously stimulate his spirit to release its contents or products, and never doubt this. The forces of the contents (products) of the spirit are what we need to achieve our desired success. That means you are absolutely responsible for the outcome of your life! This is discussed further in the next chapter.

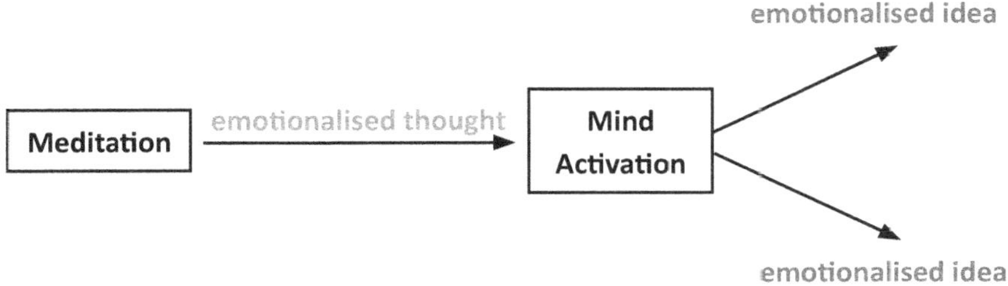

***Fig*.8: Genuine meditation involves emotionalisation of thought, which activates the mind into its subconscious state; the activated mind processed the emotional thought into an emotionalised idea that can stimulate the spirit man.**

Chapter 11
The Products of Mind Activation

Johan was not a very bright pupil in his elementary school days. His first report card showed he took the 26th position in a class of 30. He struggled with maths and just managed to pass his school certificate. Being a bit reserved he was not quick in making friends. Thus, throughout his first year in secondary school, he was more or less keeping to himself. Again, he managed to pass through the secondary school and enrolled for a course in a university. There he got involved with some bad gangs and was caught up in drugs. Soon the drugs affected him as he spent his school fees on his addiction and wayward living.

I met him in our clinic in 2001. He had contracted a sexually transmitted disease, had infected wounds all around his legs, and looked quite unkempt and carefree. Due to his wayward lifestyle, he abandoned his varsity education in his third year, just a year to his graduation. At the clinic, I tried to be a bit friendly and Johan opened up telling me his story. As at then, he had no vision and no plan for his life. I invited him to Church. There in Church he met with a certain group of professionals and businessmen. According to him, he liked the success stories of one of them, Collins, and that was the kind of thing he had desired in life.

The more he attended the professional and businessmen fellowship, the more his interest was kindled. Finally, he decided to surrender his life to Jesus and quit his wayward lifestyle. His desire to mirror his life after the success of Collins awakened a burning desire in him. All of a sudden, he could see a defined bright future. His emotions were jolted up. Each morning, Johan woke up feeling restless about his situation and was determined there must be something he could do about it.

As at this time, we had become friends. I reasoned with him the need for him to go back and finish his university degree. However, he doubted if that would be possible, considering that he had abandoned the course for about two years. We prayed about it and the final decision was for Johan to go back and seek an audience with the Head of Department. God granted him favour and he was absorbed back into the course, which he finished in one year. He immediately enrolled for his Master's degree and completed it.

As at the writing of this manuscript, Johan had finished his Master's degree, has married with a lovely family, and started a business. He is today a big importer and exporter of merchandise. He has built a company mirrored after Collins' success, and the company has branched into other fields with a brand.

Johan's story is a testimony of the power of an activated mind. His mind was inactive until he came into contact with the Christian professional and businessmen group. His meeting with Collins suddenly caused a spark in him, to start thinking seriously about his future. That was a kind of meditation. Such genuine meditation involved emotionalisation of his thought. That is, his thought life was mixed with an elated emotion that was elicited when he saw Mr. Collins' success story, the kind he had desired. His emotionalised thought activated his mind into its subconscious state to start seeking for an answer to his seeming failure in life.

When a man becomes dissatisfied with his status quo (his existing state of affairs) and start seeking actively for a way to change the state, that is a sign of an activated mind. Johan was suddenly restless and knew that he had to change and do something meaningful. But what exactly would he do? Where would he start from? As he pondered (meditated), his activated mind soon processed the emotional thought into an emotionalised idea that stimulated his spirit man to birth an insight. Johan 'saw' that he could reproduce the success of Mr. Collins in his life. Indeed, he had caught a vision of a better future to be mirrored after Mr. Collins' achievement, and an insight of what steps to take to actualise the vision; one of the first steps being to go back to the university and finish his course. The vision of a bright future that he saw triggered in him the force of faith, which pushed him into taking practical steps in pursuit of the vision, ultimately resulting in building a lovely family and the birth of his company.

Note that everything started with the activation of Johan's mind. The activated mind is the subconscious mind, which has an immense advantage – it can stimulate the spirit man to release its products, which in Johan's case were insight and faith.

PRODUCTS OF MIND ACTIVATION

In general, there are three main products that can be released by the action of an activated subconscious mind on the human spirit, and these are:

(a) Fruit of the spirit
(b) Insight
(c) Creativity

This chapter briefly discusses the Fruit of the Spirit and insight while creativity is discussed in the subsequent chapter.

FRUIT OF THE SPIRIT

One benefit of activation of the mind is that the activated subconscious mind can stimulate the heart of man to release the Fruit of the Spirit contained in the heart. The Fruit of the Spirit is articulately mentioned in the Scriptures.

> *"But the fruit of the Spirit is love, joy, peace, patience, gentleness, goodness, faith, meekness, and self-control; against such [things] there is no law" (Gal.5:22,23 MEV).*

Love, joy, peace, patience, gentleness, goodness, faith, meekness, and self-control collectively constitute the Fruit of the Spirit; they are deposits in the heart of the human spirit. The term 'Spirit' in the above Scripture is from the Greek word *pneuma*, which is also translated as the Spirit of God, spirit of man, or the evil spirit. Looking at the context of this Scripture, the '*pneuma*' here refers to the regenerated human spirit. In other words, the nine substances mentioned in Galatians chapter 5 verses 22 and 23 that collectively form the Fruit of the Spirit refer to the deposits in the regenerated human spirit. A regenerated spirit man is a recreated human spirit following the New Birth experience (see SSB Book 5).

That is, these nine substances were originally components of the human spirit at creation. Sadly, the Fall of Man in the Garden affected their expressions. Instead of love, man becomes filled with hatred; instead of peace, there is disharmony; sorrow replaces joy; fearfulness replaces faithfulness; and self-indulgence replaces self-control, etc. However, once the individual experiences the New Birth, the Fruit of the Spirit is recreated in the heart of his spirit man.

Each of the nine substances that form the Fruit of the Spirit mentioned in Galatians chapter 5 verses 22 and 23 is a force that can propel and skyrocket any man to true success in life. The forces of love and faith are among the three greatest forces that rule the world, and any man who knows and utilises them will never ever be a failure in life. These forces are some of the deposits in the heart of a man.

***Fig*.9: Each of the nine substances that form the Fruit of the Spirit is a force that can propel and skyrocket any man to true success in life.**

PRACTICE OF YOGA AND ACTIVATED MIND

In its simplest term, yoga, which originated in ancient India, is all about mind activation through meditation. When practiced genuinely, yoga does activate the mind, and such an activated mind will stimulate the spirit man, bringing about inner tranquillity, exultation, ecstasy, and physical composure, which are actually adulterated versions of the Fruit of the Spirit mentioned in the

Scriptures. In other words, yoga yields some positive dividends but which cannot be compared with the full expressions of the Fruit of the Spirit in a regenerated Christian.

At the Fall of Man in the Garden of Eden, the human spirit became dead (see SSB Book 3). As a result of the deadness of the spirit of the unregenerated person, the heart of the unregenerated man cannot release the full strength of its inherent deposits despite being stimulated by an activated mind. In other words, the forces release from the heart of the unregenerated man when stimulated by an activated mind will not be of the same strength as what the regenerated man experiences when his activated mind stimulates his spirit man.

Thus, yoga, being practised by the unregenerated persons, will at its best yield adulterated versions of the Fruit of the Spirit. Indeed, inner tranquillity, exultation, ecstasy, and physical composure that are obtained from yoga practice can never compare with the full expressions of the Fruit of the Spirit in a regenerated Christian. Oh, what joy, what peace, what love that can overwhelm and flow through the heart of a regenerated man whose activated mind stimulates his spirit man! Except you are regenerated, you won't know the genuine love of God, inner joy and peace; they are driving powers for forceful life advancement.

> *"Peace I leave with you, My peace I give to you; not as the world gives do I give to you" (Joh.14:27 NKJV).*

> *"As the Father loved Me, I also have loved you; abide in My love" (Joh.15:9 NKJV).*

> *"These things I have spoken to you, that My joy may remain in you, and that your joy may be full" (Joh.15:11 NKJV).*

My prayer is that may you become regenerated so as to experience these divine gifts that can make your life far richer than anything else (see SSB Book 5).

INSIGHT

An activated mind has one major advantage over a restful mind; that is insight. An insight is a penetrating awareness of things in an environment. There is nothing as pitiful as a man without an insight. An unwise man is a man who acquires knowledge by waiting to be told everything about a matter. However, a prudent man is one who doesn't wait to be told everything but acquires essential facts about a matter through observable inference. This observable inference is insight.

All around us, there are people who claim to be friends and of assistance but are the very people who will be ready to stab at the back. Insight helps a man to decipher fake from genuine friends. In addition, not all open doors will be beneficial; some open doors may be a trap in disguise. An insight can guide a man in the correct path to take. It was principally by insight that Johan, whose story was told in the beginning of this chapter, was able to decipher the right steps to take that changed the course of his life and made forceful advancement.

The difference between a smart student and an average student is insight. An average student meticulously follows his lecture notes, but does not sit back to have an appraisal of his progress. If he has difficulty in any subject, he simply increases his study time and his commitment to classroom attendance. However, a smart student is one with an insight. At every stage, he observes and appraises the situation. He also follows his lecture notes and commitment to classroom attendance, but learns much more through observation and drawing inferences. If he encounters difficulty in any subject, he tries to decipher the likely cause, observes other students that seem to be doing well in the course, and takes necessary steps in line with his findings.

In the school of life, we are all students. Many things that make for success in any field of endeavour are often not taught. A prudent man learns them by observable inference. For instance, the economics school teaches the theories of wealth. But if those theories do engender wealth, those economic teachers and professors would have been wealthy. However, to be wealthy, a man needs more than classroom knowledge. Insight is what opens a man to the practical school of life that make for advancement.

Indeed, if you are waiting to read and study all the books on success, attend all seminars and workshops on prosperity and the likes, in order to become a success, you'll wait too long on the floor. Great lessons that make for forceful advancement in life are often not spoken; they are silently learnt through the power of insight.

WHY SOME HAVE BETTER INSIGHT THAN OTHERS

When John D. Rockefeller decided to plunge all out and stake his life profits on the Lima Oil despite the negative messages (see chapter one), he was acting based on insight. Charles Pratt and the other executive members of the Standard Oil were insightfully blind as they couldn't see the potentials in the deal as did Rockefeller. At the end, Rockefeller's insight paid off with the Lima Oil becoming a launching pad for Standard Oil supremacy in the international oil market.

The question then is: Why did Rockefeller have a better insight than his executive board members? In other words, why do some people have better insight than others?

The answer lies in the activation of the mind. Insight is one of the products of an activated mind. A study of the history of Standard Oil shows that John D. Rockefeller was more inwardly driven than all other board members of Standard Oil. He was more motivated than all others working with him on issues pertaining to Standard Oil. As the founder, Rockefeller knew that the success or failure of the company would depend much more on him than any other person. As such, he was more motivated, more emotionally stimulated, than every other person in the organisation. It is, therefore, not a surprise that his mind was more highly activated than all others in the organisation, resulting in greater insight. That explains why he could have more unusual insight than Charles Pratt or any others in the company executive board.

That tells us a lot of information. The founder or an owner of any entity, be it a family unit, a business organisation, a social gathering, a religious organisation, is often more motivated, more emotionally stimulated than every other person in the entity because he knows the success or the failure of the entity rests squarely on his shoulders. As such, his mind would be more highly activated than every other person in that entity, and therefore have more capability for greater insight. It behoves on the founder or the owner, therefore, to communicate his vision and motivation clearly to others if there will be synergistically positive result.

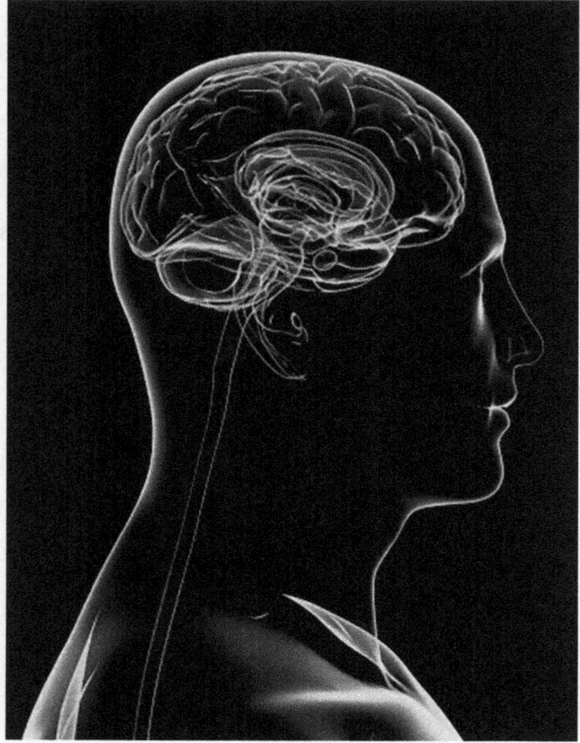

***Fig*.10: Insight is a product of stimulation of the spirit man by the activated mind.**

Vision sees the end of the project while insight sees the steps required to reach the end. Insight does this by analysing and synthesizing available facts, and thus draws inferences or conclusions from such analysis and synthesis.

Once the idea in the mind is acted upon by an appropriate emotion, the activated mind stimulates the spirit man, which begins to 'see' what hitherto he never sees. Have you wondered why it is that once you make up your mind to buy a particular phone or a car, suddenly you start noticing that model of the phone or car all around you? Why weren't you seeing them that much before you decided to make the purchase? Was there a sudden increase in the brand of that model on the street? Of course, no. The number or the brand model of the phone or the car is still the same. The only thing that has changed is that your emotions have now mixed with the purchase idea, and this activates your mind for the purchase, making you to become more consciously aware of the presence of the model. This is part of the Law of Conscious Awareness. Insight is a key component of this Law.

THREE CHARACTERISTICS OF INSIGHT

The three characteristics of an insight are:

(i) Insight is a product of stimulation of the spirit man by the activated mind.

(ii) Insight can be triggered consciously.
Since mind activation is the first step to acquisition of insight, it means meditation can be used to induce insight. That is, insight can be elicited consciously through meditation. Indeed, great insight is achieved by deeply meditating on the subject matter.

(iii) Insight reveals the steps to actualise a vision
Vision will show a man the end of a matter, insight is what breaks down the vision into workable step-by-step activities. In other

words, vision sees the end of the project while insight sees the steps required to reach the end. Insight does this by analysing and synthesizing available facts, and thus draws inferences or conclusions from such analysis and synthesis.

"The purposes of a person's heart are deep waters, but one who has insight draws them out" (Pro.20:5 NIV).

Table 2: Insight versus Vision		
	Vision	**Insight**
Futuristic sight	Sees only the end	Sees the step by step route to reaching the end
Methodology	It is received by revelation, passion, or talent analysis	It is received by meditation

CHAPTER 12
CREATIVITY – ANOTHER PRODUCT OF MIND ACTIVATION

MANY PEOPLE THINK THAT THEIR mind has nothing to do with their spirit and the spiritual world. But that is incorrect. The Scriptures show a lot of connection between the mind (soul) and the spirit. Words like 'spiritually minded,' 'carnally minded' (Rom.8:6 KJV), 'renewed in the spirit of your mind' (Eph.4:23 KJV) and the like, show such interaction between the mind and the spirit.

However, a restful inertial mind (a mind whose idea has not been emotionalised) has little or no interaction with the spiritual realm. But when activated, the subconscious mind has the capacity to interact with the unseen spiritual world. 'How does this occur?' you may wonder.

MECHANISM OF MIND-SPIRIT INTERACTION

The subconscious activated mind of a man interacts with the spirit of the man by releasing its emotionalised idea first to the heart of the spirit man. The heart is the belly of the spirit; it is like a deep well with continuous flow of water (thought).

> *"Both the inward thought and the heart of man are deep"*
> *(Psa.64:6 NKJV).*

In the heart of the spirit, the emotionalised idea from the subconscious mind triggers a sophisticated chemistry of myriads of thoughts to produce the desired answer for its problem. Thus, the heart is stimulated to conjure up an answer to the boggling question or challenge of the emotionalised idea. The conjured answer then passes to the human spirit's eido centre, where it appears as an image, making the individual to 'see' the answer.

Meanwhile, the censor of the spirit is also stimulated to weigh every answer that has been conjured up to be sure it conforms to the person's perceived moral codes (see SSB Book 1 for more information on the working of the tripartite nature of man - spirit, soul, and body).

Thus, the emotionalised idea from the subconscious activated mind does stimulate all the three components of the human spirit - heart, eido centre, and censor - to search for the answer to the question convey in the emotionalised idea. The whole process that eventually births or conjures up the required answer is what is referred to as ***inspiration***. Thus, inspiration is brought about by the subconscious activated mind stimulating the spirit man.

Depending on the question being asked, the birthed answer is wrapped and presented as an innovative thought, which is often referred to as ***creative thought***.

THE SIGNIFICANCE OF MIND-SPIRIT INTERACTION

Where the answer cannot be conjured up, the heart then passes the emotionalised idea to the eido centre of the spirit man. Thus, the eido centre, which is the eye of the spirit man, is stimulated by the emotionalised idea from the activated subconscious mind to begin to peep into the world of the spirit in search for the desired answer.

God, human spirits, angels, and demons, are all part of the spiritual world. The stimulated eido centre of a man can interact with any of these beings in the spiritual world. If the individual is regenerated in Christ, his eido centre can interact with the Holy Spirit of God to obtain an answer for his boggling question or challenge.

The stimulated eido centre of an individual can likewise interact with demonic agents for a twisted answer as often seen in occult practices. Similarly, the stimulated eido centre of an individual can interact with other human spirits to elicit the desired answer. This often happens when there is harmonious union between the individuals; such harmonious union forms the **mastermind team** that can be a well of idea generation (see **Idea Hybridisation** on page 128).

Of significant note is the fact that a highly stimulated eido centre of an individual can 'break' into the heart of another person to peep into the thoughts of that person's heart. This explains why ideas can be stolen as commonly seen among researchers and artists of various fields of human endeavours.

EXAMPLES OF MIND-SPIRIT INTERACTION

A good example was what happened in about 844 BC. Ben-Hadad, King of Syria, held a kitchen cabinet meeting during which they secretly planned a military invasion of the territory of Northern Kingdom of Israel. All security intelligence was fully observed to maintain the safety of the classified information from leaking to the enemy. However, unknown to them, the eido centre of the spirit of Prophet Elisha, by the enablement of the Spirit of God, could break into the spiritual world of the Syrians and peeped into their kitchen cabinet meeting. Hence, Prophet Elisha would send words to warn the Israelite monarch, King Jehoram the son of Ahab:

> *"Beware that you do not pass this place, for the Syrians are coming down there" (2Kin.6:9 NKJV).*

As such, the king of Israel would send spies to the place of which the Prophet of God had told him, to ascertain the claims of the Prophet. Each time, the warning of Prophet Elisha would come out to be accurate, and thus, Israel averted the military invasions of Syria several times. King Ben-Hadad of Syria was greatly troubled by this development, thinking their ranks might have been infiltrated by the Israelite spies. He investigated the situation and found out that it was Prophet Elisha that spiritually eavesdropped on their kitchen cabinet meeting.

> *"Elisha, the prophet who is in Israel, tells the king of Israel the words that you speak in your bedroom" (2Kin.6:12 NKJV).*

For someone to know what happened in the secret of his bedroom is enough reason for the Syrian king to be wary of such a man. Unfortunately, King Ben-Hadad didn't think that way. Rather he chose to go after the Prophet by sending a detachment of his military to capture Elisha, an exercise that ended in the national disgrace of the Syrian soldiers:

> *"So the bands of Syrian raiders came no more into the land of Israel" (2Kin.6:23 NKJV).*

Indeed, a highly stimulated eido centre of an individual by the emotionalised idea of his activated subconscious mind can 'break' into the heart of another person to peep into the thoughts of that person's heart, which was what Prophet Elisha did to the Syrians. For instance, some people have generated some treasured ideas, but while vacillating and delaying to take practical steps to actualise those ideas, they find out that some other persons have started to implement the same ideas. They wonder how the other persons come to know of their secret, treasured ideas since they never told anyone about those ideas.

During our campus fellowship in the university, Mr. Philip once told an interesting story. He had crafted some songs, but kept postponing recording and producing them into an album. Some of the songs came to him entirely by inspiration. He treasured the songs and kept reminding himself each day that he would develop and market them as an album 'some day.' But that 'some day' never came!

After about three years of dillydally, Philip said he was shocked to see some of the songs selling widely. He followed up with the producing musician and discovered that the musician never physically came in contact with Philip before, and that it was purely by inspiration that the musician came about the songs.

Certainly, a stimulated eido centre of an individual can 'break' into the heart of another person to peep into the thoughts of that person's heart, which was what happened between Philip and the musician. The stimulated eido centre of the musician must have broken into Philip's heart and eavesdropped on those songs. This is why once you receive a creative thought, do not delay but start to run with it!

CHARACTERISTICS OF A CREATIVETHOUGHT

A creative thought has the following characteristics:

Inspired nature

A creative thought comes as a result of the stimulation of the spirit man by an activated subconscious mind. The stimulated spirit man conjures up the needed answer from the deep rich deposits of its heart or its eido centre searches in the spiritual realm for an answer from other superior sources. The answer that eventually comes is therefore an inspired thought.

Resourceful nature

The message conveyed by creative thought is ingenious, innovative, and may even be original with the aim of providing a solution to the needed question. In other words, creative thought is the answer being sought for the posed problem. That is the power of inspiration – it seeks to provide creative solution to life problems!

This means the actively emotionalised idea in the subconscious mind should be framed in a clear concise question format for it to be able to conjure specific answers from the spiritual realm. Thus, the questions we pose forward determine the answers we receive. Great minds are often not shy in posing questions, even if they appear impossible to ask. This is because they know the quality of the questions asked determine the quality of answers generated.

Slippery nature

Creative thought may come into the stimulated heart as trickles or in a flash. A **trickled creative thought** emerges in the heart little by little over a period of time, which may be in minutes, hours, days, or even weeks and months. As the various parts come together over a period of time, the illumination will be growing and becoming clearer until the whole nature becomes visible to the heart and mind, making the individual to shout for joy: 'O, I see, I see, I see!'

Alternatively, a **flashy creative thought** comes rushing into the heart with a bang, projecting either forcefully as a tornado or as a silent rushing wind. It is much like a lightning flash in the rain so quick yet but unmistakably conveying a message.

Interestingly, whichever way it comes (as trickles or as a flash), the individual will know when the creative message appears in his heart and mind. Sadly, this is where many immature people with little or no idea of the nature of inspiration miss out; and that is where the so-called genius has the advantage. An average person, who knows little or nothing about inspiration, pays little or no attention to the creative message that appears in his heart because he never knew that such a creative thought can change his life. He is rather expecting something 'big' and utopian. However, individuals who know the nature of creative idea don't make light of such message; once they perceive an idea propping in them, they pause to reconsider and to pay more attention to it.

CREATIVE IDEAS: HOUSEWIFE'S ENCOUNTER

Mrs. Ngozi is a housewife. She knows she is quite talented in singing, but does not know how to convert her talent into a marketable venture. Each day she ponders at the question, whipping up her emotions. One day as she went about her household chores, a thought projected into her heart like a flash. Due to ignorance of creativity, she paid no attention to the message that flashed into her heart. However, any time she would be a bit quiet and contemplative, the same thought would project into her heart; again and again, but she would dismiss it off.

Then one early morning, she mentioned what was happening in her heart to her husband. Once he heard his wife, the husband shouted in surprise: "That is what we've been looking for to harness your beautiful singing talent."

That kept Mrs. Ngozi thinking. Soon she was able to rationalise more details as she contemplated on the message. She and the husband decided to start implementing their findings. The whole story was that Mrs. Ngozi started producing and writing music, and soon found a career that transformed her life from a housewife to a career woman.

Mrs. Ngozi's story is very common. Due to immaturity and ignorance, many people don't recognise and pay attention to creative thoughts that appear in their heart; hence, they don't allow their minds to process the message further. They don't realise that creative messages can be the harbinger of change, ushering in a new phase of growth and development in their lives. Because they pay no attention to it, the creative thought passes on to a more discerning heart of another person, who is more willing to utilise it to bless humanity. Obviously, at this stage one would be wondering why one has been contemplating this.

Have you walked into an arena only to realise that the very idea that kept prompting into your heart is now being implemented by another person? Possibly, due to ignorance you never knew it was a creative thought with a capacity to change your world; or, if you knew, you realise you had been indolent to let your mind process it further. The point here is that if you do nothing about a creative thought that comes into your heart, another willing heart will pick up the message! Great achievers know this, hence they discipline themselves to cultivate creative thoughts. One reason for writing this book is to unveil the nature of man. When we know how we have been wired to function, we can therefore programme ourselves to maximise our potentials and realise our heart desires. That is the plan of God for man (Jer.29:11).

BEING PREPARED FOR CREATIVE IDEAS

As stated on page 104, creative thoughts may come into the stimulated heart as trickles or in a flash. As a flash, it may come at the least expected time. Whichever way a creative thought comes, the individual must be ready at any time to grasp the message, otherwise it can be missed. Individuals with great achievements know how not to allow creative ideas slip off their hands. If you desire your ingenuity to also come alive, you must do likewise. The following are steps that should be taken in readiness for a desired creative message:

Expectancy

Great achievers live in expectancy, especially when they have important matters in consideration. Once they pose questions to their minds, they keep an open mindedness for the expected answer.

It is important for us to note that long before Henry Ford challenged his team of engineers to produce the V8 engine, his heart had conceived in 1902 the thought of making a horseless cart, an automobile, available and cheaper to all Americans. As at then, he never fully knew how this would come about. All he knew was that the vision would definitely become a reality. Thus, he lived in expectation. Then emerged the thought of 1928 in which he saw clearly for the first time the practical fulfilment of the vision. The V8 motor would fulfil his heart's vision of 1902.

Interestingly, when Henry Ford challenged his team of engineers in 1928 to produce a V8 engine, he didn't just give the instruction and go to sleep. Rather, day after day, weeks after weeks, for months and years, he kept an open mind for possible creative ideas to flash into him that would make the V8 motor a reality. He pondered, contemplated, tried and re-tried many options. The ideas came in trickles and gradually built up as he and his engineers lived and worked in expectancy. Thus, from 1928 to 1932, bit by bit the ideas kept tumbling into their hearts and their minds would rationalised each of the ideas to fish out the workable aspects.

Indeed, if you want to bring out the genius in you, live ready, live in expectation of an answer to your life question. You can't just pose a question to your mind and go to sleep. It doesn't work that way. You'll need to fuel your expectations through reading relevant books, attending seminars and workshops, and similar events. You need to identify a mentor that will constantly speak into your life and motivate you continually along the way. *"Expectation is the mother of manifestation... What you don't expect, you can't manifest,"* wrote Dr. D. Oyedepo. That is the truth.

Write down immediately

In order not to allow creative ideas to slip off your reach, jot them down immediately as each creative thought comes to you. Don't ever postpone writing it down; a creative idea is very slippery, and you wouldn't want to let it slip off your reach. Write down each rationalised idea for prompt execution.

Pause to consider

Not all thoughts will be beneficial. Indeed, in many instances, you may not know at first presentation which thought will become a productive idea until you subject the thought to mind processing.

Do not discard or wave aside a thought that comes to you. Write it down immediately; and once the environment is conducive, let your mind dwell on it for processing.

Each idea that comes into your heart must be subjected to mind rationalisation. Think and re-think. Ask yourself practicable questions about the idea such as: Is it implementable? What will it take to realise it? The more you let your mind to dwell on it, the more clarity you obtain. That is **Mind Processing**. If you have a mastermind team, bring the idea to them to get an input. As pieces come together, soon you'll have the whole picture that will baffle your expectation. Put no restriction on your mind. Let your mind *Think Big.*

PROCESSING CREATIVE THOUGHT

When a creative thought reaches the heart of the sprit man, it must still trickle down to the mind for processing into a functionally workable idea. Once creative thought passes downward to the mind, the intellectual faculty rationalises the creative thought into a creative idea. The imaginative faculty of the mind then transforms the creative idea into a pictorial format referred to as ***creative imagination***, the emotional faculty attaches the appropriate feeling that galvanises the willpower faculty to energise the body for execution. It is the execution of the creative idea that brings it into materialisation. Where the emotions are not strong enough to energise the body into action, the creative idea becomes buried in the memory faculty as dreams or mere desire.

Thus, it is not enough to receive creative thought. You need to sit down and let your mind brood over the thought. The more you reason on the creative thought, the clearer it becomes to you.

Chapter 13
The Five Steps to Creativity

FROM WHAT HAVE BEEN DISCUSSED thus far in the previous chapters, it is obvious that any person can access creative thoughts. Creative thinking is not exclusive to any individual, group, sex, age, or race. The significant import of this message is that creative thoughts can be consciously induced if we fulfil the required conditions. These required conditions are the 5 steps or levels that a man can take to transport himself from the ordinary realm into the creative realm.

STEP 1: INFORMATICS

The information age that started in the year 2000 has introduced new terminologies in our daily conversation. One of such neologised terms is informatics, which simply refers to the collation of information. The first step to creativity is the collation of information. Information is the food by which the mind feeds to grow and develop. Without this first level, the individual is incapable of rising to the next level because a poor mind is infertile and unproductive.

Level 1 is the step of information collation, but it is not just any information, rather relevant information that makes for the growth and development of the mind. Thus, Level 1 is the step by which we actively feed on the relevant food that will grow and develop our minds.

STEP 2: MEDITATION

As mentioned in the previous chapters, meditation is the process for mind stimulation. Meditation is the application of the relevant information to activate the mind. As discussed in Chapter 9, genuinely effective meditation will involve emotionalisation of thought, which has the ability to activate the mind into its subconscious state. That is, whereas Level 1 is the step for collation of relevant information, Level 2 is the step for application of the collated information to activate the mind. The power of Level 2 is so great that without it, the mind cannot rise to the next level.

STEP 3: MIND ACTIVATION

Once the mind is properly activated by the process of meditation, the mind enters into its actively subconscious state. This is the Level 3 of the Third Step to receiving creative thought. To vividly understand this state, a subconscious mind state can be likened to an electric heating system. When there is no electric current flowing into it, the heater remains dormant and of no use. But once it is connected to an electric source and the electricity is switched on to allow current to flow through it, the coils of the heater soon start burning red and generates heat. The more the electric current flows through the heater, the hotter the heat generated.

The heater is the mind; the electric current is the emotionalised thought, while the electric source is the meditation. Genuine meditation involves emotionalisation of thought (adding appropriate emotions to thought), which flows into the mind to cause the faculties of the mind to start burning red. This state of burning red is the subconsciousness of the mind. It is an active state that transforms the emotionalised thought into the heat of emotionalised ideas.

It follows therefore that without the flow of emotionalised thought into the mind, the subconscious state cannot be attained, and the mind will remain dormant just like the heater remains dormant when no electric current flows into it.

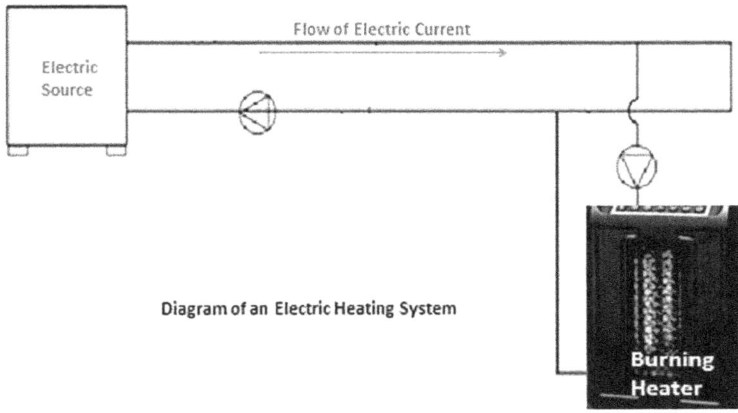

*Fig.*11: Mind activation can be likened to an electric heating system. The heater is the mind; the electric current is the emotionalised thought, while the electric source is the meditation. Genuine meditation involves emotionalisation of thought, which flows into the mind faculties to activate the mind into its burning subconscious state.

STEP 4: HEART STIMULATION

An interesting thing about the subconscious mind is that it is the 'burning' state of the mind. That is, a subconscious mind is in a state of constant agitation, crying for a release of its contents. The emotionalised thoughts that flow into and activated the mind are processed into emotionalised ideas. These emotionalised ideas in an activated mind are constantly in agitatedly burning state, which is referred to as the subconscious state. Thus, the contents of the subconscious activated mind are the active emotionalised ideas, which are released to stimulate the heart of the spirit man.

Once stimulated, the heart goes into a search for the problem conveyed by the active emotionalised ideas. The stimulated heart also awakens the eido centre and the censor of the spirit man to join in the search for the answer.

STEP 5: CREATIVE REALM

From the riches of its deposits, the stimulated heart can conjure up the desired answer, and where such an answer could not be conjured up of the heart, the awakened eido centre can peep into the spiritual world of creativity to garner creative thoughts from other superior sources.

THE LIFE OF LEONARDO DA VINCI

The life of Leonardo da Vinci (1452-1519), the symbol of medieval genius, is a good illustration of the practice of the five steps in pursuit of creative ideas for excellence in life. Leonardo was a man of great learning. He had developed his mind successfully in painting, sculpting, architecture, science, music, mathematics, engineering, literature, anatomy, geology, astronomy, botany, writing, history, and cartography. With such massive collation of information that developed his mind, he knew such massive information would profit him little without proper application. He discovered meditation to be the means for such application. Thus, he utilised the power of meditation in activating his mind.

His life clearly illustrated the power of the activated mind in stimulating the spirit man for creative ideas. Before he would embark on any assignment, Leonardo would shut himself up in a room with all lights switched off. He would concentrate his mind on the assignment, thus whipping up powerful emotions that activated his mind to stimulate his spirit man into the creative realm. He would remain locked up in that state until the solution (creative imagination) became very vivid to him.

For instance, it was reported that before Leonardo painted the Mona Lisa, described to be 'the best known, the most visited, the most written about, the most sung about, the most parodied work of art in the world,' Leonardo shut himself up for many days, depriving himself of any luxury and the presence of any human, until he could see the painting as clear as any tangible objects in his 'inner eyes.' What happened was that the meditation triggered emotionalised idea that activated his mind into the subconscious state, which stimulated his spirit man into the creative realm, from where he received creative thoughts in his heart that were then passed down into his mind for processing into creative ideas with the faculty of imagination specifically converting the creative ideas into vivid creative imaginations.

Thus, through the application of the steps of creativity, Leonardo became very successful in invention, painting, sculpting, architecture, science, and cartography. He has been variously called the father of palaeontology, ichnology, and architecture, and is widely considered one of the greatest painters of all time.

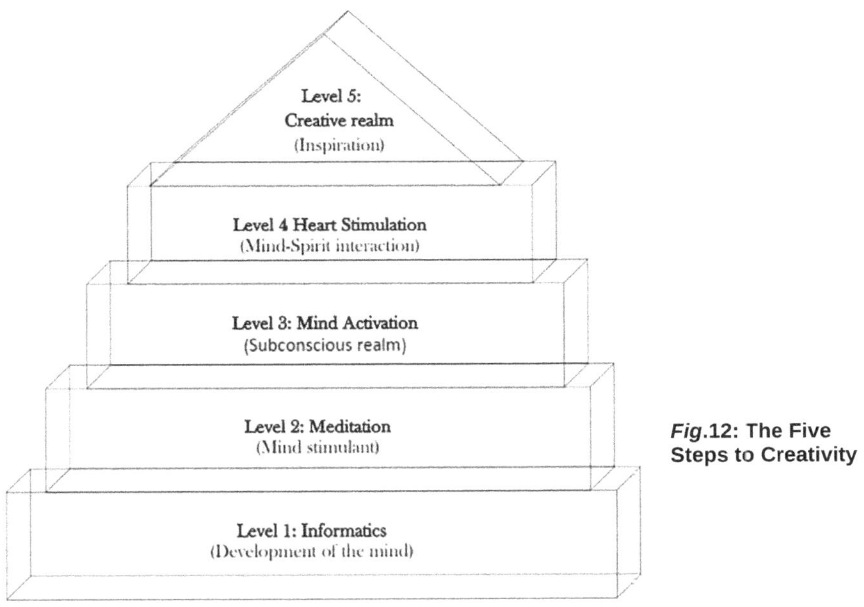

*Fig.*12: The Five Steps to Creativity

CREATIVITY – INTERACTION OF SPIRIT, SOUL AND BODY

If you followed this discussion closely, you would have noticed that these 5 levels or steps to creativity show an interaction of the three realms of human existence - the physical, mental, and spiritual realms. Steps 1 and 2 are basically the physical realm as they involve acquiring relevant information using the physical body senses and then utilising this acquired information through the process of meditation to activate the mind. Step 3 is the mental realm (the term 'mental' refers to the mind or soul). Steps 4 and 5 are the spiritual realm.

To access the creative thought means accessing beyond the physical reality into the mental and spiritual realms. Our present scientific capability can detect the physical reality to a good extent but is presently underdeveloped to be able to clearly detect the existence of the mental and spiritual realms. That we cannot detect the presence of the mental and the spiritual realms by our present rudimentary scientific knowledge does not in any way preclude the existence of these two realms. We may, tomorrow, develop up to a state in which we can correctly detect the existence of these realms and their powerful influence in pursuit of creativity.

Chapter 14
Creativity – The Secret of Genius

Individuals who know how to activate their minds to stimulate their spirit man often reap the benefits of creativity. When the five steps to creativity (mentioned in the previous chapter) are mastered and practised at will, they turn the individual into a wonder among men. This is the secret of the so-called geniuses.

THE SECRET OF ALBERT EINSTEIN'S GENIUS

Geniuses do not have unusual brains than the rest of humanity as erroneously believed by many people. For instance, Albert Einstein (1879-1955) has been the prototype of a modern genius. A German Jew, who later became an American citizen, Einstein was a theoretical physicist, who developed the general theory of relativity and photoelectric effect, a pivotal step in the evolution of quantum theory. Relativity theory and quantum mechanics constitute the two pillars of modern physics. Einstein's work influences the philosophy of science and he developed the world's famous scientific formula equation of mass-energy equivalence: $E = MC^2$.

Einstein was awarded the Nobel Prize in Physics in 1921 for his 'services to theoretical physics,' in particular for his contribution to the development of quantum theory through the discovery of the law of the photoelectric effect. Einstein published more than 300 scientific papers along with over 150 non-scientific works. In 2014, Einstein's papers, comprising more than 30,000 unique documents were made public. Einstein's intellectual achievements and originality have made the word 'Einstein' synonymous with 'genius.'

When Einstein died at 01H15 on 18 April 1955, an autopsy was conducted shortly by pathologist Thomas Stoltz Harvey in a laboratory at Princeton Hospital. Besides identifying the Einstein's cause of death to be a burst aorta (rupture of an abdominal aortic aneurysm), Dr. Harvey had gone to saw open Einstein's cranium and remove its brain contents within seven and a half hours of Einstein's death. Harvey weighed the brain and found it to be 1,230 grams, the weight which is well within the normal human range. Harvey then photographed the brain from many angles, injected 50 percent formalin through the internal carotid arteries and afterwards suspended the intact brain in 10 percent formalin for preservation. He then transferred the brain to a laboratory at the University of Pennsylvania where he dissected it into about 240 pieces (each about 1 cm^3) and encased the segments in a plastic-like material called collodion. Harvey also removed Einstein's eyes, and gave them to Henry Abrams, Einstein's ophthalmologist, while Einstein's remaining body parts were, according to Einstein's will, cremated without ceremony and the ashes scattered in secret to prevent the site becoming a place of pilgrimage.

Over the years, Dr. Harvey energetically ferried small samples of Einstein's brain across the United States to the best scientists for research studies. Harvey died at the University Medical Centre at Princeton in 2007. Three years after his death, Harvey's heirs transferred all of his holdings constituting the remains of Albert Einstein's brain to the National Museum of Health and Medicine, including 14 photographs of the whole brain (which is now in fragments) never before revealed to the public.

All the research studies so far conducted on Einstein's brain "*showed it to be within normal limits for a man his age*," as Harvey confessed to a research journalist, Steven Levy before Harvey's death (*Science, 1978; BBC World Service,* 2015). But rather than publishing these results, Harvey waited for exceptional differences to turn up; hence, now being accused by the science world of being caught up in what is referred to as the 'neuromythology' of Einstein's brain.

Indeed, we may search and keep searching and find nothing much different between Einstein's brains and any other human brain. The source of Einstein's genius transcended just the mere physical brain growth. It was the application of the steps of creativity at will that gave Einstein his continuous access to creative ideas.

Einstein might not have believed in a personal God, which is regrettable considering that his ancestral father, Biblical Abraham, was the one through whom God revealed himself to the world, yet Einstein never doubted the reality of the mental and spiritual realms. He utilised these extensively in his researches for illumination and enlightenment in obtaining creative ideas. His views adduced to this fact. For instance, he once stated the followings:

> *"The most beautiful and most profound experience is the sensation of the mystical. It is the sower of all true science. He to whom this emotion is a stranger, who can no longer wonder and stand rapt in awe, is as good as dead. To know that what is impenetrable to us really exists, manifesting itself as the highest wisdom and the most radiant beauty which our dull faculties can comprehend only in their primitive forms – this knowledge, this feeling is at the center of true religiousness." (Albert Einstein: The Merging of Spirit and Science; Haselhurst and Howie).*

In 1936 Einstein received a letter from a young girl in the sixth grade. She had asked him, with the encouragement of her teacher, if scientists pray. Einstein's reply reveals his knowledge of the existence of the mental and spiritual realms:

> *"Everyone who is seriously involved in the pursuit of science becomes convinced that a Spirit is manifest in the laws of the Universe – a Spirit vastly superior to that of man, and one in the face of which we with our modest powers must feel humble." (Einstein Albert, 1936: The Human Side - Glimpses from His Archives).*

Indeed, Albert Einstein was not ignorant about the spirituality of life. For instance, speaking on intuition, which is one of the functions of the eido centre of the human spirit (see SSB Book 1), Einstein made the following remarks:

> *"There is no logical way to the discovery of elemental laws. There is only the way of intuition, which is helped by a feeling for the order lying behind the appearance." (Where is science going? Prologue 10, Planck Max).*

> *"The intuitive mind is a sacred gift and the rational mind is a faithful servant. We have created a society that honours the servant and has forgotten the gift." (Forbes, contributor: Kasanoff B).*

Certainly, Einstein was very conversant with realms beyond the five physical senses, and he utilised the steps of creativity to develop into the bright genius we all admire.

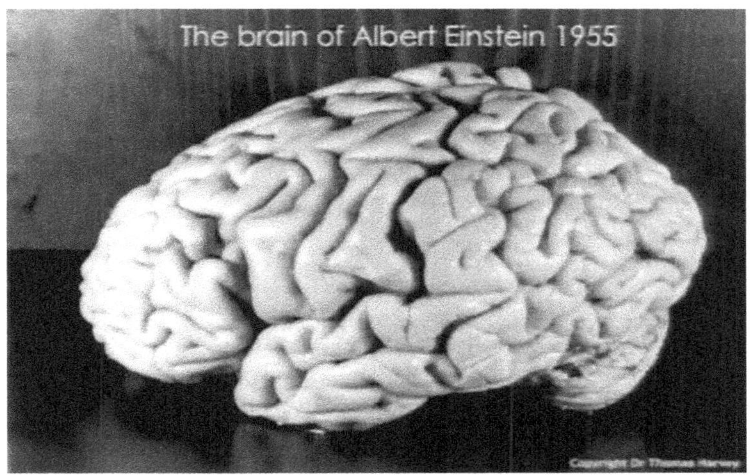

Fig.13: *Einstein's brain was preserved after his death in 1955, but this fact was not revealed until 1978. All the research studies so far conducted on Einstein's brain "showed it to be within normal limits for a man his age," as Dr. Thomas Harvey confessed to a researcher journalist, Steven Levy, before Harvey's death.*

GREAT SUCCESS - BEYOND PHYSICAL SENSES

Individuals who dwell only on the physical realm, that is, depend solely on their physical senses, are often grossly limited in their quest for success including financial success. If all you know is based on what you perceive with your five physical senses, you'll lead a miserable life and, undoubtedly, won't go far in your quest for success in life. Note, this is not a religious assertion; it is the reality of the human existence.

Interestingly, many people are acutely and remotely aware that there are more things in life than what we perceive with our five physical senses. Great success often comes from sources beyond the five physical senses. The five steps to creativity discussed in Chapter 13 finally reveal the pathway and the sources by which any individual can access creative ideas, which hitherto were the hidden secrets of the geniuses, and rise in his quest for success, advancement, and prosperity in life. These five steps to creativity, if practised consistently at will, are what can bring the ingenuity in a man to limelight.

IN SUMMARY

The prowess and dexterity of so-called geniuses are the result of the mastery of the power of inspiration. The more a man engages and utilises these five steps to creativity, the more mastery he attains, and the more readily he accesses creative thoughts that make him stand tall among his peers. Geniuses are individuals who know how to activate their minds at will to stimulate their hearts in order to harvest their creative benefits. You too can develop creative prowess if you would diligently practise the five steps to creativity!

Chapter 15
Determinants of Creativity

The strength of creative imaginations that flows into your heart and mind from the creative realm is dependent on certain conditions. In general, there are three main factors that determine how strongly and frequently we flow in creative ideas. These factors are the determinants of creativity, and they are:

- Life purpose
- Mind stimulants, and
- Idea hybridisation

(1) LIFE PURPOSE

There is nothing as powerful as working in the centre of what you are created to be. Once a man discovers his life purpose and stays in it, he gains dexterity and prowess that will never be available to him if he is pursuing any other endeavour. Working in his life purpose is the area of least resistance in the pursuit of excellence for a man; oppositions and hindrances become food for him as they fuel his resolution and passion. It is in the pursuit of life purpose that all your gifting (natural and spiritual talents) are fully maximised.

However, when a man is not in his life purpose, he strains, he labours with great angst, and he dislikes his life even though he may be making the money he envisages. But life is not just about making money. Working in your life purpose provides an avenue to make money with little or no strains, and in addition offers you fulfilment in life.

The major advantage of working in your life purpose is that it maximises your access to creative ideas. The musical exploits of people like Elvis Presley, Bob Marley, and Michael Jackson, still captivate millions of people around the world even though these artists have all died several years ago. The business ingenuity of John D. Rockefeller is still a source of inspiration to many business people around the world. The political leadership traits of Winston Churchill are still sources of motivation for many politicians in many countries. The spiritual vivacity and dexterity of Billy Graham remains a pathfinder to the Church and millions of people across the globe. Florence Nightingale and Mother Theresa still remain shining stars in the world of care and nursing. The scientific works of inventions of Isaac Newton, Albert Einstein, and Thomas Edison have shaped the way we look at the world. We can go and on about great achievements in all fields of human endeavours.

Though all these great achievers are of various races who lived at different generations, yet they all have one thing in common. They lived and functioned in the area of their dominant strength. In other words, they lived in their life purposes. Functioning in their life purposes offered them the opportunity to operate and work with least resistance. Their passion was triggered beyond measure, and such passionate emotions activated their minds to stimulate their spirit man for access into creative realms. They all knew the power of inspiration which they maximised to their benefits.

Operating in your life purpose unleashes the strongest emotions that will never be available if you were in any other endeavour. The stronger the emotional drive, the stronger the degree of mind activation and the stronger the stimulation of the heart, eido centre and censor of the human spirit to search for creative thoughts.

In addition, the fact that living in your life purpose offers the path of least resistance to success, it therefore means that a man who desires to evoke strong creative thoughts and swims in continuous flow of such creative ideas has no choice but to seek, discover, and live in his life purpose. Vision is the process for making such discovery (see Chapter 19).

(2) MIND STIMULANTS

As stated several times, meditation is the process by which emotionalised thought is generated and released to activate the mind into its subconscious state. However, merely separating oneself unto quietness to study, imagine, and utter words (which are the steps of meditation as discussed in Chapter 9) do not necessarily lead to mind activation. There are stimulants that turn our meditation contents into driving emotionalised thoughts for our mind activation. These mind stimulants can be grouped into three main types:

(a) Passion

Passion is a dominant thought in the heart and mind that craves for physical expression. Passion is a strong desire that kindles fire in the mind of men, seeking for physical manifestation. You cannot be passionate about a thing without its effect being seen physically. Passion evokes strong emotions in the mind, and such an emotionalised desire activates the mind.

Simply put, passion is a strong desire that drives a man for physical expression, and a sustained strong desire sets the tone for the direction of one's life. Indeed, our life's course tends to follow the direction of the most dominant passionate thought desire in our heart. For instance, many individuals have been lifted from poverty and despondency to affluence by reason of their hatred of poverty background. Their past poverty history kindled a pulsating desire to break away from poverty and its entanglements. In fact, the reason why children born into deprivation, poverty, and degradation tend to do much better than children born with silver spoons in their mouths is because such deprivations trigger the strongest emotionalised desire for success in them. The emotions are utilised to activate the mind, which in turn stimulate the heart to generate creative ideas for escape from the excruciating deprivations.

Furthermore, the driving force of love is a powerful stimulant for mind activation. Passionate love in the heart of a man to please a woman is a strong stimulant that can activate his mind into successful ventures. A number of stories have been told about men who, hitherto were failures in their respective ventures, fell in love with women and that changed their lives and levels of successful attainments. In addition, the drive in man for immortality is a strong desire that has activated the minds of millions, resulting in multiplication of religious belief systems.

Indeed, passionate desires of all kinds such as passions for love, wealth, health, competitive advantage, are driving stimulants of the mind. Always realise that your past experiences (whether good or bad) can be a stimulant or deterrent to the activation of your mind. It becomes a stimulant if it is a driving passion seeking for physical expression while, on the other hand, it becomes a deterrent if you allow fear to stop you from taking steps in the direction of your passion.

(b) Music

Music has been known throughout human history as a stimulant for creative idea. Music has been used to rouse individuals, groups, and even a whole nation unto a course of action. This is because music can trigger passionate emotional ideas in man, which then activate the mind into its subconscious state. The subconscious-activated mind then stimulates the spirit man to begin a search for creative ideas.

Music (whether in form of songs or poetry) are known to be strong stimulants of creative ideas in all spheres of human endeavours. Many people use music as catalyst for successful activities. God, who created man, knows the power of music. Thanksgiving, praises and worship expressed in musical forms can powerfully activate the minds of the worshippers into the subconscious state, which in turn stimulates their spirit man to interact with the spiritual world. A study of the Scriptures, both Old and New Testaments reveal one fact – most cases of divine messages received by worshippers occurred in moments of praise and worship.

BIBLICAL EXAMPLES OF MIND ACTIVATION BY MUSIC

A good example was the event of about 850 BC, relayed in Second Kings chapter 3. Three kings – Jehoram of Samaria, Jehoshaphat of Judah, and the King of Edom – went out to make war against the rebelled King Mesha of Moab. King Jehoshaphat of Judah, the godly one among these kings, wanted to know the will of God concerning the battle. Hence, Prophet Elisha was summoned for consultation.

Interestingly, Prophet Elisha first requested for music to be played to activate his mind and stimulate his spirit man to be able to hear from God. He requested: *"Send for someone who can play the harp"* (2Kin.3:15 CEV). NKJV renders Prophet Elisha's request this way: *"But now bring me a musician"* (2Kin.3:15).

Thus, a musician (a harpist) was brought to play a rousing song. As the harpist began playing, Elisha was stimulated into the prophetic realm.

> *"Then it happened, when the musician played, that the hand of the Lord came upon him" (2Kin.3:15 NKJV).*

What happened was that the music evoked passionate emotions in Prophet Elisha that activated his mind into the subconscious state, which then stimulated his spirit man to start interacting in the spiritual realm where he heard and received God's message for the kings.

The same thing could be seen in the early Church. In fact, the ministry of Apostle Paul by which Christianity spread across the entire world was launched out as a result of the activation of the mind by the instrumentality of worship.

"Among the prophets and teachers of the church at Antioch were Barnabas and Symeon (also called 'The Black Man'), Lucius (from Cyrene), Manaen (the foster-brother of King Herod), and Paul. One day as these men were worshiping and fasting the Holy Spirit said, 'Dedicate Barnabas and Paul for a special job I have for them.' So after more fasting and prayer, the men laid their hands on them—and sent them on their way" (Act.13:1-3 TLB).

The process of fasting and worship triggered strong emotional release that activated the minds of these brethren in Antioch Church. Their activated minds then stimulated their spirit man to interact with the Holy Spirit. By such interaction they could receive the divine message of consecration of Paul and Barnabas for world evangelism, which was their life purpose. That is the power of worship in musical form; it activates the minds of men and lifts the spirit man into celestial realms to interact with divinity.

WHY GOD LOVES MUSIC

Before I understood what mind activation was all about, I used to wonder why God loves music. The Scriptures give several accounts of Heaven (the Throne of God) and its rich, beautiful musical culture. The Church here on earth is filled with music. Thanksgiving, praises, and worship are in most cases expressed in music. With the knowledge of mind activation, now I understand better why God loves music.

God is a creative ingenuity; He lives and functions in the creative realm. The entire universe reveals the expression of His creative prowess. He created man in His likeness and image. Thus, man was created to function in the creative realm like God. Each human is unique; each of us is wired uniquely different from one other; at least, the uniqueness of each man's fingerprint is a testimony to this truth.

> *"I will give thanks and praise to You, for I am fearfully and wonderfully made; wonderful are Your works, and my soul knows it very well. (Psa.139:14 AMP).*

However, you cannot manifest your uniqueness by copying the lifestyle of someone else. Your uniqueness can only be realised through creative release. Creativity is what will unveil your uniqueness. When you are creative, your uniqueness is unleashed. Music is a veritable means of activating the mind into its subconscious state, and an activated mind stimulates the spirit man, which can interact with God, who is a Spirit (John 4:24). Thus, music whether in thanksgiving, praise, or worship, can lift our spirit to the spiritual realm, where we can interact with God, the true and ultimate Source of creativity.

Nevertheless, it takes a regenerated spirit through the New Birth in Christ to be able to worship God acceptably (see SSB Book 5). An unregenerated man has a dead spirit which even if stimulated by an activated mind will not be able to respond in true worship of God, hence, lacks the capacity to relate with divinity. A dead lion cannot growl.

c) Drugs

It is a known fact that many artists (athletes, musicians, soccer players, etc.) use drugs like narcotics, steroids and alcohol in various forms such as inhalation, smoking, injections, chewing and drinking. Most of these drugs are illegal in sports and music, yet they are being sought for. One major advantage these drug users derive from such drug usage is the activation of their minds. The drugs generate high euphoric emotions that activate their minds. It is this highly euphoric feeling that drives many people into usage of drugs for recreation.

Visual and auditory hallucinations with delusions, which are some evidences of mind activation, howbeit negatively, are common with most of these drugs. The drug-activated mind enters its subconscious state that stimulates the spirit man to interact with the spiritual world for inspiration. Musicians utilise this form of mind activation for heart stimulation a lot to access creative ideas.

In many parts of Africa, there is a general belief that alcoholics do have some spiritual insight; that is, some alcoholics do see into the world of the spirit in their drunken state. This won't be surprising at all because alcohol is a drug that can generate high euphoric emotions, which activate the mind into its subconscious state that stimulates the spirit man to interact with the spiritual world!

However, the medically recognised negative effects of these drugs on the body, mind, and spirit make them an unacceptable means of mind activation for heart stimulation. Why destroy your life in your quest for creativity when there are other safer stimulants that can be maximised to activate the mind for heart stimulation? The body is a gift from the Creator God and He expects us to nourish and cherish it rather than destroy it with unhealthy substances like drugs and cigarettes.

(3) IDEA HYBRIDISATION

The heart of man is capable of independent thought origination. Once stimulated by the subconscious mind, the heart begins a search for the needed answer. If it cannot procure an answer, the eido centre, which is the eye of the spirit, can peep through the spiritual realm for the answer from superior sources, and once it identifies such an answer, the eido centre can notify the heart to initiate a communication exchange to retrieve the answer.

Never doubt this truth, superior sources exist. Examples of superior sources are human mentors and spiritual beings like God and His angels. Because your heart couldn't inherently conjure up the answers you need does not mean that the answer can't be originated from other superior sources. **The Principle of Hybridisation of Ideas** is about the fusion of minds and hearts of different persons in order to produce hybrid ideas. Hybrid ideas are synergistically superior ideas. This principle is also referred to as the **Mastermind Principle**.

In other words, just as minds can interact, the hearts of different people do interact to produce hybrid ideas. In its stimulated state, the heart of an individual does search other hearts for an answer. Likewise, the eido centre can peep into the spiritual reality of others to steal an answer. The censor of the spirit man is the Policeman that makes sure the individual stays within the confines of acceptable norms while his heart and the eido centre are active searching for answers.

However, never forget that the best Person to hybridise with is the Holy Spirit. He is the Author of all creativity. He created the entire universe (Gen.1:1,2; Job 33:4). If you know Him and relate with Him intimately, He can inspire your heart with creative thoughts far beyond your thinking just as He blessed Bezaleel and Aholiab with artistic creativity (Exo.31:1-6; 35:30-35), David with creative music (2Sam.23:1,2), Solomon with creative wisdom (1Kin.3:12), Paul with creative thoughts that enabled him to write more than 60 per cent of the New Testament Scriptures (2Pet.3:15,16).

CHAPTER 16
SECTION ONE PRACTICAL STEPS

WE HAVE COME TO THE end of Section One of the book. Below is a summary of practical steps mentioned in this section:

PRACTICAL ONE: TO DEVELOP YOUR MIND, STUDY AND KEEP STUDYING

Remember, your mind determines how much success you attain in life. Develop your mind by feeding on relevant information in the area of your need. In this age of information, we swim in oceans of information. Search for information relevant to your need and educate yourself with it. Of course, the best source of information is the Bible as it contains the mind of God for humanity. When you feed on the Scriptures of the Bible regularly, your mind will grow and develop.

PRACTICAL TWO: DON'T BE RASH, LEARN TO RATIONALISE SITUATIONS

However, merely acquiring information is not enough in most cases to generate the desired success. Such information needs to be analysed and synthesised into usable format. The process of rationalisation allows the mind of man to process the acquired information into a workable solution. Rationalisation is to think over the available information, analysing and synthesising all the available facts about the information.

Rationalisation is an integral part of our humanity. We are not goats, dogs, or any other animal. We are human beings with a mind capacity for rationalisation. Most cases of frustrations are because the individuals never think deep enough. Great achievers often withdraw to search within themselves for solutions to boggling issues. That is rationalisation. Therefore, don't rush into major decisions; bring your mind capacity to bear on the project. Let your mind analyse and synthesize the situation. This is Mind Processing as mentioned in Chapter 12.

However, note that the quality of your rationalisation is a function of information available to you. The more information you imbibe in a certain field, the keener and better your rationalisation ability. Interestingly, the more you exercise your mind in thinking, the keener your mind will grow and develop. Many of life's mistakes can be avoided if individuals can learn to think through with their minds and not to rush out emotionally in decision-making. One habit every man should develop is to avoid making conclusive decision at the height of emotions. When emotions are flying too high, many decisions made at such times often turn out to be wrong and may even be regrettably too costly.

Thus, at the height of anger, it is safer to postpone important decision. Rather, move away and let the powerful throbbing emotions cool off, before you reconsider the decision. By so doing, you are giving your mind faculties the opportunity to rationalise the situation, which is very vital for your overall wellbeing and success.

Indeed, the rule of thumb for good decision making is: 'Don't be rash; process every information that comes to you.' This is referred to as mind information procession or rationalisation. The more you do this, the easier it becomes.

PRACTICAL THREE: PRACTISE SCHEDULED MEDITATION REGULARLY

If we are to act within the confines of all we know, we will be grossly limited. Our knowledge determines how far we can go in life. The more we know, the more we can advance in life. Those who know this truth, attempt to go beyond the confines of their knowledge by tapping into another realm of existence, which is the spiritual realm. Such people know that there are answers to any questions; they know that they only need to pose the correct question(s) to their mind and ascend beyond the mental realm of the mind.

Once the mind is activated into its subconscious state, it lifts beyond the mental realm to stimulate the spirit, thereby allowing the individuals to interact at the spiritual realm, where answers to all questions reside. If you desire to go beyond the limitation of the information contained in your mind, you need to activate your mind appropriately.

As mentioned in this section, meditation is the chief method by which we can activate our mind. Kenneth Hagin (1917-2003), an American preacher, regarded as the Father of the Word of Faith Movement in Christianity, once told a story of how he engaged in long sessions of prayers and fasting certain days of each week at the early stage of his ministry. In one of such occasions, he narrated how the Spirit of God spoke to him to rather spend time more in meditation than just babbling words of prayers. When he decided to obey the counsel of the Holy Spirit, Hagin said he recorded more success in his ministry in one year than in his previous five years of ministry.

That has been the story of many Christians. They spend long hours praying and fasting, and feeling 'spiritual'; yet little results. Prayers and fasting are necessities to weed off the cockroaches and tares and empower the individual; nevertheless, if done with meditation on the Word of God, the individual will make more success in his life's endeavours.

Schedule time for regular meditation, during which moment you should pose challenging questions to your mind about confronting issues. As you do this, you are activating your mind to interact with the spirit to procure answers to the boggling questions of your life. Never allow your circumstances, environment, and people to set limits to what you can think and do. No matter how great a problem is, there is often a solution out there. Challenge your mind to greater heights and you will be surprised to see how elastic your mind can be; how far you can go in life. See you at the top!

PRACTICE THE FIVE STEPS TO CREATIVITY

In summary, the practical one, two and three mentioned here are all embodied in the Five Steps to Creativity discussed in this first section of the book. The Five Steps to Creativity finally reveal the pathway and the sources by which any individual can access creative ideas, and rise in his quest for success, advancement, and prosperity in life. These five steps to creativity, if practised consistently at will, are what can bring the ingenuity in a man to limelight.

SECTION 2

HOW TO DEVELOP YOUR SPIRIT FOR EXPLOITS (THE FORCE OF VISION)

Chapter 17
The Human Spirit – the Driving Seat for Life Exploit

In the first section of this book, it has been shown that the mind can interact with the spiritual; the activated mind is what stimulates the spirit. Feeding the mind with relevant information will cause the mind to grow and develop. However, if you desire to go beyond acquired stored information in your mind, you'll need to enter the realm of the spirit.

WHY WE NEED TO KNOW ABOUT OUR SPIRITUALITY

1. We are principally spirit beings

Life on earth is not funfair, rather it is warfare. Many individuals have become victims of adverse circumstances in life because of their ignorance of the wars that besiege them. One of the worst things that can happen to an army is to be unaware of the presence of a lurking enemy. As long as you are on earth, there are battles besieging your life and even threatening your existence which are waged by relentless enemies. Many cases of misfortunes, bad luck, frustrations, diseases, poverty, are physical evidences of the wars around us.

However, most of these wars are invisible to the physical senses. They are waged at the mental and spiritual realms by unseen forces.

In fact, the majority of the woes that betide many individuals have spiritual origin. Therefore, to be ignorant of spiritual reality is to become casualties of life.

The Fire Burns of Josephine

Josephine, a 37-year-old female was admitted as a case of extensive fire burnt that affected her chest, abdomen, back, neck, and both arms in late 2013. The burnt wounds were so bad that skin grafting was done twice. Despite intensive and rigorous wound care, the conditions rather grew worse each day. Sensitive laboratory tests to identify and characterise the infective organisms were done and appropriate medications based on laboratory findings instituted; yet the burnt wounds progressively worsened. Josephine was disconsolate and depressed, and had to undergo psychotherapy.

She was a business owner with employees that worked for her. At the time she had the fire burns, her business also started depreciating. The profit margin was rapidly dwindling for no apparent reason. To make matters worse, she started having squabbles with her husband that ended in a divorce. The children were traumatised and everything appeared to be fallen apart for Josephine after more than ten years of consistent success.

The cause of Josephine's fire burns was one of great intrigues that sounded like a fairy tale. She woke up in the middle of the night, heard strange voices in her head; thereafter started feeling fire burns on her body even though there was no evidence of any naked fire in the house. The fire burnt areas spread rapidly with associated pains and she had to call for an ambulance that night to urgently transfer her to the hospital. By the time she arrived at the hospital, there were visible fire burn blisters on her. Surprisingly, her husband who slept in the same bed with her did not have any fire burns.

Josephine was not a psychiatric patient, not a substance abusing individual and had no known family history of mental disorder; she was completely mentally sound. I and other colleagues took her history when she arrived in the hospital. We contacted the ambulance that brought her to confirm the genuineness of the story.

After emergency medical treatment was given and she was stabilized clinically, Josephine was referred to a second-level hospital for specialist attention. All the doctors in this referral hospital that attended to her were stupefied by her conditions, which were really not responding to treatment.

Notwithstanding, Josephine knew her problem was spiritual, but she felt helpless not knowing what to do. Finally, she was encouraged to invite a Pastor to minister to her. The Pastor came, led her in prayers of repentance, and counselled and prayed with her. Her recovery only started following the spiritual intervention by the Pastor, and this amazed the medical team. However, I was not surprise because I had known from the first time I saw Josephine that her problem was primarily spiritual. After some weeks in the hospital, she was discharged to go home.

About a year later, Josephine's spiritual knowledge in Christ Jesus had grown quite tremendously, and with such knowledge she began to wage war against her unseen enemies. When I saw her after about two years of discharge, joy and tranquillity had been restored to her, the husband had returned to the relationship, and her business had gradually started picking up.

2. The Spiritual Controls the Physical

To an individual who knows nothing about spiritual reality, Josephine's story will sound like religious fanaticism or spiritual deception. But how can a man in his right senses ever doubt the reality of the spiritual? Josephine's story corroborates the power of the spiritual on the physical; the spiritual controls the physical. Most physical disorders have their roots in the spiritual. If you deny the reality of spiritual existence, you are undoing yourself, and you are most likely going to end up frustrated. Many individuals who deny the reality of the spiritual often end their earthly journey in bitterness, frustrations, and ill-health.

It is incontestable that the spiritual world exists. What we see with our eyes is directly or indirectly controlled by the unseen reality. The optically unseen world is far larger and wields superior influence on our physical world. As such, a man who knows and develops his spiritual life can readily control his world than the individual who lives purely in the sensual, physical realm. For more on the reality of our spiritual existence, see SSB Book 1.

3. Embodied in the spirit are forces for success

Today, many people are very ignorant of the spiritual reality. Many people don't even know that they are principally spirit beings; hence, they become victims of their ignorance. Many cases of frustration and stagnation in life occur because we don't know how to utilise our spirit being to function in the spiritual world.

Indeed, many individuals are ignorant of the truth that they are spirit beings and that there is a whole lot of rich deposits that can be drawn from the spiritual realm to fulfil their life aspirations. Surprisingly, many people think that spirituality is the prerogative of Pastors and other Church leaders. One of the chief reasons for writing the SSB Book series, of which this book is the second in the series, is to unveil the reality of the spiritual existence and to demystify the spiritual life, so that the reader can know how to draw from the rich spiritual deposits to advance his life course.

Dr. Anosia and my Medical Career

In 1990 I gained a miraculous admission into a medical school. With such excitement I began my preclinical class. The courses were arranged in such a way that some were compulsory if a student must pass to a new class. If a student failed any of these compulsory courses, he would be given a chance to re-take the exams, and if he failed again, he would repeat the entire year. If he failed the repeat year, he would be asked to withdraw from the medical school. The passing rate into clinical class was less than 25 percent; meaning about 75 percent of the total number of fresh intake would drop out in the preclinical class. Knowing this, medical students would do everything to avoid entering a lecturer's bad book.

Dr. Anosia was one of the senior lecturers in charge of one of the compulsory preclinical courses. Because I was very active in campus evangelism and Dr. Anosia strongly believed in the evolution concept, denying the existence of God, our belief systems clashed. In an attempt to convince Dr. Anosia about the reality of God and creation, he became highly exasperated, feeling that I was challenging his authority. He invited me to his office and made it very clear to me that I should forget about medical school and that I would never graduate as a doctor.

Instantly, I knew that was a threat from the devil, the enemy. Dr. Anosia was a tool from the devil to stop my career before it was birthed. While Dr. Anosia was threatening me in his office, the boldness of faith from the Spirit of God came over me, and I replied to Dr. Anosia, "You'll see my graduation." He got even angrier and asked me out of his office. I later narrated the incidence to some of my friends, and everyone was quite afraid, promising they would pray for me.

True to his word, the result of the first exam I took of Dr. Anosia's course was 47 percent instead of the minimum passing mark of 50 percent. I knew it was a direct mark-down by Dr. Anosia. I went to a Christian lecturer, who was also active in our campus fellowship, and reported the case. He looked into the matter and informed me that there was no reason I shouldn't have passed the course. However, he couldn't do otherwise to assist me because he was not of the same department with Dr. Anosia. I spoke with my friends and we all reasoned it would not be wise to apply for a remark because Dr. Anosia, who was one of the senior lecturers in that department, would definitely ensure I still fail the course.

At this stage, I knew I had to use my spiritual authority. I entered into a weekend of prayers and fasting and personal all-night prayers. I cried to God to intervene, reminding Him of the fact that He gave me the admission into the medical school. The power of the Holy Spirit is real; never, ever doubt this! At the third day of the praying and fasting, the power of the Holy Spirit came so strong on me that I started uttering strange words of authority. I decreed in prayer that Dr. Anosia would leave the department during the time I would be writing the last exams of the preclinical class.

To the glory of God, my prayers were answered. Just before we took our last exams of the course, Dr. Anosia went on a sudden sabbatical leave! By the time he was back from the leave, we had written the exams, the papers marked and the scores approved and released by the University Senate. God did it that I passed the exams so well that the cumulative average compensated for the 47 percent. I moved on to the clinical class.

I never saw Dr. Anosia again until about eight years later. It was our swearing-in-ceremony as young graduate doctors in the year 1999 during which we took the modernised Hippocratic Oath. After the induction ceremony, while taking pictures with my family members, colleagues, and friends, I looked up and saw Dr. Anosia standing at some distance. Apparently, he had been standing there for some time watching me. Immediately, I sighted him, we both started moving towards each other. I gave him a victory smile and he cheekily mumbled, "So you have made it. Congrats." We shook hands and he promptly walked away.

As I write about the incidence, I hope Dr. Anosia would read this book, and I hope he would come to realise that, indeed, there is a God, the Creator of the universe, who watches over the affairs of man, and that no man, no matter his position, is bigger than his Creator! The point here is that my dream of becoming a medical practitioner would have perished and become aborted if I did not exercise my spiritual authority.

Indeed, many bright dreams have been truncated by forces too strong against the individuals. But if only such people would tune into the spiritual realm in Christ, all things would become possible, and their losses can be turned into gains. For *"with God all things are possible"* (Mat.19:26 KJV) and *"all things work together for good to those who love God, to those who are called according to His purpose"* (Rom.8:28 MEV).

HUMAN SPIRIT – DRIVING SEAT FOR LIFE EXPLOITS

Man is primarily a spirit being, possesses a soul, and lives in a physical body. Just as the human body can be divided into systems, the human spirit, sometimes referred to as the spirit man, consists of three components - the heart, eido centre, and censor (see SS Book 1). With the eido centre of your spirit man, you can see into your future. With the heart of your spirit man, you can receive specific information on how to make the seen future become a reality. With the censor of your spirit man, you can decipher and weigh accurately between right and wrong; and know the correct decisions to make and the right steps to take. In other words, with your spirit man, you can avoid unnecessary mistakes spiritually ignorant people make and with a robust spirit, you can crush any opposition against your advancement. Indeed, your ability to make right decisions and advance in life is enhanced when your spirit man is robustly grown and well developed.

In Section One, the book discusses how the mind can be developed for exploits. However, the section makes it also abundantly explicit that the mind interacts with the spirit man to generate the exploits. The truth is that the spirit is the driving seat for any life exploits. Genuine successful living has its root in the spiritual. A man who knows how to develop his spirit man and function with the universal laws of creation will attain great success and fulfilment.

THREE GREATEST FORCES THAT RULE THE WORLD

Embodied in our spirit beings are forces that can be utilised for success. For instance, the Three Greatest Forces that Rule the World are all spiritual forces, and any man who wields them correctly will achieve the desires of his heart. However, we shouldn't forget that our spirit being releases these forces to work in our favour when our activated mind stimulates the spirit.

Thus, this section of the book analyses how we can develop our spirit being and utilise it to achieve our aspirations and do exploits. It analyses the three greatest forces that rule the world and, most importantly, how we can wield them for our benefit and the good of humanity at large. These are the forces that we use to disarm all spiritual attacks and forcefully advance our positions in life. An understanding of these three forces unveils the laws that control our universe. If you know and utilise them, you are bound to become successful in every battle that will confront you.

Chapter 18
The Force of Vision

How is it that very few people tend to have the best that life can offer while many others lead their lives struggling and meeting with frustrations, misfortunes, and stagnations?

When we were children, we all dreamt of a good and wonderful life. As we grew into teenagers, many of these beautiful dreams become fantasies and appear unrealisable. By our thirties, many people have jettisoned their dreams altogether, and in our forties many of the dreams are dead and buried, and many individuals have resigned themselves to 'fate,' boxed into corners they never dreamt of.

That is the reality of more than 90 percent of humanity. However, less than 10 per cent of individuals have dreams that never die. They go on and live their dreams and even advance far beyond their primary dreams. These few have discovered that dreams do come true.

Analysis of the few individuals whose dreams materialise reveals some significant truths. The common characteristic feature among them is that they have learnt to develop themselves for exploits. One significant area of development about them is the realisation and utilisation of the three greatest forces that rule the world. They have learnt to utilise these three forces to their advantage and the benefits of humanity. This chapter introduces the first of these forces – the Force of Vision.

HOPE IS VISION

"And now abide faith, hope, love, these three; but the greatest of these is love" (1Cor.13:13 NKJV).

The term 'hope' in the above Scripture is from the Greek term *elpis*, which literally means an 'anticipation or an expectation (abstractly or concretely).' The common contemporary term for hope is vision. Thus, most people today use the term vision instead of hope. Hope, as used in First Corinthians chapter 13 verse 13, simply means vision. What a man hopes for is what he envisions to have.

VISION – SIGHT OF THE FUTURE

Vision is simply the sight of the future. To have a vision is to see the future destination. Vision is seeing the end from the beginning. It is the hope, the anticipation of a thing.

An important trait in human nature is the crave to know the future. Every individual wants to know what the future holds for him. That explains the reason why there is always mass movement of people from one place to another seeking for fortune-tellers on the eve of every New Year. Astrology, clairvoyance, spiritism, palm reading and many other unhealthy spiritualistic practices are all over the internet, all geared towards unravelling the future. Even science is curious in knowing what the future holds. For instance, genetic mapping and sequencing of human genome is one such area of science that seeks not just to understand present human genotypic and phenotypic alignment, but also to interpret what the future holds for the human race.

Why such crave for the future? The answer is not farfetched. If you know your future, you'll confidently articulate your actions that will help you get there and you'll obviously want to avoid any stumbling block that will derange your achieving that enviable future. In other words, a man who knows the future will command enormous power in controlling circumstances.

VISION HAS POWER

Our life moves in the direction of the dominant thought within our heart and mind. This dominant thought stems from what we see and believe in. In other words, it is the vision in us that generates the dominant thought, which drives our action.

Vision is a force; it has power. Vision drives us in the direction of its flow. People have been kept alive simply because they have a vision that props them. Vision has power to quench the forces of fear, ignorance, and poverty.

THE STORY OF 72-YEAR OLD CATHERINE

Catherine was a 72-year-old grandmother that presented in our hospital during my internship as a case of complicated diabetes. She had developed ulcers in the left foot that had spread to the lower part of the left leg. By the time she presented in the hospital, the foot had become gangrenous. After due assessment with thorough laboratory evaluation, our team decided the best option was to amputate the affected leg.

Considering her age, it was decided to bring in a psychologist to prepare her for the amputation. Grandma Catherine, as she was fondly called by her family members, was a jovial and highly energetic woman. I particularly enjoyed her company while she was in our ward. What she confided in me was alarming:

"You guys want to amputate my leg," she told me. "I appreciate your kindness and care. But I have told my family that my leg will NEVER be amputated," she emphasised on 'never.'

"I know it's difficult to accept that a part of the body be removed. But if it is not done, it would become more and more complicated and worsened," I explained. This was actually not the first time we had explained the situation to Catherine and her family.

"No, you don't understand," she interjected.

"What is it that I don't understand?" I asked with so much emotion and respect.

"I had a vision. It was the vision that controlled my life. It kept me alive this number of years. Now the vision has been accomplished. What more do I want? I'm rather grateful to God for allowing me to live my vision," she replied.

"That is interesting. But do you mind sharing with me that vision?" I enquired.

"Yes, but not today and not from me, but from Clara," she finally said.

Clara is Grandma Catherine's favourite granddaughter. From the family members, I came to know that Clara was the one that Grandma always confided in.

Interestingly, Grandma Catherine signed the consent after some psychological counselling and family support. The night before the scheduled operation, we did our routine medical check-up and booked the theatre ready. Before I left the ward at about 22H30, Catherine called me: "Thank you for your care. But don't forget to speak with Clara about the vision that kept me going all these years."

"Good night, Grandma. I'll see you tomorrow," I replied.

But that 'tomorrow' only left us with the body of Grandma. She gave up her spirit, and was certified clinically dead by the team on call. It was so dramatic that I was speechless with emotional turmoil. What could that dream, that vision that sustained Catherine's life and kept her going all these years be? The good thing was that, in her methodical way (Grandma Catherina was an organised, circumspect woman), she had actually informed Clara to answer any question I would be asking. The story by Clara was quite revealing. For privacy reasons, I wouldn't be able to reproduce it here.

VISION KEEPS A MAN ALIVE

The story I got from Clara about Grandma Catherine was about the power of vision. It was such powerful force inherent in vision that drove Grandma Catherine all through the years amidst challenging times. Her vision was so real to her, and it was not surprising it all came to fulfilment. After she had accomplished her vision, Grandma Catherine felt she had accomplished her life mission, hence there was no need to keep hanging on to life. The thought of amputation finally convinced her that her mission was accomplished and it was time to vacate the world scene, and she did exactly that.

In other words, it was vision that kept Grandma Catherine alive! Vision has power. It keeps a man alive. A man with a pulsating vision cannot die!

An individual who does not have a pulsating, driving vision will end up in mediocrity. Such an individual will live below his endowments. Vision is what pulls out our strengths, forcing us to utilise our natural and/or spiritual endowments. A man with no driving vision is like a rudderless ship that is tossed about without direction and is finally destroyed by the boisterous wind. God, who made man, knows the power of vision; He inspires wise King Solomon to document in about 970 BC:

"Where there is no vision, the people perish" (Pro.29:18 KJV).

FIVE MANIFESTATIONS OF THE POWER OF VISION

In short sentences, the power of vision can manifest in five ways:

(a) Vision gives direction in life
Vision is a tale of what the future holds. Vision is the visualisation of where we are going. In short words, vision is the compass for our

lives; it defines the direction we should head to. Without vision we cannot know exactly where to go to.

(b) Vision brings focus
Vision allows the individual to focus his attention on what is needful. We live in a world of many voices; vision is what causes us to avoid distraction and focus our energy, time, and resources on our goal. Vision makes us to draw up a mission statement, set goals and objectives, which are essential if we must make success in life because they define our target and the actions required to meet the target.

(c) Vision brings stability to life
There is peace and stability when we know where we are going. A visionless man is confused and restless.

(d) Vision brings joy and health
Joy is different from happiness. Whereas both are state of mind euphoria, happiness however is elicited by physical accomplishments while joy is generated by good expectations. That is, we are happy when we buy cars, build houses, win a competition, but we become joyous when we see and know of a bright future. The anticipation of a coming bright future feels the visioner with joy.

Joy is independent of what happens around, it comes by seeing the invisible, the expected glorious end. Our heart is joyful when we are hopeful of a good thing. In other words, the degree of our joy depends on the clarity, certainty, and significance of the vision to our lives.

"we rejoice in our hope of sharing the glory of God" (Rom.5:2 RSV).

Romans chapter 5 verse 2 vividly captures the relationship between hope (vision) and joy: the hope or vision of sharing the glory of God elicits tremendous joy in the regenerated believers.

In addition, don't forget this: joy is a facilitator and an engine of good health. The more joyous you are, the healthier you'll become.

> *"A joy-filled heart is curative balm, but a broken spirit hurts all the way to the bone" (Pro.17:22 VOICE).*

The clearer and more significant your vision, the livelier your health. People suffer adversity in health due to absence of a driving vision. That was the reality of Grandma Catherine, whose story was relayed on page 147. Her vision sustained her and kept her healthy. The day she felt her vision had been accomplished and no more accomplishments needed to be attained, she kicked the bucket!

(e) Vision engenders faith
When we see where we are going, all doubts disappear. The constitution of man is that we do not doubt what we see. 'Seeing is believing' is a Law of Faith. But it is not with the optical eye; it is not with the anatomical eye of the body. It is seeing with the eye of faith. Vision is seeing the future in our inner eye, and this triggers our faith. We become irresistibly drawn in the direction of what we see.

VISION DROVETHE CHRISTIAN MARTYRS

All the Apostles of Jesus Christ (except John the Beloved), most of the Church Fathers like Ignatius of Antioch (c.35-108 AD), the third bishop of Antioch and a student of Apostle John, and hundreds of thousands of Christians were killed by governments of various generations. Many of these martyrs were given the option to renounce their faith or be killed. They refused to renounce and died for their faith. By killing them, the assailants thought they would quench out the flames of the Gospel. But such deaths became the seed for the spread of the Gospel across the world. You can read about these Christian martyrs in SSB Book 6.

The willingness of these Christian martyrs to die for their faith had baffled their executors. Why would a man die willingly for a conviction? The answer is that he is seeing something that is compelling enough for him to lay down his life. He has a vision that prompts faith, compelling him to move in the direction of his vision. Vision drove the Christian martyrs. Great faith is born from a great vision.

THE FIVE CHARACTERISTICS OF VISION

Every genuine vision usually has five characteristics:

(1) Vision comes in Raw form
At the point of reception, a vision is usually raw. Raw, because it is not yet processed or been refined (see page 236 on **Vision Refinement**).

(2) Vision evokes Passion
A characteristic feature of any genuine vision is that it drives the individual. Men and women of vision are driven to accomplishment. Vision evokes passion for accomplishing a defined task. The clearer the vision of your life, the more forcefully the passion burns in you, seeking for its physical realisation. Indeed, a genuine vision is a passionately driven force.

(3) Vision defines a Target
A vision defines a target. The target of vision refers to the object of the vision (see page 289). In other words, a vision is aimed at accomplishing a given task. Your vision is still not complete when you cannot define a target. The passion of vision seeks to achieve a target. That is, a vision is targeted task-driven.

(4) Vision comes in Outsized form
A vision is usually larger than (outsized) your present state or provisions. At the point of reception, your present financial provision, intellectual ability, physical strength (health) and/or human connections may appear quite inadequate to accomplish the vision. For instance, a student who has a dream of becoming an engineer may wonder how he can achieve this considering his poor financial background.

(5) Vision appears Intimidating
Because of its outsized nature at the point of reception, a genuine vision often appears intimidating to the ears and eyes. This is why people who hear or perceive the vision may doubt its realization and/or even mock at it. Hence, the need for you to protect yourself from these negative influences that do have the potential of killing the vision. The visioner himself, if he knows nothing about the audacity of faith, may even doubt his vision, thereby, stifling its materialization.

Therefore, if today your vision appears outsized and intimidating to you, know that it is the same with virtually all visioners at the time they received their visions. But this should not pummel you into inactivity so that you do nothing about realising the dream. The world is ruled by dreamers. Visioners are pacesetters. Dare to dream big.

VISION TROPI

These five characteristics of vision are what this book refers to as the Vision TROPI (mnemonic for: T– Target, R – Raw, O – Outsized, P – Passion, I – Intimidating). Vision TROPI is a measure of how much energy, time, and resources you will need to accomplish the object of the vision.

A vision does not fulfil itself without applied Energy, Time, and Resources, which are the three primary raw materials to accomplish a vision. No vision can be achieved without an application of these three inputs – energy, time, and resources. A vision that has the five components of Vision TROPI is one that will lay great demand on your time, energy, and resources. The stronger the Vision TROPI, the more you are tasking your potentials. In fact, any vision you have that does not have the five components of the Vision TROPI, is signal that you are undercutting and undermining your potentials. Thus, Vision TROPI is a gauge that determines how much energy, time, and resources you will need to accomplish your vision.

Chapter 19
The Three Kinds of Vision

Vision starts as a thought process. Our heart either inherently originates the thought or receives it from an external source. External sources of thought are spirit beings such as the Holy Spirit of God, Satan, demons, human spirit, etc. Whatever is the source of the thought, the significant point to remember is that vision always starts as a thought process.

Because it begins as a thought process, the heart of the spirit man plays a crucial role in the conception of vision. With his heart, the regenerated individual does have access to the thoughts of God. That is, the heart of the regenerated spirit man can perceive thought from the Creator. Likewise, the heart of the spirit man can perceive thoughts from Satan, demons, and other negative spirits. In the same manner, the heart of our spirit man can communicate with the spirits of other humans (see SSB Book 1 for more on the tripartite nature of man).

SOURCES OF VISION

As discussed in SSB Book 1, spirit beings have the ability to originate and transmit thoughts. God, Satan, demons, humans, etc. are all spirit beings, hence, can originate and transmit thought processes. Therefore, vision, which begins as a thought in the heart of a spirit being, can originate from any of these three sources:

- Positive spirit beings such as God and His angels
- Negative spirit beings such as Satan and his demons
- Human spirits

THREE KINDS OF VISION

The kinds of vision conveyed by each of the three sources vary.

(1) Genuine Vision

It is quite surprising that many people live as if they were here on earth by accident. Parents may 'accidentally' bring a child into existence; nevertheless, such a child is not an accident with God. Without divine sanction, the child would not have been conceived in the first place. This should not surprise anyone. An analysis of the conception process confirms this.

Before the outset of menopause, a woman has between 100000 to 300000 eggs (ova), and at least one ovum is released during each ovulatory cycle. Who determines which ovum should be released?

Furthermore, the released ovum is fertilised by one spermatozoon from the man. At each ejaculation, a fertile male ejaculates 2 to 5 millilitres of semen (on average about a teaspoon). Each millilitre of the ejaculated semen contains about 100 million sperm, making a total of 200 to 500 million sperm being released at ejaculation. Out of these millions, only one can fertilise the released egg! Embryogenesis has confirmed that each ovum and each sperm are unique. If a different sperm had fertilised the ovum of your mum, there would have been a different person other than you that would be born! Who determines which sperm to fertilise a certain ovum? Is it merely a chance occurrence as postulated by some propounded unproven theories?

There is a Divine Hand guiding the fertilisation process. God, in His omnipotence and omniscience, designs which sperm to fertilise a certain ovum in order to produce a certain individual. That knowledge is beyond our present comprehension. In other words, *none of us is here by accident.*

> *God does not make any product without a purpose. Everything has a purpose (Ecc.3:1).*
>
> *"The Lord has made everything for its purpose" (Pro.16:4 RSV).*
>
> *"The Lord made everything for a purpose" (Pro.16:4 CEB).*
>
> *"The Lord has a reason for everything he does" (Pro.16:4 CEV).*

That means each of us has a specific purpose in His grand design. No product ever determines its purpose; rather the manufacturer determines the purpose of the product. For instance, it is the owner (manufacturer) that determines what purpose his clothing material should serve, whether the clothing material should be made into a shirt or a trouser; the clothing material does not determine what kind of product it should become. God is our Manufacturer; we are His products. Hence, He has determined our purpose before we were born.

> *"You made all the delicate, inner parts of my body and knit them together in my mother's womb. Thank you for making me so wonderfully complex! It is amazing to think about. Your workmanship is marvellous—and how well I know it. You were there while I was being formed in utter seclusion. You saw me before I was born and scheduled each day of my life before I began to breathe. Every day was recorded in your book!"*
>
> *(Psa.139:13-16 TLB).*

> *"You made my whole being. You formed me in my mother's body [womb]. I praise you because you made me in an amazing and wonderful way. What you have done is wonderful. I know this very well. You saw my bones being formed as I took shape in my mother's body. When I was put together there, you saw my body as it was formed. All the days planned for me were written in your book before I was one day old" (Psa.139:13-16 ICB).*

Note that the last sentence (verse 16) of the Scriptures quoted above emphatically states that before you were even 'one day old' (ICB) that God has already planned 'all the days' (ICB) of your life written clearly in His book. In other words, in His book of creation, God has already detailed out the purpose of your existence. CEV and NLT render this Psalms 139 verse 16 even more succinctly as follows:

> *Even before I was born, you had written in your book everything I would do" (Psa.139:16 CEV).*

> *You saw me before I was born. Every day of my life was recorded in your book. Every moment was laid out before a single day had passed" (Psa.139:16 NLT).*

Indeed, this cannot be overemphasized: *each of us was never an accident.* God made each of us for a specified purpose. You are the masterpiece of His creation, and He has predetermined the purpose of your existence.

> *"For we are God's masterpiece. He has created us anew in Christ Jesus, so we can do the good things he planned for us long ago"*
> *(Eph.2:10 NLT).*

> *"And we know that all things work together for good to those who love God, to those who are the called according to His purpose. For whom He foreknew, He also predestined to be conformed to the image of His Son, that He might be the firstborn among many brethren. Moreover whom He predestined, these He also called; whom He called, these He also justified; and whom He justified, these He also glorified" (Rom.8:28-30 NKJV).*

That purpose for your life is part of the thought process of God. The divine thought for each man can be known, and when pursued it places the individual at the centre of divine will for his life. Such divine thought is conveyed via vision.

Genuine Vision is the process by which a man receives the thought process of God for his life. In other words, a genuine vision actually defines the individual's life purpose or destiny as originally intended by the Creator. When a man has discovered his life purpose and starts to run with it, the life of such an individual assumes a momentum that baffles people that know nothing about genuine vision.

Therefore, an individual can know his life purpose by receiving a vision from God. A good example is Apostle Paul who received a vision of what he was created to be from God on his way to Damascus (Act.9:1-28). God is the same yesterday, today, and forever (Heb.13:18). If He revealed Paul's life purpose to him, He can still do it to anyone who seeks for it.

> *"For I know the thoughts that I think toward you, says the Lord, thoughts of peace and not of evil, to give you a future and a hope" (Jer.29:11 NKJV).*

> *"Call to Me, and I will answer you, and show you great and mighty things, which you do not know" (Jer.33:3 NKJV).*

The power of vision in pursuit of meaningful existence cannot be overemphasized. Genuine vision enriches not just your life but the world at large as it unveils a man's life purpose. It is in your life purpose that all your talents are expressed. John D. Rockefeller (the first American billionaire), Thomas Edison (the inventor of the electric lamp), Edward Jenner (discovered vaccines for smallpox), Smith Wigglesworth (a world renowned evangelist), Florence Nightingale (the architect of modern nursing practice), and many others, are admired even by generations after them. A common secret in all of them is the discovery of their life purposes, which enabled them to correctly deploy their talents in their fields of passion. If they did, we can also. Genuine vision is one way a man can know his life purpose.

(2) Counterfeit Vision

Also, negative spirits like Satan and demons do also project thoughts into the hearts and minds of men. These thought processes from any of these negative spirits do not unveil the life purpose of a man. The reason is because Satan and demons were not the creators (manufacturers) of man, hence, they do not know the whole details of a man's life. Thus, thought processes obtained from negative spirits and perceived by the hearts of men only result in fake or false purposes, and therefore, the visions that unveil such false purposes are counterfeit visions.

An Example of Counterfeit Vision

An interesting event occurred in ancient Israel and is told in First Kings chapter 22. In 853 BC, Jehoshaphat, King of Judah, joined forces with Ahab, the King of the Northern Kingdom of Israel, to wage war against the King of Aram. As they prepared for war, King Jehoshaphat, being a godly man, wanted to know what the future held for them, hence, he suggested to his host, King Ahab, to inquire from Jehovah, the God of Israel, about the outcome of the approaching war. Thus, King Ahab gathered the prophets in the land together, about four hundred men, and inquired, *"Shall I go against Ramoth Gilead to fight, or shall I refrain?"* All the prophets replied in unanimity: *"Go up, for the Lord will deliver it* into the hand of the king" (1Kin.22:6 NKJV).

However, King Jehoshaphat's spirit was not convinced of the prophecy. The eido centre of his spirit man could sense that the prophecy of these prophets was not genuine, and that the vision they held was counterfeit. Therefore, King Jehoshaphat requested, *"Is there not still a prophet of the Lord here, that we may inquire of Him?"* (1Kin.22:7 NKJV).

Of course, there was a Prophet of God, Micaiah the son of Imlah, in the land, who feared no one; he spoke as directed by God, his prophetic utterances often confronted the evil works of King Ahab. For that reason, King Ahab disliked Prophet Micaiah. However, because of the insistence of King Jehoshaphat, Prophet Micaiah was sent for. The words of the prophecy of Micaiah to King Ahab are very revealing:

> *"Then Micaiah said, 'Therefore hear the word of the Lord: I saw the Lord sitting on His throne, and all the host of heaven standing by, on His right hand and on His left. And the Lord said, 'Who will persuade Ahab to go up, that he may fall at Ramoth Gilead?' So one spoke in this manner, and another spoke in that manner. Then a spirit came forward and stood before the Lord, and said, 'I will persuade him.' The Lord said to him, 'In what way?' So he said, 'I will go out and be a lying spirit in the mouth of all his prophets.' And the Lord said, 'You shall persuade him, and also prevail. Go out and do so.' Therefore look! The Lord has put a lying spirit in the mouth of all these prophets of yours, and the Lord has declared disaster against you" (1Kin.22:19-23 NKJV).*

Thus, a 'lying spirit' gave vision of conquest to about 400 prophets of King Ahab. These prophets prophesied victory for King Ahab, whereas the genuine vision was an impending defeat. The 'lying spirit' gave a deceptive, counterfeit vision, while the Spirit of God in Prophet Micaiah revealed the genuine vision.

Unfortunately, instead of King Ahab to humble himself before God and pray for mercy, he allowed pride to destroy his life. The ungodly King Ahab was enraged by the outspokenness and forthrightness of Micaiah's prophecy, and he ordered Prophet Micaiah to be incarcerated in jail. Ahab rather chose to believe the false prophecy of optimism which gave him counterfeit vision. With such high hope, he went into the battle. Sadly, he never survived the battle.

This battle of 853 BC, recorded in detail in First Kings chapter 22 verses one to 40, has been confirmed by archaeological discovery, the Kurk Monoliths, discovered in 1861. The monoliths are two Assyrian stelae that contain a description of the reigns of Ashurnasirpal II (883-859 BC) and his son Shalmaneser III (859-824 BC). The monoliths contain a description of the Battle of Qarqar, which records the Assyrian military advancement into Israel to fight Ahab's forces of 2000 chariots and 10000 foot soldiers, and Ahab was defeated and killed. From this archaeological finding, this battle that claimed King Ahab's life has been precisely and accurately dated to 853 BC.

The Danger of Counterfeit Vision

Satan and demons are real, and they do project thoughts into the hearts and minds of men. Such thought processes only produce counterfeit visions. The reason is because these negative forces are limited in their knowledge of the future. They know nothing about your future. However, they do manipulate their victims into accepting the fabricated visions they have projected.

Interestingly, the prophets of King Ahab never knew they were having a counterfeit vision with a deceptive message, and that is the usual story of the practitioners and the clients who patronise demonic spirits for visions about their lives; many people are deceived to believe that such visions are genuine. Today, palm reading, clairvoyance, astrology, ancestral worship, and many other spiritual activities abound on the internet and the mass media. People patronise them in great numbers because their predictions for their lives appear accurate.

Unfortunately, many of these susceptible clients don't realise that these spiritual practitioners utilise negative spirits. Worse of it is that these gullible individuals are unaware that the so-called accurate predictions are actually manipulations; since negative spirits can't see far into the future, they often make decisions based on extrapolations of what they hear and perceived which they utilise to manipulate their victims.

In 2015, a popular spirit medium made predictions about an important soccer tournament. The prediction was all over the print and electronic media. However, it turned out that the outcome did not match the prediction. Some of the followers of this spirit medium were disappointed. Sadly, a great number still flocked around the spirit medium.

There is danger in patronising these negative spirits. Individuals that do such expose themselves to demonic infestation; they become vulnerable to manipulative caprices of negative forces. Your Creator, God, detests any practice with negative spirits.

> *"There must not be anyone among you who passes his son or daughter through fire; who practices divination, is a sign reader, fortune-teller, sorcerer, or spell caster; who converses with ghosts or spirits or communicates with the dead. All who do these things are detestable to the Lord! It is on account of these detestable practices that the Lord your God is driving these nations out before you" (Deu.18:10-12 CEB).*

Negative spirits were created by God as angels. However, being moral agents with the ability to make decisions, they rather chose a rebellious lifestyle contrary to divine regulations for which divine punishment was meted out that wrought utter destruction of their nature (see SSB Book 3). As such, there is no truth in negative spirits; telling lies is their native language (Joh.8:44). Sorrows and heartaches are the lot of those humans that run after them.

> *"The sorrows of those who run after another god shall multiply"*
> *(Pro.16:4 ESV).*

There are evidences that curses, misfortunes, strange diseases, and untimely deaths, run in families of those that run after negative spirits. People who dabble into spiritism practices with these negative spirits often find that they are retrogressive spiritual practices.

(3) Ambition

The third kind of vision is that which originates from the human spirit, and it is popularly known as Ambition. Since man is a spirit being, man has the capacity to originate thought; in fact, all spirit beings have the inherent ability to originate thoughts in their hearts (see SSB Book 1).

Ambition versus Genuine Vision – The Story of My Career Choice

In September 1985, I was lying down on a cemented cold floor in our church, Assemblies of God, Ataba. The church building was made up of mud walls and zinc roof with a capacity for about 60 worshippers; but most times it was never full, the average attendant being about 40 (both adults and children) on Sundays. On this particular day, I was praying and fasting, enjoying a relationship with the Holy Spirit of God. Then suddenly I just knew inside of me that I was to be a medical doctor. My eyes opened spiritually, I could see myself 10 years ahead. I saw myself wearing a white gown with a stethoscope around my neck and I saw myself in a room inside a house that looked like a student hostel on a busy street. The impression was so strong in my spirit man with no any iota of doubt that God wanted me to be a medical doctor.

At this time in my life, I had never seen any medical doctor with a white coat and I had never seen a stethoscope. I was the first born of my parents. According to my father, he was living in Port Harcourt, a rapidly growing city in Nigeria. When it was time for my mum to give birth to me, my father sent my mum to Ataba, a small town, as the civil war was just over. I grew up in this small town with no exposure to hospital services.

My father was very methodological and disciplined. By his assessment of my talents, my father decided accountancy would be the best career for me. Thus, while growing, my father started programming me to be an accountant; he bought some accounting books and started drumming in my ears why accountancy was the best for my talents. Hence, I had already got used to the idea of being an accountant. However, when I came back that day from the Church and informed my dad that God spoke to me to become a doctor, he didn't take it very kindly. My dad was a strong-willed man and he loved to be in full control of any situation.

"*Where did you see God, how did He look like? Don't be ignorant, but think*," my dad thundered as I informed him of my divine encounter that day.

One thing with spiritual reality is that senses are acute and long-lasting. As I write about this experience, it's as vivid to me as it was in 1985. Despite all odds, I got an admission in the medical school just as God told me. In 1995, in our clinic years, I walked into the clinic block in a busy street in Port Harcourt. I was allocated to a room. As I entered the room, my mind started roving. I felt I had been there before! I went round the building trying to remember when I must have seen it before. Then it suddenly dawn on me that it was in a vision I had in 1985 in that mud church building! My recreated eido centre had seen the building about ten years earlier. As I stood in the room with my white coat and a stethoscope around my neck, the recollection was so acute and vivid of what I saw ten years earlier in that faraway small town, Ataba. What an experience! I raised my hands and gave thanks to God, the Father of genuine vision.

ADVICE FOR PARENTS AND GUARDIANS

If I had followed the leading of my father, I would have ended up as an accountant. That was my father's career vision for me based on his assessment of my strengths. Like every good father, my dad wanted the best for me. Unfortunately, his best was not the Manufacturer's purpose for my life. My father's assessment of my gifting fell outside the purpose for which I was created. God, who is the Manufacturer of man, purposed that I should be a medical practitioner.

Thus, if I had pursued the accountancy line of training that would have been an ambition and not the genuine vision I was created for. Vision that originates from man is an **ambition**. Often it is not a genuine vision. It is a glorified human vision that comes as a result of human thinking and assessment.

This is why parents and guardians need to be wary forcing their children and wards to choose particular careers. Parents and guardians can 'guide' their children and wards in choosing the right careers. Forcing a child to follow a certain career path can ultimately make the child to miss his genuine vision, and thus miss a life-time opportunity of really experiencing the joy of living in one's life purpose and leading an impactful existence.

But how can a parent guide his child correctly if he himself knows nothing about correct choice of career? A parent who knows nothing about genuine vision may not be able to lead his ward into his genuine vision. One of the reasons for writing this book is to simplify and demystify the nature of man. Enclosed within the human nature are fabrics that can lead a man to discover his life purpose, and hence, make correct choice of career. By the time you read through this book, your understanding of career choice will have been dramatically enhanced, and may such knowledge draw you and your wards closer to your Creator through Christ Jesus, the Author of all genuine visions.

Chapter 20
How to Know Genuine Vision

Many people claim they receive a vision from God, only to discover later that they were wrong. However, we can know if a vision is from God. That is, we can differentiate between genuine vision and counterfeit vision.

HOW TO KNOW VISION FROM GOD

There are five main differences between a genuine vision from God and a counterfeit vision from negative spirits; and they are:

(i) Genuine vision engenders Humility
A genuine vision fosters meekness or humility. In fact, it takes sincere meekness of the heart to receive a genuine vision; pride often makes it difficult for an individual to access a genuine vision. In addition, the processes to fulfil a genuine vision are enough to engrave meekness in the lives of the visioner. On the other hand, a counterfeit vision is boastful and centred on the self. That is, a counterfeit vision swims in pride.

(ii) Genuine vision is impartial
A genuine vision respects the rights, privileges, and personality of others. It detests injustice. That is, a genuine vision will not seek unfair judgment in the course of its implementation. This is not true for a counterfeit vision, which has little or no regard for equity, justice, and fair play.

(iii) Genuine vision is peaceful
A genuine vision brings peace and tranquillity to the visioner, people and environments. On the other hand, a counterfeit vision is destructive; it leaves disruption, sorrow, and sadness in its pathway.

(iv) Genuine vision is progressive
A genuine vision brings progress to you and the people around you. A genuine vision is selfless; it is helpful. However, a counterfeit vision ends up destroying people and the environment.

(v) Genuine vision is pure
A genuine vision abhors immoral conduct; there is no secretive lifestyle in a genuine vision because it ultimately comes to the open. However, a counterfeit vision thrives in immoral demeanours.

THE HIPPP CRITERIA

These five criteria, represented by the acronym HIPPP (representing Humility, Impartiality, Peacefulness, Progressiveness, and Purity), for distinguishing genuine from counterfeit visions are not the idea of psychologists or theologians, but are divine. The Holy Spirit of God spoke through James the brother of Jesus to pen down these criteria:

> *"But the wisdom that is from above is first pure, then peaceable, gentle, willing to yield, full of mercy and good fruits, without partiality and without hypocrisy" (Jam.3:17 NKJV).*

The term 'wisdom' in the above Scripture is from the Greek word *sophia*, which primarily means surpassing divine wisdom given to humans via vision. Hence, James was using *sophia* to describe the kind of wisdom that can come from God, and this wisdom is communicated as thought processes (visions) of God into the heart of men. In other words, the visions of God are divine wisdom.

The Epistle of James chapter 3 verse 17 identifies the characteristics of Sophia:

(1) pure and without hypocrisy (that is, **purity**)
(2) peaceable (that is, **peacefulness**)
(3) gentle and willing to yield (refers to **humility** or meekness)
(4) full of mercy and good fruits (refers to **progressiveness** or helpfulness)
(5) without partiality (refers to **impartiality**).

Any thought process from God must bear these five characteristics of Sophia – purity, peacefulness, humility, progressiveness, and impartiality; anything short of these cannot be from God.

For any thought process you perceive in your heart, use the **HIPPP criteria** to determine its source. *You can never go wrong by applying these criteria to determine if your vision is from God or not.*

AMBITION versus GENUINE VISION

The differences between human ambition and genuine vision are:

(a) Ambition is short-lived

Ambition often dies with the death of the visioner or after a few generations of existence. A genuine vision outlives the visioner because its Source is the eternal God, who crafted the vision within His overall eternal purpose. God's purpose is eternal, and within this eternal purpose, He has a place for each one of us. Vision is the vehicle in which He reveals your own part of this eternal purpose. However, human ambition does not recognise such eternal purpose; it only sees the short term.

> *"The counsel of the Lord stands forever, the thoughts and plans of His heart through all generations" (Psa.33:11 AMP).*

"There are many plans in a man's heart, but it is the Lord's plan that will stand" (Pro.19:21 NLV).

(b) Ambition is limiting

Ambition is crafted and often based on the dominance of a particular talent or skill. For instance, many that have a good voice naturally think they'll become musicians. However, many end up frustrated and dejected while trying to build a musical career. Having a good voice does not automatically mean you are created to be a musician; the good voice can as well be deployed in other fields.

Furthermore, ambition utilizes only a fraction of our gifting unlike a genuine vision, which ends up utilising all our gifting. At the early stage, it may begin with just a gift, but ultimately genuine vision will end up employing all of your gifts. In other words, ambition limits the expression of your abilities while genuine vision releases all the abilities you are created with.

(c) Ambition results in struggling

Many ambitious acts are as a result of the push influence from others. This is especially true for children whose parents forced them into careers to fill in some family responsibilities like family business. Such children choose the careers to please their parents, often not considering their individual gifts at all. Because they are not wired for the careers, they end up struggling and becoming frustrated.

On the other hand, if you are in your genuine calling (genuine vision), you sail through successfully despite any obstacle(s). A man in his genuine vision doesn't feel the strain of vision execution, rather he feels at ease and relaxed in the face of upheaval, mountains and may even be enjoying the heat process, while a man with ambition is most times filled with anguish.

(d) Ambition is not fulfilling

Ambition does not guarantee genuine fulfilment in life. At best, ambition can give a temporal sense of satisfaction, and it will at the long run leave the individual drained and overused. There are many people who have made substantial progress pursuing their ambition, yet they remain unfulfilled and frustrated, forcing some to resort to drugs in order to boost their emotions and changed their moods.

THE STORY OF DR. ORJI

In March 2017, Dr. Orji, a medical practitioner, while being driven across the Third Mainland Bridge in Lagos in his beautifully expensive Nissan Xterra SUV, suddenly ordered his driver to pull over. He stepped out of the vehicle and jumped off the bridge into the Lagoon on a Sunday evening. Officers from the Rapid Response Squad (RRS) and Lagos State Traffic Management (LASTMA), together with the marine unit officials of the Nigeria Police Force, attempted to rescue the doctor, deploying police boats and drones in the search and rescue exercise. Three days later, the late doctor's body was recovered from the Lagoon by the Marine Police. What really happened?

Dr. Orji was never known to have a mental disorder. No financial squabble was associated with him, and no known serious family disputes. The cause of the death of the young Dr. Orji remained a mystery despite all investigations being conducted. Accusing fingers were pointed at job dissatisfaction and medical burnout. But the truth about job dissatisfaction and burnout is that they are hinged on lack of fulfilment. Lack of fulfilment in life is a real cankerworm as it can eat deep, and it is often the product of pursuing an ambition.

On the other hand, there is no way you'll run with a genuine vision and not receive fulfilment. Many who run with their ambition suffer burnt-outs and look older than their chronological age. In comparison, genuine vision triggers inner sense of peace and tranquillity which ambition does not offer.

Chapter 21
How to Receive Genuine Vision via Revelation

One of the great questions in life that rings through the heart of every human is: 'Why am I here?' There is a drive in each of us to know why we are here on earth and how to accomplish it.

> *"God has made everything beautiful for its own time. He has planted eternity in the human heart ..." (Ecc.3:11 NLT).*

The drive is from the heart of our spirit man. As spirit beings, we are part of the grand eternal purpose of God, and as humans created in the image and likeness of God, we occupy the centre purpose of this eternal grand design. It is a drive to know the future, for in the future exists that life purpose, the blueprints, of each one of us. In fact, Good News Translation (GNT) renders Ecclesiastes chapter 3 verse 11 as:

> *"He [God] has set the right time for everything. He has given us a desire to know the future..."*

A genuine vision is a force that not only drives us into our future but opens up the future for our lives. That is, a genuine vision is the avenue by which the desired future is unveiled. Why genuine vision is very powerful is because a genuine vision reveals our life's purpose – the reason we are created. Through genuine vision, we can see the end from the beginning. Like a journey, we are either in the right or wrong path. Genuine vision points out the right path, pulling us in the pathway of what we are created to be. Therefore, knowing how to access genuine vision is of paramount significance for every human being.

There are basically three ways to receive genuine vision – **Revelation**, **Passion**, and **Talents**. This chapter discusses Revelation.

TYPES OF REVELATION

Revelation simply means unveiling of a secret; a disclosure of a thing. God does convey genuine visions as revelations to man. This revelation message can be in the form of images, sound, or impressions. Whether they are images, sound, or impressions, they all convey the thought of God to the heart of the spirit man. Most times, God uses a combination of these three – images, sound, or impressions – at the same time while passing across His message. Let's analyse a little more of each of these three forms of revelation.

(1) Revelation Images

Revelation images can be:

(a) Open Vision

An open vision is when all the bodily senses are suspended while the spirit man 'sees' physical images. That is, in open vision, the individual is completely unaware of the events around him while his spirit man sees and is engrossed with the visual images of the vision. An open vision is sometimes referred to as ***trance***. An example of an open vision was the experiences of the Roman soldier, Cornelius, and Peter. God was about to do a new thing that would change the destiny of mankind forever – the conversion of the Gentiles. Cornelius was to be the first recipient and Apostle Peter was chosen as the vehicle for the task. To convince Cornelius and Peter, God used open visions to communicate His thoughts to them (you can read up the interesting story in Acts chapter 10).

Also, Apostle John saw an open vision while he was at the Island of Patmos in about AD. 100. He later wrote down his vision in a book, the Book of Revelation, which is the last book of the Bible. In the same manner, God can reveal our life's purpose in an open vision.

(b) Closed vision

A closed vision is when only some of the body senses are suspended while the spirit man becomes aware of physical images. That is, the individual is aware of the events around him while at the same time he is seeing physical images. A good example was the appearances of Jesus after the resurrection to the disciples. For instance, when the resurrected Lord appeared to Cleopas and his friend on the road to Emmaus from Jerusalem, they saw Jesus while they were at the same time physically aware of their environment. However, they did not recognise Him until He sat down to eat with them, took the bread, said the blessing, broke the bread and gave it to them (Luk.24:13-35).

Other examples of a closed vision include the announcement of the birth of Samson to his mother by an angel of God (Judg.chpt.13), and the appearance of Angel Gabriel to Zechariah, the father of John the Baptist, and later to Mary, the mother of Jesus (Luk.1:5-38).

Gideon was a poor farmer; he never knew he had an enviable destiny of bringing liberation and providing leadership to the scattered tribes of Israel. His life purpose was to be a redeemer to his people. But he was ignorant of such lofty destiny; hence, the best he could do was a subsistent agriculture. One day he had a closed vision in which an angel of God appeared to him to unveil his destiny. When he started to walk in this revealed genuine vision he discovered he could maximise his gifting (Judg.chpt.6).

Gideon lived about 3000 years ago, but the principle behind his success can still be applied in our personal lives. Most of us are living below our potentials. Many are frustrated and stagnated because they are pursuing their ambitions instead of their life purpose. A closed vision is one way God can unveil our life purpose to us. But how does one have such an encounter? Don't drop the book, but study on and you'll find the answer.

(2) Revelation Sound

Revelation sound is when an individual hears only a voice or sound but no physical image. God does speak, and a sensitive person can hear His voice. Scriptural analysis shows that the voice of God comes in two main formats:

(a) Audible Authoritative Voice

The Audible Authoritative Voice occurs when the individual actually hears a sound with his ears. In most cases, if other people are there, they can as well hear the sound. An example was when Saul was intercepted by God on his way to arrest Christians from Damascus. A bright penetrating light shown about Saul and he heard the authoritative voice of Jesus audibly communicating with him. The people travelling with Saul heard the voice, though never understood the discussion that went on between Jesus and Saul. This was an encounter with a genuine vision that unveiled the life purpose of Saul, who later became the Apostle Paul. Without such an encounter, Saul might have lost out in eternity and his life purpose taken over by some other willing person (Act.9:1-9).

A Midnight Encounter

On 7th of July 1987, at about 12 midnight, while we were still performing burial rites of my dad who had died three days earlier, I heard a divine encounter with the Audible Authoritative Voice of God. It was in the town, Ataba, which as at then was not yet connected to the national electricity grid. Thus, the source of light we were using to keep the burial wake was a diesel-powered generator, which would be switched on from 6pm to about 10pm during the burial rites. Usually, the burial rites lasted for 7 days during which family members and sympathisers would keep a vigil with mournful songs.

Following the death of my dad, my emotions were mixed up, but the Presence of the Holy Spirit would well up in my heart, strengthening me from within. Indeed, that was when I began to fully grasp the ministry of the Holy Spirit as the Comforter. On this particular day (7th of July 1987), I was sitting in the parlour with about seven other men and women. Then unexpectedly, the Voice sounded: "Captain," calling my first name. Everyone there with me heard it. We checked among ourselves and no one called. While wondering, the authoritative Voice called again: "Captain, Captain."

The Voice sounded right through the ceiling above our head, quietly but very authoritative. The people there concluded it was a 'spirit' calling me; their superstitious beliefs made them to believe it was the spirit of my dead father. Since the electricity generator was put off about two hours earlier, some of the women there took lanterns and started searching around the compound for the 'spirit' of my dead father.

However, I knew it was the Voice of my Heavenly Father. It was a familiar Voice, the Voice of God, which I had been hearing since I became regenerated (born again) in Christ in 1983. Hence, I quickly excused myself and went to a room. When alone, I enquired: "Lord, what do you want to tell me?" The conversation that ensued changed my life permanently as it strengthened me, refocused me, and formed the basis of my life's pursuit. There in the room, God confirmed again that He wanted me to be a medical practitioner and I should not allow emotions of people to influence my judgment. Moreover, He warned me to be careful of some people (He mentioned their names) and some habits (He also mentioned the negative habits), especially now that my earthly father had died. He was so stern in His warning that it became part of my consciousness ever since.

Indeed, the Authoritative Voice of God is, in most cases, a warning of an impending doom. The biographies of individuals who walked closely with God such as Kenneth E. Hagin confirmed this. When they heard of the Authoritative Voice of God, the message conveyed is often a warning. A good Biblical example was the story of the boy Samuel and the High Priest Eli. The two sons of Eli, Hophni and Phinehas, were committing sacrileges and illicit sexual relationships that desecrated the holy priesthood office. Their father, Eli, was not firm on them, allowing them to continue their desecration. God was not happy and decided to warn Eli and his household through the boy Samuel. It was in the night when the Authoritative Voice of God came to Samuel (see 1 Sam.chpt.3).

(b) Still Small Voice:

Besides the Authoritative Voice, another form of revelation sound is the Still Small Voice, which is when the individual hears a voice in the heart of his spirit man. It is a soft, gentle Voice of God. It comes more like a quiet, whispering voice. Oh what a sweet, gentle Voice! It is one of the beauty of being regenerated (born again) in Christ. Any regenerated individual will tell you how beautiful and reassuring the Still Small Voice can be to his life. Personally, the Still Small Voice has been an inestimable treasure as it has continued to empower my life.

The Story of My Graduation Ceremony

I often tell the story of Swearing-in Day, which is when newly graduated doctors take the Hippocratic Oath of allegiance to their profession. Mine was in the year 2000. I didn't have money to buy a suit to dress up for the ceremony. At the last hours of preparation, I was disappointed by where I thought I would borrow a suit from. Hence, I made urgent arrangements to get another one from a friend. Jumping from one taxi to another, I finally arrived at the venue of the ceremony. By the time I arrived, I was a bit late with all other participants and guests just taking their seat, and my name was number one on the list of the graduating doctor. If I missed the ceremony, I'd have to wait for another whole year to join the next batch.

As I rushed into the hall, there at the door was the College Secretary, the last person no student would want to meet when he made a mistake in our medical school. Immediately I saw the College Secretary, the Still Small Voice of the Holy Spirit jerked into my heart: "Don't listen to her taunts; focus on why you are here," said the Still Small Voice. Thus, as the secretary taunted me for the lateness, I was calculatedly calm on my inside:

"Captain, you're late," said the College Secretary.

"I'm sorry, Ma" I replied.

"Stupid action," she said.

"I'm sorry, Ma" I replied.

"I can stop you from participating and you'll wait for next year."

"I'm sorry, Ma" I replied.

She continued her punishment with words, but her taunts were like water pouring on the back of a duck fowl. The lateness and the taunting would have disorganised me and the small party we had packaged for the celebration. What quieted me down completely was the Still Small Voice. Indeed, God is interested even in the smallest details of our lives.

Prophet Elijah and the Still Small Voice

After a battle for survival, due to threat to his life issued by none other but the state, Prophet Elijah ran away from the wicked Queen Jezebel. He was frustrated and despaired of life. For the next forty days, Elijah was fleeing from the wicked Queen, until he finally came to Mount Horeb.

At Mount Horeb, God unveiled the next agenda of Elijah's life purpose through a Still Small Voice revelation. Prophet Elijah heard the Still Small Voice of God, giving him three specific instructions:

- Firstly, Prophet Elijah must go back way via the Wilderness of Damascus and anoint Hazael as king over Syria
- Next, Prophet Elijah was to come into Ramoth Gilead, a Levitical city of refuge, located within the territorial allotment of the tribe of Gad, east of the River Jordan, and there and anoint Jehu the son of Jehoshaphat (not King Jehoshaphat of the Southern Kingdom of Judea), grandson of Nimshi, as the tenth king over the Northern Kingdom of Israel to exterminate the wicked dynasty of Ahab.
- Finally, Prophet Elijah was to anoint Elisha the son of Shaphat of Abel Meholah as prophet to replace; invariably, signalling the beginning of an end of Prophet Elijah's eventful ministry on earth.

Note that this insightful revelation of Prophet Elijah came via an encounter with the Still Small Voice of God. It brought tranquillity and peace to his heart and defined the next step of his life purpose. That is, the encounter with the Still Small Voice of God gave him a genuine vision (see 1 Kings 19).

The Still Small Voice is a quiet voice of God as He speaks right into the heart of the spirit man. To a spiritually sensitive individual, the Still Small Voice may sound so loud that the individual may think people around will hear, which is not usually true; only the visioner will hear the voice.

(3) Revelational Impression

Impression is a revelation that is devoid of appearance of image or sound, rather it is the direct implanting of a thought process in the heart of a man. The thought process can come as a sudden flash or as a gradual built-up into the heart, and a spiritual man picks up the signal as a heartfelt impression. Impression is also known as Perception. It is a witness, an imprint, in the heart of the spirit man, hence, sometimes referred to as Inner Witness.

An Example of Impression

An example of an impression revelation was what happened in the early Church in Jerusalem. Some members of the sect of the Pharisees who had become Christians rose up to defend the idea of male circumcision and observation of the Law of Moses by the Gentile brethren, saying, "It is necessary to circumcise them [Gentile brethren], and to command them to keep the Law of Moses" (Act.15:5 NKJV).

These uninformed Jewish Christian were secretly being gingered up by the bigoted Jewish leadership, who tried to infiltrate the Christian community with false brethren, whose goal was to create rivalry among the brethren of the young Church and hence thwart the wave of Christianity revival that was sweeping across the Roman world.

To settle this contending issue once and for all, a meeting of all the Eleven Apostles (at this time, one of the Apostles, James the Elder and son of Zebedee, was already executed by King Agrippa in AD 44) and leaders of the Church was summoned in AD 49 in Jerusalem, chaired by James the Brother of Jesus, the Resident Pastor of the Jerusalem Church. This epoch meeting is known as the Council of Jerusalem; the story is recorded in Acts of the Apostles chapter 15 (see SSB Book 6).

Apparently, the Holy Spirit was keenly monitoring and directing every step of the young Church, and the final decision reached by the Council of Jerusalem as shown by the unanimous letter that was sent out to the Gentile Churches from the Council:

> *"We apostles and leaders send friendly greetings to all of you Gentiles who are followers of the Lord in Antioch, Syria, and Cilicia...The Holy Spirit has shown us that we should not place any extra burden on you" (Act.15:23,28 CEV).*

Thus, it was the Holy Spirit that guided them to their final decision. The question is: how did the Holy Spirit guide them? The answer is in the subsequent verses:

> *"For it seemed good to the Holy Spirit, and to us, to lay upon you no greater burden than these necessary things: that you abstain from things offered to idols, from blood, from things strangled, and from sexual immorality. If you keep yourselves from these, you will do well. Farewell" (Act.15:28,29 NKJV).*

Note that there was no record of any appearance of image or sound from anywhere in the course of the meeting of the Council of Jerusalem; the Apostles and the Church leadership just perceived in their hearts the best solution for the confronting problem of the emerging Church. That is, the Holy Spirit impressed in their hearts the right decisions to be finally adopted; they all felt good with the decisions they took.

***Fig*.14: James the brother of Jesus and the first Bishop of Jerusalem addressing the Jerusalem Council in AD 49.**

Chapter 22
The Nature of Impression

In this Dispensation of Grace that we live in, impression is really the best pattern and the most common form of revelation that God communicates with humans. In the earthly ministry of Jesus, it was the most common recorded revelation.

For instance, it was by impression or perception that Jesus could know and judge correctly His relationship with His disciples (e.g. Mat.16:8; Mar.7:18; 8:17; Luk.8:46; 9:45-47). Perception was also the dominant form of revelation by which Jesus could know the evil craftiness of His critics (e.g. Mat.22:18; Mar.2:8; Luk.5:22; 20:23; Joh.6:15).

HOW DISREGARD OF IMPRESSION BROUGHT PERIL

Indeed, in the early Church, impression was also the most common revelation experience the believers had with God. The following story is a good example of impression as a way of receiving genuine vision, and how by disregarding it can lead to danger and peril.

In AD 57, Apostle Paul was arrested in Jerusalem for the course of the Gospel and jailed at Caesarea Maritima, a coastal city that then had one of the world's famous harbour built by Herod the Great in honour of Caesar Augustus. After about three years in jail at Caesarea Maritima, the headquarters of the Roman Province of Judea that was located about 70 miles (113 kilometres) from

Jerusalem, Apostle Paul was sent to Rome by sea to stand trial before Emperor Nero in AD 60.

Because there was no direct ship from Palestine to Rome, Apostle Paul with other prisoners and military officers, a total of two hundred and seventy-six people on board the ship under the Roman commander, Centurion Julius, set sail from Caesarea Maritima to Asia Minor, where they boarded a second ship of Alexandria sailing directly to Italy.

Thus, they sailed off in the Alexandrian ship, cruising with difficulty off Cnidus because of strong wind, passing the side of Crete, off Salmone, and finally came to a place called Fair Havens, which was near the city of Lasea [on the south side of Crete].

At this stage, in his heart, Paul could perceive danger ahead. He proceeded to advise the offers:

> *"Men, I perceive that this voyage will be with injury and much loss, not only of the cargo and ship, but also of our lives"*
>
> *(Act.27:10 MEV).*

In other words, based on his spiritual perception, Paul advised that they should not venture out of Fair Haven but should stay there even though the strong wind seemed to have somewhat abated. However, Julius the Roman Centurion, whose spirit man was not regenerated like Paul's and hence deaf and blind to spiritual reality, could only act by his natural senses; he was persuaded to heed the advice of the captain and the owner of the ship than Paul's advice. Moreover, winter had started brewing, and majority of the sailors supported the idea to reach Phoenix immediately and spend winter there. Thus, they pulled up the anchor and cruised off the Fair Haven of Crete.

Soon after sailing off the harbour of Fair Haven, a violent wind called *Euroclydon* (Latin: *Euroaquilo*) came rushing down from the island, and the ship was caught in it. Navigation became difficult, the ship was overpowered and could not head into the wind, and hence, left to drift about, being driven up and down on the Adriatic

Sea. For the next fourteen days the tempest erupted, the storm raged, there was no sun nor stars but blackness, and all hope of being saved was lost.

What a dramatic story! Apostle Paul perceived danger ahead, but the others who were in the ship did not. Note that Paul did not see any image nor hear any sound; he just had that inward strong knowing in his heart. That is Perception, also known as Impression or Inner Witness, which is a type of vision. Indeed, as mentioned above, perception is the most common form of vision presently among humans and the most common manner God leads His people as seen in the earthly ministry of Jesus and the experiences of the early Church. Unfortunately, many people are not aware of this fact.

THREE SIGNIFICANT POINTS ABOUT IMPRESSION

(i) Expect to be led by Impression

Many people think that when God speaks, it will be with dramatic visual images and/or sound. Waiting for images and/or sound can lead to error. There is no Scriptural evidence that urges a child of God to expect visual images and/or sound as ways of guidance from God in this era of the Church, also known as the Dispensation of Grace. Note that if God chooses to lead a man by visual images and/or sound, it is entirely by His prerogatives; that is, God may or may not choose to lead that way.

However, the Scriptures urge us to expect to be led by Impression. You have a right as a child of God to expect God to speak to you via inner witness (impression).

> *"For as many as are led by the Spirit of God, they are the sons of God" (Rom.8:14 KJV).*

The term 'led' in the above Scripture is from the Greek word *agō*, which primarily means "to move, impel, urge or influence in the inward being about a matter." The secondary meaning of the Greek word *agō* is: "to conduct someone by compelling force" as in the case of the persecution of Christians or the leading of Jesus into the wilderness by the Spirit of God:

> *"But before all these, they shall lay their hands on you, and persecute you, delivering you up to the synagogues, and into prisons, being brought [agō] before kings and rulers for my name›s sake" (Luk.21:12 KJV).*

> *"And Jesus being full of the Holy Ghost returned from Jordan, and was led [agō] by the Spirit into the wilderness" (Luk.4:1 KJV).*

In other words, when impression revelation appears in the heart of a man, the individual will suddenly becomes aware of a different interjected thought. The Holy Spirit interjects the thought of the Christian with a 'thought process.' Unfortunately, many children of God just dismiss such 'thought interjection' in their hearts because they do not know it is God communicating to their spirit. Most times, when such a Christian kneels down to pray, the same thought process will come back welling up in his heart.

THE STORY OF KENNETH HAGIN

> *"For the past three days, I had sat down to write a letter to a pastor confirming a date to hold a meeting for him. Somehow, the first day, I got about half a page written, then I tore it up and threw it into the wastebasket. The next day I did the same thing. The third day I did the same thing. Then it was the day that the Lord was here in the room talking to me" (Hagin, How You Can Be Led By The Spirit Of God, chpt.7, pp.29-30).*

The Holy Spirit was using the impression, inner witness, to guide Hagin not to hold a program in a Church. Each time, Hagin tried to write a letter to book for that Church program, he would feel a çheck' in his innermost being. Thus, for three times, he would stop the writing of the letter half-way. However, like many children of God, Kenneth Hagin did not know that the 'inward check' he had was the Holy Spirit of God guiding him not to go to go to that Church. Because of such ignorance, he disregarded the inward prompting until Jesus had to appear to him in an open vision to clarify his ignorance. During the open vision, Jesus told Hagin:

> *"The number one way, the primary way, that I lead all of My children is by the inward witness. I am going to show you how that works so you won't make the mistakes you have made in the past" (Hagin, How You Can Be Led By The Spirit Of God, chpt.7, pp.29-30).*

Then Jesus went ahead in the open vision to explain to Hagin:

> *"You see Me sitting here talking to you. This is a manifestation of the Spirit called discerning of spirits. (Discerning of spirits is seeing into the spirit realm.) This is the prophet's ministry in operation. You are seeing into the realm of the spirit. You see Me. You hear Me talking. I am bringing you, through the vision, a word of knowledge and also a word of wisdom. I am telling you not to go to that church. The pastor would not accept the way you would minister when you got there. But I am never going to lead you this way again. (He never has, and that was many years ago.) From now on, I'm going to lead you by the inward witness. You had the inward witness all the time. You had a check in your spirit. That's the reason you tore up the letter three times. You had something on the inside, a check, a red light, a stop signal. It wasn't even a voice that said, 'Don't go.' It was just an inward intuition" (Hagin, How You Can Be Led By The Spirit Of God, chpt.7, pp.29-30).*

(ii) Vision from Impression is not inferior

The revelational vision we obtain from perception (inner witness) is not inferior to any other revelation involving images and/or sound. The Holy Spirit that gives visual images and/or sound is the same Person that gives the inner witness or impression.

(iii) Impression is perceived as an inward 'check' or 'release'

The heart of a man can receive messages from the spirit world in form of thought. Such a message will produce either a 'çheck' or a 'release' in the inward being. A 'çheck' refers to an impression of discomfort while a 'release' is an impression of goodness or comfortable disposition. When there is a 'check,' it is a message of caution; it is better to halt and wait. On the other hand, a 'release' is a greenlight message to proceed.

A child of God is a regenerated person in Christ; his spirit man is born again. Hence, such a person can perceive the inner witness of the Spirit of God in him. If it is a message of danger warning, the person will have an inward 'check' anytime he thinks of the message or plans to go along with the message. For instance, in the voyage story mentioned above, Apostle Paul would have felt an impression that caused him to be very uncomfortable, an inward check, as he thought of the journey ahead, hence, he knew there was danger ahead!

If it is a message of blessing, the child of God will have a 'release' in his heart as he thinks of the event or plans to go along with the event. For instance, the impression of the Apostles and the leaders of the early Church in the Council of Jerusalem was a perception of 'goodness' in their hearts (a comfortable feeling) about their decision (Act.15:28,29).

Never forget, for any type of vision, the HIPPP criteria is the acid test to know whether it is a genuine vision. An impression that is of genuine vision will meet the five HIPPP criteria (Humility,

Impartiality, Peacefulness, Progressiveness, and Purity; see page 168).

MORAL CODES AND IMPRESSION

As discussed in detail in SSB Book 1 and mentioned several times in this book, the human spirit consists of three components or systems – the heart, eido centre, and censor (also called the conscience). Any message receives in the heart is weighed by the censor, which is the spiritual Police Officer. The censor weighs the message on the person's moral code scale. For figurative analogy, the censor picks the message, which appears as thoughts, and put it on the moral code weighing scale. If the message agrees with the man's moral codes, the censor approves it and the man perceives a 'release' deep down in his innermost being. That is, the man will feel comfortable whenever he thinks of the message.

On the other hand, if the message disagrees with the man's moral codes, the censor disapproves it and the man perceives a 'check' deep down in his innermost being. That is, the man will not be comfortable whenever he thinks of the message.

Moral codes are natural laws of life that God has written in the heart of man at creation; that is, moral codes are part of the deposits in the heart of man. Following the Fall of Man, the moral code system becomes defective, thus, producing various kinds of censor in human (see SSB Book 1). Thus, the censor (conscience) of an unregenerated man cannot perceive the full range of moral codes as originally created by God. This is why an unregenerated person can lie, cheat, commit adultery, etc. and will not feel any guilt whatsoever. This also explains why an unregenerated person will read the Bible and all he sees is religion; the Scriptures never make sense to him at all.

Indeed, an unregenerated person has a dead human spirit. The censor of such a person will not understand the things of God just as the Roman army commander, Centurion Julius, that travelled with Apostle Paul on the voyage to Rome. Messages from God were unrecognisable to the Centurion Julius' censor since his moral codes are defective and could not weigh the divine messages. It is like putting a 2000kg block on a 5kg weighing scale. Apparently, the 5kg weighing scale will be unable to weigh the 2000kg block; the 5kg weighing scale will be destroyed because of the excessive weight above its capacity. Messages from God are too weighty for the dead human spirit. Therefore, in most cases, God will speak to an unregenerated person in an easier format like visual images and/or sound. This was the case with Cornelius, another Roman army officer, whom God spoke to via images and sound when God was about to bring salvation to the Gentile family (Acts chpt. 10).

However, when a man experiences the New Birth in Christ, he is born again, recreated or regenerated (2Cor.5:17). The spirit of a regenerated man is alive, and the moral codes in his heart is fully effective as originally intended by God. Such a man can pick messages (thought processes) from the spiritual world such as from the Spirit of God. Any message that meets the standard of the moral codes in the heart of a regenerated man will appear as a 'release.' The regenerated person will feel comfortable anytime he thinks of the message or plans to go along with the message. On the other hand, any message that does not meet the standard of the moral codes in his heart will appear as a 'check,' thus, he will feel uncomfortable anytime he thinks of the message or plans to go along with the message. This is why the regenerated person feels guilty and sorrowful when he falls into sin.

Moral codes are the laws of God, later written out under divine inspiration by Prophets of God such as Moses. These written laws constitute the Scriptures, which are referred today as the Bible (see SSB Books 1 and 4). Thus, the Bible contains the words of God, which are the laws or principles of God. Therefore, when God speaks, His message received in the heart of a man, cannot contradict the Bible, which contains the moral code system.

THINGS TO BE AWARE OF

What of dreams and fleeces? God can choose to communicate genuine vision to humans via dreams and fleeces as forms of revelation. But be warned because they are not reliable means of revelation in this Dispensation of Grace that started about two thousand years ago with the birth of the Church in the Upper Room at Jerusalem!

(a) Fleeces

This is when we use swindles to determine the counsel of God. It involves asking for a sign to confirm the will of God for any situation (see Judges verses 36 to 40). Fleeces also include casting of lots (e.g. 1Sam.14:41-43; Act.1:21-26) and the use of Urim and Thumim, which were sacred stones worn in the breastplate of the Old Testament High Priest over the Ephod, to make enquiry about the will of God (e.g. Exod.28 verses 29 and 30; 1 Samuel 23 verses 9 to 13).

Fleeces were common ways God spoke to humans in the Old Testament dispensations because these people were not regenerated; they were carnal and knew nothing about the Holy Spirit. There were only three classes of people that could receive the gift of the Holy Spirit then – Prophets, Priests, and Political leaders such as a Judge or a King. The Holy Spirit would come upon individuals called into these three offices to empower them to perform the functions and meet the demands of the offices. Every other person not in these three offices was a layman as he knew nothing about the Spirit of God. Hence, God had to permit the use of fleeces, dreams and prophets to communicate His will to these laymen.

Nevertheless, in this Dispensation of Grace, the New Testament era, we can be regenerated and have the indwelling of the Holy Spirit. A regenerated spirit man can communicate directly with God; he doesn't need to go through any medium. In fact, the only time fleeces were used by the believers in the New Testament was in AD 33 before the formation of the Church; the story is recorded in Acts chapter one verses 21 to 26. The disciples met together immediately after the ascension of Jesus to Heaven to select the new disciple that would replace the fallen Judas Iscariot, who committed suicide. At this stage, the Holy Spirit was not yet poured out on them and, hence, the Church was not yet formed. Thus, the 120 believers that gathered in the Upper Room in Jerusalem for the ceremony were not yet regenerated; they were like every other Old Testament Jews. Hence, they didn't have any indwelling Holy Spirit to guide them. Therefore, they needed to rely on casting of lots to select Mathias (see SSB Book 6).

However, once they were regenerated and filled with the Holy Spirit, these 120 believers didn't need fleeces again to determine the will of God in any situation, and there was no record again of the use of fleeces by the Church.

(b) Dreams

This refers to when the individual receives pictorial and sound messages in his dream while sleeping. In this Dispensation of Grace, just like fleeces, dreams are for the spiritually immature. God still speaks via dreams, but often to someone who is yet to be spiritually mature enough to discern the voice of the Holy Spirit in his spirit man.

Most of the times, God speaks to the unregenerated, those who are not children of the Most High God, through dreams like He did to King Nebuchadnezzar (see Daniel chapter 2). God still speaks to the unregenerated people like Nebuchadnezzar these days, often with the purpose of pulling them to Himself and warn them of danger. But for a regenerated person, he should expect better communication with His Heavenly Father other than through the instrumentality of dreams.

Like fleeces, dreams are today very dangerous ways to receive visions of God. They are very prone to error. If you are sick, just watch a movie, or sleep with an empty stomach, you can have dreams, which have nothing to do with divine message. For the regenerated person, even when God has chosen to speak to you via dreams, you should confirm this through other means as discussed in this chapter.

HOW TO CONFIRM THE GENUINENESS OF ANY REVELATION

As already mentioned, every spirit being can communicate. Negative spirits (Satan and his demons) do also give revelations. They can communicate in images, sound and impression as well as manipulate dreams and fleeces to give counterfeit visions.

An authentic way to confirm any vision is that any revelation that deviates from the standards of the manual of life, the Bible, cannot be of God because God cannot kick against His words. The HIPPP criteria, discussed in Chapter 20, is a veritable tool to differentiating not just counterfeit vision but also to differentiate ambition from genuine vision.

Chapter 23
How to Receive Genuine Vision via Passion

One question often asked has been: Is it only regenerated (born again) Christians that can know their life purposes? As discussed in the two previous chapters, a genuine vision can be received from a revelation given to a man by God. Does it mean that the masses of people around the continents of the world who know nothing about Jehovah, the God of the Bible, nor the revelation visions from Him, will be unable to know and walk in their life purposes?

No, not at all. The all-wise God created man and inbuilt in him mechanisms that can direct him to discover the divine agenda for his life. One of such mechanisms is passion. There are people in the Bible who were not of the commonwealth of Israel, hence, were not of God, but walked in their life purposes by following the passion of their heart. That is, by following their genuine passions, some individuals had discovered and walked in their life purposes.

HOW HEATHEN KING DISCOVERED HIS LIFE PURPOSE

A good example was King Cyrus the Great (590-530 BC), a heathen king of Medo-Persian Empire. What is sometimes referred to as the *Edict of Restoration* that authorised the exiled Jews to return to Palestine in 538 BC and rebuild the Temple destroyed by Nebuchadnezzar described in the Bible was issued by King Cyrus. Cyrus is referred to by the Old Testament Bible as 'the anointed one' and his birth was foretold by Prophet Isaiah in about 740 BC, which was about 200 years before Cyrus conquered Babylon (Isaiah chapter 45). For more details, see SSB Book 4.

Even though he knew not Jehovah, the God of all creation, Cyrus was able to execute divine assignment, which was part of his life purpose.

> *"I am the Lord, and there is no other; there is no God besides Me. I will gird you, though you have not known Me" (Isa.45:5 NKJV).*

Because of his policies in Babylonia, Cyrus left a lasting legacy in the world. He respected the customs and religions of the lands he conquered, and he set up a very successful model of centralized administration, thereby establishing a government working to the advantage and profit of its subjects. In fact, the administration of the empire through satraps and the vital principle of forming a government at Pasargadae were the works of Cyrus, and this is the progenitor of modern provincial governance.

King Cyrus the Great is also well recognized for his achievements in human rights, politics, and military strategy, indelibly leaving an influence on both Eastern and Western civilizations. Having originated from Persia, roughly corresponding to the modern Iranian province of Fars, Cyrus played a crucial role in defining the national identity of modern Iran. He was able to accomplish this entire feat by following his passion, which placed him squarely in the divine plan for his life.

TWO KINDS OF PASSION

Passion is a sustained craving desire for a course of action. Broadly speaking, there are two kinds of passion – Positive or Negative Passion. Positive Passion is an inward drive or an intense desire in the direction of the individual's affection. That is, the individual is affectionately drawn towards a particular object, e.g. passion for teaching.

On the other hand, Negative Passion is an inward drive or intense desire in the direction of the individual's disaffection. That is, the individual is drawn in the opposite direction to the object that evoked the passion. Negative passion is an intensive desire drawn against a perceived injustice or denial, e.g. passion against financial poverty in which the individual is disaffectedly drawn against perceived financial poverty.

CHARACTERISTICS OF A GENUINE PASSION

Your passion can be an indication of what you are created for. Genuine passion has the following characteristics:

Genuine Passion is enduring

Genuine passion is one that is evoked any time the individual is exposed to a certain assault. False passion does not stand the test of time; it wanes off with time. But genuine passion is one that will keep rekindling and resurfacing once you are exposed to the assault.

Before God spoke to me to study medicine in 1985, I realised that there was always a flutter of butterflies in my tummy any time I thought of hospitals and healthcare sector in general. Passion would rise in my innermost being anytime I thought of the healthcare sector. Having grown up in a small town, I never saw a medical doctor before I had the divine encounter, yet I felt drawn to the idea of being a healthcare staff. Thus, even if I didn't receive any genuine vision, by following the passionate pull of my heart, I could have still ended up in the medical field. My dad's plan for me to pursue an accountancy career was against the passion in me. This is why parents and guardians must be sensitive to the passion of their kids and wards and not impose their opinions on them arbitrarily.

Genuine Passion evokes restlessness

Genuine passion keeps a man restless until it is satisfied. That is the power of passion. Never underrate this truth: passion is powerful; it keeps you restless until you begin to satisfy its desires.

Oh, how restless I had been in those days of late 1980s as I contemplated becoming a medical practitioner. Two years after God spoke to me to study medicine, my dad died. All human hope of ever realising the vision of becoming of a doctor appeared dead and buried since my dad was the breadwinner of the family, and there was nothing like money being saved aside, life insurance or scholarship. Moreover, the keen competition into limited number of admission in the medical schools nationally left me with no hope at all as my high school was a local one with no qualified teachers to teach the required science subjects of physics, chemistry, biology and mathematics. Thus, by all human calculations, my dream of becoming a medical practitioner was dead and buried!

However, the passion in me to become a medical doctor wouldn't accept any challenges. Many afternoons and nights I'd lose appetite for food and sleep as I tossed about meditating and ransacking my heart and mind seeking for a way forward. The passion would at times become so intense that I would start pacing about and making utterances like: "It is impossible for me not to be a doctor," "I'm a doctor and no force can stop it." Occasionally, I'd scribble these words in my jotters and diaries, some which are still with me.

Genuine passion is powerful and forceful. You are restless until you take a course of action in line with the fulfilment of your passion. This force of passion is what attracts solutions. Sadly, many people are ignorant of this truth. The force of passion is magnetic; once sent out, it goes into action searching for solutions in the physical and spiritual realms. That is part of the Law of Attraction, which states that what you passionately desire, you'll attract. This is discussed on page 224.

Genuine passion brings a release

The force of passion keeps the individual restless until the object of the passion is met. Once the goal or the object of the passion is met, a sense of fulfilment follows.

I still remember the overwhelming sense of fulfilment that ensued as I stood to take the Hippocratic Oath in January 2000 as required for all newly graduated doctors. The Registrar of the medical council requested me to repeat the words as he spelt out the terms of the oath: "I swear by....that I will fulfil according to my ability and judgment this oath..."

With such an overwhelming heart, I didn't know I was saying a different thing entirely. The hall, packed with about 2000 dignitaries from all walks of life and family members of celebrants, roared with laughter. The Registrar repeated his words, trying to correct me, but again the same statement, and again the roar of laughter. This occurred three times, and the Registrar was very understanding, he quietly asked me to calm down and enjoy the procedure. I wish he knew what was happening in me – it was a journey that started almost two decades earlier with the reception of a genuine vision in a small town, a journey that was fraught with challenges of impossible human attainment. It was a journey of faith! The sense of fulfilment was overwhelming, causing me to be oblivion of the happenings momentarily!

As you begin to take steps towards meeting the goal of your passion, an untold sense of fulfilment overwhelms you. It is not just an emotional satisfaction, but a spiritual exhalation, a release in your spirit man. Indeed, my story of becoming a medical practitioner was an interesting one. When there was no human hope of ever realising the vision, one of the desperate things I did in 1988, as I was about concluding my high school and searching for admission into a medical school, was to make a vow unto God. I had prayed:

"O God, Creator of Heaven and Earth, if You'll make me to realise my dream of gaining admission into medical school and graduate as

a medical doctor, I shall dedicate to You every single money I receive as salary in the first month I practise as a doctor."

With such passion and faith in God, do you think any force was strong enough to stop me from realising the dream of becoming a medical practitioner?

No force of poverty, deprivation, youthful exuberance or the likes, could stop the dream from being realised. Thus, in the year 2000, as I received my first salary as a medical intern, despite no other means of getting money for feeding that month, I borrowed transport money and travelled to the small town Ataba, carrying the first salary, all of it, with me. I called a brother of mine to accompany me. We went to that small Church, Assemblies of God. By now the Church had grown bigger and had relocated to a new site and the old place was overgrown with bush.

As we moved through the bush, my brother was wondering what I was doing with money in my box. On arrival at the site, I made my way to the altar where I had laid down in 1985 and received the genuine vision to become a doctor (see page 164) and which was now overgrown with thick bush. I knelt down, not minding any intruding reptiles or ants, lifted both hands to worship the God that gave me the vision and made it to become a reality. As I did that, came rushing into the heart of my spirit man was an indescribable sense of release and fulfilment. Oh, what a tranquillity! It was, indeed, an inexpressible peace and release in my being. Thereafter, I took the money to the new Pastor of the Church, explaining to him it was the fulfilment of my vow.

GENUINE PASSION – POINTER TO GENUINE VISION

Indeed, a genuine passion is a pointer to a genuine vision; it is a pointer of the problem you were made to bring solution to. A good Biblical example of passion leading to life purpose was the story of Nehemiah.

HOW GOVERNOR NEHEMIAH DISCOVERED HIS LIFE PURPOSE

In 539 BC, King Cyrus the Great conquered Babylon, and the following year, early 538 BC, still during the first year of his reign in Babylon, he issued a decree, popularly referred to as the *Edict of Restoration*, for the return of the captured Jews, thus, marking the reestablishment of Israel as a nation in the chosen Canaan Land (Palestine).

However, more than 90 years following the promulgation of the Edict of Restoration, the returned Jews could not build a nation due to stiff resistance from neighbouring states and the lack of coordinated efforts for national building. Sheshbazzar and Zerubbabel that led the first group of Jews to return to Canaan Land following Cyrus' edict met with stiff opposition that frustrated all their effort at nation building.

The Jew, Nehemiah, was the royal Cupbearer, a post equivalent to a government's Chief Chef, in the royal court of Artaxerxes, who was then the King of Persia. King Artaxerxes was a step-son to Queen Esther, the Jewish wife of King Ahasuerus, who was the father of King Artaxerxes (see SSB Book 4). Despite his privileged position, Nehemiah had a passion for the welfare of his people in Palestine.

Early 445 BC, which was the 20th year of the reign of King Artaxerxes I, some men, among whom was Hanani, a brother of Nehemiah travelled from Palestine to Persia, a journey of about 550 miles (886 kilometres). Nehemiah inquired from these travellers the welfare state of the Jews in Palestine. The reports of deprecative poverty of the Jews and the dilapidated state of the walls of Jerusalem that he heard kindled Nehemiah's passion more.

Nehemiah's passion was enduring; each day the passion seemed to be rising, reaching such a crescendo that he became restless, lost appetite and sleep. The passion drove him to be seeking God's face in prayers and fasting.

"So it was, when I heard these words, that I sat down and wept, and mourned for many days; I was fasting and praying before the God of heaven" (Neh.1:4 NKJV).

His restlessness jeopardised his current job so much that his boss, King Artaxerxes, noticed Nehemiah's new attitude.

"And it came to pass in the month of Nisan, in the twentieth year of King Artaxerxes, when wine was before him, that I took the wine and gave it to the king. Now I had never been sad in his presence before. Therefore, the king said to me, 'Why is your face sad, since you are not sick? This is nothing but sorrow of heart.' So I became dreadfully afraid, 3 and said to the king, 'May the king live forever! Why should my face not be sad, when the city, the place of my fathers' tombs, lies waste, and its gates are burned with fire?'" (Neh.2:1-3 NKJV).

Thus, as he stood before the King, he poured out his passionate plea to assist the Jews. What he finally got was quite beyond his initial expectation. The King appointed him Governor of Judah to assist in rebuilding the state of Israel. Indeed, as you follow your life purpose, you will definitely meet with progressive success, often far beyond your initial thinking.

Nehemiah discovered his life purpose through following his passion. When he arrived Palestine, he went about his job passionately, completed the rebuilding of the dilapidated state of the walls of Jerusalem in in 52 days despite stiff and relentless opposition (Neh.6:15). Nehemiah also set up programs to alleviate poverty among the Jews, established smooth systems of administrative governance that lasted for centuries, and revived the worship of Yahweh, the God of their ancestors. You can read the interesting story of how Nehemiah discovered his life purpose by following his passion in the Bible Book of Nehemiah chapters 1 and 2 (see SSB Book 4).

PASSION versus AMBITION

By now you would be wondering the difference between genuine passion and ambition. Here are the differences:

Flame of Emotion

Ambition is not enduring; its flames die with time. This is unlike a genuine passion whose flames are not extinguished. Mr. Kingsley graduated as an engineer, and by judicious application of his skills, he accumulated some wealth. However, he confided in me that engineering was not where his passion was. He had a desire to become a medical practitioner. However, after several unsuccessful attempts to gain admission examinations into medical schools, he decided for an engineering course. Though he seemed to have made some success in his current engineering career, yet down deep in his heart, the passion for medicine welled up intermittently any time he saw a doctor.

That is what passion does. Passion keeps coming up until the goal of the passion is met. That is, as long as the goal of passion is not yet met, the individual will continue to have a tug, pull, crave, yearning, or an innermost desire to fulfil it. But this is not true with ambition, which fades off with time even when the goal of the ambition is not yet attained. Thus, ambition may trigger sense of restlessness just like passion, but the emotion of ambition dies off with time even when the goal of the ambition is yet to be met.

Sense of Fulfilment

In addition, even when the goal or the object of the vision is met, ambition does not give any sense of fulfilment; rather the feeling of emptiness is evoked and deepened with each step the individual takes towards accomplishing an ambition. On the other hand, an overwhelming sense of fulfilment always ensues when the goal of a genuine passion is met.

SAUL OFTARSUS – A GOOD EXAMPLE OF AMBITION

He was born in about AD 1 in the city of Tarsus in Cilicia (in modern-day Turkey) to Jewish parents who possessed Roman citizenship, a coveted privilege that their son would also possess. In about AD 10, Saul's family moved to Jerusalem. Sometime between AD 15 and 20, Saul began his scholastic studies as a lawyer under the famous teacher, Rabbi Gamaliel. He was so zealous, energetic with a burning desire to execute his religious convictions. His passion knew no bounds as he hurled his targets into prisons and even sanctioned the death of Stephen, the first martyr of the Church in AD 35.

For him, it was an intense emotion of ambition borne from a desire for societal accolades and religious zest. His mentors were the bigoted Sanhedrin Jewish rulers, who preferred religion, traditions, and popularity than the worship of God. Like his mentors, Saul was a men-pleaser. As long as he enjoyed money and popularity, he saw nothing wrong with his despicable actions, hurling the members of the new sect, the Church, to prison and sentencing them to death (Acts chpt.9).

An analysis of Saul's vision before his conversion to Christianity shows that it was a mere ambition – the vision failed the HIPPP test as follows:

H = Humility: Saul's vision did not show any trace of humility but rather pride – Saul sought satisfaction of personal ego, which is an expression of pride.

I = Impartiality: Saul was not impartial in his judgment; Stephen never committed any offence worthy of death, yet Saul consented to Stephen's murder and imprisonment of many lawful citizens, all because he had the political power backing him.

P = Peacefulness: By his action, Saul caused mayhem in the society, breaking many homes as parents ran away seeking for cities and nations that would accommodate them.

P = Progressiveness: Saul's action did not bring any progress to himself, his people, and his nation; rather he created heartaches and afflictions.

P = Purity: Saul's action never portrayed any purity of heart, rather it smacked up indecency and religious fanaticism.

An analysis of Saul's vision shows that it was a mere ambition born of religious fanaticism, much similar to the ambition of Adolf Hitler (AD 1889-1945), the protagonist of the Second World War. When Saul later received genuine vision of his life purpose, and became known as Apostle Paul, he regretted his religious fanaticism:

> *"...I used to speak against Him [Christ], attack his people, and I was proud. But I was shown mercy because I acted in ignorance and without faith" (1Tim.1:13 CEB).*

> *"For I am the least of all the apostles. In fact, I'm not even worthy to be called an apostle after the way I persecuted God's church" (1Cor.15:9 NLT).*

Indeed, if you don't want to live in regret, let the manual of life, the Bible, be your guide and your standard of measurement. Its HIPPP test can guard us from inordinate affection, and prevent us from the fatality of counterfeit vision and unreasonable ambition. Truly, you can utilise the HIPPP test to determine if your heart's inclination is a genuine passion or a mere ambition. A genuine passion points out a person's destiny pathway.

Chapter 24
How to Receive Genuine Vision via Talents

From the previous chapters, we understand we can receive genuine vision that unveils our life purposes either through revelation or passion. The third method by which a man can receive genuine vision that unveils his life purpose is Talent.

For many individuals, of the three pathways for receiving genuine vision, talents pose the most confusing pathway. The confusion is borne mainly out of two reasons: firstly, the challenge of identification of talents and, secondly, the deployment of talents in the right career field. By the time you read through this chapter, any confusion about using talents to discover genuine vision should be settled.

DEFINITION OF TALENTS

Talents are naturally recurring patterns of behaviour that can be productively applied. That is, for any endowment to be qualified to be a talent, it must possess three characteristics:

(i) Occur naturally

Every talent is a natural endowment. Thus, a talent is a trait, which the individual is born with. In other words, these natural endowments are gifts from your Creator.

A talent is different from an acquired skill, which is sometimes referred to as Training. In other words, trainings refer to the skills you acquire through formal or informal schooling. Never be confused about this: talents and trainings are not the same. For instance, you may have a musical talent but went to an engineering school and acquired a civil engineering skill. Thus, the musical skill is a talent while the civil engineering skill is a training.

(ii) Recurrent behavioural pattern

Many people do not realise what they have as talents because they think of talents as referring to only musical skills, athletic skills, academic prowess, etc. Talents are the recurrent behavioural patterns that you are born with such as your spontaneous behaviour to relate with strangers (known as relational talent), meticulous behaviour of painstakingly going over details (analytical talent). Check yourself; if there is any recurrent pattern of behaviour that occurs naturally in you, it may be a lurking talent waiting for exploration.

(iii) Productive application

Talents are your natural skills that can be turned into assets. This is an important characteristic of talent – it can be developed and applied productively to bless the individual and humanity at large. We always admire the dexterity of a talent in display. Everyone likes the skilful display of a soccer player on the field, the voice of musical legends, the brains of inventors, etc. But what many of us do not realise is that these talents we all admire pass through the gruesome process of honing until they sparkle out productively.

THREE EXAMPLES OF TALENTS IN DISPLAY

- Walt Disney was blessed with a powerful imaginative talent. But only a few people know that he was fired from the Kansas City Star because his editor felt he "lacked imagination and had no good ideas." But that didn't daunt his efforts. Several more of his businesses failed before he finally produced the premiere of his movie 'Snow White.' He went on to redefine the world of creative visual art with his Disney World. Those supposed 'failures' were really not failures, but a honing process of his talent.

- When Sidney Poitier first auditioned for the American Negro Theatre, he flubbed his lines and spoke in a heavy Caribbean accent, which made the director to angrily tell him to stop wasting his time and should rather go and look for a job as a dishwasher. But Poitier was never discouraged; he honed his talent and eventually became a hugely successful Hollywood star. He won an Academy Award for Best Actor ('Lillies of the Field,' 1963) and helped break down the colour barrier in the American film industry.

- Stephen King grew so frustrated over his attempt to write the novel 'Carrie' that he threw away the entire early draft. But that was the grooming stage of his talent. Fortunately, his wife, Tabitha found the manuscript in the trash and took it out. 'Carrie' became a hit and launched him into a writing career that has brought him fame. His novels have since sold over 350 million copies.

THE IMPORTANT QUESTION

The important question is: Can following one's talent(s) lead an individual to his genuine vision? Can talents reveal the life purpose of an individual?

The answer is yes if we are able to identify and follow our core strengths. That is, talent can lead a man to discover his life purpose, but only if he can identify and follow his core strength. Obviously, the next questions in your mind will be: what is core strength, how is core strength related to talent, and moreover how can it be identified and followed? The following discussions reveal the answers to these all-important questions.

DEVELOPMENT OF TALENT

One characteristic feature of talents is that they all come in raw forms. Talent is one of the three kinds of raw materials that every human is born with (the other two raw materials are *time* and *resources*; resources are also known as energy). In other words, every individual is born with a certain deposit of talents as well as time and energy. Indeed, never be deceived thinking you are not endowed with talents, for no individual is born without talents.

However, being raw materials, talents need to be developed if they must yield productivity. The development process of a talent has two aspects: **honing** and **deployment**.

Talent Honing:

This is the application of relevant knowledge and skills on a talent in order to transform it into a strength. For instance, a girl who has a good voice cannot just start singing and produce a sensational musical album. Her musical talent will need to be honed. She will need to attach herself to a musical industry, learn the necessary skills that can refine her raw musical talent into strength.

Talent Deployment:

Once a talent has become a strength, it must be applied in a relevant field for it to become productive. It is the application of talent in a relevant field that is referred to as Talent Deployment.

THE STORY OF JOSEPH

I ran into Joseph, an enrolled nurse, while I was collating data for the dissertation of my master's degree. He has a natural predilection of meticulously going over details; such action occurs naturally and effortlessly to him, but not to others, hence, it is his talent, though he didn't know. He has analytical talent. He just loves and enjoys working with figures.

I encouraged him to go and acquire demographic knowledge and statistical skills that will develop his analytical talent. He gave it some thought, and then enrolled to study epidemiology. Today, he is enjoying his job a great deal. His analytical talent has been honed into a strength by the application of demographic knowledge and statistical skills on it. The strength is then deployed in the field of statistical epidemiology. If he will submit himself to continuous creative ideas (as discussed in various sections of this book), Joseph will soon become an authority in his field. Not only will the talent transform him into an authority, he can maximise it to amass financial wealth if he will acquire financial intelligence in his area of expertise.

The analytical talent of Joseph would have remained untapped and possibly unrecognised, if the talent was not honed by his epidemiological training and deployed appropriately in the field of statistical epidemiology. Thus, having and identifying your talent(s) is not enough; if the talent must become productive, it must be honed into a strength, which must then be deployed appropriately in the relevant field of endeavour. The mistake many people make is that they do not realise that a talent occurs in raw form, and will need to be honed into a strength, then deployed in a relevant field for it to become productive and useful.

WHAT IS STRENGTH?

Strength is an ability that produces consistent work of excellence. In other words, a strength refers to an ability that you are endowed with and which can be deployed in a discipline to produce excellence consistently.

THREE CHARACTERISTICS OF A STRENGTH

The followings are the three characteristics of a strength:

(a) Honed Talent

A strength is simply a honed talent. That is, a strength is a talent that has been refined by passing it through the honing process. In other words, a raw talent is not a strength. For instance, for the fact that you have a good voice does not mean that it is a strength. The good voice is a raw talent, and it needs to pass through a honing process for it to become a strength.

(b) Consistent Productivity

For a talent to be referred to as a strength, it must have been honed until it produces a particular work consistently. Thus, when the good voice is subjected to a honing process, it is turned into a strength that can produce albums of beautiful music consistently. This is why the world is filled with many musical albums that struggle to sell, many soccer players that never become soccer stars, many bright students that could not become scholars, etc. The reason is because each of these raw talents needs to pass through the crucible of refinement, the honing process, for it to become strength for consistent productivity.

(c) Productive Excellence

Depending on the degree of its refinement and whether it is deployed in the right field, a talent-turned strength can ultimately produce excellence. The more refined a strength and utilised in the right career field, the more excellent work it produces.

THE EXAMPLE OF TIGER WOODS

Tiger Woods is an African American professional golfer who is among the most successful golfers of all time. Born in 1975, Woods turned professional at the age of 20. Prior to the start of his professional career, he has an athletic talent that was born with him. He was not the most gifted of all his peers, yet he chose to develop his talent and not to allow it to lie dormant as it is the case with the majority of people. His words:

> *"People don't understand that when I grew up, I was never the most talented. I was never the biggest. I was never the fastest. I certainly was never the strongest. The only thing I had was my work ethic, and that's been what has gotten me this far" (*Black and Morrison, *The Global Leadership Challenge,* page 170*).*

At an early age, Woods identified a field of discipline in which he would acquire the necessary skills to hone and deploy his athletic talent, and that was golf. Through consistent, painstaking application, his athletic talent was groomed into strength.

Once his talent has been developed into strength, it started producing consistent work of excellence that has baffled the world of golf. He reached the number one position in the world rankings of golf players in June 1997, after less than a year as a professional, and has consistently remained so. Throughout the 2000s, Woods was the dominant force in golf; from August 1999 to September 2004 (264 weeks) and from June 2005 to October 2010 (281 weeks), Woods was the top-ranked men's golfer in the world. Woods has won 18 World Golf Championships, and won at least one of those events in each of the first eleven years after they began in 1999. His professionalism has also paid off monetarily. He has been one of the highest-paid athletes in the world. As at 2016, Woods has a net worth of 760 million US Dollars. Indeed, Woods is a testimony of the power of a talent-turned strength and deployed in a right career field.

TWO KINDS OF STRENGTH

Basically, there are two kinds of strengths:

(a) Innate Skill-based Strength

An Innate Skill-based Strength refers to strength that has been developed from talent. For instance, Mr. Joseph, whose story was mentioned above, has an analytical talent. He does not possess any athletic talent like Tiger Woods. If Mr. Joseph becomes envious of the prowess and dexterity displayed by Mr. Woods and decides to acquire golf skills like Woods', he will be using wrong skills to hone his analytical talent. Rather, by choosing to acquire demographic and statistical skills, Joseph's analytical talent was honed into good quality strength, which he has deployed in statistical demography.

(b) Acquired Skill-based strength

On the other hand, many have acquired skills not related at all with their talents, and developed these acquired skills to produce results. For instance, some have no musical talent, yet they entered into musical training and acquired musical skills by which they wrote music and made some money for themselves. That is an acquired skill-based strength.

The problem with acquired skill-based strength is that it may not be maximally productive as innate skill-based strength, and in addition, acquired skill-based strength leaves a lot of strain and struggles with little or no satisfaction at all compared with innate skill-based strength that comes almost effortlessly and produces high sense of fulfilment. Furthermore, acquired skill-based strength may not produce consistent results as innate skill-based strength.

NO TALENT IS INFERIOR

If Mr. Joseph, whose story was narrated above, made the mistake of trying to play professional golf like Mr. Woods, by sheer willpower and determination, Joseph may make some progress in golf play; however, he won't display the same degree of dexterity, prowess, and passion as Mr. Woods, and he (Joseph) will end up struggling, suffering a lot of angst and frustrations, and ultimately becoming stagnated.

This is the problem with many people. Instead of identifying their talents and hone them with relevant skills into dominant strength, they allow the lure of money and glory to determine what they do. They end up jettisoning their talents and entering fields they weren't created for, and hence, living in struggles, frustration and pains. Parents who force their children into certain careers are doing more harm than good to their children. Such children grow up living a copied lifestyle as they follow other people's pattern instead of following the masterplan for their lives as God originally created them.

Ignorance of the power of talent-turned-strength has caused many people to ignore their talents. It should be clear to everyone that no talent is inferior. God never packaged an inferior talent into anyone. What we do with our talents determines how much we reap from them. For example, many people envy the amount of money professional soccer players make these days. But it wasn't that way before. Less than 60 years ago, soccer was never a high-paying field. However, over the years the industry has been promoted and sold across the globe, thus, yielding high financial dividends. In the same way, any other industry can be promoted and marketed to yield high dividends.

In summary, how we develop and market our talents determines how much dividends we reap from them. Like Apostle Paul, you can choose to "magnify your office" (Rom.11:13 KJV). Don't ever belittle your giftings; they have the power to change your world!

Chapter 25
How to Excel with Your Talents

Prior to the industrial age in the mid-eighteenth century, metallic arrows, knives, cutlasses, machetes, and other weapons of warfare and household items were reshaped, refined, and sharpened by grinding or rubbing each one with a stone, which is called a whetstone. Sometimes the metal or even the whetstone might need to be red-heated while sharpening its edges. This process of refining and sharpening up the metal with a whetstone is called honing.

The first known use of the term 'honing' in the English language was in 1788, and it was from the old Proto-Germanic word *haino*, which means to 'sharpen or smoothen with a whetstone.' The essence of sharpening or smoothening with a whetstone is to make the material more acute, intense, or effective.

Today, there are sophisticated machines that serve the function of whetstone, and such machines can hone metals into the right diameter, shape, and size. In modern technology, the honing process allows for perfection of bore geometry, size control, final surface finish and surface structuring. The honing process provides the final sizing and creates the desired finish pattern on the interior of tubing or cylinder bores.

Just as a metal can be honed into a more refined, sharpened product, the same way our talents can be honed into strengths that will produce excellent work consistently. This is accomplished by grinding or rubbing the talents against appropriate skills; the talents are the metals while the appropriate skills are the whetstones.

THREE IMPORTANT POINTS OFTALENT HONING

To hone a talent, note the following three important points:

(a) Talent honing should be with appropriate skills

Take note that the skills for honing the talents must be appropriate; that is, the skills must be relevant. For instance, you cannot use musical skills to hone an athletic talent. Musical skills must be used to hone musical talents while athletic talents must be honed by athletic skills. Thus, if you are gifted with a musical talent, you can develop the talent by joining a musical industry where you can acquire musical skills that will develop your musical talent. It will be out of place to enter a law school to develop your musical talent.

(b) It is never too late to hone any talent

If you have identified a talent, then start immediately to hone it. You do not need to wait to secure a paid job in the industry; for instance. An individual who wants to hone his musical talent, could start by joining his church choir; as more opportunities emerge in the industry, he pursues to grab them. By all means, start doing something immediately. Indeed, it is never too late to hone a talent; age, sex, and race are never barriers to talent honing.

(c) To hone a talent requires time and energy

You need focus and dedication, which require energy, and quality amount of time to hone a talent into a strength. But once a talent is turned into a strength, it always pays its dividends, and the energy and time sacrificed will be worth it. The world always stands in awe of a talent-turned strength and deployed in the right field of industry!

***Fig*.15: Just as a metal can be honed into a more refined, sharpened product, the same way our talents can be honed into strengths. This is accomplished by grinding or rubbing the talents against appropriate skills; the talents are the metals while the appropriate skills are the whetstones.**

CHALLENGE OF MULTI-TALENTS

The uniqueness of human nature is that every human is blessed with more than one talent. For instance, you may be gifted in athletic and literary (writing) talents. Such multifarious giftings have caused the ruin of many individuals as they are divided in decision on which talent to focus and develop.

The answer to such dilemma is to concentrate on your dominant talent, and acquire skills around this dominant talent. The acquired skills should be targeted to develop or hone the dominant talent. For instance, if you are a gifted talker and you are a medical doctor, one good suggestion will be to acquire medical skills that will enable you to develop the talking talent. For example, healthcare advocacy of public health medicine will be a good discipline for such an individual. Laboratory medicine such as anatomical pathology may not fit such an individual.

PRINCIPLE OF CORE STRENGTH

Although an individual may be multitalented, yet a talent often stands out and gives greater expression, which the individual tends to lean towards to most often. That particular talent that stands out and expresses itself most often than the others in a person's life is called the Dominant Talent. Thus, a *dominant talent is the inborn recurrent behavioural pattern that stands out more conspicuously in your dealings.* In a short sentence, your dominant talent is your most recurrent natural behavioural pattern that can be productively applied.

When you focus appropriate skills, energy and time on developing and honing your dominant talent, you are said to be building on your Core Strength, and it is referred to as the **Principle of Core Strength**.

An interesting aspect of our existence is that as you develop your core strength, you will be surprised all other talents that you have will soon line up in unison to assist you in the chosen career. That is, the answer to multiple talent is the application of the Principle of Core Strength. By focusing skills, energy, and time on developing your dominant talent, all other talents of yours will line up to assist you in maximising your potential. In other words, by the application of the Principle of Core Strength, confusion is averted in a situation of multiple talents.

Chapter 26
How to Choose Right Career Using Talents

It is one thing to identify your talents; it is entirely another to know which field of career to deploy the talents. For instance, because you are gifted in artistic drawing does not necessarily mean your choice of career should be artisan craft. The artistic talent can also be deployed in civil or mechanical engineering, architecture, and the likes. Or, because you have a beautifully sonorous voice does not imply you must end up in the music industry. Sonorous voice can as well be deployed in mass communication, public health medicine, and similar fields.

Therefore, the tormenting question for many people is: which field is suitable for my talent(s)? In other words, not all career fields will allow an individual to maximise his potential. Apparently, any man will want to choose a field that allows him to maximally explore and utilise his talents. How does one determine the best field?

STARTING POINT

The correct choice of career to deploy a talent begins with the application of the Principle of Core Strength, which has been mentioned in the previous chapter. According to the principle, an individual must first determine his dominant talent and then focus on appropriate skills, energy and time on developing and honing the dominant talent into a core strength.

JUDE AND HIS DOMINANT TALENT

Mr. Jude enjoyed writing stories, and he was also a good talker, liked athletic, and a good analyser of events. As he grew up he wondered which career field to choose. Most times when discussion about careers cropped up in the class while we were in high school, Jude would say he didn't know which career field to choose.

The dominant trait manifesting in Jude's behaviour was his impulsive nature for writing stories. He could hold the class spellbound in his story tales. The writing gift was his dominant talent.

In the university, Jude studied archaeology, but he never really liked the course. Therefore, it was not surprising Jude never worked as an archaeologist. His dominant talent was pulling him; he started writing story articles for national dailies. One of the articles he wrote caught the attention of a newspaper editor, who invited him for a job interview. He was given the job, thus, he started working as a news writer for the daily. It was obvious to everyone that Jude liked his job even though his monthly salary was not much.

Being quite motivated to continue as a journalist, Jude applied for and won a scholarship to the United Kingdom for further training in journalism. He returned after the two-year postgraduate training in journalism to join the national daily. At this stage, Jude journalistic writing took a dramatic turn as everyone could see how gifted he was. He rose quickly within his organisation to become an editor.

Interestingly, still aspiring in his chosen journalism field, Jude started his newspaper corporation, and within a short period of just eighteen months, his publications have achieved national coverage with a large readership. In the journalism world, Jude's writings have become the reference points in the nation. As at the writing of the manuscript of this book, Jude wrote a great deal on sports, dedicating four pages of each publication to sports, and he featured on television, where he gave a lot of technical analysis about games.

Apparently, unknown to him, Jude was obeying the principle of core strength. He identified the writing gift as his dominant talent. By attending a school of journalism, he focused and used appropriate skills, energy and time to develop the dominant talent into a core strength that produced excellent work of consistently. By following the principle of core strength, Jude is not only utilising his writing gift in journalism, but all his other talents (talking gift, analytical talent and athletic interest) are all being utilised. Depending on his vision and faith, he can grow his corporation into a multinational conglomerate, build a school of journalism, or engage in similar ventures, and with appropriate financial literacy, he can reap huge financial opportunities.

That is what happens when an individual identifies his dominant talent, hone it into a core strength, and deploy it in an appropriate industry. Indeed, the Principle of Core Strength is the starting point to developing and maximising one's talents. Your core strength is your biggest tool to maximising your potential; a wise person will concentrate his skills, energy and time in honing his dominant talent into a core strength and avoid unnecessary distractions.

THREE SIGNS THAT SHOW CORE STRENGTH UTILISATION

In general, there are three signs that show you are using your core strengths:

(a) What you do comes almost naturally or effortlessly

Your core strength is the area of least resistance because it is natural to you; hence, its application comes almost effortlessly. Mr. Dixon is a talker; he can talk almost non-stop for hours; in fact, the longer he talks, the better it becomes. That is a talent that can be honed and deployed in the communication industry. Mr. Dixon will be making a mistake to think everybody can do likewise. A man who doesn't have that 'talking' talent will struggle to do what Dixon does.

(b) You derive sense of fulfilment in what you do

Unlike Mr. Jude Dixon is now a comedian, and he derives huge fulfilment from it. If he will continue to develop his 'talking' talent in this field and acquire financial literacy, he will grow to become an authority in his field and reap some financial benefits.

(c) What you do evokes passion in you

Must all individuals with a 'talking' talent become comedians? The answer is NO. As mentioned earlier, a talent can be deployed in many fields of endeavours. For example, other than the comedian field, the 'talking' talent can as well be deployed in journalism, nursing advocacy, law, or other similar areas. Jude deployed his own in journalism while Dixon deployed his in comedy.

The important question, therefore, is: *What determines which field a talent can be deployed?*

The answer is Passion. An individual's passion is a pointer to which field a particular talent can be deployed. If you choose a field that bears no passion for you, the talent will not be fully utilised, and you won't be able to fully maximise your potential. Passion has been discussed in Chapter 23.

DETERMINANTS OF CAREER CHOICE

To discover one's genuine vision through the principle of core strength development, talent is usually considered along with passion. Talent alone may be difficult to identify your genuine vision. When it is combined with passion, genuine vision becomes clearer. A dominant talent tells an individual what kind of strength he should develop while passion points him to the field to deploy the talent.

For instance, if your dominant talent is an analytical talent, that reveals the innate ability that God has endowed you with. However, it does not automatically mean you are to become a mathematician. An analytical talent can be deployed in other fields like medical statistics, civil engineering, accountancy and such others. To choose which field to deploy the analytical talent, you will need to analyse your true passion. A passion for working with money and a strong aversion to blood will obviously drive you to choose accountancy rather than medicine or engineering.

What this means is that a talent can be deployed in many disciplines, however, it is our passion and/or the revelation we receive that guides us to the correct field we can deploy the talent. A major secret of the success of Tiger Woods, whose story was relayed on page 211, is from his words:

> *"I wake up every day and I can't wait to go to work, and that's a gift. Not too many people have the opportunity to feel that way."*

That is passion. It was his passion that pointed him to which field of endeavour he should deploy his athletic talent. Imagine if Tiger Woods had thought, 'I have athletic gift, therefore, I could as well become a boxer!' He has undying passion for golf, and the passion guided him to the correct sports field to deploy his athletic talent.

The same story is true for all other great success in all endeavours of life. In other words, to discover genuine vision via talent pathway, you will need to know your core strength and then deploy it in the field of your passion. Once you begin to do this, you are on the right pathway for consistent production of excellence.

CHALLENGES WITH DEVELOPMENT OF CORE STRENGTH

The implication of this is that you must first identify your dominant talent for development into core strength. The main challenge with the Principle of Core Strength is, therefore, in the identification of the dominant talent. This is not that easy for many people because of some obvious reasons:

(1) Talents are discoverable

When we think we are at our best using a particular talent, we often suddenly discover another in-built talent that had been unnoticeable to us. Johnny was a good talker and he thought of becoming a comedian. But later he soon discovered he has a flare for gardening when he visited a distant uncle who had a farm; he suddenly discovered that he enjoyed planting a great deal. That caused him some confusion as he contemplated which career to pursue, and which gift was the dominant.

Often, we do not know that we have a particular gift until a circumstance forces us to use the gift. The question, therefore, is what if we are not faced with circumstances that will force out the gifts in us? Interestingly, the laws that govern creation provide the answer. One of such laws is the Law of Attraction.

The Law of Attraction

The Law of Attraction states that an individual is pulled in the direction of his persistently dominant thought. A persistently dominant thought is the principal thought process in the heart and mind of a person that continuously consumes most of his time, energy, and resources. A persistently dominant thought will ultimately dictate the pattern of behaviour of an individual, and the behavioural pattern will be seen in the person's conduct or action.

In other words, what you are apt to say and do almost impulsively is ultimately a reflection of the persistently dominant thought in your heart and mind.

According to the Law of Attraction, we are impulsively being drawn towards areas we have been wired for. The areas we have been wired for often come to us almost impulsively and appear quite naturally, and when we give them some attention, they increasingly assume dominance in our thought life. We feel some form of agitation and restlessness as we ponder over them, a signal that they are seeking for a way to be let out. Indeed, every individual is pulled towards his endowments. The problem is that many people, either out of ignorance or sheer wilful disobedience, do not pay attention to such a pull. Because such endowments often appear quite natural, many people make the mistake to think they are too common and simple to pay attention to.

For example, the fact that Jane can talk and make jokes effortlessly does not mean it is so with every person. If Jane does not realise what she has is a talent that can be developed into productive venture, she will downplay her endowment as being common and simple. Indeed, many individuals, rather than pay attention to the pull of their hearts, get busy in other people's fields. This is one sad fact about employment reality in this modern time. Working in a job has robbed many people of their potentials. Instead of carving out their individuality with their endowments, they expend their time, energy, and resources copying other people's lifestyles and end up straining themselves in a bid to make a living.

However, the wise counsel of Warren Buffett, the world's richest investor, is timely:

> *"There comes a time when you ought to start doing what you want. Take a job that you love. You will jump out of bed in the morning. I think you are out of your mind if you keep taking jobs that you don't like because you think it will look good on your resume. Isn't that a little like saving up sex for your old age? Therefore, today sit down and think. Where are you going? I insist on a lot of time being spent, almost every day, to just sit and think. That is very uncommon...I read and think. So, I do more reading and thinking, and make less impulse decisions than most people in business." [Warren Buffett: Business Insider (2015), Nasdaq (2016)].*

Living is a business, and if we must maximise our potential, we should do likewise. It is time to sit down and think out where we are heading and not just follow everyone else.

(2) Discovering Core strengths takes time and patience

Discovering the dominant talent and developing it into a core strength is a journey that requires a lot of patience and time. This is because as we grow, life's circumstances keep throwing up new challenges at us. Each new challenge is actually a lurking opportunity seeking to reveal who we are and our natural endowments.

Sadly, many people miss so many of such golden opportunities because they become reactive to the circumstances instead of analysing each circumstance to squeeze out the juice in it. Opportunity comes in disguise, mostly in an overall coat of temporal disappointment.

The Story of Florence Nightingale

Florence Nightingale (AD 1820-1910) was a young girl born to an opulent English family in Italy. At an early age, her relational talent of building friendship with a radiant smile and a charming personality was glaring. The parents thought the best thing for her was to settle down as a respectable housewife with a man of means and build a home. Having a job was regarded as an ignoble thing in Europe for any respectable woman to engage herself during Florence's days. But Florence was thinking of something else.

She felt irresistibly drawn to shower compassion on the less privilege and often wondered which career would fittingly deploy this talent. When Nightingale was 17 years old, she refused a marriage proposal from a 'suitable' gentleman, Richard Monckton Milnes, explaining that while the gentleman stimulated her intellectually and romantically, her "moral...active nature...requires satisfaction, and that would not find it in this life."

As she moved about with her parents engaging with people of prominent social standing, the pressure from the family for Florence to settle down as a wife and mother kept mounting. During that period, she found out another talent of hers, which is writing. She set about writing anything she could conjecture, paying more to work of compassion. While partly trying to escape from the persistence of the family to follow the tradition of the day for a noble woman, she decided to travel, from Rome to England, moving as far as Greece and Egypt and at the same time continuing her writing. During these periods she came to believe that God had given her a compassionate vocation that should be deployed in nursing.

After about 30 years of self-discovery, she stumbled at the Lutheran religious community, the Institution of Kaiserswerth at Kaiserswerth-am-Rhein in Germany, where she observed Pastor Theodor Fliedner and his team of trained deaconesses working for the sick and the less privileged. This was a turning point in her life as she could now see vividly that nursing rightly encapsulates the career field for the deployment of her talents. Despite strong objections by her parents, she enrolled there to study nursing for four months; the nursing training formed the basis for her later career.

After the formal nursing training, Florence felt more equipped to practise her chosen career. Three years after the training, specifically on 22 August 1853, Nightingale became employed as a superintendent nurse at the Institute for the Care of Sick Gentlewomen in Upper Harley Street, London. It was while there in Upper Harley Street that she heard a report of the poor conditions of British soldiers fighting in the Crimean War (1853-1856). Against all norms and traditions as women were never expected at the war fronts, Florence volunteered to work for the wounded soldiers at the battle front. On 21 October 1854, she and her staff of 38 women volunteer nurses that she trained, including her aunt Mai Smith, and 15 Catholic nuns, were sent to the Ottoman Empire and positioned about 546 km across the Black Sea from Balaklava in the Crimea, where the main British camp was based. They worked at Selimiye Barracks in Scutari (modern-day Üsküdar in Istanbul).

Her work in the Crimean War was what brought her the international fame as she gained the nickname 'The Lady with the Lamp' from a phrase in a report in The Times: "She is a 'ministering angel' without any exaggeration in these hospitals, and as her slender form glides quietly along each corridor, every poor fellow's face softens with gratitude at the sight of her. When all the medical officers have retired for the night and silence and darkness have settled down upon those miles of prostrate sick, she may be observed alone, with a little lamp in her hand, making her solitary rounds."

Thus, from the story, it is obvious that Florence's dominant talent was compassion. Her acquired nursing skills in the Lutheran Institution of Kaiserswerth were what honed this dominant talent into strength. In other words, the training at the institute helped to refine and develop her dominant talent. Her subsequent work as a superintendent nurse at the Institute for the Care of Sick Gentlewomen in Upper Harley Street, London, further sharpened and developed her dominant talent into core strength.

Thus, Florence had clearly identified her dominant talent, which was honed into her core strength. Her passion for the sick and less privileged defined the field to deploy this core strength, and which was nursing. By the time the war was over, Nightingale had no doubt that she had found her genuine vision.

Note that as she deployed her core strength, other talents soon lined up. Her writing talents, her relational talent that expressed in her dexterity in fostering friendship, and her innate ability of organisation and training all lined up behind the dominant talent of compassion, propelling Florence to greater heights in her chosen career. Soon a Nightingale Fund was established in 1855 for the training of nurses during a public meeting to recognise Nightingale for her work in the Crimean war.

From the Nightingale Fund, a nursing school, the Nightingale Training School was established at St. Thomas' Hospital on 9 July 1860; the school is now called the Florence Nightingale School of Nursing and Midwifery and is part of King's College London. For the school, Nightingale wrote the book *Notes on Nursing* in 1859; the book now forms the cornerstone for training of nurses in modern nursing schools across the world. In addition, because of her love for travelling, Nightingale is regarded to be the pioneer of the concept of *medical tourism*, which is the movement of people from one country to another for the purpose of obtaining medical treatment in that country.

Nightingale spent the rest of her life promoting and organising the nursing profession. Her life is a true tale of how discovering the dominant talent and developing it into core strength and then deploying it in the appropriate career of passion can lead an individual to his genuine vision, but the process needs patience as it can turn out to be a long journey.

LESSONS FROM BEZALEL URI, THE ARTISAN

A good example of how a man can discover his life purpose through talent is Bezalel Uri of ancient Israel. About 3500 years ago (in 1447 BC), God gave Moses a genuine vision via revelation about constructing a Tabernacle with its articles of worship, which would form one of the rallying points for the birth of the nation of Israel. That was no mean task. The leading artisan that would supervise such grandiose work of all-time must be able to ensure accurate construction to its finest details to meet divine perfection requirement. Bezalel was chosen to be the lead artisan. He was endowed with the required artistic talents.

> *"Then the Lord spoke to Moses, saying: 'See, I have called by name Bezalel the son of Uri, the son of Hur, of the tribe of Judah. And I have filled him with the Spirit of God, in wisdom, in understanding, in knowledge, and in all manner of workmanship, to design artistic works, to work in gold, in silver, in bronze, in cutting jewels for setting, in carving wood, and to work in all manner of workmanship'" (Exo.31:1-5 NKJV).*

The implications of Bezalel's gifting are worth paying attention to:

- Bezalel got his talents from the Spirit of God. This is evidence that our talents are gifts or endowments from God. This is confirmed by the words of Jesus in Matthew chapter 25 verses 14 to 30. Talents are part of the raw materials God has given us for profitable living.
- Through Moses, God demanded Bezalel to use his talents to construct the Tabernacle to be exactly as He had specified them. In other words, God demanded excellent job and nothing less. The lesson here is that God demands excellence in the deployment of our talents in the field of our passion. Until you start producing excellence with your talents, you are under-utilising your potentials.
- God told Moses He would put His Spirit on Bezalel in order for Bezalel to be able to produce excellent job. In other words, God promises to be with us as we deploy our talents in the relevant field of our passion. If you walk with God in deploying your talents, you will receive divine guidance just as Bezalel. With God, you can produce excellence in your career that will baffle the world!

IN SUMMARY

God has endowed us with natural gifts (talents). What we do with them determines what we get in life and our place in history. This cannot be overemphasized: each of us is blessed enormously with gifts by our Creator, and talent is one of these gifts. Sadly, many people do not know they carry gifts within themselves that can turn them into giants in their passion fields and bless humanity. Hence, they suffer in ignorance and die frustrated. The word of God remains true:

> *"My people are destroyed for lack of knowledge" (Hos.4:6 KJV).*

The essence of this book is to enlighten and guide us into what we are created to be. Therefore, if you desire to have a fulfilling success in life, discovering your genuine vision and running with it is non-negotiable. Genuine vision is what will unveil your life purpose. Following your life purpose is the path of less resistance. If you want less angst and desire to enjoy your stay on earth, you need to discover your life purpose.

Vision sets the tone and the pace for our existence. A man with no vision is a man with no direction; such a man will be lost in the crowds. Therefore, it is very worthwhile to seek for genuine vision with all your strength. The world always stands in awe of the person who has discovered his genuine vision and runs with it. Discovering your dominant talent, developing it into a core strength and deploying it in a passionate career is one pathway to receiving genuine vision that will unveil your life purpose. Truly, a talent fully deployed in a passion field is one of the wonders of our world!

Chapter 27
Section Two Practical Steps (Vision Pathway Steps 1, 2 and 3)

WITHOUT VISION, PURPOSE WILL NOT be known, and where purpose is unknown, abuse is inevitable. In other words, without vision, life becomes meaningless, for *"Where there is no vision, the people perish"* (Pro.29:18 KJV).

In the 6th century BC, God inspired Prophet Habakkuk to document five practical steps involve in pursuit of vision for anyone who desires to make the most of his earthly life-journey.

> *"I will stand my watch and set myself on the rampart, and watch to see what He will say to me, and what I will answer when I am corrected. Then the Lord answered me and said: 'Write the vision and make it plain on tablets, that he may run who reads it. For the vision is yet for an appointed time; but at the end it will speak, and it will not lie. Though it tarries, wait for it; because it will surely come, it will not tarry'" (Hab.2:1-4 NKJV).*

These five practical steps required for the pursuit of vision, detailed in the above Scriptures, are what this book refers to as the Vision Pathway, and they are as follows:

VISION PATHWAY FIRST STEP: RECEIVE A GENUINE VISION

The mind is very crucial for success because in its activated state, the mind has the ability to stimulate the spirit to release its products. One of the products of the spirit being released is the force of vision. Once a man receives a genuine vision, his life bears a new dynamism. In other words, receiving a genuine vision is the first step of Vision Pathway as clearly stated in Habakkuk chapter two verse one.

> *"I will stand my watch and set myself on the rampart, and watch to see what He will say to me, and what I will answer when I am corrected" (Hab.2:1 NKJV).*

Three Significant Points about Vision Reception

Note the following three significant points about receiving vision:

(a) It is Possible to receive Genuine Vision

Some people do wonder whether it is actually possible to know why and what you are born into this world to do. Yes, it is very possible. What and why you are created for is generally referred to as your life purpose. Your life purpose is the specific assignment you are designed to accomplish. A genuine vision reveals your life purpose. Sadly, only few people are living in their life purposes.

The main reason why many people do not discover their life purpose is simply because of ignorance. Many people do not know that they are created and wired together by God for a specific assignment. They think life purpose is more or less a religious gambit to encourage the gullible of the society. At the other extreme, many Christian leaders preach it is impossible for any man who is not a born-again Christian to discover their life purpose. But such preaching does not tell the whole truth in the Bible about life purpose.

The truth is that anybody, Christian or non-Christian, can discover his life purpose. Each human is wired with enough information that can help him discover his life purpose, and that is only if such an individual will seek diligently for it.

(b) Genuine Vision comes through Diligent Search

Life purpose is like a pearl hidden deep in the depth of the earth. It can only be unravelled through discovery.

> *"The [life] purpose in a man's heart is like deep water, but a man of understanding will draw it out" (Pro.20:5 ESV; 'life' is inserted).*

The process for discovering life purpose is vision. In other words, a genuine vision reveals one's life purpose. We can obtain a genuine vision from revelation, passion or an analysis of our talents. To obtain a genuine vision, whether through revelation, passion or an analysis of talents, requires a diligent search. Habakkuk chapter two verse one clearly shows that without an active search, vision cannot be received:

> *"I will stand my watch And set myself on the rampart, And watch to see what He will say to me, And what I will answer when I am corrected" (Hab.2:1 NKJV).*

Habakkuk chapter two verse one is an allegory, portraying the diligent search for vision. *"I will stand my watch"* refers to alertness in your spirit being. *"Set myself on the rampart"* refers to secluding yourself aside for interaction beyond the physical sensual feelings; rampart means watchtower.

In the ancient time, towers are built at the outskirts of a town, and a man would be posted there to keep watch for any intruding enemy. Ancient watchtowers are our modern radars and satellite monitors. It was required of a watchman to be vigilant always, else he would miss sighting the enemy. In the same vein, except we exercise vigilance, we would miss when a genuine vision flashes into our hearts and minds. Exercise of vigilance can be achieved by practising the Five Steps to Creativity, discussed in Chapter 13.

Thus, to receive genuine vision, you will need to 'stand on your watch, set yourself on the watchtower (rampart), and watch to see with your inner eyes what God will say to you through either revelation, analysis of passion or talents about your life purpose.'

The quickest way to obtain genuine vision is to ask from God in Jesus Name. Since He is the one that created each of us, He knows what and why we are in this world. Interestingly, God is very much willing to reveal your life purpose to you, if only you will discipline yourself to seek for it.

> *"Thus says the Lord, the Maker of the earth, the Lord who formed it to establish it; the Lord is His name: Call to Me, and I will answer you, and show you great and mighty things which you do not know" (Jer.33:2,3 MEV).*

> *"Ask and it will be given to you; seek and you will find; knock and it will be opened to you" (Mat.7:7 MEV).*

Besides seeking the face of God for revelation about one's life purpose, a man can follow his passion and analyse his talents to still obtain genuine vision that will reveal his life purpose as discussed earlier in this section.

The key word here is to seek, and seeking connotes an active process. Whether it is by asking the Holy Spirit of God, and/or analysing your passion and talents, all require diligent searching or seeking. A lazy man can never discover why and what he has been born to do in this world.

(c) Vision requires Refinement

As discussed in this section (page 152), when genuine vision is received, it is initially raw. That is, when vision thought process flashes into your heart and mind, it comes in an unrefined form. In such an unrefined form, the vision may not hold much meaning to the visioner. However, once it passes through the crucible of refinement, the vision becomes clearer and more appealing to the visioner.

As such, every vision requires refinement at the point of reception for it to be maximally productive. The Five Steps to Creativity (see Chapter 13) are the principal method for refining visions as follows:

Step 1: Informatics

The first step for **Vision Refinement** is the collation of information. After you have received a vision, you will need to acquire more facts about the vision through collation of information by reading and studying about similar visions.

Step 2: Meditation

After you collate relevant information, you take time to find out the relevance of such information to your vision. In other words, you are subjecting the collated information through mind processing, and this is meditation. As you meditate on the collated information about your vision, you will begin to 'see' the various aspects of your life purpose.

Life purpose is a journey; there is never a time you will know all about your life purpose. You know bit by bit. All you need to do is walk with what you know per time. This is why one vision encounter is often not enough to spell out all the details of our lives.

In addition, at every stage, there is need for a man to pause and check to be sure he is not deviating from the vision of his life purpose. Meditation is the practical step to achieving this. Do not get too busy to neglect separating yourself unto meditation. As you separate yourself unto scheduled meditation, your stimulated spirit will pick the information about whether you are deviating or you are on the right track. If you find out that you have deviated, retrace your steps immediately. It is never too late to make a corrective turn. Only a fool will keep doing a thing he knows is wrong and expect a right result.

Step 3: Mind Activation

As you let your mind to dwell on the collated information about the vision, new light will burst forth. The more you 'see' how significant the vision is to your life and your world, the more passionate you will be towards the vision. What is happening is that through meditation, your mind is being activated towards the vision.

Step 4: Heart Stimulation

Your activated mind will then stimulate your spirit man to begin a search for new ideas on how to run with the vision. As you see the vision in a clearer light, your emotions will be awoken, and this will rouse you into action.

Step 5: Creative Realm

In other words, the stimulation of the heart of your spirit man causes you to enter into the creative realm where creative ideas will start pouring forth on how to successfully run with the vision.

Thus, if you subject your vision to the practice of the Five Steps to Creativity, the vision will become refined (clearer). Vision refinement is a life-long exercise because each aspect of your life purpose that you discover needs to be refined continuously. The process of refinement of each aspect of your life purpose may take minutes, hours, days, weeks, months, or even years, depending on how hungry you are for success. This process of vision refinement is what Habakkuk chapter two verse one refers to as 'correction.'

"And what I will answer when I am corrected" (Hab.2:1 NKJV).

An Example of Vision Refinement

A good example of refinement of vision was the life of Dr. D. Oyedepo. He had an encounter with genuine vision in an eighteen-hour divine revelation that birthed his life purpose, which was to be a preacher of the Word of Faith for the liberation of mankind from Satanic bondage. For the next 26 months after he received the revelation, he engaged in prayer and fasting, which allowed his vision to pass through refinement, hence, bringing about clearer understanding.

Among the clearer insight Dr. Oyedepo received was the idea that to successfully preach the Word of Faith for the liberation of mankind from Satanic bondage, there is need to build not just Churches but schools as well as publication of books that will also carry the vision. Today, the ministry is not only noted for achievement in Church establishment but also in the education sector with establishment of primary, secondary, and tertiary institutions across Africa along with more than fifty publication titles of various aspects of the vision that are widely distributed in millions around the world. That is what vision refinement can accomplish in the life of a visioner!

VISION PATHWAY SECOND STEP: WRITE THE VISION

Once you have caught the vision of your life purpose, the next step to take is to immediately write the vision down.

> *"Then the Lord answered me and said: 'Write the vision'"*
>
> *(Hab.2:2 NKJV).*

The act of writing is one of the eternal gifts that God has given to humans. Writing is not just a natural invention, it is a spiritual exercise. Long before humans knew about writing, God has caused events of life to be articulated in writing. Heaven, the Throne of

God, is full of records of events that pre-existed humans. Imagine if the Scriptures (the Bible) were not written out; imagine if they were passed down to us only by words of mouth!

The point here is that writing has a spiritual connotation. Writing your vision down makes your heart and mind to accept it as 'your own vision.' Writing the vision down gives you that sense of entitlement or ownership, which is essential for your commitment. In other words, by writing it down, you are committing yourself to the vision. There is emotional exhilaration and satisfaction once you document your vision.

Moreover, documenting the vision is a way of preserving it for posterity. If you believe in your vision, you will commit to writing it down and paste it all around you where you will keep seeing it day and night! If you believe in your vision, write it down electronically or as a hardcopy and carry it along with you everywhere.

Indeed, writing the vision down is the second step of the Vision Pathway as spelt out in Habakkuk chapter 2 verse 2.

VISION PATHWAY THIRD STEP: MAKE PLAIN THE VISION

As discussed under the Five Characteristics of Vision on page 152, at the point of reception, a genuine vision comes raw and seem to outsize the resources that you have, thus, appearing intimidating to the visioner and onlookers. As such, many people give up on their visions before they have even taken the first step.

However, there is a way to go about achieving your vision. That way is the Vision Pathway. According to Habakkuk chapter two verse 2, the third step of the Vision Pathway is to 'make the vision plain.'

> *"Then the Lord answered me and said: ...make it [the vision] plain on tablets, that he may run who reads it" (Hab.2:2 NKJV).*

The phrase 'make it plain' is from the Hebrew word *baar*, which means 'to make clear,' 'to declare,' or 'to simplify.' Therefore, to 'make the vision plain' means to simplify the vision to such a form that it is practicably implementable.

THE SPECTRUM OF DREAM PURSUIT

Simplification of vision is by a process known as the *Spectrum of Dream Pursuit* (SDP).

(1) Mission

The first step of the Spectrum of Dream Pursuit is developing a mission statement (or mission, for short). A mission is a working statement of your vision. It is the purpose of the vision graphically documented in a concise format. Every vision is meant to fulfil a purpose and the concise articulation of this purpose into a working statement is what is called mission statement. That is, your mission statement must state exactly how you want to implement your vision.

Thus, vision answers the question of 'why' you want to do a thing, while mission answers 'how' you want to do it. For instance, the vision of this book is 'to develop your mind and spirit for exploit,' while the mission of the book is 'to develop your mind and spirit for exploit through the knowledge of mental development and utilisation of the spiritual forces of vision, faith, and love.' In other words, the mission statement of this book clearly defines how its vision will be carried out, which is to focus on mental development and the spiritual forces of vision, faith, and love.

(2) Goals

What is your heart indicating? It is never too late. Age is never a barrier, except you accept it as such in your mind. The vision of youth, the dreams of old age, can still be achieved even when all human hopes appear lost. To realise this, the mission of your vision must be broken down into smaller, workable steps. Goals are smaller, workable steps of the mission of a vision. In other words, when you divide your vision into practicably smaller stages, each stage is called a goal.

Goals are like the goalposts of a soccer play. We only know that a team is winning when a goal is scored. Imagine if there are no goalposts in a soccer play! The same goes for vision. You can only measure the progress you make in your vision if you set goals to attain.

The Three Principles of Goal Setting

However, before you set goals for your vision, you should be aware of three principles that govern goal setting, and these are:

(a) Goals are Personal

Each of us is different in personality trait, mental and spiritual development. Our emotional growth, health, and skill also differ. All these form who we are and determine our capacity at a given time. What constitute practicable, workable steps for you may not be practicable at all to another person at a given time. What appears easy and practicable to your colleague today may actually be too big and impracticable to you.

Consider this situation. Dr. Acu and Dr. Blema plan to start a medical business. The capital for take-off was an estimated 200 000 USD. Dr. Acu has 100 000 USD as a capital to start while Dr Blema only has 15 000 USD to start the same business. Thus, these two individuals will definitely not have the same goals. Whereas Dr. Acu will need an additional 100 000 USD, on the other hand Dr. Blema's additional sum will be 185 000 USD. Obviously, the goals Dr. Acu will set to realise his dream of owning a medical business will be different from Dr. Blema's.

Moreover, besides the difference in capital, Dr. Acu and Dr. Bema do not have the same personality trait, level of emotional growth, business acumen, etc. even though they may have the same academic qualifications. Therefore, if Dr. Blema decides to set the same goals as Dr. Acu, he may run into hitches and may end up destroying his vision of owning a medical business.

(b) Goals are Circumstantial

Goal setting is circumstantial, often taking into consideration the individual strengths, resources, and time. What is impracticable to you today may be completely practicable tomorrow. You set goals based on your circumstances, not on some other person's circumstances.

Life is like a relay race, and each of us must run in our track. Our circumstances are not equally the same. Our knowledge, experiences, and resources all count in the business arena. We all know in part. No one knows everything. We all have different experiences, which all wrap together to form who we are. Our resources and access to resources are not all the same. Goal setting takes all these into cognisance. Hence, it is stupidity to let some other person's goals to become yours knowing that you are not the same. You set your goals based on your circumstances, not based on someone else's.

That is, what constitutes one person's goals may completely be impracticable to another individual. A practicable goal is one that is tailored not only to the visioner's personality but also to his circumstances.

(c) Goals are Purposeful

Though our goals may vary, but the purpose of the goals remains the same. The purpose of goals should be to actualise the vision. In other words, goals are not set arbitrarily, they are targeted at fulfilling the mission of the vision. For instance, though Dr. Acu and Blema may set different goals, yet the purpose of their goals should be to fulfil the mission of setting up their medical businesses.

Characteristics of Goals

The truth is that most people are aware of the importance of goal setting in the realisation of their visions or dreams. But not all goals will lead you to realising your dreams. Some goals are too ambiguous and bogus to pursue. Setting a goal is an act. A successful goal setting should be a smart one.

The **SMART** acronym is a set of criteria for articulating a good plan of actions for the fulfilment of a vision. The SMART criteria were first articulated in a paper, *Management Review,* written in 1981 by George T. Doran as a guide in the setting of goals.

SMART is a mnemonic acronym for:

S for Specific – a good plan must be specific

M for Measurable – a good plan should have indicators to measure its progress

A for Assignable – a good plan must specify who will do it

R for Realistic – a good plan must state what results can realistically be achieved, given available resources.

T for Time-based – a good plan must specify when the result(s) can be achieved.

In other words, a good plan requires that the vision be broken down into attainable goals. The SMART approach constitutes a smart way of drawing up attainable goals of the vision.

(3) Objectives

Having set up your goals, next is to implement them. The steps you take to implement the goals are the objectives. Objectives are specific details of goals.

The Differences between Objectives and Goals

(a) Goals are long-term in scope

Goals are fairly long-term in scope and give an indication of what it would take for the mission of a vision to be realised. As far as possible, goals are measurable in order to monitor progress towards their achievement.

On the other hand, objectives are usually a short-term execution plans. That is, objectives define an endpoint of concern and the direction of change that is preferred. A good, clear objective should clearly describe the exact results that are being sought.

For example, the objective of a high school student with a vision of becoming a doctor will be to enrol in Mathematics, Chemistry, Physics, and Biology at the matric level. If he enrolled in Economics, Commerce, Government, and Literature, obviously he cannot be accepted in a medical school, and his vision of becoming a doctor will not be realised.

In other words, if goals are more specific than mission, then objectives are more specific than goals. Like goals, wherever possible, objectives should be quantified and should have clear time frames for their completion. This allows them to be monitored and performance managed.

(b) A goal can have many objectives

A goal can require many objectives. That is, a goal can result in multiple objectives. For example, the goal of a high school student who desires to be a doctor but having challenge in Mathematics can result in the following three specific objectives:

- allocate more study time (e.g. extra 2 hours per day) for Mathematics
- get extra three lessons per week on Mathematics
- make friendship with a student that excels in Mathematics.

(c) Objectives are flexible

Objectives are not static; they may change with time and circumstances. Setting and monitoring strategic objectives is an iterative and dynamic process, not a static procedure. The same is true with goals. A goal may change with circumstances or time. The key word is flexibility.

(d) SMART versus 3CUM

The characteristics of a goal are summarised by the acronym **SMART** while the characteristics of objectives can be summarised with the acronym **3CUM** (Complete, Controllable, Concise, Understandable, and Measurable).

Complete – a well-defined set of objectives includes 'everything that matters' in making the decision. This means taking into consideration all the environmental, social and economic outcomes that may be affected by the decision. To know whether your objectives are complete, you need to consider the range of alternatives under consideration.

Controllable – this means that the objectives include only those endpoints that can be influenced by the decision at hand.

Concise – the set of objectives should ensure that all the important consequences can be described with the fewest possible objectives and criteria, with no redundancy or double counting. Similar objectives are grouped together by creating sub-objectives that define the components of the general objectives. This hierarchical structure helps to simplify evaluation.

Understandable – objectives should be kept simple – just the thing that matters and the direction it should move in. It involves using commonly understood terms rather than scientific jargon.

Measurable – unlike goals with the SMART characteristics, objectives themselves do not always need to be measurable, but they do need to be conceptually clear enough that measures or evaluation criteria can be later defined.

Note that setting SMART goals and formulating 3CUM objectives focus your energy and quantify your outcome so that you are not just busy. Being busy alone, as most people do, is not equivalent to productivity.

THE UNCHANGEABILITY OF VISION

Vision (also known as 'dream'), Mission, Goals and Objectives form a Spectrum of Dream Pursuit. A mission is a working statement of a vision. Goals are the breakdown practicable steps of the mission, while objectives are the precise actions required to accomplish a goal; thus, objectives are the specific end-points of the Spectrum of Dream Pursuit.

Whereas objectives and goals can be changed based on changes in circumstances of the individual, mission and vision remain unchanged in pursuit of dreams. A change in vision means a change in the person's life purpose. Vision and mission carry the purpose of a thing, and any change in purpose means you have forfeited that particular thing.

For instance, the purpose of a Penicillin antibiotic is to fight bacteria. The manufacturer has this in mind and thus set out to produce the Penicillin antibiotic to fulfil that purpose, and call the Penicillin antibiotic Amoxicillin. Thus, the purpose of Amoxicillin will be reflected in the vision and mission of the manufacturer. For the vision, it can read thus: 'To produce Amoxicillin as a Penicillin antibiotic to fight bacteria.' The mission can be: 'To produce Amoxicillin as a Penicillin antibiotic to kill Gram negative bacteria and immobilise Gram-positive bacteria.'

Whereas the vision simply states the purpose of the antibiotic, which is 'fighting bacteria,' the mission elaborates further by stating what the 'fighting' means, and that is to 'kill' and 'immobilise' and even goes further to state which kind of bacteria will be killed and which will be immobilised. Thus, the mission shows the practical way that the vision will be carried out.

In other words, the purpose of producing the Penicillin antibiotic called Amoxicillin is encapsulated in the vision and clearly stated in the mission. This will guide the formulation of goals and objectives. For example, one of the goals can be: 'To produce capsules of Amoxicillin instead of tablets or suspensions.' An objective will then be: 'To produce 500 milligrams of Amoxicillin in each capsule.'

That is, one of the goals of producing Amoxicillin is to have it in capsule formulation, while the objectives clearly stated how much of the Amoxicillin will be contained in each capsule.

If, for instance, the manufacturer decides to produce a suspension instead of a capsule, his goals and objectives may change, e.g. he may now formulate 250 milligrams in 5 millilitres of suspension. Thus, to obtain 500 milligrams of Amoxicillin, 10 millilitres of the suspension will now be required. In other words, the vision and mission of fighting the bacteria will not change, although the goals and objectives will change.

On the other hand, if, for instance, the manufacturer decides not to produce a Penicillin antibiotic, but rather choose to produce a drug that will treat pain (analgesic drug). The vision will automatically change and so will the mission, goals and objectives.

In summary, whereas objectives and goals can be changed based on changes in circumstances of the individual, mission and vision remain unchanged in pursuit of dreams. A change in vision means a change in the person's life purpose. This is because vision and mission carry the purpose of a thing, and any change in purpose means you have forfeited that particular thing. Do not live your life without having a vision that is well-defined in mission statement, which must be broken down into smart goals, which in turn must be broken down into objectives that form the day-to-day practical steps to follow. By this method – the Spectrum of Dream Pursuit – vision is made plain so that the visioner and his team can run more effectively with the vision.

> *"Then the Lord answered me and said: 'Write the vision and make it plain on tablets, that he may run who reads it'" (Hab.2:3 NKJV).*

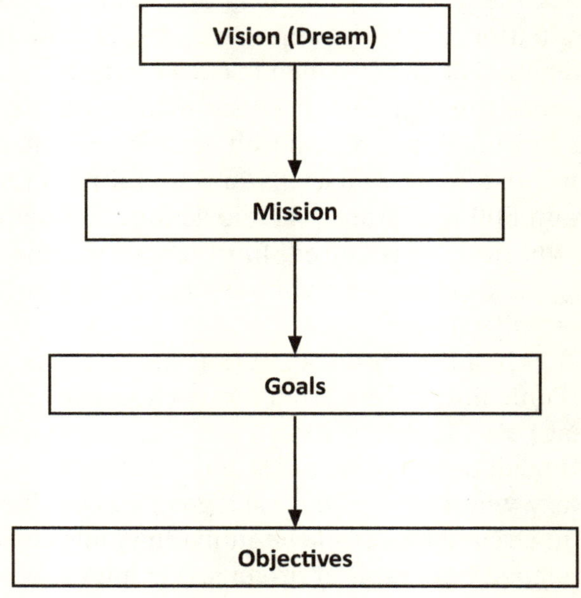

***Fig*.16: Spectrum of Dream Pursuit**

Chapter 28
Section Two Practical Steps (Vision Pathway Steps 4 and 5)

As discussed in the previous chapter, in the 6th century BC, God inspired Prophet Habakkuk to document five practical steps involve in pursuit of vision for anyone who desires to make the most of his earthly life-journey. These five practical steps are what this book refers to as the Vision Pathway. The first three practical steps have been discussed in the previous chapter. This chapter discusses the concluding fourth and fifth steps of the Vision Pathway.

VISION PATHWAY FOURTH STEP: DISCERN THE RIGHT TIME TO LAUNCH THE VISION

Note that there is a time for everything. Because you have received a genuine vision that unveils your life purpose today does not mean you are to start running with the vision immediately.

> *"For the vision is yet for an appointed time" (Hab.3:3 NKJV).*

> *"To everything there is a season, a time for every purpose under heaven" (Ecc.3:1 NKJV).*

Joseph the son of Jacob received genuine vision that spelt out his leadership and saviour roles at the age of 17 (Gen.37:1-11), yet his dreams only materialised when he was 30 years (Gen.41:46). David the son of Jesse received a divine revelation about his life purpose, which was to be king of Israel, when he was a youth (possibly at about 17 years of age) (1Sam.16:10-13; 17:33), yet he never ascended the throne until he was 30 years (2Sam.5:4). Jesus knew His life purpose from the age of twelve (Luk.2:41-50), yet He never launched out with His earthly ministry until He was 30 years old (Luk.3:23).

Why is there such Waiting Time?

The waiting time before a vision is launched out is the period of preparation. The preparation time is a period of grooming. It is a time of character development, which is the bedrock of any success! By the age of 40 years, Moses had started to sense his calling as a deliverer of his people. His life purpose was drawing him. However, he had to wait for another 40 years before he could enter into his life purpose.

Moses was born to be the deliverer of Israel, the people of God, from Egyptian bondage, which by divine timing was to last only 400 years (Gen.15:13). Thus, as the 400 years were drawing to completion, Moses was born; that is, he was born at the right time! When Moses was 40 years old, Israel's slavery was in its 390th year, remaining only 10 years!

However, Moses was ignorant of divine timing. Moses never knew that it was still 10 years to complete the stipulated 400 years of slavery. These ten years remaining were still part of the ongoing preparatory period for grooming him for his life assignment! But Moses was spiritually blind and deaf to this.

> *Who is blind but My servant, or deaf as My messenger whom I send? ...Seeing many things, but you do not observe; opening the ears, but he does not hear" (Isa.42:19,20 NKJV).*

Already, by divine enablement, he found himself living in Pharaoh's Palace, receiving leadership training that he would need to forge together the independently loose twelve tribes of Israel into a formidable nationhood. In addition, during his first 40 years of life, Moses received royal treatment in Pharaoh's household, a training he needed to build a confidently positive self-image in preparation to when he would stand in his office as the leader and saviour of his people. Moreover, he needed the boldness of faith-filled, positive self-image in preparation to when he would appear before Pharaoh, the then most powerful seat of government in the world.

Notwithstanding, by the age of 40 years, Moses' training was not yet complete. There were many character flaws in Moses that would need to be corrected for him to successfully fulfil his ministry. His self-egotism must give way to a meek spirit and his faith capacity in Yahweh, the God of his ancestors, must soar up to be able to lead his people out of the draconic bondage of Egypt.

Sadly, Moses missed the divine timing for his life. With such braggadocios self-egotism, he murdered an Egyptian in his bid to salvage his people when he was 40 years old (Act.7:23-29). That was what he thought the inner drawing he had been having was for. But he was wrong. Such misjudged decision landed him in fugitivity (Exo.2:11-22). He was a fugitive for the next 40 years.

As at the time the Israelite slavery entered its 400th year, the year the slavery was supposed to have ended as originally destined by God, Moses was 50 years, living as a fugitive in Midian. For the next 30 years, he remained a fugitive, spending a total of 40 years in fugitivity! (Act.7:30). A deliverer now a fugitive! What an irony of destiny, the experience of more than 90 percent of humanity!

However, life purpose does not die, it keeps drawing us, no matter how far we decide to flee from it. God showed Moses mercy and appeared to him in a burning bush experience. This encounter refocused Moses and brought him back into his life purpose (Exo. chpt. 3). However, this time, Moses had learnt the invaluable life lessons; never was he again too proud and self-egotistical as meekness had taken over his life.

"Now the man Moses was very meek, above all the men which were upon the face of the earth" (Num.12:3 KJV).

At this time, his faith capacity had grown tremendously as he had learnt to depend on God the one who created him for a specific purpose. He was 80 years by the time he finally stepped into his life purpose and led his people out of Egyptian bondage, an event that should have occurred 30 years earlier (Exo.7:7). Thus, instead of spending 400 years in slavery as originally intended by God, the Israelites spent 430 years during which time Moses was 80 years of age! (Exo.12:40,41)

Invaluable Lessons from Moses' Life

The story of Moses is true for billions of people around the world. Lessons from the story include:

- You are not a mistake; you are born at the right time for a specific life purpose.
- There is a right time to lunch out with your vision.
- As you meditate and grow spiritually, you can decipher the right time to lunch out.
- The waiting period before you launch out is a preparatory time.
- Immaturity can cause you to miss the right time to lunch out with your vision.
- To miss the right time to launch out is to delay the fulfilment of your life purpose.
- Even if you miss the divine timing for your life, God's mercy can still avail for you like it did for Moses.

Immaturity Delays Destiny

Indeed, there is a right time to launch out with your vision as clearly stated by Habakkuk.

"For the vision is yet for an appointed time" (Hab.2:3 NKJV).

The waiting time before launching out is the preparatory period, which is a time for grooming and empowerment. The quicker a man becomes groomed in character and empowered with the level of faith required to launch out, the quicker the right time. A man who is carefree and takes no thought for his mental and spiritual development, will remain stunted, immature, and hence, unable to enter his life purpose, for it is one thing to see and know your life purpose and another thing entirely to be able to move into it.

Indeed, immaturity in character development and spiritual capacity delays and can even kill destiny! There are giants to be overcome before you can cross into your life purpose, and you need to build up power capacity to crush the giants and step into your destiny, which the immature cannot dare.

Jesus groomed His disciples for about three-and-half years. Even after this three-and-half years of training, Jesus still instructed the disciples to wait for empowerment before they could launch out (Luk.24:49; Act.1:4-8). According to Habakkuk chapter two verse three, deciphering the right time to launch out with the vision is the fourth step of the Vision Pathway.

If you seek God in prayers, the Holy Spirit can directly speak to you about the right time to step out to implement your vision. The HIPPP Criteria can guide you safely to decipher the right time.

How to Know the Right Time to Launch Out

The HIPPP Criteria (see page 168) is a safe guard to know the right time to launch out with your vision.

H = Humility:

The right time to launch out with the vision is the time you have attained some level of character growth. One of the most important character traits that will be visible when it is the right time to launch out is genuine humility. A man who is ready to start to run with his vision will feel that sense of humility in him as he knows he cannot really make the vision successful by his sheer strength but by divine enablement and the input of others.

I = Impartiality:

At the right time, a visioner would have been groomed enough by the school of life to know how to be forthright because he knows cutting corners or taking arbitrary short-cuts will lead him and his vision to nowhere.

P = Peacefulness:

One cardinal evidence of the right time is inner peace. When he is at the right moment to launch out, the visioner feels undoubted peace within his heart anytime he thinks of stepping out with the vision. As he lets his heart and mind to dwell on the timing of the vision, an overwhelming sense of peace will envelop his inner being if the timing is right. Indeed, many visioners confirm that 'they just know' it is the right time to resign from their paid jobs and focus on their visions because they feel inner sense of tranquillity to do so.

P = Progressiveness:

This is another important indicator of the right time to step out and implement the vision. At the right time for you to start running with your vision, you will miraculously experience helping hands, which may be in cash and/or in kinds, that will assist you to launch out with the vision. I have met many friends who confirmed to me that once they were ready to step out with their visions, they started attracting favour from every corner, even from unlikely sources.

Similar thing happened to Saul son of Kish. At the time Saul was to step into his life purpose as the first king of Israel, he started meeting with favour – his lost donkey was miraculously found, he received two loaves of bread as gifts from two men, he received the gift of prophesy, and some valiant men clung to him to make sure he succeeded in his kingship (1 Sam. chpt. 10)

Indeed, one cardinal indicator of the right time to launch out with your vision is progressive favour; you will receive miraculous favours that will assist your vision once you are at the right season. The reason for this is because of the Law of Attraction. Once it is the right time, your life purpose has the capacity to start attracting attention to itself, one such attention being helpers of destiny. Your life purpose is not just for your benefits, thus, at the right time it will start to attract to itself those human and material resources that will enable it to be successful. This is why those who do not discipline themselves to discover their life purposes and run with them are harming their great destinies.

P = Purity

At the right time to launch out, the visioner experiences a kind of rebirth during which he becomes inwardly drawn away from unchastity. His vision sets him apart from all others, causing him to devote more attention to fulfilling his dream. It is like a young woman who is entering into a marriage. Once she becomes bethrothed to her lover, she separates herself from all other unholy union that can injure her marriage.

The same is true with vision. By the time the vision has reached the point of practical implementation, the visioner will start sensing a rebirth of separation from unholy acts that will injure the fulfilment of his vision. For instance, he may start having a strong sense to disconnect from some unproductive friendship, cut down on time spent watching television, cut off from unnecessary partying, and spend more time to assess and reassess his vision. Even his speech may change. This is one reason why a genuine vision can keep a man alive amidst the challenges of life.

VISION PATHWAY FIFTH STEP: THE VISION SPEAKS AT THE END

Once the vision is launched out and the visioner does not relent in his pursuit, the vision will pass through three stages of growth.

Three Growth Phases of Vision Pursuit

Vision is a plant. The vision seed is the thought process of vision in the heart of a man. Once the thought process is received (planted) and nurture continuously, it has the capacity to grow through three phases. According to Mark chapter 4 verse 28, there are three phases of growth:

First Phase: Blade Phase

The blade refers to the stalk. It first started as cotyledons, which grow to form the stem, the branches and the leaves. The stem, branches, and the leaves collectively form the stalk or the blade, hence, the blade phase is also referred to as the stalk stage.

Characteristics of Blade phase of vision:

- Requires close monitoring:
  At its infancy, your vision requires close monitoring to protect it from vision pests.
- Requires close nurturing:
  Every vision will need constant manuring and watering. You will need to continuously build up knowledge through study and training and constantly exercise the Pathway to Creativity in running with your vision. Each success should prop you to seek for ways to improve on it. Temporal defeat does not mean failure. Indeed, no force has the capacity to kill a genuine vision; the only person that can kill a genuine vision is the visioner himself. The day he gives up marks the death of his vision.

- Not very attractive stage:
  The blade phase is not an attractive stage. At the early stage, do not be despaired if no one notices your vision; when that occurs, know that your vision is at its blade phase.
- Requires efforts to cultivate to maturity
  The blade phase requires concentrated energy and time input for the vision to grow and keep growing. At this stage, the vision keeps the visioner at constant alert. Again, do not despair because you will reap the fruit of your labour if you faint not by the wayside!

> *"Do not be deceived, God is not mocked; for whatever a man sows, that he will also reap" (Gal.6:7 NKJV).*

Second Phase: Ear Phase

The ear is the flowering head of a plant. The ear phase refers to the flowering stage. It starts with budding and finally the shooting forth of flowers.

Characteristics of Ear Phase:

- Blossoming
  The ear phase is the stage of beauty. The flowers are beautiful to behold. At its ear phase, the beauty of your vision will start to radiate out as it blesses the humanity.
- Attracts all manners of insects
  Ear phase attracts both useful and useless insects. The useful insects help in cross-fertilization while the useless insects act as pests that can destroy the buds or even the entire plant. Once you vision grows into its ear phase, it will attract both useful and useless insects. Watch out for both kinds of insects. What do you do with useless insects?

Third Phase: Grain Phase

This is the phase of fruitage; it is the stage of the full kernel.

Characteristics of Grain Stage:

- Fruit bearing
  At the grain phase, the fruits are visible before everyone.
- Popularity
  Because the fruits are visible, many people will want to be identified with your vision plant.
- Last stage
  The grain phase is the last stage of growth. Thus, before you reach this phase, your vision will have to pass through the blade and ear phases.
- Perpetuation
  The grain phase set the stage for perpetuation. If the plant must perpetuate itself, its seeds contained in the fruit must not be eaten; seeds are for planting. Once sown, the seed grows through these three phases (blade, ear and grain phases) to perpetuate the plant species. Don't eat seeds with the fruit; seeds are for planting and fruit for eating! In other words, as your vision bears fruit, be wise enough to keep the seed away for replanting.

> *"Now may He who supplies seed to the sower, and bread for food, supply and multiply the seed you have sown and increase the fruits of your righteousness" (2Cor.9:10 NKJV).*

How much your vision plant will reproduce itself and bud across the world is dependent on how big your vision is. However, always remember that life purpose is to bless the entire world and not for a myopic coverage.

> *"You are the salt of the earth; but if the salt loses its flavour, how shall it be seasoned? It is then good for nothing but to be thrown out and trampled underfoot by men.*

> *"You are the light of the world. A city that is set on a hill cannot be hidden. Nor do they light a lamp and put it under a basket, but on a lampstand, and it gives light to all who are in the house.*
>
> *"Let your light so shine before men, that they may see your good works and glorify your Father in heaven" (Mat.5:13-16 NKJV).*

What you have is far bigger than what you think! A tree can become a forest if planted in the right soil and cultivate long enough for it to bud. Likewise, your vision can grow into a forest if sown in the right soil and nurtured over a period!

The Vision Speaks at the End

The grain phase is the last stage of growth; it is the phase of fruit bearing. Thus, before you reach this phase of fruit bearing, your vision will have to pass through the first and second phases (the blade and ear phases respectively), but many people are not willing to pay the price to reach this third (grain) phase of fruit bearing, hence, their visions end up being casualties of growth.

Genuine vision speaks loudest at the end as documented clearly by Habakkuk. In other words, the fifth step of Vision Pathway is the last stage of vision pursuit, and it is the grain phase of fruit bearing! It is at this last stage that genuine vision begins to speak.

> *"For the vision is yet for an appointed time; but at the end it will speak, and it will not lie" (Hab.2:3 NKJV).*

The term 'speak' in the above Scripture is from the Hebrew term *puwach,* which literally means 'to puff out,' or 'to break forth.' In other words, it is at this fifth step of Vision Pathway that a genuine vision puffs out its full beauty and begins to break forth for all to see its glory. Therefore, there is no need to give up on your vision. *"Though it [vision fulfilment] tarries, wait for it, because it will SURELY come, it will not tarry"* (Hab.2:3 NKJV), for *"through faith and patience [you will] inherit the promises"* (Heb.6:12 NKJV).

Section 3

How to Develop Your Spirit for Exploits (The Force of Faith)

Chapter 29
The Definition of Faith

Whereas vision reveals the future, faith is what brings that future into reality. Faith is one of the three greatest forces that rule the world. Faith is the power that transforms the non-materialistic future into a tangible present substance. The Force of Faith is what compelled the sighted future into reality.

Without the force of faith, the sighted future remains a dream. In other words, without the force of faith, none of your visions can become a reality. Indeed, faith is the lifeline for survival and colourful living. It is the lifestyle of God and humans created by God are wired to live like Him. To show how important faith is, Prophet Habakkuk, under divine inspiration, vividly captures its significance by this statement:

> *"the just shall live by his faith" Hab.2:4 KJV).*

This statement was repeated about 2000 years later in three separate inspired letters (Rom.1:17; Gal.3:11; and Heb.10:38). That is, to underscore the significance of faith for human survival, God caused this statement to be written down in four letters at various times. Indeed, the place of faith in the survival of a man cannot be overemphasized. This section exposes this mighty force and how you can lay hold of it to achieve your heart's desires.

SYNONYMOUS NAMES

Various authors ascribe various names to the Force of Faith. Some call it Confidence, Resolute Determination, Hot Pursuit, Trust... Whichever name you choose to call it, the truth remains that without the force of faith, nothing worthwhile can be achieved in life. Hence, it is so important that we know what faith is and how to wield this mighty force.

DEFINITION OF FAITH

Many people claim to wield the force of faith and yet fail to obtain their heart desires. To be candid, since I have come to know about this mighty force, I have not utilised the force of faith and failed to get the expected result. This is because faith does not fail. It answers to anyone who knows about it and how to wield its force. Most times, what some people refers to as faith is not faith at all.

What then is faith?

If faith is very crucial for our survival, God will not leave us in the dark about its meaning. The Scriptures succinctly defines faith in Hebrews chapter 11 verse 1.

> *"Now faith is the substance of things hoped for, the evidence of things not seen" (Heb.11:1 NKJV).*

The term 'now' in the above Scripture is a conjunction that links the previous statement (Heb.10:39) to Heb.11:1. Interestingly, Hebrews chapter 11 verse 1 has two statements joined into one compound statement as follows:

• First statement: Faith is *"the substance of things hoped for."*
The terms 'the substance' are from the Greek noun form *hypostasis*, which literally means 'structure.' The phrase 'of things hoped for' is from the Greek verb *elpizō*, which means 'to confidently expect.' Thus, the statement "the substance of things hoped for" literally means 'to confidently expect a structure.'

• Second statement: Faith is *"the evidence of things not seen."*
This statement is translated from the following Greek words:

- 'the evidence' are from the Greek word *elegchos*, which means 'proof' or 'conviction'
- 'of things' are from the Greek word *pragma*, which literally means 'thing' or 'matter'
- 'not' is from the Greek word *ou*, which is a particle for 'the absolute negative'
- 'seen' is from the Greek word *blepō*, which means 'to see with the bodily eye'

Thus, the statement "the evidence of things not seen" literally means 'convincing proof of a matter not seen with the bodily eye.' Therefore, Hebrews chapter 11 verse one has the following original words:

> *"Now faith is to confidently expect a structure, convincing proof of a matter not seen with the bodily eye."*

Table 3: The Literal Meaning of Hebrews Chapter 11 verse 1: "Now faith is *the substance of things hoped for, the evidence of things not seen*" (NKJV)		
English Translation	**Greek Version**	**Literal Meaning**
the Substance	*hypostasis*	structure
of things hoped for	*elpizō*	to confidently expect
the evidence	*elegchos*	convincing proof
of things	*pragma*	matter, thing
not	*ou*	the absolute negative
seen	*blepō*	to see with the bodily eye

An analysis of Hebrews 11 verse 1:

(a) Faith is "to confidently expect a structure"

The first thing about faith is to have a 'confidently expected structure.' This 'confidently expected structure' is also known as 'the object of faith.' In other words, if you say you have faith, then there must be something, an object, you are not just expecting, but confidently expecting. That is, you believe the object you expect will definitely arrive as you envisage.

In this generation, the meaning of the term 'belief' does not seem to have the same seriousness as it was in the first century. When you say you hold a belief, it means you have no doubt whatsoever about a thing; rather you are so confident that it will be exactly as you believe. In other words, to be 'confidently expecting a structure' is to strongly 'believe in the reality of that structure or object.'

(b) Faith is "convincing proof of a matter not seen with the bodily eye."

In addition, according to Hebrews 11 verse 1, faith goes beyond having 'a belief in a structure or an object' to having "convincing proof of a matter not seen with the bodily eye." The term matter in this statement is of great interest as follows:

- Matter is anything that has weight and occupies weight.

- The 'matter' in this second statement refers to the object of faith in the first statement.
- The 'matter' is not seen with the bodily eye (Greek blepō), but with the eye of faith, which refers to the *eido centre* of the human spirit.

The Eye of Faith

In other words, the object of faith is the matter that is seen with the eido centre of the spirit man as clearly shown by verse 13 of the same chapter 11 of Hebrews:

> *"These all died in faith, not having received the promises, but having seen [eido] them afar off were assured of them, embraced them and confessed that they were strangers and pilgrims on the earth" (Heb.11:13 NKJV).*

The term 'seen' in Heb.11:13 is from the Greek word eido, which is the eye of the spirit. It speaks about the heroes of faith like Abraham, Moses, David, Gideon, etc. who saw the promises of God from afar. They saw the promises of salvation when fallen humans will become sons of God; these promises are now fulfilled with the coming of Jesus (see SSB Book 5). In other words, with the eido centre of their human spirit they could 'see' into thousands of years (afar of) from their generation.

It is with this same eido centre (not with the bodily physical eye – *blepo*) a man sees the 'matter' (object of faith). Therefore, faith refers to seeing an object (however, not with physical *'blepo'* eye but with the spiritual *'eido'* eye), which appears so real that it forces the man of faith to start taking steps in line with what he sees. These steps he takes are the 'convincing proof of the matter not seen with the bodily eye.'

People struggle with faith because they are yet to 'see' clearly the object of their faith. When a man sees a matter, doubt about the matter ceases. However, with regard to faith, this 'seeing' is not with the *blepo*, the physical eyes, but with the eido centre (the eye of the spirit). Once you 'see' a 'matter' with your inner eye (the eido centre), you cease to doubt the physical realisation of what you 'see.' Therefore, the eido centre is the ***Eye of Faith*** with which a man 'sees' the object of his vision. This is of great significance you should never forget if you ever desire to actualise your vision.

JOE'S STORY – A CLASSICAL ILLUSTRATION

Joe was my schoolmate. He had faith to study medicine in the United States. Thus, while in high school in Nigeria, he confided in some of us about his dream. To the people around, it was a tall dream, almost an impossibility because of the huge financial involvement. Joe did not come from a wealthy family, hence, no strong financial support.

About 5 years after our high school, Joe wrote me a friendly letter from the US. He had just started his first-year studies, getting ready to enter the medical school. As at the writing of this manuscript, Joe had graduated as a medical doctor from an American university.

How Joe realised his tall dream clearly illustrates the definition of faith discussed in this chapter. Firstly, Joe had an object of faith, which was to be a medical graduate of the American university. He saw this object so clearly in his inner eye, the eido centre of his spirit man, that he had no doubt it was coming. In other words, he had a 'confidently expected structure.' To others, this was a mere wishing, but to Joe it was a real matter that would be realised.

What Joe saw with the eido centre of his spirit man drove him to start taking steps. The letters and email communication I had with Joe revealed some of the steps. He worked and saved money, did all manners of odd jobs and even got some scholarship stipends, during which time he never lost the object of his faith. What he saw kept driving him. These steps are the 'convincing proof of the matter (the object of Joe's faith – American medical graduate) not seen with the bodily eye.'

IN SUMMARY

You cannot claim to wield the force of faith when you do not meet these two conditions:

- have an object clearly visible in your inner eye
- taking practical steps as convincing proof of the object of your faith

Chapter 30
The Force of Faith

When God created the human spirit, He deposited quality substances in the heart of the human spirit. The Fruit of the Spirit is one of the rich deposits in the heart of the spirit man (see SSB Book 1). Faith is part of the Fruit of the Spirit that is deposited in the heart of the spirit man.

CHARACTERISTICS OF FAITH

The following are the characteristic features of faith:

(a) Faith is a force

Faith is not just a psychological display of emotions or a mental assent; rather it is a mighty force that can be wielded to bring the unseen object into a physical reality. Faith forces the unseen to become seen. Once it grips a man, the force of faith can catapult him from a nonentity into a wonder.

(b) Faith is spiritual

Faith is generated from the heart of the spirit man. It is one of the products of the stimulation of the spirit man by an activated mind. That is, true faith does not emanate from the mind (soulish) realm, but from the heart of the spirit man. True faith is not attained by mustering physical strength. That is, faith is not generated by the cells, tissues, organs, and systems of the body. The heart of man is the seat of faith.

Thus, every human has the capacity to wield the force of faith; God deposits faith in the heart of man at creation. Sadly, at the Fall of Man in the Garden of Eden, the human spirit became dead (see SSB Book 3). Because of the deadness of the spirit of the unregenerated person, the heart of the unregenerated man cannot release the full strength of faith as originally intended by God.

> *"And pray that we may be delivered from unreasonable and wicked men, for not all men have faith" (2The.3:2 MEV).*

For instance, many unregenerated persons believe there is God, but they lack the faith necessary to follow God's ways. Thus, I am usually not surprise whenever I see an unregenerated person with no propelling faith for true success.

However, at New Birth, the human spirit is recreated, and the Fruit of the Spirit is reborn in him. Genuine faith, which is part of the Fruit of the Spirit, towards God comes alive in such a regenerated person.

(c) Faith does grow

The nature of faith is that it can grow.

> *"We ought always to thank God for you, brothers and sisters, and rightly so, because your faith is growing more and more, and the love all of you have for one another is increasing" (2The.1:3 NIV).*

When God created the spirit man, He deposited 'a measure of faith' in each heart. A measure of faith refers to an amount, a level, or a degree of faith as clearly depicted in the inspired letter of Apostle Paul:

> *"God has dealt to each one a measure of faith" (Rom.12: 3 NKJV).*

God has apportioned to each a degree of faith [and a purpose designed for service]" (Rom.12:3 AMP).

God expects this measure of faith in us to grow. The more our faith grows, the more accomplishment we make in our destiny journey. Our destiny is like a book of many pages. To move from one page to another requires a certain degree of force. That is the force of faith. Without such force of faith, many hindering forces abound to stop us. Indeed, many have opened some pages of their lives and become stuck, not moving forward anymore. They wonder why they got stuck, not realising that they needed a higher level of faith to forcefully open into the next page.

(d) Faith is activated by vision

Vision reveals an object in the future; faith is what compelled that object into present reality. This means for faith to be generated, there must be an object of the future, refers to as the 'object of faith' or the 'confidently expected structure' as discussed in the previous chapter. The force of faith is what transforms this futuristic object into present substance.

Faith - the Link between Vision and Actuality

About 2000 years ago, Apostle Paul, under divine inspiration, concisely defines faith, showing the relationship between faith and vision:

"Now faith is the substance of things hoped for, the evidence of things not seen" (Heb.11:1 KJV).

Hebrews chapter 11 verse 1 mentions two factors: faith and hope. As discussed in Chapter 18, the common modern terminology for hope is vision; vision is the hope you want to receive. The term 'substance' in the above Scripture is from the Greek word *hypostasis*, which occurs 5 times in 5 verses in the Bible (2 Cor.9:4; 11: 17; Heb.1:3; 3: 14; 11: 1). Its rendering in Hebrews chapter 1 verse 3 is very interesting:

> *"God, who at various times and in various ways spoke in time past to the fathers by the prophets, has in these last days spoken to us by His Son, whom He has appointed heir of all things, through whom also He made the worlds; who being the brightness of His glory and the express image of His Person [hypostasis], and upholding all things by the word of His power, when He had by Himself purged our sins, sat down at the right hand of the Majesty on high" (Heb.1:1-3 NKJV).*

In this Scripture, the 'Person' refers to the incarnation of Jesus, the Word of God. God cannot be seen with the physical eye. However, the power of the Holy Spirit transformed this unseen God into a tangible, physical Person, Jesus Christ. That is, God became flesh and is called Jesus Christ (see John chapter 1). In other words, all the 'substance' [*hypostasis*] that makes up God is what is in Jesus. Thus, the optically invisible God-substance became a physical Person.

What this means is that an optically unseen substance can be transformed into a tangible physical object that can be perceived by the senses of the body. In the same manner, vision reveals an object which cannot be seen by the physical eye or perceived by the body senses. Only the inner eye of the visioner sees the object of his vision, also known as the object of faith or the 'confidently expected structure' (Greek, *hypostasis*). However, the Force of Faith is what transforms that unseen object of vision into a tangible reality for people around to see. This truth is what Apostle Paul defines in that Hebrews chapter 11 verse one as clearly rendered by ERV translation:

> *"Faith is what makes real the things we hope for. It is proof of what we cannot see" (Heb.11:1 ERV).*

Thus, without the Force of Faith, your vision will remain a dream that resides only in your heart and mind. In other words, faith is the link between your Vision and its Actuality (physical realisation)! It is, therefore, of great significance for a man to learn how to wield this might force, and which is what this section unveils.

CHAPTER 31
THE AUDACITY OF FAITH

ONCE FAITH GRIPS A MAN, it turns him into a shooting star, into an unstoppable bullet, an unconquerably indomitable force. That is the Audacity of Faith. It turns the Lilliputian into a giant, the weakling ant into a behemoth. Indeed, the force of faith is what terminates the struggles and hardship of life.

THE FORCE-LINK BETWEEN THE UNSEEN AND THE SEEN REALITY

One Scripture that shapes my life is Ephesians chapter one verse three:

> *"Blessed be the God and Father of our Lord Jesus Christ, who has blessed us with every spiritual blessing in the heavenly places in Christ" (Eph.1:3 NKJV).*

God has blessed each of His children with 'every spiritual blessing.' If God exists and the Bible is true, then Ephesians chapter one verse three is true. Of course, there is God (see SSB Bok 1) and the Bible is true (see SSB Book 4). Then why is it that many Christians are being crushed in poverty and many are wallowing in self-pity and frustration? If God has blessed each of His children and "healing is His children's bread," why are many of God's people suffering untold hardship of diseases and handicaps?

Indeed, the Bible is true and "God is no respecter of persons" (Act 10:34 KJV) and anyone of any race, tongue, and sex that meets the Scriptural requirements, such a man will reap the blessings of the Scripture. The main challenge is that many Christians do not know nor practice the Scriptures, hence, God laments: "My people are destroyed for lack of knowledge" (Hos. 4:6 KJV).

But what is this spiritual blessing that God has blessed His children with?

The term 'spiritual' in Ephesians chapter one verse three is from the Greek word *pneumatikos,* which means, 'intangible non-physical, or non-materialistic.' The Greek word for blessing in that same Scripture is *eulogia,* which literally means 'bounty by word declaration.' Other terms for 'bounty' are 'abundant gifts or abundant goods.' Therefore, 'spiritual blessing' refers to non-physical abundant gifts God has given to us by word declaration. In other words, if you are in Christ, part of your packages or inheritance is 'bounty blessings.' Truly, the day you experience the New Birth and become born-again, God has pronounced on you every abundant gift. Hence, Apostle Paul, under inspiration declares, *"all things are yours"* (1Cor.3:21 NKJV).

However, some Christians have read these Scriptures and wonder if they are really true. Some conclude they refer to life after death when the believer passes on to be with Jesus in Heaven.

Note the followings two points about Ephesians chapter one verse three:

- the blessing is spiritual
- the spiritual blessing is in the Heavenly Places

The term 'heavenly' in that Scripture is from the Greek term *epouranios*, which means spiritual or celestial. In other words, the blessing you receive from God is spiritual that is stored in spiritual realm. Thus, for an individual to enjoy the blessing, he has to transmute it from the spiritual realm into the physical realm.

The Force of Faith is what transmutes the intangible, non-material blessing from the spiritual realm to the tangible, material blessing in the physical realm. The problem with many Christians is ignorance; they do not know how to actualise this. Even worse is the fact that many individuals do not know that they have such rich blessings in Christ they can access while here on earth. As ambassadors of Christ and sons of God, we do have the right to enjoy the riches of God in Christ while still here on earth.

Vision reveals to us these riches that we have in Christ while faith enforces the riches from the spiritual into the physical realm. Indeed, His divine power has given to us all things that we will ever need for a successful living. The more of God and His laws we know, the more we will please Him and have access to the abundant riches in Him, and we can only please Him by faith (Heb.11:3). Thus, the more we know how to operate the force of faith, the more we access our blessings.

> *"His divine power has given to us all things that pertain to life and godliness, through the knowledge of Him who called us by glory and virtue" (2Pet.1:3 NKJV).*

Therefore, it is of paramount importance for an individual to learn how faith functions and how to wield its mighty force to actualise what he needs. This section of this book unveils Faith, one of the three greatest forces that rule the world, and how to wield its mighty force.

FAITH CAN BE ACTIVATED DELIBERATELY

The beautiful thing about faith is that it can be deliberately activated. Faith is not an accidental finding. Faith is not obtained by a mere wish. Faith is not wielded in an unconscious state. Rather faith is generated by a deliberate act of men to perform specific assignments. In other words, you cannot wield the force of faith and not know. Faith is a weapon for battle; no one wields this weapon and won't know it.

Because faith is activated deliberately, it means anyone can exercise it. Faith is not for a selected few. Many do not know how to generate and exercise faith because of ignorance. If they knew that their unfulfilled heart desires can become a reality by the force of faith, they would do everything it will take to generate it. Poverty, diseases, frustrations, etc. all bow at the feet of faith. The force of faith is a weapon that quenches all opposition. The Force of Faith is the Audacity of Faith.

> *"Above all, take up the shield of faith with which you will be able to extinguish all the flaming arrows of the evil one" (Eph.6:16 TLV).*

THE STORY OF DR. KEMELEY

Dr. Kemeley migrated from the Democratic Republic of Congo (DRC) to South Africa. The DRC is one of the most impoverished countries of Africa with a gross domestic product (at purchasing power parity) per capita at 773 United States Dollars, the second lowest in Africa and in the world. Dr. Kemeley had one desire, and that was to escape his poverty background and build a multimillion dollar worth of wealth. His plan was to achieve this through investment in real estate. His first target was to acquire ten properties within three years of working as an employee.

At one particular year he decided to buy 4 houses and renovate an existing old one to improve its tenant flow. Unfortunately, after evaluating his credit profile, the banks could only offer him mortgage loans of 60 to 70% on each of the four houses. He had to cough out about 1.2 million Rands to finance the houses. All he had then was just a little over R0.2 million, meaning he still required about a million Rands to foot the bill. In addition, he needed about R0.35 million for the renovation of his old house to increase tenancy. With a limited salary, where would the money come from? Who would he turn to?

Nevertheless, Dr. Kemeley was determined never to allow the capital shortage to deter him from his goal. He was given five days by the banks to accept or decline the offer. Each night, Dr. Kemeley would be up moving about the backyard of his house thinking and strategizing. But all the thinking appeared to be leading him to nowhere. He had tried to raise personal loans from all the banks he knew, but they all declined, tagging him as 'high risk.' If he accepted the bond quotation and signed the contract, the property owners would hold him liable for breach of payment in case of default, and this would leave him with enormous debts. According to him, "with butterflies in all my belly, I damned the consequences and decided to sign the contract, giving the go-ahead order to the attorneys to commence the paper works, not knowing where the money would appear from."

Interestingly, immediately he made up his mind and signed the contract of bond offer, doors started opening. One of the banks later called him and offered him a 100 per cent mortgage on one of the properties, meaning he would no longer need to pay any deposit again for that property. Another bank decided to grant him 80 per cent of the personal loan he had earlier applied for. With this 80% personal loan offer and a 100 per cent mortgage of one of the properties, Dr. Kemeley was able to raise the necessary money to pay as deposits for the four properties!

Notice the bold steps taken by Dr. Kemeley in his quest to break away from his poverty background. To migrate from the DRC to South Africa took a lot of sacrifice and effort. He had to raise the necessary finances to procure a visa, and the high currency exchange rate made it a real challenge that could have deterred anyone with no specified, clear vision. Dr. Kemeley's position was even more challenging considering that he had a wife and two infant children dependants. He knew no one in South Africa that he could turn to in the event his plan never worked out.

These challenges notwithstanding, there was nothing like failure in Dr. Kemeley's plan. All he could see was the object of his vision – to escape poverty by building real estate investments in

South Africa. His faith didn't allow him to contemplate failure at all. The force of faith generated kept driving him. He took a step of faith to purchase the houses within a span of few years of living in South Africa where many other doctors had practised for years before Dr. Kemeley's arrival; yet they couldn't dare the risk Kemeley undertook to embrace. The audacity of faith was what gripped Dr. Kemeley and kept driving him forward and upward.

Chapter 32
The Law of Faith

The force of faith is like a running tap under high pressure to let water out. However, the presence of a shut-off valve controls the flow out of the water from the tap. If it is not controlled, the water gushes out in a very berserk manner, messing up the whole area. The Law of Faith is what regulates and unleashes the force of faith in the manner that becomes productive.

The Law of Faith states that '*all things are possible for the one who has faith*' (Mar.9:23 CEB). Thus, if you know what the Law of Faith is and how to operate it, you will suddenly discover an entirely new world of existence! The story of Dr. Kemeley, presented in the previous chapter, is an interesting one. The challenges that confronted him are not uncommon. However, many people would rather throw in the towel and lose the presenting opportunities. Dr. Kemeley's experience reveals one of the laws of success – the Law of Faith.

ATTRIBUTES OF LAW OF FAITH

Faith in the heart of men operates by the Law of Faith. *A law is defined as a rule that regulates stipulated activities in a defined region.* That is, every law has the following attributes:

Every law is a rule

A rule is a legal proclamation, which may be oral or written. Simply put, a rule is a legal statement that stipulates activities. The rule in the Law of Faith states that *'all things are possible for the one who has faith'* (Mar.9:23 CEB).

If every law is a rule that stipulates activities, it means engaging in activities outside the stipulated ones is a violation of the rule and that attracts consequences. Violation of the Law of Faith brings consequences such as lack of progress, diseases, poverty, etc. Indeed, one of the laws that is utilised to achieve financial prosperity is the Law of Faith.

Every law is applicable in a defined region

For instance, the laws of a nation cannot be enforced in another sovereign nation. This means once you enter a region, the laws in that defined region becomes binding on you.

The defined region of operation of the Law of Faith is the entire universe. Universal laws are applicable in the universe, that is, in all nations. The Law of Faith is a universal law; it is applicable for all people in all nations irrespective of sex, tongue, clime, and race that live in our universe. If there are other universes beside the one we know, the Law of Faith may still be applicable because it is a spiritual law that transcends our earthly existence. God, the Creator of all and the Originator of the Law of Faith, lives and operates by faith (see Rom.4:17; Heb.11:3,6).

Ignorance of a law is not an excuse!

Ignorance of the existence of a law is not an excuse for violation of the law. For example, you cannot get into South Africa and start driving on the right-hand side of the road and cause traffic accidents with the claim that you didn't know of the South African traffic law that recognises left-hand driving. Your claim of ignorance will not suffice to set aside the penalty of the traffic offence. Similarly, ignorance of the Law of Faith does not excuse any individual from the consequences of violation. Ignorance of the operation of the Law of Faith breeds penalties such as poverty, frustration and diseases.

ORIGIN OF LAW OF FAITH

The stipulated activities of a law set the standard of behaviour. The question many naturalists often ask is: 'who sets up these natural laws that stipulates the standards of behaviour?' For example, why do we see stealing as wrong or lying as an unacceptable behaviour? Who sets up such standards?

God is a God of order, and He sets boundaries for everything He made. He created the entire universe and sets up laws for its smooth operation. As a matter of fact, some of these universal laws were the rule by which He created the universe. In other words, God is the origin of laws.

> *"Only God can say what is right or wrong. He made the Law"*
> *(Jam.4:12 NLV).*

The Law of Faith is one of the universal laws that God has established in the world. Universal laws can be natural or spiritual law. Natural universal laws only apply in the natural realm and hold no jurisdiction in the spiritual world. An example of a natural law is the law of gravity. A spiritual law has jurisdiction in the spiritual world. The spiritual world is superior in authority to the natural world (see SSB Book 1), hence, the spiritual laws wield superior authority to natural laws.

The Law of Faith is an example of a spiritual law. God is a Spirit and He operates the Law of Faith. For instance, it is by the Law of Faith that God created the universe as He "*calls into existence the things that do not exist*" (Rom.4:17 RSV). Indeed, faith is an attribute of God's nature. God operates by faith!

"By faith we understand that the universe was framed by the word of God, so that things that are seen were not made out of things which are visible" (Heb.11:3 MEV).

As spiritual beings like God, man has been inbuilt with the capacity to operate the Law of Faith just like God. Deposited in the heart of man is faith that operates via the Law of Faith by which man can utilise to control his world.

POWER OF LAW OF FAITH

Why does violation of the rule of law attracts negative consequences? The answer to this question will be clearer if we consider the process of law making. To make a law, an individual or a number of individuals will first make pronouncement, proclamation, or declaration. A pronouncement, proclamation, or declaration is a mere statement of words, which may be written or unwritten. To make the pronouncement, proclamation, or declaration binding, some level of power is imputed into the statement of words. Such power will spell out the benefits for obeying that statement of words and the consequences of violation. Once the stipulated activities in the statement are agreed upon and endorsed by the individual(s), that becomes a law for them.

In other words, every law has an inherent power. This is the imputed power that transforms the proclaimed statement of words into a legal entity called a law. Thus, without the imputed power in the proclaimed statement, the words remain mere proclamation. The imputed power is what transforms the proclaimed statement into a law.

In the same manner, God decrees a statement: *'all things are possible for the one who has faith'* (Mar.9:23 CEB). He inputs power into this statement, thereby converting it into the universal Law of Faith for all time and for all spiritual beings like man. The Law of Faith, like every other law, carries potential power, which once released causes the desired change or transformation to happen.

CHAPTER 33
THE FIVE STEPS OF THE LAW OF FAITH

There are five steps involved in the operation, exercise or application of the Law of Faith; these are the five components of the Law of Faith. Note that each of the first four steps is subject to one's voluntary initiative. That is, the first four steps can be operated at will, making faith a force that anyone who desires can activate. The last (fifth) step is automatically triggered once these first four steps are genuinely initiated. There is no way the fifth step will not be triggered once the first four are frankly initiated. Here are the five steps of the operation of this powerful Law of Faith:

FIRST STEP: HAVE A CLEAR VISION

Dr. Kemeley, whose story was told in Chapter 31, had a singular burning desire, which was the driving force of his life – to escape from his excruciating poverty background. Many first-generation wealth builders are motivated by the same desire, which is to conquer the enemy of poverty. Dr. Kemeley's vision was very clear – he saw himself conquering poverty.

Such a singular clear vision inspired him into actions. As discussed earlier, vision evokes passion or a burning desire that pushes a man into action. That is, vision triggers faith!

SECOND STEP: SET UP A DEFINITE PLAN

Dr. Kemeley's burning desire led him to developing definite plans. Most of the night thinking he engaged in was to come up with definite plans. Though unknown to him, those series of quiet night thinking constitute a form of meditation that activated his mind, which then stimulated his spirit to search out for answers. Many proposals went through his mind as he kept filtering and sieving them to obtain clear blueprints. That is, his spirit man conjured many thoughts, which were passed down to his mind for processing. His mind was able to articulate definite plans of action for implementation.

In other words, his vision generated a burning desire in him. However, only a pulsating, burning desire is not enough, definite plans of action to actualise the desire must be developed. If you are lackadaisical about developing clear plan to actualise your vision, it is obvious that the vision is not compelling enough and driving. A vision evokes burning desire or passion which drives an individual into action. A genuine vision is specific; it is forceful and driving. It forces a man to start generating plans to actualise the object of his vision.

THIRD STEP: EMBARK ON CORRESPONDING ACTION

A genuine vision is not satisfied with just making plans. It makes a man restless until definite, practical steps are taken or implemented in line with its actualisation. They are not mere steps of action, but each step is such that it brings the visioner closer to the fulfilment of his vision. In other words, each step corresponds with the desire of the vision. Each of these steps is referred to as a Corresponding Action.

This Third Step in the operation of the Law of Faith is what is popular referred to in the Christian Pentecostal/Evangelical circle as 'taking the step of faith.' It is acting or behaving exactly what the

Scriptures say on any particular issue. For instance, the Scriptures enjoin: "It is more blessed to give than to receive" (Act.20:35 KJV) and "Give, and it shall be given unto you ..." (Lk.6:38 KJV). Hence, if a man needs financial blessing, he must take the step of faith by acting on these Scriptures, which is to sow financial seeds. When he does that, he will begin to enjoy the financial blessings promised in these powerful Scriptures.

The Law of Faith is not fulfilled without corresponding action taken in line with the actualisation of the vision. Corresponding action is an important component of this law. You may have nursed a desire and developed a plan, until you take practical, corresponding steps, nothing will happen. Taking practical, corresponding step is the *'convincing proof of a matter not seen with the bodily eye'*; it is *'the evidence of things not seen"* as discussed in Chapter 29. That is, the steps you take are the proofs that you believe in what you see in your inner eye!

On arriving in South Africa, Dr. Kemeley didn't just rest and entrust his vision to fate. He started taking practical steps in line with his vision, one of which was to start looking for properties to buy even when he had no money. In fact, he got his taxi man, who often drove him around, to take him to view property layouts around the beautiful city of Cape Town. He went through hundreds of properties, searching for the ones that would meet his investment needs. On identifying the properties, his vision pushed him to start searching for where to raise finances to complete his purchases, and this led him to the banks to ask for loans.

Mathematical Analysis of Faith

Mathematics simplifies complex statements. Using mathematical symbols, what we have been discussing becomes easier to understand.

According to Hebrews chapter 11 verse one, Faith is defined as *"the substance of things hoped for, the evidence of things not seen"* (NKJV) (see Chapter 29).

That is:
Faith = the substance of things hoped for
+ the evidence of things not seen ------- (equation 1)
(Heb.11:1 English translation definition of faith)

As discussed in Chapter 29, the literal Greek meaning of "the substance of things hoped for" is "confidently expected structure." Also, the literal Greek meaning of "the evidence of things not seen" is "convincing proof of a matter not seen with the bodily eye."

Therefore, equation 1 can be re-written as:
Faith = confidently expected structure
+ convincing proof of a matter not seen with the bodily eye
(Heb.11:1 Greek literal definition of faith) ------- (equation 2)

Chapter 29 clearly shows that the "confidently expected structure" is the 'object of faith' or a 'belief' held in the heart and seen by the inner eye, the eido centre; while the "convincing proof of a matter not seen with the bodily eye" refers to the 'corresponding action' or steps taken as proof of the belief.

Therefore, from equation 2:
Faith = Belief + Corresponding Action ------- (equation 3)

That is, corresponding action is any activity done in line with your belief. The corresponding action is what the Bible refers to as 'work' (Jam.2:26). For instance, when Kemeley believed he would buy the four houses, his belief is evident by the action he took to realise it.

Therefore, from equation 3:
Faith = Belief + Work ------- (equation 4)

Mathematically, Equation 4 can be re-written as follows:
Faith – Works = Belief ------- (equation 5)

Thus, from equation 5, 'Belief' means faith without work, which James chapter 2 verse 26 refers to as being dead.

> *"For as the body without the spirit is dead, so faith without works is dead also" (Jam.2:26 NKJV).*

As stated above, 'work' refers to the steps of faith a man takes in line with his belief; it is the action or steps a man takes that correspond with his belief. In other words, without work (corresponding action), what you have is a mere belief in the heart and that amounts to nothing. Thus, any belief without a corresponding action or work will result in an abortive faith that will produce nothing. Many people, especially Christians, claim they have faith but no corresponding works; what they have is not faith but a mere belief held in their hearts and minds, hence, they remain unproductive. Genuine faith propels a man to take corresponding action.

What you believe in is what you see in your heart and mind. That is, your 'belief' (the object of faith), also known as the "confidently expected structure" is what you see in your heart and mind, and this refers to vision. Your vision is simply your pictorial belief, which is also referred to as the 'object of vision'. Thus, 'belief,' 'object of faith,' 'substance of things hoped for,' 'confidently expected structure,' or 'object of vision' refers to the same thing – vision. Your belief is what you see; if you don't believe in it, then it is not yet your vision. Thus, a mere belief is simply an inactive vision in the heart of man.

Thus, substituting 'vision' for 'belief' in equation 4 above, we have:

Faith = Vision + Work ------- (equation 6)

From equation 6:

Faith – Work = Vision ------- (equation 7)

That is, faith without work is simply an inactive vision. An inactive vision is one that doesn't rouse enough passion to thrust the visioner into action.

Summary of the Mathematical Analysis of Faith

The summary of the mathematical equations of faith discussed thus far is as follows:

Faith – Work = Belief ------- (from equation 5)
Faith – Work = Vision ------- (from equation 7)

Therefore, Faith – Work = Belief = Vision

That is, faith without work is simply a mere belief, which is an inactive vision. This is what James chapter 2 verse 26 refers to as "faith without work is dead." An inactive vision is a dead vision – it has no capacity to trigger faith in the heart of the visioner.

The visions many people had for their lives while they were young are dead by the time they entered their adulthood. The reason why these visions had died was simply because the individuals did not take steps of faith to actualise their visions. But it is never too late to take a step. Dead visions are the wishes for beggars; and if wishes were horses, beggars would ride.

Thus, without a corresponding work, the vision you see in your heart or mind remains a mere dream, a mere belief that will breed only deadness of life purpose. If you don't want to have a dead purpose of living, rise up and take a step of action TODAY in line with your vision! Do not sit still and do nothing. Take a definite step immediately, no matter how small it is; no step is insignificant when it comes to the operation of the Law of Faith.

FOURTH STEP: PRACTICE PERSEVERANCE

At the beginning, Dr. Kemeley met with seeming frustrations that would have been enough to deter anyone from taking further steps. *Success has a way of hiding under a dark cloak of frustration.* It is at this stage that many men falter, become discouraged and give up.

To avoid becoming discouraged, successful people often do this: they burn the bridge. Their attitude is: 'if I perish, I perish.'

The Inspirational Story of Queen Esther

The inspirational story of the young Queen Esther is well known in Sunday schools around the world. She was a Jew, a foreigner in the city of Susa, who in 479 BC rose to become the Queen of Persia, which was the world superpower in 5th and 4th century BC. However, her people's existence was threatened by the rising authority of the power-hungry Haman, the Prime Minister of Persia. If Queen Esther would sit and do nothing, her people would be exterminated by the grand plot of Haman.

The only course of action was for Esther to go to the king and make a passionate plea for leniency. But how could she approach the King since the Laws of Persia forbade that? The only time she could approach the king was if she was requested to do so by the king; if she took the initiative without prior consent by the king, the penalty code of the Persian Law would apply and that was death.

In such a dilemma, Queen Esther decided to act by faith. She would take the step of faith, abandon the comfort of her office and dare the unthinkable. She burnt the bridge and decided to take a step of faith to appear before the king!

> *"Go, gather together all the Jews who are in Susa, and fast for me. Do not eat or drink for three days, night or day. I and my attendants will fast as you do. When this is done, I will go to the king, even though it is against the law.* ***And if I perish, I perish"***
>
> *(Est.4:16 NIV).*

The Critical Stage

Until a man comes to the point of 'if I perish, I perish,' daring all odds, burns the bridge, the fifth step of the Law of Faith will not be attained. The fourth step is the stage of perseverance even when there is no visible thing to cheer up a man. It is the critical stage, which differentiates the man of faith from the man with just a mental belief. A faith-full man is oblivious of the scorn, obstacles, and threats in the pathway. He is ready to go on despite temporal disappointments. That is perseverance. It is to persevere in the face of seeming obstacles.

For Dr. Kemeley, he was ready to become bankrupt and even go to jail if it turned out he could not get the cash to pay as stipulated in the contract. To make sure he did not have the temptation to turn back, he burned the bridge. He left the shores of the DRC without knowing how he would survive in his new country. When he started his real estate investment, he utilised the same principle - he burned the bridge by signing the purchase contracts and asking his attorneys to proceed despite no physical money.

Until a man reaches a stage where there are no more avenues to retreat, wealth will elude him. Until he reaches a point where it is either 'I get that thing or nothing else,' that desire will remain an unfulfilled dream - a dead vision. To accumulate wealth, the rich don't accept 'NO' for an answer! That applies in all other aspects of life.

FIFTH STEP: RELEASE OF LIBERATING POWERS

Once all the requirements of the first four steps of the Law of Faith are fulfilled, the liberating powers in the law are automatically released. That is, once a man reaches the point of no return, the liberating powers in the Law of Faith are set loosed to bring the desired solutions. When Queen Esther reached that stage, the table was overturned against Haman and his schemers; the liberating powers of the Law of Faith were triggered that destroyed the evil mechanism that threatened Esther and her people!

That was exactly what happened to Dr. Kemeley. As he took a conclusive decision by signing the contract thereby irrevocably committing himself and burnt the bridge of retreat, doors of opportunities suddenly flung open. If he had not reached such a decisive, breaking point, these doors of opportunities wouldn't have opened.

Power is the ability to cause a change. As discussed above, every law is inputted with power. Inputted in the Law of Faith is power. By operating and meeting the demands of the Law of Faith, the liberating powers in the law are released to effect the change we desire. Often such powers are only released when we reach a point of no retreat. The point of no retreat is a test that must be passed before the liberating powers inherent in the Law of Faith are released. This is what many people, who claim to exercise faith, don't know. There is always an exam to pass before any promotion. In the operation of the Law of Faith, one must pass the exams before one could move on to the next level.

> *"Be assured that the testing of your faith [through experience] produces endurance [leading to spiritual maturity, and inner peace]" (Jam.1:3 AMP).*

CHAPTER 34
THE LETTER VERSUS THE SPIRIT OF THE LAW OF FAITH

IN ONE OF THE BEST-KNOWN literature plays, the Merchant of Venice, believed to have been written between 1596 and 1599, William Shakespeare narrated the story of a greedy Jewish moneylender, Shylock, who signed a contract with his arch business rival, Antonio, a merchant of Venice that if Antonio could not repay a loan, Shylock would be forced by the legal contract to have a pound of flesh from Antonio. Antonio's business suffered a temporary loss, hence couldn't repay the loan at the stated time. Shylock dragged Antonio to court, insisting for his pound of flesh.

Despite the passionate plea for mercy by Portia, who disguised as a 'doctor of the law' in a famous speech: *'The quality of mercy is not strain'd, it droppeth as the gentle rain from heaven upon the place beneath. It is twice blest: It blesseth him that gives and him that takes,'* Shylock insisted for his pound of flesh. When the passionate plea for mercy failed, Portia finally agreed that Shylock could have his pound of flesh but quickly pointed out that the agreement only sufficed for a precisely one pound of flesh, no more, no less and that no blood of Antonio should be spilled in the process, failure of which it was a violation of the law with stringent penalties according to the laws of the Venice. By this brilliant submission, Antonio's life was saved as Shylock wouldn't be able to meet the terms of the contract.

By this literature, Shakespeare popularised two terminologies often deployed in law, which are, *the letter of the law* and *the spirit of the law*. The letter of the law refers to the literal interpretation of the words of the law; that is, the letters of the law are the words of the law. The spirit of the law refers to the intent of those who wrote the law. The greedy Shylock wanted the full application of the letter of the contract law he signed with his rival Antonio, whereas the 'lawyer' argued in support of the spirit of the law. At the end, the spirit of the law won over the letter of the law.

THE LETTER OF THE LAW OF FAITH

The terms, the letter and the spirit of the law, were actually borrowed from the Bible. God unveiled His laws for mankind through holy men who wrote the Scriptures that form the Bible. The Bible is the written words of God and contains the laws of God for mankind and his universe. The Bible is written in simple language such that anyone can read and understand its letters. The letters express the principles or laws of God. As discussed in Chapter 32, inbuilt into each law or principle is power. This power is unleashed once a man fulfils the conditions stipulated by the letters of the principle. Over the generations of human existence, humanity has benefitted from the liberating powers inherent in these principles when the application terms are met. Indeed, the words of God are infallible, its principles or laws never fail.

> *"I tell you the truth, until heaven and earth disappear, not even the smallest detail of God's law will disappear until its purpose is achieved" (Mat.5:18 NLT).*

> *"Heaven and earth will pass away, but my words will never pass away" (Luk.21:33 NIV).*

The Law of Faith is one of the principles outlined very vividly in the pages of the Bible. It is inbuilt with liberating powers. Anyone, Christians and non-Christians alike, who dares to act upon the terms of this law will definitely realise the goal of his vision. That is the letter of the Law of Faith, which never fails if we apply it judiciously.

APPLICATION OF THE LETTER OF THE LAW OF FAITH BLESSES HUMANITY

(a) The Wright Brothers and the Aeroplane Invention

Indeed, the application of the letter of the Law of Faith blesses the individual who practises it. The liberating power inherent in the Law of Faith makes the letter of the law very efficacious, and men have built empires, have been rescued from various pit of despondency, poverty and diseases by the application of the letter of the Law of Faith. Virtually all achievements ever made by man are products of faith.

It took the application of the letter (principles) of faith for the Wright brothers, Wilbur and Orville, to build a machine heavier than air that flew despite the dismissing tone of academics. In fact, in 1892, the French War Ministry commissioned the scientist, Clement Ader, to build a flying machine after he had failed in previous attempts in 1872. Ader took five years to build the Avion III, which was tested on October 12 and 14, 1897, at the Sartory military base near Versailles, France. On the first day, the machine simply rolled along its circular track. Two days later, it rolled for a short distance, shot off the track, and ended up in a field. The Avion III never got its wheels off the ground, and the experiments were abandoned.

Meanwhile, Simon Newcomb (1835-1909), the foremost American scientist at the time and a Professor of Mathematics in the U.S. Navy and at Johns Hopkins, after failed successive attempts to fly, wrote:

> *"The demonstration that no possible combination of known substances, known forms of machinery and known forms of force, can be united in a practical machine by which man shall fly long distances through the air, seems to the writer as complete as it is possible for the demonstration of any physical fact to be"*
>
> *(Kelly 1943, The Wright Brothers).*

Professor Newcomb went on to write:

> *"Once he slackens his speed, down he begins to fall...Once he stops, he falls a dead mass. How shall he reach the ground without destroying his delicate machinery? I do not think that even the most imaginative inventor has yet even put on paper a demonstrative, successful way of meeting this difficulty"*
>
> *(Kelly 1943, The Wright Brothers).*

Indeed, Professor Newcomb not only proved that trying to fly was impossible, but went farther to demonstrate the 'practicability' of his knowledge. When a man of such profound scientific knowledge as Simon Newcomb had demonstrated with unassailable logic that man couldn't fly, why should the public be fooled by silly stories about two obscure bicycle repairmen who hadn't even been to college?

Yet Wilbur and Orville Wright, the two obscure bicycle repairmen, discountenanced these leading scientific reports of their day. All they had was the belief that man could fly. It was faith borne out of a clear vision in their hearts and mind. They could see clearly with their inner eyes the flight of a heavier-than-air machine. Thus, on 17th December 1903, Wilbur and Orville Wright made four brief flights at Kitty Hawk in North Carolina, USA, with their first powered aircraft, hence, invented the first successful airplane.

(b) Thomas Edison and the Electric Bulb Invention

It was the same story with Thomas Edison, who in 1878 began working on a system of electrical illumination. After many experiments, first with carbon filaments and then with platinum and other metals, Edison returned to a carbon filament. Thus, he tested and retested, refusing to quit, for ten thousand times!

> *"Thomas A. Edison 'failed' ten thousand times before he perfected the incandescent electric light bulb. That is, he met with temporary defeat ten thousand times, before his efforts were crowned with success" (Hill 1938, Think and Grow Rich, page 101).*

Finally, on 22nd October 1879, Edison invented the electric bulb, and on 31st December 1879 he hung the electric bulb at the Menlo Park, New Jersey, where the leading men of the town just ignored it and all the sceptics jeered at it, yet the lamp was the progenitor of our modern current electricity system. It was the first commercially practical incandescent light.

Edison utilised the letter (principles) of the Law of Faith; he saw clearly with his inner eye the electric bulb long before it became physically available. Hence, he knew those seeming 'ten thousand failures' were just that he was yet to get the right step to bring the electric lamp from his mind to the physical realm! Thus, he declared during an interview:

> *"I have not failed. I've just found 10,000 ways that won't work"*
> *(Thomas Edison).*

> *"I speak without exaggeration when I say that I have constructed three thousand different theories in connection with the electric light, each one of them reasonable and apparently to be true. Yet only in two cases did my experiments prove the truth of my theory" (Rutgers, Thomas Edison 1890 interview, Harper's Monthly Magazine).*

(c) Ferdinand Magellan and First Circumnavigation of the Earth

It was the practice of the principles (letter) of the Law of Faith that made Ferdinand Magellan (c. AD 1480-1521), a Portuguese explorer, to organise the expedition to the East Indies from AD 1519 to 1522, resulting in the first circumnavigation of the Earth, in spite of dissuasion and antagonism from his contemporaries.

Ferdinand was mocked and jeered at while his family wept bitterly as he entered the ship to begin his journey; they all thought he was stupid to believe that he could navigate around the world, a feat no man had ever dared as at the time. However, Ferdinand could see very clearly in his mind the fulfilment of his vision. His clear vision generated the audacious force of faith to keep moving even when all his supplies ran short. That is the application of the letter of the Law of Faith!

Indeed, all human exploits, including medical science itself, are products of the application of the letter (principles) of the Law of Faith.

THE SPIRIT OFTHE LAW OF FAITH

Behind the letters of the Scriptures is the Spirit of God, who inspired men to write down the letters. By His Spirit, God watches over His word to perform it. That is, all the laws of God are backed up by the Spirit of God. That is the Spirit of the Law.

> *"Study and read from the book of the Lord: And not one will be missing...For it is the mouth of the Lord that has issued the order, and it is his Spirit that has gathered them" (Isa.34:16 ISV).*

In other words, the Law of Faith is backed up by the Spirit of God. This is the Spirit of Faith; He is the Spirit of the Law of Faith.

> *"It is written: 'I believed; therefore I have spoken.' Since we have that same **spirit of faith**, we also believe and therefore speak'"*
>
> *(2Cor.4:13 NIV).*

THE DOMINATING POWER OF THE SPIRIT OF FAITH

Life is full of hindrances. Ignorance, fear and similar traits constantly resist man's advancement. Negative forces often deploy these tools to attack the faith of man. Many people are aware of the potency of the Law of Faith, but they just couldn't rouse themselves to apply the Law and fulfil its terms. The human nature is sometimes too weak to muster the requisite faith. As such times, faith can fail and vision turn out unfulfilled.

Some of these hindrances have stopped many people from applying the Law of Faith to their lives. People have become obstructed, stampeded, and frustrated by trying to muster faith unsuccessfully because a negative force wouldn't allow them.

A good example was Peter. He had good intention. *"Peter spoke up, 'Even if all the others reject you, I never will!'" (Mtt.26:33 CEV).* He was a professional businessperson in the fishing industry of his time, but his skills couldn't bring him much profit in life. When Peter met with Jesus, his knowledge of the principles of God, one which was the Law of Faith, opened up. He attempted to make much success with his life using the principles of success he received from Jesus, but Satan, a negative spirit, sought to destroy his faith. Satan's target was Peter's faith because Satan new once he had succeeded in destroying Peter's faith, he could get at Peter very cheaply. He launched subtle but draconic attacks on Peter's faith and almost destroyed it. But Jesus' prayer restored and strengthened Peter's faith.

> *"Simon, Simon, Satan has asked to have you, to sift you like wheat, but I have pleaded in prayer for you that your faith should not completely fail. So when you have repented and turned to me again, strengthen and build up the faith of your brothers"*
>
> *(Luk.22.31,32 TLB).*

The letter of the Law of Faith couldn't withstand the subtleties of the enemy attacks on Peter's faith. Does it mean that the letter of the Law of Faith is limited? No; not all. The Law of Faith is not limited. It is only limited by our ignorance and our ability to operate it. That is where Peter failed. Peter lacked the fortitudes to act on and fulfil the demands of the letter of the Law of Faith. Hence, he failed. He did the very thing he never wanted to do; he denied his Lord Jesus three times! (Lk.22:54-64).

At this stage of his life, Peter was ignorant of spiritual reality. He was not yet regenerated (born again) and be filled with the Holy Spirit, the very Spirit that backs up God's laws. At this stage of his life, Peter was like any other Jews, who lived only by the letters of the Law with no intercourse with the Spirit of God. Hence, he was grossly limited in knowledge and ability to muster the real force of faith. This means that his ability to operate the Law of Faith was limited.

But not long after, the same Peter was regenerated and became filled with the Spirit of God (Acts chapter 2). The Spirit of God in him now empowered Peter to begin to operate the Law of Faith in a new and higher dynamism. The same Peter could now make the lame to walk (Acts chapter 3) and challenged the bigoted religious doctors (Acts chapter 4), raised the dead (Acts chapter 9) and even his shadow could heal the sick (Acts chapter 5), all by the operation of the Law of Faith. It was no longer the same old fisherman of Galilee but a born-again Peter, with a new nature that carried the life of God.

Thus, Peter could no longer operate only by the letter of the law, but by the spirit of the law as well. The operation of the Spirit of the Law of Faith destroyed all oppositions and hindrances before him, and secured his glorious destiny as a leader in the early Church. Today, Peter's name is a household word around the globe. That is the advantage of operating by the Spirit of Faith.

SIGNIFICANCE OF THIS TRUTH

The significance of this truth can make a world of difference in one's life. Your ability to operate this powerful Law of Faith will be grossly limited if you operate only by the letter of the law. The Law of Faith is a spiritual law and man can only maximise its benefits by operating not only by the letter of the law but also by the spirit of the law. Our access to the Spirit of the Law of Faith is through regeneration and Holy Spirit baptism (see SSB Book 5).

> *"John said, 'I am just baptizing with water. But someone more powerful is going to come, and I am not good enough even to untie his sandals. He will baptize you with the Holy Spirit and with fire'" (Luk.3:16 CEV).*

Once the Spirit of Faith grips a man, he becomes irresistible. Nothing again appears impossible to him. The Spirit of Faith causes him to see life through a different prism. His view of the world takes a new dynamism. By the Spirit of Faith enablement, he can now dare the untouchable, face the forbidden, and conquer the unconquerable.

A man who comes into contact with the Spirit of Faith dominates his world; he may be unsung today, but soon he will rise to become a reference point in his field. My prayer is that may this chapter spur you enough to seek for and become regenerated in Christ Jesus, thereby having your glorious future secured through maximum operation of the Law of Faith (see SSB Book 5 for more information).

Chapter 35
The Triggers of Faith

Many individuals have attempted to make faith a religious matter. But faith is not a religious ceremony or a religious feeling. The Law of Faith is universal just as the Law of Gravity. However, unlike the Law of Gravity which is a natural law, the Law of Faith is a spiritual law, and thus, it can only be operated by spiritual beings. Animals like dolphins, elephants, lions, and dogs are not spiritual beings (see SSB Book 1), and as such, cannot operate the Law of Faith. But humans, like God, are spiritual beings, hence, can operate this law.

ANYONE CAN EXERCISE FAITH

Definitely, all persons, no matter the religion, sex, race, culture, or of any other artificial description, can operate the Law of Faith. Since man is a spirit being, a moral agent, he can operate this mighty law. The reason is that at creation, God deposited faith in the heart of each spirit man. However, this mighty force lies dormant in the heart of many people.

Individuals from all races, clime, tongues, and generations have generated great faith to accomplish great feat. There are no exploits in life without an input of faith. Thus, faith is not limited to a certain people or a religious sect. For instance, there are many people who are not conversant with the Bible, and yet have great faith in what they do. There are many parts of the world that Bible is officially restricted, yet individuals with great faith abound in these places.

In the days when Jesus walked physically on earth, He met people who had no Torah (the Law) and the Prophets, which were the Bible of those days, yet wielded enormous degrees of faith. One was the Roman military commander (Mat.8:5-13) and the other was the Canaanite woman from SyroPhoenicia (Mat.15:21-28). It was recorded about the Roman soldier:

> *"When Jesus heard this, He was amazed and said to those who were following Him, 'I tell you truthfully, I have not found such great faith [as this] with anyone in Israel'" (Mat.8:10 AMP).*

For the SyroPhoenician woman, Jesus made this statement:

> *"O woman, great is your faith! Let it be to you as you desire" (Mat.15:28 NKJV).*

What generated such great faith in these two Gentiles, the kind that was not even seen in the entire Israel that had the Torah?

VISION – THE TRIGGER OF FAITH

It was the vision of good health that drove the Roman soldier and the SyroPhoenician woman in search for answers. They believed that there must be a way out even when all circumstances pointed to the contrary. That was great faith and Jesus acknowledged it. Their faith was generated by their vision of health, and such great faith triggered the release of liberating healing powers in Jesus.

Vision is the activator of faith that has been deposited in the heart of man at creation. Vision is what triggers the dormant force of faith. That is, without vision, there can't be faith. When you see a beautiful future, a force rises in you to pursue that sighted future and bring it into reality. Vision is what reveals the beautiful future, which triggers the force of faith for the pursuit of the sighted future. Thus, faith starts with the reception of vision. As such, visions can be aptly described as being the triggering sources of faith. No vision, No faith!

ACTIVATION OF VISION-INDUCED FAITH: BIBLICAL EXAMPLE

Vision as the trigger of faith is made explicit by the inspired words of Apostle Paul:

> *"So then faith comes by hearing, and hearing by the word of God"* *(Rom.10:17 NKJV).*

The term 'hearing' in the above Scripture is from the Greek word *akoē*, which means 'to perceive with the ear' or 'audience.' That is, faith is generated in one's heart when one hears the Word of God. For the Word heard to evoke faith in the individual's heart, the Word will first create a visual image, which will then activate faith in the heart of the individual. For instance, when a sick man hears the Word of God on healing, visual images of health will be formed in his heart and be transmitted to his mind. That is, the sick man will begin to see himself in health and soundness of body without the afflicted disease. These visions of a healthy body will evoke faith in him to realise what he has seen in his heart and mind. If he will begin to take steps towards realising what he has seen, he will begin to physically experience healing.

Many people hear God's word on healing and yet do not muster the faith to physically appropriate their healing. The reason why faith is not generated in them is because the Word they heard is yet to create a vision of health they seek for. The day they 'see' in their hearts and minds the visions of health, doubt will flee away from their heart. The more they see clearly, the more determined they'll be to actualise the visions of their heart. We don't doubt what we see.

"For indeed the gospel was preached to us as well as to them; but the word which they heard did not profit them, not being mixed with faith in those who heard it" (Heb.4:2 NKJV).

In 1998 I encountered the divine word on divine health. I saw in First Epistle of Peter chapter 2 verse 24 that Jesus Christ paid the price for my sickness about 2000 years ago. If He has paid the price, it means I can no longer be sick the rest of my life. I saw very clearly that it was impossible for me to be sick in life again. With excitement, I quickly announced my findings to friends and colleagues, who thought I was being religiously fanatical. But from that day up till date, I have been living healthy with no medications whatsoever entering my body. Indeed, vision is the activator of faith.

SIZE OF VISION VERSUS SIZE OF FAITH

Therefore, the bigger the vision, the bigger the faith. A man who has a vision of creating world-renown products in his career will obviously have bigger faith than one whose vision is to become a local champion in the same career. A teacher whose heart desire is to teach and make impact in the international community will definitely not have the same size of faith as a man whose desire is to be confined within the classrooms of a village school.

Indeed, the bigger the size of your vision, the bigger the amount of faith that will be generated to meet the demands of the vision.

CLARITY OF VISION AND STRENGTH OF FAITH

If the trigger of faith is vision, it means the clearer the vision, the stronger the faith being generated. When I saw clearly that studying medicine is the will of God for my life, my faith was unleashed in the pursuit of the vision. In other words, I knew and knew beyond all doubt that it was impossible for me not to become a medical practitioner. Such conviction, which came from the clarity of the vision, roused faith in me that knew no obstacles. The obstacles of poverty, deprivations, and youthful exuberances appeared no longer insurmountable problems; with the eye of faith, they became temporal, conquerable challenges. How they would vanish away was really not a concern for consideration. My eyes were fixed on the final destination, the end-goal of my vision. I just knew that challenges would be conquered any time I met them along the vision pathway. And that was what happened!

Faith does not see problems; it sees the end of the bright future. People do wonder how Jesus could endure such hatred, animosity, torture, and cruel death from the enemies during His earthly ministry. The secret was that His eyes were fixed at the end-goal of his vision. He saw a new dawn for humanity in His ministry. Such clarity of vision fuelled His passion, the force of faith that was unleashed in His ministry.

> *"He [Jesus] was willing to die a shameful death on the cross because of the joy he knew would be his afterwards; and now he sits in the place of honour by the throne of God" (Heb.12: 2 TLB).*

Faith doesn't see obstacles; rather it sees the end-product or the goal of the vision. This is why people of faith are often accused as living a 'false' life. An outsider sees obstacles and impediments, but a man of faith rather sees the end of the matter. Hence, the outsider will accuse the faith man as not being *realistic*, and the clearer the vision, the stronger the faith being generated.

FAITH PAID TUITION FEES

I had an interesting conversation with some high school students in 2005. The school held a week-long career counselling for their graduating students, and professionals of various fields were invited to give talk about their professions as a way of enlightenment for the students' choices of careers. I was invited to also present a talk. While preparing for the talk, I felt I could communicate better with the students by sharing my story with them. An interesting conversation ensued:

"But knowing that it cost a lot of money to train, how did you raise the finances to go through medical school?" I was asked after they heard the story of how my dad, the family breadwinner, died just about the time I was to enter medical school.

"I raised the finances by faith," I replied tacitly.

"What do you mean by faith? Obviously, faith doesn't just bring money from the sky and certainly not from Heaven," one of the students interjected.

"With faith I never for once saw money as a hindrance. I just knew that at each level, a solution would appear. Honestly, I never for once thought over which avenue money would come from; I just knew that as I reached each stage, the necessary financial solution(s) will emerge."

"How?" it was like a chorus question.

"During those days, I was so charged up that all I saw was becoming a medical practitioner. How much it would cost and where the money would come from was never a concern in my mind." Continuing I said, "For instance, when I took the entrance exams and got the admission into the University of Port Harcourt medical school, I went straight to the Registrar's office to confirm the authenticity of the admission. I was given the admission letters with congratulatory message. With excitement I rushed home to share the good news, never even thought of where the money would come from. I was more excited that the first stage, admission, had been achieved. It was when I got home that I saw in one of the letters the registration and tuition fees. It was then I sat down and thought about where to raise the registration and tuition fees from," I explained.

Then I continued my explanation: "This was the way I operated all through the medical school training years. I never saw money as an obstacle, though physically there was no stand-by human source. I just knew at each stage, a solution would appear, and that was what happened all through those years."

"That is interesting," one of the students said.

I continued my explanation: "Yes, it's interesting. That was in the 1990s. Then I never knew I was only operating a law – the Law of Faith. In fact, in my final year, the university brought a new regulation that to sit for the final exams you must pay all your fees up to date. I had about two years of tuition fees in arrears. By this new regulation of the university, it meant I wouldn't be allowed to sit for my final exams. That didn't bother me at all. I went on my knees meditating and at the same time asking God for the way out. And like a flash of light, a thought interjected into my heart. The thought went thus: 'Go to the College Secretary and plead for mercy, request to sign an undertaking to pay all the arrears once you get a job. Meet the College Secretary in her home and not in the office.'

"The College Secretary is a woman of strong character. She is respected and even feared by students. Of course, I know God was speaking into my heart. In the heart of my spirit man, I could see clearly that I would write the final exams. Therefore, I sought for the house address of the College Secretary and the next evening I took off to her house. At about 7pm, I knocked on her door. Someone ushered me into a beautiful sitting room, and I waited. Soon she came out; obviously surprised to see a student at her home. She enquired why I came. I tabled my plan before her. She paused, what looked like hours to me, but it was actually a few minutes. Just then her husband joined us in the sitting room. The two looked at each other, and I could see a sign of agreement. She agreed, and issued me a letter of permission to sit for the exams."

As we concluded that day, I could see in the eyes of those students elation and a determination to focus on their vision and not on the obstacles. That is the Law of Faith. Faith focuses on the goal of the vision and not on the obstacles; it sees any obstacles as mere temporary challenges even though it may not know how the obstacles can be overcome at the time of receiving the vision.

IN SUMMARY

As we conclude this chapter, note these three important points mentioned thus far:

- vision is what triggers faith
- therefore, the bigger the vision, the bigger the faith
- the clearer the vision, the stronger the force of faith being generated.

Chapter 36
Degrees of Faith

Undoubtedly, our productivity in life is tied to our faith. With the force of faith, we engage our time, energy, and resources to achieve a level of productivity. For instance, to conquer poverty, the force of faith is required to operate the principles of wealth creation. Thus, how much wealth we accumulate will depend on our vision, which in turn determines the volume of faith we muster. A man whose vision of wealth is to accumulate a few thousands of dollars will definitely not have the same amount of faith as the man whose vision is to accumulate millions of dollars.

In any given field of human endeavour, a spectrum of achievements exists. There are low achievers, average achievers, and high achievers in any career field. A low achiever does not have the same level of faith as a medium achiever, who in turn will never have the same level of faith as the high achievers.

DETERMINANTS OF DEGREE OF FAITH

Indeed, faith is in degrees or levels. As discussed in the last chapter, what determine the level of faith a man wields are:

(a) The Clarity of Vision:
The clearer the vision, the stronger the faith being generated.

(b) The Size of the Vision:
The bigger the size of your vision, the bigger the amount of faith that will be generated to meet the demands of the vision.

This means our faith can grow. As mentioned earlier (see Chapter 30), growth is one of the characteristic features of faith.

DEGREES OF FAITH

According to the Scriptures, faith can be classified into the following levels or degrees:

(1) Dead Faith

This is a state in which an individual has no trace of faith whatsoever being generated for a given assignment. Fear, which is the opposite of faith, has taken over such an individual. Instead of focusing on the goal of his vision, his eyes rather focus on the obstacles that stand against the vision. Fear has grown so large that it paralyses the individual from exercising even the minutest degree of faith in the pursuit of his vision.

> *"Pray that we may be kept safe from worthless and evil people. After all, not everyone has faith" (2The.3:2 CEV).*

Anxiety is a manifestation of fear.

> *"And why are you anxious...if God so clothes the grass of the field, which today is alive and tomorrow is thrown into the oven, will he not much more clothe you, O men of little faith?"*
>
> *(Mat.6:28,30 RSV).*

Individuals with dead faith are very good at 'talking' but no action. They talk a lot about their visions and what could be done, but will never embark on any corresponding action that will birth the visions. Fear has paralysed their faith; hence, their visions only remain as dreams.

> *"So too, faith, if it does not have works [to back it up], is by itself dead [inoperative and ineffective]" (Jam.2:17 AMP).*

A good example was the disciples of Jesus on the Galilean sea. Many of these disciples were fishermen, hence, were accustomed to the boisterous nature of the sea. Apparently, they were acquainted with tales of loss and wanton destruction of lives and property whenever the sea became boisterous. As fishermen, they would have hoped and even prayed that they wouldn't find the sea in its ferocious state.

Nevertheless, at this particular day, they came in contact with the sea's monstrosity. The tales of woes they had heard and seen associated with the sea immediately triggered fear in them. Their eyes could not see beyond the raging sea; all they saw was perishing. Fear destroyed any iota of faith in them. The very thing they feared was right there confronting them! Practically, they had no faith whatsoever to confront the situation.

> *"He said to them, 'Why are you so fearful? How is it that you have **no faith**?'" (Mar.4:40 NKJV).*

Is that not the state of many people? Many individuals allow past events, past failures, past challenges... to define their present state. However, to show that fear is nothing but *false evidences appearing real*, Jesus rose up and challenged the boisterous sea, and calmed it down. Jesus had a vision, a destination. Going across the sea to the other side for evangelism was part of that vision. The sea was a route that would lead Him to the destination. Hence, He wouldn't allow any challenge on the way to becloud His vision. He knew how to trigger His faith and how to exercise the force of faith. And that was what He did. He spoke and the turbulence quieted down. Jesus' action was completely opposite to that of the disciples.

Faith is proactive to situations while fear is reactive to situations. Faith takes charge of a situation and does not allow it to go out of control while fear generates a feeling of helplessness. For any given assignment, never allow fear to grow to the extent as to extinguish faith completely in you. The difficulty you are currently facing has been conquered by some other person. Go and find out how he did it, and that can trigger your faith to also conquer the challenge.

(2) Weak Faith

Weak Faith is also referred to as **Little Faith** (Mtt.6:30; 8:26). Weak faith is faith that has very little force to push a vision into fulfilment. It simply means the force of faith is not strong enough to quench all oppositions that hinder the actualisation of the vision.

Weak faith is actually the state of a great number of individuals. It explains why many have started projects and abandoned them mid-way. Many have seen their bright future, which delighted their hearts. As such, they ventured out in pursuit of the bright future. But not long after, they were confronted with challenges along the way. They pushed and hit at the challenges, which remained unyielding resulting in frustration. After some attempts, they abandoned the pursuit. The vision progressively becomes halted, and finally perishes with time!

The danger with this state is that once the project is abandoned, the repercussions are overwhelming. The effect is not only limited to the situation at hand. The effect spreads little by little, infiltrating all aspects of life, resulting in generalised lethargy. A good example of this was the story of Mr. Joe.

Repercussion of Failure in Joe's Life

Joe was a bright student in his primary and secondary schools. He came out the best in his ordinary level examinations. With that feat, he gained admission into the university and enrolled as a medical student. In the medical school, he quickly came to realise that it was a stiff competition of a conglomeration of bright students from various secondary schools. In the medical school, he started having difficulty passing his exams. In his fourth year of the Pharmacology class, he failed the course. That left him with a low esteem. He took the resit exams and again failed. That sank him deeper into despair. He started feeling inadequate in the presence of his colleagues who passed the exams.

For failing the course twice, he had to repeat the whole year as stipulated by the university regulations. But instead of sitting down and re-evaluating his approach, Joe went ahead and attempted the exams, just like before. Already being pressed beyond measures, the news of another failure caused Joe temporary insanity. He was beside himself. He had just one last attempt, which was another resit exam. He took this last resit exam and again failed, and had to leave the medical school without any certificate after six years of intensive study! He was completely shattered. Throughout the year, many people thought he had become insane. He couldn't gather himself up to think of next line of action. Rather, Joe decided to secretly practise medicine without licensure. He was a quack doctor. The authorities caught up with him and he was forced to face the wrath of the law.

You may think Joe's story was too pathetic, but actually there are many people that have far worse cases. I personally tried to speak with Joe to rouse up his faith during our medical student days. But he was too despondent and cast down. That is what failure does to a man's ego. The goal of any failure is to deprive you of your faith. Each unsuccessful attempt generates more fear and despondency. Each setback causes a ripple of frustration, which if not managed properly will begin to sieve into all other areas of your life with the final goal of completely beclouding your sight of that glorious future. The final result will then be the death of your faith and the overwhelming presence of fear with the subsequent demise of the vision. Joe, a once bright student, an envy of his primary and secondary school colleagues and a pride of his teachers, had become a shadow of his former self as fear of failure took over him, not allowing him to see his vision of a bright future again. He became a victim of the fallacy of fear.

A warning: The danger is that if a weak faith (little faith) is not growing, it will ultimately lead to dead faith and great fear! But you can stop such retrogression by constantly re-ignite your vision through continuous acquisition of relevant knowledge. The actualisation or death of your vision, hence the level of faith you wield, is a function of your knowledge. What you do not know constitutes your ignorance. Fear thrives on ignorance while faith thrives on knowledge.

Weak Faith Thrives on Ignorance

Weak faith thrives on ignorance. Joe's mistake was ignorance. He was ignorant of (or chose not to act on) the fact that his methods of passing exams in the primary and secondary schools would need to be upgraded or even changed to meet with the rigours of the medical school. Smart students would have humbled themselves and befriended those students that seem to be doing well to discover their secrets.

Or, in the first place, was he supposed to be a medical doctor? Indeed, there was an obvious need for Joe to reappraise himself and his tactic. A voracious search would have led him to solutions. Joe was not created stupid; he was rather reactionary instead of being proactive. He allowed emotions to cover his sense of judgment.

I haven't heard from Joe again. If he is reading this book, I pray may he come to the understanding that it is never too late, and that he shouldn't let the fallacy of fear continue to run his life. His vision of a bright future can still be realised.

(3) Great Faith

Great faith is one that brings vision into reality. Any time your dream, no matter how small, comes to pass, that is a manifestation of great faith at work. Great faith is a proof that your faith is strong enough to quench all opposition and forcefully delivers the goal of the vision. Great faith is the force that births the goal of a vision. Great faith is a strong faith!

> *"Then Jesus answered her, 'O woman, **great** is your **faith**! Be it done for you as you desire.' And her daughter was healed instantly"*
> *(Mat.15: 28 RSV).*

Just as failure has rippled repercussion effects on a person's further exercise of the force of faith, in the same manner success has rippled repercussions on a man's faith. That is, every success achieved boosts your faith to attempt bigger and further dreams. Each success attained grows your faith astronomically just as each failure encountered grows the force of fear tremendously. For instance, when a man disciplines himself to read through and finish a book from page to page, his morale is boosted to attempt more voluminous books. Such confidence also boosts his morale not to leave other aspects of his life incomplete. That is the rippled repercussion effects of a successful accomplishment of a goal!

Never underrate the power of goal accomplishment. Each goal you accomplish boosts all aspects of your life. If you don't discipline yourself to succeed in small details (like reading books from page to page until it ends), you may not be motivated enough to pursue other bigger visions such as career visions. That is why you must accomplish any assignment you have to the best of your ability. Never leave any assignment half-done because that will cause more damage to your faith. It is better not to attempt an assignment than to leave it half-way. This is why great achievers do not rush into decisions; once they make their decisions they stick to them until they are accomplished.

Sub-Levels of Great Faith

Note that great faith is in sub-levels such as:

- Great faith (Luk.7:9)
- Exceedingly great faith (2The.1:3)
- Far-exceedingly great faith

For instance, the force of faith that helped you to complete your primary school education was a great faith. The force that helped you to complete your secondary school education was an exceedingly great faith, which was greater than the force of faith you applied in the primary school, and so on.

Indeed, faith grows, and there is no limit to how much it can grow. Each accomplishment we attain causes an incremental addition of strength to our force of faith. We keep growing in faith, and the more we grow in faith, the more exploits we realise in life. Thus, the extent of our faith is directly proportional to the size of vision we set for our live. A smaller vision will mean a smaller faith, and bigger vision will mean bigger faith.

Chapter 37
Hindrances to Operation of the Law of Faith

As LONG AS ITS DEMANDS are met, the Law of Faith does not fail as proven for all times and in all generations.

> *"For truly, I say to you, if you have faith like a grain of mustard seed...nothing will be impossible for you" (Mat.17:20 ESV).*

However, there are things that can hinder the release of the force of faith. Each of the five steps of the Law of Faith has potent hindrances that can hinder the release of the liberating powers of faith. This chapter briefly examines the common hindrances we all encounter when exercising faith.

All the hindrances to the operation of the Law of Faith can be summarised into three categories:

FIRST CATEGORY: IGNORANCE

Ignorance that hinders the practice of the First Step of the Law of Faith include:

- ignorance of what vision is
- ignorance of how to receive vision
- ignorance on how to nurse vision into fruition

A man who does not know how to receive and nurse a vision will be deficient in the exercise of faith. This is because faith actually starts with a vision. It is the vision a man has and incubates that triggers his faith. You are moved to actualise what you 'see.' Thus, to overcome the hindrance to this first step is to have a clear vision, and keep refining your vision through the practice of the Five Steps to Creativity discussed in Chapter 13.

Ignorance that hinders the practice of the Second Step of the Law of Faith include:

- ignorance of how to articulate a good plan.

While growing up in the 1980s, one of the common beliefs among Christians in the exercise of faith was: 'confess and claim it.' If you need something, all you have to do was to confess it and that will automatically become yours. Many preachers propagated this notion. Of course, many people were disappointed as what they confessed and claimed never materialised.

In those days, drawing up a plan of actions was seen as contrary to faith. Some Christians believed that planning is not being spiritual. But how wrong they were! Drawing up a good plan is actually an integral part of the operation of the Law of Faith; as discussed in the previous chapter, it is actually the second step in the operation of the law.

All the works of God were done by faith as He *"calls things into existence that do not exist"* (Rom.4:17 HCSB). Part of the operation of this faith requires thorough planning, devising or strategizing. The Creator did not just stand up and began creation. By wisdom, He had a master plan well laid out. By this wisdom, He put everything in its order.

> *"He has made the earth by His power, He has established the world by His wisdom, and has stretched out the heavens at His discretion" (Jer.10:12 NKJV).*

> *"The Lord has done what He planned..." (Lam.2:17 AMP).*

In other words, planning requires wisdom and it was by this wisdom He created the universe. Planning was part of the operation of faith of God in creation. He made laws to govern His creation, one of which is the Law of Faith (Rom.3:27). Planning is an integral part of the operation of the Law of Faith, which guarantees successful endeavour.

> *"The plans of the diligent lead surely to abundance and advantage, but everyone who acts in haste comes surely to poverty" (Pro.21:5 AMP).*

Indeed, God is not against wise planning.

> *"For the Lord, your Redeemer, and He who formed you from the womb says this, 'I am the Lord, Maker of all things, who alone stretches out the heavens, who spreads out the earth by Myself... confirming the word of His servant and carrying out the* ***plan*** *of His messengers'" (Isa.44:24,26 AMP).*

That is, devising a good plan is essential to the success of our faith. Without a good plan, we cannot know which corresponding action to embark upon in line with our vision.

The **SMART** acronym is a set of criteria for articulating a good plan of actions for the fulfilment of a vision (see page 243).

SECOND CATEGORY: NEGATIVE TONGUE

A man who operates faith will talk faith. For the force of faith to be generated, our thoughts and actions must line up with our words. Visions are the thought processes in the heart of our spirit man, plans are the proceeds of our minds, and actions are the activities of the body. That is, the three components of man – spirit, soul (mind) and body – all participate jointly in the operation of the Law of Faith.

Until the contents of the heart of our spirit, mind, and body line up with the words of our mouth, liberating powers in the Law of Faith cannot be generated. Perseverance of faith is seen in our speech. We can easily tell from a man's speech whether he is still in faith or has caved in under pressure at faith trial moments. A man persevering in faith is strong in his belief utterances even when there are no evidential proofs around him while a man whose faith is wobbly vacillates in thoughts and trembles in speech.

Perseverance in faith, which is the fourth step of the Law of Faith, is seen in our speech. Never allow your tongue to deviate from your vision. When it seems your faith is sliding, sit down and re-read the vision. That is why every vision should be written down. One reason for this is that a documented vision is like petrol garage where the visioner keeps returning to refuel his faith tank. As you re-study your vision, your faith will be rekindled.

In addition, interact with like hearts and minds, study books in line with your vision. I love autobiographies because they always contain the secrets of men and the failures of others that often prove to be invaluable lessons to be learnt. Above all, having a continuous association with the Holy Spirit of God by feeding on the Scriptures, offering prayers of all kinds with thanksgiving, praises and worship to God will keep refuelling your faith, and this will show in your daily speech. A man who never loses hope will never balk down in his faith-filled words. The mouth is the body organ for the release of the force of faith.

> *"Death and life are in the power of the tongue, and those who love it will eat its fruit" (Pro.18:21 NKJV).*

> *"Whoever guards his mouth and tongue Keeps his soul from troubles" (*Pro.21:23 *NKJV).*

You cannot have a clear vision, articulate definite plan, initiate corresponding actions and then talk defeat and expect the release of liberating power. Negative words are pests that destroy visions.

Negative words weaken the force of faith and frustrate the release of liberating power of change. Great men of faith are great talkers. A man of faith will show his perseverance by his words. He sees disappointments as mere temporary challenge; hence, maintains his possibility-positive confession of his vision.

> *"He who would love life and see good days, let him refrain his tongue from evil, and his lips from speaking deceit"*
> *(*1Pet.3:10 *NKJV).*

> *"A wholesome tongue is a tree of life, but perverseness in it breaks the spirit" (*Pro.15:4 *NKJV).*

THIRD CATEGORY: FEAR

Fear is a major hindrance that affects the operation of the Law of Faith. Fear of Failure and Fear of the Unknown are the main types of fear that inhibit a man from burning the bridge and going beyond the 'point-of-no-retreat.' But fear is like a dog; it barks from a distance; the more you retreat, the more the barking. However, once you take a step towards the dog, the dog starts retreating. Once we take a step towards our fears, the grip of fears starts crumbling. The cure for fear is action.

Moving in faith does not mean you won't feel apprehensions, fright, and tension. As humans, negative feelings of fear will be generated as you decide to lounge out. However, men of faith don't allow such negative feelings to hinder their advancement. They keep moving in spite of their fears. That is taking steps of faith. Faith is taking step in spite of fear. The more you advance, the more the negative feelings of fear recede until you get to a point where fear is totally vanquished and buried. At that point, a man stands in the full glare of faith, wielding the unstoppable, formidable weapon that guarantees success. Always remember that *F-E-A-R* is *False Evidence Appearing Real!*

The Fallacy of Fear

The hindrances have made many people to become frustrated with the exercise of their faith; they can kill the faith for a particular assignment while at the same time allows fear to grow into a monster. Thus, instead of faith, fear takes over. Fear has paralysed many people from making further attempts along the line of their vision. Because you could not muster faith for a particular course of action does not mean that you cannot command faith in other areas. The fallacy of fear is that the individual feels he has failed completely in life because he couldn't succeed in a particular assignment. Fear makes its victim to see nothing but failure.

Losing a battle does not mean losing a war. Each war is made up of several battles. When you lose a battle, it simply means the strategy employed is not good enough. Smart soldiers will want to diagnose the reason for such defeat. They see the defeat as being only temporary. Obtaining the diagnosis will equip them with the new plan to launch another combat. Losing a battle is not synonymous with failure in life, but fear makes you feel otherwise. That is the *Fallacy of Fear* which we must all guard against in our quest for success!

Chapter 38
Section Three Practical Steps

Faith is a propulsive force that pushes a man to take practical steps. In concluding this section, note the following points:

(1) What is your heart indicting?
What is your heart indicting? What vision have you conceived? The vision of your heart is the originator of the faith you will command. Faith begins with vision. Therefore, seek for a vision of your life purpose; seek to know your life purpose. Once you catch sight of your life purpose, your life will take a different meaning. Suddenly, you will feel a throbbing sense of wellbeing, a sense of significance to your world. A vision of your life purpose will evoke faith that will cause the adrenaline levels in you to soar, and you will not again need any man to prop you into action neither will you experience boredom in your life.

(2) How long will you keep postponing taking the next step?
How long will you continue in a job you never like? How long will you keep postponing taking the next step that you know is the right thing to do? Remember, the clock is ticking and time will never wait for you. Soon you will pass that stage, and what will be your story when you look back? Without a step of faith, you will remain on the same spot? Therefore, rise up and take that step of faith today.

(3) Age is never a barrier in the world of faith

Age is never a barrier in the world of faith. Do not say I am too young or I am very old. A step of faith is all that is needed today. It is never too late to make a U-turn and do the right thing.

(4) Faith means moving forward despite the threats of fear

To take that step of faith means that you move forward despite the threats of fear, and once you take that step you'll realise that what you fear was simply *False Experiences Appearing Real*. In other words, faith is to do the very thing that you are afraid of. By the time you take the step of faith in line with your vision, your eyes will open to many other opportunities. If you remain where you are today, you won't see those opportunities. Fear blindfolds and fear limits. Never allow such blindfolding limitations again in your life by taking that step of faith today.

(5) Place your journey of life in the hands of God

The surest way to strengthen your faith is to place your journey of life in the hands of God your Creator. The power of the Holy Spirit surging through your nature will propel you beyond your imaginations. God is real and He is very ready to help in times of need for anyone who cares to embrace Him. We can access the goodness of God via Jesus Christ, the Mediator between God and man, *"for there is one God, and one Mediator between God and men, the man Christ Jesus"* (1Tim.2:5 KJV) (see SSB Book 5). Jesus extends an invitation to whoever wills:

> *"Come to Me, all you who labour and are heavy laden, and I will give you rest. Take My yoke upon you and learn from Me, for I am gentle and lowly in heart, and you will find rest for your souls. For My yoke is easy and My burden is light" (Mat.11:28-30 NKJV).*

Section 4

How to Develop Your Spirit for Exploits (The Force of Love)

CHAPTER 39
THE FORCE OF LOVE

FROM GENERATION TO GENERATION, HUMANS have always been intrigued by the force of love. The story of Edward VIII (1894-1972), King of the United Kingdom and the Dominions of the British Empire and Emperor of India, who abdicated his throne for love was the twentieth century version of Shakespeare's Romeo and Juliet.

On the night of 11 December 1936, just few hours after signing the Instrument of Abdication, Edward announced his abdication decision to the surprise world in his famous worldwide radio broadcast:

> *"I have found it impossible to carry the heavy burden of responsibility and to discharge my duties as king as I would wish to do without the help and support of the woman I love"*
>
> *(The Washington Post archive).*

Edward was born into the British royal family during the reign of his great-grandmother, Queen Victoria. At the time of his birth, he was third in the line of succession to the throne, behind his grandfather and father. As a great-grandson of the monarch in the male line, Edward held the title His Highness Prince Edward of York at birth. He grew up to join the army and served in the First World War of 1914 to 1919.

Throughout the 1920s, Edward, as Prince of Wales, represented his father, now King George V, at home and abroad on many occasions. His rank, travels, good looks, and unmarried status gained him much public attention, and at the height of his popularity, he was the most photographed celebrity of his time. He developed a particular interest in science and in 1926 was president of the British Association for the Advancement of Science when his alma mater, Oxford University, hosted the society's annual general meeting.

During this period, Prince Edward did something that monarchs do not have the luxury of doing – he fell in love. He was in love with Wallis Simpson. But the relationship was not considered acceptable for royalty. Not only was Wallis Simpson an American commoner, but was also a married woman. Wallis, not measured as necessarily pretty, had a sense of style and pose that made her distinguished and attractive with radiant eyes, good complexion and fine, smooth black hair which she kept parted down the middle for most of her life, was married and divorced in 1927 from Lieutenant Earl Winfield Spencer, a pilot for the U.S. Navy. Only six months after her divorce, Wallis remarried to Ernest Simpson, a British-American businessman in the shipping line.

As part of the New Year celebration, Viscountess Thelma Furness, hosted a party on 10 January 1931 at her country house, Burrough Court, where, in addition to Prince Edward, Wallis and her husband Ernest Simpson were invited. It was at this party that Prince Edward first met with Mrs. Simpson. Edward, who had been having series of illicit affairs with married women, was to become infatuated with Mrs. Simpson, though at the initial stage he adamantly insisted to his father, King George, and mother, Queen Mary, that he was not intimate with her.

Prince Edward's relationship with Mrs. Simpson generated such grave concern in the British and American government circles in the wake of the rising Nazi Germany such that they were secretly being followed by the Metropolitan Police Special Branch, who confirmed the illicit brewing affair. King George V and Queen Mary were greatly disappointed by their son, Edward, the heir apparent to the throne, and though they met Simpson at Buckingham Palace in 1935, they later refused to receive her.

Love Story of the Century!

To some, this was the love story of the century. To others, it was a scandal that threatened to weaken the British monarchy and undermine constitutional precedence. In reality, it was the story about the power of love even though many view such power to be negatively deployed by Prince Edward and his mistress, Simpson.

At five minutes to midnight on 20 January 1936, Edward's father, King George V, kicked the bucket. Upon the death of his father, Prince Edward, ascended the throne as King Edward VIII in pomp and pageantry that captivated the world's attention. As king, Edward VIII was never himself as he felt he needed Wallis Simpson, who was still married to Mr. Simpson, to be officially recognised as his queen. Soon the king began to be late and cancelled crucial appointments, broke state and constitutional protocols. The government was increasingly becoming worried by his unprofessional attitude that threatened state security, especially considering the restiveness of Nazi Germany, and the media started insinuating many things such as Simpson being a possible German spy in the monarchy. The reason for the King's misbehaviour was attributed mainly to his frustration of not officially having Mrs. Simpson as his partner.

But such a union was a taboo since King Edward VIII, by virtue of his status, was the titular head of the Church of England, which at the time opposed the remarriage of divorced people if their former spouses were still alive. Meanwhile, Wallis Simpson, apparently intrigued by the prospects of becoming a queen, had commenced her second divorce with her husband in preparation for her third marriage to the new King Edward VIII. Realising the impracticality of his wish, King Edward grew more frustrated at each day, though still having open-secret contacts with his mistress, Mrs. Simpson. King Edward became increasingly impatient with court protocol, and caused concern among politicians by his apparent disregard for established constitutional conventions.

On 16 November 1936, the King invited Mr. Stanley Baldwin, the then British Prime Minister, to Buckingham Palace and officially indicated his desire to marry Wallis Simpson, once Simpson's divorce process was completed. However, Baldwin immediately informed him of the implication of such decision that his subjects wouldn't accept their queen to be a former wife of two living husbands.

Upon such rejection, King Edward proposed an alternative solution of a morganatic marriage, in which he would remain king but Simpson would not become queen; Simpson would enjoy some lesser title instead, and any children they might have would not inherit the throne. This proposal was presented to the British Cabinet and the Dominion governments of Australia, Canada, Ireland, New Zealand, and South Africa in pursuant of the British Empire regulation of the Statute of Westminster 1931. The then Prime Ministers of Australia (Joseph Lyons), Canada (Mackenzie King) and South Africa (J. B. M. Hertzog) rejected the proposal on the ground of their king marrying a divorcee; the Irish Prime Minister (Éamon de Valera) was indifferent and detached, while the Prime Minister of New Zealand (Michael Joseph Savage), having never heard of Simpson before, vacillated in disbelief.

With such strong opposition, King Edward VIII was presented with three options: (1) Forget any marital union with Simpson; (2) marry Simpson and retain the throne but risk en masse resignation of the British Cabinet and thereby cause constitutional crisis and weaken the apolitical stand of the royal family; and (3) abdicate the throne and marry Simpson.

By such strong bond of love for Simpson, it was clear that King Edward was not willing to give up on his relationship with Simpson for the throne, and he was not prepared to destroy the age-old monarchy of family lineage for his personal ambition. The love beats of his heart were ready to lose everything to become united with his lover. Hence, at 10H00 on 10 December 1936, King Edward VIII, surrounded by his three surviving brothers, signed the six copies of the Instrument of Abdication:

> *"I, Edward the Eighth, of Great Britain, Ireland, and the British Dominions beyond the Seas, King, Emperor of India, do hereby declare My irrevocable determination to renounce the Throne for Myself and for My descendants, and My desire that effect should be given to this Instrument of Abdication immediately"*
>
> *(The Guardian, 1936).*

To Give up All This for That!

Note what Prince Edward had to forgo and lose for the sake of his love: loss of his personal claim for the throne, permanent loss of his descendant succession claims for the throne, loss of the royal dues and entitlements from the government, banishment from the United Kingdom, and related territories. His mother, Queen Mary, with extreme emotions of anger against her first son, exclaimed:

> *"To give up all this for that" (Bradford, 1989).*

King Edward (VIII)'s abdication action seems to prove the Bible injunctions: *"love is as strong as death"* (AMP) and *"the passion of love bursting into flame is more powerful than death, stronger than the grave"* (Songs 8:6 CEV). Indeed, the passion (force) of love had gripped King Edward VIII, howbeit he misdirected the force and paid dearly for his inordinate affections.

Edward left Britain for Austria the following day after the abdication for his exile, and was later married to the divorced Ms. Wallis Simpson in a small ceremony on 03 June 1937. Prince Albert, the Duke of York, Edward's immediate younger brother, who now succeeded to the throne as King George VI in place of his abdicated brother, banned any member of the royal family from attending the wedding ceremony of Edward and Ms. Simpson.

On the eve of the wedding, Edward received a letter that stated he was not eligible to the title 'His Royal Highness,' but out of generosity the new King George VI would allow him to hold the title as the 'His Royal Highness the Duke of Windsor' but 'his wife (Simpson) and descendants, if any, shall not hold said title or attribute.' The Royal family members shunned the couple and the exile, initially thought would be for few years, lasted throughout the couple's lifetime.

Edward and his wife, Simpson, lived out most of their lives in France with no more official assignment except when Edward was made the Governor of Bahamas in July 1940, an appointment by the British government in the wake of the Second World War, believed to have been made to keep Edward far away from the Nazis German, whom Edward seemed to have some sympathy.

***Fig*.17: Wallis, Duchess of Windsor (1896-1986) and Edward, the Duke of Windsor (1894-1972), outside Government House in Nassau, the Bahamas (circa 1942). (Photo by Ivan Dmitri/Michael Ochs Archives/Getty Images)**

In France, the City of Paris provided the abdicated king and his wife, Wallis, with a house for a nominal rent, the French government exempted him from paying income tax, and the couple was able to buy goods duty-free through the British embassy and the military commissary. From the minimal allowances they received from the Royal family and with stipends as royalties from his books, *A King's Story* and *A Family Album*, which detailed the fashion and habits of the Royal Family, the couple was able to make a living.

Notwithstanding, with a heavy heart full of many questions, Edward finally died on 28th May 1972, just a month from his 78th birthday in France. The late agreement made with the royal family allowed the body to be transported and be buried in the royal cemetery in Britain. Wallis lived for more fourteen years, many of which were spent in bed, secluded from the world; she died on 24th April 1986, two months before her 90th birthday.

LOVE IS A FORCE

The story of King Edward VIII is a testimony of the force of love, which is one of the three greatest forces that rule the world – the other two being the forces of vision and faith. A man or a woman, once gripped by the force of love, is prepared to risk everything for love. He is ready to damn any consequence, even risk death, just to secure the object of his love. Knowing such mighty force, founders of legacy and institutions are always keen to know who their successors fall in love with. This is because if not managed properly, the mighty force of love has the capacity to destroy legacies and wipe off all traces of edifices that have been painstakingly laboured for and built over the years.

The force of love has the power to pull down personal edifices, nations, empires as shown by the story of King Edward VIII. Imagine the advantage Hitler, the then head of the Nazis government of Germany, would have gained by manipulating the bond of love between the King and Simpson. Actually, Hitler was quoted as boasting to transform Britain into a fascist state by scheming to manipulate the bond of love between Edward and Simpson.

FOUR KINDS OF LOVE

Love is a powerful, driving force. Unknown to many, this force is not just for sexual gratification but can be channelled into productive ventures. This section of the book unveils the different kinds of love and how their forces can be deployed for productivity.

Principally, there are four kinds of love recognised in the Scriptures:

(a) Erotica
(b) Phileo
(c) Prokope
(d) Agape

Because of the limitations of the English language, most Bible versions translate all of them as simply 'love.' However, a closer study of the Scriptures reveals these different kinds of love and their various characteristics.

Section 4 (A)

The Force of Erotic Love

Chapter 40
Sexual Energy Dissipation – Reason Many People Fail in Life

Reading such stories like the abdication of King Edward VIII, many people often wonder how strong the emotional force of love that can becloud the sense of correct judgment! In other words, does love make an individual stupid? Many men have been reported to have taken decisions which otherwise wouldn't have been possible at the height of emotions of love.

Women have influenced men to take decisions contrary to what rationalisation would agree. Napoleon Hill wrote:

> *"Man's greatest motivating force is his desire to please a woman"*
> *(Think and Grow Rich, page 192).*

Napoleon Hill further said:

> *"It is this inherent desire of man to please woman, which gives woman the power to make or break a man"*
> *(Think and Grow Rich, page 192).*

A good case was the first humans, Adam and Eve. In the Garden of Eden, an evil stranger, Satan, entered their habitation. The Stranger was soon able to deceive the woman, Eve, to disobey the divine instruction of their Father. Interestingly, the husband, Adam, was not deceived. He knew the consequences of his wife's rebellion.

> *"It was not Adam who was deceived by Satan. The woman was deceived, and sin was the result" (1Tim.2:14 NLT).*

However, Adam rather chose to follow his wife and damn any consequence. What made Adam to take such an irrational decision and damn the consequences? Obviously, it was the emotion of love! That is the driving force of erotica in a man. Erotica, also known as eros, is the love for sexual intimacy. It is one of the four kinds of love mentioned in the Scriptures. It arouses in a man the strongest willpower to damn any consequence and follow through with a course of action. It is such a tremendously mighty force that it temporarily blinds the eyes of men to see the repercussions of their decisions.

The emotion of sexual drive, indeed, transcends the bodily senses; it can warp the faculties of the mind and deaden the voice of the spirit until its target object is met. Many men and women have been driven by the sexual desire to commit actions that jeopardise their overall wellbeing. Does this mean that the force of erotica makes an individual stupid?

Though the force of erotica is a mighty force, yet God has created humans for orderliness and not for disorder. Allowing the force of erotica to run wild and unchecked often brings disorder with its consequent regrets. Many cases of sexually transmitted diseases, broken homes, shattered destinies, and premature death are clear testimonies of the negative consequence of unchecked expressions of erotica.

DISSIPATION OF SEXUAL ENERGY

In general, the sexual drive is a mighty force that runs in humans. It is believed to be the strongest of all forces that can be evoked in a man. It has made monarchs to fall prostrate before the goal of their love, and it has caused the mightiest army to sheath up their swords just to satisfy the sexual love beats.

However, some rational minds have wondered: 'Can't this mighty force be channelled into useful ventures?' Indeed, erotic love has activated the minds of men beyond measures into its sub-consciousness that in turn stimulates the heart of the human spirit for powerful creative thought flow. Great songs have been produced, great portraits have been painted, and giant scientific and technological breakthroughs have been recorded, all because of the stimulatory effect of the power of erotica.

Physical sexual gratification is just one route for channelling this mighty force. Unfortunately, many individuals do not realise this truth. Hence, they spend their youthful age dissipating this powerful energy by engaging in unbridled, rampant sexual escapades. Indeed, psychology has proven that one main reason why most people only start to achieve remarkable success after the age of forty years is that they waste their sexual energy in their earlier years. Dissipation of sexual energy is often the main reason why many people fail in life.

AN INTERESTING STUDY

Napoleon Hill made an interesting study, which he documented in his book, Think and Grow Rich. He wrote:

> *"I discovered, from the analysis of over 25000 people, that men who succeed in an outstanding way, seldom do so before the age of forty, and more often they do not strike their real pace until they are well beyond the age of fifty. This fact was so astounding that it prompted me to go into the study of its cause most carefully, carving the investigation over a period of more than twelve years.*

"This study disclosed the fact that the major reason why the majority of men who succeed do not begin to do so before the age of forty to fifty, is their tendency to dissipate their energies through over indulgence in physical expression of the emotion of sex.

"The majority of men never learn that the urge of sex has other possibilities, which transcends in importance, that of mere physical expression. The majority of these who make this discovery, do so after having wasted many years at a period when the sex energy is at its height, prior to the age of forty-five to fifty. This usually is followed by noteworthy achievement" (Think and Grow Rich, pages 182-183).

STORY OF MR. THEOPHANY

Mr. Theophany was an aspiring young man for a great destiny. He wanted to build a career in the security field. However, he had one challenge, and that was he couldn't keep his sexual thought under control. At high school, he was always having a crush from one girl to another! This affected his academic work. He managed to finish his high school, and with the certificate he enrolled in the Police Force.

Having exceptional interpersonal skills and communicative prowess, he was soon promoted through the ranks to become an inspector. His salary was modest, and for a young man it was a good supply of money for his daily needs. But his unbridled sexual life was to cause the ruin of his career. He lavished his money on girlfriends, partying on most weekends. He became a regular face in most pub joints and a popular name among the loose girls in town.

On a few occasions, information got to his superiors of his improper sexual conduct with the females. He received an official warning. Not too long thereafter, Theophany fell under the charm of a female drug trafficker, who was apprehended with drugs. The woman implicated Theophany, who couldn't prove his innocence. He was dismissed from the Police Force and jailed together with the woman.

On coming out of jail, Theophany was more cautious with the females. Nonetheless, he was yet to learn how to harness the great sexual force that ran through his system. He was still jumping from one woman to another, although this time being quite careful not to associate with those of dubious character. This lifestyle couldn't allow him to settle down and raise a home and he couldn't concentrate on his job.

It was only in his early fifties that Theophany was able to face the truth about his life. He was now more serious and started saving his money to start a family. He eventually got married and started a business. Old things seemed now to have passed away!

OVERPOWERING DRIVING FORCE OF EROTIC LOVE

To maintain moral soundness in sexual matters is a battle many people don't win. The mighty driving force of eros has destroyed many lives and killed many visions when it is unguardedly let loose. I have personally counted 86 per cent of individuals within three generations of my paternal lineage that were rendered useless and their dreams shattered because of unguarded force of sexual drive. That was an alarming number, and I thank God I knew this quite early; thus, I could ask God for help in order not to be among the victims.

Unguarded sexual behaviour leaves heartaches, frustrations, and even death in its path. It is a tale of the mighty force of sexual drive. Sexual coitus, which is the commonest expression of sexual drive, takes a high amount of energy. Human history has repeatedly shown that illicit sexual activity drains the energy that could have been utilised for more productive ventures, thereby retarding advancement in life.

The costs of engagement in illicit sexual activities are too grave for an individual who seeks to be a champion in his field of endeavour. Great names in all industries such as Rockefeller, Carnegie, Henry Ford, Thomas Edison, Florence Nightingale, etc. often have this in common: they are individuals with sexual discipline. You don't know what you lose by engaging in illicit sexual activity!

If we must realise the visions of our heart, we must learn to bridle any irrational sexual urge and channel its energy to other productive ventures. Though it is powerful and driving, yet the good thing about human nature is that man has the ability to control this mighty sexual force and channel it into furthering his life visions. This is not always easy but it is not impossible. It behoves on us then to know how to harness this mighty force for positive results and productivity, which is what this section of the book teaches.

Chapter 41
The Spirituality of Erotic Love

Because the most common, most understood, manner of expression of erotic love is carnal consummation, that is, physical sexual contact, many people erroneously think that erotic love is nothing but carnal. Thus, many people think that sexual love is simply physical with no spiritual undertones. However, a study of the Scriptures shows that erotic love is as spiritual as any of the other three kinds of love. The God who deposited agape, prokope, and phileo in the heart of the spirit man at creation, is also the One that deposited eros in man. This makes eros as spiritual as agape, prokope, and phileo.

EROS – A DEPOSIT IN THE HUMAN SPIRIT

Eros was deposited in the heart of the spirit man at creation by God. This is obvious when we consider the origin of sexual arousal. From childhood, our sexuality has already started to express itself. Sexual thought is a normal thought process even in childhood. A child distinctly knows that there is something unique about the genitalia. As he grows up, he doesn't need to see pictures of naked bodies before he entertains sexual thought.

Sexual thoughts run in our hearts even when there is no physical trigger of such thoughts. The thoughts pass into the minds for processing. The outcome of the mind procession now depends on one's past experiences, upbringing, and moral standing. A perverted mind will produce perverted sexual thought, while a disciplined mind will produce a good sexual thought.

Indeed, because of the overpowering force of erotic love, many psychologists believe man is a sexual organism. Sigmund Freud (AD 1856-1939), the Father of Pshochoanalysis, wrote:

> *"The behaviour of a human being in sexual matters is often a prototype for the whole of his other modes of reaction in life"*
> *(Sexuality and the Psychology of Love, 1963, page 25).*

In other words, erotic love is as spiritual as agape love. The implication of this is that sexual coitus is not just a bodily exercise, but it affects the mind and the spirit man. Unfortunately, many people do not realise that.

MORE ON THE SPIRITUAL NATURE OF EROTIC LOVE

A study of the Scriptures actually confirms the spirituality of erotica. The following is an interesting discussion on the spiritual nature of erotica from Scriptural view.

The Church was born in AD 33 at the Upper Room in Jerusalem following the outpouring of the Holy Spirit on the Jewish Pentecost Day. She was born amidst gross paganism and cultural barbarism of the Roman world. Hence, in the early Church some non-Jewish brethren were already married to pagan spouses before their conversion. This raised some conflict among the early Church on the relationship between these Christian brethren and their pagan spouses. However, under divine inspiration, Apostle Paul dealt with this fundamental issue that affected the early Church in his first letter to the Church in Corinth.

> *"But to the rest I, not the Lord, say: If any brother has a wife who does not believe, and she is willing to live with him, let him not divorce her. And a woman who has a husband who does not believe, if he is willing to live with her, let her not divorce him. For the unbelieving husband is sanctified [hagiazō] by the wife, and the unbelieving wife is sanctified [hagiazō] by the husband; otherwise your children would be unclean [akathartos], but now they are holy [hagio]" (1Cor.7:12-14 NKJV).*

The 'sanctification' of the marital union of the regenerated Christian and the unregenerated pagan spouse is of great significance. The term 'sanctified' in the above Scripture is from the Greek word *hagiazō*, which literally means 'to make holy.' That is, to sanctify is to be separated from profane things and be dedicated to God. *Hagiazō* is the same word used in the Gospel of Mathew chapter 6 verse 9 to hallow God's Name and the same word that is used to show the separation of Jesus unto God (see Joh.10:36; 17:17).

Hagiazō is from the root word *hagio,* which means 'holy' or 'saint' as used to designate the Holy Spirit (Mar.1:8; Joh.14:26). In other words, *hagiazō* or sanctification simply means holiness. Newer Bible translations render that 1 Corinthians chapter 7 verse 14 in modern language:

> *"For the unbelieving husband is made holy because of his wife, and the unbelieving wife is made holy because of her husband. Otherwise your children would be unclean, but as it is, they are holy" (1Cor.7:14 ESV).*

> *"For the believing wife brings holiness to her marriage, and the believing husband brings holiness to his marriage. Otherwise, your children would not be holy, but now they are holy"*
> *(1Cor.7:14 NLT).*

> *"For the unbelieving husband is made holy through the wife, and the unbelieving wife is made holy through her husband. Otherwise your children would be unclean, but now they are holy"*
> *(1Cor.7:14 TLV).*

> *"The husband who is not a Christian is set apart from the sin of the world because of his Christian wife. The wife who is not a Christian is set apart from the sin of the world because of her Christian husband. In this way, the lives of the children are not unclean because of sin, they are clean" (1Cor.7:14 NLV).*

The presence of the regenerated (born again) partner in a marital union makes the unregenerated partner and the union holy and acceptable to God. The children born from such union are holy before God because of the presence of the regenerated partner, otherwise the children will be unclean. 'Unclean' children do not refer to physical uncleanliness but spiritual state. The term unclean used for the children in that 1 Corinthian 7 verse 14 is from the Greek word *akathartos,* which means impure or unclean as used to denote 'unclean spirits' (Mat.10:1; Luk.9:42).

The significance of this becomes obvious when you understand how a Sanctuary or Temple of God is formed. Often, a sanctuary or a temple is a house just like the one Moses constructed in the wilderness on their way from Egypt to the promised Canaan. The house only became a Sanctuary or a Temple of God once the Presence of God started residing in it. In the Old Testament era, the Presence of God is carried by the Ark of the Covenant, which was also constructed by Moses under divine direction. Thus, any house that the Ark dwelt in would be transformed into a Sanctuary or a Temple of God. About 480 years after Moses, King Solomon built a house in Jerusalem (1Kin.6:1). Once the Ark was moved into the constructed house of Solomon, the house became the Temple of God.

In the New Testament era, the Presence of God is carried by the Spirit of God that lives in the regenerated believer. This makes the body of the regenerated individual a Holy Temple of God (1Cor.6:19). That is, the whole body (including the erotic genitalia) of the regenerated is holy to God. Marriage is a union of the body and the spirit of the man and his wife (Mal.2:15). The unregenerated partner, thus, shares in the holiness being carried by the regenerated spouse. Their erotic love is part of this holy union. Any child born from this union, therefore, becomes holy [*hagio*] as well.

> *"God wants husbands and wives to become one body and one spirit. Why? So that they would have holy children and protect that spiritual unity. Don't cheat on your wife. She has been your wife from the time you were young" (Mal.2:15 ERV).*

SPIRITOSEXUAL UNIFICATION

Thus, marriage with a regenerated individual is a holy matrimony. The eros of such marriage is not only spiritual but also holy. Sexual activity is, therefore, not just the union of the body genitalia of the two individuals in the activity, but also an intercourse of their spirit beings. A union of such spirits due to coital association results in *Spiritosexual Unification*. That is, the partner you have coitus with becomes unified in body and spirit with you. This explains why individuals that had sexual coitus still feel being belonged to each other even after years of separation. The coitus fuses their spirit beings together even when they are physically not in contact anymore.

Only two things can disconnect and put asunder this spiritosexual union:

• Physical death
When spiritosexual partners die, their spirits are set free from each other.

> *"A wife is bound by law as long as her husband lives; but if her husband dies, she is at liberty to be married to whom she wishes, only in the Lord" (1Cor.7:39 NKJV).*

> *"For the woman who has a husband is bound by the law to her husband as long as he lives. But if the husband dies, she is released from the law of her husband" (Rom.7:2 NKJV).*

• The Blood of Jesus Christ
Similarly, a sincere plea for God's mercy in an unwholesome sexual relationship triggers the release of the Blood of Jesus to break off the spiritosexual unification.

> *"And almost all things are by the law purged with blood; and without shedding of blood is no remission" (Heb.9:22 KJV).*

What this means is that a high level of moral discipline is required to free oneself from becoming sexually entangled outside one's marital union.

NEPHILIMS AND HUMAN SEXUALITY

The story of the Nephilims is another example of the spirituality of sexual union. About four thousand years ago, during the time of the godly man, Noah, angelic personalities, referred to as 'sons of God,' came to earth and had sexual relationship with humans, giving birth to unusual race on earth called the Nephilims (see SSB Book 3).

> *"There were Nephilim (men of stature, notorious men) on the earth in those days—and also afterward—when the sons of God lived with the daughters of men, and they gave birth to their children. These were the mighty men who were of old, men of renown (great reputation, fame)" (Gen.6: 4 AMP).*

Fertilisation of the human female gametes by the gametes of these angelic beings resulted in the birth of gigantic individuals (Nephilims) with unnatural abilities. The Nephilims were the giant and wicked men of old with various abnormal body structures. Unnatural canny for evils and wickedness soon perverted the whole surface of the earth through the activities of these individuals. Added to the fallen nature of man, evils and wickedness soon rose to their pinnacle. The pure human line with a diploid chromosome number was being threatened with extinction.

If extinct, the coming of the Seed of the woman (the Messiah) to crush the head of the Serpent as promised by God at Man's Fall in the Garden of Eden would be unrealised, and God's purpose would be defeated. Thus, God had no choice but to destroy that generation of adulterated humanity. Fortunately, the righteous man, Noah, and his household chose not to follow the wickedness and evils of their day. God wiped off the whole humanity with deluge; only Noah and his wife, their three children (Shem, Ham, and Japheth) with their wives, eight people in total, were saved to perpetuate the human race (Gen.7: 23; 9: 18, 19 NKJV).

Some theologians argue that the sons of God that fathered Nephilims were not angels, but human descendants of Seth, the son of Adam. However, a close study of the Scriptures shows that they were angels, who materialised themselves and came down to earth to have sexual relationship with the daughters of men. You can read about sons of God again in Job chapters 1 and 2, in Heaven, with the evil intruder Satan. In fact, the Book of Enoch (*Book 1 – the Watchers*), believed by some theologians to be written by Enoch, the 7th generation from Adam, gave more specific details and some of the names of these angels that fathered the Nephilims.

According to the Book of Enoch, Samyaza, an angel of high rank, was described as leading a rebel sect of angels in a descent to earth to have sexual intercourse with human females. The Book of Enoch was not canonised, hence, not grouped among the 66 books of the Bible, nonetheless, many believed Jude verses 14 and 15 were quoted from the Book of Enoch.

The point here is that angels are spirit beings. To show the spiritual nature of sexual intercourse, these angels had sexual relationship with humans that gave birth to Nephilims. Such sexual union was not in keeping with their creation. Angels are not to have sexual intercourse and cannot marry (Mat.22:30). The fallen angels that violated this divine order met with divine judgment as they were being chained in utter darkness, reserved for final judgment (Jude 1:6).

SUCCUBUS AND INCUBUS

Cases of humans having sexual intercourse with spirits abound every day. In medicine, because such phenomena, most times, do not have physical empirical supportive evidence, they tend to be given various names such as *sleep paralysis* or *unexplained hallucinations*.

In 1998, we embarked on Christian missionary outreach in a rural area of Rivers State, Nigeria, under the umbrella of the Christian medical association. Some medical students and doctors from other medical schools also joined us. It was a three-day weekend event, starting from Friday.

At about 19HOO, a young woman in her mid-twenties approached me, asking for assistance. After enquiring what nature of assistance she was seeking, she told me clearly she was being afflicted by a demonic spirit and would like us to cast out the demon from her life. The story was that the demon would come in the night and had sexual intercourse with her. During such visits, she would physically experience sexual manipulation and even reached orgasm. I quickly intimated some members of our group and we invited the woman to a quiet place to cast out the demon.

When we exercised our spiritual authority in the Name of Jesus, the demon started manifesting in the woman. Her countenance changed, her voice became baritone like a male voice, and she became very aggressive. It was there the demon claimed to have fathered two spiritual children with this woman. In summary, we had to use our spiritual authority and cast out the demon from her.

She was not the only case of sexual intimacy with demons that I have personally witnessed. Judith, a nurse, was another case. She was always scared to sleep at night because her sexual demon intruder could manifest at night. The demon was finally driven away by the authority in Jesus Name.

These sexually perverted demons are popularly referred to as Succubi (singular: Succubus, a demon that has sexual relationship with a man) and Incubi (singular: Incubus, a demon that has sexual relationship with a woman), both Latin words that mean 'to lie upon.'

Indeed, the sexual escapades of demons are well-known throughout human history. Saint Augustine of Hippo (AD 354-430) touched on the topic in De Civitate Dei ('The City of God'), in which he noted that there were too many alleged attacks by incubi to deny them. He stated,

> *"There is also a very general rumour. Many have verified it by their own experience and trustworthy persons have corroborated the experience others told, that sylvans and fauns, commonly called incubi, have often made wicked assaults upon women"*
>
> *(De Civitate Dei; 'The City of God,' AD 410, 15.23).*

Such sexual union with these demons are testimonies of the spiritual nature of erotic love, which these fallen angels (demons) became envious and wanted to share with mankind.

Chapter 42:
Five Kinds of Sexual Perversion

Erotica or eros is the romantic drive between a man and a woman for sexual gratification. It is love for sexual intimacy. Eros is a term coined after the Greek mythological god of sexuality, believed to be the mythical son of Aphrodite. The Roman counterpart of Eros was Cupid, which means 'desire.' These words have found themselves into English language as 'erotic, cupidity, and aphrodisiac,' mostly used in connection with sexuality.

The Greek Bible does not have the term eros nor erotica. Rather it uses description or expressions to refer to eros. In the Old Testament Hebrew Scriptures, sexual love or coitus is translated in English as 'know' (Gen.4:1), 'go into,' or 'lie with' (Lev.20:13). This format was also utilised by the New Testament Greek Scriptures.

LEGALITY OF EROTIC LOVE

The Scriptures (both Old and New Testaments) regard practical expression of erotic love to be divinely lawful only within the bond of marriage. Erotic love in marriage of a man to a woman is described in the New Testament as *koitē amiantos,* which means 'bed undefiled' (Heb.13:4). *koitē amiantos* literally means unsoiled or pure marital bed.

DEFILED MARITAL BED

Any expression of eros outside marriage of a man to a woman is *koitē miasma*, which literally means 'marital bed defilement.' That is, *koite miasma* is the opposite of *koite amiantos*. Thus, *koite miasma* is against the laws of God who created mankind and the universe.

FIVE MAJOR CLASSES OF DEFILED EROTICA

Various types of *koitē miasma* are clearly outlined in the Scriptures; the major five types are:

(a) Porneia

This is the practice of erotic love between unmarried people. The English language translates it as **fornication**. Porneia occurs 26 times in the New Testament Bible, e.g. Mat.5:32; Act.15:20; 1Cor.7:2.

(b) Moichao

The Greek term for the practice of erotic love by a married person outside the marital union is Moichao, which is translated in English Language as **adultery**, and it occurs 6 times in four verses in the New Testament Bible (Mat.5:32; 19:9; Mar.10:11, 12).

Two forms of *moichao* exist:

- *Moichos* is a married male person who engages in erotic love outside the marital union. The English translation is **adulterer**, and it occurs 4 times in the New Testament Bible (Luk.18:11; 1 Cor.6:9; Heb.13:4; Jam.4:4).
- *Moichalis* is a married female person who engages in erotic love outside the marital union. The English translation is **adulteress**, and it occurs 7 times in 6 verses in the New Testament Bible (Mat.12:39; 16:4; Mar.8:38; Rom.7:3; Jam.4:4; 2 Pet.2:14).

However, in many cases, *moichao, moichios*, and *moichalis* are all translated simply as adultery.

(c) Pornos

This is the practice of eros as a way of life usually as a transaction for a favour such as for material or financial gain. The English Bible translation for *pornos* is **harlotry**, fornication or **whoremonger**. Pornos occurs 8 times in the New Testament Bible, e.g. 1 Cor.5:9-11. Sometimes the Greek term *porneuō* is also translated as harlotry or fornication and occurs 8 times in the New Testament Bible (e.g. 1 Cor.6:18; Rev.2:14). Present day term **pornography** is coined from this word pornos.

(d) Arsenokoites

This is the practice of eros in which an individual engages in same-gender sexual activity. The modern terminology for arsenokoitēs is **homosexuality** (1Tim.1:10).

> *"Or do you not know that the unrighteous will not inherit the kingdom of God? Do not be deceived; neither fornicators [pornos], nor idolaters, nor adulterers [moichos], nor effeminate [malakos], nor homosexuals [arsenokoites], nor thieves, nor the covetous, nor drunkards, nor revilers, nor swindlers, will inherit the kingdom of God" (1Cor.6:9,10 NASB).*

The above Scripture mentions the four forms of eros outside a marital union – *pornos* (for both fornication and harlotry), *moichos* (adultery), *arsenokoites* (homosexuality) and effeminate. The more concise term for effeminate is Catamite (from the Greek term *malakos*]. Catamite is a practice in which a boy or a male youth engages in a sexual relationship with a man, and it was common in ancient Greek and Roman empires. Often such boys are kept as male prostitutes for the mature males as translated by NLT:

> *"Don't you realize that those who do wrong will not inherit the Kingdom of God? Don't fool yourselves. Those who indulge in sexual sin [pornos], or who worship idols, or commit adultery [moichos], or are male prostitutes [malakos], or practice homosexuality [arsenokoitēs], or are thieves, or greedy people, or drunkards, or are abusive, or cheat people—none of these will inherit the Kingdom of God" (1Cor.6:9,10 NLT).*

In addition, sexual relationship between two adult individuals of same gender (that is, man-man sexual activity or woman-woman sexual activity) is also translated as **sodomy**, which is a term coined from the prevailed practise in Sodom (and Gomorrah), dominant towns that existed about 4000 years ago during Abrahamic time (see Gen.19:1-30). Common terms in contemporary usage for sodomy are **lesbianism** (sodomy among women) and **gay** (sodomy among males).

In other words, effeminacy or sodomy are all forms of homosexuality, hence, most modern Bible translations just translate effeminacy and sodomy in 1 Corinthians chapter 6 verses 9 and 10 as simply homosexuality.

> *"Don't you know that the unrighteous will not inherit God's kingdom? Do not be deceived: No sexually immoral people, idolaters, adulterers, or anyone practicing homosexuality, no thieves, greedy people, drunkards, verbally abusive people, or swindlers will inherit God's kingdom" (1 Cor.6:9,10 HCSB).*

(e) Akatharsia

Akatharsia is the Greek word for uncleanness in the New Testament Bible. With respect to eros, it is associated with all forms of sexual pervasion, especially sexual intercourse with animals, which is known as **bestiality** in contemporary English language. Bestiality is specifically not mentioned in the New Testament Scriptures, however, the Hebrew Old Testament Scriptures denounce it in an unmistakable term.

> *"Do not have sexual relations with an animal and defile yourself with it. A woman must not present herself to an animal to have sexual relations with it; that is a perversion" (Lev.18:23 NIV).*

> *"Cursed is anyone who has sexual relations with any animal" (Deu.27:21 NIV).*

Indeed, bestiality is a pervasion of the erotic love, a form of *koitē miasma* (sexual defilement).

Chapter 43
Why Does God Hate Sexual Sins?

One question many individuals will like to ask is why does God hate sexual intercourse consented to by a man and a woman outside the marital union? If eroticism offers such a high level of pleasure, why would God frown at such pleasure? Was He not the One who created the sexual genitalia and their erotic ability?

Erotic love is often expressed via physical sexual contact (although this is by no means the only way to express eros). Like other kinds of love, eros was deposited in the heart of the spirit man at creation by the Creator God. In other words, God is the One who created man and deposited erotic love in his heart. But it was a pure eros, not tainted with any impurity at the time of creation of the human spirit. It was pure erotic love without lust or any other form of inordinate unclean cravings. Man at creation was the epitome of purity, power, and divine ingenuity. Man at creation was God's masterpiece. But at the Fall in Eden, the purity became tainted. Man's heart became defiled, as a different life known as sin began to flow through man. Sin is the life of Satan; sin is opposite to the life of God (zoe, in Hebrew) (see SSB Book 3).

Porneia, moichalis, pornos, arsenokoites, and akatharsia were never part of the pure erotic love in the heart of man at creation. If they were, the Scriptures wouldn't regard them as improper conduct against divine order. Rather, they were all the offshoots of sin that came after the Fall of Man. In other words, porneia, moichalis, pornos, arsenokoites, and akatharsia were not God's creation; they came into man as the *zoe* (the life of God) in man became replaced with sin. They were not God's original plan. Being offshoots of sin, they attract divine wrath and judgment. Indeed, sin generally attracts divine judgment because it is the complete opposite of God's creation (Eze.18:4; Rom.6:23).

This explains why God hates porneia, moichalis, pornos, arsenokoites, and akatharsia. Originally, He made expression of eros among humans to be only within bond of marriage between a man and a woman, and this is *koitē amiantos* (bed undefiled). It was God who conducted the first wedding when He joined Eve to Adam in holy matrimony in the Garden of Eden.

> *"Jesus answered, Surely you have read this in the Scriptures: When God made the world, 'he made people male and female.' And God said, 'That is why a man will leave his father and mother and be joined to his wife. And the two people will become one'"*
>
> *(Mat.19:4,5 ERV).*

Despite the way any generation of humanity may paint it, the truth remains that any other expression of erotic love outside marital union of a man and a woman is *koitē miasma* (bed defiled), and it negates divine principle and attracts negative consequences in the long run if there is no repentance.

WHY WE MUST AVOID SEXUAL PERVERSION

Sexual bed defilement or *koitē miasma* is against divine laws. For instance, porneia, moichalis, pornos, and arsenokoites negate the Principle of Agape, the Love of God. Fornication, adultery, harlotry and homosexuality do not express the love of God for humanity; rather they are all forms of expressions of selfishness. Furthermore, arsenokoites (homosexuality) and bestiality are against the Law of Procreation. If humans are only to practice homosexuality and bestiality, humanity would have been extinct. No matter how much people try to justify their actions, God's standards remain clear as distinctly shown in the Holy Scriptures.

The Scriptures refer to *koitē miasma* as sins. Every sin attracts judgment, both here and hereafter. Notable kingdoms and empires were destroyed because of such widespread *koitē miasma* practised by their citizens. The Roman Empire is a ready example of this. God is no respecter of persons, group, or race (Act.10:34,35). No matter our level of advancement in science, God still brings judgment on sins.

> *"Righteousness exalts a nation, but sin is a reproach to any people" (Pro.14:34 NKJV).*

Porneia, moichalis, pornos, arsenokoites, and akatharsia are all forms of sexual immorality or sexual sin. Of all sins, only sexual sins affect the body directly. The effect of a lie, stealing, and the likes on the body is often not seen immediately, unlike the effect of sexual sin. Destruction of homes, negative impacts on children, sexually transmitted diseases and other harmful effects are just a few of the direct impacts of sexual sins on human bodies.

> *"Have nothing to do with sex sins! Any other sin that a man does, does not hurt his own body. But the man who does a sex sin sins against his own body" (1Cor.6:18 NLV).*

In other words, besides its mental and spiritual effects, sexual sin hurts the body directly. Wisdom demands that one should flee from sexual sin. Knowing the force of an erotic love, among the many sins mentioned in the Scriptures, sexual sin is one that the Bible enjoins every wise person not just to resist, but to flee.

> *"Flee sexual immorality. Every sin that a man does is outside the body, but he who commits sexual immorality sins against his own body" (1 Cor.6:18 NKJV).*

The only way to escape from the consequences of *koitē miasma,* and all sins in general, is to repent and ask God for forgiveness in the Name of the Messiah Jesus Christ.

> *"For the wages of sin is death, but the gift of God is eternal life in Christ Jesus our Lord" (Rom.6:23 NKJV).*

God's love still exists as long as we are still here on earth. But once the earthly journey ends, the only action that awaits a sinner is the terrible, fearsome divine judgment and eternally hopeless condemnation in Hell. That is soberly fearful!

Chapter 44
The Consequences of Uncontrolled Erotic Love

From the inception of human history, sexual perversion of any kind has always come with untold consequences. The abuse of erotica impacts negatively on the three realms [mind (soul), spirit, and body] of human existence.

(1) NEGATIVE IMPACT ON THE HUMAN MIND

Destroys Creative Imagination

Erotica involves high energy consumption. Illicit sexual activity generates fear, and fear uses up energy negatively that can impede imagination, which is essential for creativity. That explains why many individuals in creative works often deny themselves of physical sexual coitus anytime they want to access the creative realm. During such moments, instead of physical sexual intercourse, they convert that vital energy into their creative works.

For instance, Jim is an artist that has done a lot of renowned paintings. Before each major artistic design, he would shut himself up in his closet, avoiding sexual contact during such a period. Once he had got the image clearly printed in his mind, he would come out of his closet and resume his normal routine. What Jim was doing was channelling his buttoned sexual energy into his creative artistry. The mighty force of erotic love can be transmuted into other worthwhile ventures rather than being dissipated by unbridled carnal sexual escapades. This is discussed in the next chapter.

Weakens the Willpower

An individual in a love-sexual relationship is a fearless individual; the absence of fear allows him to take steps, which hitherto, would be fearsome for him to dare. On the other hand, a sexual relationship that is devoid of love weakens the power of one's will for proactive action. A weak willpower for proactivity in many people is traceable to dissipation of their energy on illicit sexual activities. When such people learn to harness their sexual energy and channel it properly, their smartness and drive for proactive undertakings increase tremendously. Never, ever underrate the force of erotic love.

Negative Impact on Intelligence

Repeated engagement in illicit sexual activity distracts one's focus in life. Intelligence requires focus for analysis and synthesis, and to focus takes energy, which can be dissipated by illicit sexual activity. When a man makes the mistake of marrying outside of love, one early symptom that shows that all is not well is reduction of intelligence. The once smart guy will gradually become dull, even missing some memory tips. But if love can be restored in the relationship, such symptoms tend to disappear promptly.

Produces Poor Memory

Scientific studies have shown that continuous engagement in unloved, illicit sexual activities affects the registration, storage and retrieval of facts from the memory. Students are often aware of this. In my secondary and tertiary schooling, many serious-minded students often avoided sexual relationship during exam periods. I can still remember how many of my classmates would avoid seeing their girlfriends and sexual partners once serious professional exams were around the corner. It was an open secret among us in the medical school that some of the students that failed out of the medical schools did so because of unbridled carnal sexual expressions. A man with a low intelligent quotient but with disciplined sexual life will go very far in life than a man with high intelligent quotient but undisciplined in his sexual life.

Abnormal Emotional Development

We should never underrate the force of erotic love. It can make an individual to develop abnormal emotions if not channelled correctly. Most cases of depressions are actually due to abnormal deployment of erotic love. Women feel dumped, soiled, abused and destroyed when they engage in sexual activities with men whom they later discover have no love whatsoever for them.

Amnon was King David's first son and the heir apparent to the throne. With the assistance of his shrewd friend, Jonadab, he schemed and had an illicit sexual activity with his beautiful half-sister, Tamar. But that was a mistake that cost him not just his throne but his life also. His devastated sister was thrown into melancholic depression the rest of her life and was never able to live a normal life again (2 Samuel chpt. 13). Ultimately, Amnon was murdered for his undisciplined sexual life; he lost the throne and his unborn generation was never to be heard of! He would have been the heir of the genealogy of Jesus the Son of the Most High God. But he lost all that to sexual indiscipline in his youth. Very pathetic! That is a warning to young men and women. It always pays positively to be disciplined sexually.

Advice to the Youth

If there is any force that destroys glorious destinies of young men and women is sexual indiscipline. Illicit sexual activity has truncated the destinies of many young people prematurely. Many adults struggle with sexual discipline because they never learnt to control their sexual drive and channel it productively while they were young, hence, their lives become casualties of unbridled sexual escapades.

> *"It is good for a man to bear The yoke in his youth."*
> *(Lam.3:27 NKJV).*

> *"It is good for a man that he should bear The yoke [of godly discipline] in his youth." (Lam.3:27 AMP).*

> *"And it is good for people to submit at an early age to the yoke of his discipline." (Lam.3:27 NLT).*

The term yoke in Lamentations chapter 3 verse 27 refers to discipline. One of the most important yoke a youth should learn to bear early in life is sexual discipline. The fallen human nature poses a strong challenge to maintain sexual discipline especially at the youthful age when all the body hormones are at their peak. Nevertheless, sexual discipline is still very possible, and those who have learnt to maintain such discipline never regret their decisions later on in life.

> *"Drink water from your own cistern, and running water from your own well. Should your fountains be dispersed abroad, streams of water in the streets? Let them be only your own, and not for strangers with you. Let your fountain be blessed, and rejoice with the wife of your youth. As a loving deer and a graceful doe, let her breasts satisfy you at all times; and always be enraptured with her love. For why should you, my son, be enraptured by an immoral woman, and be embraced in the arms of a seductress?"*
> *(Pro.5:15-20 NKJV).*

Proverbs chapter 5 verses 15 to 20 refers to the discipline of sexual life. Why will a youth disperse his sexual fountains to strangers, and then live in regret? Why will a girl desecrate her sexuality and the gracefulness of her love to strangers, who only want to have carnal sexual activity with her and then dump her as a refuse dung? Proverbs chapter 5 verses 15 to 20 advises that a wise youth will focus on his destiny, get married when he is ready, and then be faithful to his sexual marital partner. This is the standard of God, and nothing less, that attracts blessing!

The Gravity of Rape

Knowing the force of erotic love and its mighty negative impact on lives when channelled negatively, makes the sin of rape a grievous one. No amount of imprisonment is commensurate with the evil perpetuated by the rape acts. Victims need God's help to be able to recover fully.

In summary, sexual energy is an enormous amount of energy. It takes the whole five faculties of the mind to be able to unleash sexual energy. That explains why individuals are often exhausted after sexual intercourse; a lot of energy is expended. When such sexual intercourse is done in the absence of love, instead of accomplishing profitability, the huge energy expended rather produces the opposite results. Never allow anyone to deceive you; the truth is that illicit sexual activity drains the energy of the mind.

(2) NEGATIVE IMPACT ON THE HUMAN SPIRIT

An illicit sexual activity affects all the three components of the human spirit as follows:

Effect on the Heart

Illicit sexual engagement dulls your spiritual fervency. A dull spirit is a lukewarm spirit; a lukewarm spirit is one that is not hot enough to propel the individual along the path of success. A lukewarm spirit is infertile. His ability to receive clear vision is deadened.

An illicit sexual activity beclouds the heart of the spirit man, thus, reducing the individual's ability to receive clear vision. As such, the individual's ability to muster faith is weakened. In other words, an illicit sexual activity weakens and ultimately destroys faith, thus, reducing the capacity for forceful advancement in life.

Effect on the Conscience

Repeated illicit sexual engagements have negative impacts on the voice of the conscience. At the initial stage, an illicit sexual activity evokes turmoil in the conscience as confusing messages are sent forth from the censor of the human spirit. The result of such confusing signals is guilt, fear, and all other negative forces that destroy faith and wasp the ability to receive clear vision. Repeated illicit sexual engagements will ultimately stifle the censor, causing it to die. A dead or seared conscience is an unproductive one. You need a sharp conscience to make sound decision and muster a strong willpower (see SSB Book 1), but repeated illicit sexual engagements destroy those abilities.

Effect on the Eido centre

An illicit sexual activity also affects the eido centre of the human spirit. The eido centre is the centre for conscious awareness; it is the centre by which we see into the spirit world (see SSB Book 1). The eido centre is the eye of the spirit. Repeated illicit sexual engagements blind the eido centre from peeping into the spiritual world. In many spiritual exercises, especially in the occult world, individuals are often advised to refrain from sexual activities during moments of spiritual vision reception. The reason is because spiritual blindness is a well-known fallout of illicit sexual engagement.

Illicit Sexual Activity Destroys Spirituality

If you want to be spiritually sound and enjoy continuous spiritual growth, avoid illicit sexual activity. Illicit sexual activities can stop the flow of the ability of God through you, and you need such divine ability (e.g. wisdom, power) to make advancement in life. Illicit sexual activities destroy one's spirituality. It can turn an individual into a reject of God. The following story illustrates this fact.

When Israel came out of Egypt in about 1447 BC, it was a nation blessed by God. Individuals and nations had tried unsuccessfully to destroy them. The powerful nation of Moab with its neighbouring country of Midian figured out that physical confrontation would never bring Israel down, but to attack their root. The Moabites knew that Israel's strength lay in its spiritual root; hence, they hired a Midianite prophet, Balaam, who had some spiritual power to place a curse on Israel (Numbers chapters 22 to 24). But because Israel's spiritual connection with God was intact, Prophet Balaam could not curse them. After several unsuccessful attempts to place a curse on Israel, Prophet Balaam exclaimed:

> *"But how can I curse those whom God has not cursed? How can I condemn those whom the Lord has not condemned?"*
>
> *(Num.23: 8 NLT).*

Being a descendant of Abraham through Midian, Abraham's son from Keturah, Balaam had knowledge of Jehovah, the God of his forefather, Abraham (Gen.25:1-4). Prophet Balaam knew one thing that would cause God to abandon His nation Israel is illicit sexual sin. Hence, the prophet counselled the Moabite and Midianite monarchs to do all they could to entice the Israelites to play harlotry with their women and idols.

Thus, the Moabites and Midianites enticed and lured Israel into illicit sexual sins. This is what is now referred to as the ***Doctrine of Balaam***. Balaam was the shrewd, money-loving, covetous prophet that gave the counsel to the Moabites and Midianites, and he paid for this crime with his life (Num.31:8,15,16).

> *"But I have a few things against you, because you have there those who hold the Doctrine of Balaam, who taught Balak to put a stumbling block before the children of Israel, to eat things sacrificed to idols, and to commit sexual immorality"*
> *(Rev.2:14 NKJV).*

As correctly predicted by Prophet Balaam, such acts provoked the anger of God against Israel, and about 24000 young Israelites perished that day. To make it worse, Zimri Salu, a clan head in Israel, brought Cozbi Zur, a daughter of a Midianite tribal chief, into his home while all Israel were mourning their loss. But Phinehas Eleazar, grandson of the High Priest Aaron, with a zeal for sexual chastity, went into the tent while Zimri was having his illicit sexual coitus with his Midianite mistress and pierced the two lovers to death with a thrust of his sword (Numbers chapter 25).

Once Phinehas did this, notice the interesting development: God instantly stopped the plaques He had sent to devour the people, and with such emotions He bestowed a special blessing on Phinehas and his descendants (Numbers chapter 25). About 20 later, the wayward Prophet Balaam was finally killed with a sword; his love of money caused him his life (Jos.13:22; 2Pet.2:15).

The lesson here is that illicit sexual sin is a tool negative spiritual forces (Satan and demons) use against the regenerated children of God. Once the regenerated man falls to such deception, he draws the anger of God. The solution is to promptly ask for God's forgiveness and flee sexual sin (1Cor.6:18).

On the other hand, another significant lesson of the Doctrine of Balaam is that a life of sexual sanctity draws God's blessing. A life committed to pursue sexual uprightness is not only envious to people and demons, but it pleases God and draws out divine blessings on the individual. That is why if you are cohabiting with a girlfriend and even have children, it is quite expedient and much pleasing to God if you will take steps to right that wrong by finding a way to officially formalise the union in marriage. Living together as boyfriend and girlfriend is sexual perversion, notwithstanding how much we try to colour and justify it.

Some laws in some nations tend to recognise boyfriend/ girlfriend cohabiting relationship as a legal sexual relationship. But such laws are made by fallen humans and will never supplant the divine requirements. Cohabiting without a proper marital tie is antagonistic to divine laws and will attract negative repercussions in the long run!

(3) Negative Impact on the Human Body

The effect of illicit sexual intercourse on the body is quite grave. Illicit sexual intercourse affects the body directly, causing untold hardship and pains. To flee from illicit sexual intercourse is the beginning of wisdom.

> *"Run away from sexual immorality [in any form, whether thought or behaviour, whether visual or written]. Every other sin that a man commits is outside the body, but the one who is sexually immoral sins against his own body" (1Cor.6:18 AMP).*

Indeed, the negative impact of illicit sexual activity on the physical body is seen in five main ways:

(a) Ill health

Sexual activity has never been free; it comes with a price. Sexually transmitted infections (STIs), some cases of impotency, cancers like cervical cancers and similar diseases are often due to illicit sexual activities. According to World Health Organisation (WHO), more than one million STIs are acquired every day worldwide; each year, there are an estimated 357 million new infections with 1 of 4 STIs: chlamydia, gonorrhoea, syphilis and trichomoniasis, and more than 500 million people are estimated to have genital infection with herpes simplex virus (HSV). More than 290 million women have a human papillomavirus (HPV) infection, and the majority of STIs have no symptoms or only mild symptoms that may not be recognized as an STI.

STIs can have serious reproductive health consequences beyond the immediate impact of the infection itself (e.g., infertility or mother-to-child transmission); STIs such as gonorrhoea and chlamydia are major causes of pelvic inflammatory disease (PID) and infertility in women.

Interestingly, the use of condoms has increasingly been promoted as the solution to the negative consequences of illicit sexual activity. Though when use correctly and consistently, condom can prevent some STDs like HIV/AIDS, yet what of the devastating impact on the mind and the spirit beings of individuals? A wise person will know that the condom alone is not a solution for the negative effects of illicit sex.

(b) Untimely death

WHO stated that STIs like herpes and syphilis can increase the risk of HIV acquisition three-fold or more, thereby increasing the mortality from HIV/AIDS. Mother-to-child transmission of STIs can result in stillbirth, neonatal death, low-birth-weight and prematurity, sepsis, pneumonia, neonatal conjunctivitis, and congenital deformities. Worldwide, over 900 000 pregnant women were infected with syphilis resulting in approximately 350 000 adverse birth outcomes including stillbirth in 2012. HPV infection causes 528 000 cases of cervical cancer and 266 000 cervical cancer deaths each year.

Sexual intercourse is never free when engaged illicitly. It can hasten your death and destroy your dreams. An individual who is sexually disciplined has a brighter prospect of long life than one with an unbridled carnal sexual activity.

(c) Family destruction

Illicit sexual activity breeds distrust which ultimately destroys the family. The aftermaths of such family disunity is untold negative impacts on both partners, especially on the children. Research studies have consistently shown that a child being raised up jointly by a mother and a father has a higher rate of success than a child from a single parenthood. Single parenthood itself puts undue strain on the single parent, and many such single parents end up developing mental breakdowns.

(d) Social disarray

Families are the basic building units of any society. Hence, destruction of family units ultimately leads to the destruction of the values and norms of the society. Such destruction often throws the society into disarray. Sexual pervasion does no good to any society. It explains why the fall of virtually all previous empires was preceded by sexual pervasion. Today, history seems to be repeating itself. The American empire appears to be steadily and progressively crumbling as sexual perversion infiltrates its environments and weakens its foundation.

(e) Generational impact

Sadly, the evil of illicit sexual intercourse does not stop with the couples involved; it passes unto the children and generations unborn. A good example of the generational impact of illicit sex is the story of Reuben, the firstborn of the Patriarch Jacob. Rueben, as the firstborn son, was entitled to double portion blessings; that is, he was meant to produce two tribes that would join the other tribes to form the nation of Israel (see Deu.21:15-17). In addition, the descendants of Reuben would be the ones to produce rulers in Israel, a kingship dynasty through which the Promised Messiah would have been born. But this was not to be so. Reuben lost all of these birth-right privileges due to an unbridled sexual life.

The Consequence of Rueben's Sexual Misconduct

In his youth, Reuben became undisciplined and had illicit sexual relationships with one of his father's concubines, Bilhah (Gen.35:22). As a result of this sexual misconduct, Rueben and his descendants lost their divine right for kingship. That is, the sexual misconduct cost Rueben's tribe the kingship, which passed on to a more morally disciplined Joseph and his descendants.

> *"The oldest son of Israel was Reuben, but since he dishonoured his father by sleeping with one of his father's wives, his birthright was given to his half-brother, Joseph. So the official genealogy doesn't name Reuben as the oldest son" (1Chr.5:1 TLB).*

Thus, Joseph took the firstborn birthright and produced two tribes in Israel – Ephraim and Manasseh. By having the birthright, the tribes of Joseph should have produced a dynasty of kings; unfortunately, no descendant from Joseph's tribes could meet up the requirements for kingship, which subsequently passed onto David of the tribe of Judah.

> *"Though Judah prevailed over his brothers, and from him came the leader [David] [and eventually the Messiah], yet the birthright was Joseph's—" (1Chr.5:2 AMP).*

The story of Reuben was, indeed, a sad one. It is a tale of what an individual can miss out just by a moment of sexual 'fun'; the fun always turns to bitterness when it is of illicit sex, and such bitterness usually propagates through descendants yet unborn. Reuben and his descendants missed the eternal genealogy of producing the Messiah!

The Wasteful Destiny of Samson

Another sad story of the of illicit sexual union is the life of Samson. Samson was among the seven people (Ishmael, Isaac, Samson, Solomon, Josiah, John, Jesus) mentioned in the Scriptures whose births and names were foretold before they were born or mentioned just at birth by God Himself (Gen.16:11; 17:19; Judg.13; 2Sam.12:25; 1Kin.13:2; Luk.1:13; Mat.1:21). That is, Samson's life purpose was quite explicit even before he was born. Sadly, engagement in unhealthy sexual behaviour cut short the fulfilment of such grandiose destiny.

Samson was born to wipe off the Philistines, Israel's greatest enemies, and establish Israel as a unified nation that would be the envy of the then known world. However, Samson's uncontrolled erotic love never allowed him to rise to his calling. He fell into an unhealthy sexual union with Delilah. He who was born a ruler, died as a blind captive in a foreign prison. What a wasteful destiny! What a tragedy of life!

***Fig.*18: Samson fell into an unhealthy sexual union with Delilah. He who was born a ruler, died as a blind captive in a foreign prison. What a tragedy of life!**

The Sad Story of Solomon

About a century after the fall of Samson, Solomon suffered similar grave loss due to indiscipline sexual life. Solomon was named at birth by God as Jedidiah, which means the 'beloved of Jehovah' (2Sam.12:25), the God of the universe. He was born as the undisputed heir apparent, even though there were many others with more qualified claims to the throne. That is, the kingship was delivered to him in a platter of gold by God Himself. He was meant to expand his father's kingdom into an empire and solidify it.

To fulfil his purpose, Solomon was equipped with unrivalled wisdom and prosperity that knew no bounds. But like Samson, he was sexually undisciplined. Instead of thinking of expansion, he was rather thinking of how to enter into more and more sexual relationships with women from all around the neighbouring nations. Instead of thinking of surpassing the greatness of Egypt (the then world superpower), which he could have easily achieved, he was talking of more marital unions. He made a history by having one thousand women as sexual partners! What was he doing with all these wives and concubines?

What a waste of time, energy, and resources! His foreign wives succeeded in turning him from the worship of the God of his fathers. Solomon, the beloved of Jehovah, became a builder of shrines for heathen gods. God forbid that such should ever happen again! And so, Solomon died a wretched man, losing 83.33 per cent of his kingdom to his arch-rival, Jeroboam (1 Kings Chapters 11 and 12).

His foreign wives succeeded in turning him from the worship of the God of his fathers. Solomon, 'the beloved of Jehovah,' became a builder of shrines for heathen gods. What a waste of time, energy, and resources!

***Fig*.19: Solomon the son David was equipped with unrivalled divine wisdom and prosperity that knew no bounds. But he was sexually undisciplined, having one thousand women as sexual partners, who led him away from God into idolatry that destroyed his kingship!**

WARNING FOR US ALL

Indeed, no one should ever underrate the mighty force of erotic love. When used negatively, it has brought strong men down and humiliated great minds; it has destroyed the lives of many women and has caused great monarchs to abdicate their thrones.

Many lives and properties have been wasted and destinies have been shattered because of unhealthy sexual unions. These are warnings for us all!

CHAPTER 45
HOW TO DISCIPLINE YOUR SEXUAL LIFE

IGNORANCE IS A GRAVE DISEASE; however, it is not an excuse. Ignorance of the truth that sexual drive can be put into other productive uses beside physical sexual intercourse is the major cause of dissipation and wastage of this vital force of life. Many young people are ignorant of the fact that a great sexual drive is a blessing for high level of productivity. Great creative achievers in all fields are usually blessed with great libido.

However, these achievers have learnt how to turn this great force in them into creativity, thereby shining forth in their chosen fields. Leonardo da Vinci, Thomas Edison, Franklin Roosevelt, Michael Jackson, Andrew Carnegie, Donald Trump are notable achievers in their various fields with great libido. How were these achievers able to harness their strong sexual drive into notable achievements? The followings summarise what they did:

(1) NEVER SUPPRESS SEXUAL DRIVE

Sexual drive is among the strongest desires that can be evoked in a man. Because of the abuse of such inward force in its expression, many religious fellows and moralists have advocated that sexual desire be suppressed or be killed outright; they tend to perceive sexual drive as a green snake in a green field. To the chagrin of such individuals, the more they try to annihilate sexual desire in them, the more it rears up its head, pulling many of them down into despicable acts that, once made public, bring great shame, regrets, and pains.

Nonetheless, what we should all know is that humans are sexual organisms. The sexual drive, in its natural state, is not evil. It is a blessing by the Creator that can be put into productive venture. Sexual drive is like a dam, which can be kept in check as long as the water has not yet reached the brim. However, unless the water finds an outlet, it soon reaches the brim and breaks down the walls of the dam, forcing an outlet. That is what happens when a man tries to suppress or kill sexual drive. He may succeed for a time, but soon the drive will force an outlet that can become detrimental. That explains the various cases of sexual misconducts commonly found among religious persons and moralists that profess celibacy.

The lesson here is never attempt to suppress or kill sexual drive. Rather learn how you can harness its force for productivity.

(2) COMMITMENT TO A LIFE PURPOSE

Harnessing of sexual energy starts with having a specific purpose or goal for pursuit. Do you have a vision? If you do, your vision will spell out your purpose. Does the purpose evoke passion in you? When you wake up each morning do you feel passionate about that purpose? Where are you heading in your studies, career, business, family, and spiritual life? Do you have specific goals well written out for each of these areas of your life? If you do, then you are on to a good start in harnessing your sexual energy.

Dissipation of sexual energy is avoided when an individual has a course in life to which he is committed. If there is nothing you live for, you won't have an object to direct your embodied energy. Indeed, if you look around your neighbourhood, you'll realise that many individuals who waste their sexual energy are people who are not committed to something in life. Finding a course of action and committing your time, energy, and resources unreservedly into it is the sure way to harness one's sexual energy.

(3) USE SEXUAL DRIVE TO TRIGGER CREATIVE IMAGINATION

As you move about your daily activities, sexual desire will start to build up. What arouses sexual feeling? Science is yet to completely elucidate the exact mechanism by which sexual drive is aroused. Sexual drive is the presence of the erotic love in humans, and erotic love is a deposit in the heart of a man. That is, erotic love is not just biological, it arises from the heart and triggered by mental and biological factors. Therefore, just the study of the biology of sexuality will not give the full answers about sexual drive.

In general, three groups of factors have been associated with arousal of sexual desire:

• *Hormonal factors:*

A number of chemicals called hormones have been associated with sexual drive. The four main hormones implicated in sexual drive are testosterone, oestrogen, progesterone, and oxytocin, and they are commonly referred to as sex hormones. The most dramatic is testosterone, which is secreted mostly in the testicles in men and ovaries in women. The testosterone is more abundant in males, hence, often referred to as male hormone. Oestrogen is more abundant in females than males and is believed to be less aggressive in arousing sexual drive than testosterone. Also, it has been found that oxytocin stimulates sexual desires in females, and the oxytocin levels in women are at their highest during sexual activity. The effect of oxytocin on male sexual desire is still ambiguous.

The exact mechanism by which these sex hormones cause sexual arousal is not known. Possibly, they are metabolised into other products like dopamine, and as these metabolic products increase, sexual drive is increased proportionally. What informed this idea are the levels of dopamine and prolactin found in the blood after an orgasm. When orgasm occurs during sexual coitus in men and women, dopamine levels have been found to fall dramatically, more quickly in men and more gradually in women. In addition, both men and women experience prolactin increase after orgasm. Women naturally have more prolactin than men, so the effect of prolactin spike after orgasm is more pronounced in men than in women.

The fall in dopamine and the increase in prolactin are believed to have some explanation with the temporal fall in sexual drive that occurs after an orgasm. The dramatic fall of dopamine and the sharp rise in prolactin are believed to be the reason why a man suddenly loses sexual drive immediately after orgasm. On the other hand, the slow decline of dopamine and the relative rise of prolactin level is believed to explain why women have only slight loss (sometimes none at all) of their sexual drive after they reach orgasm.

This is what we know scientifically for now; tomorrow we may know better as more research works progress. But note that both Dopamine and Prolactin are hormones that are produced naturally in the body before, during, after, and independent of coitus.

A woman's desire for sex is most often correlated with her menstrual cycle, with many women experiencing a heightened sexual desire in the several days immediately before ovulation, which is her peak fertility period that normally occurs two days before until two days after the ovulation. This period has been associated with changes in a woman's testosterone levels. Testosterone levels have a direct impact on a woman's interest in sex. Testosterone levels rise gradually from about the 24th day of a woman's menstrual cycle until ovulation at about the 14th day of the next cycle, and during this period the woman's desire for sex increases consistently. The 13th day is generally the day with the highest testosterone levels. In the week following ovulation, the testosterone level is the lowest and as a result, women will experience less interest in sex.

Also, during the week following ovulation, progesterone levels increase, resulting in a woman experiencing difficulty achieving orgasm. Although the last days of the menstrual cycle are marked by a constant testosterone level, women's libido may boost as a result of the thickening of the uterine lining which stimulates nerve endings and makes a woman feel aroused. Also, during these days, estrogen levels also decline, resulting in a decrease of natural lubrication of the vagina.

For men, no cyclical rhythm has been associated with testosterone. What is generally known in the medical world is that a low testosterone may mean low sexual drive, and vice versa. However, many people with low testosterone but high sexual drive have been found. The often quoted idea that the levels of testosterone start to decline from late teenage is also being disputed because there are many men who have strong sexual drives all through their lives into their late 80s. The truth remains that hormonal factors are not alone in arousing sexual drive.

• *Genetic factor*

Another area of interest in the study of sexuality in humans is the genetic factor. Some families tend to have stronger sexual drives than others. Interestingly, even within a specified family, some members tend to have higher sexual drives than other members of the same family. Is there a gene that codes for sexuality? This is also not well known scientifically.

The gay movement has been trying but unsuccessfully to prove that homosexuality is genetic and hereditary, but science is far from confirming this. The truth remains that porneia (fornication), moichao (adultery), pornos (prostitution/pornography), arsenokoites (homosexuality), or akatharsia (sexual uncleanness like bestiality) is a choice and not hereditary. One chooses his sexual orientation, but God who created humans have spelt out clearly what is acceptable and what is not, and will definitely bring every deviation to divine judgment at His own time.

• *Environment Factors*

Your environment here refers to all the external conditions that impinge directly or indirectly on you. It includes family upbringing, peer pressure, religious belief, school system, etc. It is a well-known fact that all these factors play a major role in sexual drive. Interestingly, these factors impact on sexual drive through their effect on the mind and the heart. A negative impact is when an environmental factor attempts to stifle sexual drive or when it encourages unbridled physical coitus. As mentioned above, to stifle or kill sexual drive only results in harmful effects on the individual while to leave sexual drive to run wild results in wastage of the vital energy.

In today's world, various environmental factors encourage unbridled sex. Pornography is everywhere and readily available, causing many people to lower their moral virtues. But researched works pouring in have consistently been showing the negative effects of porn on the sex drive of young people. Studies show that more and more men are suffering from 'sexual anorexia' and are unable to get erections because of addiction to internet porn.

The Negative Effect of Internet Pornography

For instance, a survey of 28000 internet porn users found that many Italian males started an 'excessive consumption' of porn sites as early as 14 years old. After daily use in their early to mid-20s, they become inured to 'even the most violent' images. The effects of developing their sexuality largely divorced from real-life relationships are gradual and devastating. 'It starts with lower reactions to porn sites, then there is a general drop in libido and in the end it becomes impossible to get an erection,' Carlo Foresta, head of the Italian Society of Andrology and Sexual Medicine (SIAMS), told reporters. However, the condition is not irreversible and a proper recovery is possible.

Apparently, this study would indicate that testosterone alone is not responsible for the male sex drive as the participants in this study were young and healthy with presumably normal hormone levels. It attests to the influence of environmental factors on sexual drive. Environmental factors do not affect just the body, they also influence the mind (soul) and the heart of the spirit man, which is the seat of all the four kinds of love, including the erotic love. A dysfunction of the mind and the heart will thus produce negative effect on one's sexuality.

(4) COMMIT TO A LIFE OF SEXUAL DISCIPLINE

Sexual energy keeps you keen and interested in life. It helps spur you on to greater achievements if channelled correctly. To maintain and build on strength, you will need to commit to a life of sexual discipline. One sure way people try to build discipline is by preventing their weaknesses. The following are veritable steps to handling your weakness:

- ***Become conscious of them***

Don't pretend the weaknesses aren't there. Acknowledge their presence.

- ***Know the costs of the weaknesses***

Always bear in mind what the dire consequences that can result by yielding to the weaknesses. Many young fellows couldn't maintain sexual chastity because of ignorance of the consequences that come with unbridled sex life and ignorance of the power of sexual energy that can positively change their lives and their unborn children. Let the fear of the consequences of weakness indulgence be the beginning of your wisdom.

- ***Set gate-keepers to checkmate them***

Billy Graham (1918-2018) is a household name around the world. He was an American evangelist, believed to have reached wider audience across the globe in the twentieth century than any other human in any field. Interestingly, Evangelist Graham recognised his three weaknesses and put men in charge of these three areas, which he coined 3G – glory, gold, and girls.

Successful people often put boundaries around them to demarcate what they should and shouldn't do. For instance, a male doctor whose weakness is sexual misconduct should possibly not employ a female secretary and should keep chaperon whenever he attends to female patients. Be wise and set boundaries around you.

• *Avoid a luring environment*

Also, during moment of sexual tension, by all means avoid an environment that will lure you into physical coitus. Never allow any temptation to dissipate this vital sexual energy in you. Always remember the negative consequences that follow and the blessings that come with positive sexual harnessing.

• *Interact with the greater*

No matter the type and category of your weakness, there are men and women who have similar weaknesses but have grown above them. Associating with such great minds is a sure rapid way to outgrow your weakness. That is one reason why mentorship is crucial to our success.

• *Feed on the Word of God*

The Word of God is the food for the human spirit. The manual of life, the Bible, carries the Word of God. As you feed on it, you will be empowered to grow above your weakness and be built up. In addition, the power (anointing) of the Spirit of God that is present in the Word of God, can break every mistake and any other challenge that might confront you as you run with your genuine vision. Prayer and fasting should be a normal way of life. Great spiritually minded individuals have scheduled prayer/fasting moments during which time they discipline their body and allow their spirit and soul to have fellowship with the Creator God, the Ultimate Source of success. If you do likewise, you'll grow up spiritually and mentally strong with new physical vivacity.

CHAPTER 46
THREE PRACTICAL WAYS TO HARNESS SEXUAL ENERGY FOR PRODUCTIVITY

THE FOLLOWINGS ARE THREE PRACTICAL ways on how to harness the mighty sexual energy:

(1) STIMULATE YOUR MIND WITH THE SEXUAL ENERGY

To harness the mighty sexual drive, the sexual energy must be applied to stimulate the mind into creative imagination. To achieve this, the first step to take is to avoid environmental factors that negatively affect sexual drive. Avoid pornography. Keep off from porneia, moichalis, pornos, arsenokoites, or akatharsia. They kill the sexual drive. If you are married, stick to your spouse.

Then, when sexual tension mounts, instead of running to look for a sexual partner or engage in masturbation, you purposefully turn your attention to a specific, passionate, non-sexual activity. In other words, let your mind dwell on that particular passionate activity of your life at such moment of sexual tension. For example, if you are a writer, focus your attention on a topic of passion, and begin to write.

As sexual tension mounts, some may want to take a short walk, allowing their mind to dwell on their passionate work. If you are a laboratory scientist, this is the time to let your mind to go wild searching for solutions to the laboratory problems. If you are a musician, it is this time of sexual tension that you let your mind search around for creative tunes. If your interest is to build spiritual strength, take your Bible and speak its promises to your life and work. This applies to any area of endeavour.

What you are doing is practising mind stimulation. This is the Level 2 of the Five Steps to Creativity (see page 109). One of the strongest stimulants of the mind is the desire for love, and of the four kinds of love, eros is the most potent stimulant of the mind. By wilfully transferring your focus from physical coitus to a passionate work in the height of sexual tension, you are stimulating your mind with the sexual drive.

However, at the initial stage of practising this mind stimulation with the sexual energy, it will be a bit of a struggle to master the process of mind stimulation if the individual is one who has been living all his life having sexual coitus at any moment of sexual tension. But as he keeps at it and refuses to be give up trying, even if he fails the first few attempts, he will begin to see positive results and will start experiencing a new found energy and creativity unknown to him before. That is the power of sexual harness, which some refer to as ***sexual transmutation***.

(2) LEARN TO ISSUE COMMAND

If the sexual tension for illicit sexual gratification appears to be overwhelming and out of control, speak to your body, command it to obey you and it will be quiet. If you are regenerated in Christ, use the Name of Jesus to command quietness to your body, mind, and spirit. This process of speaking to your body is an essential aspect of the sexual energy harness. It is known in psychology as Autosuggestion (see page 82), and it is part of the Level 2 of the Five Steps to Creativity.

I stumbled at this knowledge in my late teen age. As I was walking down the busy Mile One Market, Diobu, Port Harcourt in 1989, sexual tension started mounting in me that afternoon. I tried to let my mind dwell on some Biblical promises, but my mind was not concentrating. Out of frustration, I blurted out, "*I command you, sexual tension, to be quiet within me now, and peace be still in Jesus Name.*" I was surprised to see that as soon as the words went out of my mouth, the tension started to wane off. I stood there by the roadside and contemplated on what had just happened. 'So I can control it with my tongue!' I observed. That was new to me then. From thence, I have learnt the use of my mouth in harnessing sexual energy.

(3) RECOIL FROM DISTRACTIONS

As you focus your sexual tension on your work of passion and repeatedly speak to your body, mind, and spirit, gradually the tension will start to cool off, and with it will spark off a new sense of zest, passion, energy, and inspiration you might not have known before. You'll be surprised how your mind will easily slip into a creative mood and your spirit will swim in inspiration. At this stage, intelligent people recoil from all forms of distractions and focus their energy on their assignment.

Metaphorically, at this stage you are 'making love with your assignment.' If it is an assignment of great interest, you'll see a high level of dedication and speed in the pursuit of the assignment. At this stage, your mind and spirit, if aligned properly, enter the realm of inspiration. It is the stage of creative imagination. It is the stage when the individual begins to relate with the subconscious world of imagination, and may even enter the spiritual realm of creativity. To meet up with the speed of creative outflow, some individuals will start to jot down all the important points as they rapidly flow out. In other words, keep pen and paper handy!

Section 4 (B)

The Force of Phileo Love

CHAPTER 47
THREE CATEGORIES OF PHILEO LOVE

PHILEO IS AN EXPRESSION OF kind affection towards a person or an object. Simply put, phileo is love for companionship. It occurs many times and in various forms in the Bible. Generally, Phileo love can be grouped into three categories:

(1) PHILOS GROUP

Philos refers to a friend or bond of affectionate friendship. It occurs 29 times in the New Testament Scriptures. It is a mutual respect or consideration between two people.

Three types of Philos are known:

(a) Philia

This is a bond of affection between two people of equal status. The two equal people are called friends. Thus, philia is love between friends. It often involves the feelings of loyalty among friends, camaraderie among team mates, and the sense of sacrifice for the sake of the friendship bond of love. It occurs once in the New Testament Scriptures (James 4 verse 4). The love that existed between David and Jonathan was a good example of Philia (1Sam.18:1-4).

(b) Philostorgos

This is also called Consanguineal Philos, and it refers to the kinship love or the mutual respect between family members such as the bond of love between parents and their offspring, between grandparents, nephews, aunts, uncles, etc. Philostorgos is sometimes just shortened as **Storgos** or **Storge**. Some people think that storgos is a completely different category of love, but a closer study of it shows that it is actually a form of Philos, however, in this case it exists among family members. It is a friendship of love between family members. In the Scriptures, it is used in Romans 12 verse 10.

(c) Philotheos

This is also known as Divine Philos or Theophilos (also spelt as Theophilus), and it refers to the mutual love between the Heavenly Father and His children. In other words, it is a bond of friendship between the Father God and His children. It is an expression of the fatherhood love of God for His children.

Jesus' prayer outline, popularly known as the Lord's Prayer that He taught His disciples, starts with "Our Father in Heaven" (Mat.6:9 HCSB). What Jesus was teaching is that God is not just a Creator, but also a Father, who seeks for a bond of mutual love with His children. That is the Theophilos. The second epistle of Paul to Timothy refers to children of God with divine philos in their hearts as "lovers [philotheos] of God" (2Tim.3:4 KJV).

Abraham enjoyed that level of affection [philotheos] with God. It was a mutual affection of trust.

"And the Lord said, Shall I hide from Abraham that thing which I do; seeing that Abraham shall surely become a great and mighty nation, and all the nations of the earth shall be blessed in him? For I know him, that he will command his children and his household after him, and they shall keep the way of the Lord, to do justice and judgment; that the Lord may bring upon Abraham that which he hath spoken of him" (Gen.18:17-19 KJV).

In turn Abraham trusted in God and he was called the Friend of God:

"And the Scripture was fulfilled which says, "Abraham believed God, and it was accounted to him for righteousness." And he was called the friend [philos] of God" (Jam.2:23 NKJV).

Thus, theophilos is a mutual affectionate friendship between two individuals, Father God and man.

(2) PHILAGATHOS

Philagathos is love for good things of life. It is the desire to identify with anything good. Human nature is such that we are attracted to beauty, pleasure, and success. We don't want to be associated with ugliness, pains, and failure. That desire for associating with a perceived beauty, pleasure, and success is a form of phileo known as Philagathos.

Note that Philagathos is different from prokopean love. Whereas Prokope is a drive to make progress in life, Philagathos is a drive to be identified or be seen with an already known success, beauty or pleasure. That is, an individual with Prokopean love desires to be the object of success while Philagathos does not want to be the success but rather wants to be identified with the individual who is successful.

Philagathos is most especially expressed by the female gender. Most women have a natural predilection to ravel and bathe in the streams and euphoria of success, beauty, and pleasure of others. When we were young kids, we used to make boast of any family member perceived to be successful. That is Philagathos; it is an innate drive in man to be associated with success. The Scriptures refer to an individual who expresses Philagathos as "a lover of good men" (Tit.1:8 KJV).

(3) PHILOXENOS

Philoxenos is the drive to contribute positively to the welfare of others in the society. Simply put, it is the love for the welfare of others, a drive to make the society better; Titus chapter 1 verse 8 refers to it as love for hospitality. Philoxenos is now known in English language as Philanthropy.

The term philanthropy is derived from two Greek terms *philos*, which simply means 'loving or friendship' and *anthropos*, which means 'human being.' Thus, Philoxenos or Philanthropy is simply the love to provide care for a fellow human.

ABNORMAL DISPLAY OF PHILEO

Phileo love is one that is commonly abused. The fallen nature of man has subverted the pure phileo that God deposited in man at creation. Hence, various abnormal displays of phileo are seen, which include:

(a) Philargyros
This is covetousness, which is unlawful crave for what is not yours (2Tim.3:2).

(b) Philautos

This is selfishness or lover of own self without consideration for others (2Tim.3:2).

(c) Philedonos

This is lust or excessive love for pleasures or fun beyond the confines of an acceptable standard of behaviour (2Tim.3:4). Philedonic love will prefer good times to the worship of God; Philedonic individuals love fun far more than the love for God. That is, philedonic individuals are lustful and often engage in erotic flirtations. Philodonos is an abuse of philos and erotica.

Origin of Abnormal Phileo

When God created man, He deposited love in the heart of the spirit man, among which is Phileo. Sadly, the Fall of Man was what adulterated the nature of man so that instead of the pure deposits of phileo and other forms of love, the heart of man now expresses abnormal love patterns such as Philargyros, Philautos, and Philedonos

The solution for an abnormal phileo is to make a decision not to continue in such engagements and become regenerated in Christ.

Chapter 48
The Force of Phileo Love

Phileo, like all other forms of love, is one of the deposits in the heart of man at creation. It is God that created man and deposited phileo love in the human heart. The essence of such love deposit is to enrich the life of man and make his pursuits colourful and grandiose. However, the Fall of man in the Garden of Eden weakened the force of love in man. Nonetheless, we can still see the power of love in display when an individual has learnt to utilise it. Below is a brief discussion of the power of the various forms of phileo love.

THE FORCE OF PHILAGATHOS

Expression of Philagathic love seems to be most common with the female folk. Along with the force of Erotic love, the force of Philagathos is known to drive a man into success. The force of Philagathic love is behind the common saying: 'behind every successful man is a woman.' The desire of a man to give his spouse a better life has driven many a man into success.

THE FORCE OF PHILIA

Philia, which is the philosic love among friends, is a known source of healthy competition. A man whose friend is building some degree of success will be stimulated to do likewise. Indeed, many men have been lifted from despondency and frustration by developing friendship with an individual of a higher calibre. Discipline, dedication, and sacrifice, which are the qualities for true and lasting success, have been instilled into many individuals through the power of Philiac association.

Reading this book is a way of philosic association with the author and the principles in them, and these have the power to lift your thought life to higher terrestrial for higher success. In fact, great achievers do not underrate the power of association, hence, they chose who should be their friends and what books to study. Friendship is by choice and not by force. Spending money, energy and time to read stories of havocs on the pages of newspapers often do not edify; great achievers do not spend their time, energy and resources in such frivolities. Life on earth is short, and wise people invest their time, energy, and resources rather than wasting them. By associating with great minds, a man learns how to build on the habits that make for great success.

BLOOD THICKER THAN WATER: THE FORCE OF PHILOSTORGOS

From another angle, philos among family members is a strong bond of union. It is often said, 'blood is thicker than water,' which is true, partly due to the consanguineal philos among family relatives.

The Story of Grandma Josephine

An event happened in the year 2000 in a hospital that I worked in. It was about Ms. Josephine. She was aged 76, and was admitted for complications of diabetes and hypertension. She was on admission for about one month, but her conditions were not improving. Mr. Joe was her son, apparently her favourite child. But the challenge was that Joe, who was a businessman, was not in the country. Grandma Josephine always talked fondly of Joe, requesting that he should be contacted immediately. Joe was contacted, and he cancelled all other engagements to return to the country to see his mum, who by now had lapsed into a coma.

The coma lasted for almost a week as the medical team battled to save her life. Suddenly, one morning Grandma Josephine opened her eyes and whispered that her son Joe would be coming soon and she would see him. That sudden recovery baffled everyone. Truly, Joe arrived that same day. Went to the bedside of Grandma Josephine. Even though she was weak and frail, but you could see an elation and twinkles in the eyes of Grandma Josephine.

Like the Biblical patriarchs, Grandma Josephine blessed Joe and other family members, and then gave up the ghost in the hands of her son, Joe. What a sight! It was the tale of the power of the human spirit!

It was apparent that Grandma Josephine's desire to see her beloved son, Joe, was what kept her alive. That was the force of Consanguineal Philos or Philostorgos.

FORCE OF PHILOTHEOS

God seeks for friendship with man, whom He has made in His image and likeness. It is like a father who, not only wants to make decisions that will guard and guide his children into success, but also wants to enjoy a bond of friendship, a mutual respect with them. Such mutual love is the theophilos or philotheos. That was what Abraham enjoyed and regenerated individuals can enjoy that too.

Imagine being a friend of God. That would allow you into the secrets of God! Imagine what such privilege can do in the life of a man! Sadly, not every regenerated individual enjoys divine philos. That is, not all God's children enjoy theophilos. Many of God's children only practise agape love which, indeed, is a powerful force that can lift any man to as far as he can envision and muster faith. However, much more is divine philos, which allows you into divine secrets that can open a man to another realm of existence, a realm where mortality is swallowed up by divinity. It is a realm where you are practically a god on earth in which what you say holds.

As a friend of God, you will share in the majesty of divinity just as true friends share oneness. God is not just the Creator but also the Supreme King of the universe. By becoming His friend, you share in the majesty of divine royalty. Since kings rule by words, in the same way by having divine philos, your words will rule both the spiritual and physical worlds, what you decree is what will be established. That is the force of theophilos or philotheos.

In the Scriptures, besides Abraham, a number of individuals also enjoyed divine philos. Moses, Joshua, David, and Paul all radiated theophilos.

> *"The Lord spoke with Moses face to face, just as a man speaks with his friend" (Exo.33:11 HCSB).*

> *David was called 'a man after God's heart' (1Sam.13:14).*

> *"After removing Saul, he made David their king. God testified concerning him: 'I have found David son of Jesse, a man after my own heart; he will do everything I want him to do'"*
> *(Act.13:22 NIV).*

How does one become a Friend of God? Two processes are involved: regeneration and trust. Regeneration is the process of new birth in Christ Jesus that transforms a man into a child of God (see SSB Book 5), while trust is simply complete faith in God. Trust in God means you are willing to do anything He tells you. When you are wrong, you own up to that and not become defensive. A good example was King David. He had implicit trust in Jehovah. He was ready to follow every divine instruction. When he made mistakes like every other mortal, he genuinely repented. His heart panted after God. This was completely opposite to the lifestyle of his predecessor, King Saul.

King Saul was more interested with the encomiums and accolades of men. He was a king who loved to be politically correct even when he knew his stand was against divine instruction. How then could mutual trust exist between him and God? At the end, God regretted ever making him king (1Sam.15:11). Note that by human standards, King Saul appeared, on the surface, more like a humane monarch than King David. After all, before he was disposed from his kingship, he never committed adultery and murder like King David. But God looked into the heart. He knew our frames that we are humans. He looked for a heart that would be ready to trust him completely. That was the advantage of David.

Trust is earned. It is something that develops in the course of a relationship. If we want to enjoy theophilos, we need to earn God's trust. This starts with a relationship: Father-son relationship, which is only possible through the process of regeneration in Christ. At regeneration, you'll become a New Creature, a child of God, following which you'll need to grow to know your privileges, rights, and responsibilities in God. As you commit to them, you will grow in theophilos love towards God.

FORCE OF PHILOXENOS (PHILANTHROPY)

In each nation, not everyone attains the same level of success. In every society, there are classes. Man has propounded and practised a number of systems of governance to address such inequalities that exist in the classes of humanity. Capitalism, communism, fascism, socialism and other political systems are systems invented to eradicate inequality and establish an egalitarian society. However, no matter how much we try, socioeconomic classes and inequalities persist. No one system has the solution to all human maladies; each system has its strengths and weaknesses.

With such a reality, the force of philoxenic love (often known as philanthropy) is a veritable avenue of reaching out to the weak and the less endowed. Philanthropy is a way of allowing energy and resources to flow among the ranks and classes in a society. Through philanthropy, we express our common human heritage, our love for fellow humans.

The Story of University of Chicago Formation

Genuine philanthropy releases happiness for both the giver and the recipient of the philanthropic love. A good point was the founding of the University of Chicago in 1889 through the philanthropic gesture of John D. Rockefeller. Chernow (1998) aptly captured the mood of the occasion in his book, *Titan – the Life of John D. Rockefeller.* He wrote:

> *"After all these excruciating dilatory tactics, the campaign for a Chicago college or university reached a surprisingly swift climax on a clear spring morning in May 1889.*
>
> *"After breakfast, the two men [Rockefeller and Frederick T. Gates] strolled to and fro before the Rockefeller house on Fifty-Fourth Street. After months of stalling, Rockefeller said he was ready to provide 400000 USD – considerably short of the figure he had quoted to Harper six months before. When Gates rejected this as insufficient, Rockefeller raised the ante to 500000 USD. Once again, Gates spurned the offer, citing the advantages of Rockefeller contributing the majority of the money. Gates held out for a stunning 600000 USD contribution – equal to 9.5 million USD today [1998] – which was predicated upon another 400000 USD being raised from other sources. Eager to commit this historic pledge to paper, they went down to Rockefeller's office where he put his promise in writing.*

"The next day, clutching this paper, Gates rose before the Baptists in the Tremont Temple in Boston. Rumours had circulated about the gift, creating a tingling mood of expectation. 'I hold in my hand,' Gates thundered, 'a letter from our great patron of education, Mr. John D. Rockefeller.' A groundswell of cheers surged from the floor. 'A letter in which, on the basis of the resolutions adopted by our board, he promises that he will give six hundred thousand dollars–' At this point, pandemonium erupted, with clergymen waving their handkerchiefs, whistling, and applauding. Driven to ecstasy by this earthly bounty, one minister on the podium flung his hat heavenward, while another theologian sprang to his feet and praised 'the coming to the front of such a princely giver... It is the Lord's day...As an American, a Baptist, and a Christian I rejoice in this consummation. God has kept Chicago for us; I wonder at his patience.' On this note, the ecstatic holy men rose up to offer a lusty rendition of 'Praise God from Whom All Blessings Flow.' Overnight, for all his infamy in business, Rockefeller wore a golden nimbus in the eyes of many Baptists" (Chernow, 1998: Titan – The Life of John D. Rockefeller, pages 312, 313).

Indeed, *"it is more blessed to give than to receive"* (Act.20:35 KJV), because the philanthropic gift brings untold happiness and blessings to the giver and great relief to the recipient. Undeniably, you won't know the other side of bliss if you don't engage in philoxenic love. The practice of it destroys selfishness and opens the individual up to the benevolence of humanity. God, Himself, is a great giver, and He wants us to give in order to enrich our lives.

If there is one law of prosperity that a man shouldn't forget is the Law of Seedtime and Harvest. What you give multiplies back to you. The Scriptures enjoin:

"Cast your bread upon the waters, for you will find it after many days" (Ecc.11:1 NKJV).

The words of the Master Jesus succinctly put this:

> *"Give, and it will be given to you: good measure, pressed down, shaken together, and running over will be put into your bosom. For with the same measure that you use, it will be measured back to you" (Luk.6:38 NKJV).*

Section 4 (C)

The Force of Prokopean Love

Chapter 49
The Features of Prokopean Love

PROKOPEAN LOVE IS LOVE FOR progress or advancement in life. Prokopean is from the Greek word *prokopé*, which literally means: 'advancement by chopping down whatever impedes progress.' Prokope occurs 3 times in 3 verses in the New Testament Bible (Phi.1:12, 25; 1Tim.4:15).

Prokope is also known as Eudoo in the New Testament Bible. Eudoo, which is a Greek term that means 'prosperous and expeditious journey,' occurs four times in 3 verses in the New Testament (Rom.1:10, 1Cor.16:2, and 3Joh.1:2). The traditional Greek term for *prokopé* or *eudoo* is *epitychia*, which literally means a desire for success.

ORIGIN OF PROKOPEAN LOVE

When God created the human spirit, He deposited love, which includes the prokopean love, in the heart of the human spirit. In fact, speaking under divine inspiration, Apostle John spelt this thought very clearly in his epistle to Gaius, possibly a leader in the early Church:

> *"Beloved, I wish above all things that thou mayest prosper [euodoō] and be in health, even as thy soul prospereth [euodoō]"*
> *(3Joh.1:2 KJV).*

Note it is God's utmost desire that we function maximally by progressively moving from one level of success to the other. That is growth, which is a characteristic of humans. We are designed for endless progress. That is how God created humans to function.

The desire to seek for a better life is innate in all humans. It is the yearning of the heart of man for advancement. When a child is born, the expected desire is that he will not remain a baby but will grow through the various phases of infanthood and adolescence into adulthood. It is the desire of all parents that their children will become more successful than they are. Such a desire is the expression of the deposited prokopean love in the heart of the spirit man.

Life has never been kind to those individuals who attempted to stifle this voice of their spirit man crying for advancement. History has consistently shown that individuals who attempt to asphyxiate or smother this voice ended up living a miserable life.

The human spirit is a progressive spirit. God created the earth in a raw form. In the trees, God buries wood for furniture, in the sand is hidden beautiful glasses, in the animal skin is hidden clothing fabrics, etc. Through the didactic power of the human spirit and the mind, humans can convert the earth's raw materials into finished products for his survival and pleasure. For instance, God created the earth and buried in it crude ores such as petroleum. Extracted petroleum in its raw form benefits very little. However, through technology, the crude petroleum is transformed into finished products like gasoline for energy need, plastic for plastic works, and other derivatives.

That is, deposited in the human spirit is the creative capacity that can transform these raw materials into useful products. Refining and making of products is a continuous process. Each generation builds upon the works of the predecessors, as such there is room for a continuous improvement. The desire for such a continuous improvement and advancement emanates right deep from the heart of the spirit man. It is the cry for the expression of prokopean love.

CHARACTERISTIC FEATURE OF PROKOPEAN LOVE

The characteristic feature of prokopean love is the desire for prosperity. Simply put, prokopean love is the love for success, prosperity or advancement in life. For instance, a sick man's hope is to be well; nobody wants to remain in ill-health. That is an expression of the prokopean love. It is the love for a better life – better relationship, increasing material prosperity. Prokopean love is all about continuous improvement and advancement in the quality of life.

Any man who claims to be disinterested in success is not being true to his heart because the desire to progress beyond where we are at each point in life is an inbuilt nature of man.

CHAPTER 50
THE FORCE OF PROKOPEAN LOVE

PROKOPEAN LOVE IS A DRIVE for advancement; it causes a man to risk everything he has to advance a cause. It is a driving force that pushes a man to stretch himself, and as he stretches out he discovers there is no limit to his advancement; the only limit being his vision and faith.

There are always barriers to overcome and giants to be slain on our path of progress. Due to ignorance, these barriers and giants have stopped many people from advancing and making further progress. Even when you stop advancing due to a perceived barrier, yet nudging at the corner of your heart is that desire to make progress. That is the prokopean love for advancement. The fact that you still have the nudge even when you feel being pummelled and pounded to a pulp is a testimony that the human nature is inbuilt with the desire for endless advancement.

TODAY'S SUCCESS IS TOMORROW'S OLD-FASHIONED

When an individual stops advancing, his past records will soon become obsolete, old-fashioned, and might even become irrelevant. In the early 1970's, we had a headmaster, Mr. Nkpukrankpu. He was well respected because of his good conduct and knowledge as the headmaster of the primary school, and he prided himself in that status. He would proudly wear his shirt, well ironed and lined with a charcoal pressing iron, and neatly tucked into khaki short knickers and with a leather belt made from a crocodile skin, one of great value in the post-colonial era.

Mr. Nkpukrankpu qualified with an ordinary level certificate, which was a prodigious attainment at the time! Sadly, Mr. Nkpukrankpu never sought to improve his academic qualification. In 1978, a younger teacher with a Bachelor of Education degree was posted to the school to replace Mr. Nkpukrankpu. Though everybody liked Mr. Nkpukrankpu, nobody could do anything to the contrary. Mr. Nkpukrankpu had to step down as headmaster for this new teacher.

In the same manner, when we stop making progress, our past success becomes obsolete and, in many cases, irrelevant, and will have to step aside for a newer, superior success. Today's success is tomorrow's old-fashioned, if not built upon. The only way we remain continuously relevant is by making continuous progress. Old age is not an excuse in the school of success (see Psalm.92:12-14). Many people have achieved great success even at old age. For instance, Anna Mary Robertson Moses, better known as Grandma Moses, began her prolific painting career at 78, and one of her paintings sold for 1.2 million USD in 2006. Harland Sanders, popularly known as Colonel Sanders, was 62 when he franchised Kentucky Fried Chicken (KFC) in 1952, which he would sell for 2 million US dollars 12 years later.

Prokopean love is that desire for endless progress. When channelled properly, prokopean love becomes a tool for 'advancement by chopping down whatever impedes progress.'

CHANNELLING PROKOPEAN LOVE FOR PROGRESS

The force of prokope needs to be channelled properly for it to result in the desired progress. To do this, note the followings:

Definite target

The force of prokope becomes beneficial when it is directed to a specific target. Having a desire to make progress is not enough to lead to advancement; all humans have such desires. But there must be a target, a well-defined object that prokopean love can be focused on. This establishes the significance of vision. The force of vision is what reveals the object – the target, to which prokopean love can be directed.

Emotionalised thought

Vision creates a defined object in the heart and mind of a man. Such object of vision is what triggers the desired force of faith that compels a man to take steps in line with the vision of his heart (see Chapter 30). However, the force of faith only becomes maximally stimulated when it is mixed with an appropriate emotion. Prokope is what generates the appropriate emotion. As discussed in Chapter 10, the emotionalised thought is what activates the mind into its subconscious state that can stimulate the spirit man for creativity.

For example, every sick man desires to be free of the sickness. In other words, health is his vision. With the force of vision, he can begin to see wholeness of body. This vision is what will trigger his faith that will compel him to start taking appropriate steps to actualise his desire. But why does he desire to be whole and healthy? May be, he wants to be strong enough to provide the needed leadership and material substances for his family. The crave to take care of his children and spouse can evoke so much emotions in him that will drive him to do all he can and knows well to become.

This crave for a better life is the prokopean love, which evokes the appropriate emotions that can skyrocket the dynamism of faith into an unstoppable force.

Napoleon Hill wrote:

> *"...all thoughts which have been emotionalised (given feelings) and mixed with faith, begin immediately to translate themselves into their physical equivalent or counterpart. The emotions, or 'feeling' portion of thoughts, are the factors which give thoughts vitality, life, and action...Not only thought which have been mixed with Faith, but those which have been mixed with any positive emotions, or any of the negative emotions, may reach, and influence the subconscious mind" (Think and Grow Rich, page 48).*

Dedication

For Prokopean love to become profitable, the application of its force requires total dedication to the object of the vision. When the force of faith, mixed with an appropriate emotion stimulated by prokopean desire for advancement, is consistently directed against the resistance to the vision, the resistance often crumbles with time. Dedication has three attributes: patience, total commitment and persistence. A man who is not ready to pay the price of dedication can never see his heart's desires becoming materialised. Indeed, application of the force of prokopean love for advancement requires patience, total commitment and persistence.

EXAMPLE FROM TIMOTHY

Timothy was from the Lycaonian city of Lystra in Asia Minor, born in about AD 17 to a Greek father. His grandmother, Lois, and his mother, Eunice, both Jews, were eminent for their piety and faith in the local Christian assembly (2Tim.1:5). From this godly family,

Timothy imbibed good Christian conduct. When he met Apostle Paul, who became his mentor, Timothy learnt about the three forces that rule the world – hope (vision), faith, and love:

- Timothy received a clear vision for his life at a very tender age (1Tim.4:14).
- Faith was continuously being generated in him to fulfil the object of his vision (2Tim.1:5).
- The force of prokopean love (along with agape) kept driving him in the actualisation of the vision.

Apostle Paul clearly told him that the actualisation of that vision requires total commitment, persistence and patience, the three attributes of dedication.

> *"Give your complete attention to these matters. Throw yourself into your tasks so that everyone will see your progress [prokopē]"*
> *(1Tim.4:15 NLT).*

Truly, there is no man who will be dedicated in the pursuit of an assignment by having total commitment, persistence, and patience that will not rise to the top in the chosen field. That is the force of prokope. From a layman, Timothy rose to become the first Bishop of Ephesus, under whom over 80 per cent of Ephesians and a majority of dwellers of the entire Asia Minor turned from paganism to Christianity in less than 70 years of Church history.

Timothy was so dedicated to his assignment that at the age of 80 years, he suffered martyrdom. In the year AD 97, some miscreants attempted to revive the dead worship of the goddess Diana in Ephesus by embarking on a pagan procession, accompanied by impious ceremonial sacrifices and songs. The 80-year-old Timothy approached the procession and tried to preach the Gospel of love to these lost souls. But the organisers instead orchestrated a riot, seized the Bishop, dragged him through the streets, and finally stoned him to death (see SSB Book 6 for more details of the life of this dedicated servant of God).

Section 4 (D)

The Force of Agape Love

CHAPTER 51
THE DEFINITION OF AGAPE LOVE

AGAPE LOVE OCCURS 259 TIMES in the New Testament; 116 times as its noun form *agape* and 143 times as the verb form *agapaó*. It is occasionally translated in older English versions such as the King James Version of the Bible as charity.

Agape is called the love of God.

> *"Now hope does not disappoint, because the love [agape] of God has been poured out in our hearts by the Holy Spirit who was given to us" (Rom.5:5 NKJV).*

Agape is also known as the love of Christ.

> *"Who shall separate us from the love [agape] of Christ? Shall tribulation, or distress, or persecution, or famine, or nakedness, or peril, or sword?" (Rom.8:35 NKJV).*

AGAPE LOVE DEFINED

Agape is simply *'a devotion to the principles of God.'* The central point in agape love is divine principles. Divine principles are simply the expressions of the nature of God. These expressions are what we call divine laws. In other words, divine principles are the divine laws which express divine nature. For instance, God hates injustice of any kind (Pro.21:3; Heb.1:8,9). That is His nature. Hence, any divine law of justice is only an expression of the justice nature of God. Agape love seeks to satisfy the requirements of these divine laws or principles, and that means agape love actually seeks the nature of God.

Divine principles are the basis on which God centres His works; they are the laws which God used to create and sustain His creation. Our universe is created using divine principles, which constitute the laws of the universe. Some of the laws of science are simply the discovery of these universal principles utilised in the formation of the universe.

God makes life easy for man by causing these divine principles to be written out in words. The principles of God are expressed in His words. The words of God are contained in the Bible. Thus, agape love is a commitment to following the principles of God in the Scriptures.

DUAL NATURE OF AGAPE

Agape love, which is devotion to divine principles, has two faces: the Creator devotion and the Creature devotion.

Creator Devotion:

God is the Creator of all things. God created the universe. Man is created by God: "we are the workmanship of God" (Eph.2:10). His principles compel God to be devoted to the works of His hand. He didn't just create and leave everything to do as occasion demands. No; not at all. God's principles commit Him to His creatures.

> *"Certainly the Lord watches the whole earth carefully and is ready to strengthen those who are devoted to him" (2Chr.16:9 NET).*

Can you remember the feeling of ownership that fills your heart when you draw the money you have laboured for to buy a valuable item for yourself? Do you remember that feeling of ownership for the house or car you bought? That feeling is often expressed in your devotion to the car or the house. That sense of devotion makes you to care for and protect your house or car; you won't entertain an untoward behaviour that threatens to damage the house or car you laboured to purchase. This sense of devotion is akin to the agape love in the heart of God for His creatures.

Because we are the works of His hands, God loves [agapao] us. He cherishes us. He won't allow us to be destroyed by the Enemy of man, Satan. Sadly, about 6000 years ago man fell to the deceit of Satan, and disobeyed God in Eden. This caused man to be cut off from God and ceased to belong to Him (man no longer God's children). To be cut off from God is also known as spiritual death. Because spirits don't die, any spirit cut off from God will ultimately exists in a world that is devoid of God. That world is Hell. Hell is a world that is devoid of God the Author of life. That is, Hell has no life whatsoever. It is a place of utter darkness, eternal misery, anguish, and all other expressions of lifelessness. Man was doomed for an eternity in Hell.

But God is agape. "*God is love* [*agape*]" (1Joh.4:8,16 KJV). That is, God's heart is full of agape towards the works of His hands. This agape love in the heart of God would not allow Him to let the spiritually dead man to be eternally dumped in Hell. He incarnated as human and came down to earth to rescue the fallen man from eternal damnation.

> *"God clearly shows and proves His own love for us, by the fact that while we were still sinners, Christ died for us" (Rom.5:8 AMP)*

Jesus Christ is the Son of God that came in human flesh. He walked on earth physically about 2000 years ago. He endured grave hatred, animosity, rejection, and finally subjected to the worst kind of death by His own people, the Jews, and the government of the then controlling empire, the Roman Empire. But what offence had He committed? None that His accusers could justify. Yet He was condemned as a criminal. He had the spiritual power and authority to counter such antagonism. Instead, He willingly submitted Himself to such cruel torture and death. But why? Because He knew His blood is the only thing qualified to atone for the sin of man and restore him to his Maker. In other words, Jesus' death was not for any wrongdoing of His, but purely for the sake of man!

What such a degree of devotion! What a commitment! It is the agape love of God that pushed Him to do that. It is a devotion of God to the works of His hand. Only a fool will doubt such a degree of love; the fact that one man willingly chose to die for another person is the highest expression of devotion.

> *"For God so loved the world that He gave His only begotten Son, that whoever believes in Him should not perish but have everlasting life. For God did not send His Son into the world to condemn the world, but that the world through Him might be saved" (Joh.3:16,17 NKJV).*

Creature Devotion

When God created the human spirit, He deposited many qualities in the heart of the spirit man. Love is one of the qualities deposited in the heart of man by God. Agape love is specifically the relationship link between the Creator God and His creatures. It is the love in the heart of a man that makes him to commit and devote to the One he sees not with his optical eyes.

Sadly, at the Fall of man, the spirit man died spiritually. Thus, the ability of the spirit man to express agape love towards his Creator becomes deficient. A fallen man has no more devotion or commitment to his Maker. He may want to make such devotion, but he'll find himself fallen short of that. This was the story of many Israelites in the Old Testament. To devote to God is to follow God's principles. The Israelites fell short of that.

In many instances, the fallen man even hates his Creator because he no longer perceives and does not know Him. The fallen spirit man is dead to any spiritual reality, and he cannot relate with the invisible Spirit that created him. The Enemy of man, Satan, has infiltrated man's heart to hate the God that made him. That explains why some persons refer to themselves as atheists and Satanists; they dislike and even hate God.

Despite this fallen state of man, His divine nature compels God to still seek for man's rescue from eternal doom; by His divine wisdom God has made provisions for man to be reconciled to Him. That is an expression of agape.

However, being moral beings, we have the right to choose to reject or accept God's reconciliatory measures. If we choose to be reconciled to God through the shed blood of Christ, we will become God's children through regeneration just as it was before the Fall. By the process of regeneration, the Spirit of God will shed abroad in our heart that lost agape love. Because it is imputed into man's heart at regeneration, agape love is also called the Love of the Spirit (see Romans chapter 15 verse 30). The Spirit of God will empower us to love (agapao) God as our Maker and Father.

> *"For we know how dearly God loves [agapao] us, because he has given us the Holy Spirit to fill our hearts with his love [agape]" (Rom.5:5 NLT).*

THE DIFFERENCE BETWEEN AGAPE AND THEOPHILOS

Note that theophilos, which is a philos love (see page 394), is different from agape. Whereas agape is a devotion to divine principles, theophilos is a mutual affectionate friendship between two individuals, Father God and man.

Agape demands authoritative theocratic obedience to divine laws while philos is respect for each other's views. In modern language, agape love is an exercise of authoritarianism while philos is egalitarianism. Agape is a display of Sovereignty Right of the Creator while theophilos is a display of the friendly fatherhood heart of God.

THE EXPRESSIONS OF AGAPE LOVE

Agape love expresses itself in two main ways:

(a) Agape love seeks to please God

To be devoted to God's principles is to seek to please God because the principles of God are the expressions of the nature of God. In other words, devotion to the principles of God is the will of God. An agape-filled heart is committed in carrying out the will of God. A man whose heart is shed abroad with agape love has one singular desire, and which is to please the God who created him. The more he does the will of God, the deeper the sense of his fulfilment. An agape-filled heart enjoys devotion to the principles of God; the principles of God being the divine laws or commandments.

> *"If you love [agapao] Me, keep My commandments"*
> *(Joh.14:15 NKJV).*

> *"He who has My commandments and keeps them, it is he who loves [agapao] Me" (Joh.14:21 NKJV).*

> *"If you keep My commandments, you will abide in My love [agape]"*
> *(Joh.15:10 NKJV).*

As a result of such commitment to obeying the principles of God, a heart filled with agape hates anything that damages his devotion to his Creator. Sin is simply a life pattern that is opposite to the life of God. All that seek to damage devotion to the Creator are encapsulated in that single word, 'sin.' In other words, agape hates sin.

(b) Agape love seeks no harm to what God has created

Agape love will not intentionally harm a fellow human being because he knows every human is created in God's image and likeness. Rather Agape love will seek the welfare of humankind.

> *"Love does no harm to a neighbour; therefore love is the fulfilment of the law" (Rom.13:10 NKJV).*

Thus, agape love seeks to please God and it seeks no harm to what God has created. These two expressions of agape love constitute the totality and finality of the laws of God:

> *"You shall love [agapao] the Lord your God with all your heart, and with all your soul, and with all your strength, and with all your mind and your neighbor as yourself" (Luk.10:27 MEV).*

Chapter 52
The Fifteen Characteristics of Agape Love

AGAPE LOVE IS UNIQUE. THERE is no individual who will allow agape love to dominate him that won't be turned into a champion in his field. Agape love is domineering and conquering. But how do we identify or recognise agape love? First Corinthians chapter 13 verses 4 to 7 mention fifteen characteristics or attributes of Agape love, which are:

(i) Agape love is patient
(ii) Agape love is kind
(iii) Agape love is not envious
(iv) Agape love is not boastful
(v) Agape love is not proud
(vi) Agape love is not rude
(vii) Agape love is not selfish
(viii) Agape love is not quick tempered
(ix) Agape love is not evil seeking
(x) Agape love keeps no record of wrongdoing
(xi) Agape love enjoys truth
(xii) Agape love is always supportive
(xiii) Agape love never loses faith
(xiv) Agape love is hopeful
(xv) Agape love endures all things

AGAPE LOVE COVERS OVER A MULTITUDE OF SINS

Note Attribute (X) above that says: 'Agape love keeps no record of wrongdoing.' First epistle of Peter chapter 4 verse 8 throws more light on this attribute:

> *"Above all, love [agape] each other deeply, because love [agape] covers over a multitude of sins" (1Pet.4:8 NIV).*

The modern rendering of Epistle of Peter chapter 4 verse 8 is: *"love [agape] wipes away many sins"* (CEV), or more clearly, *"love [agape] will cause people to forgive each other for many sins"* (EXB).

Keeping records of wrongs is an unnecessary weight that has negative effects on not just the body (health), but also on the soul (mind) and the spirit of the individual. I heard about a man who recorded down major wrong doings of his wife and children. He painstakingly jotted them down in his diaries. That was totally against the principle of agape love and will never allow a family to grow and make progress. Agape love wipes away a multitude of sins.

Indeed, about 2000 years before the birth of the Church, Solomon was inspired to pen down the same words of Apostle Peter and Paul.

> *"Hatred stirs up strife, but love covers all sins" (Pro.10:12 NKJV).*

In general, an individual with agape love is straightforward and transparent, and without hypocrisy in his dealings (see Rom.12:9). Within the ambit of God's commandments, the agape love in his heart seeks to build up other people and not to destroy them (see 1Cor.8:1).

Fig.20: Agape love shows kindness.

An individual with agape love is straightforward and transparent, and without hypocrisy in his dealings. Within the ambit of God's commandments, the agape love in his heart seeks to build up other people and not to destroy them.

AGAPE LOVE NOT STUPIDITY

Agape love makes a man wise. Contrary to what many outsiders think, a man that is filled with the love of God is very knowledgeable about the nature of man. Such a man knows when to insist on rightness and when to withdraw. He knows when to push and when to pull back. He is an embodiment of divine wisdom.

In about AD 31, after seeing the mighty miracles and good nature of Jesus, the crowd became emotional and wanted to impose kingship on Jesus. However, filled with agape love, Jesus knew the nature of man. He didn't allow the praise and accolades to dissuade him from His life purpose. Thus, on seeing the exhibit of carnal emotions of the crowd, Jesus quickly withdrew.

> *"When the people saw the sign He had done, they said, 'This really is the Prophet who was to come into the world!' Therefore, when Jesus knew that they were about to come and take Him by force to make Him king, He withdrew again to the mountain by Himself"*
> *(Joh.6:14,15 HCSB).*

AGAPE LOVE FULFILS DIVINE LAWS

The summary of the characteristics of agape love is that the practice of agape love fulfils all the divine laws. The Old Testament Ten Commandments are fulfilled by the practice of agape love.

> *"Owe no one anything except to love one another, for he who loves another has fulfilled the law. For the commandments, 'You shall not commit adultery,' 'You shall not murder,' 'You shall not steal,' 'You shall not bear false witness,' 'You shall not covet,' and if there is any other commandment, are all summed up in this saying, namely, 'You shall love your neighbour as yourself.' Love does no harm to a neighbour; therefore, love is the fulfilment of the law*
> *(Rom.13:8-10 NKJV).*

AGAPE LOVE IS FOR PRACTICE

Contrary to what some people think, agape love is not a religious emotional exhibition. Agape love is a devotion to the practice of divine principles. Agape love is for practice. If you claim to have agape love in your heart, it must show in your activities. Any emotional expression without the practical application of divine principles is not an agape love. Mere singing and dancing are not agape love. Agape love is for practice.

> *"He who has My commandments and keeps them, it is he who loves [agapao] Me" (Joh.14:21 NKJV).*

AGAPE LOVE CAN GROW

Agape love in its purest form expresses all the 15 characteristics or attributes mentioned above. However, most of the times we don't measure up in all of these 15 attributes, but the goal for any regenerated individual should be to fully express all these fifteen attributes at any point in time.

As you grow in your knowledge of God, these 15 attributes of agape love will increasingly become more and more expressed in your life. In other words, God expects us to grow in agape love.

> *"We ought always to thank God for you, brothers and sisters, and rightly so, because your faith is growing more and more, and the love [agape] all of you have for one another is increasing"*
>
> *(2The.1:3 NIV).*

The question is, therefore, how do you know if the agape love in your heart is growing? The growth of agape love is an increase devotion to the principles of God, and such increase devotion is shown by increasing expression of the fifteen attributes of agape love. If you lack the expression of any of the attributes, it is advisable you pause and ask God for grace to express it. A stunted growth will not project an individual far in the race of life. This truth becomes obvious when you consider the force of agape love in the quest for success.

Chapter 53
The Force of Agape Love

AGAPE LOVE IS A DOMINEERING force that can drive a man beyond his natural ability. Contrary to what some people think, the practice of agape, the love of God, is not synonymous with weakness. Indeed, agape love is overpowering and driving. The following are some of the ways agape love can drive a man into stupendous degrees of success:

(A) AGAPE EMPOWERS FOR CREATIVITY

Agape love is a relationship link between God and man. When an individual practices agape love, it allows God to unleash His creativity in him. The heart of such a man that practices agape love will rise in tune with divinity, a relationship that engenders creative insights. It is simply impossible for a man to be filled with agape love and not be creative. If you claim you practice agape love, it will show in the works of your life; creativity will be seen all over you.

Indeed, creativity is a cardinal product of agape love. The reign of Solomon was the zenith of prosperity in the Kingdom of Israel. Such degree of prosperity started with the man Solomon. He loved and practised the principles of God.

> *"Solomon showed his love for the Lord by walking according to the instructions given him by his father David..." (1Kin.3:3 NIV).*

Solomon's father, King David, was a man filled with understanding. David taught his son the importance of practising the principles of agape love, which Solomon obeyed. The result was the unleashing of creative wisdom on Solomon. Such creative wisdom was the genesis of good governance and prosperity that was attained in his reign. Solomon wrote:

> *"When I [Solomon] was a son with my father [David], tender and the only son in the sight of my mother [Bathsheba], he taught me and said to me, Let your heart hold fast my words; keep my commandments and live. Get skilful and godly Wisdom, get understanding (discernment, comprehension, and interpretation); do not forget and do not turn back from the words of my mouth"*
> *(Pro.4:3-5 NKJV).*

Solomon's fall started when he abandoned the lifestyle of agape love and engaged in practices that were contrary to the principles of God. In other words, a man cannot genuinely practise agape love and not be creative and prosperous; it's simply impossible. The practice of agape has the ability to lift an individual from the gutters to the height his vision and faith can carry.

Example of Creative Invention by Agape Love

In 767 BC, Uzziah ascended the throne of the Southern Kingdom of Judah. He reigned up to 740 BC. During the first half of his reign, Uzziah devoted himself to the practice of agape under his spiritual mentor, Zechariah the High Priest. Here is the recorded account of his story:

"After the death of King Amaziah, the people of Judah crowned his son Uzziah king, even though he was only sixteen at the time. Zechariah was Uzziah's advisor and taught him to obey God. And so, as long as Zechariah was alive, Uzziah was faithful to God, and God made him successful. Some of his skilled workers invented machines that could shoot arrows and sling large stones. Uzziah set these up in Jerusalem at his defense towers and at the corners of the city wall. God helped Uzziah become more and more powerful, and he was famous all over the world" (2Chr.26:1,5,15 CEV).

King Uziah's life was the story of a man who was taught and practised the principles of agape love, and as he did it, he prospered to the extent he became the first king to invent missile machines of war; his prosperity and military prowess brought him worldwide fame.

Such feats can be repeated at any time and at anywhere because principles do not change. God with His principles is no respecter of persons; if it profited Solomon and Uzziah, it can profit anybody. Agape love is the practice of divine principles, and such practice does engender creativity and prosperity at any time and at place.

(B) AGAPE LOVE BANISHES CONFUSION

The practice of agape love allows the individual to easily access clear divine instructions on any issues of life. Because he is in oneness with divinity, the agape-filled life enjoys divine direction. This is one secret that makes individuals who practice agape to become wonders in their environments and generations.

When people think he is down and no way of escape exists, the agape-filled individual suddenly springs up in another direction contrary to what onlookers think. The agape-filled individual is like wind that cannot be grasped but keeps blowing and meandering onwards and forwards no matter the impediment.

> *"The wind blows where it wishes, and you hear the sound of it, but cannot tell where it comes from and where it goes. So is everyone who is born of the Spirit (Joh.3:8).*

To be 'born of the Spirit' is to be regenerated through the New Birth in Christ, and the heart of the regenerated person is filled with the agape love of God. Such an agape-filled person is like a wind that onlookers find it difficult to understand and predict! An agape-filled heart has easy access to continuous revelation (vision), which triggers faith in him at any point in time. Such a person is not confused at any stage of his destiny journey because he knows what to do. Indeed, an individual who practices agape love is on his way to becoming a wonder!

(C) AGAPE LOVE INCREASES ABILITY

An agape-filled individual is unconquerable, he is indomitable. The secret is because he draws strength from divinity. You cannot practise agape and not secure the love of the Father. Agape love is a relationship link between man and his Creator. The man who practises agape love has access to the strength of God. Drawing on this enormous strength increases his faith beyond measures. Such amplified faith commands great exploits at all times despite stiff opposition.

Indeed, the agape-filled life is like an inflatable ball that cannot be pushed and kept under a pool of water, rather it will always bounce back to the surface.

(D) AGAPE LOVE GUARANTEES HEALTH AND LONGEVITY

An agape-filled heart is devoid of acrimony. His heart is pure and he has a clear conscience. Purity of heart and clarity of conscience are drivers of bodily health. Many cases of hypertension, diabetes, stroke, kidney diseases, and others are expressions of impure hearts and unclean consciences. You cannot harbour grudges against your neighbour and expect to live very healthy. Grudges are one of the spiritual impurities that poison the spirit man; such impurity of heart and conscience have negative repercussions on the individual's health. If you want to be healthy and live long, the practice of agape love can guarantee you that!

(E) AGAPE LOVE PROTECTS

An agape-filled life is an untouchable fellow. Throughout the six thousand years of human existence, onlookers usually think the individual who practises agape love is a weakling, and some attempt to take advantage of him, only to discover to their hurt that a fence of protection surrounds the individual.

Lot learnt the practice of agape love from his uncle, Abraham. He sought and lived in the beautiful towns of Sodom and Gomorrah. But the citizens of these towns were reprobate, having no regard for godly principles. Lot was being choked by the ungodly lifestyle of these citizens, who thought he was a weakling because he never followed their heinous, immoral lifestyle.

At a certain day, the citizens wanted to take advantage of Lot when he had two visitors. But to their chagrin, they discovered Lot was not the weakling they thought he was; a divine protection surrounded him and his household. At the end, Lot and his family were rescued from such an ungodly situation, but the ungodly people were destroyed.

> *"But at the same time the Lord rescued Lot out of Sodom because he was a good man, sick of the terrible wickedness he saw everywhere around him day after day. So also the Lord can rescue you and me from the temptations that surround us, and continue to punish the ungodly until the day of final judgment comes"*
> *(2Pet.2:7-9 TLB).*

Truly, agape love in the heart of man guarantees divine protection. This protection is not docile but active. It is like a two-edged sword that can cut asunder anyone who falls on it. Agape-filled individual will not go about looking for trouble. However, because he engenders success through the practice of agape love, he will attract all shades of jealousy and antagonism from miscreants. But such antagonism is quelled down by the force of faith that works through agape love. Indeed, people have been known to die and perish away for confronting an agape-filled life unjustly. This is because the practice of agape love makes the individual an apple of God's eye. No one thrusts a finger in God's eye and does not suffer the consequences.

> *"For thus says the Lord of hosts... he who touches you touches the apple of His eye" (Zech.2: 8 NKJV).*

In other words, the practice of agape love attracts God's rewards. It pays immensely to be devoted to divine principles, which is the practice of agape love.

> *"God is not unjust; he will not forget your work and the love you have shown him as you have helped his people and continue to help them" (Heb.6: 10 NIV).*

(F) AGAPE IS UNCONQUERABLY DRIVING FORCE OF PROPULSION

God's love in the heart of men is a driving force of propulsion. Agape love in the heart of man is the devotion or commitment towards the principles of God. It is not just a plastic commitment or devotion, but an unconquerable propulsive force.

A man who practises agape is not weak at all as some may think; rather such a man is a propulsive jet that keeps advancing and crushing all oppositions. This sort of strength often baffles those who know nothing about the working of agape love. That explains why many Christian leaders are maligned and attacked by the society. The society thinks a Christian with a heart filled of agape love should be docile and weak, but when it sees an unrivalled strength, the society becomes baffled and resorts to undue criticism and attack.

How wrong the society can be? The majority opinion does not necessarily mean correct opinion. Popular opinion does not always mean right opinion. Agape love seeks to please only one Person, God and His principles, and when such a desire conflicts with the society's opinion, a man with agape love is not afraid to go alone, and he will eventually be the winner because agape love is domineering and dominating. Indeed, agape love evokes such a high degree of devotion to the principles of God that baffles those who never experience it.

THE STORY OF MY ZEAL

Once the Spirit of God evokes agape love in a heart, the individual becomes a driving force in the pursuit and advancement of the cause of God. The individual zeal is fired up beyond words. When agape love gripped my heart in 1983, my family thought I was going crazy. My father was completely surprised by my zeal for God. It took the centre of my life, driving me in an unusual manner. Soon the zeal began to circulate about and infect other hearts. Agape love is infectious. I was at my early teenage life. But agape love is not age restricted. The zeal soon began to affect both young and old. A revival started in our local church, Assemblies of God, because of this zeal. The zeal soon overflowed into other churches around with a galvanising revival, and it soon became the talk of the day. The whole town of Ataba was being invaded by the zeal.

By 1990, the zeal had grown quite deeply in the town that some elders began to threaten us for destroying their ancestral worship places and traditions. I remember one particular night when some youths in the town, instigated by some disgruntled elders, assaulted us and attempted to burn down our local church building. The zeal kept growing and many lives have been completely turned around because of that zeal.

ROMAN WORLD AND DOMINEERING AGAPE LOVE

Never ever underrate the driving force of agape love. It is a propulsive force that knows no limitation. It is the strongest force that an individual will ever experience in life. It is this force of agape love that a mere 120 individuals, who never went through any formal training in any human institution and who without shooting any arrow or utilising the barrel of guns, yet could conquer the world with the Gospel within 80 years of the pouring out of agape love in their hearts. That was the story of the formation of the Church of God in about AD 33 at the Upper Room in Jerusalem in Palestine where 120 people gathered together (Acts chapters 1 and 2).

According to history, within 80 years following the event of AD 33, major cities across the world were already converted to Christianity. For example, over 80 per cent of the citizens of the Asian city of Ephesus (the fourth greatest city in the world in the New Testament era, after Rome, Alexandria in Egypt and Antioch of Syria) were already members of the Church by about AD 80. By the

Fig.21: The remains of the Ancient City of Ephesus

By AD 325, the year of the First Council of Nicaea, the entire sphere of human activities such as the constitutions, calendar dates and times, healthcare delivery, were already dominated by the principles of the Gospel. What the Jews who had the Torah Scriptures could not achieve in 2000 years of the giving of the Law through Moses, the Church was able to achieve in less than 350 years. The Jews failed primarily because their hearts were not filled with the propelling force of agape love, which the Church embodies (see SSB Book 6 for more on Church history).

In other words, agape love is like a propeller of an engine that moves a ship. All through the generations of human existence, agape love is known to propel a man forward and onward when it is practised. The darkness of hatred and evil can never overpower agape love. Evil may appear to reign temporarily, but ultimately agape love conquers and dominates it.

That was the secret of Christianity, which started with individuals regarded as the lowliest class in the society, but like the mustard seed grew, and still growing, to dominate the entire realms of human existence. Indeed, Agape love is an unconquerably driving force of propulsion.

AGAPE LOVE: THE GREATEST OF THEM ALL

> *"And now abide faith, hope, love, these three; but the greatest of these is love [agape]" (1Cor.13:13 NKJV).*

A man may not know anything about hope (vision) and faith, but if he practises agape love, he is bound to make progress in life. Agape love promotes. A man may be inaccurate in the operation of the forces of vision and/or faith due to ignorance, but if he should practise agape love, he can still command some measure of exploits. An example was Cornelius, a Roman soldier in the town of Caesarea. He practised welfare (almsgiving) and prayers, which are parts of divine principles. Apparently, he knew a little about genuine vision from God or faith-powered lifestyle. Moreover, being a non-Jew, he was not a partaker of the blessings of the Abrahamic covenant.

Nevertheless, Cornelius practised agape love by being devoted to the principles of welfare and prayers. The practice of agape love never goes unnoticed; it always stands as a memorial before the Presence of Divinity.

> *"Your prayers and your acts of charity have gone up as a memorial before God" (Act.10:4 NET).*

The practice of agape love attracted the attention of God to Cornelius. In response, God despatched an angel to Cornelius to give him specific instructions on how to become regenerated; hence, empowered for more productivity. It was an eventful development that culminated in the salvation of the entire household of Cornelius in about AD 37, who by that act entered into history as one of the first Gentiles (non-Jews) to become a Christian. Much more than that, the conversion of Cornelius changed the dogma and the parochial minds of the Jewish Church leaders in Jerusalem, thereby setting a stage for a more aggressive worldwide evangelism.

THE PRACTICE OF AGAPE IS FOR YOUR GOOD

God created the universe and reserves the right of sovereignty, which includes enactment of laws. However, His laws are not grievous or burdensome, but they are for the good of all. He knows how He has created us and if we submit ourselves in obedience to His laws, we enjoy the blessings that follow such obedience. That is agape love.

> *"For this is the love [agape] of God, that we keep his commandments: and his commandments are not grievous" (1Joh.5:3 KJV).*

> *"For this is the love [agape] of God, that we keep His commandments. And His commandments are not burdensome" (1Joh.5:3 NKJV).*

The summary of the issue is that if any man desires to enjoy life here on earth, he will need agape love to be shed abroad in his heart, and needs to practice this agape love. The practise of agape love is for your good.

> *"Keep my commands and live, and my law as the apple of your eye" (Pro.7: 2 NKJV).*

> *"Obey my commands and you will live. Guard my teachings as you would guard your own eyes" (Pro.7: 2 NIRV).*

Chapter 54
Section Four Practical Steps

The four kinds of love – erotica, phileo, prokope, and agape – have some basic characteristics, which are as follows:

(1) Practise of Love is a Choice

The practise of love is a choice. A man can choose to love or choose to hate. Hatred and unforgiveness are unnecessary weights in the quest for life's success. They are undue burdens that retard progress and can grow to destroy the carrier. They will slow down the pursuit of your life purpose. Remember, you have an allotted, limited time here on earth. Why carry such unnecessary burden? The choice of love is always a right choice because it engenders peace and progress.

(2) Practising Love Brings Personal Help

By practising love, you are actually helping yourself. The human nature is created to love and not to hate. Deposited in the heart of each spirit man is the Fruit of the Spirit, of which love is a cardinal feature. When we love, we make progress in health and material advancement. The opposite is true when we hate. Hatred is evil; it does kill. Therefore, each day of your life, make it a duty to extend a loving hand to someone in need; by so doing, you will experience exhilarating joy and contentment that hatred never gives.

(3) Societal Ills can be Righted by Love

Many ills in the society can be righted if we all chose love instead of hatred. Families will be better and our society will prosper if we choose to love. Remember, pure erotica will seek healthy sexual union, phileo will seek to advance brotherhood, prokope will seek for continuously positive personal advancement, and agape will seek to please God. In summary, all these four kinds of love will seek not to destroy but to build up. Therefore, choose not to follow the part of destruction, rather choose healthy advancement.

(4) Sin Weakens the Forces of Love

Sin weakens and even adulterates the efficacy of the forces of love. Sin destroys your ability to effectively wield the forces of love. In other words, sin drains the energy of your mind, weakens the force of your spirit man, and sickens your body. Thus, a wise man will be wary of intentional sin.

(5) The Spirit of God can Rekindle Love

However, note that God is the One who deposited all the four kinds of love in the heart of man. When you notice hatred instead of love bubbling in your heart and mind, you can ask God for forgiveness and for His assistance. The Spirit of God does shed abroad the love of God in our heart. The Spirit of God can rekindle love in us. He can turn your hatred into love; a wicked heart into a good one.

(6) Love – the Driving Force for Success

Hatred is an unnecessary weight and it limits an individual's speed for success. Hatred causes internal tensions and untold health calamities such as hypertension, stroke and similar infirmities. On the other hand, a life of love produces peace and inner tranquillity, which are necessities for reception of genuine vision. A peaceful heart is one that can easily ascend realms of creativity for success. Therefore, choose this day to love instead of to hate. Even if an individual chooses to hate you, be smart enough to choose to love.

(7) Love is Not Stupidity

To love does not mean you must expose yourself to the ridicule and harmfulness of hatred. If a man chooses to hate you and intends to harm you, you should protect yourself. Still do not harbour hatred or ill-will towards such a man.

> *"You have heard that it was said, 'You shall love your neighbour and hate your enemy.' But I say to you, love your enemies, bless those who curse you, do good to those who hate you, and pray for those who spitefully use you and persecute you, that you may be sons of your Father in heaven; for He makes His sun rise on the evil and on the good, and sends rain on the just and on the unjust. For if you love those who love you, what reward have you? Do not even the tax collectors do the same? And if you greet your brethren only, what do you do more than others? Do not even the tax collectors do so? Therefore you shall be perfect, just as your Father in heaven is perfect" (Mat.5:43-48 NKJV).*

However, be smart and be wise. *"Behold, I send you out as sheep in the midst of wolves. Therefore be wise as serpents and harmless as doves"* (Mat.10:16 NKJV). Always seek to protect yourself against the injustices of the hatred of the wicked, for *"the whole world lies in wickedness"* (1Joh.5:19 MEV). Remember, love is not stupidity.

The Conclusion

Chapter 55
Three Greatest Forces that Rule the World – Their Relationship

Success in any field starts with a vision. The vision in a man's heart triggers the force of faith required to bring the object of the vision from the dreamland into the physical reality. Love is what lubricates the vision and fuels the faith, making the object of the vision and its actualisation process very beautiful and attractive. Indeed, these three – vision, faith and love – are the greatest forces that rule the world.

> *"And now abide faith, hope, love, these three..." (1Cor.13: 13 NKJV).*

Hope is vision; what a man envisions is what he hopes for (see page 146). Thus, the above Scripture can be re-written:

> *"And now abide faith, vision, love, these three..."*
> *(1Cor.13: 13 NKJV).*

The term 'abide' in First Corinthians chapter 13 verse 13 actually means 'to last or endure forever' as translated in the newer Bible versions such ICB, EXB and NCV.

> *"So these three things continue forever [endure; remain]: faith, hope, and love" (1Cor.13:13 EXB).*

That is, these three – faith, hope (vision) and love – abide forever. They do not change with age. We may change their names;

nevertheless, they remain the same in all generations. They are the principles which were utilised in creating and making of products. For instance, it was the forces of vision, faith and love that God applied in the creation of man as shown below:

Vision: First God envisioned the man He wanted to make. Man was envisioned in the heart of God. When He said, *"Let us make man in our image, after our likeness..."* (Gen.1:26 KJV), God was only speaking forth what He saw in His heart and mind.

Faith: Having envisioned man, God went ahead and created man by faith. It took faith to put all the parts of man together to form a tripartite being. It took faith for God to completely deposit full dominion of ownership of earth on man. In modern terms, God took the risk of relinquishing all authority over the earth to man at creation. From the human perspective, that was a big risk, but that is what faith is all about!

Love: God could take such a big risk because of His love for man. It was love that made Him to entrust all dominion in man's hand. Even when man failed Him, love still drove Him to incarnate to earth as Jesus Christ to salvage man and restore man's stolen dominion.

What this means is that vision, faith, and love are the greatest forces that rule our world, and a wise man will, therefore, want to know how to utilise these three forces for his advantage. Every other principle or law of success hinges on these three forces. Napoleon Hill enumerates 13 principles for wealth generation in his classic book, *Think and Grow Rich.* If you take time and review all these 13 principles, you will discover that they are all based on these three forces of vision, faith, and love. That applies to all other aspects of life. In fact, there is no principle of success that is not based on these three forces. Truly, vision, faith and love are the three greatest forces that rule the world!

SUCCESS SPECTRUM – REQUIRED QUALITIES FOR SUCCESS

Indeed, hope (vision), faith, and love form a threefold cord that cannot be broken. When the three are fused together they generate a mighty irresistible power that can forcefully enthrone a man in life. Maximised success is attained when these three forces of vision, faith, and love are wielded together for a defined purpose. In other words, faith, vision, and love form a success spectrum.

Second epistle of Peter chapter 1 verses 4 to 7 are interesting Scriptures that reveal the recipe for success in life:

> *"He has given to us exceedingly great and precious promises, so that through these things you might become partakers of the divine nature and escape the corruption that is in the world through lust. For this reason make every effort to add virtue to your faith; and to your virtue, knowledge; and to your knowledge, self-control; and to your self-control, patient endurance; and to your patient endurance, godliness; and to your godliness, brotherly kindness; and to your brotherly kindness, love" (2Pet.1:4-7 MEV).*

Verse 4 refers to promises or the objects of vision; that is, verse 4 informs that we have been given *"exceeding great and precious promises."* In other words, we need to know what we have been given by God. Vision is what unveils those 'exceeding great and precious promises.'

Verses 5 to 7 unveil all the eight forces that are required to make the promises (vision) become reality. These eight forces are *faith, virtue, knowledge, temperance, patience, godliness, brotherly kindness, charity (love)*. Note that they start with Faith. That is, verse 5 reveals the faith tool upon which all other requirements are built upon.

The spectrum ends with love (agape). That is, verse 7 concludes with agape love. In other words, the success recipe is a spectrum that starts with vision, utilises faith to build all others, and ends with love. The more you grow in these qualities that form the success spectrum and exercise them, the more successful you will become in your life's pursuits.

"For as these qualities are yours and are increasing [in you as you grow toward spiritual maturity], they will keep you from being useless and unproductive ..." (2Pet.2:8 AMP).

CONCLUSIVE THOUGHTS

Life on earth is a journey. We all don't have the same route to follow. Sadly, many are travelling on the wrong routes, on other people's paths; hence, they suffer great anguish. Vision points you in the direction of your own path, faith empowers you to walk in that path, while love lubricates and makes the path smoothly beautiful.

Faith and vision only function maximally in the atmosphere of love. Genuine Vision reveals your life purpose; Faith generates the thrust to actualise the life purpose, while Love beautifies the life purpose for it to be attractive.

These three forces - vision, faith, and love - can be likened to a fruit. Vision is the seed in the fruit that will give birth to more fruits when planted. Faith is the sap that flows through the tree into the branches and nourishes the tree and causes fruits to appear. Love is the juicy flesh of the fruit. Without the flesh, the seed will be exposed to the harsh environment and the sap that nourishes the fruit to keep it growing will pour out and dissipates, not achieving its purpose. In the same manner, without love, the vision seed will be exposed and become vulnerable to the harsh attacks by wicked forces, who always want to destroy any good seed. Without love, the faith sap will dissipate and run dry. Love is what gives colour and beauty to life's pursuits. That is, faith and vision work maximally in love.

From another analogy, a heart filled with love is restful; such an individual is at peace with himself. You need such inner tranquillity to receive genuine vision and trigger mighty faith (1Tim.1:5). Such peace of heart allows the mind and the heart of the spirit man to access the realm of creativity. It is not possible to be at maximum creativity in the absence of a peace of heart and mind. Love grants you that conducive atmosphere for accessing the realm of creativity.

Sadly, in our world today and in many lives, hatred has replaced love, and as such weakness has taken over strength. Consequently, many bright dreams have been buried. As Myles Munroe famously stated:

> *"The wealthiest place in the world is not the gold mines of South America or the oil fields of Iraq or Iran. They are not the diamond mines of South Africa or the banks of the world. The wealthiest place on the planet is just down the road. It is the cemetery. There lie buried companies that were never started, inventions that were never made, bestselling books that were never written, and masterpieces that were never painted. In the cemetery is buried the greatest treasure of untapped potential"*
>
> *(The Cable, 2014: Memorable Munroe Quotes).*

The evil of hatred seems to pervade and antagonise the good. That has been the age-old conflict. It is the Great Conflict between good and evil that shapes the destiny of humanity in all sectors – healthcare, financial, educational, entertainment and other sectors. More about this age-old conflict between the forces of good and evil, and the progressive unfolding destiny of humanity are vividly captured in SSB Book 3.

Bibliography

For Section 1:

Accardi M. (2016) "Power to the People: Happy Birthday to the Ford Flathead V8" [Online] Available from: http://www.allfordmustangs.com/2016/03/31/power-to-the-people-happy-birthday-to-the-ford-flathead-v8/ (Accessed: 27 September 2016).

BBC World Service (2015) "The strange afterlife of Einstein's brain." William Kremer, BBC (British Broadcasting Corporation), World Service, 18 April 2015. [Online] Available from: https://www.bbc.com/news/magazine-32354300 (Accessed: 23 September 2018).

Beals G. (1999) "The Biography of Thomas Edison." [Online] Available from: http://www.thomasedison.com/biography.html (Accessed: 20 May 2017).

BrainyQuote (2016) "Bible Quotes." [Online] Available from: http://www.brainyquote.com/quotes/keywords/bible.html (Accessed: 10 October 2016).

Carson B. and Murphey B. C. (1992). In: Think Big – Unleashing Your Potential for Excellence. Zondervan: Grand Rapids, Michigan, USA.

Chernow R. (1998). In: Titan – the Life of John D. Rockefeller, Sr. Random House, Inc.: New York, 1998, p. 230.

Correa E. J. (2016) "Digestive System of Goats." Julio E. Correa, Associate Professor and Extension Animal Scientist, Alabama A&M University. Alabama Cooperative Extension System. [Online] Available from: http://www.aces.edu/pubs/docs/U/UNP-0060/UNP-0060.pdf (Accessed: 29 September 2016).

Edison Innovation Foundation (2012) "Thomas Edison – Man of the Millennium." [Online] Available from: http://www.edisonmuckers.org/thomas-edison-man-of-the-millennium/ (Accessed: 20 May 2017).

Einstein Albert (1936). In: Albert Einstein, The Human Side – Glimpses from His Archives. Princeton: Princeton University Press, pp. 32-33. [Online] Available from: https://books.google.co.za/books?id=2fswAAAAQBAJ&pg=PA32&redir_esc=y#v=onepage&q&f=fals (Accessed: 09 September 2018).

Forbes (2017) "Intuition Is the Highest Form Of Intelligence." Bruce Kasanoff, Forbes Contributor, Feb 21, 2017, 05:45am. [Online] Available from: https://www.forbes.com/sites/brucekasanoff/2017/02/21/intuition-is-the-highest-form-of-intelligence/#586335563860 (Accessed: 09 September 2018).

GoatGuide (2016) "Goat Anatomy." [Online] Available from: http://thegoatguide.com/caprine-goat-information/goat-anatomy/ (Accessed: 29 September 2016).

Haselhurst G and Howie K. (2012) "Albert Einstein: God, Religion & Theology – Explaining Einstein's understanding of God as the Universe / Reality." [Online] Available from: http://www.spaceandmotion.com/albert-einstein-god-religion-theology.htm (Accessed: 04 November 2015).

Hill, Napoleon (1938). In: Think and Grow Rich. USA: The Ralston Society, Meriden, Conn. (Accessed: 06 September 2016).

King, Martin Luther Jr. (1963). "Address at the Freedom Rally in Cobo Hall." A speech delivered by King, Martin Luther Jr. at Detroit, Michigan on June 23, 1963. The Martin Luther King, Jr. Research and Education Institute, Stanford University. [Online] Available from: https://kinginstitute.stanford.edu/king-papers/documents/address-freedom-rally-cobo-hall (Accessed: 21 September 2018).

Kremer W. (2015) "The strange afterlife of Einstein's brain." BBC World Service, 18 April 2015. [Online] Available from: http://www.bbc.com/news/magazine-32354300 (Accessed: 04 November 2015).

Levy Steven (2015) "I Found Einstein's Brain." [Online] Available from: http://www.stevenlevy.com/index.php/about/einsteins-brain (Accessed: 04 November 2015).

Lichfield J. (2005) "The Moving of the Mona Lisa." The Independent, Saturday 2 April 2005. [Online] Available from: http://www.independent.co.uk/news/world/europe/the-moving-of-the-mona-lisa-530771.html (Accessed: 06 October 2016).

McNicholl G. (2005). In: How to Build Ford Flathead V-8 Horsepower, pp. 77–78. [Online] Available from: https://books.google.co.za/books?id=ItB4Tg8IYLYC&pg=PA77&redir_esc=y#v=onepage&q&f=false (Accessed: 27 September 2016).

Planck Max (1932). In: Where is science going? A book, first published in 1932, by Nobel Prize-winning German physicist Max Planck. [Online] Available from: https://archive.org/stream/whereissciencego00plan_0/whereissciencego00plan_0_djvu.txt (Accessed: 09 September 2018).

Science (1978) "Brain that rocked physics rests in cider box." Science editorial, 1978; 201:696.

Simkin J. (2015) "Henry Ford." 1997-2015 Spartacus Educational Publishers Ltd. [Online] Available from: http://spartacus-educational.com/USAford.htm (Accessed: 14 December 2015).

Sorensen C. E. and Williamson S. T. (1956). In: My Forty Years with Ford. Norton: New York, USA. [Online] Available from: https://lccn.loc.gov/56010854 (Accessed: 27 September 2016).

Severson A. (2010) "The Ford Flathead V8 and the Fall of Henry Ford." [Online] Available from: http://ateupwithmotor.com/model-histories/ford-flathead-v8/ (Accessed: 27 September 2016).

STR (2017) "Albert Einstein Quotes on Spirituality." STR – Simple to Remember. [Online] Available from: https://www.simpletoremember.com/articles/a/einstein/ (Accessed: 04 August 2018).

Suetonius C. T. In: The Lives of the Twelve Caesars: the Life of Nero. Loeb Classical Library, 1914 [Online] Available from: (Accessed: 28 September 2016). [Online] Available from: http://penelope.uchicago.edu/Thayer/E/Roman/Texts/Suetonius/12Caesars/Nero*.html#37 (Accessed: 28 September 2016).

Wells A. B. (2016) "Standard Oil Whiting Refinery." Bruce A. Wells, Executive Director, American Oil & Gas Historical Society, 1201 15th Street, NW, Ste. 300, Washington, DC 20005. [Online] Available from: http://aoghs.org/products/standard-oil-whiting-refinery/ (Accessed: 28 September 2016).

Woo-Choong K. and Louis K. (1992). In: Every Street is Paved with Gold: Success Secrets of a Korean Entrepreneur. Times Books International, 1992, 199 pages. [Online] Available from: https://www.cse.iitk.ac.in/users/amit/books/woo-choong-1992-every-street-is.html (Accessed: 10 March 2018).

For Section 2:

BBC (2016) "Florence Nightingale: Saving lives with statistics." [Online] Available from: http://www.bbc.co.uk/timelines/z92hsbk (Accessed: 16 July 2016).

Bible Charts (2012) "Distances from Jerusalem Distances from Jerusalem" [Online] Available from: http://www.biblecharts.org/biblelandnotes/Distances%20From%20Jerusalem.pdf (Accessed: 10 August 2018)

Bio (2016) "Florence Nightingale Biography." [Online] Available from: http://www.biography.com/people/florence-nightingale-9423539 (Accessed: 16 July 2016).

Biography (2017) "Tiger Woods Biography: Golfer (1975–)." [Online] Available from: https://www.biography.com/people/tiger-woods-9536492 (Accessed: 06 June 2017).

Black S. and Morrison (2014). In: The Global Leadership Challenge. Routledge: Abingdon, United Kingdom, 11 Jul 2014. [Online] Available from: https://books.google.co.za/books/about/The_Global_Leadership_Challenge.html?id=e9YABAAAQBAJ&redir_esc=y (Accessed: 24 September 2018).

Boardman J. (1994). In: The Cambridge Ancient History IV: Persia, Greece, and the Western Mediterranean, C. 525-479 B.C. Cambridge: Cambridge University Press.

Business Insider (2015) "Warren Buffett thinks working just to beef up your résumé is like 'saving up sex for your old age'" Business Insider, Nov. 11, 2015, 2:44 PM by Myles Udland [Online] Available from: https://www.businessinsider.com/warren-buffett-on-resume-building-2015-11?IR=T (Accessed: 12 August 2018).

Business Insider (2017) "29 famous people who failed before they succeeded." [Online] Available from: http://www.businessinsider.com/successful-people-who-failed-at-first-2015-7/#ile-developing-his-vacuum-sir-james-dyson-went-through-5126-failed-prototypes-and-his-savings-over-15-years-22 (Accessed: 05 June 2017).

Cleveland Clinic (2017) "The Female Reproductive System." [Online] Available from: https://my.clevelandclinic.org/health/articles/the-female-reproductive-system (Accessed: 02 June 2017).

Cook E. T. (1913). In: The Life of Florence Nightingale, vol 1, p 237.

Fisch H. (2017) "The Male Biological Clock." [Online] Available from: http://www.harryfisch.com/the-male-biological-clock.html (Accessed: 02 June 2017).

Gill J. C. and Gill G. C. (2005). "Nightingale in Scutari: Her Legacy Reexamined." Clinical Infectious Diseases, 40 (12): 1799–1805. [Online] Available from: http://cid.oxfordjournals.org/content/40/12/1799 (Accessed: 16 July 2016).

Golden M. J. (2004). In: Ancient Canaan and Israel: New Perspectives. ABC-CLIO, 2004, p.275. [Online] Available from: https://books.google.co.uk/books?id=yTMzJAKowyEC&lpg=PP1&pg=PA275#v=onepage&q&f=false (Accessed: 06 August 2018).

Greenspahn E. F. (2008). In: The Hebrew Bible: New Insights and Scholarship. NYUPress,2008,p.11.[Online]Availablefrom:https://books.google.co.uk/books?id=inRKaf_To5sC&lpg=PP1&pg=PT29#v=onepage&q&f=false (Accessed: 06 August 2018).

Hagin E. K. (1989) "Chapter 7 Number One: The Inward Witness." In: How You Can Be Led By The Spirit Of God. USA: Kenneth Hagin Ministries, 1995 edition, pages 29-30. [Online] Available from: http://www.tukcu.org/wp-content/uploads/2017/07/How-to-be-led-by-the-holy-spirit.pdf (Accessed on: 09 August 2018

Nasdaq (2016) "Warren Buffett: Take a Job That You Love." Nasdaq, April 22, 2016, 01:15:16 PM EDT By Brian Flores, GuruFocus. [Online] Available from: https://www.nasdaq.com/article/warren-buffett-take-a-job-that-you-love-cm610294 (Accessed: 12 August 2018).

Olawoyin O. (2017) "Body of doctor who jumped into Lagos Lagoon recovered." The Premium Times, Nigeria, March 22, 2017. [Online] Available from: http://www.premiumtimesng.com/news/top-news/226846-breaking-body-doctor-jumped-lagos-lagoon-recovered.html (Accessed: 01 June 2017).

Sahara Reporters (2017) "How Medical Doctor Jumped Into Lagos Lagoon." Sahara Reporters, New York, March 20, 2017. [Online] Available from: http://saharareporters.com/2017/03/20/how-medical-doctor-jumped-lagos-lagoon (Accessed: 01 June 2017).

Sounes H. (2004). In: The Wicked Game: Arnold Palmer, Jack Nicklaus, Tiger Woods, and the Story of Modern Golf. New York: Harper Collins, pp. 120-121, 293 (Accessed: 06 June 2017).

For Section 3:

Clarke A. C. (1962). In: Profiles of the Future. Harper and Row: New York, 1962. pp. 2-3.

Doran G. T. (1981). "There's a S.M.A.R.T. way to write management's goals and objectives." Management Review. AMA FORUM. 70 (11): 35–36.

Foresight Institute (2018). "Erroneous Predictions and Negative Comments Concerning Scientific and Technological Developments." Originally taken from a Congressional Research Report on Erroneous Predictions and Negative Comments Concerning Scientific and Technological Developments, CB 150, F-381, by Nancy T. Gamarra, Research Assistant in National Security, Foreign Affairs Division, May 29 1969 (revised). [Online] Available from: https://www.foresight.org/news/negativeComments.html (Accessed: 26 March 2018).

Hagin K. E. (1972). In: I Believe in Visions. USA: Rhema Bible Church, 2nd edn., pg. 23.

IMF (2017) "World Economic Outlook Database, April 2017." IMF – International Monetary Fund; database updated on 12 April 2017. [Online] Available from: http://www.imf.org/external/ns/cs.aspx?id=28 (Accessed: 08 June 2017).

Israel P. (2000). In: Edison: A Life of Invention, John Wiley & Sons. [Online] Available from: (Accessed: 15 August 2018). [Online] Available from: http://www.jhalpin.com/metuchen/tae/israel.htm (Accessed: 15 August 2018).

Kelly C. F. (1943). In: The Wright Brothers: A Biography Authorized by Orville Wright. Pickle Partners Publishing, 07 February 2017, 226 pages.

Kelly C. F. (2014). "A Study in Human Incredulity" [Online] Available from: http://www.wright-brothers.org/History_Wing/Aviations_Attic/They_Wouldnt_Believe/They_Wouldnt_Believe_the_Wrights_Had_Flown.htm (Accessed: 26 March 2018).

Miller G. (2011). In: Voyages – To the New World and Beyond, p. 30, University of Washington Press, First American edition, 2011.

Hill, Napoleon (1938). In: Think and Grow Rich. USA: The Ralston Society, Meriden, Conn. (Accessed: 06 September 2016).

Rutgers (2016). In: Thomas A. Edison Papers, The Edisonian - Volume 9 Fall 2012. Rutgers, the State University of New Jersey, USA, on Thomas Edison's 1890 interview, reported in *Harper's Monthly Magazine.* [Online]

Available from: http://edison.rutgers.edu/newsletter9.html (Accessed: 15 August 2018).

Rumerman J. (2013) "Efforts at Powered Flight During the Last Decade Before the Wright Brothers' [Online] Available from: https://www.centennialofflight.net/essay/Prehistory/Last_Decade/PH5.htm (Accessed: 26 March 2018).

Smart Goals Guide (2016) "What is a Smart Goal?" [Online] Available from: http://www.smart-goals-guide.com/smart-goal.html (Accessed: 08 June 2017).

For Section 4:

About.com (2015) "King Edward VIII Abdicated for Love." [Online] Available from: http://history1900s.about.com/od/1930s/a/kingedward.htm (Accessed: 27 August 2016).

Augustine (AD. 410). In: The City of God, 15.23. [Online] Available from: http://www.documentacatholicaomnia.eu/03d/1819-1893,_Schaff._Philip,_2_Vol_02_The_City_Of_God._Christian_Doctrine,_EN.pdf (Accessed: 18 June 2017).

Bartleby.com (2017) "St. Timothy, Bishop and Martyr." Rev. Alban Butler (1711-73). The Lives of the Saints, volume I: January 24, 1866. [Online] Available from: http://www.bartleby.com/210/1/241.html (Accessed: 21 June 2017).

Bowcott O. and Bates S. (2003) "Car dealer was Wallis Simpson's secret lover", The Guardian, London, Thursday 30 January 2003 09.43 GMT. [Online] Available from: https://www.theguardian.com/uk/2003/jan/30/freedomofinformation.monarchy3 (Accessed: 27 August 2016).

Bradford S. (1989). In: King George VI. London: Weidenfeld and Nicolson.

Broad L. (1961). In: The Abdication: Twenty-five Years After. A Re-appraisal, London: Frederick Muller Ltd, pp. 4–5.

Bullivant S. B., Sellergren S. A., and Stern K., et al. (2004) "Women's sexual experience during the menstrual cycle: identification of the sexual phase by noninvasive measurement of luteinizing hormone." Journal of Sex Research. 41 (1): 82–93 [Online] Available from: http://www.tandfonline.com/doi/abs/10.1080/00224490409552216 (Accessed: 22 September 2016).

Enoch. In: Book 1: Watchers. Academy for Ancient Texts, Timothy R. Carnahan. Retrieved 14 August 2012. [Online] Available from: http://www.ancienttexts.org/library/ethiopian/enoch/1watchers/watchers.htm (Accessed: 16 June 2017).

Feloni R. (2014) "20 People Who Became Highly Successful After Age 40." Business Insider, 09 September 2014, 3:50pm. [Online] Available from: http://www.businessinsider.com/people-who-became-successful-after-age-40-2014-9/#rland-sanders-better-known-as-colonel-sanders-was-62-when-he-franchised-kentucky-fried-chicken-in-1952-which-he-would-sell-for-2-million-12-years-later-17 (Accessed: 06 September 2016).

Hill, Napoleon (1938). In: Think and Grow Rich. USA: The Ralston Society, Meriden, Conn. (Accessed: 06 September 2016).

Jiang M., Xin J., Zou Q., and Shen, J. W. (2003) "A research on the relationship between ejaculation and serum testosterone level in men." Journal of Zhejiang University. Science.4 (2): 236–240. [Online] Available from: http://link.springer.com/article/10.1631%2Fjzus.2003.0236 (Accessed: 22 September 2016).

Lichterma G. and Haltzman S. (2004). In: 28 Days: What Your Cycle Reveals about Your Love Life, Moods, and Potential. USA: Adams Media Corporation, 01 Nov 2004, pp.281 pages

Notable Quotes (2016) "Sigmund Freud Quotes." Sigmund Freud – Sexuality and the Psychology of Love. [Online] Available from: http://www.notable-quotes.com/f/freud_sigmund.html (Accessed: 19 September 2016).

Orthodox Christian Church (2017) "Apostle Timothy of the Seventy." [Online] Available from: https://oca.org/saints/lives/2013/01/22/100262-apostle-timothy-of-the-seventy (Accessed: 21 June 2017).

Padfield D. (2016) "The City Of Ephesus In Bible Times." Online] Available from: http://www.biblelandhistory.com/turkey/ephesus html (Accessed: 01 September 2016).

Roberts D. M. (2011) "Ancient Ephesus and the New Testament: How our knowledge of the ancient city of Ephesus enriches our knowledge of the New Testament." [Online] Available from: http://www.patheos.com/blogs/markdroberts/series/ancient-ephesus-and-the-new-testament/ (Accessed: 01 September 2016).

Roya.Uk (2016) "The home of the Royal Family." Edward VIII, Broadcast after his abdication, 11 December 1936 (PDF), Official website of the British monarchy, retrieved 1 May 2010. [Online] Available from: https://www.royal.uk (Accessed: 27 August 2016).

Scutti S. (2013) "Male Sex Drive: Is the Mighty Testosterone Alone Responsible for Libido?" IBT Media Inc., 13 June 2013, 04:33pm. [Online] Available from: http://www.medicaldaily.com/male-sex-drive-mighty-testosterone-alone-responsible-libido-246793 (Accessed: 22 September 2016).

Sigmund Freud (1963). In: Sexuality and The Psychology of Love page 25. New York: Simon & Schuster Inc.: New York. [Online] Available from: https://books.google.co.za/books?id=CkgpiGbERY4C&pg=PA25&lpg=PA25&dq#v=onepage&q&f=false (Accessed: 26 August 2018).

The Cable (2014) "Memorable Munroe Quote." [Online] Available from: https://www.thecable.ng/wealthiest-place-earth-cemetery-—-memorable-munroe-quotes (Accessed: 16 July 2018).

The Guardian (1936) "King Edward renounces the throne. Abdication effective tonight. Duke of York succeeds. 'The King never wavered.'" [Online] Available from: https://www.theguardian.com/uk/1936/dec/11/queenmother.monarchy (Accessed: 26 August 2018)

The London Gazette (1936). "The London Gazette Extraordinary." The London Gazette, Issue no. 34349, p. 8111, 12 December 1936. [Online] Available from: https://www.thegazette.co.uk/London/issue/34349/page/8111 (Accessed: 27 August 2016).

The Washington Post (1986) "The Duchess of Windsor Dies at 89." J.Y. Smith, The Washington Post archive, April 25, 1986. [Online] Available from: https://www.washingtonpost.com/archive/politics/1986/04/25/the-duchess-of-windsor-dies-at-89/527355f5-b283-441c-b892-a5d35c0a341f/?utm_term=.f186a660a751 (Accessed: 26 August 2018).

Tolman D. L. and Diamond L. M. (2001) "Desegregating Sexuality Research: Cultural and Biological Perspectives on Gender and Desire." Annual Review of Sex Research. 12 (33): 33–75.

WHO (2016) "Fact sheet: Sexually transmitted infections (STIs)." WHO – World Health Organisation, updated August 2016. [Online] Available from: http://www.who.int/mediacentre/factsheets/fs110/en/ (Accessed: 19 September 2016).

www.ingramcontent.com/pod-product-compliance
Lightning Source LLC
Chambersburg PA
CBHW032031080426
42733CB00006B/55

9780620812337